Archeology of the Florida Gulf Coast

Southeastern Classics in Archaeology, Anthropology, and History

Southeastern Classics in Archaeology, Anthropology, and History
Jerald T. Milanich, Series Editor

Each volume in this series is a nineteenth- or twentieth-century
scholarly work still used today by students of the native American societies
and the colonial period of the southeastern United States.

Archeology of the Florida Gulf Coast, by Gordon R. Willey

Early History of the Creek Indians and Their Neighbors, by John R. Swanton

Space and Time Perspective in Northern St. Johns Archeology, Florida, by John M. Goggin

Archeology of the Florida Gulf Coast

Gordon R. Willey

with a new preface by the author

foreword by Jerald T. Milanich, series editor

University Press of Florida
Gainesville · Tallahassee · Tampa · Boca Raton
Pensacola · Orlando · Miami · Jacksonville

First published in 1949 by the Smithsonian Institution,
Smithsonian Miscellaneous Collections, Volume 113
Printed in the United States of America on acid-free paper

03 02 01 00 99 98 6 5 4 3 2 1

Library of Congress Cataloging-in-Publication Data

Willey, Gordon Randolph, 1913–
Archeology of the Florida Gulf Coast / Gordon R. Willey;
with a new preface by the author; foreword by Jerald T. Milanich.
p. cm. — (Southeastern classics in archaeology, anthropology, and history)
Originally published: Washington: Smithsonian Institution, 1949, in series:
Smithsonian miscellaneous collections.
Includes bibliographical references.
ISBN 0-8130-1603-7 (alk. paper)
1. Gulf Coast (Fla.)—Antiquities. 2. Excavations (Archaeology)—
Florida—Gulf Coast. 3. Florida—Antiquities. 4. Indians of North
America—Florida—Gulf Coast—Antiquities. I. Title. II. Series.
F317.G8W55 1998
975.9'901—dc21 97-46484

The University Press of Florida is the scholarly publishing agency for the State University System of Florida, comprising Florida A&M University, Florida Atlantic University, Florida International University, Florida State University, University of Central Florida, University of Florida, University of North Florida, University of South Florida, and University of West Florida.

University Press of Florida
15 Northwest 15th Street
Gainesville, FL 32611
http://nersp.nerdc.ufl.edu/~upf

CONTENTS

PAGE

LIST OF PLATES

(All plates at end of book.)

LIST OF FIGURES

LIST OF MAPS

LIST OF TABLES

Sherd classification

FOREWORD

What makes a classic? Why are some books and articles as useful today as when they were first written? For archaeologists, anthropologists, and historians interested in the native American cultures of the southeastern United States and the events of the colonial period, classics are references that contain ideas and knowledge essential to research. Some classics helped to shape a field of study, others developed the fundamental taxonomies used today, and still others offer basic building blocks of information that can be used to fuel theoretical models. Many classics exhibit all these characteristics. All are publications that active researchers cannot live without.

In my own personal research library I have a number of southeastern classics and I consult them frequently. They are the books my students covet and which I guard zealously, for scholarly as well as financial reasons. Classics—if one can still find them at all—can cost a pretty penny!

The knowledge published in classics continues to endure. Unfortunately, many of the books themselves have been less fortunate. Originally published in paperback with non-acid-free pages and bindings, in limited printings, or in hard-to-find journals, some of them have become rare indeed.

The Southeastern Classics Series will put back into print books and articles deemed by scholars to be timeless treasures, resources we all use, but which are difficult to find or, in some cases, have literally disappeared. As someone who loves books and could not wait for the Bookmobile to visit my neighborhood during the summers of my youth, I am very pleased to be a part of this project.

This first volume in the series might well serve as the answer to the question "What is a classic?" Gordon R. Willey's *Archeology of the Florida Gulf Coast* is a book as important today as it was when it was first published half a century ago. *Archeology of the Florida Gulf Coast* appeared at a time when archaeological research in the southeastern United States was nearing the end of a decade and a half of robust growth. (It also appeared at a time when federal agencies were spelling "archaeology" without the second "a" preferred today, forever creating a headache for compilers of bibliographies.) The first book-length, single-authored synthesis in Florida archaeology to be published, Willey's reference work no doubt influenced other archaeologists to write similar summary overviews for other regions in Florida. Several would appear on the heels of Willey's treatise.

It was clear to those archaeologists—Willey included—that out of syntheses comes progress. Summarizing what was known provided a foundation on which future scholars could build. In the case of *Archeology of the Florida Gulf Coast,* it was a tactic that worked better than anyone might ever have predicted in 1949.

The impetus for the Gulf Coast volume came from a trip Gordon Willey took to northwest Florida in 1938. He returned in 1940 to undertake fieldwork in the Panhandle region. After several more years, and having received a firsthand knowledge of the archaeology of Georgia and the Lower Mississippi Valley, Willey realized that the Florida Gulf Coast cultural and ceramic sequences were germane to understanding not only the native cultures of Florida but those of the adjacent southeastern states from Louisiana to Georgia. That is one reason *Archeology of the Florida Gulf Coast* is such a classic and why it was chosen to kick off our new series; it is not only valuable for students of Florida archaeology, but for archaeologists working in other regions of the Southeast as well.

Secure in his belief that such a book would be a contribution to southeastern archaeology, Willey undertook a multi-year study of what was known about the Florida Gulf Coast, the eighteen counties from Alabama to Charlotte Harbor, Florida, including inland regions 20–100 miles away from the coast. I suspect it turned out to be a bigger project than he originally had envisioned. Available by that time were all the publications of Clarence B. Moore, describing his many excavations along the Gulf Coast from 1900 to 1918, as well as a relatively large number of excavations undertaken (but never written up) in the 1930s under the auspices of federal relief archaeology programs. To use the information from these latter projects, Willey had to analyze the relevant collections and collate them with the extant field notes; he then included the site reports in his 1949 synthesis.

In addition to contending with the pre–1940s, there was new information to interpret as well. Willey's own excavations had to be reported, and other Florida archaeologists—John Goggin, John Griffin, and Ripley Bullen—were digging up new data even as he labored to make sense of the old.

But he did it. *Archeology of the Florida Gulf Coast* reports on many Gulf Coast excavations for the first time, and it integrates old and new into a cogent overview of the native coastal cultures. It also provides detailed descriptions of the artifacts and other traits used to define and interpret those cultures.

As Willey noted at the time, *Archeology of the Florida Gulf Coast* was not meant to be the "final word." In 1949 there was still very much to learn. In writing about some areas and cultures he was hindered by a lack of information because radiocarbon dating was not yet available to provide absolute dates. Today, in many instances, we can fill in those gaps and we can correlate an impressive array of radiocarbon dates with *Archeology of the Florida Gulf Coast,* making it an invaluable reference.

As a young archaeologist just out of graduate school at Columbia University, Gordon Willey wrote a classic. It was only the beginning of a number of other book-length classics that he has written about the precolumbian cultures of Central and South America, as well as Florida. He also has authored well-received introductory overview volumes on North and Central America and on South America. Perhaps the most published archaeologist in the world, Gordon Willey has been recognized and honored as the doyen of North, Central, and South American archaeology. Gordon Willey himself is a classic.

Now retired as Bowditch Professor from Harvard University, Dr. Willey has embarked on a new career as a novelist, an undertaking in which he also is enjoying great success. I recommend a trip to your local bookstore to buy *Selena,* his first novel, a tale about archaeology and intrigue on the northwest Florida Gulf Coast. It too may become a classic.

Jerald T. Milanich
Series Editor

PREFACE TO THE 1998 EDITION

That my monograph *Archeology of the Florida Gulf Coast* (Smithsonian Institution, 1949) is still deemed worthy of reprinting, almost fifty years after its original publication date, is naturally gratifying to me. I think that the primary merit of this book derives from its position in the history of Florida archaeology.

The first interest in the prehistoric remains of Florida began with exploratory surveys and diggings in the nineteenth and early twentieth centuries. These climaxed with the many excavations and publications of Clarence B. Moore (1894 through 1918), as well as the well-known classificatory-descriptive ceramic study by William H. Holmes (1903), which incorporated substantial Florida material. All of this represented, in effect, the first major phase of Florida archaeology. Ancient mounds and sites were located and excavated; materials from them were described and illustrated. Moore, whose excavation procedures, in the tradition of his time, were somewhat "rough and ready," was nevertheless extraordinarily conscientious in publishing good photographs of much of what he found. Holmes's fine eye for style and well-ordered, systematic approach laid the groundwork for subsequent ceramic typological studies. Florida archaeology had thus "come of age" in what can be considered its exploratory and initial descriptive stage.

By the 1930s, however, archaeology in the eastern United States had moved on to concerns of cultural taxonomy and chronology. My *Archeology of the Florida Gulf Coast* was primarily an attempt at chronological ordering. In the summer of 1940, along with my colleague Richard Woodbury, I had conducted stratigraphic testing in a number of northwest Gulf Coast midden sites (Willey and Woodbury, 1942). The data obtained from these tests enabled us to set up a chronology of ceramic complexes extending from Spanish Contact times to the earliest pottery of the area. Later, while on the staff of the Smithsonian Institution in the 1940s, I was able to supplement these data with others from unpublished excavated materials that were available at that institution. In sum, I tried to bring together all that was known or available about Florida Gulf Coast archaeology at that time and to present this in the framework of a relative cultural chronology. In my introduction (p. 1), I state, "If this work serves as a general stock-taking and as a base of departure for future researchers it will have fulfilled its purpose." I think that it has. It provided a beginning or a "platform" for the second major phase of Florida Gulf Coast archaeology, the phase of chronological ordering, or "type-space-time systematics."

Those who have followed me have modified and added to this structure; and, as of now, I think it would be fair to say that much of this second phase has been completed. Today, Florida's archaeologists are turning to other concerns, to what might be considered a third phase in the development of their discipline, characterized by attempts to interpret the archaeological record in ways aimed at expanding the cultural contexts involved as well as understanding the processes of cultural change and growth.

Let me add one final word. Back in 1949, when *Archeology of the Florida Gulf Coast* first appeared, a distinguished senior colleague remarked, "That book has set Florida archaeology back fifty years!" (This was a fairly frequent form of criticism in the archaeological discourse of the day.) Now, with 1999 almost upon us, I can only remind my younger colleagues that they are essentially back up to the starting line; and I encourage them to "go for it," and "full speed ahead!"

Gordon R. Willey
Bowditch Professor, Emeritus
Harvard University

ARCHEOLOGY OF THE FLORIDA GULF COAST

By GORDON R. WILLEY

Bureau of American Ethnology, Smithsonian Institution

(With 60 Plates)

INTRODUCTION

PURPOSE OF STUDY

The purpose of this report is to provide a complete and integrated synthesis of the archeology of the Florida Gulf Coast to the present date. It is both a field report of unpublished excavations and a compilation and reinterpretation of previous archeological work in the area. I have attempted to show how recent archeological investigations along this coast give the clues which enable us to incorporate the results of almost a century of earlier digging into such an over-all reconstruction. This by no means implies that I pretend to have written the "final word." As in most other parts of the southeastern United States and the Americas, the archeology of Gulf Florida is in its initial stages of synthesis. If this work serves as a general stock-taking and as a base of departure for future researches it will have fulfilled its purpose.

The orientation of the report is historical reconstructive. Specifically, it is a reconstruction of the skeletonized time-space systematics of prehistory. Within the Gulf Florida area I have attempted to show the succession of cultures and culture growth throughout several centuries of past time. In conclusion, I have also tried to indicate something of the contacts and interplay between these prehistoric Gulf Florida cultures and those of neighboring areas. The spatial and temporal arrangement of cultural forms or types which is the framework for such a reconstruction submits to demonstration and is, I think, reasonably well proved. Beyond this realm of the demonstrable, several lines of speculation are pursued. One is also historical and concerns origins and diffusions; the others relate to population density, time duration, and cultural trends. The nature of each, as it is followed, marks it as speculative and exploratory as opposed to evidential and established. In offering these speculations I have tried to explain the factors which have guided my choice of interpretations.

DEFINITION OF THE FLORIDA GULF COAST AREA

The Florida Gulf Coast archeological area is comprised of a coastal strip which extends from Perdido Bay on the northwest to Charlotte Harbor on the southeast (map 1). The inland extent of the area varies from 20 to about 100 miles. All the counties of northwest Florida are included as is a bordering strip of south Alabama and southwest Georgia. Southward along the peninsula the area is made up almost entirely of the coastal counties.

Ecologically the area is valid as it is all a part of the Gulf Coastal Plain. There are some physiographic, soil, vegetational, and climatic variations; but, relatively speaking, these present no striking differences. The area also has an adequate cultural validity. Thomas, in his mound surveys, included all of Florida in a greater lower southeastern or Gulf area (see Kroeber, 1939, pp. 102 ff., for a simplification of the Thomas groupings). Holmes (1914, pp. 420-424) placed all of Florida and adjacent south Georgia in a Georgia-Florida area, pointing to over-all similarities in pottery types, stone artifacts, and burial mounds. Wissler (1938, p. 268) includes Florida along with Georgia and the Carolinas in a South Atlantic archeological area. All these areal classifications are similar in that Florida is treated as a whole, or grouped with portions of other States, to create a large area of which the Florida Gulf Coast is but a part. The narrowing of archeological culture areas and the increased number of subdivisions in those previously projected has followed as a natural result of additional research and increased knowledge, particularly with reference to culture sequences. M. W. Stirling (1936) was the first to subdivide the greater Florida area and to delineate a Gulf Coast area. Stirling's Gulf Coast area was defined as: ". . . . the area of Florida draining into the Gulf of Mexico, as far south as the Caloosahatchee River." With minor revisions and qualifications this is the Gulf Coast area as it is accepted today. Goggin's recent (1947b) definition of Florida culture areas has modified the southern boundary, bringing it north to Charlotte Harbor. Goggin has also drawn more definite eastern boundaries separating the Gulf Coast area from those of the central and eastern parts of the peninsula. The area as it is defined in this report and presented on map 1 follows the Goggin revisions.

A degree of arbitrariness in the definition of the area is not denied. The realities of natural environment and prehistoric cultural distributions have been modified or approximated to suit our purpose and convenience. The southern boundary is quite definite and

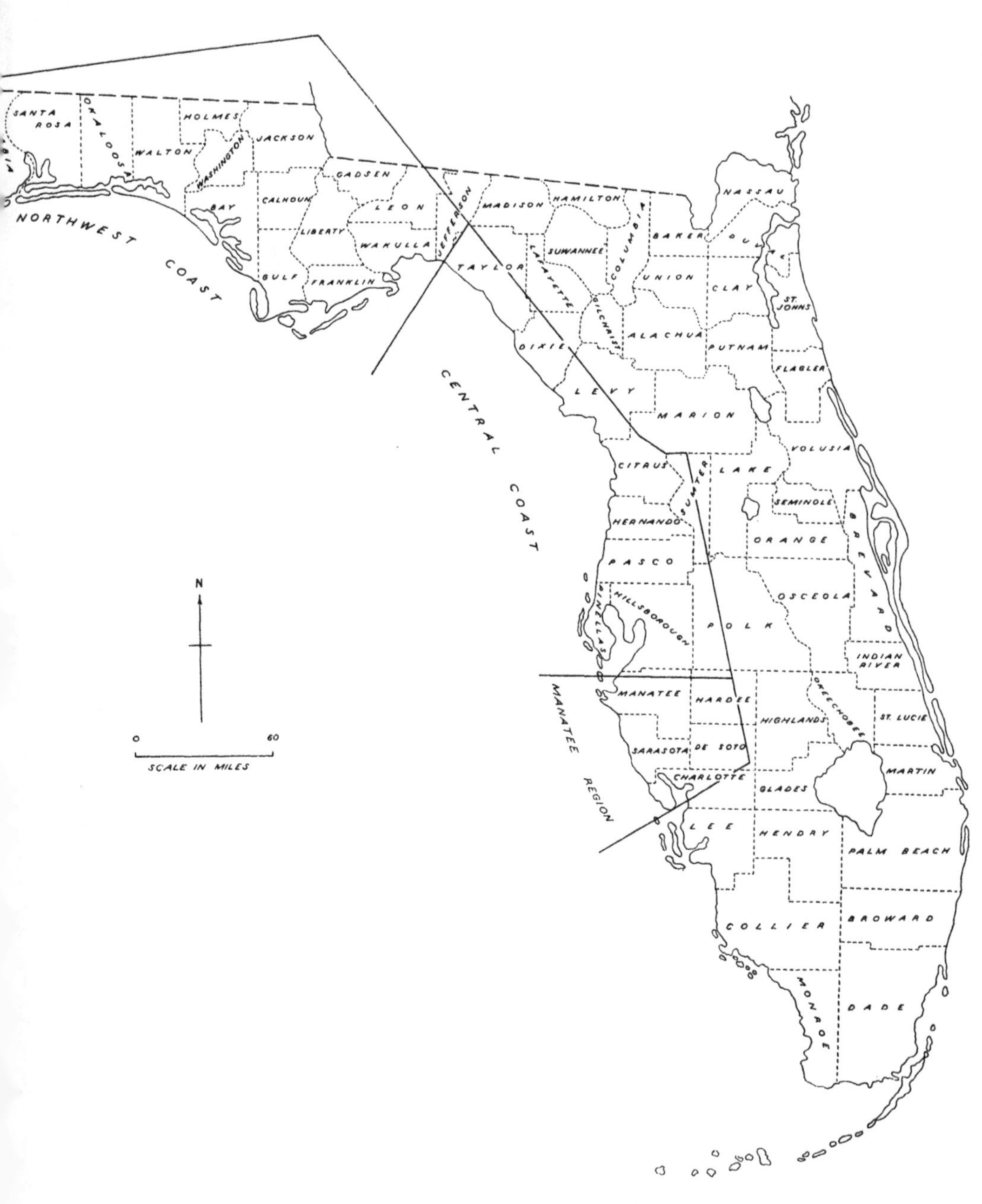

MAP 1.—Florida counties and the Gulf Coast archeological area.

has a substantial basis both in natural environment and culture types. South of Charlotte Harbor the climate is subtropical, and the archeological culture of the Glades area, as it is called, differs markedly from the Gulf Coast. To the east the lines are less sharp both as to environment and prehistoric cultures. There is more shading of one type into another. Nevertheless, differences have been observed (Goggin, 1947b; n.d. 2). The northern boundary is, perhaps, our weakest as the archeological picture in south Georgia and south Alabama is only hazily recognized. I am inclined to think that here the Florida Gulf Coast culture area might eventually be extended inland for a greater distance than we have indicated in this paper. Westward the boundary is also largely arbitrary. Close similarities are known to exist between the Florida Gulf Coast and southern Louisiana and Mississippi. There are also differences. Presumably a division could be made somewhere along the Alabama or Mississippi coast, but, at the present time, we do not know where it could most accurately be placed.

The Florida Gulf Coast has unity as an archeological culture area in that it has been the locale in which the same archeological patterns and fusions of these patterns have persisted over a considerable span of time. There are observed, however, a number of secondary differences in these patterns which are reflected in subarea variations of cultures. These subareas are referred to here as "regions." Three such regions have been formalized by Goggin (1947b; n.d. 2). These are, from north to south, the northwest coast, the central coast, and the Manatee region. The northwest coast includes all of Florida and adjacent Alabama and Georgia as far east as the Aucilla River on the border of Jefferson and Taylor Counties; the central coast extends from that division point down to the southern end of Tampa Bay; and the Manatee region takes in the southernmost counties of the area going as far south as Boca Grande Pass, Charlotte Harbor (see map 1). Although the three regions are closely united during all culture periods, and virtually identical during some, there are period-to-period differences. Of the three the northwest and central coastal regions are most similar to each other, and the Manatee region is the most divergent. This matter of regional differences is considered in detail in the ensuing sections of this report.

PROCEDURES OF CLASSIFICATION

The formulation of culture periods.—Archeological data offer almost limitless possibilities for the classificationist. A classification is an arbitrary procedure; the grouping or categorizing of phenomena reflects the attitudes of the classifier toward his data rather than any inherent "truths" in the materials themselves. In view of this it is incumbent upon the classifier to define his particular attitudes or the ends for which his classification is but the means.

In establishing the culture "periods" as the major classificatory device of this report we are operating with the basic assumption that culture changes through time. The culture period is the means of measuring and describing cultural forms, both material and nonmaterial, as these have existed in a time continuity. Ideally, this period-to-period change should be uniform throughout the geographical area of study; however, few culture areas of any size display such time-depth regularity. The Florida Gulf Coast approximates it but does not fully attain it; to accommodate these spatial variations in the time continuity of the cultures of the area we have devised the above-mentioned subareal divisions for the regions.

Lacking any satisfactory means of establishing an absolute time scale by which to measure and segment the prehistory of the Gulf Coast we have defined these culture periods by their own content. Certain qualitative and quantitative cultural features have thus come to symbolize a cultural period. Both the period and the complex of features are designated by the same name. The particular points in the time continuum which have been selected as the dividing lines between a period and its predecessor or successor have been chosen in an attempt to emphasize certain trends and changes in the prehistoric developments. For example, the appearance or disappearance of a pottery type or the shift from mound to cemetery burial have been capitalized upon as markers on the time scale.

The primary method by which the culture continuum has been arranged and given direction from early to late has been stratigraphy. This has been continuous rather than discontinuous stratigraphy and has effected a correlation between arbitrary depth in refuse deposits and cultural succession. This method was successfully employed on the northwest coast, and its results have been extended by comparison and inference to the central coastal and Manatee regions. In the northwest each of the culture periods in that region was first established upon the presence of certain pottery types and upon the percentage configuration of these types in a particular stratigraphic depth context. By this it is meant that the simple presence of a pottery type is not always enough to denote a specific period; its association with other types and its percentage relationships with these types in context were more often the significant factors.

It will be seen from this that the culture periods, as they were first defined, were essentially ceramic periods. The general availability and stratigraphic occurrence of pottery made it the handiest media for our purpose. Furthermore, the assumption that pottery is one of the most sensitive reflectors of culture change seems substantiated in the Gulf Coast area where its observable changes progressed at a much more rapid rate than did those of other prehistoric manufactures or mortuary customs. The period constructs as first outlined by ceramic stratigraphy were tested and expanded by projecting them against the broader archeological background of the area. The ceramic stratigraphies of the northwest coast were compared with pottery series from burial mounds and cemeteries in the same region and with burial-mound collections of the central coast and the Manatee regions. The final results of this were much fuller definitions and characterizations of the culture periods.

Pottery classification.—As the basic time guide pottery has been described and classified in accordance with a definite system. The basis of this system is its smallest classificatory unit, the *type*. The concept of the type as used in this report follows procedures of definition which are current in the archeology of the southeastern United States. The function of a pottery type is as an historical tool. It is conceived of as an abstraction based upon a specified range of constructional and artistic variables which are recognized in a group of pottery specimens. To be of value in the solution of historical problems each type must have a definable time and space position. Krieger (1944, pp. 272-273) has made the point that this time-space position of the type must be demonstrable by archeological data and not in terms of "logical" assumptions or unproved hypotheses of culture development.

As the type is thought of as representing a number of combinations of techniques in manufacture, materials, form, and decorative features it is obvious that not all of these features, or modes (see Rouse, 1939), will appear on any one specimen but will tend to fall in a normal frequency of occurrence curve for the type. The degree of allowable variation within a type follows no set rules. It has, however, been a principle to establish a new type when any material, form, or style variation is found to have temporal, spatial, or associative significance. This has been the general intent in the present report although there are some exceptions.

Type nomenclature has followed Southwestern procedures, now also in use in the Southeast. This is to let the names of sites or geographical areas which are associated with a certain type be used as the "designant name." Techniques of pottery decoration serve as the second name. Where necessary an intermediate modifying term is introduced. Thus, the type name Swift Creek Complicated Stamped is composed of the type site designant, "Swift Creek"; the decorative term, "Stamped"; and the modifying adjective, "Complicated."

The classificatory term of the next order is the *series*. I have introduced this in the present report as a means of grouping together a number of types which bear a very obvious relationship to each other. Usually companion types in the same series have about the same temporal and spatial distribution although minor differences may exist on this point. The series is named after one or more prominent types which compose it. For example the Weeden Island Series consists of Weeden Island Plain, Weeden Island Incised, Indian Pass Incised, Keith Incised, and a number of other closely related types. In this report I have consistently excluded types from a series if identity of paste and temper was lacking. Thus, the Papys Bayou Series types, although clearly related to the Weeden Island Series in decorative technique and design, have been set apart as a separate series because of a difference in ware qualities.[1]

The most inclusive classificatory term in the pottery classification system is the *complex*. A complex is synonymous with culture period in that it represents the group of pottery types or the various series of types that occur together in the same general area at the same time. Thus, the Weeden Island Complex is composed of several series and each series consists of several pottery types. It is, of course, possible for types of two different complexes to be contemporaneous. It must be remembered that the cultural development of the Florida Gulf Coast was a continuum and the actual picture was a dynamic one. The dying types of one complex or period may have overlapped in time with the inception of types of a new period and complex. Actually, they were contemporaneous for a time, but they have, for purposes of description and analyses, been made static and classified as components of one complex or the other.

Techniques of decoration such as incision, punctation, stamping, rocker-stamping, etc., are well known and common throughout Southeastern and Eastern literature. Similarly, material and con-

---

[1] This difference in ware was demonstrated to have distributional significance.

structional terms need no glossary qualification as the range found in Gulf Florida is about the same as that encountered elsewhere in the eastern United States. Vessel forms, however, are extremely varied and in many cases unique to the Florida Gulf. For this reason, a vessel form classification is added as an appendix to the section on "The Culture Periods," following the various pottery type descriptions (see pp. 496-506). This classification has been formulated after a thorough review of the C. B. Moore publications, the Moore museum collections, and other Gulf Florida ceramic collections.

Descriptive classifications.—With the exception of the pottery, all artifacts are classified by an informal descriptive system. For example, projectile points are listed by blade and haft form and size; stone celts are usually referred to as "pointed polled" or "rectangular"; copper ornaments as "bicymbal ear spools of copper," etc. Similarly, such features as mounds are designated with self-evident descriptive terms such as "rectangular flat-topped temple mounds" or "circular, conical burial mounds." In general, the lack of sufficient numbers of artifact specimens, the absence of adequate provenience data, or an extremely limited number of forms or variations of an artifact or feature made formal systematic classification unnecessary.

I. THE NATURAL AREA

GENERAL CHARACTERIZATION

The area of this study (see map 1) a strip approximately 50 miles wide which extends around the Gulf Coast of Florida from Perdido Bay on the Alabama-Florida line to Boca Grande Pass, Charlotte Harbor, in the southwestern part of the peninsula, is a part of the Gulf Coastal Plain of the eastern United States. In general, there are two physiographic types in the area, the flat marine terraces of the coast and the rolling hills which lie several miles inland. The dominant vegetation pattern is that of the southeastern mesophytic evergreen forest; however, this is interspersed with swamps, marshes, and hammock lands of oak and other hardwoods. Year-around climate is mild to warm, with hot, wet summers and relatively dry winters. There is a gradual increase in summer heat and rainfall, proceeding from the northwest to the southeast. Drainage is rather poor, owing to the low-lying terrain and the height of the water table. Most of the rivers that flow into the Gulf are short, although there are some exceptions to this in the cases of the major rivers whose headwaters are far to the north in the uplands of Alabama and Georgia. Along the northwest coast there are several large, well-protected bays into which many of the streams drain. There are fewer of these bays on the west coast, with Tampa and Charlotte Harbors being the only important exceptions.

GEOLOGY, SOILS, VEGETATION, AND CLIMATE

The Florida Plateau is an ancient geologic feature which today is only partially above the waters of the south Atlantic and the Gulf. It dates back at least to the Paleozoic when it was a part of the old land mass of Appalachia. During the Upper Cretaceous the entire plateau was covered by the sea. Afterward, in the Cenozoic, the Florida shoreline underwent many shiftings, but it was never submerged to any great depth nor, correspondingly, was it ever raised very high above the water level. Sedimentation during the Cenozoic was from the Piedmont Plateau and was predominantly limestone, especially during the Eocene and Oligocene. Miocene deposition combined sand and limestone and the later epochs sand and clay.

The topography, soils, and vegetation of Gulf Florida can be divided into a number of small zones which differ from each other in varying degrees. In west Florida, large portions of Escambia, Santa Rosa, Okaloosa, Walton, Calhoun, and Gadsden Counties make up the west Florida pine hills. This zone lies back away from the coastal flats and extends on into Georgia and Alabama. It is composed of red-orange clay hills. Rivers are numerous and there are occasional swamps. Open forests of long-leaf pine are the characteristic vegetation cover. A similar upland is the Knox Hill country in Walton and Washington Counties. A little to the east of this in Holmes and Washington Counties, is the west Florida lime-sink region, a low-lying area of thin soils with open forests of pine. Solution of underlying limestone has produced ponds and swamps around which hardwoods and cypress cluster. To the northeast, in Jackson County, is a region known as the Marianna red lands. This is red-clay hill country but with numerous limestone outcrops and natural caverns. The soil here is rather rich. Another particularly favorable area for agriculture is the Tallahassee red hills in Leon County. This is upland covered with short-leaf pine and deciduous trees. Around Tallahassee there are several large, shallow lakes, the result of river channels dissolving out the underlying limestone and causing the valley floors to sink below the level of the outlets. The valleys are large and broad-bottomed, the lakes extremely shallow, and the land the richest in Gulf Florida. The Tallahassee red hills are surrounded by another topographic-vegetation zone, the middle Florida hammock belt, an alternately hilly and flat region with moderately good soils.

South of the hills, but not a part of the immediate beach country, are the Apalachicola flatwoods, embracing parts of Gulf, Calhoun, Liberty, Franklin, and Wakulla Counties. This is a rather poor lowland sustaining pine, palmetto, and wiregrass, and dotted with cypress ponds. An exception to this topography is a series of high bluffs forming a narrow strip along the east bank of the Apalachicola River from Bristol to the Georgia border. Other zones occupying a similar transition place between the clay-hill uplands and the coast proper are the Bellair sand region of Leon and Wakulla Counties and the Wakulla hammock region of that county. Here the soils are deep sands and not well suited to agriculture. The middle Florida flatwoods, farther to the east and south in Taylor, Lafayette, Alachua, Marion, and Levy Counties, are comparable to the Apalachicola flatwoods in soils, lack of topography, shallow lime-sink depressions, and sluggish streams. These middle Florida flatwoods lie back about 20 miles from the coast.

North and east of the middle Florida flatwoods, stretching from Georgia southward through Madison, Hamilton, Suwannee, Gilchrist, Alachua, Marion, Sumter, and Pasco Counties, is the peninsular lime-sink region. This is a profusion of low hills and basinlike depressions resulting from limestone solution. Rivers and swamps are scarce but springs or underground streams common. The country is covered with pine except along occasional streams and in the deeper limestone sinks where hardwoods grow. The soil is sandy but can produce good crops.

The actual coastal strip, varying from 5 to 20 miles or so in width, can be divided into three zones: (1) In west Florida, from Escambia Bay to the Ocklockonee River there is a topography of simple beach dunes and marshes. Beaches are wide and composed of fine sand. (2) South and east of this, from the Ocklockonee to Tarpon Springs, the shore is marshy. Along this coast the water for a long way out into the Gulf is quite shallow and large waves do not reach the shore, preventing the formation of smooth sandy beaches. In many places along this stretch there are limestone outcrops at the water's edge. (3) South of Tarpon Springs, down to Charlotte Harbor and beyond, the outer bars are sandy beaches, but the protected inner shores are lined with mangroves. The beaches or marshy shore, as the case may be, are backed up by several miles of flat pine lands, marshes, and hardwood hammocks. Neither in the northwest nor the west is this type of terrain suitable for agricultural production.

From Gordon's Pass southward, a region lying out of the Gulf Coast area as we have defined it, mangrove swamps line the outer as well as the inner shore.

Climatic variation in the Gulf Coast area can best be schematized from the following figures based upon three weather stations: one, in the extreme west at Pensacola; another, near the center of the coastal area at Apalachicola, and a third in the extreme south at Fort Myers. The Pensacola station gives average temperatures for January of 53° Fahrenheit and for July of 80°; there are 300 days to the annual growing season; and rainfall is 57 inches annual with 4.6 inches in a maximum spring month and 7.5 inches in a maximum summer month. The Apalachicola station shows temperatures of 55°-81°; 305 growing days; and 57 annual inches of rain with 3.5 inches for a maximum spring month and 7.7 inches for a similar summer month. Fort Myers has a temperature variation between January and July of 64° and 81°; growing days per year exceed 335;

and with 52 annual inches of rainfall the maximum spring month is 2.2 inches while the maximum summer month is 8 inches. These figures show that while there is more annual rain in the northwest, there is a greater summer precipitation in the south. Semitropical to tropical conditions prevail in the southern part of the area for several months each year. On the whole, the climate and precipitation are well suited for corn and other crops that are best adapted to a mild, relatively dry winter and a hot, wet, and humid summer.

LIFE POTENTIALITIES

The potentialities of the Gulf Coast area for human exploitation on a preindustrial level are definitely restricted. Although climate and soils are generally favorable to heavy native vegetation, the soils and drainage near the coast are, for the most part, unsuited for intensive agriculture. Mixed sandy soil which is best for crops is found only in small scattered patches along the coast; the more plentiful pure sandy soils and organic soils require modern cultivation techniques for successful production. Inland, in the hilly country, especially in the north, as has been noted, there are many sections where agriculture now flourishes and undoubtedly did so in the past. Today, corn, beans, and sweetpotatoes, as well as many other food crops, are grown in abundance in these uplands but less successfully in the flat lands.

The native resources of the Gulf Coast were, however, quite ample to offer subsistence for a small and well-distributed population. Previous to European settlement, it was a region of wild game, such as deer, bear, panther, wildcat, fox, opossum, raccoon, skunk, muskrat, and rabbit. In early historic times buffalo were found as far east and south as western Florida. Turkey, duck, various sea birds, fish, turtle, alligator, and mollusks were extremely plentiful. The natural conditions of the Gulf Coast waters were, in fact, ideally suited for the breeding of shellfish. Oysters breed only where a combination of shallow, salt-water shoals and river deltas obtain. The few large and many small rivers emptying into the Florida Gulf offer these conditions to a degree that is unmatched almost anywhere else in Atlantic North America. It is believed that a rising sea level in the later geologic history of the Florida peninsula created more of these coastal shoals and marshes resulting in more mollusks. Today, marine foods remain one of the principal economic resources of the coast although there are sections where oysters and clams are no longer extant. The prehistoric refuse middens contain numerous fish and animal bones as well as shell.[2]

In addition to the fauna, wild plum, crabapple, blackberry, cherry, persimmon, huckleberry, and swamp chestnut grew in profusion and served as supplementary diet.

Native materials for building and for artifactual use were limited to wood, shell, bone, and flint. Stone, other than flint, limestone, or soft coquina and occasional sandstones, was lacking. Metals, such as copper and galena, were not present.

Communication on the numerous streams or along the coast in the places protected by offshore bars was reasonably easy and rapid by canoe.[3]

---

[2] Identification of such remains from the old village middens excavated in 1940, at Carrabelle, Mound Field, Sowell, Fort Walton, Gulf Breeze, and Lake Jackson, revealed the following species:

Mammals: Opossum (*Didelphis virginiana*); racoon (*Procyon lotor*).
Fish: Sea drum (*Pogonias cormis*); jack fish (*Caranx hippos*).
Turtles: Box turtle (*Terrapene major*); mud turtle (*Kinosternon* ?); gopher tortoise (*Gopherus* ?).
Birds: Florida cormorant (*Phalacrocorax auritus*).
Shells: *Polynices duplicate; Rangia cuneata; Chione cancellata; Pecten irradians; Englandia rosea; Fasciolaria tulipa; Oliva sayana; Ostrea virginica; Melongena corona; Arca sectiocostata; Strombus pugilis; Murex fulvescens; Busycon contrarium.*

This is only a partial list of prehistoric fauna from the area.

[3] This section on "The Natural Area" is based upon first-hand observation and upon the following references: Cooke, C. W., and Mossom, S., 1929; Fenneman, N. M., 1938; Goggin, J. M., 1948b; Harper, Roland M., 1914; Kroeber, A. L., 1939; Martens, J. H. C., 1931; U. S. Department of Agriculture Yearbook, 1941.

II. HISTORY OF ARCHEOLOGICAL RESEARCH: 1846-1946

EARLY INVESTIGATIONS

The period of contact and conquest in Florida begun in 1513 by Ponce de León and continued through Spanish, French, and English colonization, came to an end with the cession of Florida to the United States in 1819. The country remained wild and semipopulated for several decades after this, but by 1850 the Indian was no longer looked upon as a serious problem for the settler but rather an object of curiosity. Archeology, as distinct from general exploration, began in this second half of the nineteenth century. With the widespread stimulation of interest in the ancient past of the New World, following the rediscovery of the Mayan ruins of Yucatán and the explorations of the mounds of the Ohio Valley, notes and comments on the antiquities of Florida began appearing in the scientific journals of that time.

Aside from William Bartram who in the 1770's made his celebrated journey through north Florida, traveling as far west as Mobile (Bartram, 1940), the first published accounts of Gulf Florida archeology appeared just before the Civil War. In the 1830's and 1840's the small towns along the west coast of Florida were established and the region was more thoroughly explored. Two naturalists, J. H. Allen (1846) and T. A. Conrad (1846), primarily interested in making conchological collections, visited and described the large shell middens near the mouth of the Manatee River in the middle 1840's. Both these men were of the opinion that the huge shell deposits were the result of natural wave action. As Allen states: ". . . . their immense quantity precludes the idea of their having been accumulated by the aborigines of the country." In 1854, in Schoolcraft's monumental though somewhat uneven "Indian Tribes of the United States, Part III," there is a discussion of aboriginal pottery from the "low mounds of the Gulf Coast" (Schoolcraft, 1854, pt. III, pp. 77 ff.). The collection under consideration was submitted to Schoolcraft by a Mr. Hitchcock who had obtained it in the field, in the vicinity of Apalachicola Bay, in 1841. The data are not sufficient to locate the site. Typical burial mounds are described as being 12 to 18 feet high and 30 to 50 feet in diameter; they were constructed of black soil and sand, and were encircled with trenches (the borrow trenches). Shell middens are also mentioned as a distinct type of site. Such features as artificially perforated or "killed" pottery, clay pipes, lump galena, and metal are listed as coming from the mounds. The art style of the pottery was classified, in conception and skill, as intermediate between Mexico and the northeastern United States. Apparently Schoolcraft's plate 45 is the first illustration of Gulf Coast archeological pottery. The sherds shown are of the Fort Walton culture period.

The distinguished anthropological scholar Daniel G. Brinton visited Florida in 1856-57, and, although he spent most of his time on the St. Johns River, he made a quick trek to the Gulf Coast from where he reported large mounds in Marion and Alachua Counties, along the Suwannee River, and as far south as Charlotte Harbor (Brinton, 1859). Brinton, too, marked the distinction between shell middens and sand mounds, and in a later paper (1867) he called attention to the great shell refuse heap on the Crystal River. This Crystal River report was based upon the field observations of F. L. Dancy, at that time State Geologist of Florida. Dancy located the shell mound at 4 miles upstream on the Crystal.

Another distinguished scientist of about the same time, Jeffries Wyman, described a shell mound at Cedar Keys, apparently the great midden pile reported on by various parties since that time (Wyman, 1870).

In 1869 R. E. C. Stearns studied the shell deposits around Old Tampa Bay, on Point Pinellas, and at Cedar Keys. He commented upon the distinction between the shell heaps, which were refuse middens, and the purposefully built sand burial mounds (Stearns, 1870, 1872).

The first description of excavations on the Gulf Coast was offered by an army surgeon, G. M. Sternberg, in 1876. He lists two shell mounds, one at Bear Point, Ala., and the other at Anerierty's Point, Fla., on Perdido Bay, both of which he recognized as middens. His excavations were principally directed toward a sand burial mound at the first location, a tumulus some 12 to 15 feet high and 100 feet in diameter. Sternberg's listing of burials and artifactual remains is the most detailed up to that date.[4] Sternberg also excavated in both the shell midden and the big platform mound at Fort Walton at the eastern end of Santa Rosa Sound. He does not, however, describe the site under this name (Sternberg, 1876). Both Bear Point and Fort Walton were the scene of later archeological activities by Clarence B. Moore and others.

---

[4] A Francis H. Parsons, of the U. S. Coast and Geodetic Survey, obtained a large collection from this mound in about the year 1889. Holmes (1903, p. 105) refers to this, but, apparently, Parsons never published on his findings.

There were a number of other rather desultory attempts at investigation in the 1870's, none of which were very fully reported. Calkins (1877-1880) described some excavations by a Lt. A. W. Vogdes in Tampa Bay shell mounds. This work was done in 1876 (see also Vogdes, 1879), and only the finding of human skeletons is reported. Vogdes also dug into the big shell refuse at Cedar Keys. Charles Rau reported upon a gold effigy woodpecker ornament found in a mound, along with pottery and human bones, in Manatee County (Rau, 1878). C. J. Kenworthy, making a boat trip from Key West to Cedar Keys in 1877, listed shell mounds between the Crystal and Homosassa Rivers and others around Orange Lake in Alachua and Marion Counties. Kenworthy also evinced considerable interest in the artificial canals on Pine Island, in Charlotte Harbor, and the large shell mounds in this same vicinity (Kenworthy, 1883). Henry Gillman (1879) excavated a burial mound northeast of Santa Fe Lake, Alachua or Putnam Counties, and found painted and punctated pottery, a stone ax, and two human skulls which he believed to have been filled with calcined human bones from other parts of the cremated bodies.

A somewhat different note was struck in Florida studies by Ecker's paper published in 1878. His "Zur Kenntniss des Körperbaues früherer Einwohner der Halbinsel Florida" was the first serious attempt at physical anthropology for the area. It is in the central European tradition of the period. Measurements and descriptions of crania from a sand mound in Cedar Keys region are presented in great detail and with exemplary orderliness. All fall within the brachycephalic and mesocephalic ranges. Like so much scientific industry of its kind it is rendered sterile by a virtually complete lack of cultural data concerning the skeletal material in question. Ecker was not to blame for this, however, as the material was gathered by others in 1871.

In the Smithsonian Annual Reports for 1879, 1881, and 1883, S. T. Walker (1880a, b, 1883, 1885) gave reasonably thorough accounts of his observations and excavations on the Pithlochascootie River, on the Anclote River, at John's Pass, at Maximo Point, in Old Tampa Bay, at Shaw's Point at the mouth of the Manatee River, at Cedar Keys, and on the northwest coast. At the Cedar Keys site he conducted some crude stratigraphy and noted changes in pottery types by depth, but, unfortunately, included no good descriptions or illustrations of his ceramic material. In the northwest, Walker visited and excavated some of the sites later investigated by Moore. These include Escribano Point, Fort Walton, and Hogtown Bayou, all between Pensacola and the eastern end of Choctawhatchee Bay.

Walker was the best Florida archeologist of his time. Obviously influenced by the cultural evolutionism of his day, he had some awareness of the principles of culture growth as interpreted through archeological remains. In this way, he had a generalized interest in chronology although his attempts to demonstrate it from his field work were not systematized. His descriptions of materials recovered were fairly full although he did not completely itemize his findings. In this he is the equal of Moore who was to follow him in the area some 20 years later. Walker's total contribution was, however, much more limited than Moore's.

After Walker, little of consequence was achieved in Gulf Coast archeology until almost the turn of the century. F. LeBaron, in making a trip from Orlando to Charlotte Harbor in connection with explorations for a steamboat route through Florida, saw a small mound near Fort Myers on the Caloosahatchee and described the artificial canal through Pine Island in Charlotte Harbor (LeBaron 1884). James Bell described six sand mounds in the vicinity of Gainesville, Alachua County. Most of these mounds contained nothing in the way of artifacts or burials, but in one he found secondary burials and pottery which, from his description, may have been of the Weeden Island style (Bell, 1883). M. H. Simons, of the U. S. Navy, published a brief account of shell-midden keys, mounds, and artificial canals from the southern end of Charlotte Harbor. Simons also explored the Caloosahatchee River for a distance of 25 miles inland but reported no archeological sites (Simons, 1884). James Shepard, in making a few investigations around Tampa, gathered a collection of stone and shell tools as well as potsherds. Among the sites he mentions are Rocky Point, 5 or 6 miles west of Tampa, the Culbreath site on the shore of old Tampa Bay, and the Bull Frog mound at the mouth of the Alafia River several miles below Tampa. Shepard was a good observer and interested in the natural resources that were available to the primitive inhabitants of the area. He pointed out that all the marine shells which he saw corresponded with live species now inhabiting the nearby waters and that chalcedony and quartz were available at a location about 5 miles below Tampa in the form of silicified geodes (Shepard, 1886). G. F. Kunz described in considerable detail a flat rectangular gold pendant and a silver ornament, one from a mound on the west side of Lake Apopka, Sumter County, and the other from a mound near Tampa. Kunz was careful to point out in the case of the gold object that it was found deep in the mound in association with the bones of "hundreds of Indians" and was not, therefore, a later intrusion (Kunz, 1887).

Much of this survey work of Walker, LeBaron, Bell, and others was assembled by Cyrus Thomas in his exhaustive mound survey of the eastern United States (1891). Although little more than a catalog of county, location, and type of Indian site, this work served to bring together for the first time a skeleton outline of just what had been accomplished in archeological research in Gulf Florida as elsewhere. Thomas' field agent, Rogan, excavated two mounds in Alachua County and these operations are described by Thomas in the Twelfth Annual Report of the Bureau of American Ethnology (1894).

Work on a much larger scale than heretofore reported was undertaken on the Gulf Coast by F. H. Cushing and party at Tarpon Springs in 1896. This was a prelude to the later and more famous excavations at Key Marco in the Glades area keys. A small sand mound, known as the "Safford mound," was thoroughly excavated and was found to contain over 600 human skeletons as well as a large amount of pottery. This was a Weeden Island Period mound, and Cushing's work, for the first time, drew considerable attention to this very distinctive style of pottery. Cushing and party also excavated in a mound at Finley Hammock, 9 miles northwestward of Tarpon Springs. Unfortunately, the Tarpon Springs material was never reported upon in detail, although a few years later some pottery specimens were illustrated by Holmes (1903). In the brief preliminary report (Cushing, 1897) Cushing offered some very colorful theories with regard to the nature of the mound construction, the disposition of burials, and the general cultural affiliations of the builders of the Safford mound. Of all the early Florida Gulf investigators he was the most given to extreme speculation.

In connection with Cushing's cruises to Key Marco he made a number of interesting observations among the keys in Charlotte Harbor, Pine Island Sound, and Caloosa Bay. This region of the keys is the borderland between the Gulf Coast and Glades archeological areas as they have been defined in more recent times. The phenomena which Cushing saw and described here are somewhat more typical of the south than the north. He was considerably impressed by the artificial or semiartificial terracing, the platforms, and the mounds on the shell-refuse-covered keys at Demorey, Josselyn's and Battey's Landing, and he described these in some detail, including photographs and drawings (Cushing, 1897).

A contemporary of Cushing, Thomas Featherstonhaugh, reported on some mounds and mound excavations in central Florida at about the same time (Featherstonhaugh, 1899). These were near Lake Apopka and Lake Butler in Lake and Orange Counties. Although this region is as close to the east coast as it is to the Gulf, the pottery which Featherstonhaugh found in the mounds pertains to the Weeden Island Period. Featherstonhaugh's account is fairly complete but lacks illustrations. Fortunately, his material is available in the United States National Museum.

From this brief summary, it is obvious that the period between 1850 and 1900 was not a brilliant one in Gulf Florida archeological research. Archeology as a profession in the United States was in its infancy, and techniques in the field as well as manner of presentation of data were undeveloped. Of all of the men named, only Brinton, Wyman, and Cushing could be considered professionals, and of these three only Cushing worked to any extent in the Gulf area. Of the entire group, S. T. Walker shows up the best, as far as Gulf Florida studies are concerned, and he was an interested layman. Most of the accounts are merely the casual relations of educated men, naturalists, doctors, military and naval officers, lawyers, and engineers who had an appreciation for both natural and human history. The fact that much of this material was published at all was due to the stimulation by Powell and Thomas, of the Bureau of American Ethnology, who were encouraging responsible persons in all sections of the country to make investigations and to communicate some record of these to the Smithsonian Institution. Similarly, the editors of the American Naturalist and the American Antiquarian encouraged their readers to report their archeological findings.

Of various unpublished investigations of the period there is almost nothing known except where museum collections exist. With the passage of time old correspondence is lost or forgotten and artifact collections often scattered or separated from any provenience data that may once have accompanied them. As the Gulf Coast was less thickly settled then than now, it is not likely that there was as much unrecorded digging and "pothunting" previous to 1900 as afterward. I would imagine that a good proportion of the gentlemen of "scientific bent" of the last century made, at least, some brief published entry of their activities.

The solid results of the "early investigations" are these: The great number of aboriginal remains of the Gulf Coast were made known to the scientific world. These were accurately grouped, as far as we can yet tell, into functional categories of burial mounds, house platform mounds, refuse piles, and the canals, terraces, basins, etc., of the keys below Tampa. Some knowledge was gained as to the nature of the artifacts found in the Gulf Coast sites, although this knowledge was not systematized and very few illustrations of artifacts were published. From the discovery of European trade materials some of the mounds were identified as post-Conquest while others, without such objects inclusive, were considered wholly aboriginal. It was generally conceded that the sites and remains were those of the Indians or the ancestors of the Indians who occupied Florida at the coming of the Europeans. The controversy as to "Indians versus a mysterious race of Mound Builders" was not fought out on the Florida scene, but the outcome of the dispute which raged farther to the north seems to be reflected in most of the statements of the men writing on the Florida Gulf.

THE SURVEYS OF CLARENCE B. MOORE

In volume of work accomplished and in amount of published data Clarence B. Moore ranks as an outstanding investigator in the Florida field. Earlier workers carried on their researches rather sporadically and published only brief notices in the scientific journals. Moore, through sheer dint of effort, persistence, and thoroughness in covering the ground, brought a certain system into Florida studies. By faithfully publishing his findings he has left an invaluable record that forms the groundwork for any synthesis of Florida prehistory. In method and sense of problem, it is true, he differed but little from most of his predecessors or colleagues. Moore introduced no new point of view to Southeastern studies; his contribution was of a quantitative rather than qualitative value. His interests were in phenomena themselves, in their appearance and diversification, rather than in any scheme into which they could be placed. He had little appreciation of chronology and took only casual note of geographic distributions. Nor was he scrupulously careful to itemize all features, burials, and artifacts in the sites that he excavated.

He was aware of the ethnohistoric contacts of the early Spaniards on the Gulf Coast, and he occasionally mentioned the European explorers in connection with a particular vicinity in which he was carrying out explorations. There was no attempt, however, definitely to "document" a site in terms of historical incidents. Similarly, allusions are made to the early historic tribes of the area without any systematic effort to identify tribes with archeological sites. Like many of his contemporaries, Moore was impressed with the value of physical anthropology and made and recorded various observations on the skeletal material found in the mounds. These observations included pathology, head form, size and shape of long bones, and cranial deformation. They are not metrically or systematically presented, nor are they, except for a general statement on cranial flattening, synthesized for the area or any part of the area. On most of his trips he was accompanied by a Dr. M. G. Miller, a medical man, who aided in the task of identifying and commenting upon human skeletal material. In other lines Moore also sought specialists' advice. Rocks and minerals were turned over to geologists for classification, metals were analyzed, and even soil samples and potsherds were microscopically examined. Unlike many of his colleagues, Moore was not given to sweeping speculations, at least in these Florida reports. Occasionally he offered a theory, often concerning the use or function of some archeological object or feature. Sometimes he pointed out what seemed to him similarities between one of the specimens uncovered during his survey and artifacts from other parts of the Southeast or, rarely, the Americas at large. But, generally, his work was factual and not conjectural.

Moore made his first excursion into Gulf Florida in the winter of 1900. Previous to this, he had been surveying and excavating sites in the St. Johns drainage of east Florida, but the remarkable finds which Cushing (1897) uncovered in the muck at Key Marco at the head of the Ten Thousand Islands attracted his attention to the west. Much of Florida was still a wilderness at that time, and land transportation was difficult in the thinly settled regions. Because of this, Moore's surveys were conducted by boat. Beginning at Clearwater Harbor, north of Tampa Bay, Moore's party, consisting of associates, ship's crew, and laborers, proceeded southward. Excavations were made at mounds and shell piles within Tampa Bay, on the Little Manatee and Manatee Rivers, in Sarasota Bay, in Pine Island Sound, on the Caloosahatchee River, and, finally, south into the islands and keys. The southern extent of this survey of 1900 was the Chatham River of Cape Sable. Within the Gulf Coast archeological area the sites he investigated range from Four Mile Bayou to Indian Hill in Hillsborough County. He critically examined Cushing's (1897, pp. 338-339) claim for truncated pyramids faced with conch-shell masonry and successfully disproved it. In general, Moore considered it a very unsuccessful season as he was unable to locate anything comparable to Cushing's "Court of the Pile-Dwellers." The 1900 survey was published as "Certain Antiquities of the Florida West Coast" (1900).

In the following year, survey was resumed but in the extreme northwest, on Perdido Bay. The first site explored was the "Mound at Bear Point," Baldwin County, Ala. Moving eastward Moore investigated and recorded 16 mound or cemetery sites. The season of 1901 was terminated on the southern side of Choctawhatchee Bay at Hogtown Bayou, Washington County, Fla. These excavations are described and the materials from the sites are illustrated in Moore's "Certain Aboriginal Remains of the Northwest Florida Coast," Part I (1901). In 1902 Moore continued his survey, beginning at St. Andrews Bay which lies next in order to the east of Choctawhatchee Bay. The first site was on West Bay Creek, a small stream flowing into St. Andrews Bay from the west. Proceeding eastward along the coast, 52 sites, mostly sand burial mounds, were excavated and reported upon during this second season in northwest Florida. The last and most southeasterly site was the "Mound near the Shell-Heap," Levy County, Fla., just south of the mouth of the Suwannee River. The area covered during 1902 included St. Andrew's Bay, the Bay of St. Joseph's, Apalachicola Bay, St. George's Sound, Ocklockonee and Apalachee Bays, and Deadman's Bay. A detailed account of this work is given in "Certain Aboriginal Remains of the Northwest Florida Coast," Part II (1902).

In 1903 Moore continued by moving south from the region of the mouth of the Suwannee as far as Tampa Bay, thus completing his first inspection of the entire Gulf Coast area. He began in the north at "Fowler's Landing" on the Suwannee, and, after a brief 50-mile trip up that river, went southward, concluding at Long Key, an island fronting Tampa Bay. From north to south he surveyed the lower reaches of the following rivers, as well as the intervening coastal stretches: the Waccasassa, Withlacoochee, Crystal, Homosassa, Chassahowitzka, Wekiwachee, Pithlochascootie, and Anclote. This season's account appeared as "Certain Aboriginal Mounds of the Florida Central West Coast" (1903).

Supplementary investigations were made in 1903 on the Apalachicola River which drains into Apalachicola Bay. On this waterway, from the Gulf to the point of confluence of the Flint and Chattahoochee Rivers, 14 mound sites were excavated, ending with "Mounds at Chattahoochee Landing" in Gadsden County, Fla. These 14 mound sites are discussed in Moore's "Certain Aboriginal Mounds of the Apalachicola River" (1903).

In 1904, after an unfortunate beginning on the Kissimmee River in interior Florida, north of Lake Okeechobee, Moore returned to the west coast to make excavations in the vicinity of Charlotte Harbor and to the south. He eventually rounded Cape Sable, visited various southern keys, and put in at Miami on the east coast. This account is given in his "Miscellaneous Investigations in Florida" (1905).

Still later, in 1906, Moore went farther up the greater Apalachicola drainage, on the Chattahoochee and Flint Rivers, respectively. Twenty-one sites, mostly burial mounds, were opened on the Chattahoochee in Florida, Alabama, and Georgia. The northernmost site was in Muscogee County, Ga., just below the city of Columbus. However, the presence of burial mounds and an essentially Floridian type of culture were not met with beyond 50 miles from the Gulf Coast. On the Flint River, in Decatur County, Ga., Moore dug four sites. The Chattahoochee and Flint excavations are the subject of a paper appearing in 1907 with the title "Mounds of the Lower Chattahoochee and Lower Flint Rivers."

At about this same time, a brief period of excavation at Crystal River, in Citrus County on the west coast, terminated the explorations of the Florida Gulf for a good many years. These excavations are reported on as "Crystal River Revisited" (1907). Moore had, previously, examined the burial mound at Crystal River in his west coast survey of 1903.

From 1906 until 1918, Moore was occupied elsewhere in Florida and the Southeast, but early in 1918 he made a final visit to northwest Florida which he summed up in "The Northwestern Florida Coast Revisited," published in the same year. The 1918 investigations included 9 mounds on the Choctawhatchee River, 13 sites on Choctawhatchee and St. Andrews Bays; 4 sites on the Apalachicola River in Florida and Georgia, and 10 sites along the coast between St. George's Sound and the "Greenleaf Place," Citrus County.

Most of Moore's excavations were in small sand burial mounds and although he often mentions shell middens and other refuse areas near or in association with the mounds he seldom excavated these. An occasional cemetery drew his attention, and in several instances he sampled pyramidal platform mounds of the sort considered as temple or house substructures. Moore also mentions the excavation of small, low, circular or oval sand mounds in which no burials or purposefully placed artifacts were found. This type of mound was usually located near a burial mound, and the author considered them as domiciliary mounds, presumably erected by the builders of the burial mounds.

Moore attempted no stratigraphic excavations on the Gulf Coast, and his conclusions are not primarily concerned with relative chronology. In his earlier work on the St. Johns River he had discussed the temporal relationships of the ceramics and other artifacts from the various layers of the great shell deposits in that area. Following Wyman (1875), he pointed out evidences of nonpottery levels underlying pottery-bearing strata, of intermediate fiber-tempered pottery levels, and of top levels showing decorated sand-tempered pottery. In his west Florida work he failed either to find or to look for indications of sequence. Perhaps this was because nearly all the pottery of the Gulf area which Moore encountered has a general resemblance to the upper-layer pottery of the St. Johns and he neither expected nor tried to distinguish periods in what he considered to be a single horizon. Nor did Moore make any serious effort at classification, either of sites or of pottery. He recognized close similarities among all the burial-mound sites from Pensacola to the region of Tampa Bay, and it is now clear that this was a sound observation. Yet, in spite of many important features held in common throughout the area, there are many easily recognizable differences, especially in the pottery of the various sites. Some of these distinctions in ware and pottery types were known to him, for, along with Holmes, he saw a divergence in style between pottery of the Mobile-Pensacola district and that of the Apalachee Bay region. He was also well aware of the importance of European trade goods inclusive in a burial mound or grave. This makes it seem strange that he should have missed the suggestive correlation of European objects being found only in sites which contained pottery of Mobile-Pensacola or Mississippian affiliations.

Moore's conclusions deal with minor problems of distribution of selected traits. In his 1901 report he emphasizes the "mixed" nature of the cultures of the Choctawhatchee Bay district, pointing to the Lower Mississippi Valley ware, Georgia stamped ware, and characteristic Florida pottery all within this one region. The trait of basal perforation of funerary vessels, or the "killing" of pottery, was briefly examined upon an areal basis, and Moore advanced the hypothesis that this idea was Floridian, or at least had its first focus there after being transplanted from an unknown source. He concluded that the pottery in northern peninsular Florida with ready-made mortuary perforations was a refinement of the original idea of breaking or "killing" a mortuary vessel and was more limited in distribution and later in time.

Comparing his 1900 and 1901-02 field seasons, Moore (1902) calls attention to the fact that pottery in the burial mounds of peninsular Florida is neither equal in quality to that of the northwest coast nor does it occur as abundantly. He notes, in addition, that the custom of placing pottery with the dead does not obtain on the lower southwest coast of the peninsula or on the east coast. The custom of urn burial is observed in the northwest, and cremation, or partial cremation, is mentioned as being exceedingly rare in northwest Florida as compared to the Georgia coast. Of the mounds inland, on the Apalachicola River system, Moore concludes his 1903 report with the fact that these sites closely resemble those of the Gulf coast.

After Moore's work between the Suwannee River and Tampa Bay (1903), he drew some comparisons between the west coast and the northwest. He pointed out that no urn burials, no general deposits of earthenware found in blackened sand in mounds, no cranial flattening, no prefired "killed" pottery, and almost no pottery vessels modeled after life forms were found below the "bend" of the State. But west coast burial mounds were numerous and similar to those of the northwest. Pockets of calcined human bone in the mound were met with in both regions. The general ceramic pattern was much the same, with graceful incised and punctated pottery, some complicated stamped, and abundant check stamped. Finally, he notes, with surprise, the presence of solid copper artifacts well to the south.

THE CLASSIFICATORY STUDIES OF W. H. HOLMES

W. H. Holmes was the first man of considerable intellectual stature to bring his talents seriously to bear upon the problems of Florida Gulf Coast archeology. Not primarily a field investigator, nor a Florida area specialist, his impress has, nevertheless, been the greatest of any of those of his time upon the later generation of archeologists. Holmes worked with the artifact collections gathered by others, and his energies were chiefly directed toward injecting order into the great mass of ceramic materials that had been brought to the museums of Washington and Philadelphia. He was one of the first to visualize Florida prehistory as but a part of the larger fabric of the Indian past of the eastern United States. With him, Florida archeology, for the first time, moved away from a consideration of discrete phenomena toward a comprehension of broad categories of related phenomena.

In his introduction to the "Earthenware of Florida: Collections of Clarence B. Moore," an analysis of the Moore and other collections as of 1894, Holmes (1894a, p. 105) states:

> Exploration has not yet gone far enough on the peninsula of Florida to give archaeologists a firm grasp on the problems of its prehistoric art. The general nature and range of the remains are pretty well understood, as they form no

marked exception to the rule in this latitude, but little has been done in the study of those details that must be relied upon to assist in assigning the art remains to particular tribes and stocks of people, in correlating them with culture features of neighboring regions and determining questions of chronology.

By this, Holmes demonstrated a grasp of the essentials of: (1) archeological-tribal correlations; (2) correlations with other areas or extra-areal cross ties; and (3) culture chronology. To that time none of his predecessors or colleagues had equaled him in understanding, or in any event clearly formulating, these principles.

And again (Holmes, 1894a, p. 105) he pointed the way toward modern methods with:

It is on ceramic evidence perhaps more than any other that we must depend for the solution of problems of time, people and culture, and to this branch of investigation the most careful and painstaking attention must be given.

In both his Florida study and in his monumental "Aboriginal Pottery of the Eastern United States" (Holmes, 1903), Holmes stressed geographical groupings of ceramics. In defining these ceramic areas he considered it necessary to evaluate a number of characteristics or a complex of features which distinguished the ware of one such area from another. Form, temper, method of manufacture, and decoration were all taken into account. Nor was Holmes unsophisticated in his conception of the validity or usefulness of his major pottery provinces. He makes it quite clear that within a given area there might be pronounced ceramic diversity due to a number of complicating causes such as differences in culture period or the intermingling of different ethnic groups upon the same time horizon. Nor were the areas absolutely defined, for, as he says, "limitations of these varieties (in pottery), geographically or otherwise, are not well-marked, one grading imperceptibly into the others, features combining in such ways that many specimens occur that cannot be definitely assigned to any one of the groups" (Holmes, 1894a, p. 111). But the importance of this first step, difficult as it was, was indisputable, and Holmes did not hesitate to make it.

Along the Gulf in northwest Florida Holmes recognized three major ware groups: the "Mobile-Pensacola," the "Apalachicola," and the "Appalachian" (Holmes, 1903, pp. 104-114). The Mobile-Pensacola group was based upon the Parsons collections from the sand mound at Bear Point, Ala., on Perdido Bay, on the Moore collections from the same site, and on Moore's other collections from Choctawhatchee Bay. The vessels are well described and well illustrated, and the classificatory group is a good one. It is, essentially, the same material that makes up the Fort Walton Period ceramic complex. Holmes, however, had no chronological evidence to support his classification. He did, though, draw comparisons between the Mobile-Pensacola Ware group and the pottery of southern Alabama, of Tennessee, and of Mississippi. Similarities were demonstrated in vessel forms and decorations, particularly the skull and hand designs, eagle and rattlesnake designs, and the frog-effigy bowl. From the vantage of a more recent point of view, it is clear that Holmes visualized this ware group as the strongly Middle Mississippian and late Lower Mississippi Valley influenced styles which are outstanding along the western Gulf Coast. The Fort Walton, or Camp Walton, collections were also lumped by Holmes into the Mobile-Pensacola group. At Point Washington, a little farther east, he felt that there were significant differences between the predominantly three-lined incised styles of that site and the Mobile-Pensacola group as a whole; at the same time he recognized their very great similarities.

Between the Choctawhatchee Bay and the Apalachicola River he noted a lessening of Mobile-Pensacola Ware and an increase in what he called Apalachicola Ware.[5] This latter group is what is now considered as the Weeden Island ceramic complex. Holmes thought it peculiarly Floridian but showing interesting analogies to both the Caribbean Islands and Yucatán. He also observed the more immediate connection with the pottery from the Florida west coast site of Tarpon Springs or Safford which Cushing recovered. The presence of complicated stamped pottery in this section also helped to distinguish it from the Mobile-Pensacola-Choctawhatchee region. The inland Georgian affiliations of the complicated stamped pottery were appreciated by Holmes, but at the same time he was also puzzled by the design elements which were, to him, similar to those of the West Indies. In a separate paper (Holmes, 1894b), he advanced a hypothesis for West Indian-Southeast contact as expressed in the stamped pottery designs.

Concerning the Moore collections between St. Andrews Bay and Cedar Keys, Holmes felt that there was a gradual shading off from the pottery groups of west Florida into those of the peninsula. He is not very clear about this, probably because the relatively minor stylistic differences within the Weeden Island Complex are more difficult to synthesize and clearly point up than the sharp contrasts between the Mobile-Pensacola (Fort Walton) and the Apalachicola (Weeden

[5] This study was based in part on a collection from Gulf County given to the U. S. National Museum in 1893 by C. H. B. Lloyd. (U.S.N.M. Nos. 155318-155329.)

Island) groups. Holmes also was aware that pottery of the Mobile-Pensacola group was found all along the northwest coast and as far south as Tampa.

As indicated, the Holmes area classification of pottery still has significance for archeological research on the Florida Gulf. Some of the problems that bothered Holmes have been resolved in terms of period differences. Finer and more exact regional and subregional break-downs have been made in the Florida ceramic data. Extra-areal affiliations have come to be more clearly understood as a result of additional work both in and out of Florida. On the other hand, many of the questions raised by Holmes, such as the hints of Middle American or Caribbean resemblances, have not yet been explained to the satisfaction of the archeologist.

THE PROBLEM OF EARLY MAN IN GULF FLORIDA

As in most parts of the United States some claims for "Early" or Pleistocene man have been made for the Florida Gulf Coast. The status of these finds has never been completely settled, but the original materials and data were so sparse that proof for the occurrence of Early man on the west side of the Florida peninsula must await new finds.

In 1871 J. G. Webb, of Osprey, Fla., sent a number of human bones to the Smithsonian Institution accompanied by the data of their discovery. They had been found on Sarasota Bay and, presumably, were from intentional burials. They were uncovered at 3 to 4 feet below the surface and were imbedded in soft ferruginous rock. Subsequently, a number of other human bones were discovered and described from the same general region. Some of the outstanding scholars of the day visited the area, and in 1887 Angelo Heilprin, the geologist, published an account of human finds made at Hanson's Landing, Sarasota Bay. The remains of a human skeleton were observed exposed in a low bank of ferruginous sandstone along the shore. The human bone was fossilized, being completely replaced by limonite. Heilprin's attempts to correlate this sandstone bed in the geological scale were not successful, but he believed the bones to be inclusive in the bed and the whole to be of a great age. Joseph Leidy (1889), who was also interested in the Hanson's Landing discovery, pointed out that the bones did not differ from modern human bones but withheld comment on the geological evidence. A critical note on the geology was injected into the discussions, however, by W. H. Dall, writing in 1887. It was his contention that rock formation proceeded at a much more rapid rate in this part of Florida than was generally believed. The fact that the natural springs of the Sarasota region contained considerable iron in solution was held to be the cause of the consolidation of gravel, sand, and shells into a sort of rapid-forming pseudocoquina. Dall noted that a potsherd had been found imbedded in such a conglomeritic mass of material in a find made near an Indian shell mound on the Webb estate. It was his further observation that the human bone remains reported by Heilprin from nearby Hanson's Landing were encased in a similar formation and that they were of recent age.

Hrdlička tackled the problem of Early man in west Florida several years later (1907). After a careful description and analysis of finds from Osprey and Hanson's Landing he ruled out the possibilities of a Pleistocene or early dating. Somatologically, he pronounced all the remains to be American Indian. His critique of the geology, supported by a statement from the geologist T. Wayland Vaughan, follows that of Dall. He held that the skeletons were all recent Indian burials that had subsequently, and within a relatively short time, been covered and impregnated with ferruginous sediments.

That the bones are well within the range of those of American Indians does not surprise us in the light of more recent developments in Pleistocene and early postglacial archeology in North America. This is to be expected. The case of the Osprey bones appears to devolve upon the geological interpretation of the find situations. The fact that they were imbedded in stone was the single factor in bringing them to attention. No distinctive artifacts of any kind were found in association with any of the skeletal remains nor were there correlations with extinct fauna. The evidence and arguments adduced to date indicate that the rock formation surrounding the bones could have developed in a very short time. For the present, the claims for Early man in west Florida are unproved.

SUBSEQUENT WORK

Following the studies of Moore and Holmes there was no concerted field program on the Florida Gulf Coast until the beginning of the Federal Relief Archeological Projects in 1933, but a number of minor investigations were reported upon in the interim period. R. D. Wainwright described some miscellaneous diggings at Palma Sola, Sarasota, and on Bokeelia and Pine Islands at about the same time that Moore was concluding his work (Wainwright, 1916, 1918). In 1923-24 Dr. J. W. Fewkes, assisted by M. W. Stirling, excavated a burial mound at Weeden Island, on Tampa Bay, for the Bureau of American Ethnology. This Weeden Island investigation proved to be of considerable significance as it became the basic datum or the type site of the Weeden Island culture. A collection quite comparable to that which Cushing recovered from the Safford mound was acquired at Weeden Island (Fewkes, 1924). Shortly after the termination of the Weeden Island work, D. I. Bushnell made a brief survey of the Pinellas Peninsula and gathered a few surface specimens from several other sites in the same region (Anon., 1926). At the other end of the Gulf Coast, on Santa Rosa Sound, T. M. N. Lewis made excavations in a small burial mound located about 18 miles east of Pensacola (Lewis, 1931). Midway down the coast, near Crystal River, F. G. Rainey excavated what appeared to be a mound or cemetery on Buzzard's Island (Rainey, 1935).

In 1929 and 1930, several years before the Federal Relief Projects began, Stirling, as Chief of the Bureau of American Ethnology, returned to Florida and conducted a survey and series of small excavations at Palma Sola, Shaws Point, Horr's Island, on the Withlacoochee River, and at Safety Harbor (Stirling, 1930, 1931). The latter site on Old Tampa Bay has become, like Weeden Island, a type station for a culture complex and period. As a follow-up to these personally directed field surveys, Stirling then maintained over-all supervision of the Smithsonian Federal Relief excavations at Perico Island and on the Little Manatee River, both in Manatee County, at the Thomas mound in Hillsborough County, and at the Englewood mound, Sarasota County. The immediate field supervisors in this work were M. T. Newman, Preston Holder, and D. L. Reichard (Stirling, 1935). These Relief Program undertakings of the Smithsonian began in 1933 and were terminated in 1936. They are treated, along with the Weeden Island and Safety Harbor excavations, in the present paper under the section, "Excavations on the West Coast: 1923-1936."

After the Smithsonian withdrew from the field, the Florida State Board of Conservation continued Relief-financed archeology under the supervision of J. Clarence Simpson, of the Florida State Archaeological Survey. Simpson made additional excavations at the Thomas mound and also conducted work at the Spender, Cagnini, Branch, Lykes, Snavely, Jones, and Picknick mounds. Very brief notices of this work have been published in the Biennial Reports of the Florida State Board of Conservation (see Anon., 1937 and 1939a). As a byproduct of his archeological interests Simpson has published an interesting and useful little summary of sources of stone in the

Florida Gulf Coast area which were used by the Indians in the manufacture of both chipped and ground stone artifacts (see Anon., 1939b, and Simpson, 1941).

The present author and R. B. Woodbury made a surface survey and a number of stratigraphic tests in northwest Florida (Willey and Woodbury, 1942). This field work was done in 1940 and is reported on in full in this paper under "Excavations on the Northwest Coast: 1940." Following Stirling's lead, the emphasis in this survey was upon sequence determination of pottery styles, the relating of these sequences to neighboring areas and sequences, and the analysis and interpretation of previously excavated and published or unpublished data from the Gulf Coast.

A number of very recent surveys and test excavations have been made in the area. In 1946 J. G. Griffin and Hale G. Smith, working under the auspices of the Florida Park Service, conducted a quick survey along the northwest coast. This was done chiefly by way of examination of the area although surface collections were made at a number of sites. Griffin and Smith also made test diggings at the Lake Jackson site in Leon County and the Scott Miller place in Jefferson County (Smith, Hale G., 1948). Their findings at these sites should add much to the sketchy data presented in this paper on these two stations. As this report is being written Griffin is resurveying the important Safety Harbor site in Pinellas County and opening new test trenches in the mounds and middens of that group. In connection with Griffin's Park Service work it is hoped that R. P. Bullen will survey and study mound and village sites along the lower Chattahoochee River this coming winter (1948-49). Coextensive with Griffin's program, Dr. John M. Goggin made surface surveys at Cedar Keys, Shaws Point, on the Withlacoochee River, and in Alachua County during the summer of 1947. Goggin had made previous trips to some of these regions in 1944. During the present summer (1948), Dr. A. J. Waring, Jr., explored sites in Citrus County and tested a midden heap near the mouth of the Chassahowitzka River. This last site, from preliminary reports, may be one of the most significant in the archeology of the preceramic periods for Florida. The need for continued archeological research in Gulf Florida is recognized by all these men and others interested in the area (see Stubbs, 1940; Sleight, 1943). The establishment of a division of archeology within the Florida State Park Service (1946) and of a chair of anthropology at the State University at Gainesville (1948) indicate that present interests and research trends will be continued in good hands.

Mention should also be made of reference material in the way of numerous collections and a considerable correspondence from various interested persons, many of whom live along the Florida Gulf Coast. These individuals are referred to in various places throughout this report. Some of this correspondence is now in custody of the Smithsonian Institution and many of the collections are accessioned in the division of archeology, United States National Museum. Other significant collections of Gulf Coast materials are in the Heye Museum of the American Indian, Peabody Museum of Harvard University, Peabody Museum of Yale University, the R. S. Peabody Foundation of Andover, Mass., the University Museum of Ann Arbor, Mich., the University Museum of Philadelphia, and the Florida State Museum at Gainesville.

In addition to the actual field work, the period of 1918 to the present produced a number of summary and general papers on Florida archeology, all of which, to a greater or less degree, touch upon the Gulf Coast. Taken in chronological order, the first of these is Hrdlička's "Anthropology of Florida," published in 1922. This study was, in part, based upon a field trip which the author made in 1918 around the southern end of the Florida peninsula; but, in greater part, Hrdlička drew upon Moore's data and Moore's skeletal collections from the various Gulf Coast mounds. As a synthesis, the work is principally concerned with physical anthropology rather than archeology.

Another summary paper, but one more archeologically and ethnohistorically oriented, was published by Rhea M. Smith in 1933. This is a competent statement of what was known of Florida prehistory as of that date, although there is no attempt at synthesis or integration of the data into any scheme.

In 1936, as a result of the several seasons of field work along the Gulf, Stirling published his "Florida Cultural Affiliations in Relation to Adjacent Areas." This short paper defined what the author considered to be the four major cultural regions of the State in terms of pottery wares. The method is comparable to that used by Holmes; however, in addition to the trial definition of areas, Stirling also pointed to chronological relationships between two of the dominant pottery styles of the Gulf Coast, the earlier Weeden Island and the later Safety Harbor. This sequence relationship, the first for Florida in terms of described styles, was based upon associations rather than stratigraphy. Cross similarities between Safety Harbor and other late periods in nearby areas, such as Georgia, were established; and, in addition to this, the associations of European trade artifacts with

Safety Harbor sites, but never with Weeden Island sites, gave added proof of the chronological relationship between the two.

Other brief papers, following along similar lines, are those of the present author (Willey, 1945, 1948a), Goggin (1947b),[6] and J. W. Griffin (n. d.).

Going somewhat farther afield are the papers by Greenman (1938) and Willey and Phillips (1944) which treat of Gulf Coast prehistory in relation to other cultural manifestations outside of Florida, and the syntheses by Ford and Willey (1941), J. B. Griffin (1946), and Martin, Quimby, and Collier (1947) which attempt to place the Florida Gulf Coast in terms of the total chronological and developmental framework of the eastern United States. The same approach, but from another geographical quarter, is seen in the papers of Gower (1927), Rouse (1940), Stone (1939), and J. W. Griffin (1943), where the authors are interested in the problem of West Indian and Middle American influences into the Gulf Coast and other parts of Florida.

The trends in recent archeological research along the Florida Gulf have been in keeping with those of American archeology in general. In short, the definition of the details of culture complexes and the tracing of these through time and space have been the primary objectives. We are currently engrossed in this phase of prehistoric study in Gulf Florida, and as investigations progress it is possible to comprehend the local scene more satisfactorily against the larger background of eastern North America. At the same time, a new level of research effort is anticipated in that the archeologist will soon be in a position to go forward from the attained platform of time-space formulations toward an understanding of culture growth and process.

THE ETHNOHISTORICAL STUDIES OF JOHN R. SWANTON

As archeology in its most restricted sense gives us only a partial picture of culture history, a summary of the development of Florida prehistory would be incomplete without taking into account the important strides made in the ethnography and history of the region. This ethnohistoric material has been compiled and interpreted in able fashion by John R. Swanton. In his long and distinguished career

[6] Even more recently (spring 1948) Goggin (n. d. 2) has completed a Florida-wide summary treating with the relations of prehistoric cultures to their natural environment (Ph.D. thesis, Yale University).

in the field of Southeastern studies Swanton has consistently worked to bring clarity and integration out of a complex assortment of ethnohistoric and linguistic sources. His two principal researches that deal with the Gulf Coast area of Florida (Swanton, 1922, 1946) are works of critical scholarship. In Gulf Florida as in other parts of the Southeast Swanton's tracings of tribal movements during the sixteenth, seventeenth, and eighteenth centuries, his ethnographic descriptions, and his linguistic analyses have provided the starting points for the archeologists who are following him.

III. EXCAVATIONS ON THE NORTHWEST COAST: 1940

INTRODUCTION

In the summer of 1940 an archeological survey of the northwest coast of Florida was conducted by the writer assisted by R. B. Woodbury. These investigations were under the auspices of the Department of Anthropology, Columbia University, and were financed jointly by Columbia and by the National Park Service of the United

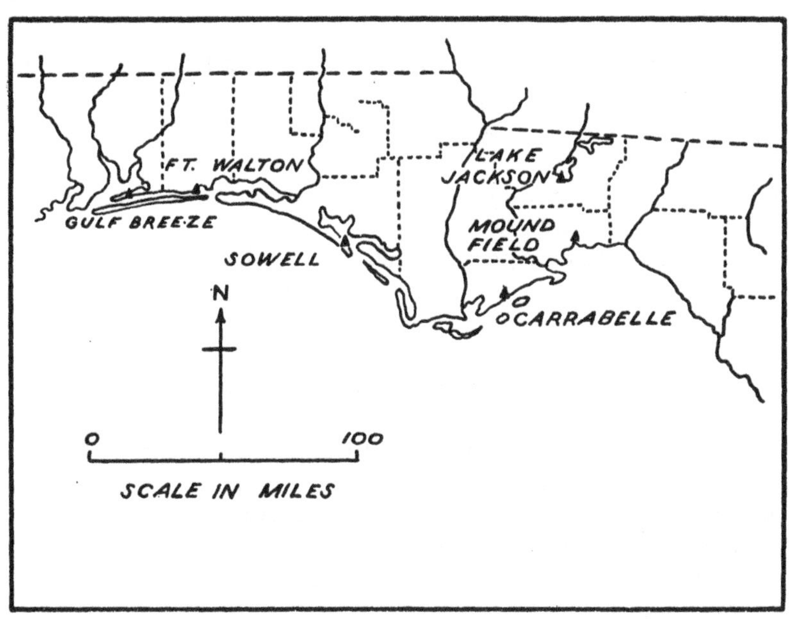

MAP 2.—The northwest Florida Coast, showing sites excavated in 1940.

States Department of the Interior. At that time both the writer and Woodbury were graduate students of anthropology at Columbia. Taking the field on the first of June, surface survey and test excavations were pursued until mid-August. In this 2½-month period 87 sites were visited and studied briefly in the region between Pensacola and St. Marks; 6 of these were excavated stratigraphically (see map 2). As it is these excavations on which the ceramic and cultural chronology of Gulf Florida is essentially established, the present section of this report demonstrates these several stratigraphies in some detail.[7]

Because of the crucial nature of this sequence data for the analyses and interpretations that are to follow, it is placed here, near the beginning of the report. The pottery types that are the principal media for measuring culture change through time, and that are listed only as names in the tabulations of sherd counts and percentages, are described in detail in connection with the cultural periods of which they are characteristic in a subsequent section of this report. Methodologically, this presentation is the reverse of the actual procedure of investigations. In making the survey, the analyses of Moore and Holmes, the ceramic chronologies outlined in neighboring areas, and the inferences to be drawn from a consideration of these were the first points of departure from which trial classifications and tentative groupings of the data were projected. These hypotheses were then checked by a seriation of the surface pottery collections from all the surveyed sites. The final substantiation and correction of the pottery periods and their chronological order were the test excavations which are presented here.

The excavations were primarily concerned with ceramic stratigraphy and test pits were laid out at each site with this in mind. Burial mounds and cemeteries were not excavated. No burials were discovered in any of the refuse digging, nor were any structural features, such as house floors, post-mold patterns, or house mounds uncovered or explored. A very few nonpottery artifacts, mostly chipped-stone projectile points or tools, were recovered from the stratigraphic tests. These were too scarce in any one excavation or in any one site to compute stratigraphic percentage trends. Together with similar artifacts gathered in the surface survey, they are identified as to period and incorporated in the several descriptions of the section on "The Culture Periods."

CARRABELLE, FRANKLIN COUNTY (FR-2)

Description of the site.—In his 1918 report Moore (pp. 557 ff.) describes what he calls an "Aboriginal Cemetery near Carrabelle":

> About 1.5 miles north-northeast from the town of Carrabelle, on the Gulf Coast, is a low ridge . . . covered with scrub and scattered pine, having its

[7] The principal type sherd collection, together with the nonceramic artifacts from the 1940 survey, are stored in the archeological laboratory, Department of Anthropology, Columbia University. The remainder of the materials are at the National Park Service Museum at Ocmulgee, Macon, Ga.

> eastern extremity almost enclosed by a small, shallow, fresh-water pond somewhat in the form of a horseshoe. This ridge is of white sand on the surface, darkened by vegetal deposit and the charcoal of fires that have spread over it. Below the white sand, which is from four inches to one foot in depth, is yellow sand of uniform shade.

Moore cut a trench through the east end of the ridge and discovered several deposits of whole and broken pottery on the yellow sand or in it. No material was found at a greater depth than 20 inches. The remains of two cremated human burials were also found in the yellow sand. No other human skeletal material was uncovered.

From this description, which is rather unlike any of the other sites that Moore explored along the Gulf Coast, it appears as though cremated burials and mortuary deposits of pottery, both broken and "killed" by perforation, were placed in the natural sand of the ridge at superficial depths. Possibly a low artificial sand mound was built over the burials, but this cannot be satisfactorily determined from Moore's data. That Moore was correct in his assumption that this site was a cemetery or burial place seems to be borne out by the absence of any amount of black detritus or shell-midden refuse.[8]

In the 1940 survey some test excavations were made at a midden site on the edge of the city of Carrabelle (map 3). At that time it was our opinion that the site which we excavated was not a part of, or near to, the site described by Moore (Willey and Woodbury, 1942, p. 238, footnote 45), but in again reviewing the notes it seems at least probable that our site and Moore's are the same. The site is about one-half mile from the present center of town in an easterly rather than a north-northeast direction. It is located on a low ridge about 75 meters back from the Gulf beach. The northeastern end of this ridge is surrounded by a swampy lowland, tallying in some respects with Moore's description of a "shallow, fresh-water pond somewhat in the form of a horseshoe." Because of modern development we were unable to excavate in the eastern or northeastern portions of the ridge; these are now house sites of a pleasant suburb. Fortunately, on the west side of the ridge, on the Keith property, there was a vacant area, and the northwest corner of the ridge was similarly unoccupied. Permission was obtained for excavations in these portions. Test digging here, as well as an examination of the banks of a railroad cut (see map 3) which has bisected the ridge, revealed abundant black earth and shell midden.

---

[8] See section on "Review and Analysis of Gulf Coast Sites," Carrabelle Site, pp. 267-268.

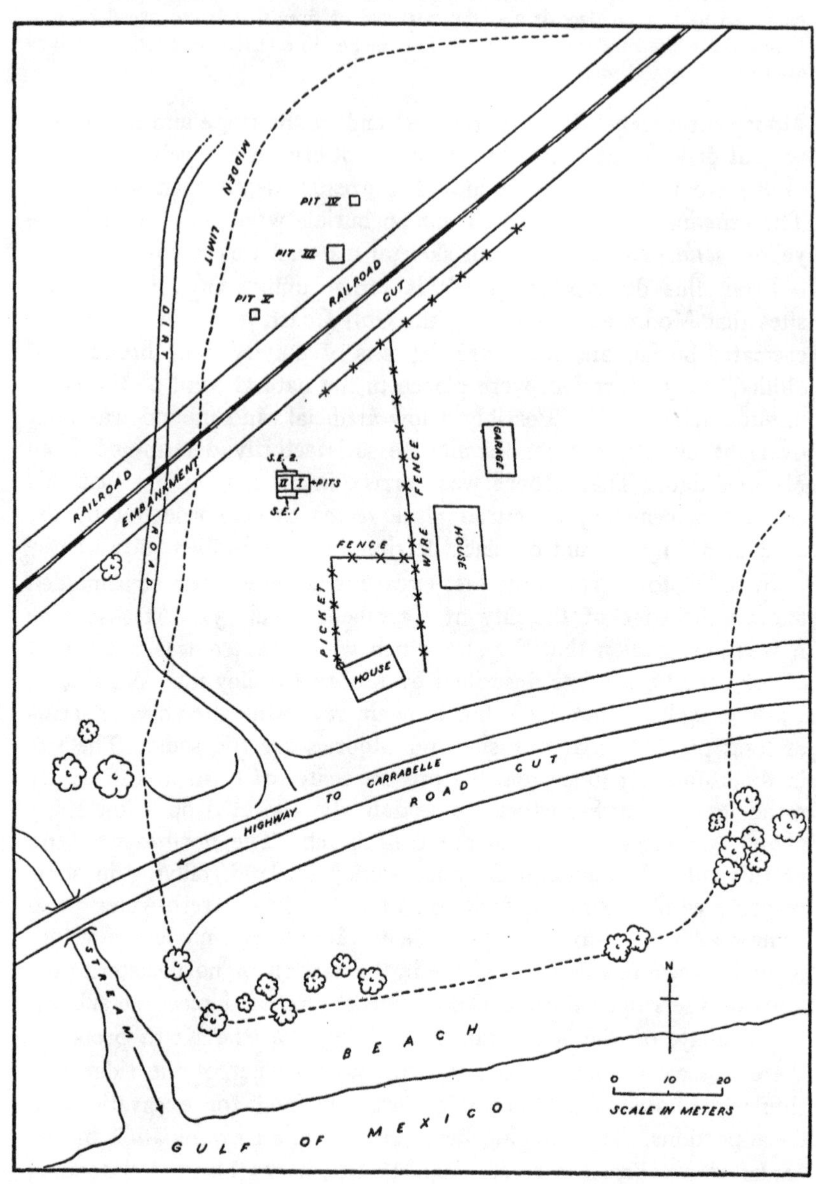

MAP 3.—The Carrabelle site, Franklin County (Fr-2).

The general conformation of the site accords with Moore's description, and it seems likely that Moore's direction of "north-northeast from the town" was in error. If the site was located on the Gulf beach, within 1 or 2 miles of the city, it could not possibly have been in a northerly direction, and the location which we visited is the most likely spot. The difference in the nature of the deposits which Moore encountered and those which we noted might well be due to the fact that his excavations were confined to the eastern or northeastern section of the ridge which had been reserved by the Indians as a burial place. Our observations and excavations, on the other hand, were contained within the old habitation ground.

The Carrabelle site, as it appears today, is situated on a ridge paralleling the beach for about 200 meters. The ridge is approximately 75 to 100 meters wide. It lies just above a paved subsidiary highway which connects as a small side loop with U. S. Highway 319. This highway cuts along the southern edge of the site, between the ridge and the beach, exposing shells, midden, and sherds. The modern houses referred to are built on the crest of the ridge, and back of the houses the railroad cut slices through the ridge on a northeast-southwest axis. In most places the refuse averages about 1 meter in thickness. On the western edge of the ridge the ground drops away rapidly to a small drainage which empties into the Gulf, passing first under a railroad bridge and then through a highway culvert. A little side road comes into the highway from the north, following along the west side of the ridge and coming up over one corner of it just before it joins the pavement.

The midden, shell, and sherds did not extend the full length of the ridge but occupied the western or southwestern half of it. Cultural debris was also found in the flat between the ridge and the beach, and some sherds were picked up as far away as the high-tide line (see map 3). A surface collection of pottery was gathered from the railroad banks, the highway cut, the beach flats, and the top of the ridge on both sides of the railroad excavation. The low, marshy area to the north and east of the ridge was covered with deep grass and other vegetation so that surface pottery would not have been visible; however, it is extremely unlikely that the site occupation ever extended down into this terrain. The sand ridge on which the site is located is an ancient dune formation rising above the surrounding lowlands. Several hundred years ago, at the time of Indian occupation, the surrounding marshes may have been flooded regularly by the tides. Even in more recent times, as Moore has remarked upon, water stood in the basin at one end of the ridge.

Excavations.—Tests pits I and II and the two supplementary excavations were put down in the vacant lot near the west end of the ridge. There is no record of modern building in this space, and the spoil dirt from the railroad excavations has not been thrown back over the banks but taken a few hundred meters farther to the west to serve as fill for a low gulley. All other indications were that the small western section where excavation was possible was an undisturbed deposit.

The four tests were dug contingently so that when the work was completed they formed one large excavation (see map 3). Pit I (a 3- x 3-meter pit) was oriented to the cardinal directions, and pit II was later excavated immediately to the west. The supplementary excavations 1 and 2 were made prior to the excavation of pit II, and they were for the purpose of exposing pit II as a stratigraphic block on the north and south as well as the east side. Both pits and both supplementary excavations were excavated by arbitrary 10-centimeter levels.

The first level of pit I (0–.10 meter) was composed of packed shell and very black midden with abundant sherds. In levels 2 and 3, down to .30 meter below the surface, the midden concentration lessened, but a gray, charcoal-stained sand continued to yield sherds. In level 4 (.30–.40 meter deep) there was a continued decrease in midden richness and color. Shells were scarcer although all types, including oysters, small clams, conchs, and scallops, were still found. At the bottom of this level small, dark organic concentrations remained in the southwest and northeast corners of the pit. The final level, 5, was excavated from .40 to .60 meter below the surface, and exhausted this refuse. The upper portion of the level was of gray sand, slightly stained with organic and charcoal color; the lower part of the level was clean red-brown loam, completely sterile except for a few shells. The southwest quadrant of the excavation was taken on down to .90 meter below the surface before closing the pit.

Supplementary excavation 1, on the south side of the isolated stratitest block that was to be pit II, was excavated in .10-meter levels down to .80 meter below the surface, a total of 8 levels. It differed from pit I only in that the midden and shell concentration at the top were a little deeper. Its surface dimensions were 1 meter north-south by 4 meters east-west. Supplementary excavation 2, on the north side of pit II, had the same surface dimensions as supplementary 1. Supplementary 2 was not as rich, and the last level, 6, yielded only one or two sherds. The excavation was continued to .80 meter, terminating in sterile red-brown loam.

Pit II (3 x 3 meters) was excavated to a depth of .80 meter, being removed in 8 levels. Carefully working in from the three sides which were exposed by pit I and the two supplementary excavations, the removal of the levels was well controlled and an accurate picture of the physical strata obtained (pl. 1, top). Soil conditions were very similar to those of pit I. Shell and midden concentration at the top gave way to midden-stained gray sand and finally to sterile loam.

Profiles of the faces of pit I and pit II are shown in figures 1 and 2. They may all be generalized as follows: a top stratum of hard-packed shell and black midden, varying from .10 to .30 meter in thickness; a secondary stratum of gray sand and midden; in some places, a third stratum of lighter gray sand with only a little organic coloring; and basal reddish sand or loam. There are a few intrusive pockets reaching from either the midden concentration or the gray, sandy midden into lower strata, but these are not numerous enough or do not appear to be large enough to have greatly churned the deposits. The dip and strike of the strata are slight although the various beds have small irregularities. The soil profiles are those of the average thin occupation site for the Florida coastal area. Packed debris has mixed with the natural gray top sand of the region and has stained the sand for several centimeters in depth. The pure rubbish concentration is a small band at the top.

Test pits III, IV, and V were all located on the north side of the railroad cut in a small grove of trees. On this side of the tracks there is no present-day occupation. All pits were put down in the crown of the slope in the deepest part of the refuse. Pit III (a 3- x 3-meter pit) (see map 3) was excavated down to .80 meter below the surface, each level .10 meter in depth. The top level (0-.10 meter) had very little shell, a number of sherds, and consisted of brownish midden mixed with humus. Levels 2, 3, and 4, down to .40 meter deep, passed through black midden rich in sherds but with only scattered shells. At the bottom of level 5 (.40-.50 meter deep) thick shell deposits were mixed with the black midden, and a fire area was noted. Shell continued through level 6 (.50-.60 meter deep) but diminished in level 7 (.70-.80 meter deep). In the bottom level (.70-.80 meter deep) there was little shell and few sherds. The bottom of the pit showed clean gray sand dotted with a few organic spots which might possibly be post molds. A small additional test revealed that red-brown sand underlay the gray sand at a depth of .90 to 1 meter (see fig. 3).

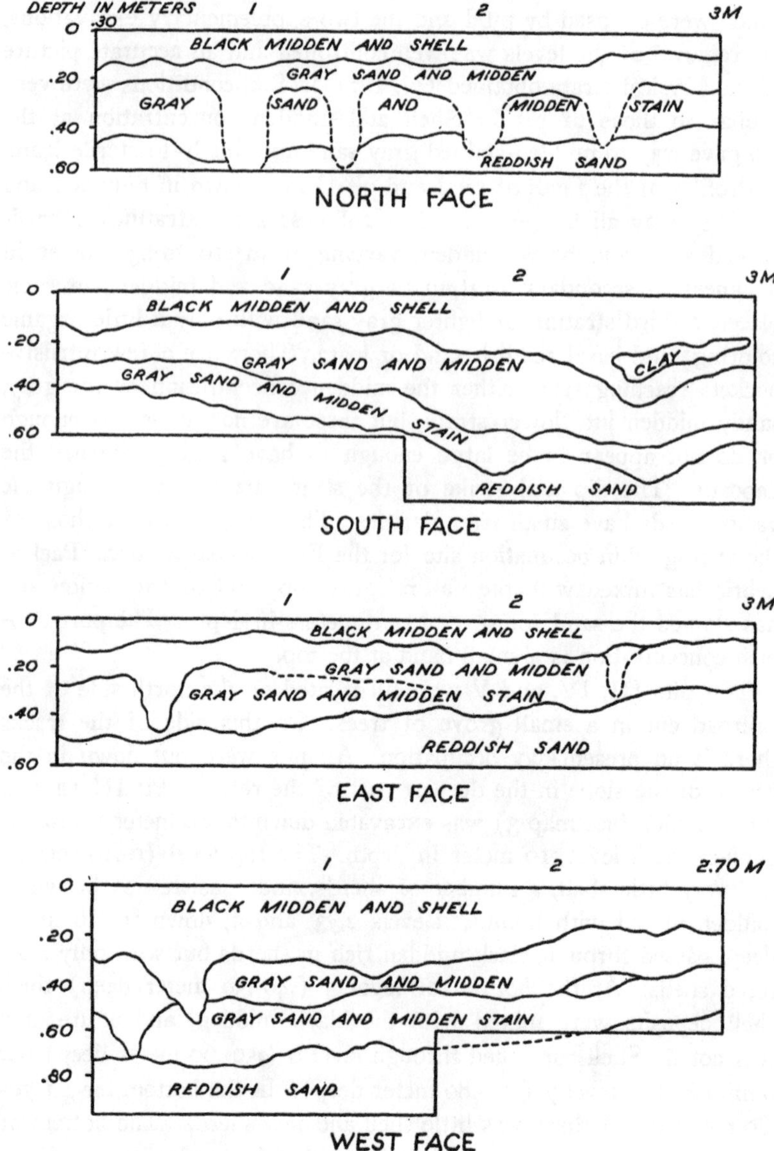

FIG. 1.—Pit I soil profiles, Carrabelle (Fr-2).

Pit IV was a small (1.50 x 1.50 meters) test made just a few meters to the northeast of pit III. Levels 1 to 6 (0-.60 meter deep) penetrated mixed rich black midden and shell with the shell being slightly more concentrated toward the bottom of this zone. Level 7 was made 20 centimeters deep, going from .60 to .80 meter, and in this level gray

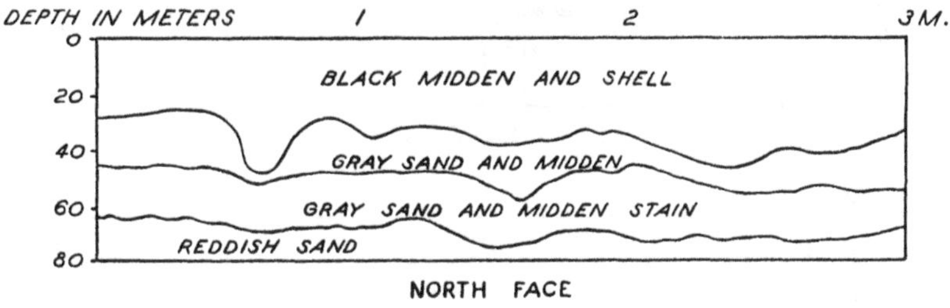

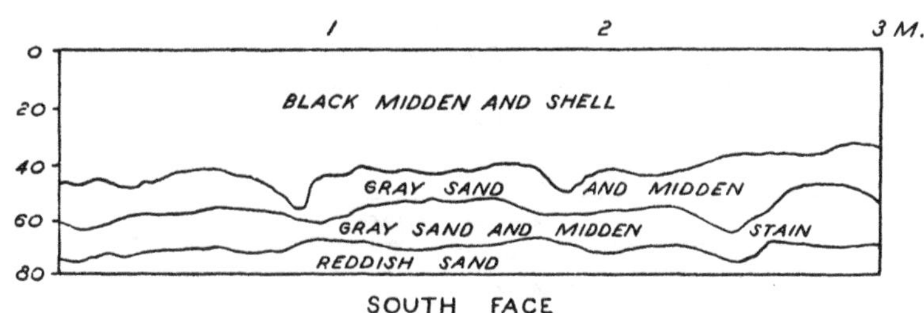

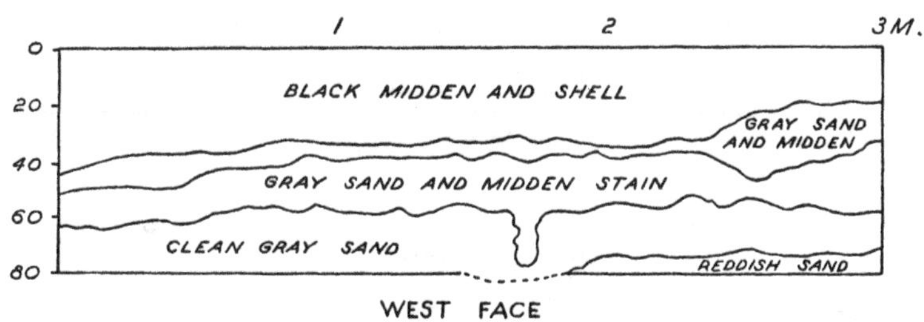

FIG. 2.—Pit II soil profiles, Carrabelle (Fr-2).

sand began to replace midden and shell. The pit ran out into sterile sand in level 8 (.80-1.00 meter deep).

Pit V, another 1.50- x 1.50-meter test pit, was located about 25 meters south and west of pit III. The refuse at this point was exhausted at the bottom of the 6th level (.50-.60 meter deep). Sherds were plentiful except in the bottom level. There were almost no shells in the pit. A brown midden and humus was slightly less than .30

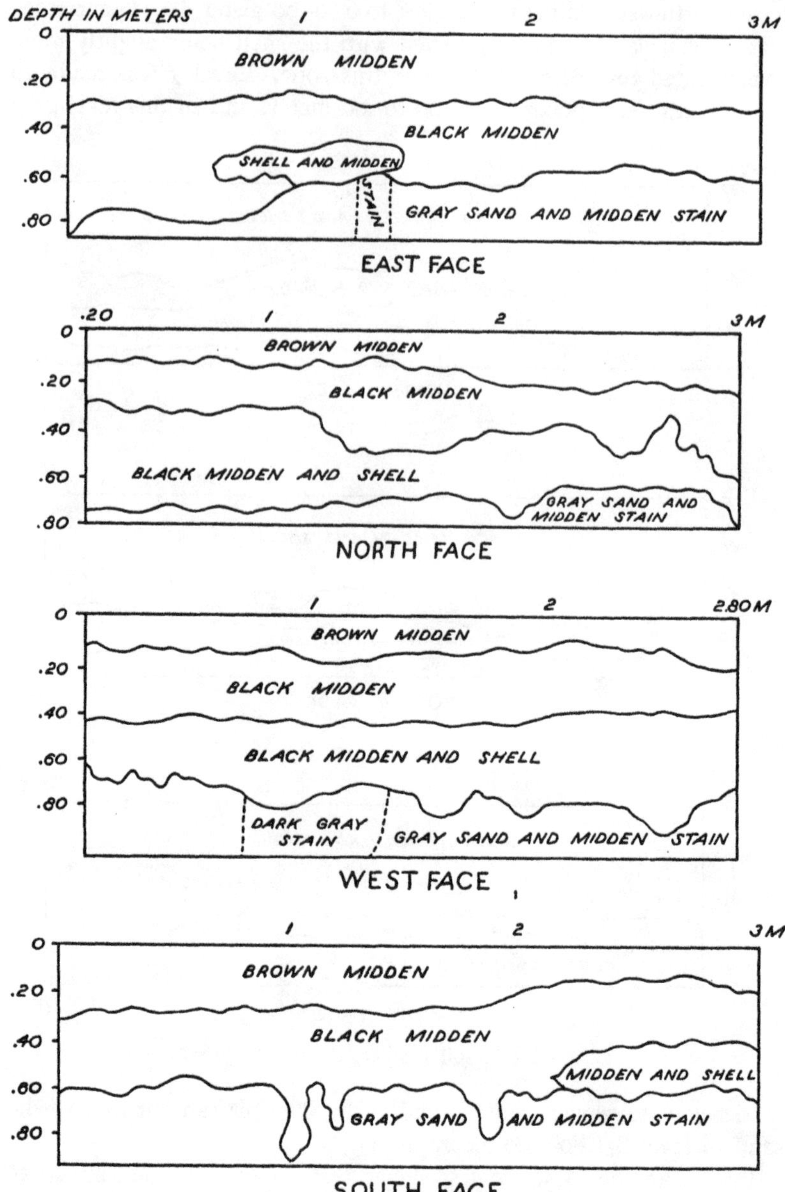

FIG. 3.—Pit III soil profiles, Carrabelle (Fr-2).

meter deep; black midden extended from here to the .50-meter point and gradually shaded off into gray and then reddish sand.

The soil profiles on the north side of the railroad track differ from those on the south side in that the midden concentration is deeper and can be divided into an upper brownish zone and a lower black zone. Shells, though not as abundant as they are in the top two levels of the pits south of the railroad are fairly plentiful in the lower portion of the black midden zone. Below the midden and shell there is a zone of gradual transition from the dark occupation layer to the natural sand of the ridge. (See fig. 3 for profiles of pit III.) As in pits I and II, there is nothing in the profiles of pits III, IV, and V to indicate an interval of nonoccupation for this part of the site.

Stratigraphy.—In pits I, II, and the supplementary excavations there is a marked complementary relationship in the vertical distribution of the pottery types. This is keynoted by the two types, Swift Creek Complicated Stamped and Deptford Linear Check Stamped. (See tables 1 and 2 and the graphs on fig. 4.) In pits I and II, Swift Creek Complicated Stamped is 40 percent of the total number of sherds for the top levels. There is a gradual diminution of the type toward the bottom of both pits. In pit I Swift Creek does not occur in the two bottom levels, and in pit II it occurs in those levels only in very small quantity. Deptford Linear Check Stamped, on the other hand, shows a numerical and percentage increase in the bottom levels of both pits. Compared to Swift Creek, there are not, proportionately, many Deptford sherds in either pit. It is extremely significant that those few which are present should be, with few exceptions, in the lower levels. The supplementary excavations show approximately the same percentage changes in this regard as the test pits.

Occurring in small percentages in the same levels as the Swift Creek Complicated Stamped are three other complicated stamped types: Crooked River Complicated Stamped, New River Complicated Stamped, and St. Andrews Complicated Stamped. On the whole, their sporadic distribution in the various levels seems to indicate their temporal affinity to Swift Creek. Typologically, they are also more closely related to the family of complicated stamped wares rather than to the Deptford pottery. The supplementary excavation 1, vaguely suggests that New River Complicated Stamped is a little earlier than the other two.

Paralleling the vertical distribution of Deptford Linear Check Stamped is Deptford Bold Check Stamped. This is best shown in pit II. However, the other pits show Deptford Bold as being well

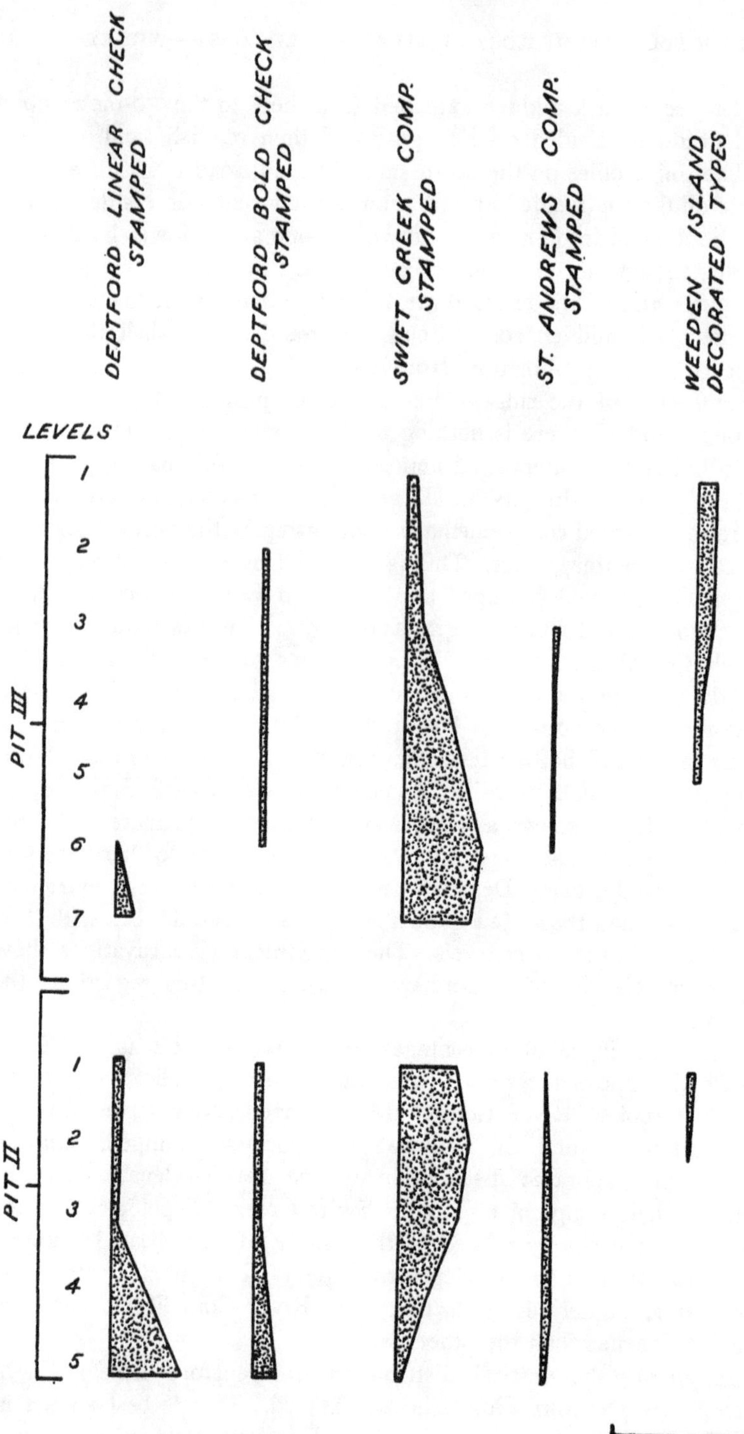

FIG. 4.—Graph on pottery stratigraphy, pits II and III, Carrabelle (Fr-2).

TABLE 1.—*Sherd classification of pits I and II, Carrabelle (Fr-2)*

(Percentage occurrence by level given in italics)

Levels	Weeden Island Plain	Weeden Island Incised	Carrabelle Punctated	Swift Creek Complicated Stamped	Crooked River Complicated Stamped	New River Complicated Stamped	St. Andrews Complicated Stamped	Franklin Plain	Gulf Check Stamped	West Florida Cord-marked	Deptford Linear Check Stamped	Deptford Bold Check Stamped	Deptford Simple Stamped	St. Simons Plain	Smooth Plain	Residual Plain	Unclassified	Total sherds by level
Pit I, Carrabelle																		
1	1	....	....	116	5	....	2	6	2	2	1	1	1	....	13	82	....	....
	.004	....	....	*.487*	*.021*	....	*.008*	*.025*	*.008*	*.008*	*.004*	*.004*	*.004*	....	*.054*	*.344*	....	238
2	....	....	....	46	4	1	3	1	1	....	1	3	1	....	7	32	3	....
	....	....	....	*.446*	*.038*	*.009*	*.029*	*.009*	*.009*	....	*.009*	*.029*	*.009*	....	*.067*	*.307*	*.029*	103
3	....	....	....	3	2	3	4	....	1	1	13	2	....	....	5	9	2	....
	....	....	....	*.066*	*.044*	*.066*	*.088*	....	*.022*	*.022*	*.288*	*.044*	....	....	*.111*	*.20*	*.044*	45
4	....	....	....	....	1	....	....	....	2	....	5	....	....	....	....	....	1	....
	....	....	....	....	*.111*	....	....	....	*.222*	....	*.555*	....	....	....	....	....	*.111*	9
5	....	....	....	....	....	....	....	....	1	....	11	3	1	1	....	....	4	....
	....	....	....	....	....	....	....	....	*.047*	....	*.523*	*.142*	*.046*	*.047*	....	....	*.190*	21
																Pit total		416
Pit II, Carrabelle																		
1	4	1	2	208	11	2	1	3	2	1	2	8	....	....	12	257	13	....
	.007	*.001*	*.039*	*.394*	*.020*	*.003*	*.001*	*.005*	*.003*	*.001*	*.003*	*.015*	....	....	*.022*	*.487*	*.024*	527
2	2	1	....	118	5	....	4	4	2	....	3	4	....	1	14	73	6	....
	.008	*.004*	....	*.497*	*.021*	....	*.016*	*.016*	*.008*	....	*.012*	*.016*	....	*.004*	*.059*	*.308*	*.025*	237
3	....	....	....	36	6	1	3	2	....	....	....	1	....	....	5	27	11	....
	....	....	....	*.391*	*.065*	*.010*	*.032*	*.021*	....	....	....	*.010*	....	....	*.054*	*.293*	*.119*	92
4	....	....	....	21	3	....	4	....	3	2	19	10	1	....	....	23	7	....
	....	....	....	*.228*	*.032*	....	*.043*	....	*.032*	*.021*	*.206*	*.108*	*.01*	....	....	*.239*	*.076*	92
5	....	....	....	3	2	3	1	....	3	....	37	12	....	....	1	5	2	....
	....	....	....	*.043*	*.029*	*.043*	*.014*	....	*.043*	....	*.536*	*.173*	....	....	*.014*	*.072*	*.029*	69
6	....	....	....	1	....	....	....	....	....	....	3	1	....	....	....	....	....	....
	....	....	....	*.20*	....	....	....	....	....	....	*.60*	*.20*	....	....	....	....	....	5
																Pit total		1,022

TABLE 2.—*Sherd classification of supplementary excavations 1 and 2, Carrabelle (Fr-2)*

(Percentage occurrence by level given in italics)

Levels	Weeden Island Plain	Weeden Island Incised	Swift Creek Complicated Stamped	Crooked River Complicated Stamped	New River Complicated Stamped	St. Andrews Complicated Stamped	Santa Rosa Stamped	Franklin Plain	Gulf Check Stamped	West Florida Cord-marked	Deptford Linear Check Stamped	Deptford Bold Check Stamped	Deptford Simple Stamped	St. Simons Plain	Smooth Plain	Residual Plain	Unclassified	Total sherds by level
Supplementary excavation 1, Carrabelle																		
1	3 *.021*	....	54 *.394*	3 *.021*	....	2 *.014*	....	....	....	....	3 *.021*	3 *.021*	....	....	3 *.021*	64 *.467*	2 *.014*	137
2	....	2 *.028*	32 *.47*	....	....	1 *.014*	....	....	1 *.014*	....	1 *.014*	....	....	....	2 *.028*	28 *.411*	1 *.014*	68
3	....	....	37 *.493*	1 *.013*	....	1 *.013*	....	2 *.026*	....	....	2 *.026*	8 *.106*	....	....	....	23 *.306*	1 *.013*	75
4	....	....	33 *.471*	....	1 *.014*	....	....	....	....	1 *.014*	5 *.071*	3 *.042*	....	....	2 *.028*	25 *.357*	....	70
5	....	....	9 *.30*	....	1 *.033*	....	....	1 *.033*	....	1 *.033*	12 *.40*	3 *.099*	1 *.033*	....	....	2 *.066*	....	30
6	....	....	3 *.130*	....	4 *.173*	....	1 *.043*	....	....	....	7 *.304*	5 *.217*	....	....	....	....	3 *.130*	23
7	....	....	2 *.25*	....	2 *.25*	....	....	....	1 *.125*	....	....	1 *.125*	....	....	....	2 *.25*	....	8
8	....	....	1 *.333*	....	....	....	....	....	....	....	1 *.333*	1 *.333*	....	....	....	....	....	3
																Pit total		414
Supplementary excavation 2, Carrabelle																		
1	1 *.009*	1 *.009*	55 *.540*	....	1 *.009*	1 *.009*	....	2 *.018*	....	....	2 *.018*	3 *.027*	....	....	3 *.027*	36 *.33*	4 *.036*	109
2	....	....	38 *.641*	....	....	....	....	3 *.048*	....	....	....	1 *.016*	....	....	2 *.032*	15 *.254*	....	59
3	....	....	8 *.38*	....	....	....	....	1 *.047*	....	....	3 *.141*	2 *.094*	....	....	....	7 *.333*	....	21
4	....	....	6 *.107*	....	....	....	....	....	19 *.333*	....	14 *.25*	6 *.107*	1 *.017*	....	1 *.017*	6 *.107*	3 *.054*	56
5	....	....	2 *.333*	....	....	....	....	....	2 *.333*	....	1 *.166*	1 *.166*	....	....	....	....	....	6
6	....	....	....	....	....	....	....	....	1 *.20*	....	....	....	....	2 *.40*	....	2 *.40*	....	5
																Pit total		256

scattered throughout the pits from top to bottom and not showing the high frequency for the lower levels as is the case with Deptford Linear.

Gulf Check Stamped seems to occur sporadically and at all depths except in supplementary excavation 2 where it occurs only in the three bottom levels. West Florida Cord-marked and Deptford Simple Stamped are found occasionally in these pits, but neither type is numerically strong enough to give any patterning of occurrence by levels. Four sherds of St. Simon's Fiber-tempered Plain appeared, three of these in the lowest levels of pit I and supplementary excavation 2. A single fragment of the distinctive type Santa Rosa Stamped came from level 6, a little over halfway to the bottom of supplementary excavation 1.

In both supplementary excavations, and one of the test pits, scatterings of Weeden Island Plain, Weeden Island Incised and related incised and punctated types were found in the topmost levels. Smooth Plain and Franklin Plain were also found toward the top but were not quite as superficial as the Weeden Island types. Residual (sand-tempered) Plain was found in all levels, but it definitely had its highest frequency at the top and faded toward the bottom.

Pits III, IV, and V, on the north side of the railroad cut, averaged a much greater number of sherds per excavation than pits I and II and the supplementary excavations. The midden being somewhat deeper undoubtedly accounts for part of this, but as pits III, IV, and V are all in Weeden Island Period refuse, the greater abundance of pottery in this later period is also a factor. In examining the pottery count data (tables 3 and 4 and graphs on fig. 4) for these excavations one is struck with the complete absence of Deptford Linear Check Stamped, the marker type for the Deptford Period, and the only occasional presence of Deptford Bold Check Stamped. Swift Creek Complicated Stamped is found in all levels of all pits, and maintains an inverse and complementary frequency relationship to Weeden Island Plain, Weeden Island Incised, Carrabelle Incised, Carrabelle Punctated, Tucker Ridge-pinched, Keith Incised, and Indian Pass Incised, all types of the Weeden Island Period.

Smooth Plain is found in almost all levels with some indication of its being a little more common in the upper than in the lower part of the midden. Residual Plain follows the same trend as in pits I and II, increasing toward the top. In the Weeden Island levels of pits III and IV this is more marked than it was in the Swift Creek Period levels of pits I and II. Residual Plain is 60 to 70 percent of the total sherds for the top three levels of pits III, IV, and V.

TABLE 3.—*Sherd classification of pits III and IV, Carrabelle (Fr-2)*

(Percentage occurrence by level given in italics)

Levels	Weeden Island Plain	Weeden Island Incised	Carrabelle Incised	Carrabelle Punctated	Keith Incised	Indian Pass Incised	Tucker Ridge-pinched	Swift Creek Complicated Stamped	Crooked River Complicated Stamped	St. Andrews Complicated Stamped	Basin Bayou Incised	Franklin Plain	Gulf Check Stamped	West Florida Cord-marked	Mound Field Net-marked	Deptford Linear Check Stamped	Deptford Bold Check Stamped	Smooth Plain	Plain Red	Residual Plain	Unclassified	Total sherds by level
Pit III, Carrabelle																						
1	15	14	....	7	1	3	....	7	....	....	....	....	....	....	....	....	....	....	....	181	....	228
	.065	*.061*	....	*.030*	*.004*	*.013*	....	*.030*	....	....	....	....	....	....	....	....	....	....	....	*.792*	....	....
2	33	21	14	11	....	3	....	39	....	....	....	....	....	6	2	....	1	45	1	267	1	444
	.074	*.047*	*.031*	*.024*	....	*.006*	....	*.087*	....	....	....	....	....	*.013*	*.004*	....	*.002*	*.101*	*.002*	*.601*	*.002*	....
3	32	21	7	25	2	3	1	60	....	2	....	1	....	....	....	....	2	18	1	348	6	529
	.058	*.038*	*.013*	*.046*	*.003*	*.005*	*.001*	*.112*	....	*.003*	....	*.001*	....	....	....	....	*.003*	*.033*	*.001*	*.650*	*.010*	....
4	4	4	....	1	....	1	....	72	....	1	....	....	....	....	....	....	2	7	1	151	....	244
	.016	*.016*	....	*.004*	....	*.004*	....	*.295*	....	*.004*	....	....	....	....	....	....	*.008*	*.028*	*.004*	*.618*	....	....
5	84	1	1	1	....	....	....	158	....	3	2	....	....	....	....	2	1	*.5*	....	128	2	....
	.215	*.002*	*.002*	*.002*	....	....	....	*.407*	....	*.007*	*.005*	....	....	....	....	*.005*	*.002*	*.012*	....	*.329*	*.005*	388
6	5	....	....	....	....	....	....	94	....	2	....	....	....	....	....	....	3	7	1	54	....	....
	.03	....	....	....	....	....	....	*.566*	....	*.012*	....	....	....	....	....	....	*.018*	*.042*	*.006*	*.325*	....	166
7	....	....	....	....	....	....	....	8	....	....	....	....	....	....	....	2	....	1	....	6	....	....
	....	....	....	....	....	....	....	*.47*	....	....	....	....	....	....	....	*.117*	....	*.058*	....	*.352*	....	17
8	....	....	....	....	....	....	....	2	....	....	....	....	1	....	....	....	....	....	....	2	....	5
	....	....	....	....	....	....	....	*.40*	....	....	....	....	*.20*	....	....	....	....	....	....	*.40*	....	....
																				Pit total	....	2,021
Pit IV, Carrabelle																						
1	19	12	2	9	1	....	4	24	....	....	....	....	....	....	....	....	....	24	3	200	....	298
	.063	*.04*	*.006*	*.033*	*.003*	....	*.013*	*.08*	....	....	....	....	....	....	....	....	....	*.08*	*.013*	*.671*	....	....
2	7	1	....	3	....	....	4	3	....	....	....	....	....	....	....	....	....	3	2	65	....	88
	.079	*.011*	....	*.034*	....	....	*.045*	*.034*	....	....	....	....	....	....	....	....	....	*.034*	*.022*	*.738*	....	....
3	6	....	4	5	....	....	3	24	....	3	....	....	1	....	....	....	1	....	1	108	1	....
	.036	....	*.024*	*.03*	....	....	*.018*	*.146*	....	*.018*	....	....	*.006*	....	....	....	*.006*	....	*.006*	*.658*	*.006*	164
4	1	....	....	1	....	....	....	45	....	1	....	....	....	....	....	....	1	5	....	51	1	106
	.009	....	....	*.009*	....	....	....	*.42*	....	*.009*	....	....	....	....	....	....	*.009*	*.046*	....	*.476*	*.009*	....
5	1	....	....	....	....	....	....	36	....	2	....	....	....	....	....	....	....	3	....	38	....	80
	.012	....	....	....	....	....	....	*.45*	....	*.025*	....	....	....	....	....	....	....	*.037*	....	*.475*	....	....
6	1	....	....	....	....	....	....	27	....	1	....	....	....	....	....	....	1	1	....	19	....	50
	.02	....	....	....	....	....	....	*.54*	....	*.02*	....	....	....	....	....	....	*.02*	*.02*	....	*.38*	....	....
7	....	....	....	....	....	....	....	56	....	3	....	....	....	....	....	....	....	6	....	35	....	100
	....	....	....	....	....	....	....	*.56*	....	*.03*	....	....	....	....	....	....	....	*.06*	....	*.35*	....	....
8	....	....	....	....	....	....	....	14	1	1	....	....	....	....	....	....	....	3	....	6	....	25
	....	....	....	....	....	....	....	*.56*	*.04*	*.04*	....	....	....	....	....	....	....	*.12*	....	*.24*	....	....
																				Pit total	....	911

Of the Complicated Stamped types, other than Swift Creek, that were seen in pits I, II, and the supplementary excavations, only St. Andrews Complicated Stamped is found in pits III and IV. In neither pit is it found in the two upper levels. Six West Florida Cord-marked and two Mound Field Net-marked sherds are in level 2 of pit III, but no others of these types appear.

The generalizations involving ceramic sequence that can be made from the Carrabelle excavations are these: In the group of pits south of the railroad cut (pits I, II, and supplementary excavations 1 and 2) Deptford Linear Check Stamped, in rather small amounts, underlies, and is earlier than, the main bulk of the Swift Creek Complicated Stamped type. Occurring in small amounts, Deptford

TABLE 4.—*Sherd classification of pit V, Carrabelle (Fr-2)*

(Percentage occurrence by level given in italics)

Levels	Weeden Island Plain	Weeden Island Incised	Carrabelle Incised	Carrabelle Punctated	Swift Creek Complicated Stamped	Deptford Bold Check Stamped	Smooth Plain	Residual Plain	Unclassified	Total sherds by level
1	2	2	....	1	10	....	....	47	....	62
	.032	*.032*	....	*.016*	*.161*	....	....	*.758*	....	....
2	2	2	1	1	4	....	....	29	....	39
	.051	*.051*	*.025*	*.075*	*.102*	....	....	*.743*	....	....
3	9	2	....	6	11	2	....	84	1	115
	.077	*.017*	....	*.052*	*.095*	*.017*	....	*.730*	*.008*	....
4	5	2	....	....	25	....	1	41	....	74
	.067	*.027*	....	....	*.337*	....	*.013*	*.546*	....	....
5	....	....	....	....	14	....	2	15	2	33
	....	....	....	....	*.424*	....	*.060*	*.454*	*.060*	....
6	....	....	....	....	5	....	1	5	....	11
	....	....	....	....	*.454*	....	*.090*	*.454*	....	....
								Pit total		334

Linear Check Stamped and Deptford Bold Check Stamped are found in most all levels of all excavations. There is a suggestion that Deptford Bold Check Stamped has a longer range upward in time than Deptford Linear Check Stamped. Also, Deptford Bold has an earlier inception than any of the Complicated Stamped types. Three complicated stamped types, Crooked River, New River, and St. Andrews, are contemporary with Swift Creek in pits I and II and related excavations.

In the group of pits north of the railroad track (pits III, IV, and V) Weeden Island types are superimposed upon Swift Creek types in much the same fashion that Swift Creek overlies Deptford in the southern excavations. Of the minority types, New River and Crooked River Complicated Stamped do not occur in the northern group of pits. St. Andrews Complicated Stamped does occur, as does Deptford Bold Check Stamped. As there is little doubt that the rubbish sectioned by the northern pits is later than that of the southern pits, there is an inference here that St. Andrews Complicated Stamped is slightly later than New River or Crooked River Complicated Stamped. Also, Deptford Bold Check Stamped has a clearly later time range than Deptford Linear Check Stamped. Conversely, Gulf Check Stamped, of which only one sherd occurs in the northern group of pits and that in a bottom level, would seem to be temporally related to the Deptford Period and the earlier half of Swift Creek.

Franklin Plain belongs almost entirely to the earlier half of the Swift Creek Period. Smooth Plain is late Swift Creek and Weeden Island in time; and Residual Plain steadily increases from almost no occurrences in the Deptford Period to a numerically predominant position in Weeden Island. The position of West Florida Cord-marked and Mound Field Net-marked pottery is indefinite, but the small amounts found seem to be later than the Deptford Period.

Although Fort Walton and Wakulla Check Stamped sherds were found in the surface collection from this site, none were recovered from the excavation.

Classification of surface sherds from Carrabelle

Fort Walton Complex	
Fort Walton Series:	
Fort Walton Incised	6
Lake Jackson Plain	2
Safety Harbor Incised	1
Weeden Island Complex	
Weeden Island Series:	
Weeden Island Incised	13
Weeden Island Plain	43
Carrabelle Incised	11
Carrabelle Punctated	16
Keith Incised	5
Indian Pass Incised	2
Wakulla Check Stamped	15
Santa Rosa-Swift Creek Complex	
Complicated Stamped Series:	
Swift Creek Complicated Stamped	125
Crooked River Complicated Stamped	1
St. Andrews Complicated Stamped	9
Gulf Check Stamped	8
West Florida Cord-marked	2
Franklin Plain	1

Deptford Complex

Deptford Series:	
Deptford Linear Check Stamped	8
Deptford Bold Check Stamped	15
Deptford Simple Stamped	6
Miscellaneous	
Plain Red	5
Smooth Plain	10
Residual Plain	325
Indeterminate stamped	21
Other unclassified	1
Total sherds	651

MOUND FIELD, WAKULLA COUNTY (WA-8)

Description of the site.—Mound Field is located in the southeastern section of Wakulla County, 2.7 miles inland from the small beach settlement of Shell Point (map 2). The region is sparsely populated, heavily grown with scrub oak and pine, and the midden and mound are difficult to find without a local guide. The shell midden is situated on a small rise of ground in a swamp (pl. 2, bottom). Sherds, shells, and black organic matter cover most of the eminence which is approximately 100 x 200 meters in extent. A few holes, dug within the last 2 or 3 years, indicated the depth and richness of the deposit. A surface collection was gathered from around these old excavations and elsewhere on the midden.

On another rise in the swamp, some 50 meters from the occupation area, was a sand mound which had been excavated by Moore during his survey of this part of the northwest coast. In 1902 he described the site as follows (pp. 306 ff.):

> The mound, very symmetrical, was in hammock land on the border of cultivated ground known throughout the region as the Mound Field.
>
> The mound had a height of about 9 feet above the surrounding level, though a measurement taken when the mound was in process of demolition, from the summit plateau, to undisturbed sand at the base, gave an altitude of about 11 feet.
>
> The outline of the base was circular, with a diameter of 61 feet. Across the summit plateau was 15 feet. A graded way about 15 feet wide joined the mound on the west, making the slope less steep on that side than on the others. The length of the causeway before union with the margin of the mound was 18 feet.

Upon excavation Moore found several burials and a large mortuary deposit of pottery in the east side of the mound.[9] Moore does not record excavations in the midden site, nor does he mention it.

[9] See section on "Review and Analysis of Gulf Coast Sites," Mound Field site, p. 294.

Excavations.—Test pit I was located just north of the wagon-track road by which it was possible, in dry weather, to take a car into the midden site (see map 4). Excavation of the 3- x 3-meter pit was by 10-centimeter levels. The first .20 meter was brown midden and humus, slightly sandy and intersected by occasional small roots from nearby bushes. Sherds were numerous in these top levels. Animal and fish bones were abundant in level 2 (.10-.20 meter deep).

In level 3 (.20-.30 meter deep) a fire area appeared in the center of the pit, shell was abundant, and animal and fish bones came out in large quantities. Root disturbance had completely disappeared. As in levels 1 and 2, this level yielded a great many sherds. Level 4 (.30-.40 meter deep) carried the pit down through a fire and ash area. The color of the midden, though still brownish, was darker at this depth and the shell content increased. Level 5 (.40-.50 meter deep) continued with ample sherds and increasing shell. As in level 4, the midden continued dark, almost black. Animal and fish bones were about as common in levels 4 and 5 as above.

Levels 6 and 7 (.50-.70 meter deep) were much alike in appearance and sherd yield. Both showed more shell and sand than the levels above, and the number of sherds from each was about the same. In level 8 (.70-.80 meter deep) sherds were somewhat scarcer and the midden soil sandier. In level 9 (.80-.90 meter deep) only 51 sherds were obtained from the slight sprinkling of shell and midden on top of the pure sand of the natural ridge. With this level the refuse abruptly ended. (See fig. 5 for profiles of pit I.)

Pit II, a 3- x 3-meter excavation located on another midden hillock 70 meters southeast of pit I (see map 4) gave results similar to those of pit I. The midden played out sharply at .80 meter below surface. Sherds were very plentiful from level 1 through level 6 with a great concentration in levels 3 and 4 (.20-.40 meter deep). In levels 1 and 2 (0-.20 meter deep) the midden was brown in color, animal and fish bones were plentiful, but there was little shell. With the midden growing blacker in levels 3 to 5 (.20-.30 meter deep) oyster, conch, and clam shells appeared along with animal and fish bones. Levels 6, 7, and 8 grew sandier with increasing depth. Profiles of pit II are shown in figure 6.

In addition to the two test pits, two small supplementary tests were made at other locations on the site. The first of these was a small hole made near the southern limit of the site (see map 4). The midden at this point was .80 meter deep, virtually the same as that where the principal test pits were made. A small collection of sherds, animal bone, and shells were made from this supplementary excava-

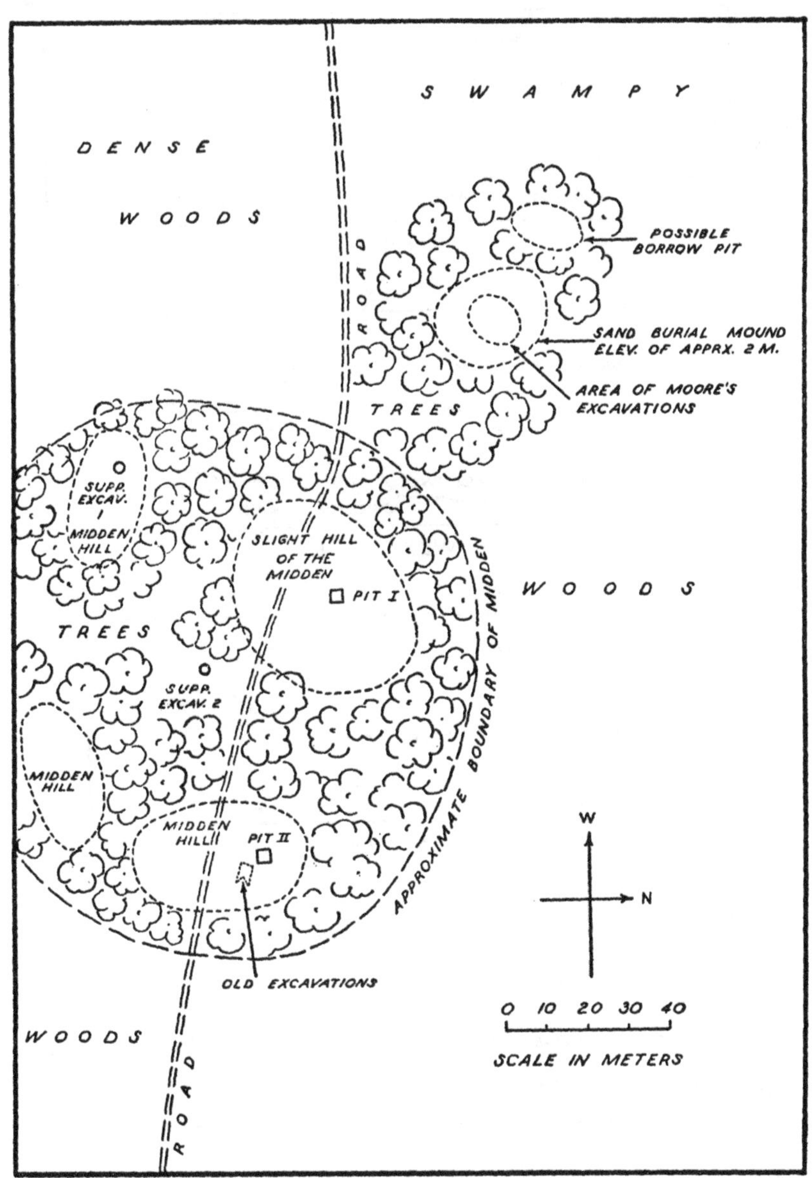

MAP 4.—The Mound Field site, Wakulla County (Wa-8).

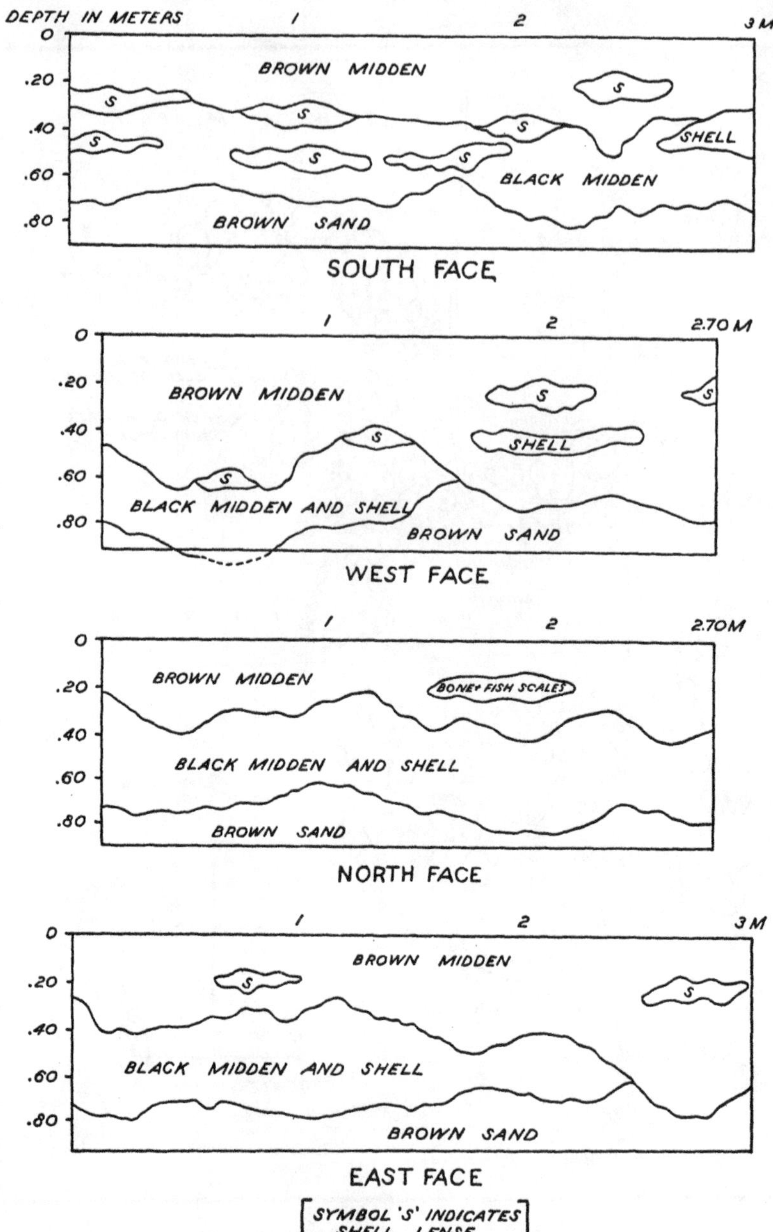

FIG. 5.—Pit I soil profiles, Mound Field (Wa-8).

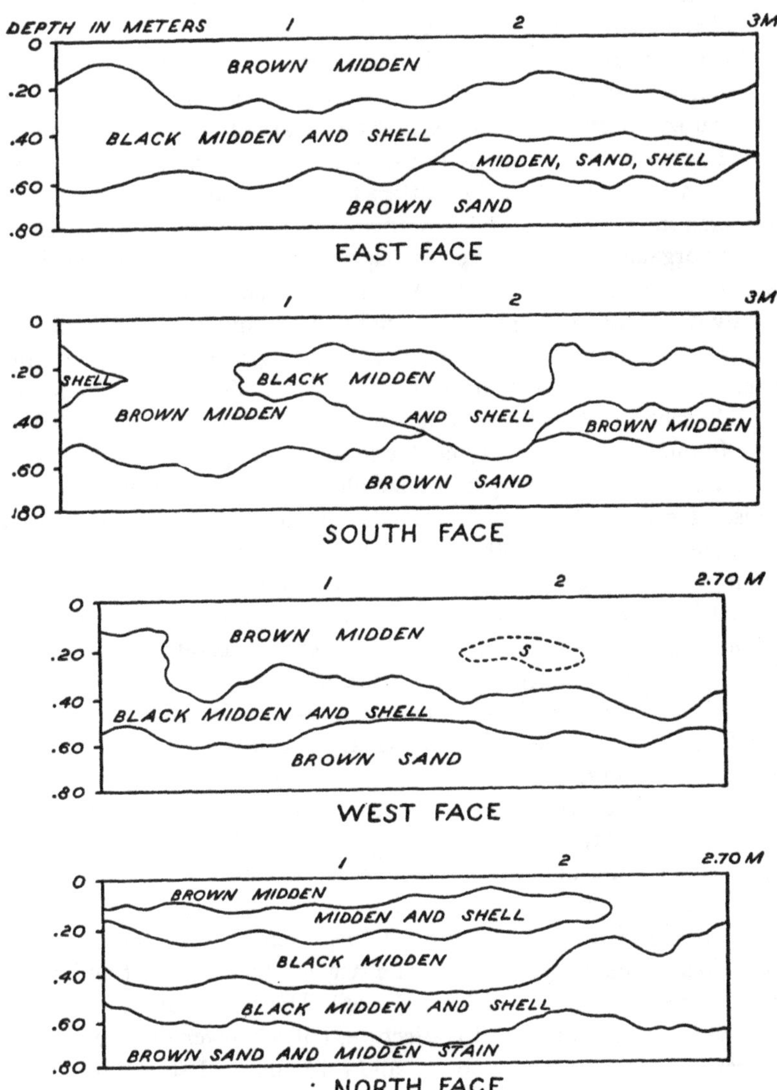

FIG. 6.—Pit II soil profiles, Mound Field (Wa-8).

tion although they were not removed in arbitrary levels. The second supplementary test location is also indicated on map 4. No evidence of midden material or sherds was found in this excavation which was abandoned at .40 meter below the surface.

Stratigraphy.—At Mound Field an upper and a lower section of the midden can be distinguished, although there is nothing in the physical soil profiles to indicate that any marked lapse of time intervened between these two sections. The upper organic midden was brownish in color with only scattered shells or small lenses of shell pocketed in the matrix. The lower section of the refuse was darker, a black organic material mixed through with scattered shells and thick bands of concentrated shells. Animal and fish bones seemed to be evenly distributed through both sections of the midden. At Carrabelle, a similar condition was noted except that the greatest shell concentrations tended to underlie the black organic midden, making a threefold division of the refuse at that site. The phenomenon of the difference in midden coloring may be due to weathering, with the upper and relatively more exposed part of an old village area turning lighter. This, of course, does not explain the greater abundance of shell in the lower levels. At both Mound Field and Carrabelle, this shift from concentrated shell to refuse relatively free of shell is accompanied by a ceramic change from Swift Creek (below) to Weeden Island (above). A possible subsistence change is suggested by this difference in the content of the refuse strata.

Pit I at Mound Field had a total of 4,789 sherds, an amazing number from an excavation 3 meters square and less than 1 meter deep. The concentration of pottery fragments in the refuse, averaging approximately 500 sherds per .10-meter level, offers an adequate sampling for a study of ceramic change. The richness of the refuse, coupled with the undisturbed appearance of the profiles of the test pits, all marked with horizontally laid, elliptical lenses of shell, offset the thinness of the deposit. Mound Field, like most of the other village sites of the northwest Florida coast, is small in extent and probably represents only a small population. The length of time the site was occupied is a matter of conjecture, but whatever this was it was a period of sufficient duration to allow for marked shifts in pottery styles.

A study of the graph on figure 7, and an inspection of table 5, reveals a significant division in the decorated pottery for pit I. The types Weeden Island Incised, Carrabelle Incised, and Carrabelle Punctated all group in the upper six levels. Although the latter two types occur in such small percentages that it is difficult to be sure, there appears to be an increase in incised types toward the top of the refuse. Opposed to these incised types is the type Swift Creek Complicated Stamped. Swift Creek, with occurrences averag-

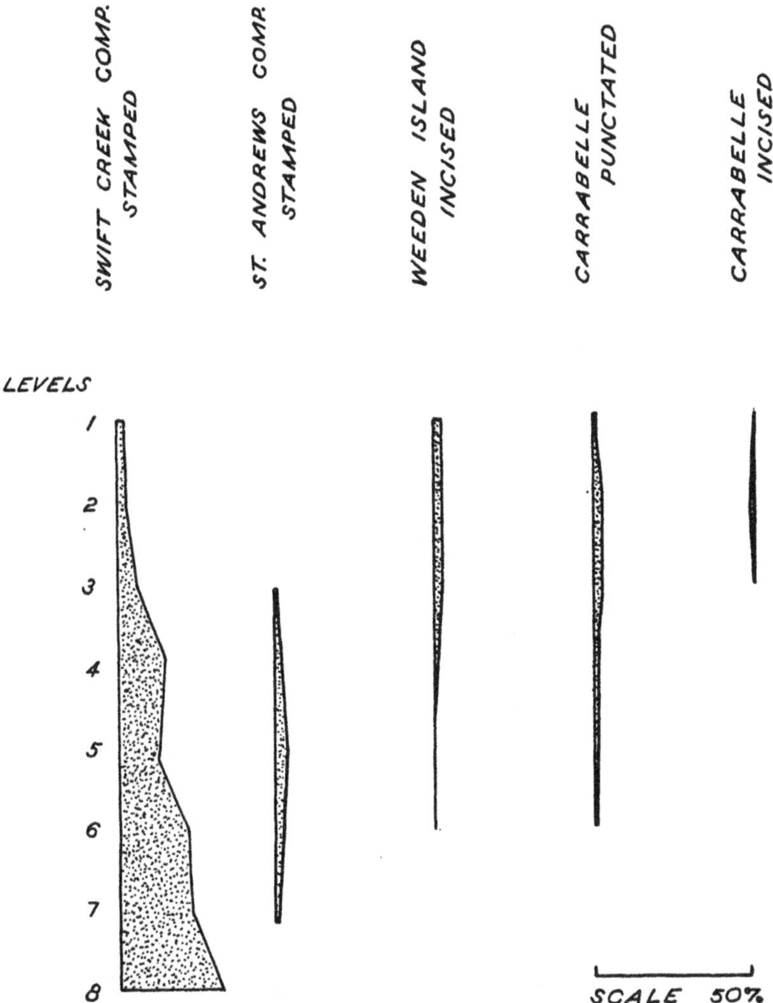

FIG. 7.—Graph on pottery stratigraphy, pit I, Mound Field (Wa-8).

ing over 25 percent of the total number of sherds in each of the four lowest levels, gradually dwindles toward the top of the midden where it makes up only 1 percent of the total sherds for level 1. The types Keith Incised and Indian Pass Incised, occurring in small quantities and sporadically, follow the distribution of Weeden Island

TABLE 5.—*Sherd classification of pits I and II, Mound Field (Wa-8)*

(Percentage occurrence by level given in italics)

Levels	Weeden Island Plain	Weeden Island Incised	Carrabelle Incised	Carrabelle Punctated	Keith Incised	Indian Pass Incised	Tucker Ridge-pinched	Wakulla Check Stamped	Swift Creek Complicated Stamped	Crooked River Complicated Stamped	St. Andrews Complicated Stamped	Mound Field Net-marked	Deptford Bold Check Stamped	Plain Red	Smooth Plain	Residual Plain	Unclassified	Total sherds by level
Pit I, Mound Field																		
1	26	7	2	2	1	....	....	....	5	....	....	....	....	....	....	460	6	509
	.051	*.016*	*.004*	*.004*	*.0019*	....	....	....	*.010*	....	....	....	....	....	....	*.937*	*.012*	....
2	82	39	15	23	3	2	....	....	35	....	....	....	2	1	40	1443	5	1,690
	.047	*.023*	*.007*	*.013*	*.001*	*.001*	....	....	*.020*	....	....	....	*.001*	*.001*	*.023*	*.853*	*.005*	....
3	31	12	1	8	1	....	....	....	42	1	1	....	....	8	11	344	1	439
	.080	*.028*	*.002*	*.018*	*.002*	....	....	....	*.042*	*.002*	*.002*	....	....	*.018*	*.028*	*.783*	*.002*	....
4	25	3	....	1	....	....	....	....	68	2	1	1	....	....	48	345	....	494
	.050	*.006*	....	*.002*	....	....	....	....	*.143*	*.004*	*.002*	*.002*	....	....	*.093*	*.769*	....	....
5	13	....	....	2	1	....	1	....	72	3	8	....	....	....	22	255	....	377
	.034	....	....	*.005*	*.002*	....	*.002*	....	*.111*	*.007*	*.026*	....	....	....	*.068*	*.676*	....	....
6	16	1	1	3	....	....	....	....	131	....	2	....	....	....	25	305	....	484
	.032	*.002*	*.002*	*.006*	....	....	....	....	*.268*	....	*.004*	....	....	....	*.051*	*.630*	....	....
7	17	....	....	....	....	....	....	....	143	....	1	....	....	....	8	352	....	521
	.032	....	....	....	....	....	....	....	*.274*	....	*.002*	....	....	....	*.015*	*.675*	....	....
8	10	....	....	....	....	....	....	....	73	....	....	....	....	....	10	131	....	224
	.044	....	....	....	....	....	....	....	*.328*	....	....	....	....	....	*.044*	*.584*	....	....
9	3	....	....	....	....	....	....	....	15	....	....	....	....	....	1	32	....	51
	.057	....	....	....	....	....	....	....	*.285*	....	....	....	....	....	*.019*	*.639*	....	....
																Pit total	......	4,789
Pit II, Mound Field																		
1	29	18	2	10	....	3	....	6	14	....	....	....	....	....	1	647	2	732
	.033	*.024*	*.002*	*.013*	....	*.003*	....	*.008*	*.019*	....	....	....	....	....	*.001*	*.883*	*.002*	....
2	41	15	6	4	2	....	....	1	10	....	....	....	....	....	18	531	6	635
	.064	*.022*	*.009*	*.006*	*.003*	....	....	*.001*	*.015*	....	....	....	....	....	*.036*	*.836*	*.009*	....
3	80	22	8	12	2	2	1	2	9	....	....	....	....	....	61	982	3	1,184
	.067	*.017*	*.006*	*.009*	*.001*	*.001*	*.0007*	*.001*	*.007*	....	....	....	....	....	*.051*	*.829*	*.001*	....
4	70	7	1	7	....	....	....	....	12	....	4	....	....	9	66	897	5	1,078
	.064	*.006*	*.0009*	*.006*	....	....	....	....	*.010*	....	*.003*	....	....	*.008*	*.061*	*.822*	*.004*	....
5	72	5	2	15	....	1	....	....	....	....	....	....	....	3	12	636	2	748
	.096	*.006*	*.002*	*.019*	....	*.001*	....	....	....	....	....	....	....	*.003*	*.016*	*.850*	*.002*	....
6	50	....	8	9	....	....	....	....	29	....	1	1	....	....	26	485	3	613
	.082	....	*.013*	*.014*	....	....	....	....	*.046*	....	*.001*	*.001*	....	....	*.042*	*.791*	*.004*	....
7	19	....	....	....	....	1	....	....	33	....	....	....	....	....	3	226	....	282
	.067	....	....	....	....	*.003*	....	....	*.117*	....	....	....	....	....	*.010*	*.801*	....	....
8	2	....	....	....	....	....	....	....	21	....	....	....	....	....	2	57	....	82
	.014	....	....	....	....	....	....	....	*.256*	....	....	....	....	....	*.014*	*.695*	....	....
																Pit total	......	5,354

Incised and the two Carrabelle types. Crooked River Complicated Stamped and St. Andrews Complicated Stamped, related in technique of ornamentation to Swift Creek, have a somewhat intermediate distribution in the rubbish, not appearing at the top or bottom.

The plain types, which make up the bulk of the pottery, per level, do not show clear-cut vertical distributions. Weeden Island Plain occurs all the way to the bottom, although it is possible that it decreased slightly from top to bottom, an action paralleling Weeden Island Incised and related types. It would appear that Weeden Island Plain, at least as far as the Mound Field midden is concerned, had its inception somewhat earlier than its related decorated types. Smooth Plain shows no significant percentage changes or trends from top to bottom. Residual Plain, the category which includes all undecorated, sand-tempered body sherds, does decrease gradually from top to bottom. This decrease can most easily be attributed to the opposite and complementary behavior of Swift Creek Complicated Stamped. The Swift Creek mode of decoration was, in many cases, an over-all application of stamped designs to the vessel, while Weeden Island and related types restricted the decoration, as a rule, to the upper portion of the vessel body. This gives a greater plain sherd count for Weeden Island Period levels.

Pit II is little different from pit I. The same relationships obtain between the incised types and Swift Creek Complicated Stamped. There is a suggestion that the rubbish of pit II began and ended a little later than that of pit I. Only in the bottom level of pit II is there a really high occurrence of Swift Creek, while Wakulla Check Stamped, a type characteristic of a later phase of Weeden Island, occurs in small numbers in the three top levels.

In brief, the Mound Field midden excavations indicate a Swift Creek Period and a Weeden Island Period occupation, falling in that chronological order.

Classification of surface sherds from Mound Field

Weeden Island Complex	
Weeden Island Series:	
Weeden Island Incised	2
Weeden Island Plain	13
Santa Rosa-Swift Creek Complex	
Complicated Stamped Series:	
Swift Creek Complicated Stamped	4
Crooked River Complicated Stamped	1
St. Andrews Complicated Stamped	1

Miscellaneous

Smooth Plain	2
Residual Plain	106
Total sherds....	134

SOWELL, BAY COUNTY (BY-3)

Description of the site.—The Sowell midden and burial mound are on the west side of St. Andrews Bay, about 1 mile west of Bear Point, Bay County. This location (map 5) is approximately 60 and 70 miles west of the Carrabelle and Mound Field sites. The midden and mound are among several in the immediate vicinity. The mound was excavated by Moore (1902, pp. 167 ff.) who describes it as follows:

> The height of the mound was 4.5 feet; the basal diameter, 50 feet. A great depression whence the sand for the mound had been taken was at its southern margin.

Moore recovered several burials accompanied by a mortuary deposit of pottery.[10] He makes no mention of the associated shell midden.

The midden site, which today is clear of scrub oak, fronts along St. Andrews Bay and lies a little over 1.5 miles below the new St. Andrews Bay bridge of U. S. Highway 98. The area of shell and potsherds extends back from the water's edge for 40 or 50 meters. Along the bay shore its extent is 100 to 125 meters. The mound site excavated by Moore lies a few hundred meters distant in a dense scrub oak thicket.

Excavations.—Unfortunately, the midden site at Sowell had recently been gutted by commercial shell-gathering operations, so that our 1940 excavations were limited to a very few places in the site which had not been disturbed. Pits I and II were both very shallow (see map 5 for pit locations). Both pits were 3 x 1.5 meters in surface dimensions. Pit I was excavated in three levels, the first two of 10 centimeters each and the last of 20 centimeters, making a total depth of .40 meter. The pit was located on what had apparently been the edge of the thickest shell and midden deposit. The two upper levels showed sand mixed with fragments of shell and gray organic stain. The bottom level gradually shaded off into sterile reddish-brown sand which gave no evidence of former disturbance. Pit II was carried down in five 10-centimeter levels. It was almost identical to pit I in the nature and depth of the refuse.

[10] See section on "Review and Analysis of Gulf Coast Sites," Sowell site, p. 231.

Both pits averaged about 40 to 50 sherds per level except for the bottom levels.

Pit III (1.50 x 1.50 meters square) was located in a part of the

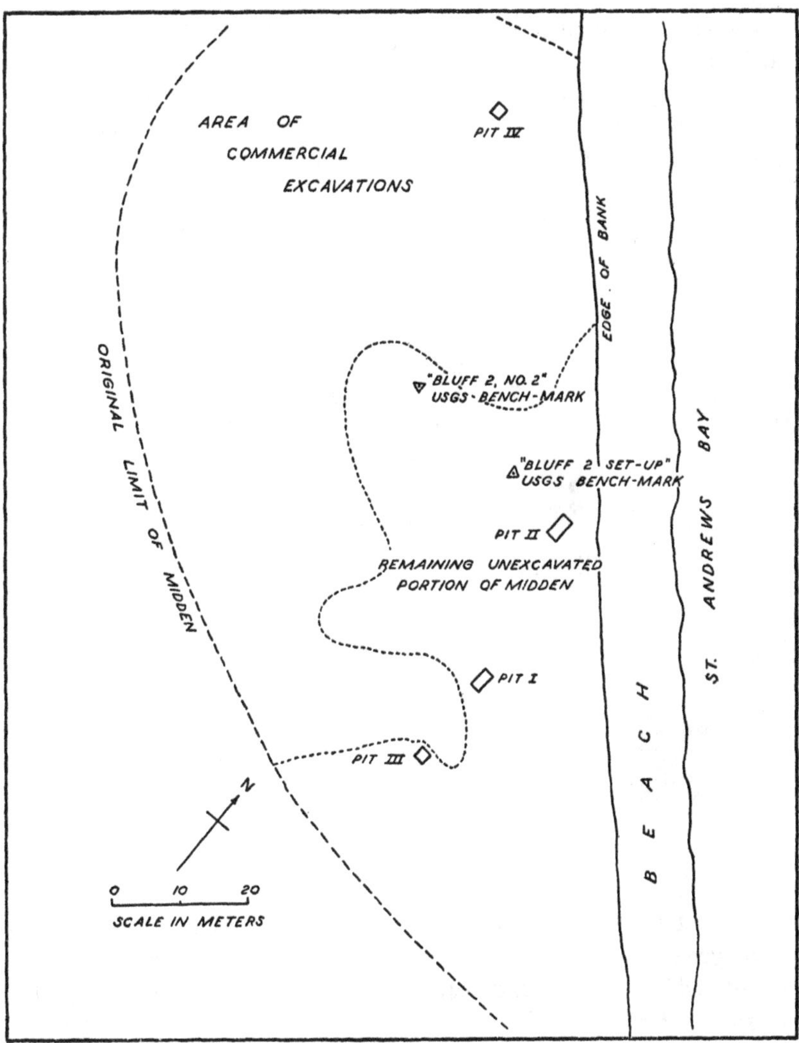

MAP 5.—The Sowell site, Bay County (By-3).

midden that appeared deeper than those sections where pits I and II had been placed. Some small trees at the spot had discouraged the shell excavators from clearing out this portion of the site. The first two levels of pit III (0-.20 meter) yielded over 100 sherds and the soils were a mixture of humus, broken shell, and sand. In levels 3 and 4 (.20 to .40 meter deep) sherds continued, but the sandy refuse showed very little shell or organic material. In level 5 (.40 to .50 meter deep) the soil was sandy, and there were very few sherds. Thinking the midden was giving way into undisturbed sand, the sixth level was made deeper (.50 to .80 meter deep), and, rather abruptly, dark midden and compact shell showed up again with an increased number of sherds. In levels 7 and 8 (.80 to 1.00 meter deep) the darker midden and shell continued, but in level 9

TABLE 6.—*Sherd classification of pits I and II, Sowell (By-3)*

(Percentage occurrence by level given in italics)

Levels	Fort Walton Incised	Lake Jackson Plain	Pensacola Plain	Weeden Island Plain	Weeden Island Incised	Carrabelle Incised	Wakulla Check Stamped	Swift Creek Complicated Stamped	Smooth Plain	Residual Plain	Unclassified	Total sherds by level
						Pit I, Sowell						
1	6	2	2	3	....	1	13	....	....	48	1	76
	.074	*.025*	*.025*	*.037*	....	*.012*	*.171*	....	....	*.631*	*.012*	....
2	4	....	....	....	....	....	8	....	....	26	2	40
	.100	....	....	....	....	....	*.200*	....	....	*.650*	*.050*	....
3	....	....	....	1	....	....	3	....	1	3	....	8
	....	....	....	*.125*	....	....	*.375*	....	*.125*	*.375*	....	....
										Pit total		124
						Pit II, Sowell						
1	2	1	....	1	2	....	11	....	5	61	1	84
	.022	*.011*	....	*.011*	*.022*	....	*.131*	....	*.059*	*.072*	*.011*	....
2	1	....	1	4	....	....	10	....	....	19	....	35
	.028	....	*.028*	*.114*	....	....	*.285*	....	....	*.542*	....	....
3	....	....	....	3	....	....	4	....	1	28	....	36
	....	....	....	*.084*	....	....	*.111*	....	*.027*	*.777*	....	....
4	7	1	2	....	3	....	2	1	....	38	1	66
	.106	*.015*	*.030*	....	*.045*	....	*.030*	*.015*	....	*.575*	*.015*	....
5	....	1	2	1	....	....	1	1	....	19	3	28
	....	*.071*	*.142*	*.071*	....	....	*.071*	*.071*	....	*.678*	*.213*	....
										Pit total		249

(1.00 to 1.10 meters deep) shell began to disappear, and the midden color grew fainter. The bottom level (1.10 to 1.20 meters deep) exposed reddish sterile sand below gray-white sand. Only one profile is shown from pit III, the southwest face. This cross section is typical of the pit (see fig. 8).

Pit IV (1.50 x 1.50 meters) was located at the opposite end of the site from pit III, near the water's edge. The top level (0-.10 meter deep) was in sandy midden and broken shell. From level 2 to level 6, inclusive (.10-.70 meter deep), the midden was black and mixed with whole shells. In level 8 (.70-.80 meter deep) reddish subsoil showed up very abruptly. The pit was carried down another .10 meter, but the refuse was obviously no deeper. In each level, with the exception of 8, approximately 100 sherds or more were recovered.

Stratigraphy.—Of the four pits excavated at Sowell only pit III shows any appreciable change in pottery type frequencies from top to bottom (see table 7 and fig. 9). The type Wakulla Check Stamped displays a gradually expanding upward trend in the midden.

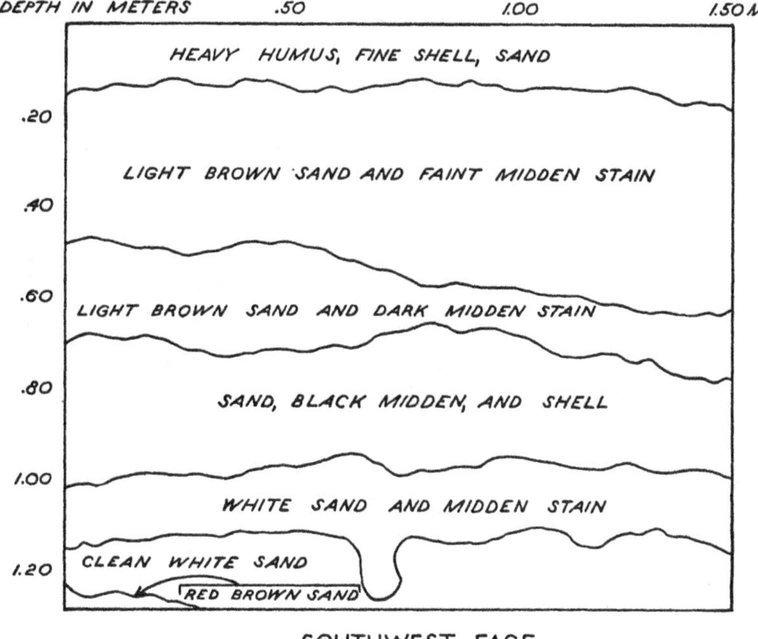

FIG. 8.—Pit III soil profiles, Sowell (By-3).

Weeden Island Incised and Weeden Island Plain occur with slightly greater frequency in the middle levels. The four sherds of Swift Creek Complicated Stamped that are present come from the three bottom levels. Fort Walton Incised and Lake Jackson Plain are both found only in the upper levels.

In pit IV there is also evidence for Fort Walton Incised, Lake Jackson Plain, and Pensacola Plain being late (see table 7). There is, however, in this pit little or no substantiation for the increase of Wakulla Check Stamped in the upper levels or of the presence of Swift Creek in the lower levels.

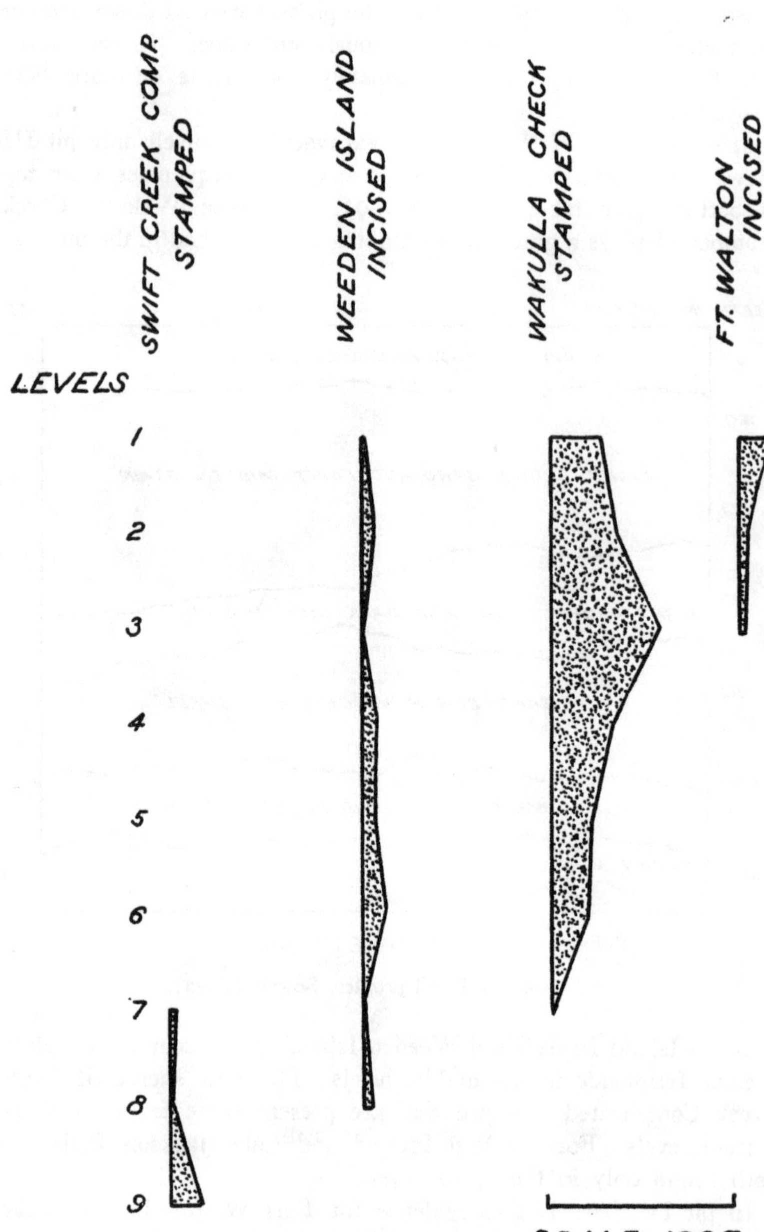

FIG. 9.—Graph on pottery stratigraphy, pit III, Sowell (By-3).

TABLE 7.—*Sherd classification of pits III and IV, Sowell (By-3)*

(Percentage occurrence by level given in italics)

Levels	Fort Walton Incised	Lake Jackson Plain	Pensacola Plain	Leon Check Stamped	Weeden Island Plain	Weeden Island Incised	Carrabelle Incised	Carrabelle Punctated	Indian Pass Incised	Tucker Ridge-pinched	St. Petersburg Incised	Wakulla Check Stamped	Swift Creek Complicated Stamped	West Florida Cord-marked	Plain Red	Smooth Plain	Residual Plain	Unclassified	Total sherds by level
Pit III, Sowell																			
1	12 *.157*	2 *.026*	....	....	1 *.013*	1 *.013*	....	....	....	....	....	19 *.25*	....	....	....	2 *.026*	39 *.513*	....	76
2	2 *.038*	....	....	....	2 *.038*	4 *.076*	....	....	....	....	....	17 *.333*	....	....	....	1 *.019*	23 *.45*	2 *.038*	51
3	2 *.03*	....	....	....	1 *.015*	....	....	....	....	....	....	38 *.584*	....	....	....	3 *.045*	19 *.292*	2 *.03*	65
4	....	....	....	....	2 *.057*	2 *.057*	....	....	....	....	....	11 *.314*	....	....	....	4 *.114*	15 *.428*	1 *.028*	35
5	....	....	....	....	....	1 *.047*	....	....	....	1 *.047*	....	5 *.238*	....	....	....	3 *.142*	11 *.523*	....	21
6	1 *.013*	....	....	....	4 *.052*	7 *.095*	....	....	....	....	....	16 *.219*	....	....	....	22 *.301*	23 *.315*	....	73
7	....	....	....	....	7 *.142*	....	....	....	....	2 *.04*	....	1 *.02*	1 *.02*	....	....	6 *.122*	29 *.591*	3 *.06*	49
8	....	....	....	....	4 *.058*	1 *.058*	2 *.117*	....	....	....	....	....	....	....	....	3 *.175*	7 *.409*	....	17
9	....	....	....	....	....	....	....	....	....	....	....	....	3 *.129*	2 *.086*	....	3 *.129*	14 *.608*	1 *.043*	23
																	Pit total		410
Pit IV, Sowell																			
1	5 *.035*	....	1 *.007*	2 *.014*	1 *.007*	4 *.028*	1 *.007*	....	....	....	....	48 *.336*	2 *.014*	....	....	....	79 *.552*	....	143
2	9 *.047*	1 *.005*	2 *.01*	1 *.005*	8 *.042*	2 *.01*	1 *.005*	....	....	....	1 *.005*	45 *.239*	....	....	1 *.005*	3 *.015*	110 *.585*	3 *.015*	188
3	2 *.013*	....	2 *.013*	....	2 *.013*	4 *.026*	....	....	1 *.007*	....	....	56 *.373*	....	....	1 *.007*	10 *.066*	68 *.453*	4 *.026*	150
4	1 *.005*	1 *.005*	....	....	2 *.011*	1 *.005*	1 *.005*	....	....	....	....	84 *.469*	1 *.005*	....	....	19 *.106*	65 *.363*	3 *.02*	179
5	....	....	....	....	2 *.018*	5 *.045*	....	4 *.036*	....	1 *.009*	....	29 *.263*	2 *.018*	....	....	9 *.081*	57 *.518*	1 *.009*	110
6	....	....	....	....	4 *.096*	....	....	2 *.047*	....	1 *.023*	....	3 *.071*	....	....	....	12 *.285*	20 *.476*	....	42
7	....	....	....	....	....	....	....	....	....	....	....	....	....	....	....	3 *.100*	....	....	3
																	Pit total		815

Pits I and II are both shallow, and all types seem to be fairly well mixed through nearly all levels (see table 6). In pit II, Wakulla Check Stamped does show an increase at the top, and the only Swift Creek sherds come from the two lowest levels. This, however, is offset by the presence of Lake Jackson Plain and Pensacola Plain sherds in the bottom of the pit.

The case for ceramic stratigraphy at Sowell, based essentially upon pit III, is not as conclusive as at Mound Field or Carrabelle. There are, nevertheless, indications of a number of the same sequential changes in pottery types which were found in the two previously excavated sites. Sowell was the first site excavated at which the type Wakulla Check Stamped obtained in dominant percentages. Its high frequencies of occurrence in the upper levels of pit III accord with its small occurrence in the top three levels of pit II of the Mound Field site. The small amounts of Fort Walton Period pottery coming from the upper levels of pit III at Sowell are in line with the late position in which sherds of this complex were found at other sites, and their presence argues that the area of the site sampled by pit III has not recently been disturbed to any profound depth.

The physical strata revealed in pit III are not analogous to the sequences of soil types seen in the Carrabelle and Mound Field pits. The band of midden and compacted shell at .50 to .90 meter in pit III at Sowell was not associated with an intensive Swift Creek occupation, and the overlying refuse, rather than being rich brown or black midden, was sand only slightly discolored by organic debris. The pit III deposition can best be interpreted by considering it as a continuous cultural accumulation in spite of the lighter sandy zone superimposed on the deep shell and midden layer. This sandy stratum is not clean sand, and it does not appear to have been water-carried or wind-blown.

The pottery sequence at Sowell overlaps with the later stages of the sequences at Carrabelle and Mound Field. Whereas both Carrabelle and Mound Field stratigraphies close with a ceramic period characterized by a mixture of Weeden Island and Swift Creek types, the Sowell pit III sequence shows Swift Creek Complicated Stamped only in the lower levels. In the upper levels Weeden Island is associated with a new stamped type, Wakulla Check Stamped. Fort Walton Period sherds occur superficially.

Classification of surface sherds from Sowell

Fort Walton Complex	
Fort Walton Incised	4
Weeden Island Complex	
Weeden Island Series:	
Weeden Island Incised	3
Weeden Island Plain	41
Carrabelle Incised	6
Carrabelle Punctated	6
Keith Incised	2
Tucker Ridge-pinched	2
Wakulla Check Stamped	117
Swift Creek Complicated Stamped	9
Deptford Complex	
Deptford Bold Check Stamped	2
Miscellaneous	
Smooth Plain	24
Plain Red	6
Residual Plain	270
Indeterminate stamped	12
Other unclassified	7
Total sherds	511

The above collection is supplemented by another from the Sowell site which was collected many years ago by R. E. C. Stearns. The Stearns collection is in the Peabody Museum, Yale University. It is tabulated below:

Fort Walton Complex	
Lake Jackson Plain	4
Weeden Island Complex	
Weeden Island Series:	
Weeden Island Incised	3
Weeden Island Punctated	2
Weeden Island Plain	26
Carrabelle Incised	6
Carrabelle Punctated	12
Indian Pass Incised	1
Tucker Ridge-pinched	2
Wakulla Check Stamped	24
Thomas Simple Stamped	7
Swift Creek Complicated Stamped (Most of these are Late Variety.)	9
Mound Field Net-marked	2
West Florida Cord-marked	1
Miscellaneous	
Residual and Smooth Plain	well represented
Total sherds	99

FORT WALTON, OKALOOSA COUNTY (OK-6)

Description of the site.—In the modern community of Fort Walton on Santa Rosa Sound, near the entrance to Choctawhatchee Bay, is one of the largest Indian mound and village sites in northwest Florida (map 2). In 1883 (Walker, 1885, pp. 860 ff.) S. T. Walker, who made investigations at the site described it:

> The sound here is only about one-fourth of a mile in width, and navigation is obstructed by numerous bars and shoals, which were once covered by oyster beds, though at present the oyster is entirely extinct in both bay and sound. On the east is Choctawhatchee Bay, and northwest lies a large branch of Garnier's Bayou. Several bold springs of excellent water break out of the bluffs, and a small fresh-water stream empties into the sound here and once passed through the center of town. The largest mound and shell heaps are situated near this stream and in the neighborhood of the finest of the springs. The position of the largest domiciliary mound in this portion of the State is marked by a large shell heap on the bluffs above the largest spring. This shell heap, which was converted into a fort by the Southern army during the civil war, is about 12 feet high, with a base about 200 feet in diameter. About 400 yards nearly due north of this heap, situated in a dense thicket of bushes and small trees, is the mound in question. It is covered with a growth similar to that around it, and so dense and tangled is the growth of vines, briers, and bushes upon it that it is difficult either to measure or explore it. Its estimated height is 25 feet, its length 250 feet, and its width 135 feet. The measurements were taken along the top which is nearly level; of course, the base is much greater. The sides are very steep, and on the south side is a sloping roadway leading to the top.

Walker reports that many excavations had been made in the mound prior to his visit.[11] He made a few cursory diggings in the mound but found little. He did, however, make the observation that the mound was constructed of alternate layers of shell-midden refuse and clean sand. According to his account human burials had been placed on the top of a shell layer and covered with sand. The other evidences of human occupation in the area which Walker noted are as follows:

> West of the great mound are many small circles of shells covered with soil, from 40 to 60 feet in diameter, and the earth is covered with fragments of broken pottery. Over a space reaching from the great mound to the beach, one-fourth of a mile in width, and extending along the beach for nearly a mile, are shell heaps of all shapes and sizes, from a mere bed a foot in thickness to large heaps 12 and 15 feet high. In the fields, the crops are growing in beds of shell, and the furrows are full of broken pottery and fragments of clay figures.

In 1901 Moore, who carried out extensive excavations in the big flat-topped mound, described the site with greater accuracy (see

[11] See also Sternberg, 1876, pp. 282-292.

Moore, 1901, pp. 435 ff., "Mounds at Walton's Camp, Santa Rosa Sound, Santa Rosa County, Fla."). Moore also mentions the shell heap at the water's edge. His measurements of the big mound are: height, approximately 12 feet; base, 223 feet (east-west) by 178 feet (north-south); summit platform, 179 by 135 feet. The discrepancy in the height measurement between Moore and Walker may be due, in part, to unrecorded excavations in the mound between 1883 and 1901; but it is more likely that Walker's estimate was considerably in excess of the actual height. Today, the mound stands just about 12 feet above the surrounding flat land.

Moore also describes a graded way or ramp approach, which can still be seen, on the south side of the mound. Other features of the area listed by him were a sand mound about one-quarter of a mile west of the big mound and various small mounds in the immediate neighborhood. The sand mound, which had been excavated before his visit, was investigated, and Moore concludes that it was erected for domiciliary purposes; test diggings in the other small mounds showed only midden refuse.

Moore's main interest, however, was in the large mound. He states:

> During our investigation 11 men dug for 7 days. This digging consisted of trenching at various points to determine the construction of the mound; the removal of a large part of the summit plateau to a depth of from 3 to 5 feet; the investigation of much of the marginal portion on the northern side of the mound.

Like Walker, Moore reports the structure of the mound to have been built by successive layers or mantles of sand or shell. Near the top of the southeastern slope of the mound he found a great many burials accompanied with pottery vessels. In the central part of the mound, on the summit, in a shell deposit, were a number of burials unaccompanied by pottery. In all instances, the burials in the Fort Walton mound were relatively superficial. Moore reports none at over a depth of 3 feet. A number of pottery bowls and jars were taken from the mound, in connection with some of the burials. Virtually all of these belong to the Fort Walton Period. An analysis of this material is presented in a subsequent section of this report on "Review and Analysis of Gulf Coast Sites" (pp. 213-214).

In preparing a plat and estimated contour map of the Fort Walton midden area which we excavated in 1940 (map 6) the big mound was found to be exactly 200 meters from the water's edge rather than one-quarter of a mile as given by Walker. There is no longer a great shell heap on the shore of the sound; apparently large sections of this deposit were built over, leveled off, or destroyed in recent

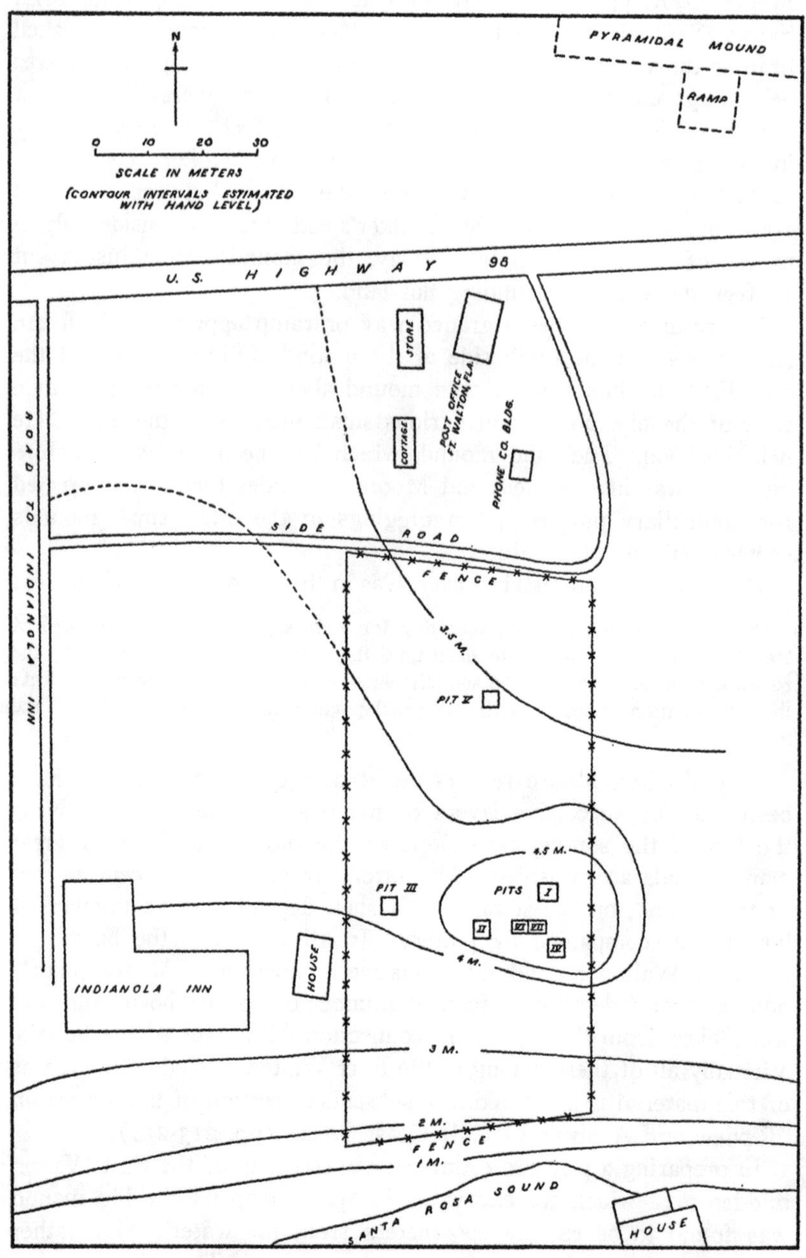

Map 6.—The Fort Walton site, Okaloosa County (Ok-6).

years. Remnants of it remain, however, and many of the houses fronting the shore have been built on the midden ridge. The Indianola Hotel (see map 6) has been built over what was probably the largest of these shell eminences, probably the one referred to by both Walker and Fewkes. Just to the east of the hotel there is a vacant, fenced lot on which there is a hillock of shell which rises about 1.5 meters above the surrounding lot. Most of our test excavations were made in this hillock, as this was the most likely appearing spot available for sampling.

Excavations.—Pit I (a 3- x 3-meter cut) was situated on the slightly sloping western flank of the small rise of shell mentioned above. The first three levels of the pit (0-.30 meter deep) cut through small clam shells. Sherds were numerous, averaging about 200 per .10-meter level. From level 4 to level 8, oyster and clam shells were evenly mixed, with the sherd yield remaining heavy down through level 7. In level 8 (.70-.80 meter) sherds were scarce. Below level 8 clam shells again predominated. In level 12 (1.10-1.20 meters) most of the pit was in yellow, sterile sand with only a little midden and shell in the northeast corner. With refuse disappearing, the pit was closed at a depth of 1.40 meters below surface (see fig. 10 for pit soil profiles).

Pits II and III (both 3 x 3 meters) were made in the flat area west of the hummock where pit I had been located (map 6). In neither pit was the rubbish over .40 meter deep. Underneath the humus was a thin zone of shell (mostly clam with a few oyster); below the shell and midden was a transition zone of gray sand and organic stain. A few sherds were found in this transition layer. The basal yellow and reddish sand appeared in both pits at .50 meter below the surface. Pit V was very similar to pits II and III in content. Located in the flat area north of the hummock, it showed only a very few centimeters of shell midden, and the red-yellow sand of the original terrain was exposed in less than .40 meter. These three tests indicated that, as far as the area available for excavation was concerned, only the shell concentration on the east side of the lot was deep enough to give results, and that the surrounding flat had only a very meager occupation layer.

For this reason, the remainder of the pits, numbers IV, VI, and VII, were all made in the hummock near pit I. Pit IV (3 x 3 meters) was situated on the southwestern flank of the knoll. Sherds were found as deep as level 14 (1.30-1.40 meters below the surface). They were, however, not as numerous as in pit I, the count averaging about 50 fragments per level in the first five levels; half that number be-

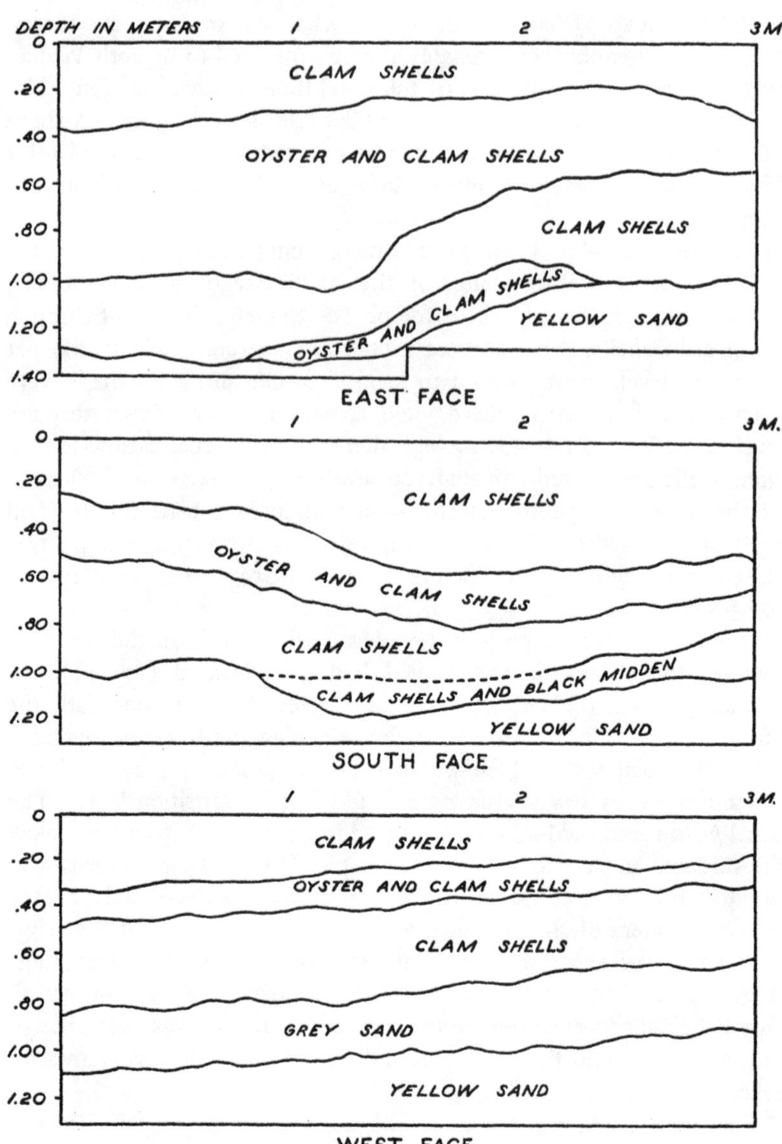

FIG. 10.—Pit I soil profiles, Fort Walton (Ok-6).

low .50 meter; and from .80-1.40 meters deep there were only 10 sherds or so for each .10 meter of refuse. The strata in pit IV were more evenly bedded than in pit I, and from appearances it suggested better possibilities for accurate stratification of pottery types. The first level (0-.10 meter) cut through the sandy humus and broken shell scattered over the top of the ground. Below this oyster and clam shells were about evenly mixed down to .30 to .40 meter. From .40 to .70 meter deep, clam shells were common, but below this all shell gradually decreased, and the pit proceeded through gray sand stained with midden and charcoal. Yellow sand began to appear in the two lowest levels (1.20-1.40 meters) (see fig. 11 for profiles of pit IV).

Pits VI and VII were placed between pits I and IV on the west slope of the hillock. They were each laid out 3 meters east-west by 2 meters north-south, with the eastern end of pit VI joining the western end of pit VII to make a single trench 6 meters long and 2 meters wide. Sherds were almost as numerous in these two cuts as in pit I, especially in the top half-meter. In pit VII, as could be expected from its position, the phenomenon of clam shells, then clams and oysters, with clams again below was observed. In pit VI, farther out toward the edge of the concentration, most of the shells were clams and the actual shell zone was not as thick as in pit VII (see fig. 12 for profiles of pits VI and VII). As in the other pits, gray and white sand mixed with midden and charcoal was found below the shell. Sherds continued down into this soil, but were not numerous. Yellow, sterile sand appeared in the twelfth level of each pit (1.10-1.20 meters).

Stratigraphy.—The problem of stratification of pottery types at Fort Walton is more complex than at Mound Field, Carrabelle, or Sowell. To begin with, we may disregard pits II, III, and V as being all too shallow and apparently too badly mixed to be of any value in arriving at conclusions of pottery sequence. In pits II and III it is of interest, however, to note that the few Pensacola Plain and Fort Walton Incised sherds were all found near the top of the refuse. Except for this, these particular pit collections are little more than surface data (see tables 9 and 11).

The most reliable evidence for ceramic sequence comes from pits IV, VI, and VII, excavations in the shell hillock or rubbish concentration on the east side of the lot. Even here, the story is not as clear as at Mound Field or Carrabelle. All three of these pits, as well as pit I, show a few late period fragments of Fort Walton Incised or Pensacola Plain in the upper two to four .10-meter levels.

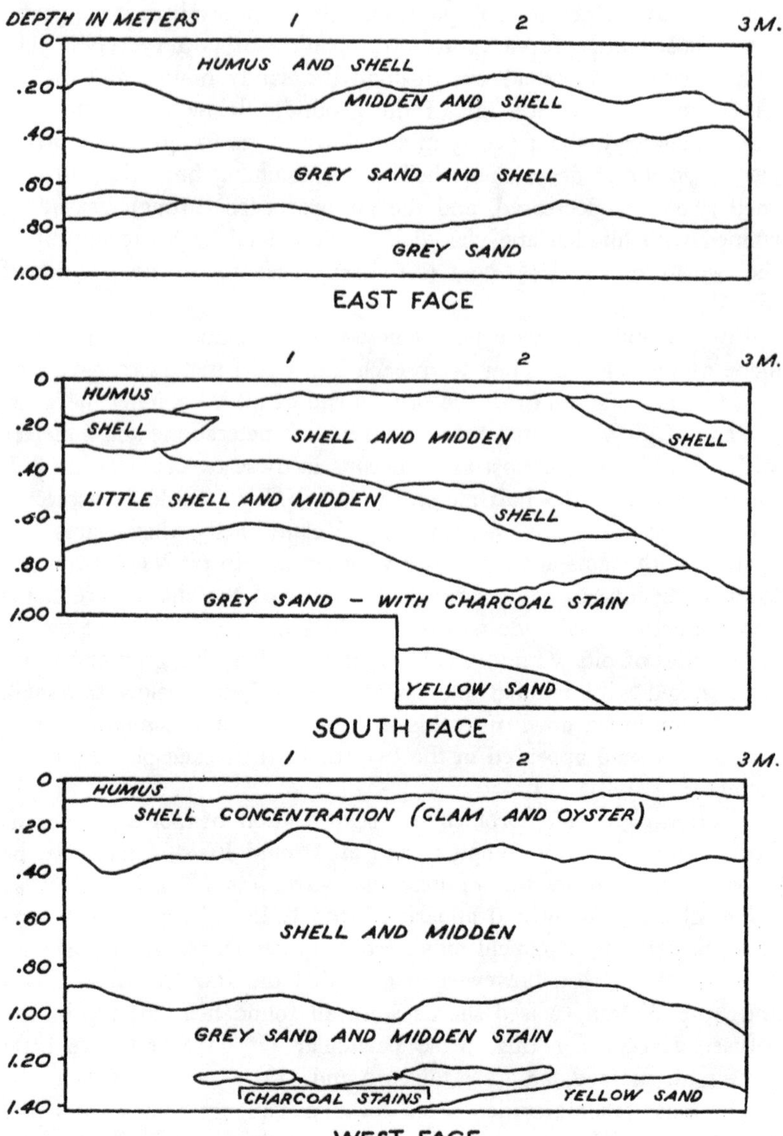

FIG. 11.—Pit IV soil profiles, Fort Walton (Ok-6).

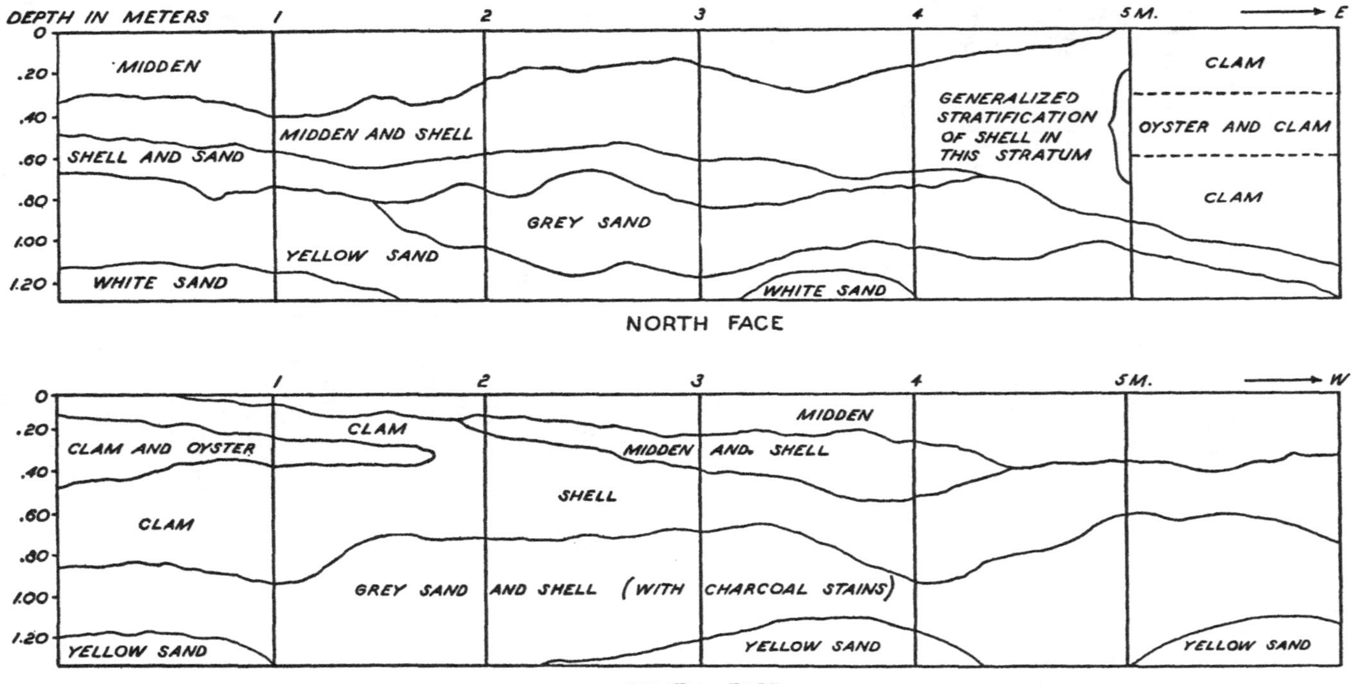

FIG. 12.—Pits VI and VII, soil profiles, Fort Walton (Ok-6).

Presumably these few pieces represent the final occupation at this part of the Fort Walton village midden. In the earlier periods, all the pits in the shell concentration differ in that each pit seems to have revealed a slightly different span of ceramic history. In pit VII, Weeden Island Period decorated sherds and Wakulla Check Stamped occur throughout the upper two-thirds of the pit: Swift Creek Complicated Stamped runs from top to bottom but is more frequent in the lower levels; and Basin Bayou Incised, Santa Rosa Stamped, and Alligator Bayou Incised are only in the lower half of the pit. The few Deptford Bold Check Stamped sherds present are also in the lower part of the refuse (see table 13).

In pit VI (see table 12) a similar condition obtains except that Weeden Island decorated types and Wakulla Check Stamped are grouped a little higher in the pit; Swift Creek Complicated Stamped does not go all the way to the top; the Santa Rosa, Basin Bayou, and Alligator Bayou types are found in the middle levels; and Deptford Bold Check Stamped and Deptford Simple Stamped are mainly in the bottom levels. That is, with the exception of a late sprinkling of Fort Walton types, the refuse in pit VI does not extend as late in time as that of pit VII and goes back a little earlier.

In pit IV there are very few Weeden Island sherds, either of the decorated or of Weeden Island Plain, and the few that were found all came from the upper one-quarter of the pit. The same is true of Wakulla Check Stamped. Swift Creek Complicated Stamped, Santa Rosa Stamped, Alligator Bayou Stamped, and Basin Bayou Incised are found, principally, in the middle levels. There are not many decorated sherds in the lower one-third of the pit, but the few present are Deptford Bold Check Stamped, Deptford Simple Stamped, and a scattering of Santa Rosa pieces. Quite clearly, the bottom of pit IV extends down into an earlier part of the deposit than either pits VI or VII (see table 10).

Pit I (see table 8) is approximately in the same time range as pit VI, but the evidence for stratification is not as clear as in the other pits. A shell-tempered sherd (Pensacola Plain) was found as deep as level 9 (.80-.90 meter) in pit I, suggesting that this part of the refuse had been disturbed. A review of the profiles for the various pits will also show that the shell and midden strata in pit I lie in poorer conformity than those of the other pits. This last may account for the more scrambled distribution of types, as all the arbitrary levels were excavated parallel to the horizon.

By arranging pits VII, VI, and IV in a descending series of that order, a complete sequence, covering all the materials excavated by us at Fort Walton, may be generalized (see graphs, fig. 13). Such

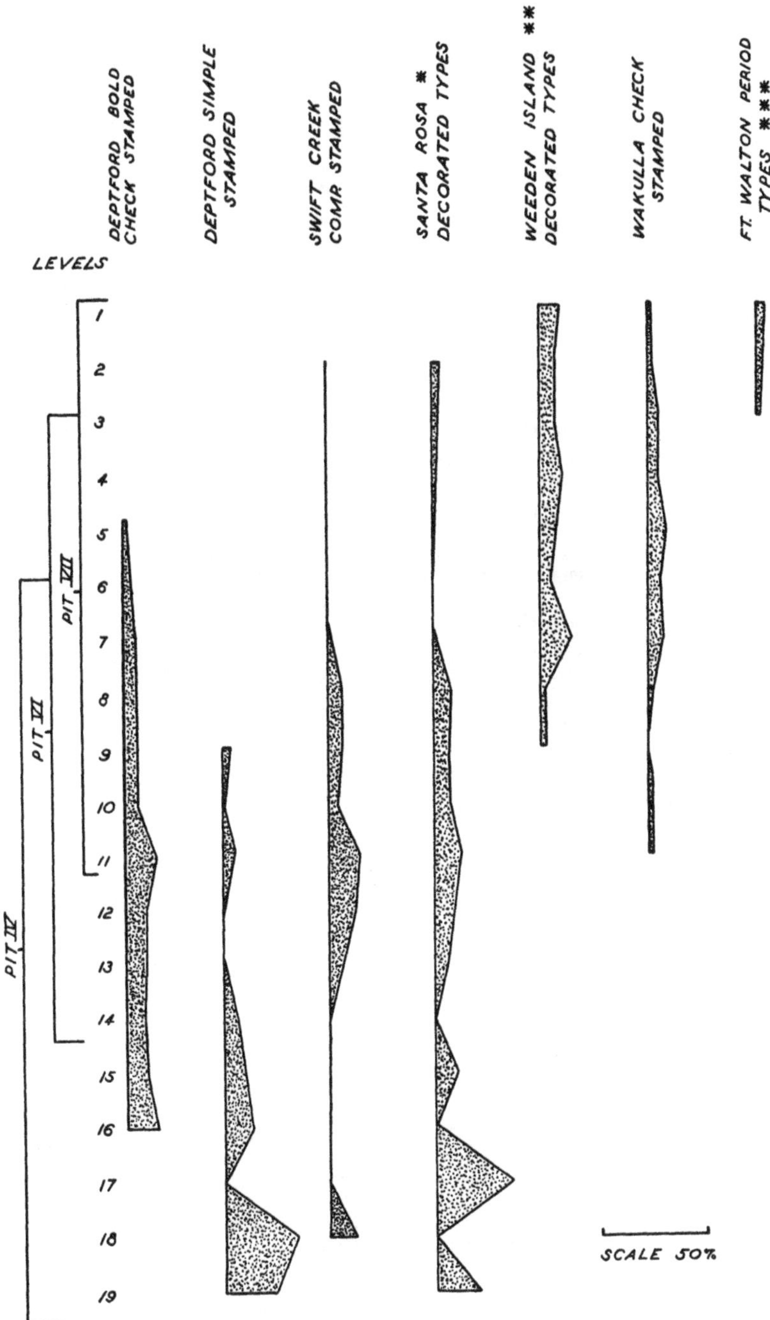

FIG. 13.—Graph on pottery stratigraphy at Fort Walton (Ok-6). Pits IV, VI, and VII are combined. (* Includes Santa Rosa Stamped, Basin Bayou Incised, Alligator Bayou Stamped. ** Includes Weeden Island Incised and Carrabelle Punctated. *** Includes Fort Walton Incised and Pensacola Plain.)

TABLE 8.—*Sherd classification of pit I, Fort Walton (Ok-6)*

(Percentage occurrence by level given in italics)

Levels	Leon Check Stamped	Weeden Island Plain	Weeden Island Incised	Carrabelle Incised	Carrabelle Punctated	Keith Incised	Indian Pass Incised	Tucker Ridge-pinched	Wakulla Check Stamped	Swift Creek Complicated Stamped	Santa Rosa Stamped	Basin Bayou Incised	Alligator Bayou Stamped	Franklin Plain	West Florida Cord-marked	Mound Field Net-marked	Plain Plaited Fabric Impressed	Deptford Linear Check Stamped	Deptford Bold Check Stamped	Deptford Simple Stamped	Plain Red	Smooth Plain	Residual Plain	Unclassified	Total sherds by level
1	....	3	2	6	8	....	....	2	4	....	....	....	....	....	....	....	....	....	....	....	....	2	123	6	157
	....	*.019*	*.012*	*.039*	*.051*	....	....	*.012*	*.026*	....	....	....	....	....	....	....	....	....	....	....	....	*.012*	*.783*	*.039*	....
2	....	7	3	6	26	1	1	1	3	1	....	....	....	....	1	....	3	....	....	....	....	12	183	5	255
	....	*.027*	*.011*	*.023*	*.101*	*.003*	*.003*	*.003*	*.011*	*.003*	....	....	....	....	*.007*	....	*.011*	....	....	....	....	*.048*	*.717*	*.018*	....
3	2	13	7	7	14	....	....	....	....	2	....	....	3	....	3	....	1	....	....	....	....	10	174	1	237
	.008	*.054*	*.03*	*.03*	*.058*	....	....	....	....	*.008*	....	....	*.012*	....	*.012*	....	*.004*	....	....	....	....	*.042*	*.725*	*.004*	....
4	....	4	6	4	11	2	....	1	....	2	....	....	1	....	2	2	....	....	....	....	....	5	127	....	169
	....	*.023*	*.034*	*.023*	*.065*	*.011*	....	*.006*	....	*.011*	....	....	*.006*	....	*.011*	*.011*	....	....	....	....	....	*.029*	*.751*	....	....
5	....	8	3	1	15	1	1	....	....	2	1	1	....	....	....	1	....	....	....	1	1	5	135	3	179
	....	*.046*	*.017*	*.005*	*.081*	*.005*	*.005*	....	....	*.011*	*.005*	*.005*	....	....	....	*.005*	....	....	....	*.005*	*.005*	*.027*	*.748*	*.017*	....
6	....	8	1	3	12	....	....	....	1	1	....	....	....	....	....	....	....	....	1	....	....	3	168	....	198
	....	*.044*	*.006*	*.016*	*.066*	....	....	....	*.006*	*.006*	....	....	....	....	....	....	....	....	*.006*	....	....	*.016*	*.848*	....	....
7	....	7	9	....	13	....	2	....	....	2	....	1	....	....	....	....	....	....	....	....	....	9	156	4	203
	....	*.035*	*.044*	....	*.064*	....	*.009*	....	....	*.009*	....	*.005*	....	....	....	....	....	....	....	....	....	*.044*	*.768*	*.02*	....
8	....	2	4	....	5	....	....	1	....	....	....	....	2	....	....	....	....	....	....	2	....	5	43	....	64
	....	*.031*	*.062*	....	*.078*	....	....	*.015*	....	....	....	....	*.031*	....	....	....	....	....	....	*.031*	....	*.078*	*.671*	....	....
9	....	1	....	....	3	....	....	....	....	....	....	....	....	....	....	....	....	....	....	....	....	....	37	2	44
	....	*.022*	....	....	*.066*	....	....	....	....	....	....	....	....	....	....	....	....	....	....	....	....	....	*.84*	*.044*	....
10	....	....	....	....	2	....	....	....	....	....	....	....	....	....	....	....	....	....	....	....	....	1	27	2	32
	....	....	....	....	*.062*	....	....	....	....	....	....	....	....	....	....	....	....	....	....	....	....	*.031*	*.843*	*.062*	....
11	....	....	1	....	....	....	....	....	....	1	....	....	....	....	....	....	....	....	1	....	....	1	25	1	30
	....	....	*.033*	....	....	....	....	....	....	*.033*	....	....	....	....	....	....	....	....	*.033*	....	....	*.033*	*.888*	*.033*	....
12	....	....	....	....	1	....	....	....	....	....	....	....	....	....	....	....	....	....	....	....	....	....	25	....	26
	....	....	....	....	*.039*	....	....	....	....	....	....	....	....	....	....	....	....	....	....	....	....	....	*.961*	....	....
13	....	1	....	....	....	....	....	....	....	....	....	....	....	....	....	....	....	1	....	....	....	....	11	....	13
	....	*.076*	....	....	....	....	....	....	....	....	....	....	....	....	....	....	....	*.076*	....	....	....	....	*.843*	....	....
14	....	....	....	....	....	....	....	....	....	....	....	....	....	....	....	....	....	....	....	....	....	....	1	....	1
	....	....	....	....	....	....	....	....	....	....	....	....	....	....	....	....	....	....	....	....	....	....	*1.00*	....	....
																							Pit total		1,608

TABLE 9.—*Sherd classification of pits II and III, Fort Walton (Ok-6)*

(Percentage occurrence by level given in italics)

Levels	Fort Walton Incised	Weeden Island Plain	Weeden Island Incised	Carrabelle Punctated	Wakulla Check Stamped	Swift Creek Complicated Stamped	Santa Rosa Stamped	Basin Bayou Incised	Alligator Bayou Stamped	Franklin Plain	Deptford Linear Check Stamped	Deptford Bold Check Stamped	Deptford Simple Stamped	Smooth Plain	Residual Plain	Unclassified	Total sherds by level
Pit II, Fort Walton																	
1	....	1	2	1	8	2	....	....	....	2	....	....	....	....	130	1	153
	....	*.006*	*.013*	*.006*	*.052*	*.013*	....	....	....	*.013*	....	....	....	....	*.851*	*.006*	....
2	....	1	2	....	7	1	....	....	....	2	....	1	....	3	70	1	90
	....	*.011*	*.022*	....	*.077*	*.011*	....	....	....	*.022*	....	*.011*	....	*.033*	*.778*	*.011*	....
3	....	....	....	....	....	1	....	....	1	....	....	....	....	1	36	5	44
	....	....	....	....	....	*.023*	....	....	*.023*	....	....	....	....	*.023*	*.818*	*.113*	....
4	....	....	....	1	....	....	....	....	....	....	....	....	....	....	6	1	8
	....	....	....	*.125*	....	....	....	....	....	....	....	....	....	....	*.75*	*.125*	....
5	....	....	....	....	....	....	....	2	....	....	....	....	....	....	5	....	7
	....	....	....	....	....	....	....	*.286*	....	....	....	....	....	....	*.714*	....	....
															Pit total	....	302
Pit III, Fort Walton																	
1	1	12	3	5	23	....	....	2	....	....	....	....	....	3	140	6	199
	.005	*.060*	*.015*	*.025*	*.115*	....	....	*.01*	....	....	....	....	....	*.015*	*.703*	*.03*	....
2	1	7	12	5	8	....	....	....	....	....	....	....	....	3	93	1	140
	.007	*.05*	*.086*	*.036*	*.128*	....	....	....	....	....	....	....	....	*.021*	*.664*	*.007*	....
3	....	2	2	1	4	....	....	2	....	1	....	1	5	1	37	1	57
	....	*.036*	*.036*	*.018*	*.070*	....	....	*.036*	....	*.018*	....	*.018*	*.088*	*.018*	*.650*	*.018*	....
4	....	1	....	....	17	....	1	1	....	3	....	4	....	5	24	3	59
	....	*.017*	....	....	*.288*	....	*.017*	*.017*	....	*.051*	....	*.068*	....	*.085*	*.407*	*.051*	....
5	....	....	6	....	1	1	....	....	1	....	1	3	....	1	9	....	23
	....	....	*.261*	....	*.043*	*.043*	....	....	*.043*	....	*.043*	*.13*	....	*.043*	*.391*	....	....
															Pit total	....	478

a sequence is consistent within itself and checks fairly well with the stratigraphic data from the other excavated sites. The alignments of the levels of the three pits follow the frequency patterns of the various marker types. The occurrences of Weeden Island Incised and Carrabelle Punctated, Wakulla Check Stamped, and the Santa Rosa-Swift Creek types were matched across from pit VI to pit VII, resulting in level 1 of pit VI being correlated with level 3 of pit VII. In a similar manner the occurrences in pit IV were compared with those of pit VI; and level 1 of pit IV was correlated with level 4 of pit VI and level 6 of pit VII. This gave a total of 19 levels with considerable overlap among the pits. Percentage of types for each level were then computed on the basis of the "greater" levels where there were instances of overlap. For instance, "greater" level 6, composed of level 1, pit IV, level 4, pit VI, and level 6, pit VII, combines the sherds of all these levels, totaling 371. The Weeden Island decorated types for this combined level are then totaled to 19, an occurrence of .048 percent of the combined or "greater" level.

Gross and simplified as this system is, the various types and type complexes fall into easily recognizable trends of vertical occurrence.[12] Two periods, first the Santa Rosa-Swift Creek, and later the Weeden Island, are substantially documented. The Fort Walton Period is not well represented, but enough sherds were found to prove occupancy of that time, and these sherds are similar or identical to the vessels which Moore found with the burials in the big pyramidal mound. The Deptford Period is only suggested in the bottom levels. Deptford Linear Check Stamped, the marker type for the period, was not found in significant quantity at Fort Walton. The Carrabelle stratification would indicate that Deptford Bold Check Stamped and Deptford Simple Stamped have a later occurrence than Deptford Linear Check Stamped, and, also, that they are found in small numbers in dominantly Swift Creek Period levels. Such would seem to be the case at Fort Walton where only the "tag-end" manifestations of the Deptford Period were observed.

---

[12] The greatest weakness, in this case, is not the inspectional and subjective matching of the levels from one pit to another, but the relatively small numbers of decorated sherds, and total sherds, in most of the lower levels of the pits. Thus, the high occurrences, expressed on the graph in figure 13, of Swift Creek Complicated Stamped and Basin Bayou Incised, in level 19, are based upon one sherd each.

TABLE 10.—*Sherd classification of pit IV, Fort Walton (Ok-6)*

(Percentage occurrence by level given in italics)

Levels	Pensacola Plain	Leon Checked Stamped	Weeden Island Plain	Carrabelle Incised	Carrabelle Punctated	Wakulla Check Stamped	Swift Creek Complicated Stamped	St. Andrews Complicated Stamped	Crooked River Complicated Stamped	Santa Rosa Stamped	Basin Bayou Incised	Alligator Bayou Stamped	Franklin Plain	West Florida Cord-marked	Deptford Bold Check Stamped	Deptford Simple Stamped	Smooth Plain	Residual Plain	Unclassified	Total sherds by level
1	3 *.057*	....	....	....	2 *.038*	....	....	....	....	....	....	....	....	....	....	....	1 *.019*	44 *.845*	2 *.038*	52
2	1 *.019*	....	3 *.056*	1 *.019*	....	3 *.056*	....	....	....	....	....	1 *.019*	....	....	2 *.037*	....	8 *.150*	33 *.622*	1 *.019*	53
3	....	....	....	....	....	....	2 *.047*	....	....	2 *.047*	2 *.047*	2 *.047*	1 *.023*	....	2 *.047*	....	....	30 *.714*	1 *.023*	42
4	....	....	....	....	....	....	5 *.108*	....	....	2 *.043*	1 *.021*	....	....	....	3 *.065*	3 *.065*	4 *.086*	26 *.565*	2 *.043*	46
5	....	....	....	....	1 *.025*	....	....	....	1 *.025*	1 *.025*	1 *.025*	1 *.025*	1 *.025*	1 *.025*	....	1 *.025*	3 *.078*	26 *.666*	2 *.051*	39
6	....	1 *.037*	1 *.037*	....	....	1 *.037*	2 *.074*	....	....	2 *.074*	....	1 *.037*	....	....	1 *.037*	2 *.074*	2 *.074*	14 *.518*	....	27
7	....	....	....	....	....	....	....	....	....	2 *.045*	2 *.022*	4 *.09*	....	....	4 *.09*	....	....	31 *.704*	1 *.022*	44
8	....	....	....	....	....	....	1 *.025*	....	....	2 *.051*	....	3 *.078*	....	....	2 *.051*	....	2 *.051*	24 *.615*	5 *.130*	39
9	....	....	....	....	....	1 *.111*	....	1 *.111*	....	....	....	....	1 *.111*	....	1 *.111*	1 *.111*	....	3 *.333*	1 *.111*	9
10	....	....	....	....	....	....	....	....	....	....	1 *.090*	....	....	....	1 *.090*	1 *.090*	....	8 *.727*	....	11
11	....	....	....	....	....	....	....	....	....	....	....	....	....	....	1 *.142*	1 *.142*	1 *.142*	3 *.427*	1 *.142*	7
12	....	....	....	....	....	....	....	....	....	1 *.100*	3 *.300*	....	1 *.100*	....	....	....	....	5 *.50*	....	10
13	....	....	....	....	....	....	1 *.111*	....	....	....	....	....	....	1 *.111*	....	3 *.333*	....	2 *.222*	2 *.222*	9
14	....	....	....	....	....	....	....	....	....	....	1 *.125*	1 *.125*	1 *.125*	....	....	2 *.250*	....	2 *.250*	1 *.125*	8
																		Pit total		396

Classification of surface sherds from Fort Walton

Fort Walton Complex	
Fort Walton Incised	1
Pensacola Series:	
Pensacola Incised	1
Pensacola Red	1
Pensacola Plain	10
Weeden Island Complex	
Weeden Island Series:	
Weeden Island Incised	5
Weeden Island Plain	13
Carrabelle Incised	3
Carrabelle Punctated	8
Keith Incised	1
Tucker Ridge-pinched	2
Wakulla Check Stamped	19
Santa Rosa-Swift Creek Complex	
Swift Creek Complicated Stamped	13
Basin Bayou Incised	1
Deptford Complex	
Deptford Series:	
Deptford Bold Check Stamped	2
Deptford Simple Stamped	1
Miscellaneous	
Plain Plaited Fabric Impressed	1
Plain Red	1
Smooth Plain	1
Residual Plain	177
Unclassified	3
Total sherds	264

TABLE 11.—*Sherd classification of pit V, Fort Walton (Ok-6)*

(Percentage occurrence by level given in italics)

Levels	Fort Walton Incised	Pensacola Plain	Weeden Island Plain	Carrabelle Punctated	Tucker Ridge-pinched	Wakulla Check Stamped	Crooked River Complicated Stamped	West Florida Cord-marked	Plain Red	Smooth Plain	Residual Plain	Total sherds by level
1	....	....	....	....	2	1	....	....	....	....	37	40
	....	....	....	....	*.050*	*.025*	....	....	....	....	*.925*	....
2	1	....	1	1	....	2	....	1	....	2	50	61
	.016	....	*.016*	*.065*	....	*.033*	....	*.016*	....	*.033*	*.821*	....
3	....	1	....	2	....	....	1	....	1	1	23	29
	....	*.034*	....	*.069*	....	....	*.034*	....	*.034*	*.034*	*.793*	....
4	....	....	....	....	....	....	....	....	....	1	8	9
	....	....	....	....	....	....	....	....	....	*.110*	*.890*	....
										Pit total		139

TABLE 12.—*Sherd classification of pit VI, Fort Walton (Ok-6)*

(Percentage occurrence by level given in italics)

Levels	Fort Walton Incised	Pensacola Plain	Weeden Island Plain	Weeden Island Incised	Carrabelle Incised	Carrabelle Punctated	Keith Incised	Tucker Ridge-pinched	Wakulla Check Stamped	Swift Creek Complicated Stamped	Crooked River Complicated Stamped	Santa Rosa Stamped	Basin Bayou Incised	Alligator Bayou Stamped	Franklin Plain	West Florida Cord-marked	Deptford Bold Check Stamped	Deptford Simple Stamped	Plain Red	Smooth Plain	Residual Plain	Unclassified	Total sherds by level
1	....	2	1	2	2	1	....	....	2	....	....	....	....	....	....	....	....	....	....	....	45	2	57
	....	*.035*	*.017*	*.035*	*.035*	*.017*	....	....	*.035*	....	....	....	....	....	....	....	....	....	....	....	*.759*	*.035*	....
2	....	3	2	....	....	2	....	....	2	....	....	....	....	....	....	....	....	....	1	1	33	....	44
	....	*.068*	*.045*	....	....	*.045*	....	....	*.045*	....	....	....	....	....	....	....	....	....	*.022*	*.022*	*.750*	....	....
3	3	4	6	5	....	1	1	3	20	1	....	....	....	....	....	....	....	....	....	3	85	3	135
	.022	*.029*	*.044*	*.037*	....	*.007*	*.007*	*.022*	*.148*	*.007*	....	....	....	....	....	....	....	....	....	*.022*	*.622*	*.022*	....
4	....	....	6	4	....	5	....	....	22	1	....	....	....	....	1	....	....	....	1	7	143	8	198
	....	....	*.030*	*.020*	....	*.020*	....	....	*.111*	*.005*	....	....	....	....	*.005*	....	....	....	*.005*	*.035*	*.722*	*.040*	....
5	....	....	3	8	....	7	....	....	5	2	....	1	2	....	....	....	1	....	....	5	79	....	113
	....	....	*.052*	*.141*	....	*.123*	....	....	*.087*	*.017*	....	*.008*	*.017*	....	....	....	*.008*	....	....	*.087*	*.699*	....	....
6	....	....	1	....	....	3	....	....	1	1	1	2	3	....	....	....	....	....	....	2	44	1	59
	....	....	*.016*	....	....	*.033*	....	....	*.016*	*.016*	*.016*	*.033*	*.033*	....	....	....	....	....	....	*.033*	*.745*	*.016*	....
7	....	....	....	....	....	1	....	....	....	....	....	....	1	2	....	....	....	....	....	5	26	....	35
	....	....	....	....	....	*.028*	....	....	....	....	....	....	*.028*	*.057*	....	....	....	....	....	*.141*	*.742*	....	....
8	....	....	1	....	....	....	....	1	1	....	....	1	....	2	....	....	....	....	....	....	14	1	21
	....	....	*.047*	....	....	....	....	*.047*	*.047*	....	....	*.047*	....	*.094*	....	....	....	....	....	....	*.666*	*.047*	....
9	....	....	....	....	1	....	....	....	....	1	....	....	....	....	....	....	1	1	....	....	1	2	7
	....	....	....	....	*.142*	....	....	....	....	*.142*	....	....	....	....	....	....	*.142*	*.142*	....	....	*.142*	*.285*	....
10	....	....	1	....	....	....	....	....	....	3	....	....	....	....	....	1	1	....	....	1	4	3	14
	....	....	*.071*	....	....	....	....	....	....	*.215*	....	....	....	....	....	*.071*	*.071*	....	....	*.071*	*.286*	*.215*	....
11	....	....	1	....	1	....	....	....	....	1	....	....	....	....	....	....	1	....	....	....	5	....	9
	....	....	*.111*	....	*.111*	....	....	....	....	*.111*	....	....	....	....	....	....	*.111*	....	....	....	*.555*	....	....
12	....	....	1	....	....	....	....	....	....	....	....	....	....	....	....	....	....	....	....	....	2	1	4
	....	....	*.250*	....	....	....	....	....	....	....	....	....	....	....	....	....	....	....	....	....	*.50*	*.250*	....
																					Pit total		696

TABLE 13.—*Sherd classification of pit VII, Fort Walton (Ok-6)*

(Percentage occurrence by level given in italics)

Levels	Pensacola Plain	Leon Check Stamped	Weeden Island Plain	Weeden Island Incised	Carrabelle Incised	Carrabelle Punctated	Keith Incised	Indian Pass Incised	Wakulla Check Stamped	Swift Creek Complicated Stamped	Santa Rosa Stamped	Basin Bayou Incised	Alligator Bayou Stamped	Franklin Plain	West Florida Cord-marked	Mound Field Net-marked	Plain Plaited Fabric Impressed	Smooth Plain	Residual Plain	Unclassified	Total sherds by level
1	2	....	1	2	....	7	....	1	1	....	....	....	....	....	1	....	....	3	78	3	101
	.020	....	*.030*	*.020*	....	*.070*	....	*.010*	*.010*	....	....	....	....	....	*.010*	....	....	*.030*	*.078*	*.030*	....
2	1	1	7	3	2	4	1	2	2	1	....	....	2	....	4	....	1	8	68	4	111
	.009	*.009*	*.063*	*.027*	*.018*	*.036*	*.009*	*.018*	*.018*	*.009*	....	....	*.018*	....	*.036*	....	*.009*	*.072*	*.612*	*.036*	....
3	....	....	3	....	3	9	....	....	4	1	....	....	1	....	1	1	....	7	98	3	131
	....	....	*.022*	....	*.022*	*.068*	....	....	*.031*	*.007*	....	....	*.007*	....	*.007*	*.007*	....	*.053*	*.748*	*.022*	....
4	....	....	6	4	1	13	....	1	2	....	....	....	....	....	....	1	....	2	86	1	117
	....	....	*.053*	*.034*	*.008*	*.113*	....	*.008*	*.017*	....	....	....	....	....	....	*.008*	....	*.017*	*.735*	*.008*	....
5	....	....	2	2	2	9	....	....	1	2	....	....	....	....	....	....	....	6	99	1	125
	....	....	*.016*	*.016*	*.016*	*.072*	....	....	*.008*	*.016*	....	....	....	....	....	....	....	*.048*	*.792*	*.008*	....
6	....	....	5	6	....	2	....	3	1	1	....	....	....	....	....	....	....	8	88	6	121
	....	....	*.041*	*.049*	....	*.016*	....	*.024*	*.008*	*.008*	....	....	....	....	....	....	....	*.067*	*.65*	*.048*	....
7	....	....	10	7	2	4	1	....	1	....	....	....	....	....	1	2	....	1	45	....	75
	....	....	*.133*	*.093*	*.026*	*.053*	*.013*	....	*.013*	....	....	....	....	....	*.013*	*.026*	....	*.013*	*.600*	....	....
8	....	....	1	....	....	3	....	....	1	5	1	1	....	....	....	....	....	2	50	2	67
	....	....	*.014*	....	....	*.045*	....	....	*.014*	*.074*	*.014*	*.014*	....	....	....	....	....	*.028*	*.744*	*.028*	....
9	....	....	....	....	....	1	....	....	....	2	....	2	1	....	....	....	....	....	30	....	36
	....	....	....	....	....	*.027*	....	....	....	*.055*	....	*.055*	*.027*	....	....	....	....	....	*.833*	....	....
10	....	....	1	....	....	....	....	....	....	1	....	....	....	3	....	....	....	....	14	3	23
	....	....	*.043*	....	....	....	....	....	....	*.043*	....	....	....	*.130*	....	....	....	....	*.608*	*.130*	....
11	....	....	....	....	....	....	....	....	....	1	....	....	1	....	1	....	....	....	....	....	4
	....	....	....	....	....	....	....	....	....	*.250*	....	....	*.250*	....	*.250*	....	....	....	....	....	....
																			Pit total		911

GULF BREEZE, SANTA ROSA COUNTY (SA-8)

Description of the site.—On the south or Santa Rosa Sound side of the peninsula which separates Pensacola Bay from the sound there are a number of midden accumulations. Four of these middens, visited by the survey in the summer of 1940, are grouped together in the space of about 2.5 to 5 miles from the western end of the peninsula. One of these sites, about 4 miles from the end of the peninsula, has been designated as the Gulf Breeze site (map 2) after a little summer resort not far from the Pensacola Bay bridge. It is on the property held permanently as a United States Naval Reservation. In 1940 a temporary CCC side-camp, from Foley, Ala., was established near the spot.

Actually, along the shore of the sound the midden sites are so numerous that they virtually consist of a continuous occupation. Describing this country in 1883, S. T. Walker writes (1885, p. 859):

> In proceeding east the first shell heaps are met with at Dr. Rotherford's place, about 2 miles east of the old Government Live Oak Plantation. Immense beds of shell and the usual indications mark this as the former residence of a large population. The slopes of the hills are covered with irregular beds of shell from 2 to 6 feet in thickness, which occupy an area of several acres.

As near as can be determined this is in the general vicinity of the Gulf Breeze site.

This site is on the low bank back of the beach, some 2 meters above sea level at high tide. Outcroppings of shell and black midden, about .50 meter deep, can be observed along the top of this bank which is undergoing erosion. Like most of the land along the sound it is thickly grown with scrub trees and underbrush, and the best possible estimate on the extent of the immediate deposit would be about 40 meters in diameter. Although the surface was overgrown, it was possible to gather a sherd collection from along the bank.

Excavations.—Six test pits were put down at the Gulf Breeze site within a radius of less than 10 meters (map 7). Pit I (3 x 3 meters) was representative of the others in soil content. The upper soil zone was composed of brown sand, humic stain, and a little shell and midden. Below this top layer was the main midden and shell zone. This was, in turn, underlain by a gray, midden-streaked transitional zone; then by gray-white natural sand; and, finally, by reddish sand. The tangled mat of many roots (living and dead) of trees and bushes was noted down to a depth of at least .50 meter or part way through the concentrated shell and midden layer.

Sherds were plentiful in all levels of pit I down to .70 meter below the surface. In the eighth level, it was necessary to take the pit down to 1.10 meters to recover sherds from a pocket of midden which extended downward from the west corner. This pocket, upon

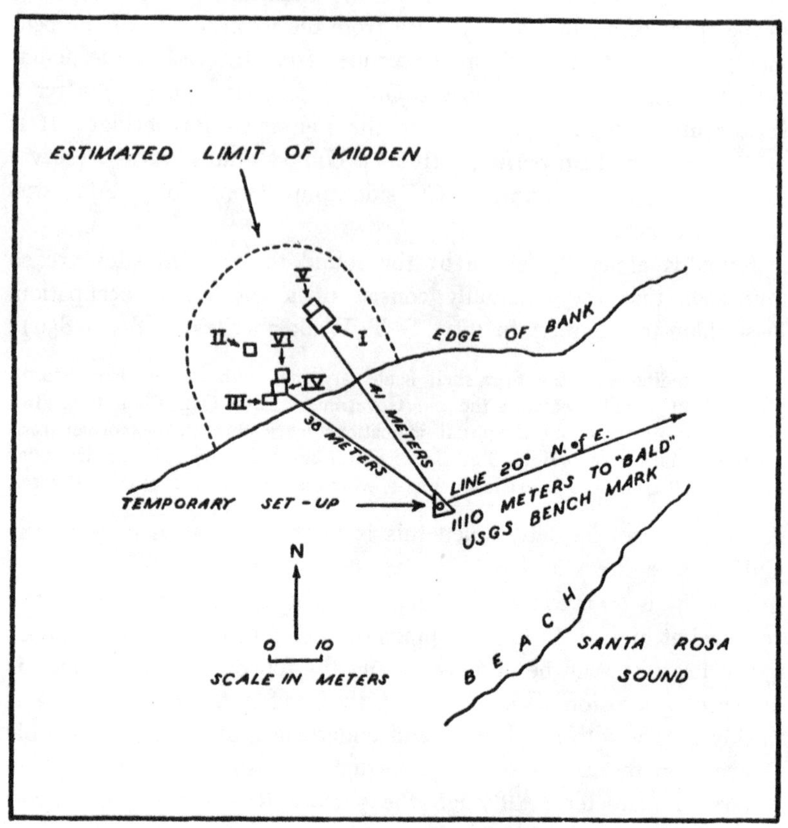

Map 7.—The Gulf Breeze site, Santa Rosa County (Sa-8).

further excavation, proved to be an old refuse pit containing black soil, shells, and several sherds. All the sherds taken from it were cataloged with the material of level 8 (.70-1.10 meters), although the actual limits of the refuse pocket extended to 1.80 meters below the surface.

There were not many sherds in pit II (1.50 x 1.50 meters). Seven levels were removed, all .10 meter in thickness except the last which extended from .60 to .90 meter. Pit III (1.50 x 1.50 meters) yielded more sherds than pit II and was excavated in 8 levels, down to .80 meter below the surface. Pit IV (2 x 2 meters) was excavated to .70 meter below the surface for a total of seven levels. Sherds were fairly numerous, averaging about 50 for each of the upper levels. Pit V (2 x 2 meters) was carried down to .90 meter in eight levels, the last level being .20 meter in thickness. There were almost as many sherds in this pit as in pit I, an average of well over 50 per level with the exception of the lower and semisterile levels. Pit VI (2 x 2 meters square) went to a depth of .85 meter below the surface, the last and sixth level going from .50 to .85 meter. The sherd yield was about the same as that of pit IV.

Stratigraphy.—An examination of the tables for the various excavations at Gulf Breeze (see tables 14, 15, 16) does not reveal any significant vertical changes. The refuse was thin, although no thinner than that tested at Carrabelle, where definite stratigraphic results were forthcoming. Small amounts of shell-tempered (Pensacola Series) and other Fort Walton Period types are seen in the topmost levels of pits II, III, IV, and V. Occasional shell-tempered sherds were also found in the lower levels in pits I and VI. Pottery of the Weeden Island Complex is conspicuous by its absence. Only one or two possible Weeden Island sherds were recovered out of all six pits. No Deptford Linear Check Stamped was present and only a half dozen Deptford Bold Check and Deptford Simple Stamped sherds were scattered through various levels of the different pits. Swift Creek Complicated Stamped ran almost from top to bottom of all pits. In association were the incised and rocker-stamped types of the Santa Rosa Series, including Santa Rosa Stamped, Santa Rosa Punctated, Basin Bayou Incised, and Alligator Bayou Stamped. In pits II, III, V, and VI there is a suggestion that these last-mentioned four types may have a slightly earlier range than the Swift Creek Complicated Stamped; but on present evidence this is so vague and inconclusive that it can hardly be considered.

The site would appear to have been occupied at a relatively early date, during the Santa Rosa Swift Creek Period. The several shell-tempered sherds, the majority of which were found in the upper levels, imply some Fort Walton Period activity at the site after an interval of no occupation.

TABLE 14.—*Sherd classification of pits I and II, Gulf Breeze (Sa-8)*

(Percentage occurrence by level given in italics)

Levels	Fort Walton Incised	Lake Jackson Plain	Pensacola Incised	Pensacola Plain	Safety Harbor Incised	Weeden Island Plain	Weeden Island Incised	Carrabelle Incised	Swift Creek Complicated Stamped	St. Andrews Complicated Stamped	Santa Rosa Stamped	Basin Bayou Incised	Alligator Bayou Stamped	Franklin Plain	Deptford Bold Check Stamped	Deptford Simple Stamped	Smooth Plain	Residual Plain	Unclassified	Total sherds of level
Pit I, Gulf Breeze																				
1	1 *.013*	....	1 *.013*	....	1 *.013*	....	1 *.013*	....	6 *.083*	....	1 *.013*	2 *.027*	....	1 *.013*	....	2 *.027*	....	55 *.763*	1 *.013*	72
2	1 *.009*	....	....	2 *.019*	....	....	....	....	9 *.089*	....	1 *.009*	2 *.019*	1 *.009*	3 *.029*	....	....	2 *.019*	80 *.792*	....	101
3	....	1 *.021*	....	....	....	....	....	....	7 *.149*	....	1 *.021*	2 *.042*	....	....	....	....	1 *.021*	35 *.744*	....	47
4	....	....	....	1 *.010*	....	....	....	....	10 *.107*	2 *.021*	1 *.010*	1 *.010*	6 *.064*	1 *.010*	....	....	6 *.064*	63 *.677*	1 *.010*	93
5	....	....	....	....	....	....	....	1 *.017*	8 *.137*	....	....	1 *.017*	....	....	....	....	1 *.017*	47 *.810*	....	58
6	....	....	....	1 *.016*	....	....	....	....	9 *.150*	....	....	....	....	1 *.016*	....	....	4 *.064*	44 *.733*	1 *.016*	60
7	....	....	....	....	....	....	....	....	1 *.045*	....	....	2 *.091*	1 *.045*	1 *.045*	1 *.045*	1 *.045*	....	12 *.545*	3 *.136*	22
8	....	....	....	2 *.025*	....	....	....	....	3 *.038*	....	2 *.025*	....	3 *.038*	1 *.038*	....	2 *.038*	....	50 *.649*	11 *.140*	77
																		Pit total		530
Pit II, Gulf Breeze																				
1	....	....	....	....	....	....	....	....	2 *.047*	....	....	....	....	....	....	....	....	19 *.904*	....	21
2	....	....	....	....	....	....	....	....	2 *.117*	....	....	....	....	....	....	....	....	15 *.882*	....	17
3	....	....	....	3 *.073*	....	....	1 *.024*	....	2 *.048*	....	....	....	....	....	....	....	3 *.073*	31 *.756*	1 *.024*	41
4	....	....	....	....	....	....	....	....	1 *.142*	....	....	1 *.142*	....	....	....	....	....	5 *.714*	....	7
5	....	....	....	....	....	....	....	....	1 *.071*	....	1 *.071*	1 *.071*	1 *.071*	....	....	....	....	9 *.642*	1 *.071*	14
6	....	....	....	....	....	1 *.333*	....	....	....	....	....	....	....	....	....	....	....	2 *.666*	....	3
7	....	....	....	....	....	....	....	....	....	....	....	1 *.500*	1 *.500*	....	....	....	....	....	....	2
																		Pit total		105

TABLE 15.—*Sherd classification of pits III and IV, Gulf Breeze (Sa-8)*

(Percentage occurrence by level given in italics)

Levels	Lake Jackson Plain	Pensacola Plain	Swift Creek Complicated Stamped	St. Andrews Complicated Stamped	Santa Rosa Stamped	Basin Bayou Incised	Alligator Bayou Stamped	Santa Rosa Punctated	Franklin Plain	West Florida Cord-marked	Deptford Simple Stamped	Smooth Plain	Residual Plain	Unclassified	Total sherds by level
Pit III, Gulf Breeze															
1	....	....	4	....	....	....	....	....	....	....	....	....	14	....	18
	....	....	*.222*	....	....	....	....	....	....	....	....	....	*.777*	....	....
2	....	1	4	1	....	2	....	1	....	1	....	1	38	2	51
	....	*.019*	*.078*	*.019*	....	*.039*	....	*.019*	....	*.019*	....	*.019*	*.745*	*.039*	....
3	....	....	4	....	1	....	1	....	2	....	2	3	31	....	44
	....	....	*.090*	....	*.022*	....	*.022*	....	*.045*	....	*.045*	*.068*	*.704*	....	....
4	....	....	7	4	1	....	....	....	1	....	....	2	27	2	44
	....	....	*.159*	*.090*	*.022*	....	....	....	*.022*	....	....	*.045*	*.613*	*.045*	....
5	....	....	1	....	5	....	5	....	....	....	....	1	13	....	21
	....	....	*.047*	....	*.238*	....	*.047*	....	....	....	....	*.047*	*.619*	....	....
6	....	....	2	....	7	....	4	1	....	....	....	3	13	1	31
	....	....	*.064*	....	*.225*	....	*.129*	*.033*	....	....	....	*.096*	*.419*	*.033*	....
7	....	....	....	....	3	....	1	....	....	....	....	....	2	1	7
	....	....	....	....	*.428*	....	*.142*	....	....	....	....	....	*.285*	*.142*	....
8	....	....	....	....	....	....	....	....	....	....	....	....	3	....	3
	....	....	....	....	....	....	....	....	....	....	....	....	*.100*	....	....
													Pit total	....	219
Pit IV, Gulf Breeze															
1	....	1	....	....	....	....	1	....	....	....	....	....	12	....	14
	....	*.071*	....	....	....	....	*.071*	....	....	....	....	....	*.857*	....	....
2	3	3	5	....	....	1	....	1	1	....	....	....	41	....	55
	.054	*.054*	*.090*	....	....	*.018*	....	*.018*	*.018*	....	....	....	*.745*	....	....
3	....	1	4	2	....	1	....	....	3	....	....	1	41	....	53
	....	*.018*	*.075*	*.037*	....	*.018*	....	....	*.056*	....	....	*.018*	*.773*	....	....
4	....	....	11	....	7	....	....	1	1	....	....	2	35	1	58
	....	....	*.189*	....	*.120*	....	....	*.017*	*.017*	....	....	*.034*	*.603*	*.017*	....
5	....	....	....	....	5	1	....	....	2	....	....	....	11	....	19
	....	....	....	....	*.263*	*.052*	....	....	*.105*	....	....	....	*.578*	....	....
6	....	....	....	....	....	....	....	....	....	....	....	....	4	....	4
	....	....	....	....	....	....	....	....	....	....	....	....	*1.00*	....	....
7	....	....	1	....	....	....	....	....	....	....	....	....	....	....	1
	....	....	*1.00*	....	....	....	....	....	....	....	....	....	....	....	....
													Pit total	....	204

TABLE 16.—*Sherd classification of pits V and VI, Gulf Breeze (Sa-8)*

(Percentage occurrence by level given in italics)

Levels	Lake Jackson Plain	Pensacola Plain	Swift Creek Complicated Stamped	St. Andrews Complicated Stamped	Santa Rosa Stamped	Basin Bayou Incised	Alligator Bayou Stamped	Santa Rosa Punctated	Franklin Plain	West Florida Cord-marked	Deptford Simple Stamped	Plain Red	Smooth Plain	Residual Plain	Unclassified	Total sherds by level
Pit V, Gulf Breeze																
1	1	1	3	....	....	1	....	1	....	....	....	....	....	60	....	73
	.013	*.013*	*.040*	....	....	*.013*	....	*.013*	....	....	....	....	....	*.821*	*.013*	
2	....	1	7	....	....	1	2	....	1	....	....	....	3	110	....	125
	....	*.008*	*.056*	....	....	*.008*	*.016*	....	*.008*	....	....	....	*.024*	*.880*	....	
3	....	1	5	....	6	2	....	....	....	....	....	....	7	52	....	73
	....	*.013*	*.065*	....	*.078*	*.026*	....	....	....	....	....	....	*.091*	*.712*	....	
4	....	....	7	....	1	4	3	1	1	1	....	....	12	64	1	95
	....	....	*.073*	....	*.010*	*.042*	*.031*	*.010*	*.010*	*.010*	....	....	*.026*	*.676*	*.010*	
5	....	....	3	....	2	1	....	1	3	....	....	2	4	52	1	69
	....	....	*.042*	....	*.028*	*.014*	....	*.014*	*.042*	....	....	*.028*	*.056*	*.753*	*.014*	
6	....	....	2	1	1	....	....	....	....	....	....	....	1	25	1	31
	....	....	*.064*	*.032*	*.032*	....	....	....	....	....	....	....	*.032*	*.806*	*.032*	
7	....	....	1	....	....	....	....	....	1	....	....	....	2	16	....	20
	....	....	*.050*	....	....	....	....	....	*.050*	....	....	....	*.100*	*.800*	....	
8	....	....	....	....	....	....	....	1	....	....	....	....	1	....	....	2
	....	....	....	....	....	....	....	*.500*	....	....	....	....	*.50*	....	....	
														Pit total	....	488
Pit VI, Gulf Breeze																
1	....	....	3	....	....	....	....	....	1	....	....	....	1	27	3	35
	....	....	*.085*	....	....	....	....	....	*.028*	....	....	....	*.028*	*.771*	*.085*	
2	....	1	7	....	....	2	1	1	1	....	....	....	1	56	1	72
	....	*.013*	*.097*	....	....	*.027*	*.013*	*.013*	*.013*	....	....	....	*.013*	*.775*	*.013*	
3	....	....	6	....	4	2	2	....	1	....	....	....	4	32	....	51
	....	....	*.117*	....	*.076*	*.039*	*.039*	....	*.019*	....	....	....	*.076*	*.627*	....	
4	1	1	8	....	2	....	1	....	2	....	....	1	3	35	....	54
	.018	*.018*	*.148*	....	*.037*	....	*.018*	....	*.037*	....	....	*.018*	*.055*	*.648*	....	
5	....	....	....	....	1	1	1	....	1	....	3	....	....	35	....	42
	....	....	....	....	*.023*	*.023*	*.023*	....	*.023*	....	*.071*	....	....	*.833*	....	
6	....	....	....	....	....	....	....	....	....	....	....	....	....	8	....	8
	....	....	....	....	....	....	....	....	....	....	....	....	....	*1.00*	....	
														Pit total	....	262

Classification of surface sherds from Gulf Breeze

Fort Walton Complex	
Fort Walton Incised	1
Pensacola Series:	
Pensacola Incised	5
Pensacola Plain	36
Weeden Island Complex	
Tucker Ridge-pinched	1
Santa Rosa-Swift Creek Complex	
Santa Rosa Series:	
Alligator Bayou Stamped	1
Santa Rosa Stamped	4
Complicated Stamped Series:	
Swift Creek Complicated Stamped	10
St. Andrews Complicated Stamped	1
West Florida Cord-marked (Early Variety.)	1
Franklin Plain	2
Miscellaneous	
Residual Plain	56
Unclassified	9
Total sherds	128

LAKE JACKSON, LEON COUNTY (LE-1)

Description of the site.—Four and one-half miles north of Tallahassee, Fla., in Leon County, there is an impressive mound group (map 2) of six, or possibly seven, mounds.[13] The topography of the immediate setting is a natural lake shore or valley backed immediately to the west of the site by sloping but high bluffs (pl. 3, top). The lake valley stretches northward for about 10 miles and is surrounded by similar bluff and rolling hill formations. At present the lake is little more than a shallow marsh, and, according to old inhabitants of the region, it has been receding for a number of years. Oak and gum trees form a screen along the lower slopes of the bluff around the lake, and cover, or partially cover, some of the mounds. A large part of the area immediately surrounding the mounds has at one time been under cultivation.

Physiographically, the region is a part of the "Southern Pine Hills," a gently rolling red clay formation which begins some 20 to 30 miles inland from the coast. Jackson is one of several lakes in the

[13] Previous to 1940, the only direct reference to the site in the literature, to the best of the author's knowledge, was Boyd, 1939, p. 272.

Tallahassee region formed by the solution of underlying limestones. In general, the Tallahassee region has a greater physiographic resemblance to the red clay hill country of parts of south Georgia than it does to the sandy coastal strip of Florida. The superiority of the soil in this hill country, as compared with the sandy soil of the coast, is attested by modern agriculture which is flourishing around Tallahassee. This present-day condition undoubtedly reflects the aboriginal situation, and, in part, explains the presence of such a large mound center in this region when there are none on the immediate coast.

The mound group is located on the southwest shore of the lake on a small inlet known locally as "McGinnis' Arm." All six or seven of the mounds can be enclosed in an area measuring approximately 450 meters north and south and 375 meters east and west. Six of the mounds are, or were, in all probability, truncated pyramids. Mounds 3 and 6 still preserve this shape, but the others no longer retain their original contours which have been blurred by erosion accelerated by promiscuous digging. The accompanying plan (map 8) exaggerates the shape of all the mounds, as measurements were taken from points estimated to be the corners of the bases and summit platforms.

Mound 2 is much the largest of any of the six, having an estimated height of about 8 meters and base measurements of 65 x 48 meters. What may have been a ramp slopes down from the summit on the northeast side. Viewed from the top, the mound appears to be five- rather than four-sided. Together with mounds 3, 4, and 6, mound 2 forms a quadrangle which is roughly oriented to the cardinal points with mound 2 being on the north. Mound 4 is second in size and is on the west. The base of mound 4 measures 34 x 43 meters, but the height is only about 3 to 4 meters, Mounds 3 and 6, on the south and east, are each about 3 meters high. Mound 6 is particularly well formed, oblong and steep-sided (pl. 3, bottom).

A little to the south of mounds 3 and 4 is mound 5, also approximately 3 meters in height. The summit of this mound seems to be triangular; however, it has been badly scarred by excavations into the top and sides. To the north, a good distance apart from the other mounds, is mound 1, the smallest of the pyramidal mounds. It measures only 21 by 20 meters at the base and is approximately 2 meters high.

The old excavations in the sides of the mounds reveal something of the nature of their construction. All are topped with red clay mantles, and in some, successive clay mantles with intervening beds of sand or midden fill are discernible. Near mounds 2 and 4 are large depressions suggesting borrow pits. There is little doubt that the six mounds are of the platform or substructure type, and future excavations, if they are carried out, will probably reveal house patterns on the various clay mantles.

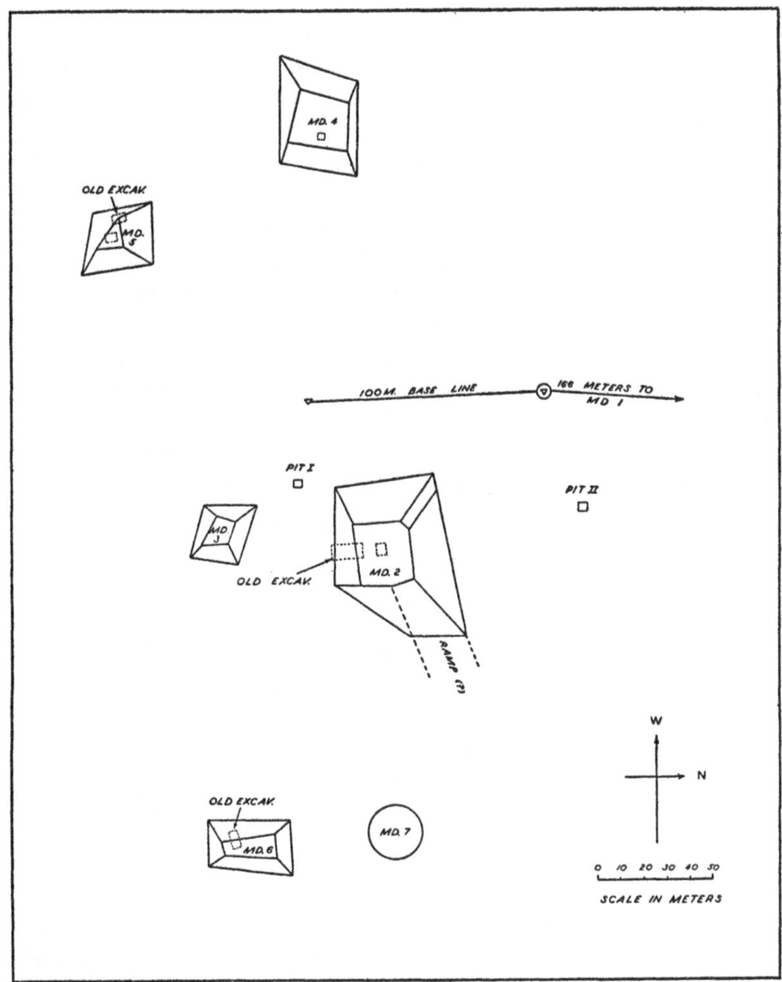

Map 8.—The Lake Jackson site, Leon County (Le-1). The conformation of the mounds is highly stylized.

A few meters to the north of mound 6 is a small, low, circular rise which we have termed mound 7. Not more than a meter high, its artificiality can only be proved by excavation. Although it may be a burial tumulus, the possibility that this low hummock is a house mound is increased by the fact that a small stream flowing nearby has cut through a portion of a baked clay floor.

The area surrounding the mounds is, with few exceptions, covered with sherds. A surface collection was made at large over the site and from concentrations on and around mounds 1 and 2 and the area between these mounds.

Excavations.—Two 3- x 3-meter test pits were made at Lake Jackson in the village area (map 8). Pit I was located about 20 meters south of the southwest corner of the mound. This area, between mounds 2 and 3 appeared, from surface inspection, to be covered with a heavy alluvial layer deposited by a small stream which once ran between the two mounds and then turned northeastward to empty into the lake. It was thought that at such a spot the probable village refuse would be sealed in and protected by the alluvium. Level 1 of pit I was carried down to a depth of .30 meter below the surface. At this depth, sand wash mixed with recent dark brown humus was exposed, and a few eroded sherds were found. In level 2 (.30-.45 meter) the soil appeared the same, and no more sherds were encountered. A small test hole was put down in one corner of the pit at this depth to see if the midden zone lay below the sand and silt. Between .45 and .70 meter consolidated sandy clay and specks of charcoal were observed. Below this was a thinner zone of clean sand which was again underlain by clay and traces of charcoal. Under this second band of clay, clean light brown sand was followed down to 1.40 meters below the surface before the pit was abandoned. It seems likely that the midden, if it existed between mounds 2 and 3, had been scoured away by the action of the stream, or was buried at a considerable depth.

Pit II, on the north side of mound 2, 60 meters or more from the mound, was situated in the midst of an intensive occupation area. The surface, which not long in the past had been plowed, was covered with sherds. In this pit the first level, .10 meter deep, contained 100 sherds. Working in .10-meter arbitrary levels, the first two or two-and-a-half levels were plow-disturbed, and the sherds found were very small fragments. Beginning in level 3 (.20-.30 meter), the soil became more compact, and the color of the midden deepened in intensity. Sherds were most numerous in level 3. Level 4 (.30-.40 meter) revealed undisturbed black midden. A few briquette fragments came out of this level, and there was a small patch of partly burned yellow clay on one side of the pit floor. In level 5 (.40-.50 meter) the midden was much lighter, and the sherd yield dropped to about one-quarter of either of the two previous levels. In level 6 (.50-.60 meter) only a few streaks and spots of dark midden stain showed up in the red-brown loam. It is possible that some of the spots may be post molds, but the excavated area was too small to determine an alignment. Level 7 (.60-.85 meter) was a small test in one quadrant of the pit. In this test, a yellowish calico-clay marl was revealed in an uneven stratum below the loam, but no sherds or other evidence of human occupation were found.

TABLE 17.—*Sherd classification of pit II, Lake Jackson (Le-1)*

Levels	Fort Walton Incised	Lake Jackson Plain	Safety Harbor Incised	Lamar Complicated Stamped	Plain red	Residual Plain	Unclassified	Total sherds by level
1	7	3	2	..	..	85	3	100
2	6	2	1	..	..	136	2	146
3	15	7	2	1	1	181	3	210
4	13	5	1	2	..	155	1	177
5	6	..	..	..	..	34	..	40
6	4	7	..	..	..	23	..	34
						Pit total		707

Stratigraphy.—The pit II excavations showed the same pottery types as the surface collection from the site. The rich but thin midden gave no indications of a percentage stratification of types (table 17). The site, on the basis of the tests and the other collections, belongs to the Fort Walton Period of Gulf Coast occupation, and it is undoubtedly one of the largest mound centers of the late period in northwest Florida. It is possible that earlier materials than those of the Fort Walton Period may be found at the site with intensive excavation.

Classification of surface sherds from Lake Jackson

Fort Walton Complex
- Fort Walton Series:
  - Fort Walton Incised.................................... 21
  - Lake Jackson Plain.................................... 5
- Safety Harbor Incised.................................... 2
- St. Petersburg Incised.................................... 1

Miscellaneous
- Brushed (possibly Walnut Roughened)..................... 1
- Residual Plain 188
  (These are undoubtedly body sherds of the Fort Walton Series.)

Total sherds.... 218

CONCLUSIONS

In briefly analyzing and characterizing the successive culture periods of northwest Florida and their ceramic identities we begin with the earliest (see fig. 14). This is the Deptford Period which is characterized by the appreciable occurrence of the type Deptford Linear Check Stamped. This type is the most distinctive of all the Southeastern check stamped types, and its appearance cannot easily be confused with other types. The evidence for the Deptford Period comes from the stratigraphic tests at Carrabelle where Deptford Linear Check Stamped is the dominant type in the lower levels of four of the tests made in the Carrabelle midden. It is associated with Deptford Bold Check Stamped, Deptford Simple Stamped, Gulf Check Stamped, and small amounts of Swift Creek Complicated Stamped. At Carrabelle, and in other excavations Deptford Bold Check Stamped, Deptford Simple Stamped, and Gulf Check Stamped are found in later contexts where Deptford Linear Checked Stamped is absent.

The Santa Rosa-Swift Creek Period is distinguished by the ascendancy of Swift Creek Complicated Stamped (Early Variety); and the coeval appearances of St. Andrews Complicated Stamped (Early Variety), New River Complicated Stamped, and Crooked River Complicated Stamped (Early Variety). Deptford Bold Check Stamped, Deptford Simple Stamped, and Gulf Diamond Check Stamped occur only in small quantities. The type Franklin Plain enjoys its greatest popularity along with the rise of the complicated stamped pottery. Plain, sand-tempered body sherds, never a large part of the sherd counts from Deptford Period levels, are more common during the Swift Creek Period than previously. At Carrabelle, levels overlying the Deptford Period and underlying those showing Weeden Island decorated pottery best represent this period. The lowest levels at Mound Field also fall into the Santa Rosa-Swift Creek Period. Around St. Andrews Bay and to the west the make-up of the Santa Rosa-Swift Creek Period differs somewhat from the pottery complex seen in the middle levels at Carrabelle and the lower levels at Mound Field. In addition to the early complicated stamped types, Santa Rosa Stamped, Basin Bayou Incised, Alligator Bayou Stamped, and Santa Rosa Punctated appear. These types are also found to the east of St. Andrews Bay, but seem to be more common to burial mounds in which they are found as far east and south as Pinellas County. The Santa Rosa and Alligator Bayou Stamped types are the result of a technologically different surface treatment, being produced by a rocker rather than a

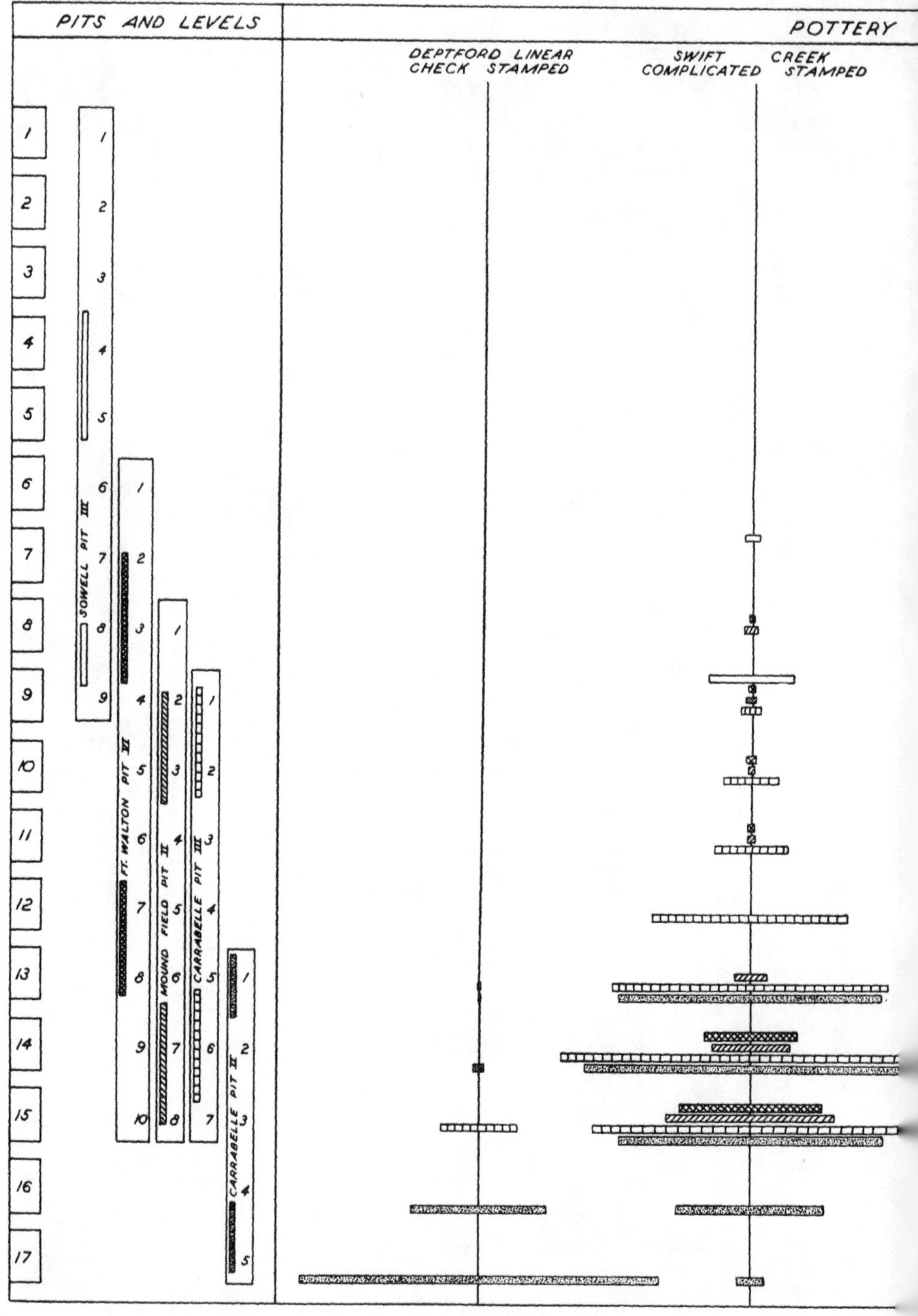

FIG. 14.—Graph showing interrelationships of ceramic stratigraphy amo

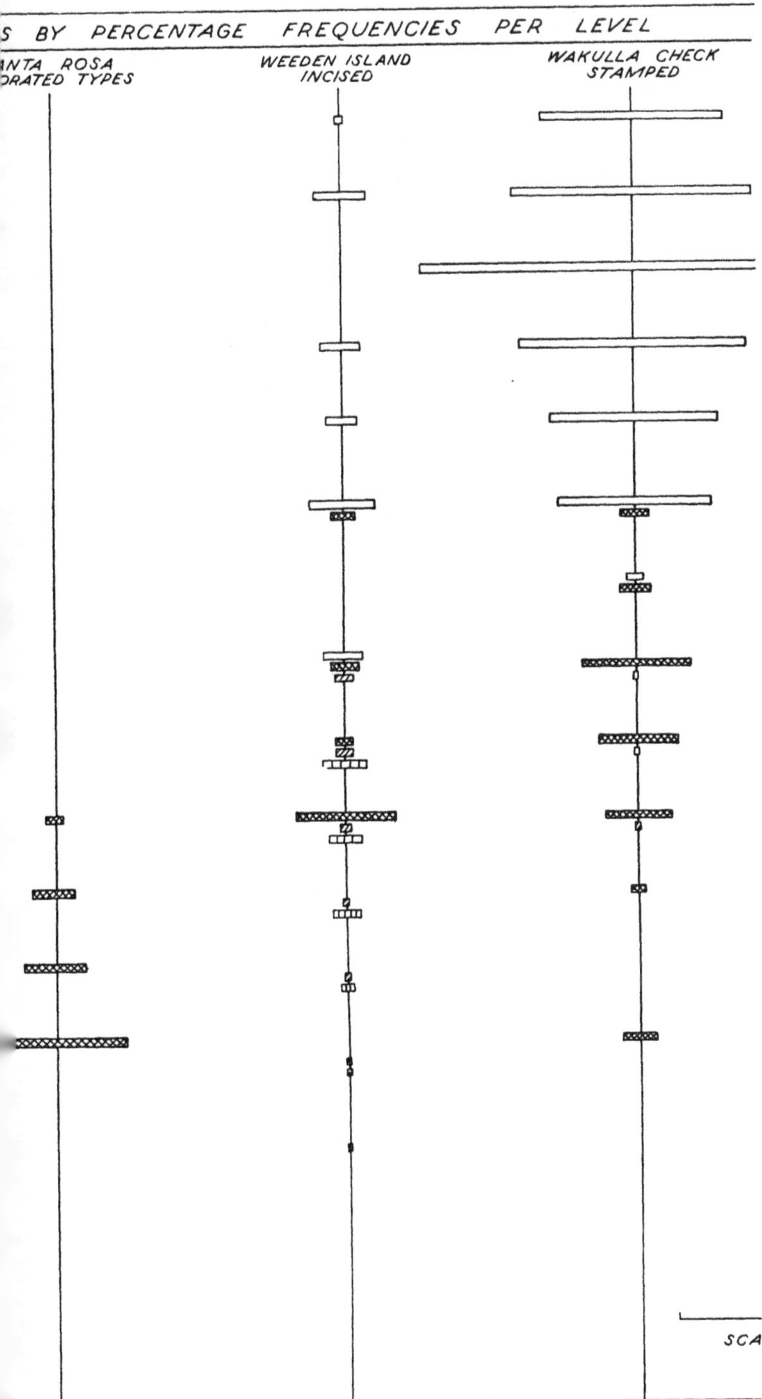

s sites of the northwest coast. Stratigraphic pits at Carrabelle, Mound Fie

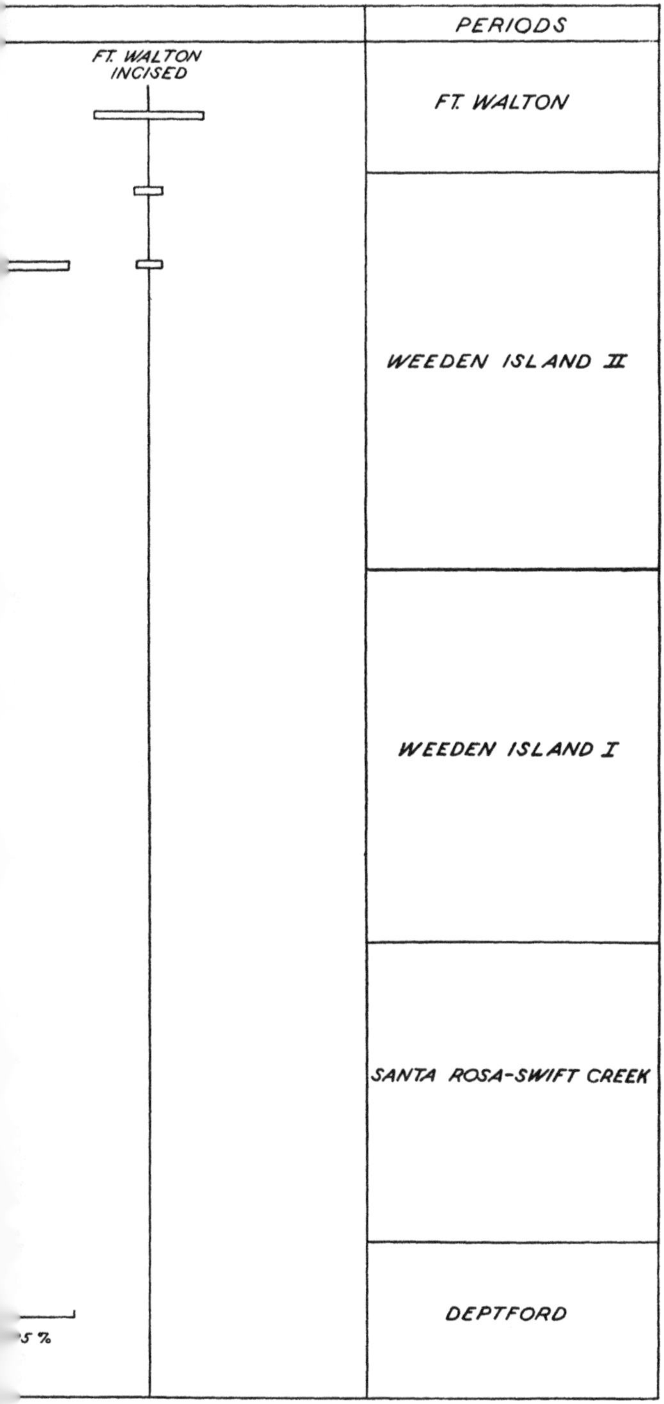

FT. WALTON INCISED

PERIODS
FT. WALTON
WEEDEN ISLAND II
WEEDEN ISLAND I
SANTA ROSA-SWIFT CREEK
DEPTFORD

5 %

owell, and Fort Walton are interdigitated.

flat stamp, and they bear obvious relationship to the Marksville pottery of the lower Mississippi Valley and the Hopewell style of Ohio. Basin Bayou Incised and Santa Rosa Punctated also reflect this general relationship. The lower levels at Fort Walton and the bulk of the midden at Gulf Breeze are representative of the Santa Rosa-Swift Creek Period in the west.

The appearance of Weeden Island Incised, Carrabelle Incised, Carrabelle Punctated, Indian Pass Incised, Keith Incised, Tucker Ridge-pinched, and Weeden Island Plain defines the beginning of Weeden Island. Plain, sand-tempered body sherds are most numerous during the Weeden Island Period, in part the result of the limited surface decoration area of the Weeden Island style vessels. Swift Creek Complicated Stamped is still present in quantities in this period but is undergoing changes as the result of the impact of the new Weeden Island influence. This modified type is referred to as Swift Creek (Late Variety). An early Weeden Island, or what we are calling Weeden Island I, is seen at Mound Field and in the upper Carrabelle levels. At Sowell, most of the midden seems to be Weeden Island II in time. This second stage of Weeden Island is characterized by Wakulla Check Stamped, a small square check stamped typed which occurs in great quantities compared with the decorated Weeden Island types. Swift Creek Complicated Stamped (Late Variety) is definitely on the wane during the Weeden Island II Period, although there is evidence of some overlapping of Swift Creek and Wakulla in the middle and upper levels of the Fort Walton test pits.

The beginnings of the Fort Walton Period are denoted by the occurrences of Fort Walton Incised, Lake Jackson Plain, Pensacola Incised, and Pensacola Plain. The last-named types, both shell-tempered, are common to the west of St. Andrews Bay. At Sowell, Fort Walton, and Gulf Breeze a small proportion of the sherds were of the Fort Walton types. These came exclusively from upper levels. Only at Lake Jackson, a site purely or predominantly of the Fort Walton Period, did we find Fort Walton refuse in any depth or abundance.

IV. EXCAVATIONS ON THE WEST COAST: 1923-1936

INTRODUCTION

This section treats of those excavations that were made under the direction of the Bureau of American Ethnology, Smithsonian Institution, between the years 1923 and 1936 (map 9). Of all the sites discussed only Weeden Island has been previously published upon in any detail (Fewkes, 1924). In this account some material, heretofore not published, is presented from the Weeden Island site. Safety Harbor, which was excavated by Stirling, is presented here for the first time as a site report. The remaining sites, investigated under Stirling's general direction, were a part of a joint Federal Relief Archeological Survey sponsored by the Bureau of American Ethnology and the State of Florida. Some of these had been briefly summarized in a preliminary account (Stirling, 1935).

The location of this group of west coast sites is at the boundary of two of the cultural regions of the Gulf Coast area, the central coast and the Manatee regions (see "Introduction," pp. 2-3). The majority of the sites are within the Manatee region, and those in the central coast region lie just north of the line. For practical purposes they fit best, as a total group, in the Manatee region in that most of them show traits of the peripheral blending between the Gulf Coast and the Glades area to the south. (See Willey, 1948a).

This discussion of site excavations from this part of the Gulf Coast is placed immediately following a similar presentation of basic data for the northwest coast region. These lower central coast and Manatee region excavations differ from those of the northwest in that they are, for the most part, investigations of burial mounds rather than refuse middens. Consequently, the problems of ceramic sequence are not as effectively resolved. In spite of this it is possible, by inferences drawn from the northwest coast, to arrange this group of mounds in chronologic order.

The preparation of these west coast site reports is based upon the examination of collections and upon the field notes and verbal information of the various field supervisors. The Weeden Island analysis was written from the Fewkes report (Fewkes, 1924), from unreported collections, and from information given me by Dr. Stirling. Safety Harbor excavations are described from verbal information given by Dr. Stirling, from a brief published preliminary note (Stir-

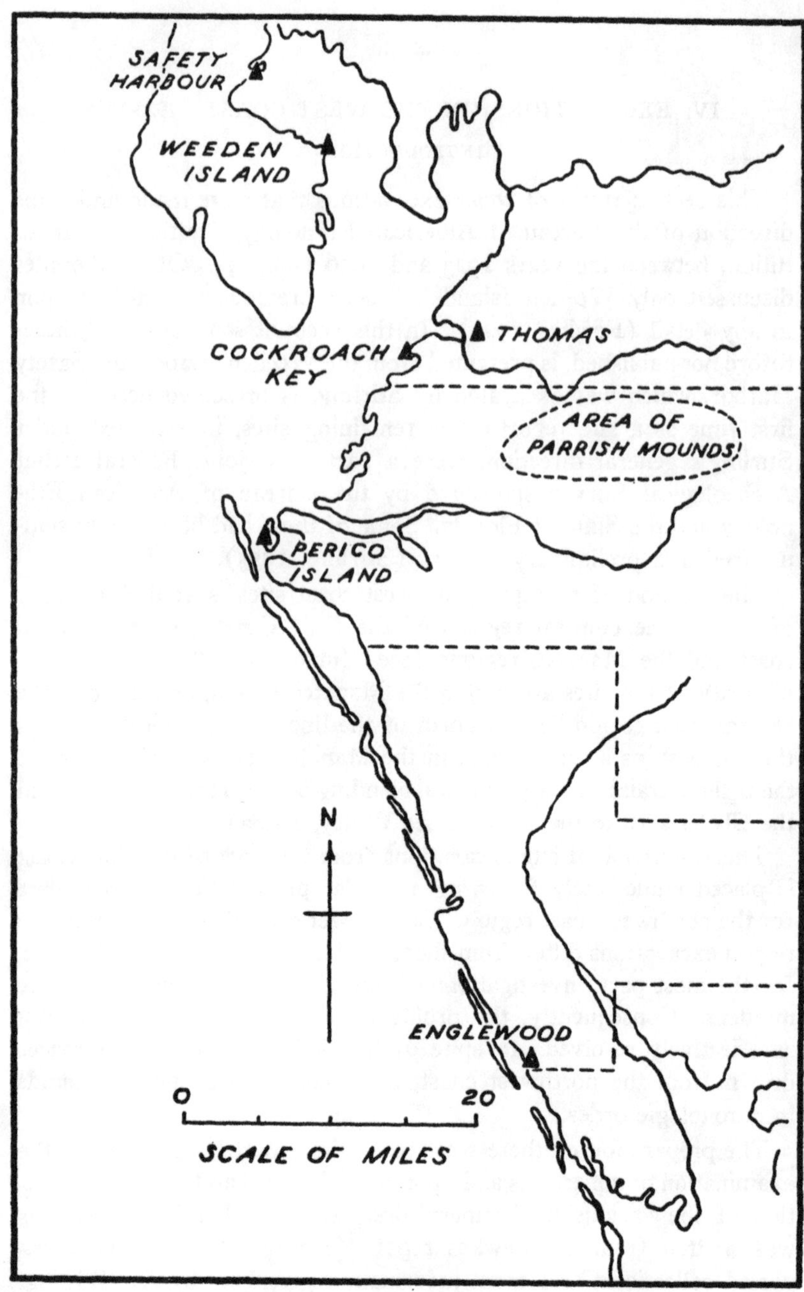

MAP 9.—The Florida west coast between Tampa Bay and Charlotte Harbor, showing sites excavated in 1923-1936.

ling, 1931), and from the collections. The Thomas mound and Cockroach Key field notes were prepared by Preston Holder, the excavator. An additional set of notes, on the Thomas mound, covering a short period of work in 1937, were submitted by J. Clarence Simpson. Dr. Marshall T. Newman gathered the data on Perico Island and the Englewood mound, the two sites under his immediate charge. The work and notes at the Parrish mounds were maintained by Lloyd Reichard.

Collections from all these sites were studied in the United States National Museum. In most cases, however, these collections represent only a portion of the material actually taken from the sites during excavations. This is specifically discussed in the report on each of the sites.

Pottery and artifact types are listed or discussed in context only so far as they serve for period identification of a site or to differentiate certain features within a site. Nonceramic artifacts are, in some cases, described in more detail than the pottery. Both are more fully treated in the subsequent sections of this report which summarize and define the cultural complexes and periods of the Gulf Coast.

Where data permit, a brief summation of the physical anthropology for each site is included along with the site excavation report. This information has been extracted from Hrdlička's "Catalog of Human Crania in the United States National Museum Collections" (1940).

WEEDEN ISLAND, PINELLAS COUNTY (PI-1)

Introductory review.—The Weeden Island cluster of shell middens and sand mounds is one of several sites on the southwestern shore of Old Tampa Bay not far from the city of St. Petersburg (map 9). Geographically, Weeden Island is a peninsula rather than a true island and projects out into the bay on the north side of a small body of water known as Papy's Bayou. S. T. Walker's investigations (Walker, 1880a) in the neighborhood of Tampa Bay may have taken him to Weeden Island, although J. W. Fewkes (1924, pp. 1-3), who later excavated the burial mound at the site, is uncertain if the mound group described by Walker from Papy's Bayou is the same site. In any event, the Weeden Island burial mound which Fewkes and party excavated in 1923-24 had not been previously touched by Walker, Moore, or any of the other earlier investigators.

Dr. Fewkes published an account of his Weeden Island excavations in 1924. This was entitled "Preliminary Archeological Explorations at Weeden Island, Florida" (Fewkes, 1924). Although the Fewkes account is obviously not a complete record, it is not possible to expand it greatly from the materials and data now extant at the United States National Museum [14] and in the Bureau of American Ethnology. Virtually all of the whole or restored vessels now in the National Museum are those also illustrated in the 1924 paper. A sherd collection now available was not illustrated or tabulated by Fewkes and is presented in this discussion; however, few nonceramic artifacts are in the Museum Weeden Island collections that were not illustrated or mentioned in the original report.

Rather than to present new information, the purpose of this analysis of Weeden Island is to review this key type site in Florida archeology so that the original data may be reappraised in the light of more recent findings.

Site description and excavations.—The excavations of 1923-24, conducted in the field by Stirling, Reichard, and Hedberg, included numerous test pits and trenches made in the various mounds on the Weeden Island property and the more complete investigation of the burial mound. About one-third of the latter was removed. From these excavations Fewkes concluded that the group represented a single village unit, and he defined four types of mounds or works comprising such a unit. The first type is the refuse pile, mainly composed of shell and fragmentary artifacts, but no complete vessels. The largest mound at Weeden Island is such a rubbish dump. Two other types (between which I can discern no real difference) are both domiciliary mounds. These are small hummocks of sand, shell, and midden which contained no burials or ceremonial deposits of any sort. Fewkes found no post-mold patterns or other direct evidences of superimposed buildings on these mounds so that his statement that they were house substructures is inferential. There is, however, evidence to support Fewkes' assumption in that Moore's excavations at more northerly sites of the Weeden Island culture occasionally revealed sterile sand mounds in group association with a typical burial mound. The fourth type listed by Fewkes is the small sand burial mound.

The burial mound at Weeden Island was approximately 4 feet in height and circular in outline. Fewkes was of the opinion that the mound was a natural tumulus of wind-blown sand which was selected by the inhabitants of the site for burial purposes because its soft, unresistant nature was easily penetrated by the crude implements the Indians employed for grave digging. This seems extremely unlikely.

---

[14] Weeden Island collections are numbered 325671, 326944-326981, 369387-369390 in the U. S. National Museum catalog.

In view of all the data gathered by Moore and others on Weeden Island burial mounds of the Gulf Coast it is more reasonable to assume that the mound was raised as a burial covering over the dead.[15] Fewkes describes the stratification or structure of the burial mound as follows:

> Three layers, irregular in thickness, often lacking definite lines of separation, can be differentiated in Weeden Mound, but two of these are very evident, situated stratigraphically one above the other and distinguished by the nature of their contents. The third or uppermost is naturally modern or deposited since the locality was abandoned for burial purposes. It is penetrated by roots of trees and gives every sign of having been formed by blown sand and reveals nothing of Indian manufacture; in other words, it seems to have formed after the Indians had ceased to use this mound for a cemetery. Its depth averages about 4 inches and is fairly continuous over the mound so far as it has been excavated. Immediately below this superficial deposit came the first of two strata which are supposed to indicate two successive occupations. The shallowest burial in this stratum was little more than 4 inches below the surface. . . . Down to a depth of 3 feet we have at all intervals numerous fine examples of crania. Skulls and skeletons occur in numbers until we reach the lower portion of this stratum. The skeletons found through this layer were in bunches or bundles hastily deposited in their graves and destitute of a covering of any kind. . . . .
>
> Apparently a considerable time elapsed between the use of this place as a cemetery in the interval between the deposit of the lower stratum and the next in order. This is shown in places by black deposits of vegetable matter. The pottery of this layer is as a rule finely decorated and better made than that of the layer below. . . . . (Fewkes, 1924, pp. 10-11.)

Stirling has recently clarified this somewhat and has placed a different interpretation upon the total mound and submound deposition.[16] According to his observations, the bottom layer referred to by Fewkes was the old original ground surface. This was covered with a zone of humus and decayed organic matter. In the natural sand and humus of this old surface a number of burials had been made in small, round pits which were lined with oyster shells. Sherds, one whole vessel (see Fewkes, 1924, pl. 4, A and D, pl. 21, C), and various other artifacts, came from the old surface stratum. Over this old cemetery the artificial mound of sand was later constructed. Disregarding the thin, 4-inch weathered or wind-blown top layer of the mound which Fewkes has described, Stirling divides the mound proper into an upper and lower zone. Physically these zones were not easily discernible, but the nature of the burials found in the two zones distinguished them from each other and from the old ground surface beneath the mound proper. In the upper zone, virtually all of the burials

[15] Dr. Stirling, who was in immediate charge of the excavations, is of the opinion that the tumulus was a man-made mortuary.

[16] Personal communication, 1947.

were of the secondary vertical bundle type; single skulls and long bones without associated crania were also present. As opposed to this, the lower zone burials were mainly primary and extended. A third mode of burial was then found in the round pits in the old surface beneath the mound. These were primary and tightly flexed.

Physical anthropology.—Thirteen adult male and 22 adult female skulls were examined from the Weeden Island burial mound (Hrdlička, 1940, pp. 341 and 375). Only two of the females showed any evidence of artificial deformation. This was slight-to-moderate lateral-occipital. Male skulls were underformed. The average male cephalic index is 81.34 with a range of 76.0 to 87.9. Female average is 81.84 with a range of 77.4 to 88.8.

Provenience of these skulls, with relation to mound proper (Weeden Island context) or submound (Glades Culture context), is not known.

Pottery.—Only a few vessels and sherds are illustrated in the Fewkes (1924) report, but a very great amount of ceramic material was taken from the mound excavations. Most of these unreported specimens were sherds of which only a few have been saved.

The pottery illustrations in the published report (Fewkes 1924) are representative in the sense that they show that the ceramic complex from the mound is quite definitely Weeden Island in culture and period. Its selection as the type site is, indeed, justified. At the same time, the illustrated collection is selective on two counts. First, Fewkes selected whole or nearly whole vessels to be photographed; second, he appears to have exercised a certain esthetic judgment, thereby slighting some pottery types. From the preliminary report one would get the impression that check stamped and complicated stamped types were quite rare at Weeden Island. The reverse, however, is the case. Hundreds of stamped fragments, as well as incised and punctated pieces, were found in the mortuary mound. Similarly, adequate samples of the simpler, plain pottery from the old ground surface or submound level are not shown.

In this last connection, both Fewkes and Stirling state that pottery was found at all depths throughout the mound as well as in the submound level. They are quite clear in identifying the Weeden Island style pottery only with the mound proper where it had been placed as a mortuary offering. Fewkes also maintained that pottery was not as abundant in the submound as in the mound proper and that this submound pottery was of a crude sort, quite different from that of the Weeden Island Complex found above. Stirling verifies this from memory; but, unfortunately, sufficient pottery samples are no longer available from the submound stratum to prove definitely this stratification. Only one specimen, a large plain bowl (Fewkes, 1924, pl. 21, C), is designated as coming from this old level. This bowl is of the type Glades Plain.

The illustrated pottery in the Fewkes report (1924) has been classified below according to the types which have been set up for the Weeden Island Complex at large. In most cases these photographs have been checked against the original specimens, now on display in the National Museum.

Pl. 9 .... All Weeden Island Punctated.
Pl. 10, E .... Weeden Island Zoned Red.
Pl. 11 .... Papys Bayou Punctated.
Pl. 12, A .... Wakulla Check Stamped.
Pl. 12, C .... Weeden Island Period sherds.
Pl. 12, B, D, E........... Unclassified.

Pl. 13 (2), A............. Weeden Island Punctated.
Pl. 13 (2), B............. Weeden Island Plain.
Pl. 14, A .... Weeden Island Punctated.
Pl. 14, B .... Unclassified complicated stamped.
Pl. 15, A .... Indian Pass Incised.

Pl. 17, A-D .... Weeden Island Punctated.
Pl. 17, E-G .... Weeden Island Incised.
Pl. 18, A, B.............. Weeden Island Punctated.
Pl. 18, C-F .... Weeden Island Incised.
Pl. 19, A-F .... Weeden Island Punctated.

Pl. 20, A-D .... Weeden Island Punctated.
Pl. 20, E, F.............. Pinellas Incised.
Pl. 21, B .... Weeden Island Period sherds.
Pl. 21, C .... Glades Plain.
Pl. 21, E .... Weeden Island Plain.

The sherd collection now in the United States National Museum, and with one or two possible exceptions not previously illustrated by Fewkes, has been classified according to the same ceramic types as those applied to the illustrated vessels. All these sherds came from the body of the mound. It will be noted that no Glades Complex pottery is included. However, in addition to the Weeden Island Period pottery, which forms the bulk of the collection, a few pieces of Englewood and Safety Harbor Period styles were also present. It is possible that the Englewood types represent a continuity with the Weeden Island, and they may have been manufactured at about the same time as there is reason to believe that the Englewood Period immediately follows out of and overlaps with the Weeden Island in the Tampa Bay-Charlotte Harbor section. On the other hand, it seems unlikely that the few Safety Harbor fragments also represent this continuity. It is more reasonable to believe that these specimens come from a later occupation of the site during which time a few typical sherds of the period were dropped on the mound or possibly placed with a later burial into the body of the mound. There is, unfortunately, no exact provenience for these few Safety Harbor sherds.

The following tabulation is for the Weeden Island collection:

Weeden Island Complex	
Weeden Island Series:	
Weeden Island Plain	23
Weeden Island Incised	52
Weeden Island Punctated	49
Weeden Island Zoned Red	11
Keith Incised	26
Carrabelle Incised	82
Carrabelle Punctated	2
Indian Pass Incised	15
Hillsborough Series:	
Hillsborough Shell Stamped	7
Ruskin Dentate Stamped	15
Complicated Stamped Series:	
Tampa Complicated Stamped	11
Sun City Complicated Stamped	12
Old Bay Complicated Stamped	25
Swift Creek Complicated Stamped (Late Variety)	3
Wakulla Check Stamped	101
Thomas Simple Stamped	5
St. Petersburg Incised	5
Papys Bayou Series:	
Papys Bayou Punctated	27
Little Manatee Series:	
Little Manatee Zoned Stamped	3
Biscayne Series:	
Biscayne Plain	5
Biscayne Check Stamped	22
Englewood Complex	
Lemon Bay Incised	11
Combination Biscayne Check and Sarasota Incised	1[17]

[17] A sherd of Sarasota Incised from the Weeden Island burial mound is illustrated by Bushnell (Anon., 1926, fig. 126). This piece was not in the collection studied.

Safety Harbor Complex	
Safety Harbor Series:	
Safety Harbor Incised	8
Pinellas Plain	3
Pinellas Incised	15
Pensacola Series:	
Pensacola Plain	5
Miscellaneous	
Smooth Plain	7
Unclassified Incised and/or Punctated	8
Indeterminate Stamped	2
Total sherds	562

Artifacts.—Except for a very few shell and stone tools now on display in the United States National Museum no nonceramic artifacts were available for this study. A number of such artifacts were found in the mound, however, and Fewkes illustrates a few of these in his report (Fewkes, 1924, pl. 21,A). This illustration includes two large, triangular-bladed, stemmed projectile points of chipped stone, some plummet-shaped objects, and a number of perforated coquina-stone sinkers.

Fewkes (1924, pp. 21 ff.) considers the nonceramic materials from the mound under the heading, "Shell Objects from the Lower Layer." On reading through this, however, it will be seen that the artifacts which he discusses may have come from any location within the mound as well as from the "Lower Layer." It is, of course, quite probable that the shell artifacts were most common in the submound stratum, and for this reason Fewkes may have been inclined toward such a subheading. Certainly many of the shell tools which he describes in this section are of types most commonly associated with the Glades culture. If the submound stratum does represent the Glades Complex, as there is reason to believe from the pottery evidence, such a distribution of the shell tools would be consistent with the site occupation and structure. Shell artifacts which might reasonably be expected to be found in a Glades culture context, and which Fewkes lists, are celts, conch hammers or hoes, and chisels or adzes. In addition to these, others which could be Weeden Island, as well as Glades, in their cultural associations are conch-shell drinking cups, shell pendants or plummets, shell beads, miscellaneous bone artifacts, and coquina sinkers.

The following artifacts from the Weeden Island burial mound were noted in the museum display collections:

Shell picks or hammers (*Busycon contrarium*)	7
Conch-shell cup or dipper	1
Shell disks	2
Shell bracelet	1
Shell pendants or plummets	2
Miscellaneous worked shells.	
Coquina-stone perforated sinkers	2

Summary.—The Weeden Island burial mound is one of a mound group located on Old Tampa Bay. The other mounds of the group are rubbish heaps and, seemingly, artificial sand mounds which may have been the bases for temples or other prehistoric buildings made of perishable materials. About one-third of the burial mound was excavated by Dr. J. W. Fewkes, assisted by Dr. Stirling, Mr. Hedberg, and Mr. Reichard, during the winter of 1923-24. In a brief report (1924), Fewkes has discussed the composition of the mound and its contents. In his opinion the mound was a natural eminence which had been used by the Indians as a burial place at two different prehistoric periods. From what is known of burial mounds on the Florida Gulf Coast, and from the comments of Stirling who directed most of the investigation, it seems much more likely that the Weeden Island burial mound was artificially constructed. According to Stirling, mound structure and burials within the structure took the following form. Flexed primary burials were found in the submound level or original ground surface beneath the mound proper. These burials were in small, round pits which had been lined with shells. Extended primary burials were found in the lower zone of the sand mound proper; and secondary burials, mostly of the vertical bundle type, came exclusively from the upper zone of the mound proper.

Both Stirling and Fewkes agree that the submound stratum contained little pottery and that this was simple and crude. The one available specimen from this stratum, a large food bowl, is of the type Glades Plain. Nearly all of the pottery, both vessels and sherds, which came from the mound proper is of the Weeden Island Complex. Shell tools, typical of the Glades Complex, including hafted conch weapons or hammers and celts, were found in the excavations, and it appears as though these came from the submound level. Unfortunately, this provenience for the shell tools, which would be of importance in substantiating the presence of a Glades archeological complex underlying the Weeden Island Period mound, is not verifiable.

Fewkes concluded that the remains from the submound were those of a people related to the primitive Ciboneys of Cuba. This group, he felt, were driven out by a people coming from the north with a more typically Southeastern, or even Muskogean culture. Leaving aside the ethnic identifications and the suggested relationships to the West Indies, there seems to be a very definite possibility that the Weeden Island burial-mound site is a stratified one. This stratification can be expressed by saying that the old submound surface depositions and burials represent a manifestation of the Glades archeological culture which centers principally in south Florida but that the mound proper was built and used during the Weeden Island II Period. The lack of more material, particularly from the submound, and of more complete records, preclude a definite conclusion on this stratigraphy. Future excavations at the site may give such conclusive results.

THOMAS, HILLSBOROUGH COUNTY (HI-1)

Description of the site.—The Thomas site, Hillsborough County, consists of a sand mound and an extensive shell midden located on the north bank of the Little Manatee River not far from the mouth of the stream (map 9). The mound is listed by Moore (1900, pp. 358-359) as "Mound near Little Manatee River, Hillsboro County." However, the present owner is Rupert W. Thomas (as of 1936), and the site and mound are now commonly known by his name.

The region in the neighborhood of the mouth of the Little Manatee River and Tampa Bay is typical of the central west coast of the Florida peninsula. The gray sandy soil is generally quite sterile and supports only a growth of palmettos, water-oak, pine trees, and occasional cabbage palms. The littoral of the bay is fringed with a heavy growth of mangroves, through whose root action innumerable small keys have been built up of a heavy black silt. The bay is shallow and placid, except during times of high winds, and is admirably suited for navigation in small boats. Fresh water is available from numerous springs on the mainland, and the country must have supported a large fauna in pre-Columbian times.

The shell midden on the Thomas property extends for about 60 meters along the shore of the river bank. It has been almost completely removed by dredging operations, and no excavations were attempted in this part of the site. Its location along the stream bank and its proximity to the sand mound suggest that the midden area and the mound were, respectively, the habitation place and the mortuary of the occupants. The mound lies 70 yards (65 meters) north of the shell midden, away from the water's edge. It was approximately 65 feet (20 meters) in diameter and 6 feet (2 meters) in height. The form was a roughly truncated cone. In composition it appeared to be wholly of sand, and excavation bore this out except for a scattering of black, shell-less midden layers along the northern and northwestern sides at a depth of over 3 feet (1 meter) below the surface. The mound showed evidence of considerable disturbance along its north edge, and this checks with Moore's descriptions of his excavations in the mound. The following comment is from Moore's account:

> The mound, irregularly circular and rather rugged as to its surface, has a base diameter of about 58 feet, a height of 6 feet. From the southwest side of the mound an aboriginal canal, almost straight, runs a distance of 238 feet to the water. Leaving the mound the canal is 64 feet across, converging to a width of 36 feet at its union with the water. The canal, in common with the field through which it runs, has been under cultivation, and consequently is irregular as to sides and bottom. The maximum depth is now 3 feet 3 inches, though, according to Mr. Hoey, 20 years ago, when he first came to the place, the sides were steeper and the canal about 2 feet deeper, so that high tides entered the field until a dam was placed across the mouth of the canal.
>
> Beginning in the marginal part of the northeast side of mound, a trench 35 feet across at the beginning was run 29 feet in to the center of the mound, where the trench had converged to a width of 9 feet. The mound was of pure white sand, unstratified. At the very outset burials were encountered. In all, 112 burials were met with, classing as such human remains with which the cranium was present and omitting a limited number of bones found loose in the mound.

Excavations.—Excavations under the sponsorship of the State of Florida and the Smithsonian Institution were begun on the Thomas mound late in the fall of 1935 and were terminated January 30, 1936. Preliminary survey revealed no trace whatsoever of the canal recorded by Mr. Moore; however, continued cultivation and plowing in the 30-year interval could easily account for its complete obliteration. Coming in from the northern periphery of the mound were evidences of Moore's earlier trench. In addition, there were a few other miscellaneous "pot holes" at various places on the mound surface. Preceding excavation, a grid system, 100 x 100 feet, was staked out over the mound at 5-foot intervals, and elevations were taken for each 5-foot intersection. Two trenches, 5 feet wide and 100 feet long, were opened along the western and northern edges of the mound. Potsherds were found in great numbers on these two peripheries. No burials were uncovered, however, until excavations proceeded farther into the body of the mound.

Excavation was continued in progressive 5-foot strips, along both the north and west sides of the mound, and by smaller units of 5-foot blocks. Depth of excavation, which was carried to undisturbed soil, ranged from 18 inches to 60 inches, depending upon the location in the mound.

Potsherds, plain and decorated, were found throughout, although they seemed to be most concentrated in two layers. Both of these layers extended from the peripheries to the center of the mound; and at the center they were located at depths of 24 to 36 inches and 42 to 50 inches respectively. The total pottery count for the mound was 7,746 sherds and vessels.[18] Twenty-one specimens were partial vessels or restorable vessels, including a complete and undecorated "toy" pot and an undecorated "utility" vessel. Pottery fragments were found nearby and surrounding burials in the mound. Direct association of mortuary pieces with individual skeletons could not be conclusively proved but was suggested in some instances.

The present account of the Thomas mound is based chiefly upon the excavation notes, materials, and other data submitted by Preston Holder. This covers the period of work in late 1935 and early 1936. Subsequent to this J. Clarence Simpson, representing the Florida State Geological Survey, returned and excavated the remaining portions of the Thomas mound that had been left undisturbed by Holder. This later investigation was made during the months of June to August in 1937. A copy of Mr. Simpson's field notes and two study photographs of materials recovered from the mound are on file at the Bureau of American Ethnology.[19] In the following discussions the observations and data on the Simpson excavations will be separately designated.

In addition to the final excavations in the Thomas mound proper, Simpson made several exploratory trenches in what were probably nearby piles of shell refuse, quite likely the midden at the water's edge. Burials were found in some of these exploratory trenches, and several artifacts and potsherds were also recovered. None of the latter are illustrated in the photographs or described in detail; hence, it is impossible, from available data, to determine the period of the burials or rubbish.

Mound structure.—Near the northern edge of the mound, at a depth of 42 to 50 inches below the surface, was an intermittent layer of black midden, the only strikingly distinct stratum or "lensing" in the mound which could be differentiated from the sand. The most intensive section of the above-mentioned lower pottery stratum, a small zone 28 x 36 inches in diameter and 4 to 5 inches thick, was found associated with this black midden layer.

---

18 As recorded by Holder during the 1935-36 season.

19 Simpson has published a very brief account of the 1937 work at the Thomas mound. (See Anon., 1937, pp. 109-116.)

Concerning the possibility of an inner mound the field notes state:

While suggestions appeared in the field to support a thesis for the existence of two mounds, one of which was an older underlying mound about 20 to 30 feet in diameter with a rise of perhaps 2 feet which had subsequently been covered over by the present mound, it is doubtful that the evidence recovered will warrant such an hypothesis. The evidence of definite (physical) stratigraphy was disappearingly faint.

As will be noted, the ceramic evidence from the mound does not help verify the presence of an inner mound culturally distinct from the upper or outer mound.

Burials.—There were 137 human burials in the portion of the mound which Holder excavated, almost the entire western half. These are in addition to the 112 burials which Moore had previously recovered from other sections of the mound and the 170-some removed by Simpson during the final excavations, a grand total of approximately 419. Careful burial data were assembled upon 112 of the 137 burials discovered by Holder, the remaining 25 of this group being hastily removed at the close of his operations at the site in order to facilitate excavation to the lowest levels of the final blocks.

Most of the burials which Holder found were in the southwestern quarter of the mound. In addition, he uncovered a smaller burial concentration in the west-central to northwest section. Most of the primary interments which he recorded were found in this west-central group at a depth of 50 to 62 inches below the surface. Only one secondary burial was observed by Holder at this lower depth; and conversely, only one primary burial was recovered in the upper part of the mound.

The following is a summarization of the burial types found in the Thomas Mound (after Holder):

Secondary burials		
Vertical bundle	59	(see pl. 4, top, right)
Horizontal bundle	33	
Group vertical bundle	3	(individuals)
Aberrant secondary burial	1	
Primary burials		
Flexed	6	(see pl. 4, top, left)
Semiflexed	3	
Primary (disturbed)	1	
Cremation	1	
Isolated skulls	3	
Too decayed for identification	2	
Total burials	112	

Secondary burials in addition to those classified	25
Miscellaneous bone pile	?

Aside from possible associations of pottery fragments with individual burials no artifacts were found in immediate association with the bones. A few instances of charcoal, as though from an in situ fire, were seen in connection with burials, and occasional scraps of calcined human bone were found in or near the charcoal. One burial lay below some limestone rocks.

Simpson's data on the 1937 excavations confirm the above observations. He mentions both full-flexed and semiflexed primary burials and secondary bundles of the vertical and horizontal types as well as single skulls. In several cases there is notice of cremation or partial cremation. As in the earlier excavations it was seen that the primary burials were more often met with in the lower levels of the mound.

Physical anthropology.—Most of the skeletal material was in a very poor state of preservation, precluding a thorough analysis of the burials on the basis of age and sex, but some data were obtained. There were 18 adult males (over 20 years of age); 5 adult females; 6 adults (not sexed); 3 female youths (12 to 20 years of age); and 2 children (3 to 12 years of age).

Because of the very poor condition of the bones only 10 skulls, or partial skulls, were saved. Seven of these were sent to the United States National Museum. The field notes make only one reference to physical characteristics, describing three skulls. These crania showed pronounced prognathism, heavy supraorbital ridges, low and abruptly curving noses, low foreheads, and heavy and foreshortened mandibles. They are mesocephalic to brachycephalic. Associated long bones are described as heavy and somewhat short.

One case of what seems to be slight artificial deformation (occipital) was noted.

The feature of a severely fractured left temporal was observed on six skulls, and there was one instance of a crushed right temporal.

Pottery.—Pottery fragments were removed from the mound in arbitrary small levels from the 5-foot square excavation blocks; or they were removed from other specific locations where possible burial associations were encountered. The 7,746 sherds and restorable vessels which Holder took from the mound were divided into two gross lots, and one-half of the material was shipped to the United States National Museum [20] in Washington for study while the other half was presented to the State of Florida. Only a very primary classification of "plain pottery," "decorated pottery," and "stamped pottery"

[20] U.S.N.M. Nos. 384130-384291, 384312-384313.

was made in the field prior to the division. Further discards were made at the National Museum preparatory to storage; hence, the collection treated here is considerably smaller than the original lot obtained from the excavation. Eleven hundred forty-three sherds were examined and classified in the National Museum. This number is supplemented by a smaller collection of sherds which is now in the Florida State Museum and which was classified during the summer of 1947 by Dr. John M. Goggin. This second collection is appended separately below. Presumably, it is a part of the material obtained by J. Clarence Simpson in the 1937 excavations at Thomas.

The Thomas collection compares favorably with that from the Weeden Island burial mound in that it is also quite typical of the Weeden Island Complex. The Weeden Island, Hillsborough, and Complicated Stamped Series are all well represented, as is the type Wakulla Check Stamped. These are marker types for the Weeden Island Period, particularly for Weeden Island II as it has been defined from the northwest coast. Chalky or temperless ware is more common at Thomas than at Weeden Island proper, although this may be due to selective discarding from the latter site. Biscayne types are numerically strong, and the Papys Bayou Series, which parallels the Weeden Island decorated types, but on the soft paste, occur in considerable quantity. The Little Manatee types, also of the soft, chalky ware, are present here as they were at Weeden Island. A significant difference between the two sites is in the plain wares. The residual type, Smooth Plain, is fairly abundant at Thomas but nonexistent at Weeden Island. Again, this may be due to selective discarding as might also be the frequent appearance of the types Glades Plain and Belle Glade Plain at the Thomas mound but not at Weeden Island. On the other hand, the Glades and Belle Glade types at Thomas may possibly be correlated with the primary burials found in the lower levels of the mound. If so, this would be somewhat comparable to the mound superposition at Weeden Island, with a Weeden Island Period mortuary constructed over an earlier burial place of the Glades culture.

Such a stratification at Thomas seems less likely, however, than for Weeden Island. At the Weeden Island burial mound, primary, flexed burials and Glades type ware are said to have had a 100-percent correlation with the submound stratum. Only absolute material proof is lacking. At the Thomas burial mound there is more available evidence, but it does not reinforce such a separation and correlation. In the first place, the lower stratum at Thomas seems to have been part of the artificial mound, not the old original ground surface as at Weeden Island. Further, although the examination for stratigraphy was based upon only about one-seventh of the total number of pottery specimens found in the mound, these available specimens were from locations in all parts and depths of the tumulus. One such distinction was noted, but this was with relation to the few Safety Harbor Period sherds which were found not far below the mound surface and, presumably, represent a later intrusion into the Weeden Island Period structure.

Thus, if the Thomas site is not a stratified one we are left with the possibility that the Glades and Belle Glade Plain types were contemporaneous associations with the Weeden Island types and a part of the mixed ceramic complex of the people who built the mortuary mounds. This interpretation would not be too far out of line with what we know of Glades and Belle Glade wares. Weeden Island sherds were found in association with Glades and Belle Glade pottery at the Belle Glade site (Willey, n. d.). This being the case, a mixture of the two pottery styles and wares at any other site would be in order. As will be seen farther along, the type Glades Plain, with slight modifications, seems to have had an extremely long life span on the Gulf Coast in the Manatee region. There is every reason to believe that it had a temporal extension from pre-Weeden Island up to historic times.

The following is a classification by types of the available pottery from the Thomas:

Weeden Island Complex	
Weeden Island Series:	
Weeden Island Plain	102
Weeden Island Incised	154
Weeden Island Punctated	187
Weeden Island Zoned Red	14
Keith Incised	12
Carrabelle Incised	11
Carrabelle Punctated	1
Indian Pass Incised	4
Tucker Ridge-pinched	1
Hare Hammock Surface Indented	4
Hillsborough Series:	
Hillsborough Shell Stamped	19
Ruskin Dentate Stamped	6
Ruskin Linear Punctated	29
Complicated Stamped Series:	
Tampa Complicated Stamped	38
Sun City Complicated Stamped	26
Swift Creek Complicated Stamped (Late Variety)	26
Old Bay Complicated Stamped	2

Type	Count
Wakulla Check Stamped	66
Combination Wakulla and Weeden Island Punctated	1
Thomas Simple Stamped	10
Papys Bayou Series:	
Papys Bayou Plain	14
Papys Bayou Incised	5
Papys Bayou Punctated	44
Papys Bayou Diagonal-incised	2
Little Manatee Series:	
Little Manatee Zoned Stamped	9
Little Manatee Shell Stamped	2
Little Manatee Complicated Stamped	3
St. Petersburg Incised	5
Biscayne Series:	
Biscayne Plain	56
Biscayne Check Stamped	67
Biscayne Red	32
Glades Complex	
Glades Series:	
Glades Plain	91
Belle Glade Series:	
Belle Glade Plain	8
Perico Plain	10
Safety Harbor Complex	
Safety Harbor Series:	
Safety Harbor Incised	8
Pinellas Plain	1
Pinellas Incised	1
Miscellaneous	
Smooth Plain	57
Fabric-marked	3
(Sand-tempered, close-meshed textile-like fabric, probably plaited. Produces heavily roughened surface.)	
Unclassified Incised and/or Punctated	5
Indeterminate Stamped	4
Total sherds	1,143

Potsherds were also found in abundance in the mound during the 1937 excavations. Two whole vessels (pots with slightly flaring orifices) of plain ware, blackened by fire and "killed," were discovered. Other sherds illustrated in Simpson's study photographs include a fragment of a human-effigy vessel in the Weeden Island style (very similar to fragments found by Holder), a red-painted sherd, and a duck-head effigy broken from a vessel.

There is a collection of sherds from the Thomas mound in the Florida State Museum at Gainesville which is, apparently, the bulk of the decorated sherds recovered by Simpson. I have not seen the collection, but it has been classified by Dr. John M. Goggin who has kindly turned this classification over to me. It is appended below:

Weeden Island Complex	
Weeden Island Series:	
Weeden Island Incised	8
Weeden Island Punctated	48
Weeden Island Zoned Red	10
Carrabelle Incised	1
Carrabelle Punctated	2
Hare Hammock Surface Indented	2
Ruskin Dentate Stamped	4
Thomas Simple Stamped	3
Complicated Stamped Series:	
Swift Creek Complicated Stamped (Late Variety)	10
Tampa Complicated Stamped	2
Wakulla Check Stamped	22
Papys Bayou Punctated	1
West Florida Cord-marked	1
St. Johns Series:[21]	
St. Johns Check Stamped	24
St. Johns Plain	12
Dunns Creek Red	12
Glades Complex	
Belle Glade Plain	28
Safety Harbor Complex	
Safety Harbor Series:	
Safety Harbor Incised	17
Pinellas Incised	10
Miscellaneous	
Pasco Plain	8
Plain Red	13
Residual Plain	14
Unclassified	7
Total sherds	259

Artifacts.—The few artifacts, other than pottery and pottery fragments, that came from the mound were scattered through it at vari-

[21] The St. Johns Series is essentially the same as the Biscayne as far as these types are concerned, and it has been used by Goggin here where I have used Biscayne to cover the same material in the Holder collection.

ous depths and with no recognized associations with other artifacts or features of the mound. These are:

Chipped stone:
- Projectile points:
  - Stemmed, triangular blade, nublike stem 1
    (Length 3.5 cm.)
  - Stemmed, triangular blade, broad straight stem 1
  - Others recovered by Simpson 13
    (These were illustrated in the study photographs. Ten are stemmed; 3 are unstemmed. All are large to medium in size and crudely chipped. Blade shapes include the equilateral triangle, the elongated triangle, and the large ovate triangle. Most of the stems are straight and broad with flat bases, although two have bases which are slightly fish-tailed. The 3 unstemmed points are all long (averaging about 5 cm.) and narrow. Two are triangular; the other is ovate-triangular.)
- Drills 2
  (One of these recovered by Holder and the other by Simpson.)
- Scraper 1
  (Recovered by Simpson. Appears to be a round type, suitable for hafting.)

Ground stone:
- Plummets or pendants:
  - Fragment of plain pendant 1
  - Fragment of bird-effigy pendant 1
  - Complete plain pendants 4
    (Recovered by Simpson. Three are simple, smoothed pebbles tapered and grooved at one end; the other is more carefully formed, grooved at one end and with a large bulbous expansion at the other.)
  - Complete duck-effigy pendant 1
    (Recovered by Simpson.)
- Tubular beads ....several
  (Recovered by Simpson. The longest is 5 cm. in length, 1.4 in diameter. All are well-polished cylinders.)

Shell:
- Conch columellae 4
- Worked clam shells 16
- Fragments of worked shell 7
- Conch cup or bowl 1
- Beads cut from conch columellae 7
  (Recovered by Simpson.)

Miscellaneous:
- Shark's teeth ....several
  (Recovered by Simpson. One included in the study photographs appears to have had side notches near the base which could have facilitated hafting.)

Various animal, bird, reptile bones.
(Not in U. S. National Museum.)

European: (All recovered by Simpson.)
Metal:
Silver pendant 1
(Square, measuring 10 cm. on a side. There are two small perforations at the center of one edge. A large circular, hemispherical boss (6.5 cm. in diameter) is the only decorative feature.)
Tubular silver bead (rolled sheet)...................... 1
Glass beads ....approx. 200
(Seed beads of blue and white.)

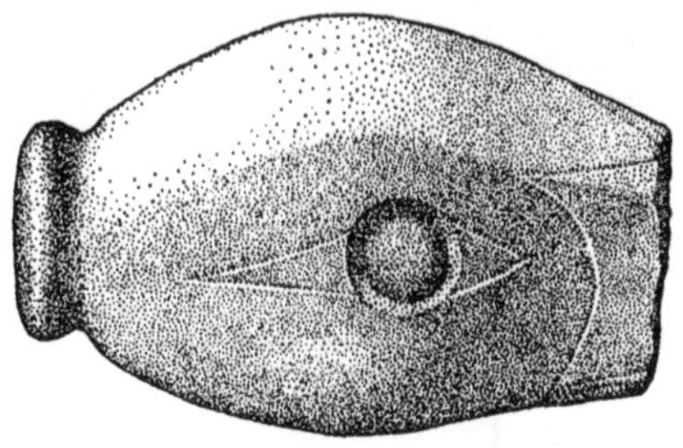

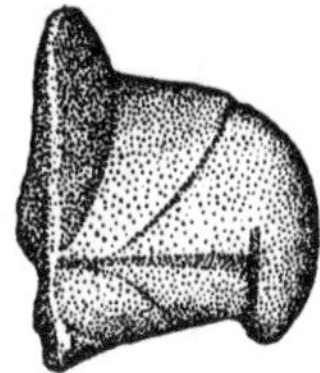

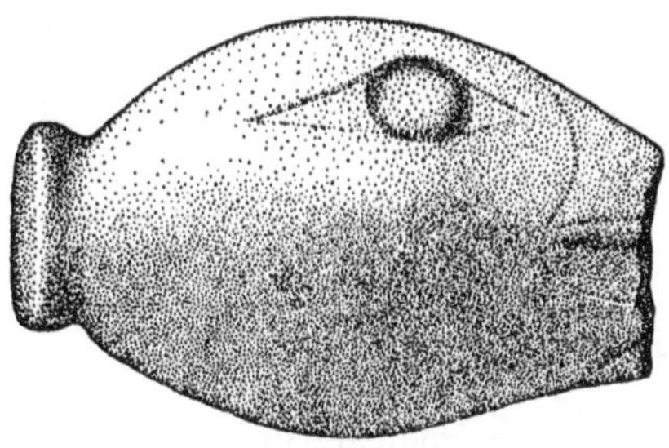

FIG. 15.—Bird-effigy stone pendant fragments from the Thomas mound (Hi-1). *Left:* Two views of fragment found by Moore (redrawn from Moore, 1900, fig. 3, p. 359); *right:* beak fragment found in 1935-36. (Actual size.)

The fragment of the stone bird effigy from the Holder collections is in the United States National Museum. It is made of brown porphyry and excellently carved. Moore (1900, p. 359) found a head fragment of a pendant, carved in the same tradition, in the mound during his period of excavations there. He describes and illustrates it as being made of fine-grained sandstone and measuring 5.5 cm. in length. The beak fragment is about 2 cm. long. (See fig. 15.)

The silverwork and beads which Simpson found in the Thomas mound are as puzzling as the bits of looking glass recovered by Moore.

These additional finds are clear proof of postcontact materials having been placed in the body of the mound. I have suggested that the objects of European origin described by Moore were probably later intrusives into the mound, and this seems to be the best explanation for the silver and glass beads. Judging from their appearance they are the types of ornaments favored by the Indians of the Safety Harbor Period.

Not mentioned in any of the excavation accounts are two metal objects of special interest. Presumably, these came from the Thomas

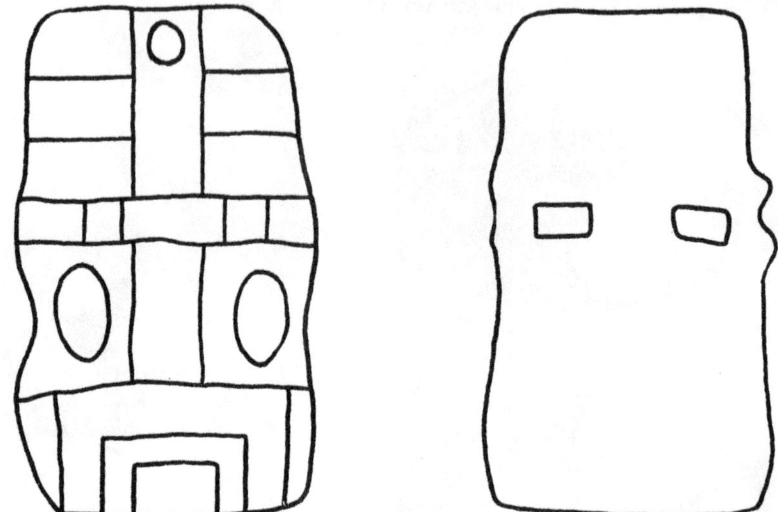

FIG. 16.—Ceremonial tablets of metal from the Thomas mound (Hi-1), Hillsborough County. *Left:* Copper; *right:* silver. (Height of tablets 4.5 cm.) (After tracings made by M. W. Stirling.)

mound or so they are listed in the Florida Geological Survey Museum at Tallahassee. One is of copper, the other silver. From what we know of other similar objects in Florida it is likely that they are postcontact in time. The silver specimen is almost certainly made from European-introduced metal, the copper one possibly so. They are little tabletlike objects of a very characteristic form. Goggin (1947a) has interpreted them as objects of a cult which had its origins in south Florida.[22] The copper specimen is 4.5 cm. high and about 2.8 cm. wide. It is flat and medallionlike. A rather complex design is engraved on one side (fig. 16, left). The silver tablet is

[22] See also John W. Griffin, 1946, for a discussion of these ceremonial "tablets."

almost exactly the same size. It bears no engraved ornamentation but is perforated with two rectangular holes in a fashion characteristic of many of the "tablets" (fig. 16, right).

Summary.—The Thomas mound was obviously built and used solely for purposes of a mortuary. Most of the pottery of the mound dates from the Weeden Island II Period of the Florida Gulf Coast. Characteristic of that period, deposits of sherds and vessels (broken or "killed") were placed in the mound in great patches or layers, and other sherds were scattered through the sand. The pottery appears to have been placed in the mound as a communal offering for all the inhumations, and it is not, convincingly, found in immediate association with individual burials. A few artifacts of stone and shell were also recovered from the mound fill. A few Safety Harbor Period sherds were found together, not far below the surface, and it seems probable that they represent a later intrusion. Moore's finds of two bits of looking glass and blue glass beads, located near burials in the mound (Moore, 1900, p. 359), are curious and may belong in the same category of intrusive deposition. In no other instance does the writer know of a case of association of European trade objects with Weeden Island pottery; however, in west Florida European trade goods are often found as companion artifacts with Safety Harbor Period vessels and sherds.

Besides the few Safety Harbor sherds, whose presence seems satisfactorily explained, the only other non-Weeden Island ceramic component in the mound is a number of sherds of the Glades and Belle Glade Series. Two possibilities exist here. One is that the Glades and Belle Glade material came from an old inner mound level, for which there is some slight physical evidence in the mound structure, and, therefore, precedes the Weeden Island component at the site. The other is that Glades and Belle Glade Plain pottery, known to be in part coeval with the Weeden Island Period, represents a component associated with the Weeden Island at this site. The depth distribution data on pottery from the total mound would appear to support the second hypothesis as Glades and Belle Gladé types were found, along with Weeden Island types, in all parts of the mound structure, arguing for contemporaneity rather than separation.

It was noted that there was a correlation of burial type with depth. Bundle burials and single skulls were usually found in the upper part of the mound; primary burials were encountered in the lower part. However, as stated, the distribution of the pottery types within the mound does not offer any sure correlations with upper- and lower-level burials.

ENGLEWOOD, SARASOTA COUNTY (SO-1)

Description of the site.—The Englewood mound is named after the small town of Englewood, Fla. (map 9), which is situated on the Gulf Coast about 50 miles south of the Little Manatee River (see Stirling, 1935, pp. 383-385) and 15 miles north of Charlotte Harbor. In 1934 the property on which the Englewood mounds were located belonged to the Tylor and Darling Realty Company and to Edward Rich. The mound is not far from the east shore of Lemon Bay, one-half mile south of the town.[23] It lies in Sarasota County .4 mile north of the Sarasota-Charlotte county line. Two other aboriginal features are in the immediate vicinity. One-third of a mile to the northwest of the mound is a shell ridge, lying along the shore of the bay. It seems likely that this ridge was the village location of the people who built the mound, although this has never been demonstrated. About 200 yards (180 meters) to the northwest, between the mound and the shell ridge, is a second sand mound, somewhat larger than the one investigated. Excavations were not undertaken in either the shell ridge or the second mound; but local reports indicate the second mound to have yielded several burials to sporadic digging. That it is a mortuary, such as the mound investigated, is quite likely.

The Englewood mound with which we are concerned was 110 feet (about 33 meters) in diameter and 13 feet (about 4 meters) in height. In the opinion of the excavator the mound was originally slightly higher and, presumably, conical or dome-shaped in form and circular in outline. Superficial pitting and erosion had, however, given it irregular contours and proportions. In some of these old pits, dotted over the surface of the mound, fragments of human bone and potsherds were exposed. Two very large, and apparently old, concavities were in evidence at the northwest and east margins of the mound. It is likely that these were borrow pits from which the Indians took the sand to build the mound.

The mound was covered with tall grasses and bushes and surrounded by pine flatlands. All vegetation was cleared from mound surface before excavations commenced (pl. 5, top).

Excavations.—Excavations, under State of Florida and Smithsonian sponsorship, were begun by Dr. Marshall T. Newman in mid-April of 1934 and concluded by him in mid-June of the same year. During these 2 months the mound was completely removed with digging operations proceeding down into sterile soil over the entire mound area. Excavation control was established in 5-foot intervals

[23] This is probably the site referred to by Moore (1900, p. 362).

along both north-south and east-west axes. Beginning on the south edge, a trench 5 feet wide and 40 feet long was the initial cut. This was carried down into the original subsoil. From this first cut exploration was carried north by similar 5-foot trenches with the excavation being steadily lengthened on both east and west ends as the center of the mound was approached. Owing to the increased height of the mound profiles, and the loose, soft quality of the sand, it was necessary to use a "step" technique in the central part of the mound. Although the greater portion of the digging operations were made from the south side, similar trenching was also begun on the north side of the mound.

During the work, all artifacts, features, and burials were located horizontally and vertically within each 5-foot square. Burials were found in all parts of the mound and in a large submound pit located beneath mound center. In addition to the 263 numbered burials, fragmentary bits of human bone suggest that a total of somewhere near 300 individuals were buried in the mound. Thousands of pottery fragments were found scattered through mound fill and on the original ground surface. Of these, 381 specimens were shipped to the United States National Museum where they were available for this study. Included among them were several whole or restorable vessels. Other artifacts were not found in great numbers. Stonework was exceedingly scarce. A few shell tools were recovered, and dozens of conch shells, whole and broken, were found throughout the mound.

Mound structure.—Excavation by progressive 5-foot cross trenches revealed two mounds rather than one: an interior or primary mound, and a superimposed or secondary mound. The presence of the inner primary mound was first suspected at the 30-foot-line profile, and was further revealed by a partial capping of pure white sand which was clearly defined in the 45-foot-line profile. A break in the original ground surface sod line indicated the submound pit which had been covered by the primary mound. (See map 10 and fig. 17.)

The story of mound construction, in brief, can be recapitulated as follows. A large, shallow pit was first dug through the sod and weathered zone down into the sterile yellow sand of the subsoil. This pit roughly measured 50 feet north-south and 15 to 25 feet east-west. The outlines of the pit, although irregular, were more or less an elongated oval. In depth, the excavation varied from 1 to 2.5 feet. The old ground surface had probably been an occupation area previous to the digging of the pit, for the dark, organic stratum revealed under the mound was thicker and blacker than is customary for a humus line in this sandy soil (pl. 5, bottom). Burials were placed in the pit and covered by a stratum of red ocher several inches thick. Above this, red ocher mixed with sand was deposited to form a slight mound over the pit and burial. The remainder of the primary mound was then completed over the pit. This mound had a diameter of approximately 50 feet and a maximum height of 5 feet. It was composed mainly of dark brown sand with a thin surface coating of white sand.

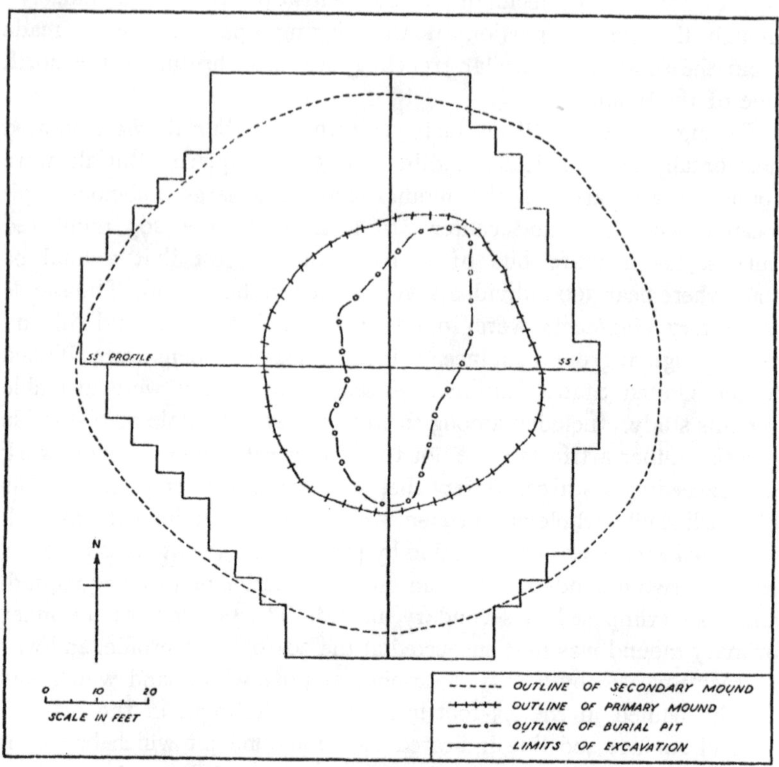

Map 10.—Plat map of Englewood mound (So-1) excavations.

This last was undoubtedly taken from the weathered zone immediately below the black midden humus. At some later date the secondary mound was built over the primary, completely covering the earlier mound and greatly extending the total mound dimensions. From the physical appearance of the mound profiles it would seem that a very brief span of time elapsed between the building of the primary and secondary mounds. The cultural evidence from the two mound levels tends to support this view.

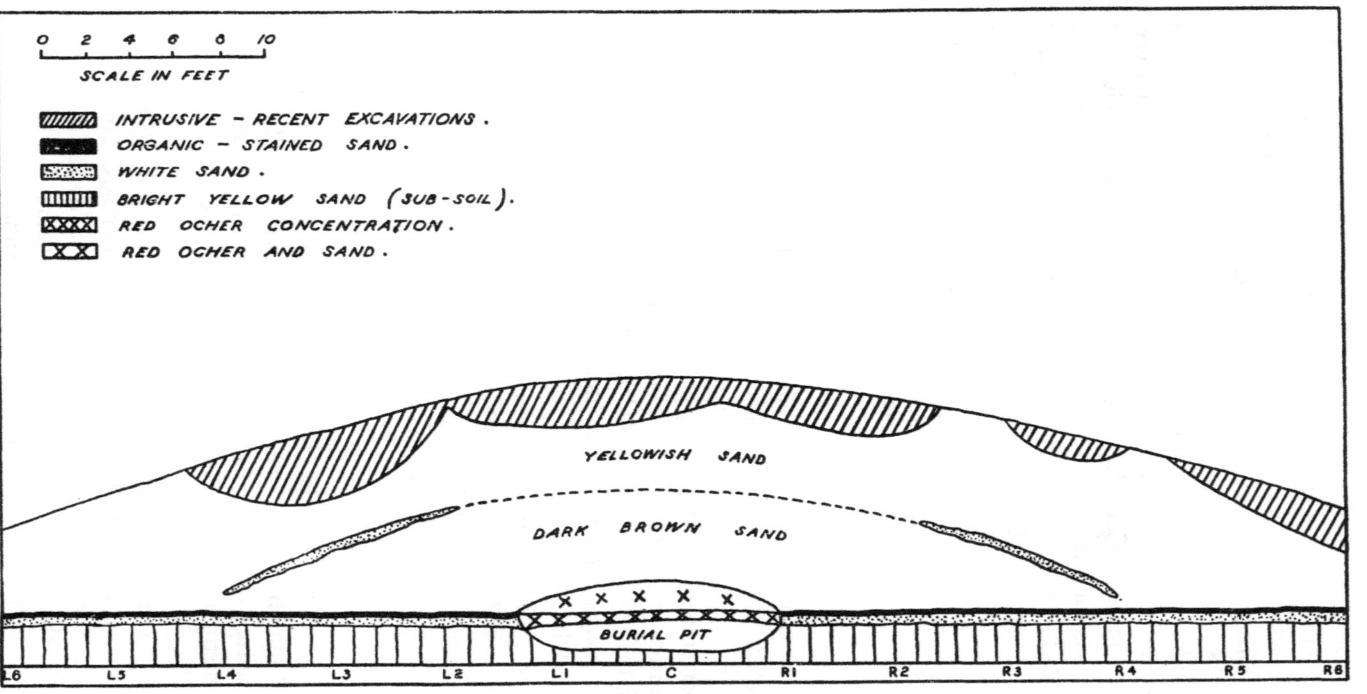

FIG. 17.—Profile on the 55-foot line, Englewood mound (So-1).

Burials.—The remains of at least 124 individuals were recovered from the burial pit under the primary mound. All were closely packed and in several cases the bones were badly mixed. In addition to this, the condition of preservation of bone material in the mound was extremely poor so that only a mere dozen skulls were salvaged from the remains of the 263 burials recorded from the entire mound. Hence, the identifications of burial type or burial position were extremely tentative. Considering all interments, which included a skull and various long bones as "bundle" or "bunched" burials, and individual skulls (with or without mandibles) as "single skulls," the total for the burial pit beneath the primary mound can be divided as follows:

34 bundle burials (pl. 6, bottom)
87 single skull burials
3 undetermined
—
124

It is possible that the "3 undetermined" burials were flexed and articulated, although this is not certain. Otherwise, all burials in the burial pit were secondary, and, presumably, were stripped of flesh and dismembered before being placed in the grave.

From the original ground surface under the primary mound, in the soil of the primary mound, and at all depths in the soil of the secondary mound, 139 more individuals were uncovered. These may be accounted for as:

35 bundle burials
78 single skulls
16 flexed (or semiflexed) burials
9 undetermined
1 fragment of a skeleton
—
139

Sixteen of the burials (flexed) were primary interments (pl. 6, top). Nine others may have been. The presence of these primary, flexed burials outside of the burial pit is the only outstanding feature which distinguishes the burials of the burial pit from those of the mound levels.

Pottery sherds and other objects were found associated with, or very near, burials, both in the pit and in the mounds. No differences in ceramic types were noted among the sherds found near burials in the pit, in the primary mound, or in the secondary mound. It is possible that with the remains of so many individuals crowded into the small space of the mortuary mound, the associations of pottery and artifacts with specific burials may have been fortuitous. In this connection, it must be pointed out that no complete or restorable pottery vessel or shell artifact was found in immediate association with any burial.

Pottery.—All the pottery from the mounds, original ground surface, and burial pit has been grouped together and classified as a single provenience unit. Tentative arrangements of types under the headings of "primary mound," "secondary mound," and "burial pit" gave no clue to cultural stratigraphy within the total mound. A total of 381 pottery specimens, both vessels and sherds, were studied by me in the United States National Museum.[24] In addition to this sample, two smaller collections were classified by Dr. John M. Goggin who has very kindly made his results available to me for use in this report. Both of these collections are from the 1934 season of excavations and are, apparently, a part of the share of the materials given to the State of Florida. One collection is in the Florida State Museum at Gainesville; the other was very recently discovered by J. W. Griffin in the Geology Museum at Florida State University, Tallahassee. I am also advised by Dr. Newman, the former field archeologist at Englewood, that several thousand plain potsherds from the excavations were discarded in the field. It should, thus, be kept in mind that the samples of Englewood pottery tabulated below are but a small fraction of the total pottery found in the mound.

The bulk of the decorated pottery from the Englewood mound belongs to the Englewood Complex, including the distinctive Englewood types, Englewood Incised and Sarasota Incised. Weeden Island and Safety Harbor types are also present, and I am inclined to interpret the mixture of these three pottery complexes as the result of true association rather than separate occupation or utilization of the mound. If this interpretation is correct the Englewood Complex would seem to occupy an intermediate period position between the earlier Weeden Island and the later Safety Harbor cultures. The continuity of the three periods and complexes is also indicated in the intrinsic nature of the pottery types as well as by their associations, for Englewood Incised and Sarasota Incised are related to both Weeden Island and Safety Harbor in surface decoration, ware quality, and vessel form.

It could be argued that the distinctiveness of the Englewood types is a function of geographical position as much as separateness of time

---

[24] U.S.N.M. Nos. 383165-383189.

period. Lying well to the south, the Englewood site may have been too remote to have felt the full force of the Mississippian-influenced Fort Walton Complex which is strongly registered in Safety Harbor sites in Hillsborough and Manatee Counties. In fact, the two loop-handled sherds listed in the tabulations are the only ones which could remotely be considered Fort Walton or Mississippian-inspired. However, as a counter to this argument, pottery from the vicinity of Arcadia, in De Soto County, almost as far south as Englewood, does have Mississippian affinities and strong resemblances to Safety Harbor. Furthermore, while most or all Safety Harbor sites contain European trade goods, it should be noted that the Englewood mound does not. In brief, the ceramic and associative evidence implies an intermediate time position between Weeden Island and Safety Harbor for the Englewood Complex.

As a final ceramic note, it should be mentioned that Glades Series pottery is present in strength at the Englewood site and that its presence also is undoubtedly the result of association rather than separate occupation. This is further evidence for the long life span of types such as Glades Plain, and gives added support to the hypothesis expressed earlier that the presence of Glades types in Weeden Island context at the Thomas mound is associative rather than temporally distinct.

The National Museum collection from the Englewood mound may be classified as follows:

Englewood Complex	
Englewood Series:	
Englewood Plain	22
Englewood Incised	19
Sarasota Incised	29
Lemon Bay Incised	21
Miscellaneous:	
Diagonal incised zone below rim, with strap or loop handles.	2
Biscayne Series:	
Biscayne Plain	29
Biscayne Check Stamped	100
Biscayne Roughened	2
Biscayne Cord-marked	9
Weeden Island Complex	
Weeden Island Series:	
Weeden Island Plain	2
Weeden Island Punctated	1
Carrabelle Punctated	5
Keith Incised	1
Payps Bayou Series:	
Papys Bayou Punctated	19
St. Petersburg Incised	5

Glades Complex
Glades Series:
Glades Plain 87
Miami Incised 1

Safety Harbor Complex
Safety Harbor Series:
Safety Harbor Incised.. 21
Combination Safety Harbor Incised and Simple Stamped...... 2

Miscellaneous
Smooth Plain 2
Unclassified Incised and/or Punctated.. 2

Total sherds.... 381

The Florida State Museum, Gainesville, collection is classified as follows:

Englewood Complex
Englewood Plain 22
Biscayne Series:
Biscayne Check Stamped.. 11
Biscayne Plain 4
Biscayne Cord-marked 2

Weeden Island Complex
Weeden Island Plain.. 1
Wakulla Check Stamped.. 3

Glades Complex
Belle Glade Plain.. 3

Miscellaneous
Unclassified 3

Total sherds.... 49

The collection from the museum at Tallahassee is classified as follows:

Englewood Complex
Englewood Plain 7
Sarasota Incised 3
Biscayne Series:
Biscayne Check Stamped.. 20
Biscayne Plain 9
Biscayne Red 3

Weeden Island Complex	
Carrabelle Punctated	1
Wakulla Check Stamped	1
Little Manatee Zoned Stamped	1
Papys Bayou Series:	
Papys Bayou Plain	6
Papys Bayou Punctated	6
Glades Complex	
Belle Glade Plain	20
Miscellaneous	
Unclassified	1
Smooth Plain	1
Total sherds	79

Artifacts.—Artifacts and various materials and objects that were placed in the mound and therefore have some cultural significance include:

Chipped stone:	
Flint chips or nodules	5
Shell:	
Conch dippers or cups (pierced)	2
Hoe (*Busycon contrarium*)	1
Miscellaneous conchs and clams.	
Miscellaneous:	
Iron oxide pellets.	
Red ocher lumps.	
Charcoal deposits.	
Shark teeth	2

Summary.—The Englewood mound was built in two stages. The first, or primary, mound stage was made to cover and commemorate a mass pit burial which had been made into the original ground surface. The second, or secondary, mound stage was larger in extent and volume than the first mound and covered it completely. The two mounds were made of different colored sand, and, in addition, they were easily distinguished from each other by a layer of white sand which had been put down as a surface mantle on the primary mound. No old sod line had formed upon the primary mound, and it is believed that very little time had elapsed between the building of the first and second mounds.

Burials, all secondary, were massed together in the burial pit under the primary mound. Additional burials were found in the primary mound and in the secondary mound. Most of these were secondary interments, but a few were primary, flexed burials. Pottery had been "killed" or perforated and placed in the mound as accompanying mortuary goods. There was no clear-cut evidence of whole vessels being found with individual burials. Most of the complete, or nearly complete, pottery bowls and jars were found on the old ground surface near the southern edge of the mound. Small piles of sherds, red ocher, shells, and minerals were found near some of the skeletons, and perhaps the association was intentional.

The pottery from the Englewood mound can be divided into four pottery complexes: the Weeden Island, the Englewood, the Safety Harbor, and the Glades. The interrelationships among the various styles represented in these complexes indicate that they were all present in the mound as associated rather than temporally distinct ceramic groups. The Englewood Complex is numerically predominant as far as decorated material is concerned. Stylistically, this Englewood pottery assumes an intermediate position between the Weeden Island and Safety Harbor Complexes, and it has been deduced that it is chronologically intermediate in time between the two. Strong Mississippian ceramic influences and European artifacts are both absent from the ceramics and contents of the mound. As both of these elements are present in typical Safety Harbor Period mounds, it seems to be reasonable to place Englewood as pre-Safety Harbor although overlapping slightly with Weeden Island and Safety Harbor Periods.

Like Weeden Island sites in the Manatee region, the ware of the Englewood Complex and the Weeden Island Complex breaks down into two categories: sand-tempered and chalky. The chalky Biscayne Series of types is well represented in the mound, and there are also several sherds of the Weeden Island chalky type, Papys Bayou Punctated.

Finally, it should be noted that the bulk of the plain ware in the collection is of the type Glades Plain of the Glades Complex. There are some regional or period differences in this Glades Plain type as it is found at Englewood, but on the whole it is impossible to distinguish it from Glades Plain as the type is found farther south into the Glades area. Its occurrence at Englewood indicates that the type has a long life span extending from Weeden Island or pre-Weeden Island to later times in the Manatee region.

SAFETY HARBOR,[25] PINELLAS COUNTY (PI-2)

Description of the site.—The Safety Harbor site, near the head of Old Tampa Bay in Pinellas County, is situated on a little spur

[25] This site is also called Phillippi Hammock or Phillippi's Point (Walker, 1880a, pp. 410-411). It is generally believed to be the Tocobaga capital of the sixteenth and seventeenth centuries.

of land which extends out into the bay at a point about 1.5 miles north of the town of Safety Harbor (map 9). The waters of the bay have gradually encroached upon the site so that a long sandspit which extends eastward from the principal mound, and is now subject to tidal action, was formerly dry land and a part of the village to which the mound belonged. This principal mound is a flat-topped, rectangular shell mound, presumably an artificial platform for a temple or building. It measures about 70 feet square and is somewhere between 15 and 20 feet high. At distances of 50 and 100 yards west of this large mound are two tumuli of shell. These are circular and dome-shaped and may be midden piles. The burial mound at the site lies 400 yards west of the big flat-topped mound. It is approximately 80 feet in diameter and 10 to 12 feet high.[26] Previous to the Bureau of American Ethnology excavations it had been considerably dug over, and the old pits revealed that the mound had been composed chiefly of sand.

Excavations.—Permission to excavate was given to Dr. Stirling in 1930 by Col. Thomas Palmer, owner of the property. Excavation centered mainly on the burial mound which was removed in about one-quarter of its area down to subsoil base. It was revealed that the burial mound had been built up in successive stages of sand layers. Burials were of the secondary type and were placed without any particular order throughout the mound. Over 100 were removed in the course of excavations. Pottery was found principally in a mortuary deposit on mound base near the edge of the mound. Many of these vessels were intentionally perforated or "killed." A few additional sherds were also scattered through the sand fill of the mound structure. All European artifacts, such as silver tubular beads and an iron ax, were found associated with burials in the upper portion of the mound. No comparable trade materials were found with the lower burials or in the mortuary deposit on mound base.

Some small test diggings were also made in the area between the platform mound and the burial mound. This was the village occupation area of Safety Harbor, and in the following lists of pottery and artifacts, materials from this zone of the site are designated as "Safety Harbor Village" to distinguish them from those of the mound.

Physical anthropology.—The skeletal material from the Safety Harbor burial mound was examined by Hrdlička (1940, pp. 339-340

[26] All these distances are estimates given to me by Dr. M. W. Stirling, June 1947.

and 373). In the 27 males and 23 females studied there was no definite example of cranial flattening. The cephalic index for males ranged from 73.7 to 85.5 with an average of 80.3. The cranial mean height index on males, on the basis of 11 skulls, had an average of 87.7. Among the females the cephalic index range was 74.6 to 87.7, averaging 81.8. Cranial mean height index, on the basis of 10 skulls, had an average of 86.3.

Pottery.—Two small pottery sherd collections, one from the Safety Harbor burial mound [27] and one from the village site,[28] were examined. These collections represent the totality of the decorated pottery found at the sites, plus a few samples of the plain types. In the burial mound, the bulk of the pottery, from mound base, belongs to the Safety Harbor Series. These are the types Safety Harbor Incised and Pinellas Plain and Incised. Presumably this was the intentionally destroyed mortuary pottery of the tumulus. In addition, a few sherds of the Biscayne and Glades Series also came from the mound.

As compared to the Englewood mound, the pottery from Safety Harbor shows appreciable Mississippian influence. The types Pinellas Plain and Pinellas Incised are closely related to the Fort Walton and Lake Jackson types of northwest Florida. These types were found in the Safety Harbor village as well as the mound, and the village excavations also yielded some typical Fort Walton Incised fragments as well as one sherd painted red-on-buff with finely pounded shell as temper. In total, the Safety Harbor ceramics, from both the mound and village, appear to be later than those of the Englewood mound. Added to the strong Mississippian influences which are present at Safety Harbor, is the absence of any Weeden Island Period types such as those found at Englewood. These Weeden Island sherds at Englewood implied a temporal overlap with the earlier period, an implication lacking in the Safety Harbor collections. Then, intrinsically, the Safety Harbor Series types are stylistically degenerate. Their manufacture is poor; the designs are badly conceived and slovenly executed. This, coupled with the fact that they bear a very definite relationship to Englewood and Weeden Island types, suggests a decline in the ceramic art which took place with the European contact period.

In connection with the Safety Harbor pottery, it should be noted that Glades Plain and Biscayne Check Stamped continue into the Safety Harbor Period.

---

[27] U.S.N.M. Nos. 351513-351525.

[28] U.S.N.M. Nos. 351526-351536, 362378-362386.

The pottery from the Safety Harbor burial mound may be classified as follows:

Safety Harbor Complex	
Safety Harbor Series:	
Safety Harbor Incised	30
Pinellas Incised	28
Pinellas Plain	43
Biscayne Series:	
Biscayne Plain	2
Biscayne Check Stamped	11
Glades Complex	
Glades Series:	
Glades Plain	15
Miscellaneous	
Unclassified Incised and/or Punctated:	
Deep, horizontal incised lines, Biscayne paste	1
Total sherds	130

The pottery from the village site area at Safety Harbor is classified as:

Safety Harbor Complex	
Safety Harbor Series:	
Safety Harbor Incised	5
Pinellas Incised	1
Fort Walton Series:	
Fort Walton Incised	4
Leon Check Stamped	3
Biscayne Series:	
Biscayne Plain	1
Biscayne Check Stamped	3
Miscellaneous	
Cord-marked	1
Red-on-buff, shell-tempered	1
Unclassified Incised and/or Punctated:	
Broad incised lines, sand-tempered	3
Random dot punctations, sand tempered	1
Total sherds	23

The Florida State Museum at Gainesville has a small collection from Phillippi Hammock, or Safety Harbor, which was classified by Dr. John M. Goggin. This collection was presumably gathered from the surface of the site, but there are no further accompanying data. It contains Safety Harbor Series sherds, a few Biscayne and Glades types, including Belle Glade Plain, and differs from the National Museum collections only in the presence of a few pieces of Pasco Plain. Besides the sherds, there are also some fragments of Spanish olive jars, a brass plummet, and some shell plummets and *Busycon* picks.

Artifacts.—A quantity of artifacts, particularly chipped-stone weapons and tools, were found in the village site. A few were also obtained from the burial mound. The chipped-stone artifacts are made of impure flint, most commonly of a white-gray color. This material occurs natively in the vicinity of Tampa Bay.

The following artifacts were taken from the burial mound:

Chipped stone:	
Projectile point	1
(3 x 6.5 cm., straight, broad stem, long, ovate-triangular blade.)	
Ground stone:	
Plummet of limestone	1
(5 cm. long, 3 cm. in diameter, grooved at one end.)	
Shell:	
Hammer or pick (*Busycon contrarium*)	1
Cup or dipper (*Busycon contrarium*)	1
Miscellaneous scrap	13
European:	
Iron axes	2
Sheet-silver ornament	1
Sheet-silver tubular bead	1

The following artifacts came either from the excavations in the village area or from surface collections made in that area:

Stone:	
Projectile points:	
Small, stemless, triangular blade	13
Large, stemless, triangular blade	6
Fish-tailed	2
Large, expanded-based, side-notched	4
Small, expanded-based, side-notched	1
Large, straight or contracted stemmed, triangular or ovate-triangular blade	12
Knives or projectiles:	
Large, round-based	1
Large, square-based	1
Large, stemmed, single-notched	1
Fragments (basal portions)	3

Scrapers:	
End scrapers	5
Long, side scrapers	13
Round, side scrapers	10
Elongated, turtle-back	2
Large, round, turtle-back	1
Triangular	2
Drill	1
Graver	1
Unfinished, broken, or rejected objects	57
Flakes:	
Worked	30
Unworked	78

Bone:

Incised piece of deer long bone	1
(Small fragment, 3 cm. long with single incised line running longitudinally.)	

Shell:

Celts, concave variety, unfinished (?) (*Busycon contrarium*)	4
Hammer (*Busycon contrarium*)	3
Cup (*Busycon contrarium*)	1
Plummets or pendants, single-grooved	2
Pierced *Eontia ponderosa* shells	10
Miscellaneous worked sections of flat shell	11
Miscellaneous conch columellae sections	24

European:

Olive-jar fragment	1
Clay-pipe fragment	1
Clay pipes	2
(One has simple bowl and stem with ridges for ornamentation; other is green glazed and bowl is human effigy head facing away from smoker.)	

Summary.—The Safety Harbor site, on Old Tampa Bay, is a mound complex consisting of a large, flat-topped mound, presumably a temple base, a burial mound, and several acres of shell-midden deposit. Excavations were made into the burial mound and the village, the latter being the designation for the area of midden between the big mound and the burial mound. The pottery in both locations was essentially the same. Mortuary deposits of pottery were found on the base of the burial mound. These were intentionally perforated vessels of the Safety Harbor ceramic series. Sherds were also found in the mound fill. A great many burials were discovered in the course of the mound excavation. These were all of secondary type and had been placed in all parts of the mound. It also appeared as though the mound had been built up in several stages, as distinct layers in the sand composition were discernible; however, from the nature of the material within the mound it is almost a certainty that no great lapses of time separated any of these building stages.

From the stylistic nature of the pottery, from the ceramic associations and lack of associations, and from the presence of European artifacts in the upper levels of the mound, it can most reasonably be argued that the Safety Harbor burial mound was built in a late period of prehistoric to early historic occupation of the Tampa Bay district. Unlike the Englewood site, no Weeden Island types were associated at Safety Harbor. On the other hand, Mississippian influences, presumably making their way down from the northwest part of the peninsula via the Fort Walton and Leon-Jefferson cultures, are strong in Safety Harbor. It would appear as though the Safety Harbor Period is slightly later than the Englewood and considerably later than the Weeden Island Period.

As with Englewood, a number of features characteristic of Weeden Island culture are retained. The most striking of these is the burial complex of conical or rounded sand mounds, secondary burial, and "killed" mortuary pottery. The pottery, though of different types, is in the same general tradition of incision and punctation as that of Weeden Island and Englewood. Similarly, associated wares with the two earlier periods also continue on into Safety Harbor. The Glades Plain type and the various types of the Biscayne Series are examples of this.

The large collection of flint points, knives, and scrapers from Safety Harbor is not so atypical as the other site collections might indicate. In most cases, few such artifacts were placed in the burial mounds, and at Weeden Island, Thomas, and Englewood only the burial mounds were extensively excavated. The great bulk of the chipped-stone artifacts at Safety Harbor came from the village occupation midden. Both small, stemless, triangular points and much larger and heavier stemmed and side-notched types appear. Scrapers of various types are also abundant.

Addenda.—During the month of August 1948 J. W. Griffin and R. P. Bullen conducted a series of excavations at the Safety Harbor site. We await their full report on this work with interest. In April 1949 Mr. Bullen very kindly furnished me a detailed letter covering several features of this work and giving me Mr. Griffin's and his permission to include this synopsis in my own report. I am in the debt of both of these colleagues for their generous offer.

The Florida Park Service excavations were made at several locations at the site, but perhaps the most interesting were those in the summit of the big pyramidal or flat-topped mound. Bullen relates that 19 squares, each measuring 5 x 5 feet were put down in the mound summit to an average depth of about 5 feet. Profile data from these cuts indicated that the mound was built in stages or layers. Post molds were observed, although no house patterns were obtained. A total of 2,698 potsherds were taken from these mound cuts and of this number 2,455 were of the type Pinellas Plain. Other types included: Pinellas Incised, Safety Harbor Incised, Lake Jackson Plain, Belle Glade Plain, St. Johns Check Stamped, St. Johns Plain, Jefferson wares, and Spanish sherds. The latter two types were concentrated in the top 18 inches of the mound. This distribution would seem to indicate that European occupation and Leon-Jefferson influence were confined to the later stages of site occupation. Triangular points, lanceolate and stemmed points, scrapers, a plummet, grindstones, and a large grooved boulder came from the mound summit excavations as did a quantity of bone pins and shell tools.

Griffin and Bullen also dug in the village area in a location which they describe as about 250 feet west of the big main mound. Presumably, this is in the area of the shell midden piles which Stirling mentioned as being 50 to 100 yards west of the big flat-topped mound. The refuse averaged about 2 feet in depth, and there were many refuse pits and post molds in the debris, although no house rings or squares could be made out. Out of 4,708 sherds, 4,562 were Pinellas Plain. Other Safety Harbor Complex and related types were the same as those from the big mound. Spanish pottery fragments were confined to the upper portion of the debris. Triangular projectile points were found to have an upper and later distribution than the stemmed types. Miscellaneous shell, bone, and stone tools and artifacts also came from these village diggings.

Although we will have to await full analysis for a definite statement, this recent work appears to substantiate thoroughly and to supplement the earlier excavations.

PARRISH MOUND 1, MANATEE COUNTY (MA-1)

Description of the site and excavations.—This mound was excavated during the early winter of 1933 by Lloyd Reichard. It has been reported on, in brief, by Stirling under the heading "Little Manatee River, Manatee County, Mound No. 1" (Stirling, 1935, pp. 378-379). There is very little to add to Stirling's preliminary description of the site and the work done there. To recapitulate quickly, the following are the essential facts available:

The mound is a low sand hummock of artificial construction which measures 5 feet in height, 44 feet north-south, and 38 feet east-west. A depression on the south edge of the mound probably is the ancient borrow pit. The general location is at a point approximately 16 miles north and east of the little community of Parrish, Manatee County (map 9). It is in section 12, Township 33 S., Range 20 E. A few old excavations were in evidence on the mound surface before the 1933 excavations were begun. None of these appear to have penetrated through the body of the mound to the old ground surface. Twenty-seven human skeletons, all buried in a secondary manner, were recovered during the excavations. Mr. Reichard was also informed that an earlier excavator had removed some 16 skeletons from the old diggings in the mound a few years previous. Pottery was found at various locations throughout the mound. Several whole, or nearly whole, vessels were revealed which had, apparently, been put in the mound as intentionally perforated mortuary offerings. These did not seem to be placed with specific burials. In addition to the pottery, several projectile points of chert or flint came from the mound as well as a number of shell artifacts. Objects of European manufacture, such as colored glass beads, olive-green glazed pottery, copper, brass, silver, and gold-sheet ornaments, were met with in all parts of the mound. Unlike the pottery, these were associated with individual burials.

Pottery.—The mound dates from the Safety Harbor Period. This seems supportable in view of the fact that one of the nearly whole, and intentionally destroyed, vessels which had been placed in the mound as a mortuary offering is of the type Pinellas Incised. Three other vessels were also found in the body of the mound. One of these was a complicated stamped pot. This vessel is very similar to Lamar Complicated Stamped, a late period type in central and south Georgia. Its appearance this far south is surprising, but its temporal position is consistent. The other two vessels were bowls: one Glades Plain, the other Belle Glade Plain.

The sherd collection from the mound contained Safety Harbor types. In addition, Biscayne sherds, both Check Stamped and Plain, and Glades and Belle Glade Plain appear. The appearance of these types may possibly indicate a period mixture in the mound. If so, this could be explained as earlier (Glades Complex) sherds having been taken up with the fill, presumably from an old occupation area, and included in the mound built by people of the Safety Harbor Period. On the other hand, we have seen Glades Plain in association with Safety Harbor types at the Safety Harbor site, and the Glades Plain and Belle Glade Plain in Parrish mound 1 may be a true association. The nearly complete Glades Plain and Belle Glade Plain vessels taken from the mound, where they had apparently been placed as a mortuary offering, would seem to verify this latter interpretation.

The collection examined[29] from the Parrish mound 1, including both sherds and whole vessels, is classified as follows:

Safety Harbor Complex	
Safety Harbor Series:	
Pinellas Plain	31
Pinellas Incised	1
Biscayne Series:	
Biscayne Plain	1
Biscayne Check Stamped	10
Glades Complex	
Glades Series:	
Glades Plain	21
Belle Glade Series:	
Belle Glade Plain	112
Miscellaneous	
Lamar Complicated Stamped	1
Total sherds	177[30]

Artifacts.—Most of the nonceramic artifacts from Parrish mound 1 were of European manufacture or ultimate origin. This includes beads and ornaments of glass, pottery, and metals. There is little doubt that the gold and silver objects were made by the Indians from Spanish treasure. Goggin (n.d. 1) describes rolled-gold cones from the Bee Branch 1 site on the Caloosahatchee River some 20 miles upstream from Fort Myers. These are similar or identical to the one found in Parrish mound 1. In the Glades area they definitely date with the Glades III-C Period, the European contact phase of south Floridian prehistory. The copper ear ornament from Parrish 1 differs from those found in Florida mounds of earlier periods; it is a disk with an attached hollow-button center. It seems likely that this object was made from imported rather than native American

[29] The U. S. National Museum collections from this mound and from the other Parrish mounds are cataloged as Nos. 383190-383238.

[30] Additional sherds from Parrish mound 1 were recently discovered by J. W. Griffin in the museum, Florida State University, Tallahassee. These, classified by Dr. J. M. Goggin, are: 13 Belle Glade Plain; 3 Biscayne Check Stamped; 6 Pinellas Plain.

metal. Ear disks of this type are also characteristic of the late Glades III Period of south Florida (Goggin, n.d. 1).

There are no shell tools in the collection, the only shell artifacts being the cups or dippers made of conch shell. Ten projectile points were recovered, all stemless and either medium-size or small.

The nonceramic artifacts taken from Parrish mound 1 are subsumed as follows:

Stone:
- Projectile points:
  - Unstemmed, ovate with flat base........................ 4
    (Thin, well made. Three are of quartzite, one of chert. Range from 5.5 to 4 cm. in length and average 2 cm. in width.)
  - Unstemmed, triangular 6
    (Well shaped, but surface not as finely dressed as above-listed type. One large point 6 x 2.6 cm.; three long, narrow, thick points 3.7 x 1.4 cm.; two small points 2.6 x 1.6 cm.)

Shell:
- Conch-shell cups or dippers (fragments).................... 3
- Worked-shell fragments 3

European:
- Pottery with olive-green glaze............................ 10
- Seed beads of glass............................several hundred
  (Dark blue, light blue, white, yellow. Thickness 1 mm., diameter 2 to 3 mm.)
- Small beads of glass...........................several hundred
  (Opaque: yellow, blue, white, dull red, black; translucent: green, amber, blue, lavender. About 2-3 mm. thick and 3-4 mm. in diameter.)
- Large beads of glass....................................several
- Pentagonal green glass bead................................ 1
  (1.5 x .9 cm.)
- Pendant of green glass...................................... 1
  (2.5 x 1.2 cm., flattened in cross section. Suspended by a thin loop at top. Made from European glass by Indians (?).)
- Rolled tubular beads of sheet silver........................ 3
  (3 mm. in diameter and 2 to 3.5 cm. in length.)
- Copper ear ornament.. 1
  (6 cm. in diameter and paper-thin except for center. On one side is button-nub center, 2.2 cm. in diameter. On opposite side the center is raised and pierced. Thus, button on one side and swelling on other form a hollow chamber.)
- Rolled cone of gold... 1
  (Formed by double sheeting of very thin gold of semiconical shape which has been forced down inside a similar piece made of a single sheet. Length 4.6 cm.)

Miscellaneous:

Bone or tortoise-shell comb fragments[81] 2

(Bases about 2 cm. wide and teeth spaced at intervals of 5 mm. Questionable as to whether these are of aboriginal manufacture, in imitation of European forms, or are European.)

Summary.—Parrish mound 1 is a low burial tumulus made of sand. Secondary burials, 27 in number, were found in various parts of the mound. Several are reported to have been removed by previous excavators. Several whole vessels, intentionally perforated as mortuary offerings, were found in the mound fill. These had been placed as general grave goods rather than as offerings for specific burials. Sherds, a few shell cups, and a number of objects of European manufacture or European derivation were also taken from the excavations. The last were found as accompanying mortuary gifts or accoutrements with individual burials.

The whole pottery vessels from the mound were Safety Harbor and Glades Complex types. It is likely that the latter were contemporaneously made and associated with the Safety Harbor types. The sherds from the mound fill belong to the same ceramic complexes as the vessels. The presence of the European trade goods and the metal derived from European sources at Parrish mound 1 helps to verify the Safety Harbor Period dating of the mound.

PARRISH MOUND 2, MANATEE COUNTY (MA-2)

Description of the site.—This mound is located 5 miles north of the Parrish-Wauchula road at a point about one-half mile south of the south fork of the Little Manatee River. The site is briefly described by Stirling (1935, pp. 379-381) as "Little Manatee River, Manatee County, Mound No. 2." It is a tumulus of sand without surrounding or nearby midden material or other evidences of human occupation. When first visited it was covered with a growth of short-leaf pine, oak, and scrub bushes, the usual vegetation typefying the high sand flats of this section of the State. The north-south axis of the mound measured 63 feet, the east-west axis 65 feet. The height of the mound was approximately 6 feet above the surrounding ground. Shallow depressions, presumably the borrow pits, were seen contiguous to the mound on its south and west sides. The north side of

---

[81] Moore, 1910, fig. 15 (p. 286) illustrates a similar, although decorated, comb taken from a mound on Murphy Island, St. Johns River. This comb came from a distinctly post-Columbian context, being associated with a superficial burial deposit of glass and iron artifacts.

the mound sloped rather steeply, while the other sides presented more gradual and longer slopes. A number of old excavations in the crown of the hummock made it difficult to appraise the original shape of the surface. That the mound may have had a flat, platform surface at one time is implied by the structure within it which was discovered upon excavation.

Excavation, structure, and burials.—Permission to excavate was given by the owner, T. W. Parrish, and work was begun under Mr. Reichard in January of 1934. A number of artifacts, among them conch-shell cups or vessels, a flint point, and a number of potsherds were recovered from superficial depths of only a few inches under the mound surface. From the first, charcoal was observed to be extremely plentiful. As excavation proceeded the source of the charcoal became clear. The remains of a charred wooden structure were uncovered and numerous cremated burials associated with charcoal deposits were found scattered through the mound.

Mound structure was complicated, and its reconstruction in terms of past mortuary and other activity is open to varied interpretations. Briefly, the facts are these. On the mound base, and below it, at a depth of 5.5 to 7 feet below the mound summit was a large circular pit. This pit, about 1.5 feet deep, was filled with charcoal, the remains of cremated or partially cremated human bones, and several accompanying artifacts. It was either a crematory pit for mass cremations or the repository of cremations made elsewhere. The first explanation seems the more likely. Over this pit was a mound of light-colored sand which, at varying depths, contained the remains of secondary, cremated burials, primary cremated burials, and secondary noncremations. Near the present surface of the mound, associated with the layer of charcoal, were the evidences of a wooden structure. This building or enclosure had been made by placing posts into the mound at intervals of approximately 6 inches. The posts were completely charred on their outer, buried surfaces, but their interiors were decayed to a fine, brown powder. Individual posts ranged from 5 to 10 inches in diameter. The structure was rectangular or trapezoidal in shape, being just slightly over and under an average of 25 feet on a side (see map 11). That the building was constructed on top of the mound could be determined from the fact that the bottoms of the posts, which were imbedded from 4.5 to 5 feet deep in the sand, followed the contour of the mound.

Additional interesting details of the structure or enclosure include a reinforced corner. This was at the southeast of the building where the row of posts, single elsewhere, had been doubled. The doubling had been accomplished by setting the posts in a staggered arrangement so that posts of the inner row were placed opposite the interstices or openings between the posts of the outer row. This reinforcement extended for 6 feet along one wall and 7 feet along the other. Within this reinforced corner was a dense deposit of charred wood, ashes, and semiburned human bone. Other structural details were a number of charred timbers found lying horizontally on the mound just below the surface. It is possible that these were sills or stringers that were used to bind the base of the building. It is also possible that these timbers represent the fallen and burned upper sections of the posts or they may be the remains of burned roof timbers.

The burials located at various depths in the mound were mostly below what had been the floor level of the structure on top of the mound. Of the 41 individual skeletons, or partial skeletons, from the Parrish mound 2 all but seven were found under the enclosure. It is not clear whether these were inhumations made during the building of the mound or if they were excavated later into the mound summit. Reichard, the field investigator, is inclined to the latter opinion. It should also be mentioned that the number 41 is undoubtedly much too low for the actual number of persons buried in the mound. At least double that number must have been buried in some form or other in the total tumulus. The great number of badly burned bones in the basal charcoal pit, as well as in the southeast corner of the mound summit structure, would probably account for a great many other individuals.

Burial form, as stated, was, in the majority of cases, secondary and cremated. Of the 34 distinguishable burials under the enclosure, 32 were secondary cremations and 2 were simple uncremated secondary interments. Outside the walls of the enclosure, but still in the body of the mound, were seven more cremations. Five of these were of the secondary type, but two were individuals who had been cremated in primary form in situ. These latter two, found at respective depths of 4 and 3.5 feet below mound surface, had been burned in small pits. These pits, either made during the building of the mound or excavated afterward, were lined with small logs. The body had then been placed in the pit in a slightly flexed position and covered with more timbers. When the funeral pyre had been reduced to embers, the graves had been filled in with sand, and the logs, completely reduced to charcoal, were all in place.

Many of the cremated secondary burials, and one of the in situ cremations, were accompanied by artifacts such as shell cups and flint points. In one case, part of a pottery bowl was directly associated with some cremated remains. There were also instances of European artifacts in association with, or nearby, other cremation burials.

In addition to the burials excavated by Reichard, Wesley Parrish, living in the vicinity, reported that earlier excavators had taken three human skulls from the mound.

An analysis of these data lead most easily to the following conclusions as to the nature and history of the mound construction. An original crematory pit was excavated on the old ground surface and a considerable number of bodies were burned in this pit. Over the pit the circular mound of sand was heaped up to a height of about 6 feet. This mound building may have been accomplished over quite a period during which time the various cremated burials, both secondary and in situ, were placed in the fill; on the other hand, the mound may have been piled up in a single, rapid operation with the burials made later. In any event, after it was built it was obviously used as the base for a building constructed of wooden posts. This building or enclosure may or may not have been roofed over. In one corner of the building there was either a crematory platform or an altar for the bones of the dead (see map 11). It may be that bodies or skeletal remains were cremated here purposefully and subsequently buried in the mound. The other interpretation, that of a bone repository, coincides with the known southeastern practice of keeping the denuded bones of dead tribal dignitaries in hampers or boxes within the mound temples. If this was the case at Parrish mound 2, the charred mass of bones in the corner of the structure or temple could be the result of the complete burning of the structure which thus destroyed the bone cache that had been placed on a platform or altar. The destruction of the temple mortuary by fire may have been a purposeful ceremonial act, or it may have been accidental or the result of warlike depredations. The results would have been much the same. That the structure was burned seems indicated by the charring of what was the outer surface of the wall posts and by the scattered charred timbers found at what was approximately the floor level of the structure. That the lower portions of the wall posts did not burn completely through is to be expected in that they were imbedded in the sand of the mound.

Pottery.—No complete vessels from the mound were found in the excavations conducted by Reichard, but Stirling, in his preliminary report states:

> A very interesting owl-effigy water bottle of a familiar lower Mississippi type was taken from the central part of the mound during a previous excavation. (Stirling, 1935, p. 380.)

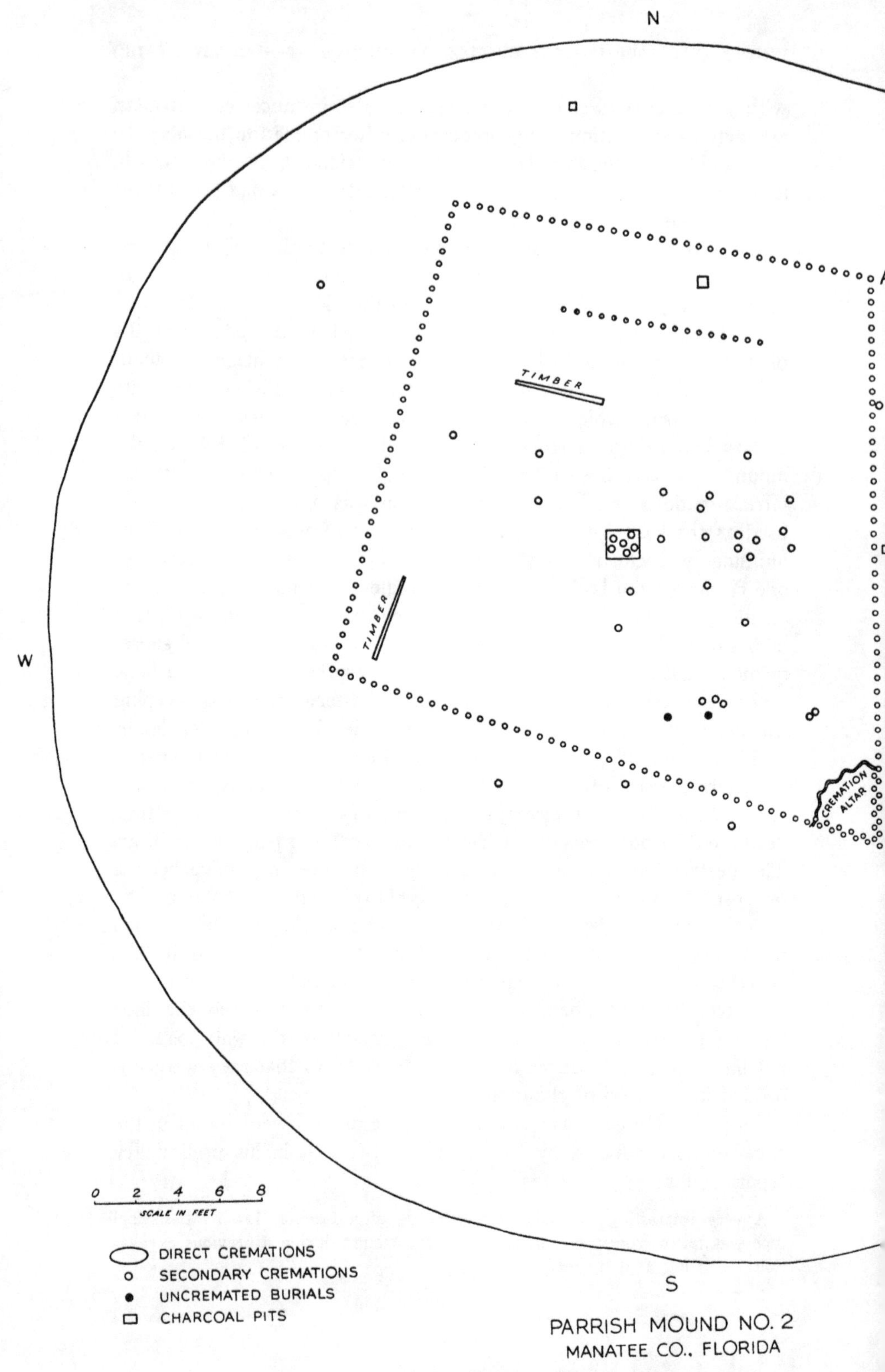

PARRISH MOUND NO. 2
MANATEE CO., FLORIDA

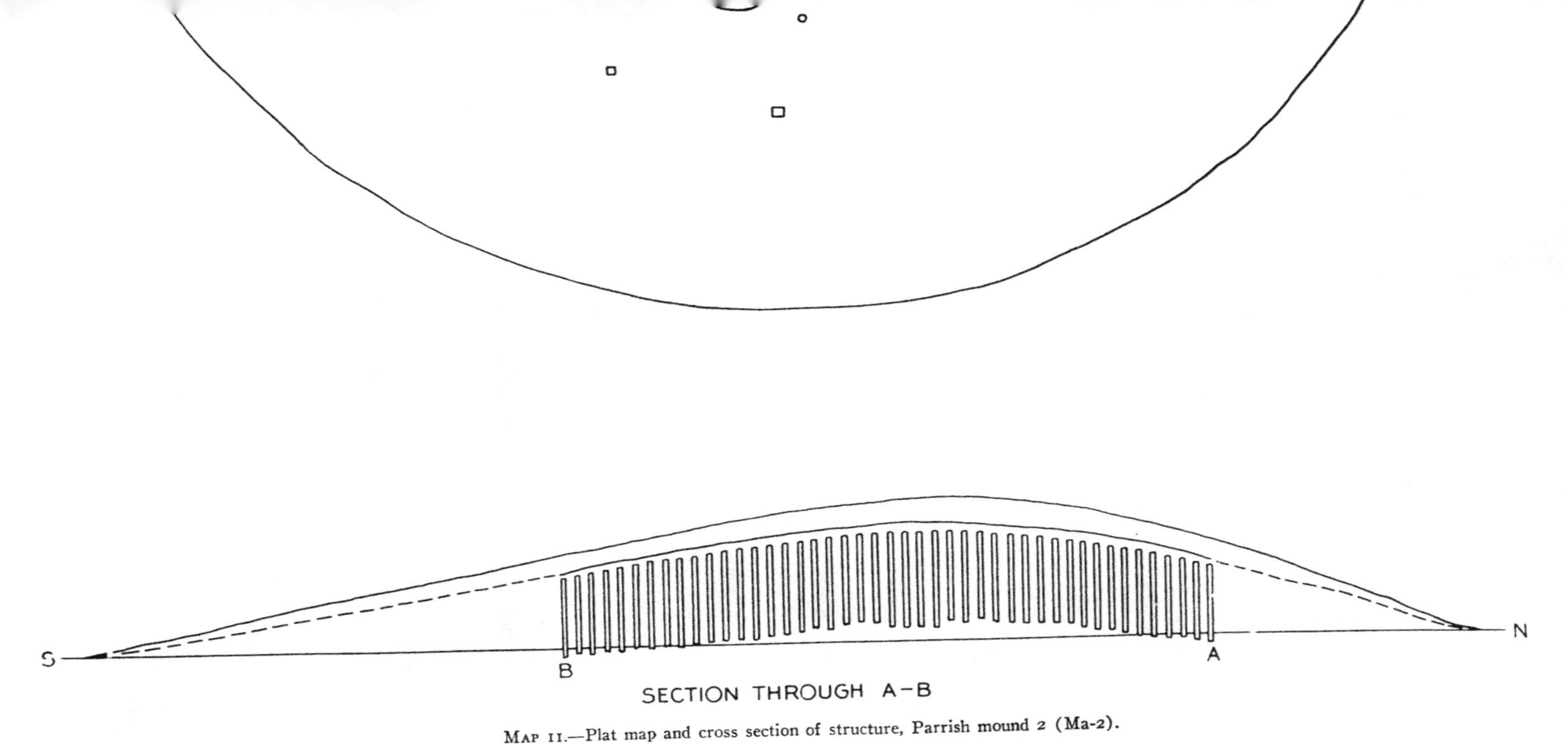

Map 11.—Plat map and cross section of structure, Parrish mound 2 (Ma-2).

Such a piece as he describes would be chronologically consistent with the Safety Harbor sherd types found in the mound fill. Again Belle Glade Plain and Glades Plain are present. The mound undoubtedly dates from the Safety Harbor Period and is contemporaneous with Parrish mound 1. The presence of the Glades Complex types raises the same question as it did in Parrish mound 1, and the probabilities favor their association with the Safety Harbor Period rather than earlier materials accidentally included in the body of the mound.

Pottery vessels and sherds from Parrish mound 2 are tabulated as follows:

Safety Harbor Complex	
Safety Harbor Series:	
Pinellas Plain	18
Pinellas Incised	22
Glades Complex	
Glades Series:	
Glades Plain	1
Belle Glade Series:	
Belle Glade Plain	17
Total sherds	58

Artifacts.—The nonceramic artifacts from Parrish mound 2 are of the same general categories and types as those from mound 1. Projectile points are stemless; conch-shell cups are present but shell tools are scarce; and European trade goods were included in the mound. The latter are less common than in mound 1, but three small seed beads and a bone or tortoise-shell comb, all identical with those from mound 1, were recorded.

Because of the accident of preservation resulting from the burning of the structure within mound 2 a few carved wooden specimens and some rope or cordage were recovered (pl. 59, *m-q*). These are almost certainly of aboriginal make.

Nonceramic artifacts from Parrish mound 2 are tabulated as follows:

Stone:	
Projectile points:	
Unstemmed, small triangular	3
(Between 2 and 3 cm. in length.)	
Tubular bead (?)	1
(3.4 cm. long x 1.2 cm. in diameter. Hole is biconically drilled.)	
Plummet	1
(Crudely worked, single-grooved. Measures 4.7 x 2.8 cm.)	

Shell:

Conch cups or dippers.................................... 4
("Killed" or perforated.)

Conch pick (*Busycon contrarium*)........................ 1

Circular beads 2
(2 cm. in diameter and about 5 mm. thick.)

Wood:

Carved fragments (charred)............................... 2
(One piece has close-spaced incised lines. The other has deep central indentation encircled by a ridge; this, in turn, is enclosed by a spiral ridge which is ticked off with close-spaced notches. The total design on the second piece measures 2.2 cm. in diameter.)

Textile:

Cordage or rope (charred)....................several fragments
(Appears to have been made from hair.)

European:

Seed beads of glass...................................... 3
(Light blue and white.)

Brass pendant 1
(Length 2.2 cm. Appears to be of European make and design. See plate 59, *b*.)

Miscellaneous:

Bone or tortoise-shell comb.............................. 1
(Similar to combs from Parrish mound 1.)

Summary.—Parrish mound 2, a small sand tumulus, was built both as a mortuary mound and as a base for a building. On the original mound base was a large crematory pit in which bodies of the dead had been burned. A mound was built over this pit and cremated secondary remains were placed in the body of the mound. In addition, a few primary burials were cremated in situ, in small log crypts, in the mound. As a final phase in the building and use of the mound, a near-rectangular wooden building or enclosure was placed upon the mound top. This was constructed of posts placed next to each other in the sand. This structure appears to have been burned. In one corner of the building there was a raised platform. This platform may have been a crematory altar or it may have been the place where the chests or hampers filled with the bones of the honored dead were placed for safekeeping. In either event, with the burning of the building, probably a temple, a great many charred human bones were left on this raised platform of sand.

The number of burials in the mound is subject to conjecture. Of the 41 distinguishable burials all but 2 had been cremated. These were secondary bundle burials. Because of the scattered placement of the cremations and the advanced stage of decay of the bones it is likely that the mound actually held the remains of many more individuals than it was possible to record.

The pottery found in the mound and the association of the European trade objects dates the site in the Safety Harbor Period.

PARRISH MOUND 3, MANATEE COUNTY (MA-3)

Description of the site.—This mound is located in the flat open timberland northeast of Parrish, Manatee County. The site was briefly described by Stirling (1935, pp. 381-382) as "Little Manatee River, Manatee County, Mound No. 3." It is in the northwest quarter of section 27, Township 33 S., Range 19 E. Before excavation the mound was covered with a stand of pine and oak. The mound proper measured 68 feet on both cardinal axes, being nearly perfectly circular. It was approximately 7 feet in height but had been dug over, especially in the crown. These old excavations encompassed an area of about 30 feet in diameter but did not appear to be profound. The mound proper was encircled, horseshoe-fashion, with an embankment on the south, west, and east sides. This embankment continued northward from the mound for about 150 feet where both arms eventually tapered off into the level of the surrounding ground. The embankment was of uniform width (30 feet) and height (3 feet), and it was separated from the mound by a gulley or depression some 17 feet wide and 2 feet deep. The form of the embankment is strikingly reminiscent of semicircular earthworks found in Glades area sites of what is, presumably, the Glades III Period. Big Mound City, in Palm Beach County, is a good example (Willey, n.d.).

Lying off to the southeast of the mound, at distances of 75 and 100 yards are two small, circular mounds.

Excavations and burials.—The mound was excavated down to original mound base. It was composed of sand and was without distinctive structural features. Burials were met with in all parts of the mound fill. Of the 212 recognizable burials, all but one were secondary bundle burials of the horizontal bundle type. The interments had been made, probably during the construction of the mound, by placing a horizontal bundle of long bones in the sand and then setting the skull just above the bones. It is quite likely that there were considerably more than the counted number of 212, as many places in the mound fill appeared to be spots where virtually complete decomposition of burials had been effected. It is also probable that the earlier diggings in the mound removed a number of skeletal remains.

With the burials were found shell artifacts, flint points, pottery bowls, and an occasional artifact of European manufacture. These latter were chiefly glass beads. The pottery vessels, and some of the conch-shell cups, which were specifically placed with an individual burial, were sometimes perforated or "killed" and put just over or above the skull.

The one exception to the secondary burials was a cremation found just below the surface of the mound at a depth of 12 inches. Its position and the accompanying grave artifacts imply that it was a late interment. With the cremation were glass beads, several pieces of iron, probably gun parts, and two flint projectile points.

Although the two small mounds nearby were excavated, no artifacts or burials were found.

Pottery.—Two Safety Harbor Incised, one Lamar Complicated Stamped, one Glades Plain, and one Pasco Red complete, or nearly complete, vessels were taken from the mound. This assemblage of mortuary ware places Parrish mound 3 as a Safety Harbor Period mound along with mounds 1 and 2. The sherd collections are essentially consistent with this dating. Safety Harbor types are numerous, additional Lamar Complicated Stamped specimens were found, and Biscayne types appear in small percentages. As in Parrish mounds 1 and 2, both Glades Plain and Belle Glade Plain are present in appreciable amounts. This association in three mounds makes it seem almost certain that the Glades Complex types existed simultaneously with the Safety Harbor wares. The single Pasco Red vessel is an interesting specimen. This is a large, flattened-globular bowl, 32 cm. in diameter and 21 cm. high. It has been tempered with limestone or coquina, more likely the latter. The individual tempering particles were large and have leached out in many places on the surface. The red slip, applied and fired to the exterior, is of a dark shade.

The one inconsistency with the Safety Harbor dating of Parrish mound 3 is the Papys Bayou Punctated specimen, or specimens. These nine sherds of what is obviously and unmistakably a Weeden Island Complex type appear to have come from the same vessel. As there is no evidence of an earlier Weeden Island mound or village area in the vicinity of Parrish 3, the most likely explanation is that the specimen was a hold-over or "antique" from earlier times which was placed in the mound as an offering.

The vessels and sherds from Parrish mound 3 have been classified as follows:

Safety Harbor Complex	
Safety Harbor Series:	
Safety Harbor Incised	3
Pinellas Plain	21
Pinellas Incised	33
Biscayne Series:	
Biscayne Plain	5
Biscayne Check Stamped	6
Weeden Island Complex	
Papys Bayou Series:	
Papys Bayou Punctated	9
Glades Complex	
Glades Series:	
Glades Plain	4
Belle Glade Series:	
Belle Glade Plain	24
Miscellaneous	
Pasco Red	1
Lamar Complicated Stamped	4
Plain Red	1
Unclassified:	
Fingernail Punctated on Biscayne-type paste	1
Total sherds	112[32]

Artifacts.—The artifacts from Parrish 3 are similar to those from Parrish 1 and 2 in many respects. European materials were recovered in the form of the ubiquitous trade beads as well as some iron tools and weapons. Conch-shell cups or bowls were the only shell artifacts. The chipped-stone projectiles are large or medium-size and stemmed. This last differs from the Parrish mounds 1 and 2 where the projectiles were unstemmed.

The following are the nonceramic artifacts from Parrish mound 3:

Stone:	
Projectile points:	
Unstemmed, small triangular (Length, 2.7 cm.)	1
Stemmed, triangular blade, large (Length over 5 cm.)	3

[32] Additional sherds from Parrish mound 3 were recently discovered in the museum, Florida State University, Tallahassee, by J. W. Griffin. These, classified by Dr. J. M. Goggin, are: 3 Biscayne Check Stamped; 7 Belle Glade Plain; 4 Residual Plain; 1 Jefferson Complicated Stamped (?).

Stemmed, triangular blade, small 3
(Length 3.5 to 4 cm., stems straight or tapered.)
Stemmed, ovate-triangular blade, large 1
(Length 6.8 cm., straight stem.)

Knives or projectiles:
Unstemmed, ovate-triangular, flat base 1
(Well but not finely chipped. Length 13 cm., width 4.5 cm.)
Unstemmed, ovate-triangular, fish-tail base 2
(Fragmentary specimens.)
Projectile rejects 4
(All appear to have been intended for medium-size, stemmed points.)
Scrapers:
Round turtle-back 1
(3.2 cm. in diameter.)
Elongated turtle-back 2
(About 5 cm. in length.)
Plano-convex rejects 2
Worked flakes 4
Kaolin lumps 2
(Plano-convex in shape and about 10 x 5 x 3 cm.)
Red ocher lump 1

European:
Iron objects:
Chisellike artifacts 2
(6 and 14 cm. in respective length.)
Sword or knife-blade fragment 1
(13 cm. in length.)
Gun-barrel (?) 1
(5 cm. in length, obviously fragmentary.)
Miscellaneous small fragments 5

In addition to the materials studied, 14 conch-shell bowls, many of them intentionally perforated, sandstone abrading hones or stones, and additional European glass beads are also reported from Parrish mound 3.

Summary.—Parrish mound 3 was 7 feet high and surrounded by a horseshoe-shaped embankment. Like the other Parrish mounds it was made of sand and had been constructed for mortuary purposes. Of the 212 recognizable individual burials all but one were secondary bundles. The exception was cremated and, from its position in the mound, was indicated to be a late intrusive interment.

Although European artifacts were relatively scarce in this mound, and many of them were found in association with the single cremated burial, the pottery from the mound fits the Safety Harbor Complex and Period. As at Parrish 1 and 2, Glades wares and Biscayne wares were found in association with the Safety Harbor types. The one dissenting feature in the ceramic tabulations is the small group of Weeden Island Period sherds. These seem best explained as a hold-over or "antique" piece.

PARRISH MOUND 4, MANATEE COUNTY (MA-4)

This site is a mound about 300 yards northeast of Parrish mound 3, just to the south of the Parrish-Wauchula road. It was not described by Stirling in his 1935 preliminary summary. The mound is rather imposing, as it stands above the flats some 4.5 or 5 feet. It measures 80 feet on both cardinal axes. The form is symmetrical, and there were only a few old excavators' pits noted in its surface. The mound was trenched along the south side and no evidence of cultural debris, other than a few flint chips and some pieces of charcoal, was observed. Its composition was, however, artificial and man-made. Presumably it was a habitation or temple-substructure mound.

PARRISH MOUND 5, MANATEE COUNTY (MA-5)

Description of the site.—This mound was reported upon briefly by Stirling (1935, p. 383) under the heading of "Little Manatee River, Manatee County, Mound No. 4." Its location is in the area northeast of Parrish just to the north of the Parrish-Wauchula road. It is on the property of Nicodemus Keen in the northwest quarter of section 23, Township 33 S., Range 21 E. Mr. Keen gave permission to excavate. The mound is on open woodlands and stands about 7 feet above the flat, although Mr. Keen was of the opinion that its height had diminished within the past 60 years. This degradation is probably the result of plowing, as the mound surface had been farmed in the recent past. In this connection Mr. Keen recalled plowing up a pottery vessel with stamped decoration from the mound. Unfortunately, this specimen was not available.

Before excavation the mound was symmetrical, approximately circular, and measured about 80 feet across. Its original shape is uncertain; the best guess is that it was conical or dome-shaped. The intrusions or old excavations in the mound appeared to have been inconsequential.

Excavations and burials.—The body of the mound was of sand, much like the other Parrish mounds. No evidences of structural sequence in its building were distinguished during the excavation. Sherds, charcoal, fragments of human bone, red ochre stain, an occasional flint artifact, shark teeth, and a stone plummet were taken from various depths and locations in the fill.

Burials were also scattered through the body of the mound. Eighty-nine inhumations were recorded, but these were in such a poor state of preservation that it is most probable that there were many more individuals buried in the mound. Burial position, because of advanced decay of the bones, was difficult to determine, but secondary treatment seems to have been the rule. Some of the bone remains appeared not to have been burned nor to have been in any way associated with fire; however, there were many cases where the bones were very definitely burned as though by partial cremation. In some of the latter, evidences of fire, charcoal and burned sand, were seen in direct contact with the bones, so that the placing of a small fire with a secondary burial, at the time of its deposition in or on the mound, is inferred. In a few instances, flint points or conch shells were noted in direct association with individual burials.

Pottery.—Of the very few sherds found in Parrish mound 5, only three are of much use as time diagnostics. These are the two Carrabelle Incised fragments, which are good Weeden Island Period types, and the single sherd of St. Petersburg Incised which is found in both Weeden Island and Englewood contexts. The mound is tentatively placed as Weeden Island. The Biscayne and Glades types are of little help in the dating, but their occurrence with Weeden Island types is commonplace.

The collection examined from Parrish mound 5 has been classified as follows:

Weeden Island Complex
- Weeden Island Series:
  - Carrabelle Incised 2
- St. Petersburg Incised.................................... 1
- Biscayne Series:
  - Biscayne Plain 1
  - Biscayne Check Stamped.................................... 7
  - Biscayne Roughened 1

Glades Complex
- Glades Series:
  - Glades Plain 5

Miscellaneous
- Residual Plain 1

Total sherds.... 18

Artifacts.—The only nonceramic artifact studied from Parrish mound 5 was a plummet of gray diorite (?). This object is beautifully polished, grooved at one end, and has a flat, tablike nub above the groove. In addition, Stirling (1935, p. 383) lists fragments of conch shell, probably pieces of shell cups or bowls, and a shark tooth as coming from the mound.

Summary.—This was a sizable mound of sand which had been constructed solely for purposes of burial. All the burials encountered at different levels in the mound fill were apparently of the secondary type, although decay of the bone was so advanced as to make identification of burial type difficult. Eighty-nine individuals were counted, but many more may have been put into the mound during its construction. In many instances the bones were partially burned, and there were evidences of fires having been made on or near the individual burials.

On the basis of the few potsherds found in the mound it is tentatively identified with and dated in the Weeden Island II Period.

COCKROACH KEY, HILLSBOROUGH COUNTY (HI-2)

Description of the site.—Following the excavations at the Thomas mound, this unit of the Smithsonian-State of Florida Federal Relief-sponsored archeological survey transferred its activities to a small key 3 miles south of the mouth of the Little Manatee River (map 9). The key is variously known as "Indian Hill,"[88] "Indian Key," and "Cockroach Key." The latter name was selected by the excavator in his field reports and is used throughout this paper. Although Moore, who excavated on the key in 1900 (Moore, 1900, pp. 359-362), recorded it as "Indian Hill," that name is not used here because of its identity with or similarity to various site names not only in Florida but throughout the Southeast. On the Hillsborough County map, Cockroach Key is simply referred to as "Unsurveyed Island No. 1," in section 20, Township 32 S., Range 18 E.

The key is separated from the mainland by about 300 meters of tidewater flats. Prior to the building of a county causeway the distance between the shore and the island was said to be about three-quarters of a mile. With the exception of the north side, a fringe of mucky mangrove swamps surrounds the island. All portions of the key that extend above the water line appear to be artificial in origin, consisting of discarded shells of edible shellfish. As shown on the

---

[88] S. T. Walker refers to the site by this name (Walker, 1880b, p. 418).

contour map (map 12), it is composed of a series of terraces rising to two major mounds; the higher is 35 feet (roughly 10 meters) above the average high-water level, and the other is slightly less.

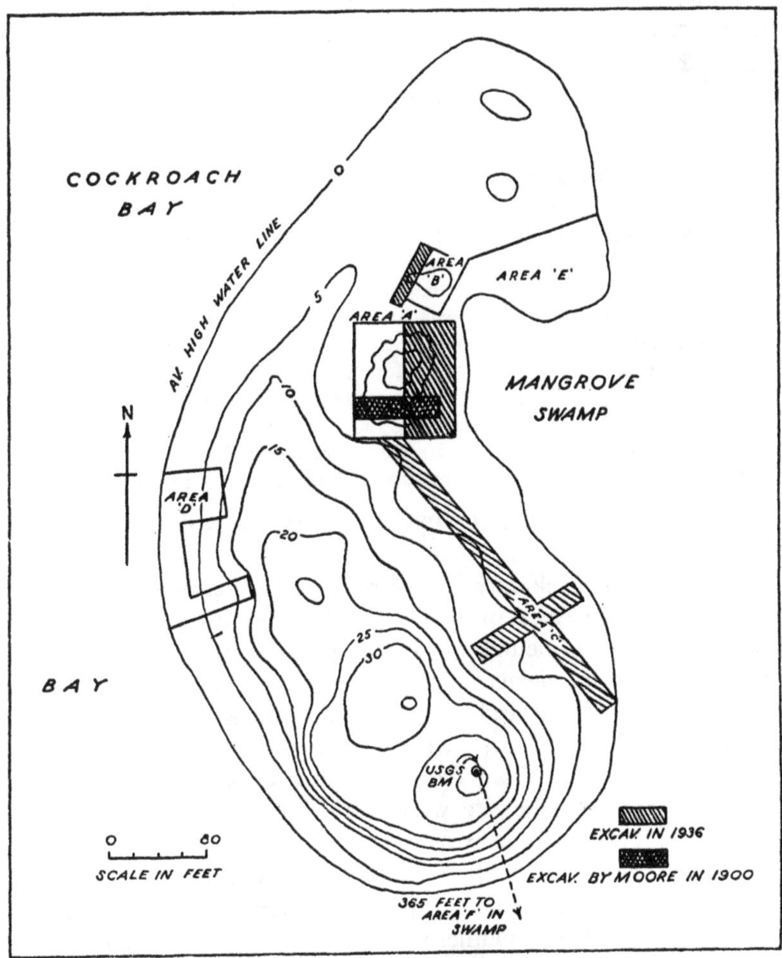

Map 12.—Excavations at Cockroach Key (Hi-2). The letters indicate the excavation areas or units referred to in the text.

There is also a smaller shell burial mound (indicated on the contour map as area A) which is about 15 feet above water level. In the mangroves to the southeast of the main body of the key is another small artificial shell mound in which some exploratory excavations were made (indicated as area F). Along the western shore of the key, about 5 feet above high-water level, there is a flow of brackish water at one point; this may at one time have been a fresh-water spring.

Moore's description of Cockroach Key tallies very closely with its appearance in 1936 (see pl. 8, center). In the winter of 1900, upon his visit to the site, he wrote:

> About 3 miles down from Tampa Bay from the mouth of the Little Manatee River is an island known as Indian Hill (Cockroach Key), probably 8 acres in extent, almost covered by an aboriginal deposit of shells, including oyster, clam, conch, and cockle. . . . Part of the shell deposit is made of irregular mounds and ridges. At one extremity, however, the deposit rises steeply, forming a great heap seemingly composed of three mounds with depressions between. . . . The largest of these heaps has a height of 30 feet above the surrounding shell deposit and 36 feet 7 inches above water level. We believe, after personal inspection of the majority of Florida shell heaps and careful inquiry as to the rest, that the shell deposit at Indian Hill exceeds in height any in the State, though considerably greater altitudes for other sites have been given by writers who base their assertions upon estimate. . . . Close to the great shell heap is another, also of shell, very symmetrical, with upward slope of 28 degrees in places. This mound [see Moore, 1900, fig. 4, p. 362], oblong with rounded corners, extends 76 feet in a NE. and SW. direction. Its minor diameter is 55 feet; its height above the general level of the surrounding shell is 12 feet 4 inches.

This last mound which Moore describes is clearly the burial mound or area A of the present report.

Excavations at Cockroach Key were begun on February 1, 1936, and concluded in mid-April of that year. Preston Holder, field supervisor at the Thomas mound, was in charge of the work; Louis Symmes of Riverview, Fla., owner of the site, gave permission to excavate. Before digging commenced, a topographic map was prepared for the entire key. The map (map 12) was originally contoured in 2.5-foot intervals and ranged from the water level to 35 feet above water level. Six areas of the site were marked on the contour map for excavation. These include areas A, B, C, D, and E on the key proper, and area F, the small shell mound rising above the tidal flats 100 meters or so to the southeast. No excavation was planned for the great shell mass at the southern end of the key. Here were the two high hummocks of shell and a third hummock which was 25 feet above the water level. Although these eminences were probably artificial, and chances for stratigraphy were greatest here, the engineering difficulties of digging at great depth into semicompact shell piles were too formidable. It was decided to concentrate on the burial mound (area A) and to test further the island deposits at the peripheries where the depth of shell was not profound.

Area A excavations.—A rectangle, 95 feet north and south and 110 feet east and west, was laid out over the burial mound and designated as area A (see pl. 8, bottom). This area was subdivided into 5-foot squares as a system of excavation control, and a little over one-half of the area was excavated in these 5-foot sections. This includes the entire eastern half of the burial mound plus a strip along its southern edge. Work was, unfortunately, halted before complete excavation of the mound could be accomplished. On the south side of the mound the trenches made by Moore in 1900 were encountered and reexcavated. These remaining evidences of his excavation were approximately 15 feet wide and 70 feet long.[34] The present excavations were carried somewhat deeper than was Moore's original cut, and at nearly all points area A was excavated down to the water table which was about 2 feet deeper than the water line as indicated on the topographic map (map 12). In all places, shell, refuse, and occasional artifacts were found at and below the water table. The original muck or sand base of the key was never located; thus it is to be surmised that the cultural debris continued on down for several additional feet. Complete excavation to the oldest levels would have been possible only with pumping equipment.

Mound structure of area A.—Of his excavations into this burial mound Moore says:

> At the southwest end of the mound a trench was run in from the margin 21 feet, converging from 41 feet at the beginning to 20 feet at the end. The mound was built of layers of small oyster shells and strata of crushed shell and blackened debris. During the excavation, human remains were met with at 17 points and in other places while caving the sides of the excavation at the end. No remains lay at a greater depth than 4 feet, while the majority were just beneath the surface. With three exceptions the burials consisted of parts of disarranged skeletons. Two skeletons lay much flexed, on the side; the other, face down and partly flexed. No artifacts were with the remains.
>
> At one end of this mound lay in numbers small shells (*Strombus pugilis*) with two perforations for a handle, in the body whorl below the periphery and much chipped and worn at the beak. These and similar shells, lying here and there over the entire deposit, had doubtless served as hammers, probably to open shell-fish for food.

Excavation of over half of the total content of the Cockroach Key burial mound revealed that Moore's trench had by no means penetrated the full depth of the artificial deposits composing the tumulus. Three distinct strata or superimposed mounds were discovered, and from the exposed cross sections it could be seen that Moore's cut had

---

[34] As will be noted, this does not check well with the dimensions given by Moore (1900, pp. 359 ff.).

gone through only the outer mound mantle (fig. 18). Holder cut through the mound, at center, to a total depth of 15 feet, the point at which the water table precluded further excavation. Beginning at the bottom with this arbitrary base line the three exposed mounds are recorded as "primary," "secondary," and "tertiary." The primary mound, as it is seen above the water table, is 1.5 feet thick on the peripheries and 4 feet thick at the center. Its shape must have been a low hillock or dome. In composition it is horizontally stratified in alternate bands of shell, heavy black midden or decayed organic

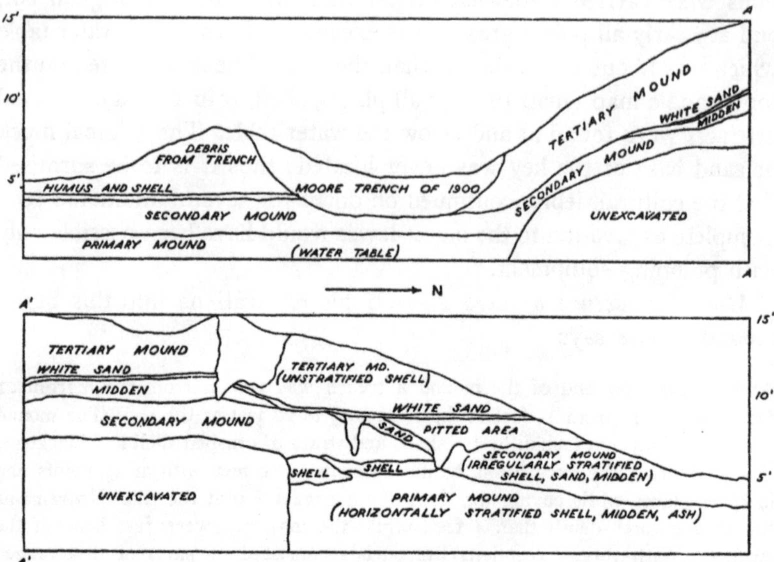

FIG. 18.—Profile of mound in area A, Cockroach Key (Hi-2). This is a cross section through mound center on a north-south line. Vertical lines of the drawing, A-A and A'-A', conjoin to complete the cross section.

matter, sand lenses, and occasional pockets of ash. The even bedding and nature of the mound material (cultural debris) argue that the structure is not a mound in the artificial sense but a midden heap built up by gradual accumulation. This is further attested by the absence of burials from the primary mound except in the peripheries where they are intrusive from mound levels above. The majority of the artifacts recovered from area A were taken from the primary mound.

The secondary mound is irregularly stratified as compared with the primary mound. In cross section it presented a "loading" type of structure rather than the elongated, lenticular bands of rubbish that are more apt to characterize the occupational deposit. It was made up of shell, sand, and sand and midden deposits. Ashes, or evidences of fires, are lacking. Its total thickness is about 2 feet with less variation between the peripheries and the center than in the case of the primary mound. On the crest of the secondary mound several inches of concentrated midden suggest that the summit was occupied after the mound had been built, and that, possibly, a sod or humus line had also developed. Above the midden and possible humus, and also extending down the flanks of the secondary mound, was a thin layer of pure white "topsoil" sand. This narrow band of white sand varies between 1 and 2 inches in thickness. It may have been an artificial capping or, possibly, the result of storm or hurricane deposition. Burials were found inclusive within the secondary mound, implying that the essential function of this layer was a mortuary one.

The tertiary mound was 3 to 4 feet thick on the crest and tapers considerably toward the peripheries. It was most clearly distinguishable from the other two mound mantles, as it was composed of pure, unstratified shell. Burials were found at all depths in the tertiary mound, and it was presumably built as a burial place.

Burials in area A.—A total of 224 burials were encountered in all the mound mantles. This includes 3 primary group burials and 3 secondary group burials. Two of the secondary group burials had as many as 15 and 10 individuals in them, respectively (pl. 8, top). Two hundred eighteen burials were solitary interments. Unfortunately, the multiple structure of the mound was not discovered until over half of the burials were removed. Because of this no tabulations of burial types for the secondary and tertiary mounds were included in the field notes. As has been mentioned, there were no inclusive burials in the primary mound, and all interments were in the two upper mounds. Over 50 percent of the burials were young children or infants. Of these, the excavator estimated that 90 percent were found in the tertiary mound. The additional fact that the adult burials in the tertiary mound showed, in numerous cases, bone pathology suggests that epidemic disease was a factor in the high infant mortality during the late stage of the mound construction.

Burials from the mound in area A are tabulated as follows:

Primary:	
Full-flexed, horizontally placed (pl. 4, center)	84
Full-flexed, upright position	2
Semiflexed, horizontally placed	10
Extended, horizontally placed	1
Probable primary burials	94
Group burials	3

Secondary:	
Bundle (pl. 4, bottom)	15
Single skull	12
Group burials	3
Total....	224

The secondary bundle burials encountered were not of the same type as those discussed from the Thomas mound. Little care was given to the placement of the long bones in the Cockroach Key burial mound. In those few instances where the bones had been carefully "bundled" the long bones were placed above the skull. The horizontal type of bundle burial at the Thomas mound was formed by placing the long bones below the skull. Occasional bundle burials at Cockroach were found without skulls, being no more than a pile of leg and arm bones.

Pottery from area A.—Over 300 pottery specimens were recovered from all locations and depths of the excavations. All but one of these were sherds. This remaining specimen was a bowl of plain ware which had, apparently, been purposefully perforated or "killed." No vessels were found in immediate association with burials in the mound. The field accounts describe the pottery as being nearly all plain ware of an exceedingly crude quality, with check-stamped surface treatment as the only exception. Most of the plain ware was the sand-tempered, gray-to-black pottery of the Glades or Belle Glade Series. A third ware type present in the mound is the light-weight, chalky Biscayne Series pottery. All fragments with check-stamped surface decoration were of this series (Biscayne Check Stamped).

Of the original sherds, 340 were plain and 18 check stamped. Ninety-three of these sherds are now available for study in the United States National Museum.[85] From this sample it is reasonable to assume that all the sand-tempered plain pottery described by Holder in the field notes, and subsequently discarded, belonged to the types Glades Plain, Belle Glade Plain, and, possibly, Pinellas Plain. Similarly, without much doubt, the discarded sherds of the soft, chalky ware were the type Biscayne Plain.

Concerning the 23 sherds of the type Pinellas Plain, it should be pointed out that none of the typical rim projections or handles, usually characteristic of this type, were recorded for the Cockroach Key collection. The ware quality was, however, identical with that of Pinellas Plain sherds as these are found at Safety Harbor.

---

[85] The National Museum catalog numbers for these, and all other Cockroach Key collections, are 384292-384311.

The following pottery was classified from Cockroach Key, area A:

Glades Complex
- Glades Series:
  - Glades Plain 11
- Biscayne Series:
  - Biscayne Plain 1
  - Biscayne Check Stamped 18
- Belle Glade Series:
  - Belle Glade Plain 40
- Okeechobee Series:
  - Okeechobee Plain 1

Safety Harbor Complex
- Safety Harbor Series:
  - Pinellas Plain 23

Total sherds.... 93

Artifacts from area A.—Artifacts listed in the field catalog as coming from various depths and locations of the burial mound in area A are described and enumerated as follows:

Pottery:
- Pendant 1

Stone:
- Flint scrap 1
- Fragments of carved stone pendants or plummets 2

Shell:
- Conch-shell celts 2
- Gouges or chisels 3
- Hammers or picks 79
- Hoes 2
- Scrapers 3
- Conch columellae 22
- Miscellaneous worked conch shell 1
- Worked oyster shell 1

Bone:
- Dagger of deer bone 1

  (This specimen is not in the National Museum collection, but was presented to the State of Florida. The dagger is 20.5 cm. long, 3.5 cm. broad, and 1.7 cm. thick at base. It tapers to a flat but sharp point. It is two-edged and bears an engraved decoration combining both geometric and naturalistic (?) elements. Only one side was so ornamented. Near the top the dagger has been pierced by a small, circular hole.)
- Bipointed projectile points 2

  (These are in the National Museum. They measure 9.5 and 10.5 cm. in length, respectively. Both are roughly cylindrical and pointed at the ends.)

Human humerus with shark-tooth point imbedded in bone...... 1
(Left humerus of young woman with point imbedded in coronoid depression. This specimen, now in National Museum, was found with one of mass secondary burials. Although the point is firmly imbedded in bone it is not likely that growth continued after injury.[86] The shark-tooth point is about 4.5 cm. long and has a round notch cut in one side near base. Although referred to as a point it is possible that the tooth was set in a toothed club and became dislodged from the club after striking and sticking into the bone.
Fragment of petrified bone................................ 1

Except for the artifacts so indicated in the lists, plus two fragments of worked shell, none of the above specimens are in the National Museum or were available for this study.

Summary of area A.—The mound in area A appears to have been a burial tumulus built in two stages upon an earlier hill or crest of occupational debris. The primary mound was not a burial place, and from its physical appearance in cross section was the result of slow occupational accretion. The secondary mound was built up by small "loadings" of refuse, sand, and shell. Burials were placed in the mound during its construction. The upper few inches of the secondary mound is composed of dark organic matter which suggests that the surface was once again used as a habitation area. Over the organic layer is a thin capping of pure white sand. This may be beach sand which was put down as a purposeful capping to the mound prior to the erection of the tertiary mound, or it may be beach sand blown onto the mound. The latter seems the less likely, but if it was the case it may indicate a period of desertion between the building of the secondary and tertiary mounds. The tertiary mound, though made up entirely of discarded edible shellfish, was an intentionally constructed layer in which many burials were made.

Primary burials were much more numerous than secondary burials, although several of the latter did occur and three mass secondary burials, or large piles of human bone, were encountered. Nearly all of the primary burials were flexed or semiflexed. No recording of burial types by mound level was made, but a greater incidence of child burials and bone disease was noted for the tertiary mound. This may indicate diseases of an epidemic or contagious sort during the late history of the mound site.

Pottery sherds and shell artifacts were scattered all through the mound in considerable numbers. A few bone implements were also found. All may have been accidental inclusions rather than mortuary goods. The one exception to this was a bowl of the type Biscayne

[86] Opinion of Dr. T. Dale Stewart, U. S. National Museum.

Plain which had been intentionally destroyed or "killed." Belle Glade Plain and Glades Plain were common types. Biscayne Checked Stamped, as well as Biscayne Plain, was also present in the mound. There is one hint of ceramic stratigraphy. Of the available sherds in the small sample collection it was noted that all the Biscayne ware types, all the Pinellas sherds, and all the Belle Glade sherds except one came from a depth of 30 to 36 inches below mound surface, a relatively superficial depth and totally within the tertiary mound. The remainder of the sherds now at hand, which are the Glades Plain fragments and one piece of the type Belle Glade Plain, are described as coming from "various units in area A," implying inclusion of lower as well as upper level. This bit of information, slight though it is, would tend to corroborate a stratification and to suggest that the Biscayne, Belle Glade, and Pinellas types had made a relatively late appearance at the area A mound.

The shell hammers referred to are undoubtedly the complete, or near-complete, conch shells which have been pierced through the body of the whorl with two holes for hafting. The natural small end of the shell shows various types of sharpening and marks of use. These were listed as the artifact type most frequently met with in area A, as well as in all the other excavation areas on Cockroach Key. A few other shell tools, or fragments of tools or artifacts, and some bone artifacts made up the remainder of artifacts taken from the burial mound. Both pottery and artifacts were most common in the primary mound level.

Area B excavations.—Area B was a rectangle, 40 x 45 feet, laid out to the northwest of area A. The rectangle and the excavations within the rectangle were oriented northeast-southwest. The shell refuse in this spot was mounded only to a low rise, a foot or so above the surrounding ground level and only 6 feet above the water line. A 10-foot strip along the northwest side of the rectangle was the only portion excavated. This was a trench 55 feet long, extending 10 additional feet beyond the southwestern limits of the rectangle. Excavation proceeded through shell refuse down to the water table and was discontinued. Pottery sherds, shell and bone artifacts, shell, animal bones, and rubbish were noted at all depths. At a depth of 2 feet below the surface, in the southwest end of the trench, six post holes were discovered in clean shell. These were traced downward for an additional foot where they disappeared. No other structural details, such as evidences of a house floor, hearths, more post holes, or burned Wattle were encountered. The six post holes were arranged in a semicircle, or segment of a circle, which measured 10 feet in diameter. The posts had been unevenly spaced at distances ranging from 2 to 4 feet. This was the only trace of a structure found in any of the Cockroach Key excavations.

Pottery and artifacts from area B.—The following list comprises the field catalog of materials taken from the trench excavation in area B:

Pottery:

- Plain sherds 292
  (Only six of these sherds were available for study; five are Glades Plain, one Belle Glade Plain.)

Stone:

- Projectile point 1
  (Squared stem, long barbed shoulders. The length is about 11 cm.)

Shell:

- Hammers or picks 181
- Celts, flat-surface variety 2
  (*Strombus gigas*[87] celts, rectanguloid to trapezoidal in outline. The broad end has a prepared cutting edge. The other sides and both surfaces are carefully trimmed and smoothed. The complete specimen is 14 x 5 x .8 cm.)
- Celts, concave-surface variety 5
  (*Busycon contrarium* celts, trianguloid or rectanguloid in form. Cutting edge at broad end. Sides carefully trimmed but surfaces unworked.)
- Chisels or gouges 5
- Pendants or plummets 3
  (One fragment available for examination.)
- Beads 4
  (Circular in form, diameter 2.5 cm. and thickness 1 cm. Perforation slightly off center. Other three specimens not available.)
- Columellae 91
  (Four fragments examined. All have worked, smoothed butt ends.)
- Miscellaneous worked shells 3

Bone:

- Knife 1
- Fishhooks 2
- Projectile points 10
  (Nine examined. These are bipointed type. Three are complete and range in size from 4 to 11 cm.)
- Tubular bead 1
  (Crudely cut section of bird bone, 1.5 cm. in length and 1 cm. in diameter.)
- Fragment of turtle-shell pendant 1
  (Simple, pierced fragment.)

---

[87] Shell identifications from this site by Dr. Harald A. Rehder, U. S. National Museum.

Only the specimens described in the above list were available for study in the United States National Museum.

Area C excavations.—Area C was a long trench system which begins contingent to the south side of area A and extends to the southeast for 285 feet. It was 15 feet wide. At a point a little southeast of the midpoint of the trench another trench of the same width intersects the main trench. This subsidiary trench was 100 feet long, and its eastern extremity almost reached to the water line. The area C system of trenches explored the flat section of the key lying to the northeast of the three great shell hills. Excavation was carried down, in all sections of the trench, to the water table. At no place was the depth of the cultural refuse exhausted.

Pottery and artifacts from area C.—The following list comprises the field catalog of materials taken from the trench system designated as area C:

Pottery:
- Plain sherds 285

Stone:
- Projectile point 1
  (Stem small, rounded, and shoulders straight. Length 8 cm., width at base 4 cm. Chipping crude but evidence of pressure retouch.)
- Sandstone anvil 1

Shell:
- Hammers or picks 150
- Beads 2
- Celts 2
- Pendant or plummet 1
  (Made from columella. Has length of 10 cm. and diameter of 1.6 cm. Tapers at each end and is grooved at each end.)
- Columellae 89
  (Six specimens in which butt end has been cut off and smoothed.)

Bone:
- Awls 2
  (Splinter awls from deer bone. Both are flat with flat, sharp points. Measure 8 and 5.5 cm. respectively.)
- Turtle-shell pendants 3

Only those specimens specifically described in the above list were available for study in the United States National Museum.

Area D excavations.—Area D was an irregular plot which was marked off on the extreme west-central part of Cockroach Key. It extended for 120 feet along the shore, and back from the shore for as much as 75 feet. In this area several random tests were put down in the refuse. All were carried to the water table, and in no case were the artifact-bearing shell deposits exhausted.

Pottery and artifacts from area D.—The following list comprises the field catalog of materials taken from the test excavations made in area D:

Pottery:	
Plain sherds	243
Shell:	
Hammers or picks	821
Columellae	9
Hoe	1
Beads	11
Fragments of worked shell	2
Clam shell, pierced (*Venus* shell.)	1
Bone:	
Fragment of worked bone	1
Fossil shark tooth	1
Other:	
Bead made of resin (?)	1

Area F excavations.—Exploratory tests were made in the small shell deposit situated over 100 meters to the southeast of Cockroach Key. This was designated as area F. Conditions of refuse, depth of deposit, and materials encountered were much the same as in the various excavations made on the main key.[38]

Pottery and artifacts from area F.—The following list comprises the field catalog of materials taken from the test excavations at area F:

Pottery:	
Plain sherds	12
Shell:	
Hammers or picks	391
Columellae	6

Surface collection from Cockroach Key.—Previous to excavation on the main key a number of artifacts were gathered from the surface. None of these were forwarded to the United States National Museum, but they are listed in the field catalog as given below. From

[38] Area E marked off but not excavated.

this brief description, the materials found on the surface seem to be very much of a type with the subsurface collections.

Pottery:	
Plain sherds	31
Shell:	
Hammers or picks	1014
Columellae	3
Fragments of worked shell	25
Oyster shell, worked	1

Summary of Cockroach Key.—The Cockroach Key site, 3 miles south of the mouth of the Little Manatee River, on the southern reaches of Tampa Bay, is one of the big shell-midden sites on the Gulf Coast of Florida. Although only a portion of its tremendous bulk has been explored, it appears to represent a culture which is significantly different from the Weeden Island, Englewood, or Safety Harbor Complexes, all of which are well known from the Tampa Bay section. This complex has been designated the Glades culture (Goggin, n. d. 1; Willey, n. d.), and its affinities are to the south with the Glades archeological area. The characteristic ceramics of the Glades culture are the Glades Series types. These are crude, black-to-gray, sand-tempered vessels of simple open bowl shapes. Both plain and incised and punctated types are known, but of these only the type Glades Plain was found in Cockroach Key. In addition, types of the Belle Glade Series, a variant ware found typically at Belle Glade on Lake Okeechobee (Willey, n. d), and the Biscayne Series are often found associated with the sand or grit-tempered Glades types. This seems to be mainly true of the later phases of Glades culture, and the presence of Biscayne types at Cockroach Key implies that at least a part of the site belongs to the last of the Glades periods, Glades III. A hint of stratigraphy in area A suggests that the tertiary mound in that location may date from this period.

An abundance of shell implements is another characteristic Glades trait. These include, principally, conch hammers or picks, chisels or gouges, celts, and various tools made from the centrum or columella of the conch shell.

There are indications, such as the stratigraphy at Weeden Island proper (see pp. 107-108), that at least one phase of the Glades culture is earlier than the Weeden Island Period in the Tampa Bay vicinity. This does not apply to all phases of the Glades culture, however, as Glades II and Glades III Periods have been demonstrated to be coeval with Weeden Island and even Englewood and Safety Harbor. The most likely chronological relationships between the Glades culture and those of the Gulf Coast are that the latter, as they are represented in the region between Tampa Bay and Charlotte Harbor, overlie an early Glades culture (Glades I) and continue parallel with Glades II and III Periods. It is likely that the earlier levels at the Cockroach Key site, such as the primary refuse mound in area A, may have been Glades I or Glades II in time.

From the nature of the shell refuse which covered the entire key, it is to be supposed that the people who lived at Cockroach Key were primarily a fishing group who lived upon the abundant shellfish found in nearby waters. Animal bones mixed through the shell show that hunting was also important. One cannot conceive of horticulture having been very important on such a small, shell-covered island. Maize may, of course, have been grown on a small scale, or, possibly, farm plots could have been maintained on the nearby mainland.

Animal bones from the midden identified by Preston Holder, the excavator, include:

deer	alligator	mullet
opossum	sting ray	drumfish
rabbit	3 kinds of turtle	cetacean vertebrae
wildcat	birds	
raccoon	shark	

A summary of the invertebrate fauna, as determined by Prof. Robert Webb of the University of Tampa, is as follows:

Pelecypods:

Cardium magnum	*Ostrea frons*
Cardium isocardia	*Ostrea virginica*
Chama macrophylla	*Ostrea* cf. *haytiensis*
Crassitella floridana	*Ostrea* cf. *sculpturata*
Venus mercenaria	*Chlamys dislocatus*
Modiola tulipa	*Carditamera* sp.

Gastropods:

Fulgur perversum	*Fasciolaria tulipa*
Strombus pugilis	*Crepidula fornicata* (sic)
Melonogena sp.	*Sigaretus perspictiva*
Fasciolaria gigantea	*Natica* sp.

PERICO ISLAND, MANATEE COUNTY (MA-6)

General comments on the archeology of Manatee County.—In conjunction with the excavation program at Perico Island, the field supervisor, Dr. M. T. Newman, conducted a hurried survey of aboriginal sites in Manatee County. The survey was made for the purpose of locating sites and taking general descriptive notes. Surface collections or test excavations were not made. Fifty-one sites were recorded. Most of them were small sand mounds, presumably burial places; but several habitation sites are included in the total. Of interest for this report are Newman's generalizations about the type of sites visited and their environmental settings. The following statements, with a few minor revisions, are taken from that writer's field notes made at the close of the Manatee County survey.

(1) The mounds are not often situated in groups. Usually, mounds are found singly. Occasionally, there may be three or four mounds within a rather large radius of one-quarter of a mile or over.

(2) Sites are well-distributed throughout the county, particularly along the waterways. There are not as many mounds along the Manatee River as one might expect, except near the mouth on Tampa Bay. Mounds may be located either on sand ridges or in the flat.

(3) A number of characteristic things are found to be generally true in regard to the coastal mounds of this county. All along the coast, at intervals, are shell-midden accumulations. Large shell habitation mounds, such as the Shaws Point mound and the large Perico Island habitation mound, are characteristic of the coastal region. Very often there is a sand or shell burial mound in connection with the habitation mound. There may even be a sand or shell ridge running from the habitation mound to its burial place as is the case in the Shaws Point mound, the Perico Island mound, and the Johnson shell mound on Terra Ceia Island.

As indicated by the above, the Perico Island site is a large dwelling and burial place with such elaborations as a shell ridge connecting the burial mound with the habitation midden. Cockroach Key, to the north in Hillsborough County, is, except for the feature of the connecting shell ridge, very much like the big shell-midden and burial-mound sites of the Manatee County coast. From the standpoint of physical appearance alone, it would appear that with such sites as Perico and Cockroach Key we are dealing with a culture that is markedly different from either Weeden Island or the sites of the late period in this region.

Description of the site.—The Perico Island site is situated on the western side of that island not far from the city of Bradentown, Manatee County (map 9). The site is a complex composed of two sizable shell middens, a small shell and sand burial mound, and a cemetery area. The mounds lie between 60 and 125 yards back from Sarasota Bay which fronts the site along the west side (see map 13). The larger of the two shell middens is the most northerly; this deposit is approximately 300 yards long (north-south) and 40 yards wide (east-west). At its southern terminus a lower, narrower ridge of shell extends southwestward for 150 yards. This shell ridge ends at the burial mound (pl. 7, top, left).

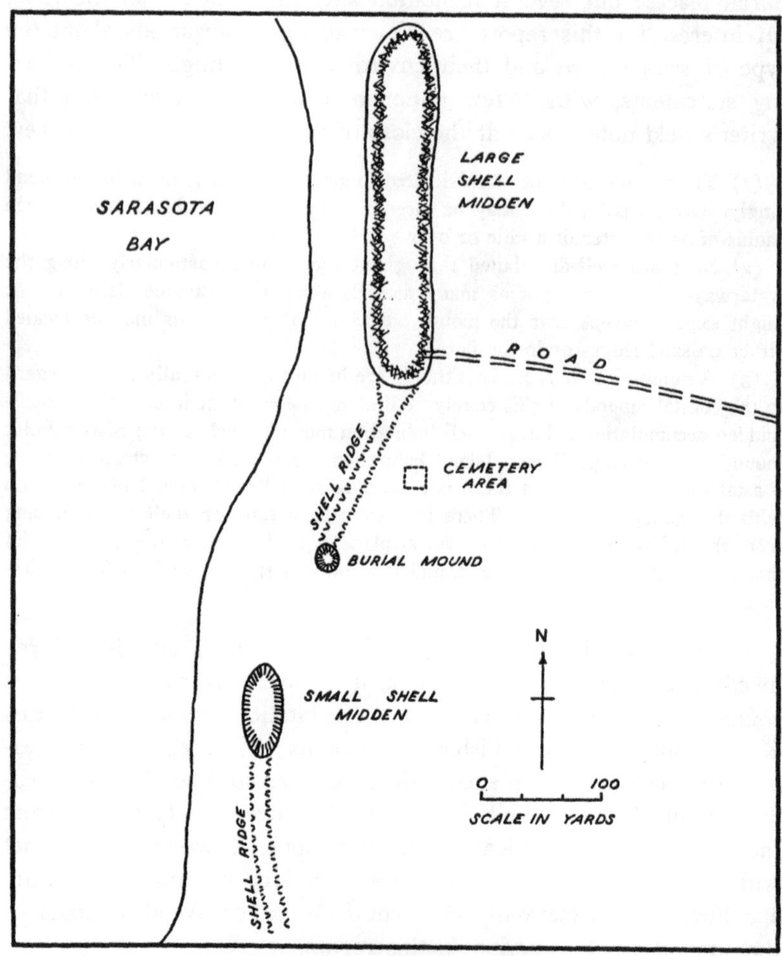

MAP 13.—The Perico Island site (Ma-6).

The burial mound is 60 feet in diameter, dome-shaped, circular, and at its highest point was almost 5 feet above the surrounding flats. Continuing southwestward from the burial mound is the smaller of the two shell middens. Like the larger, its long axis is oriented along the beach, almost true north-south. Its over-all length is 80 yards and its width 30 yards. The highest point is only a little higher than the burial mound, being 5.5 feet above the beach flats. At one time, however, before the removal of much of the shell for commercial purposes, this midden was said to have been much higher.

The middens are practically surrounded by marshlands, and high tide reaches to their western edge. They appear to be particularly large concentrations on a more or less continuous ridge of shell refuse. This ridge extends for about one-third of a mile south of the midden mounds proper, and at intervals it is dotted with other similar but smaller knolls or concentrations.

The remaining unit of the Perico Island site is the cemetery (pl. 7, bottom, left). This was discovered by the presence of shell showing up on the surface of the marsh in the area between the burial mound and the larger midden mound. It lies about 65 yards south of the southern end of the larger midden and about 40 yards east of the shell ridge which connects the burial mound to the larger midden mound. Excavation demonstrated the cemetery area to have a diameter of approximately 40 feet.

Three units of the site were excavated by Dr. M. T. Newman in the winter of 1933-34. These were the burial mound, the smaller midden, and the cemetery. In the following discussion they will be referred to under these names.

Excavation of the burial mound.—The burial mound at Perico was completely excavated by a profiling technique, working in from the north and west faces (pl. 7, center, left). All artifacts and burials were located by a coordinate system. The fill of the mound was sand mixed with shell, animal bone, ash, potsherds, and general detritus. Layers and lenses of relatively pure shell were noted at various levels of the mound. Rather than representing midden accumulations these shell layers were apparently carried in for mound construction as they were invariably found to be sterile of sherds and other cultural material. Sherds and artifacts were, instead, present in the sand fill, suggesting that this refuse material had been piled up for the express purpose of building a mortuary tumulus and that the fill had been carried in from a nearby village area. On the base of the mound there was a hard conglomerate made up of ash, burned shell and animal bone. Possibly this was an old occupation area on which the mound had been built. The conglomeritic quality of the deposit at the base of the mound is probably due to the fact that the salt-water table comes up into the mound base.

Burials were found from the original ground level throughout the body of the mound, and these were all inclusive. One hundred eighty-five primary, flexed skeletons were recorded. The burial position was true, tight flexure, with the legs drawn up under the chin, the arms flexed, and the hands sometimes over the face (pl. 7, top, right). The position of the head was on its side.

Artifacts of consequence were lacking in the mound. Numerous plain sherds and a few decorated sherds were found in the fill, but these were obvious accidental inclusions in the building material and not mortuary objects. In addition to the pottery, pieces of cut deer bone, polished tortoise shell, and broken flint projectiles were found. A single intentionally perforated conch-shell bowl may have been a mortuary artifact.

As a part of the rubbish, animal and fish bones, particularly the latter, were very abundant.

Pottery from the burial mound.—The pottery from the mound is predominantly of the Glades Complex and appears to represent Glades culture in its earliest stages, probably the Glades I Period. Only three plain Biscayne Series sherds were included in the collection, and, notably, Biscayne Check Stamped is absent. The two Deptford Check Stamped sherds, especially one with a tetrapodal support, are similar or identical to Deptford pottery from the northwest Florida coast. The complicated stamped sherd has the appearance of one of the early types within the complicated stamped tradition, St. Andrews Complicated Stamped.

As an assemblage, the material could easily be dated as a Glades I collection, with the Deptford and early complicated stamped sherd verifying this chronological position by establishing a cross date with such periods as Deptford and Santa Rosa-Swift Creek in northwest Florida. Whether or not the material is a contemporaneous association is, of course, unproved. The sherds appear to have been gathered up along with midden debris for the purpose of building the mound. As such they may not represent a true period assemblage. Nor can the building of the mound be considered as dating from the Glades I Period. All that can assuredly be advanced is that the mound was built either in Glades I times or afterward.

The pottery from the Perico burial mound has been classified below.[89] This represents the entire collection taken from the mound, without discards.

Glades Complex
Glades Series:
Glades Plain 482
Perico Series:
Perico Plain 8
Biscayne Series:
Biscayne Plain 3

Deptford Complex
Deptford Bold Check Stamped 2

Miscellaneous
Unclassified Complicated Stamped 1
(Sand-tempered, large concentric diamond designs with each unit 5.5 cm. long. Has general appearance of Swift Creek tradition of complicated stamping. Resembles the type St. Andrews Complicated Stamped.) —
Total sherds.... 496

Artifacts from the burial mound.—Nonceramic artifacts were extremely rare in the burial mound. Nothing of diagnostic value was recovered.

The following nonceramic artifacts were taken from the Perico burial mound:

Stone:
Flat fragment of worked stone 1
(5 cm. in diameter, 1 cm. thick, is slightly concave on one surface from grinding.)
Projectile point:
Unstemmed, triangular 1
(7 cm. long.)
Knife:
Unstemmed (fragment of butt end) 1

Shell:
Conch cup, "killed" or perforated 1

Miscellaneous:
Animal, fish, bird bones.

Excavation of the smaller shell midden.—A trench 25 feet long and 5 feet wide was put down from the eastern periphery of the mound and carried in to the north-south central axis (pl. 7, center, right). No other excavations were attempted. Both the appearance of the deposit, upon cross section, and the nature of the materials recovered, demonstrated the mound to be a midden deposit. There

[89] U. S. National Museum catalog numbers for this and other Perico Island collections are 383972-384055.

was considerably more shell in the smaller shell midden than in the burial mound. Like the burial mound, ash, burned animal bone, and burned shell were found at the base. This basal ash stratum was sterile of any cultural material. A large quantity of plain sherds, a few decorated sherds, and an occasional ground-stone, bone, or shell tool were found in the shell strata. A possible differentiation of shell was noted in that conch shell was plentiful on the periphery, but farther into the mound, and presumably deeper, only oyster shell was present.

Pottery from the smaller shell midden.—The principal difference between this assemblage and that from the burial mound is the large proportion of the type Perico Plain which appeared in the midden excavations. A few sherds of this type were noted in the burial mound but they were not numerically important as compared with the Glades Plain type. Unfortunately, we have no stratigraphic data available for the midden excavations, and it is impossible to say whether the Perico Series, a limestone-tempered pottery, is earlier or later than the Glades Plain. It is reasonable to expect such a time differentiation in view of the near absence of the Perico Plain type in the burial mound. Speculating upon the problem, it is most likely that Perico Plain is a later innovation at the site. The demonstrated early appearance of Glades Plain as the first pottery of the Glades area supports this hypothesis. The Perico Series types may be a local development which appeared at the close of Glades I Period. The fact that some of them are incised, in the same general technique of Glades decorated types although differing in design, suggests a correlation in time with the Glades II Period.

The 15 fiber-tempered sherds are unmistakable and are identical with the types St. Simons Plain (Caldwell and McCann, 1941, p. 51) from the northwest coast and the Georgia Coast or Orange Plain of the St. Johns River district (Griffin, J. B., 1945, p. 220). Presumably, these sherds must come from an early part of the site. It is possible that they are contemporaneous with Glades I Period, or they may even be earlier.

The two chalky-ware sherds with the incised decorations are similar in type of design to the type Perico Incised. This incised design has an interesting resemblance to the decoration on the type Orange Incised of the fiber-tempered-ware series of the St. Johns River area. (See J. B. Griffin, 1945, pp. 218-223.) In the St. Johns area, at South Indian Fields, Brevard County, a chalky ware with incised decorations seems to develop out of the earlier fiber-tempered Orange Incised (Masius, n. d.). This later incised type has been designated as St. Johns Incised. The two incised chalky sherds from Perico may be of this type.

The pottery from the Perico smaller shell midden is classified below. This is a complete collection from the excavations conducted by Newman.

Glades Complex	
Glades Plain	229
Perico Series:	
Perico Plain	281
Perico Incised	7
Perico Linear Punctated	5
Biscayne Series:	
Biscayne Plain	13
Miscellaneous	
St. Simons Plain	14
Incised (fiber-tempered)	1
Unclassified	2
(St. Johns Incised (?). Has Biscayne paste, geometric decoration.)	

Artifacts from the smaller shell midden.—Only a few artifacts were taken from the midden excavations; however, some of these are quite diagnostic of the Glades culture, such as the shell celts, the bipointed bone projectile, and the bone dagger.

Stone:	
Hammerstone, flattened-spheroid of limestone (5 cm. in diameter.)	1
Pitted hammerstone or anvil (Sandstone. Trianguloid, 7 cm. on a side and 3 cm. thick. Deep pit on one surface; other surface concave and dotted with percussion pits. Edges have been used for hammering.)	1
Red ocher (lump)	1
Bone:	
Dagger (point fragment)	1
Bipointed projectile point, short variety (4.2 cm. long.)	1
Shell:	
Celt, concave-surface variety (*Busycon contrarium,* length 11.5 and 10 cm.)	2
Celt, flat-surface variety (*Strombus gigas* (?), ovate and rectangular, measure 9.5 and 9 cm.)	2
Worked columella	1
Cup, "killed" or perforated	1
Miscellaneous:	
Cut deer bone scrap.	

Excavation of the cemetery.—This excavation proved exceedingly difficult. The ground was soft, being gray, wet sand with only a little admixture of shell. The burials were all very shallow, the deepest recovered being found at only 27 inches below the surface.

Working in from two trench faces, 43 skeletons were taken from the area. These were preserved to a condition of almost rocklike hardness, probably as the result of immersion in salt water. They were not, however, mineralized. All skeletons on which it was possible to determine position were tightly flexed (pl. 7, bottom, right). They tended to be buried in groups of from three to six. They had been placed in small pits and the pits had been lined with and covered by shells.

A few potsherds and a flint scraper were found in the cemetery. Presumably these were accidental inclusions.

Pottery from the cemetery.—Of the very small collection of sherds from the cemetery area only a single fragment of Glades Plain remains in the National Museum collections.

Artifacts from the cemetery.—A pebble hammer and a stemmed projectile, reworked as an end scraper (length 7.6 cm.) were the only artifacts found in the cemetery area.

Physical anthropology.—The crania from the cemetery area and from the burial mound at Perico Island were grouped together into a single series in the craniometric study which Hrdlička made on this material (Hrdlička, 1940, pp. 342-343 and 375-377). Among the males (37 crania) Hrdlička noted five instances of slight lateral-occipital or occipital flattening. In all instances this is apparently the sort of deformity that could occur from accidental causes. Among the females (60 crania) he noted four examples of asymmetry or slight flattening comparable to that observed in the males. There was one case of moderate occipital flattening.

Male cephalic index averaged 79.5 with a range of 74.0 to 87.2. Mean height index average was 85.6 with a range of 82.0 to 91.6. Female cephalic index average was 80.7 with a range of 74.3 to 89.1. Mean height index for females averaged 86.3 with a range of 78.8 to 91.5.

Summary of Perico Island.—The Perico Island site is comprised of four archeological units: a burial mound, two shell middens, and a cemetery area. The burial mound, cemetery, and the smaller of the middens were excavated in the winter of 1933-34. The burial mound was found to be composed of shell, sand, ash, and general cultural detritus. It was constructed purposefully for burial. It contained at least 185 primary, flexed burials, virtually no mortuary artifacts, a quantity of debris potsherds in the fill, and a few nonceramic artifacts. The smaller shell midden was composed mostly of shell. A sample cut in this part of the site produced several hundred potsherds and a few other artifacts. The cemetery area, located in flat ground in the sand, yielded 43 human skeletons also primary and flexed. The burials had been placed in small pits lined with shells.

The pottery from the burial mound is an assemblage of what appears to be Glades I Period material with a few extraneous sherds that relate to the Deptford and Santa Rosa-Swift Creek Periods of northwest Florida. That this assemblage represents a contemporaneous lot of material is open to doubt in that the sherds were accidental inclusions in the rubbish of which the mound was built.

The ceramics from the smaller midden also can be assigned to the Glades Complex, but there is a marked difference from the burial mound in that over one-half of the midden sherds are of a type called Perico Plain. Perico Plain, a limestone-tempered type, has resemblances to Glades Plain, the principal Glades Complex type, in vessel and rim forms. Associated with it are several sherds of incised pottery, Perico Incised and Perico Linear-punctated. Although there is no stratigraphic information for the smaller midden excavations, it is offered as a speculation that the Perico Series types are later innovations at the Perico site, and that a horizon of virtually 100 percent Glades Plain probably precedes it. Farther south, in the Glades area proper, incised types mark the appearance of the Glades II Period. Although these Perico decorated types are not the same as the Glades Series incised types, it is suggested that their appearance indicates the beginning of a comparable time period at the Perico site. It is noted that they bear a resemblance to the Glades incised types in technique of decoration and to the Orange Series fiber-tempered ware of the St. Johns River in decorative motifs.

A surprising find in the smaller midden were the 15 sherds of St. Simons (fiber-tempered) ware. These bear close relationship to the few fiber-tempered sherds of the northwest Florida coast, the Georgia coast, and to the Orange Series ware of the St. Johns. Their appearance indicates that some part of the midden site is very old, being chronologically correlated with Deptford or, possibly, pre-Deptford levels. Such levels in the Perico site may show a mixture of fiber-tempered ware and Glades Plain or they may show only fiber-tempered pottery. The chronological questions raised by the study of these collections cannot be answered without further excavation in the middens of the area.

Only in the smaller midden were there sufficient nonceramic artifacts to aid in cultural identification. Here the shell tools and bone artifacts fall into the Glades cultural complex rather than that of Weeden Island, Englewood, or Safety Harbor.

To conclude briefly, Perico Island represents an early Glades-type occupation in many ways similar to that glimpsed at Cockroach Key and in the submound level at the Weeden Island site. This variant of the Glades culture in the Manatee region will be referred to hereafter in this report as the Perico Island Period. At Perico, Glades pottery, probably of the Glades I Period, is associated with a few Deptford and Santa Rosa-Swift Creek pieces. There are also indications that a local development of the Perico Island Culture continued at the site paralleling Glades Period II.

CONCLUSIONS

The sites.—The sites excavated between Tampa Bay and Charlotte Harbor in the 1923-36 period are of two principal types. The first type, which is represented by the greater number of excavations, is the sand burial mound. In some instances shell middens, or rather refuse accumulations, were found near these burial mounds, but these were usually relatively small deposits. The second type of site is the deep and extensive shell midden. Burial mounds may be found in association with these middens, but these are composed of shell and detritus rather than sand. As will be pointed out in summation, these two types of sites are culturally distinct. It will be recalled that the differentiation between the two, the sand burial mound and the great shell refuse heaps, was one of the first significant observations made by early students of archeology in the general Tampa Bay coastal region (Brinton, 1859; Stearns, 1872).

As is obvious from the foregoing discussions, the first type of site, the sand burial mound, is present in three cultural complexes. These are the Weeden Island, Englewood, and Safety Harbor cultures. All have in common the feature of burial within a conical mound of sand built expressly for that purpose. They also share the trait of secondary burial as the dominant mode of disposal of the dead. In connection with the burials, it was the general custom to place a mass deposit of ceremonially broken or "killed" pottery in the mound. This pottery was not associated with any individual burial but seemed to be a communal offering to the dead. Nonceramic artifacts were sometimes found in the mounds, and, on occasion, these were directly associated with individual skeletons or skeletal remains.

The Weeden Island mounds are the Weeden Island burial mound, the Thomas mound, and Parrish mound 5. At Weeden Island proper Fewkes (1924) lists a number of domiciliary mounds and refuse heaps as a part of the total mound group complex. These domiciliary mounds were not carefully investigated, and it is not clear as to just how they differ from refuse accumulations. Presumably they were substructure or temple mounds. At the Thomas site a large shell midden lay only a few meters distant from the burial mound. No additional features were reported in connection with Parrish mound 5. The burial mounds at all three sites were roughly circular in outline and conical or dome-shaped. They ranged from 50 to 100 feet in diameter and from 4 to 7 feet high. Human burials were found in all parts, from mound base virtually to the surface. Between 200 and 300 burials were taken from the Weeden Island burial mound, 419 from the Thomas mound, and 89 from Parrish mound 5. No convincing physical stratigraphy was noted in the body proper of any of the three mounds. A change in the mode of burial during the Weeden Island Period may be indicated in two of the mounds, Weeden Island and Thomas. In both, primary burial, either extended or flexed, was the rule in the lower part of the mound while secondary treatment, including bundles and single skulls, was much more common in the upper portion. There was nothing, in either case, to substantiate any other cultural change paralleling this change in burial form. It should be noted that, with reference to the Weeden Island mound, this discussion of burial stratigraphy has not taken into account the premound or submound burials over which the Weeden Island mound was constructed. This premound level is culturally quite distinct from Weeden Island and is discussed below.

Cremation was rare in the Weeden Island Period mounds, occurring once at Thomas and being unrecorded at Weeden Island. In Parrish mound 5 there were several instances of burned secondary burials or partial cremations, apparently made in situ. This partial burning of the bones after they had been placed in the mound has been observed in other Weeden Island sites farther north along the coast (Willey, 1945, p. 235). The conventional mass deposit of "killed" mortuary ware was found on mound base at both Weeden Island and Thomas but not in Parrish mound 5.

The second of the three culture complexes, represented by the sand burial mound, is the Englewood. This culture is known chiefly from the type site near Sarasota, Fla. There were two burial mounds at the site, but only one was excavated thoroughly. The other has, however, been reported locally as containing burials. Some few hundred meters from the mound, along the bay front, is a shell midden of modest size. The Englewood mound was 110 feet in diameter and 13 feet high. The interior structure of the mound was revealed as a small inner mound over which the larger outer mound had been built. The inner mound had been constructed over a shallow burial pit. Apparently, very little time had elapsed between the construction of inner and outer mounds. One hundred twenty-four secondary burials were taken from the basal burial pit, and 139 secondary and primary burials were found in the mound fill of the inner and outer mounds. Of this latter group only 16 were definitely primary interments; all these were flexed in form. In spite of the physical evidence of mound stratigraphy, no cultural correlations with this superimposition of mounds was observed. A large mortuary deposit of "killed" pottery was found on the mound base.

The third culture associated with the sand burial mounds is the Safety Harbor. The sites belonging to this culture and period that were investigated include Safety Harbor proper and Parrish mounds 1, 2, and 3. The Safety Harbor site, on Tampa Bay, is much the most imposing of the four sites. Besides the burial mound, the site consists of a fairly extensive shell midden and a large, flat-topped pyramidal temple-type mound. The Safety Harbor Period burial mounds are dome-shaped and range from 40 to 80 feet in diameter and from 5 to 10 feet in height. The Safety Harbor burial mound and Parrish 1 and 3 were simple heaps of sand containing from 30 to over 200 burials. No complexities of structure were observed. Burial was uniformly secondary, and in only one case was there evidence of cremation. Parrish mound 2 was more complex in structure. It appears to have served two functions: that of a mortuary tumulus, like the other mounds, and also as a base for a special building. Under the mound, in the original ground surface, was a crematory pit filled with ash, charcoal, and burned human bones. The mound had been built over this pit to a height of 6 feet and a wooden building or enclosure of wooden posts had then been built on the mound summit. This building had been burned. In one corner of the rectangle was a platform of sand which had been used either as a seat for the storage of the bones of the dead or, possibly, as a crematory altar. It was impossible to determine the number of individuals represented by the burned bones in the submound pit or by the mass of bones on the raised sand platform, but throughout the body of the mound were the remains of 37 cremated burials and 2 uncremated bundle burials. The remains of two bodies that had been partially cremated in situ were found in burned, rectangular log crypts.

At Safety Harbor and Parrish mound 1 deposits of "killed" pottery were found on the mound base; at Parrish 3 this pattern differed in that vessels were often "killed" but were sometimes found inverted over or near individual burials rather than put into a common deposit. No special ceramic offerings of any sort were found in Parrish 2, the mound with the superimposed burned temple or building. In all the Safety Harbor mounds other artifacts, of shell, stone, or of European manufacture, had been placed with individuals.

The three sites, or site components, of the other type of site, the great shell middens and shell burial mounds, have been recognized as a local manifestation of the Glades culture which we have termed the Perico Island Period. These are the Perico Island site near Bradentown, Cockroach Key just off the delta of the Little Manatee River, and the premound level at the Weeden Island burial-mound site in Tampa Bay. All three sites are on islands or near-islands off the marshy shore. All were habitation places and all were burial places. At Weeden Island the premound level was an old midden and cemetery that preceded the later Weeden Island Period occupation of the site. Perico consists of several shell middens, a cemetery, and a burial mound. Cockroach Key is a giant midden with a burial mound located on one part of it. At both Perico and Cockroach Key the burial mound was made of shell and general village refuse rather than sand. In the Perico burial mound 185 primary flexed burials were recovered; there was no other burial type. At Cockroach Key 224 burials were taken from the mound. Most of these were primary and flexed although a few were secondary bundle burials. The Cockroach Key burial mound had been built in two stages and it is very probable that the secondary interments belonged to the latter level of mound construction.

At Perico, a number of primary flexed burials were also found in what was designated as the cemetery area. This was in flat ground near to but separate from the burial mound. These burials were unaccompanied by grave artifacts, but they were characteristically placed in small shell-lined pits. The situation is paralleled by the findings at Weeden Island in the premound level. Here, the burials were primary and flexed and had been interred in shell-lined pits.

At none of the three sites were any artifacts or pottery associated in the mounds or cemeteries with the dead, either individually or as group offerings.

Ceramics and artifacts.—The pottery from all these sites falls into four principal complexes, and it is from these that we have arrived at and first defined the culture complexes and periods. These are the Weeden Island, Englewood, Safety Harbor, and Glades pottery groups. In all the sites there is some evidence of mixture of pottery types of these different complexes. In some instances this mixture is, presumably, fortuitous or intrusive; in other sites the mixture seems to indicate a degree of contemporaneity.

The pottery from the three Weeden Island Period sites is typical of that inventoried from other Weeden Island type mounds in Florida. The sand-tempered, well-made Weeden Island Series types occurred in quantity at both Thomas and Weeden Island proper. Parrish mound 5 yielded only a few sherds, but these were typical of the Weeden Island ceramic complex. The most common Weeden Island types are Weeden Island Plain, Weeden Island Incised, Weeden Island Punctated, Weeden Island Zoned Red, Carrabelle Incised, and Keith Incised. Wakulla Check Stamped was also abundant in the mounds. Less common, but present, were the complicated stamped series found in Weeden Island sites in northwest Florida. One type, the Late Variety of Swift Creek Complicated Stamped is present at both Weeden Island proper and at Thomas. In addition, Sun City, Tampa, and Old Bay Complicated Stamped are typical of the region of Tampa Bay. Other characteristic central coastal types not found in quantity in the north are Ruskin Dentate Stamped, Ruskin Linear Punctated, and Hillsborough Shell Stamped. Another distinctive characteristic of the southern Weeden Island sites is the presence of considerable quantities of the soft, chalky Biscayne Series ware. Biscayne Check Stamped, and Biscayne Red are two common types. The Little Manatee Series is closely related to the Biscayne; and, paralleling the Weeden Island Series of types, in both decorative motives and vessel forms, is a chalky-ware series I have designated as Papys Bayou. The Papys Bayou Series pottery shows the blending of two ceramic histories, the Weeden Island and the Biscayne.

Besides the types of the Weeden Island Complex, and those of the Biscayne Series which are commonly associated, a few sherds of the Englewood, Safety Harbor, and Glades Complex types were found in the Thomas and Parrish 5 burial mounds. The Glades types, Glades Plain, Belle Glade Plain, and Perico Plain, may have a contemporaneous relationship with the Weeden Island Complex. There is a question here of type identity. As all these Glades types in question are plain, and embrace very simple forms, it is sometimes difficult to be sure of type identification. Their similarity with the Glades types, as these have been found in south Florida, is readily recognizable although the sherds found at Thomas and Parrish 5 may be regional variants of the more typical Glades ware of the south. In any event, they are typologically distinct from the Weeden Island Complex although found in association with it. The few Safety Harbor Complex sherds found at both Weeden Island and Thomas are assumed to be later intrusives. At Thomas they were associated with artifacts of European origin and were superficially placed in the mound.

The Englewood pottery complex is composed of sand-tempered types like Englewood Plain, Englewood Incised, and Lemon Bay Incised and soft ware of the Biscayne Series. Sarasota Incised is a chalky-ware type seemingly related to both traditions. Stylistically, there is a feeling of relationship to both Weeden Island and Safety Harbor, and their association in the mound at Englewood bears this out. A number of Weeden Island types were present as were a quantity of Safety Harbor Complex types. Rather than representing an earlier occupation and a latter intrusion. I am inclined to believe that these types were found in association with the Englewood Complex material as a result of a continuity into and out of the Englewood Period. Also present in the Englewood mound were a quantity of Glades Plain sherds. The problem here is similar to that confronted with the appearance of Glades Complex types in the Weeden Island Period sites. The pottery appears to be a variant of Glades Plain, differing slightly from that found in south Florida and also from the Glades Plain sherds recovered from the Thomas and Parrish mounds. From the amount found, plus the fact that it was scattered throughout the mound, it is likely that its presence is associative rather than intrusive.

The four Safety Harbor Period mounds were characterized by such types as Safty Harbor Incised, Pinellas Plain, and Pinellas Incised. Biscayne ware was also present, and vessels of the type Lamar Complicated Stamped, a late prehistoric and historic horizon type in Georgia, were taken from Parrish mounds 1 and 3. Glades Plain and Belle Glade Plain were also represented in these mounds. The Belle Glade Plain sherds are identical with those from the Glades region; the Glades Plain, as in the Weeden Island and Englewood Period mounds, is a very slight variant. The only ceramic find definitely out of line came from Parrish mound 3. This was a group of sherds, undoubtedly from a single bowl, of the characteristic Weeden Island type, Papys Bayou Punctated. Its appearance in this context is difficult to explain. I am inclined to think that its association with Safety Harbor materials was the result of its being retained as an "antique" piece.

The available ceramic finds from Cockroach Key and premound Weeden Island were rather limited so that very little can be said concerning the pottery of the Glades Complex as far as these two sites are concerned. Only a single vessel of Glades Plain remained from the Weeden Island premound level. At Cockroach Key the pottery from beneath the artificially constructed layers of the burial mound was either Glades Plain or Belle Glade Plain with no other types recorded. This seems to have been the situation in the parts of the Cockroach Key midden that were tested. In the artificial layers of the burial mound, however, both Biscayne Check Stamped and Pinellas Plain, the latter a Safety Harbor type, were present in addition to the Glades and Belle Glade types. This suggests an early, pure Glades pottery horizon at the Cockroach Key site with a later occupation, contemporaneous with the burial mound, that had ceramic cross ties with Safety Harbor.

More pottery was available for study from Perico Island. The bulk of this from the Perico burial mound was Glades Plain with a few Perico Plain and Biscayne Plain sherds associated. Also in the burial mound fill were two sherds of the type Deptford Bold Check Stamped and one fragment of complicated stamped that closely resembled the early northwest Florida type, St. Andrews Complicated Stamped. It should be remembered, however, that the pottery in the Perico Island burial mound was all in the form of sherd material that had been included in the refuse fill of which the mound was constructed. Because of this its reliability in dating the structure is not the equivalent of the pottery collections from any of the sand burial mounds of the Weeden Island, Englewood, or Safety Harbor Periods. From the Perico Island shell midden Glades Plain and Perico Series types were also obtained, but the relative proportions were considerably changed from the occurrences in the burial mound. Over half of the midden pottery was the Perico Series limestone-tempered plain or decorated ware. Several Biscayne Plain sherds were in the midden collection along with two incised sherds of Biscayne soft ware that are reminiscent of the early fiber-tempered pottery of the St. Johns River area. Fifteen fiber-tempered sherds made up the Perico midden lot. These last are identical with the St. Simons ware of the Georgia coast or the Orange Series pottery of the St. Johns.

Nonceramic remains were not plentiful in any of the mounds or middens. A considerable number came from Fewkes' Weeden Island excavations, but there is a difficulty here of determining which artifacts are of the Weeden Island Period and which came from the premound Glades culture. By comparison with other Weeden Island Period mounds we can, however, reasonably assume that medium-size stemmed triangular or ovate-triangular projectile points of flint, plain or duck-effigy stone plummets, conch-shell beads, and conch-shell cups are representative of the Weeden Island Period at the site. At the Thomas mound a number of medium and large flint points resembled those from Weeden Island proper. Most of these are stemmed, but a few are unstemmed. Stone plummets, tubular stone beads, conch-shell vessels, and shell beads were also found at Thomas. Fragments of shell vessels and a polished-stone plummet were among the very few artifacts taken from Parrish mound 5, the remaining Weeden Island Period site of the group.

In the Englewood mound only conch-shell vessels, ceremonially perforated like the pottery vessels, and a single *Busycon contrarium* shell hoe, drilled for hafting, were recovered. The shell vessels are the same as those from the Weeden Island mounds.

Projectile points of chert and chalcedony are more common in the Safety Harbor than in the Weeden Island Period mounds or in the Englewood mound. There is considerable variation in these. Both stemmed and unstemmed categories are represented, as well as a few fish-tail bases. There are many large triangular or ovate-triangular bladed points as well as small stemless triangulars. In addition, scrapers, knives, and drills were found in some of the sites. A ground-stone plummet, comparable to those from the Weeden Island mounds, came from the Safety Harbor burial mound and shell plummets were present in some of the Parrish mounds. Conch shells were utilized to make cups, beads, celts, and picks. These latter two are made from the *Busycon contrarium.*

Artifacts of European provenience, or at least derived from European sources if reworked aboriginally, came from all four Safety Harbor Period mounds. Iron tools, silver, olive-jar fragments, and clay pipes were found in the upper part of the Safety Harbor burial mound while glass beads, copper, gold, silver, iron, bone combs, and olive-jar sherds were taken from the Parrish mounds.

Nonceramic artifacts from the midden refuse at both Perico Island and Cockroach Key include shell tools or weapons such as conch-shell hammers or picks, shell celts of the *Strombus* and *Busycon* varieties, shell plummets and beads, bipointed bone projectiles, bone daggers, and bone awls. Some of these types, quite characteristic of Glades culture, also came from the pre-mound level at Weeden Island.

Evidence for chronology.—Throughout this discussion relative chronology has been implied by the word "period" and by statements referring to the continuity of one ceramic type or series of types out of another. The evidence for arranging the cultural complexes of the Manatee region into a time sequence is largely inferential and associative rather than direct. In all the excavations there was no first-class instance of demonstrable stratigraphy or superposition of cultures. Nevertheless, we know from the stratigraphic work done on the northwest coast, and presented in the preceding section, the general outlines of chronology in Hillsborough, Manatee, and Sarasota Counties.

One of the principal leads into the problem of sequence is the Weeden Island culture. Weeden Island sites are known from the entire Gulf Coast of Florida, from Pensacola to Charlotte Harbor.[40] Chronologically, Weeden Island has been placed in the northwest Florida sequence as following out of the Santa Rosa-Swift Creek Period and preceding the Fort Walton Period. By extension, the Weeden Island sites of the Manatee region must be roughly coeval. In the north, Weeden Island I and Weeden Island II divisions were formulated on the basis of changes in pottery types and percentage occurrences of these types (Willey and Woodbury, 1942, fig. 26). This division was more successfully applied to stratigraphic investigations in refuse middens than to mortuary mounds. The presence of both complicated stamped types and Wakulla Check Stamped in the Weeden Island and Thomas burial mounds dates these, in terms of the northern sequence, as definitely Weeden Island II and, possibly, also as Weeden Island I.

The Safety Harbor culture apparently centers in the Tampa Bay section of the Gulf Coast. Its southern extension may be as distant as Charlotte Harbor, and it seems likely that there is a northward continuation of Safety Harbor from Tampa Bay along the coast. Just where it separates from or merges with the late period of the north, Fort Walton (Willey and Woodbury, 1942, fig. 26, pp. 244-246), is not yet clear. Its time position is securely established as late. Its close stylistic affiliations with Fort Walton and the consis-

[40] The site of Cayo Palu (Ch-1), in Charlotte Harbor, is, apparently, the southernmost Weeden Island burial mound.

tent association of European trade objects in Safety Harbor mounds and village sites admit no other conclusion. The superficial occurrence of Safety Harbor sherds, along with European artifacts, in the Thomas mound is additional evidence, of a more direct nature, for the temporal priority of Weeden Island. Further correlations with north Florida substantiate the time position of Safety Harbor. It has been noted that in northwest Florida some Fort Walton sites have shown European artifacts while others have not. However, a still later period in the north has been defined for the region around Tallahassee. Hale G. Smith (1948) has termed this the Leon-Jefferson Complex, and preliminary studies indicate that it dates from the seventeenth and early eighteenth centuries. There are many parallels between Safety Harbor and Leon-Jefferson ceramic types. Leon-Jefferson is definitely a Spanish Mission-Indian culture; trade objects of European manufacture are commonplace. From these correlations an equation of Leon-Jefferson with Safety Harbor, certainly the latter half of Safety Harbor, is the logical reconstruction.

The distribution of the Englewood Complex is unknown. Presumably, it extends no farther south than Charlotte Harbor, but there are few data on its northward extension. Its sequence position is less well established than that of Weeden Island or Safety Harbor. Stylistically, Englewood pottery is akin to Weeden Island though distinctive. Where Weeden Island is basically a curvilinear style, Englewood is rectilinear. The vessel forms, the execution of the decoration, and the ware quality are superior to Safety Harbor but more limited than and inferior to Weeden Island. Unlike Safety Harbor, there are virtually no Fort Walton or Mississippian features in the Englewood pottery. A single strap handle is the exception to this. This small bit of evidence, plus the association of both typical Weeden Island and Safety Harbor types in the Englewood Mound, lead to the tentative conclusion that the time position of Englewood is intermediate between Weeden Island and Safety Harbor.

In attempting to date the Perico Island Period variant of the Glades culture in the Manatee region we are confronted with the situation of a cultural continuum that is essentially foreign to the Weeden Island-Englewood-Safety Harbor tradition. As Goggin has pointed out (Goggin, n.d.1), there seem to be several period phases of Glades culture. The premound level at Weeden Island obviously antedates the Weeden Island culture in the Tampa Bay locale. This is direct superposition evidence of a sort. At Perico, the association of the Deptford and the early complicated stamped sherds are evidence for equating the Glades Culture with the Deptford and Santa Rosa-Swift Creek Periods of northwest Florida. The fiber-tempered pottery in the Perico midden may indicate that the site was, in part, coeval with the fiber-tempered pottery horizon of the Eastern Archaic as represented on the St. Johns River or the Georgia coast. Lacking stratigraphy in the Perico midden, and acknowledging the possibility of a fortuitous association of sherds in the fill of the burial mound, it is admitted that cross-dating with fiber-tempered pottery, with Deptford, or with Santa Rosa-Swift Creek is not ironclad. But in the absence of any Weeden Island types, or later types, in either mound or midden it is reasonably safe to assume that the Glades culture at Perico was earlier than the Weeden Island culture in this same general region. As such, a Deptford or Santa Rosa-Swift Creek correlation would be approximately correct.

As for later continuations of a Glades-like culture, the mound at Cockroach Key, at least in its upper levels, offers some proof for this. Biscayne Check Stamped and Pinellas Plain at this site are clues to a possible contemporaneity of Glades culture with Safety Harbor. It will be remembered that at Englewood and in the various Safety Harbor sites the Glades pottery types, such as Glades Plain and Belle Glade Plain, were fairly frequent. Similarly, Safety Harbor sites also showed shell tools reminiscent of Glades types.

From all this we can say in summary that the Perico Island-Glades culture was present sometime previous to the advent of the Weeden Island into the Tampa Bay-Charlotte Harbor sector, that a Glades-type culture continued coeval with Weeden Island in the same region, and that it may also have paralleled the Safety Harbor development. Whether or not it lasted this long as a separate cultural entity, we know that it had a very definite influence upon the Safety Harbor culture.

Geographically, the Perico Island Period variant of the Glades culture relates to the whole Glades area of south Florida, and its appearance in Tampa Bay is its apparent northwesternmost extension. Goggin (n.d.1) has subdivided the Glades culture of the south into three major periods, Glades I, II, and III. At some sites, such as Belle Glade near Lake Okeechobee, trade sherds of Weeden Island, Englewood, and Safety Harbor Periods have been found in Glades III levels. These cross finds, in addition to those discussed from the Perico Island site, serve to correlate the Glades continuum with the sequences of the Gulf Coast.

The accompanying chart (fig. 19) summarizes the chronology of the Manatee region of the Gulf Coast as it has been covered in the

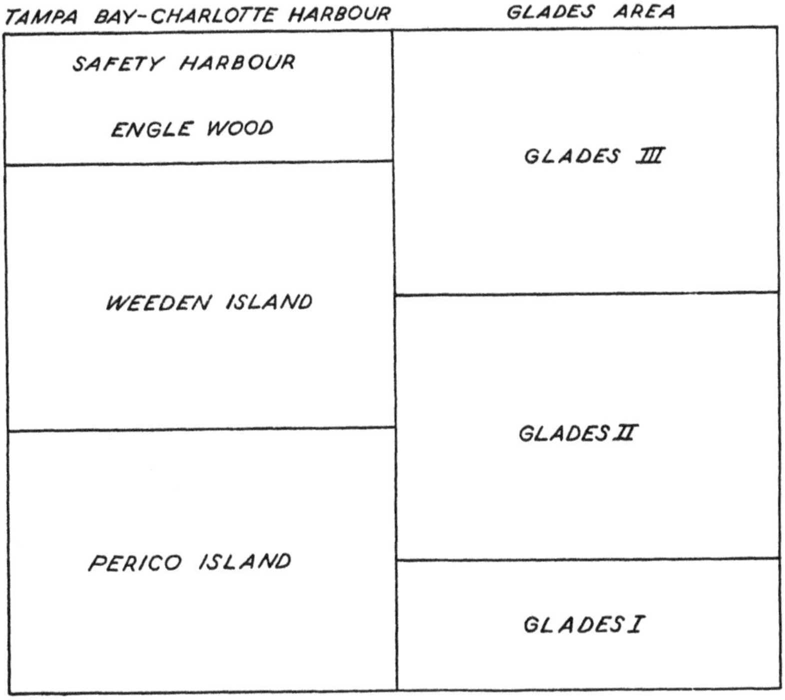

TAMPA BAY-CHARLOTTE HARBOUR
GLADES AREA
SAFETY HARBOUR
ENGLE WOOD
GLADES III
WEEDEN ISLAND
GLADES II
PERICO ISLAND
GLADES I

Fig. 19.—Chart of culture sequence in the Tampa Bay-Charlotte Harbor or Manatee region, showing period relationships to the Glades area.

group of sites discussed above. Because of the intimate connection of the Manatee region cultures with those of the Glades area a parallel column of the Glades culture periods has been placed along side.[41]

[41] These equations between the two columns have also been expressed by Goggin (1947b, fig. 12).

V. REVIEW AND ANALYSIS OF GULF COAST SITES

INTRODUCTION

The number of controlled archeological excavations in the Gulf Coast area is not large. The principal ones have been treated in the two previous sections of this paper. Nevertheless, there is a large body of excavation data and numerous site materials in the earlier literature, in museums, and in private notes and collections. In any attempt at thorough summary, analysis, and synthesis of the prehistory of the Florida Gulf this material must be taken into account. These scattered data and collections are not only a great reserve of scientific raw material but stand unique in that there is little likelihood that they can be duplicated in quantity by future field research. At the middle of the twentieth century a very great part, I should say well over half, of the archeological sites of all types on the Gulf Coast of Florida have been seriously damaged or completely destroyed. Perhaps inland from the coast the prehistoric resources are not so depleted, but it is certain that most of the more readily accessible mounds and middens along the shore have been exhausted. The only way to make the best of this loss is to "reclaim," by inference and interpretation, whatever can be salvaged at the present time.

We have seen how the stratigraphic excavations on the northwest coast have isolated and placed into continuity several cultural complexes or culture periods for that region. By seriation, association, and extrapolation a similar sequence of culture periods has been erected on the west coast in the Manatee region between Tampa Bay and Charlotte Harbor. A certain coincidence in these two sequences is also observable. The purpose of the present section is to describe and analyze sites from the entire Florida Gulf Coast area and to extend the cultural identifications and chronological order derived from the recent northwest and west coast excavations to these other sites. In this way it is expected that the content of the successive cultural periods now sketchily outlined will be greatly enriched and that the story of cultural development and cultural change for the total area will be more fully understood.

The data at hand are diverse and uneven as to detail and accuracy. In some ways the diversity is to our advantage. Most of the earlier excavations in the area, particularly those of Moore, were of burial mounds. Some of the later studies, especially the 1940 survey, have been directed at village sites. These two bodies of data complement each other in providing information both as to burial and ceremonial customs and as to more routine community life. In many cases it has been possible to assemble potsherd and artifact classifications from specific village midden areas that were almost certainly related to certain burial mounds which Moore had opened nearly 40 years before. In other cases, unfortunately more frequent, the unevenness of the data has worked against us. For example, fairly large random sample collections were made of surface potsherds on a great many midden sites in the northwest in the attempt to obtain a representative picture of the ceramic complex characterizing each site. These collections have been carefully classified, tabulated, and the tabulations presented so that they may be compared to the stratigraphic and other tabulations of pottery from the excavated sites; but most of the burial-mound accounts of pottery are nowhere near so systematically or fully presented. For the Moore sites we have had to rely upon illustrations of pottery or the examination in museums of small and partial samples from these sites. Percentile treatment of pottery types for site seriation or comparison has in this way been rendered impossible.

In spite of these and other difficulties, the results have been promising, and, I think, a reasonable degree of assurance characterizes most of the site analyses and identifications that are made in this review. Throughout, I have tried to evaluate by emphasis or qualification the particular cultural and period placement of each site. What seemed to me the essential facts about each mound, midden, cemetery, or isolated unit collection have been set down for inspection. Ceramics have been utilized as the chief indicator in placing a site, and the assumption has been that midden pottery, as it has occurred in the stratigraphic cuts of the excavated sites, has approximately contemporaneous relationships with mortuary pottery found in graves or mounds. Certain cultural lags and quantitative emphases may be operative in the case of mortuary wares. I do not, however, think that these have been marked enough to throw us off by any appreciable amount in the gross site dating. In fact, now that we have a better perspective on Gulf Coast prehistoric cultures, there is little doubt that each cultural period was sufficiently homogeneous so that the ceremonial and funerary pottery did not differ greatly from the utilitarian wares. Site dating has depended to a lesser degree upon other artifact types, burial forms, and the physical structure of the sites themselves. Usually these data have fallen in line with the ceramic periods to give convincing over-all correlations. When data have conflicted, ceramic evidence has been given the greater weight, but in each case the discrepancy is pointed up and the pertinent facts presented.

The sites considered in this review include those surveyed by Woodbury and myself in 1940. All these lie within the range of the northwest coast between Escambia and Jefferson Counties. Moore's exhaustive surveys have also been analyzed both from the literature and from supplementary museum collections. In many instances the Moore data and our own have been combined in the study of a site. Other sources of information are minor survey accounts and miscellaneous museum collections.

Sites are presented by a simple geographical order in groups of counties. This order runs from the northwest, at Pensacola, to the south and east, terminating at Charlotte Harbor. Those sites in adjacent Alabama or Georgia which are treated are placed in this geographical succession according to their locations. There has been no attempt made in this section to group sites by chronological period or cultural similarity. Such a treatment has been reserved for the succeeding section on "The Culture Periods." The accompanying maps (maps 14-20) indicate the locations, or approximate locations, of the reviewed sites. In some cases there were conflicts among authorities or lack of information as to exactly where a site was located; in other instances there was no more than the information, "a few miles north of . . . . ," etc. For these we make very generalized map locations, usually indicating them by a site number only, without an accompanying dot. Sites are keyed to the maps by numbers, and the numbering series begin anew for each county so that, for example, the designation "Fr-11" in the text corresponds to site number 11 on the Franklin County map. Site names used follow the literature, where available, or present local geography.

BALDWIN COUNTY, ALABAMA

Bear Point (Ba-1).—Sternberg (1876) refers to a sand burial mound and nearby shell midden at Bear Point on Perdido Bay, Baldwin County, Ala. He describes the mound as ranging from 6 to 15 feet in height, being circular in outline and about 100 feet in diameter. Moore (1901, p. 423) gives a more accurate location for a mound at Bear Point which he excavated with his usual thoroughness. This mound described by Moore was 150 yards northwest of the point proper (see map 14). It was circular in outline and had a flat summit top. Moore gives the basal diameter as 80 feet and the average height as about 7 feet. It is likely that Sternberg and Moore described and excavated the same mound as both refer to the varied height, one side being much higher than the other, and both mention that the mound was built against a natural slope. Furthermore, although Sternberg includes no illustrations, the ceramics and artifacts described by him

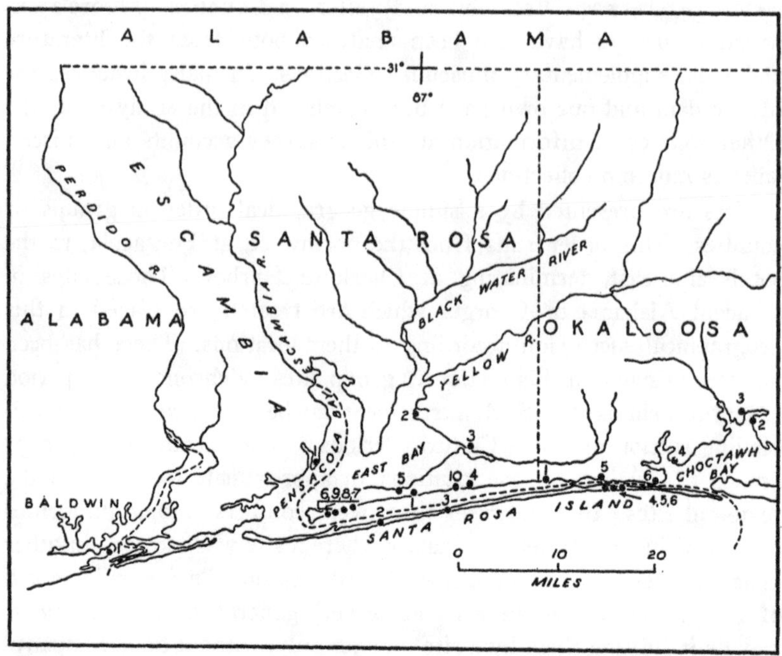

MAP 14.—Site map of western Alabama and Escambia, Santa Rosa, and Okaloosa Counties. Sites indicated by numbers.

as coming from the mound check very closely with the descriptions and pictures offered by Moore.

Judging from Moore's description, the Bear Point mound was constructed in two principal layers, one overlying the other. It had, seemingly, been built as a substructure mound. All 44 burials and the complete pottery vessels in the mound were found in the second or were recovered from pits which had their inception in this upper mound layer and had penetrated into the lower level. Burials are all described as secondary. Quite often the remains of more than one individual were placed in the same grave pit as when two or more skulls were found together. Bunched or bundle burials were a common form as were single isolated skulls. In several instances skulls, accompanied by both aboriginal and European artifacts, had been placed beneath inverted pottery bowls.

Pottery and other artifacts were found both in accompaniment with individual burials and without burial associations. These last seem to have been placed in the mound as caches, being distinguishable from potsherds and arrow points accidentally scattered through the mound fill. Chipped-stone projectile points, ground-stone celts, hones, pebble hammers, discoidal stones, hematite and limonite ore, and shell beads and pins were the nonpottery artifacts. Both Moore and Sternberg attest the presence of European artifacts in indubitable association with the burials. These include iron nails, metal tools, sword fragments, glass beads, silver buttons, copper or brass objects, and coins. Moore describes one of the coins which may be of significance in establishing a date for the site.

> . . . . ; an undated silver coin of Spanish-Mexico, which, we were informed at the United States Mint, was struck by Charles and Joanna between 1521 and 1550 A.D.; . . . . (Moore, 1901, p. 426.)

Moore lists incised, plain, check stamped, and complicated stamped sherds as coming from the mound fill, and also mentions loop handles and shell-tempered polished black ware. These last are Fort Walton period features. Moore's pottery illustrations (Moore, 1901, pp. 426-429) can readily be typed. In several instances the actual vessels have been examined either at the Museum of the American Indian, Heye Foundation, or Peabody Museum, Harvard University. They are classified below:

Fort Walton Complex
- Pensacola Series:
  - Pensacola Plain .... Fig. 3
  - Pensacola Incised .... Figs. 1, 2, 5, 6, 7
  - Pensacola Three-line Incised.......................... Fig. 4
  - Handles and adornos.............................. Fig. 10

Besides the material gathered by Moore, there is a small sherd collection in the United States National Museum, without catalog number, which is marked "Bear Point Alabama." It has been classified as follows:

Fort Walton Complex
- Fort Walton Series:
  - Fort Walton Incised.................................... 3
  - Lake Jackson Plain..................................... 1
- Pensacola Series:
  - Pensacola Incised 36
  - Pensacola Plain 17
  - Pensacola Three-line Incised............................ 6
- Moundville Engraved 12

Total sherds.... 75

As Sternberg stated that the pottery from the shell middens surrounding the mound was of the same type as that found in the mound, and as the small National Museum collection falls completely within the range of the Fort Walton Period, it seems quite likely that this collection comes from the original Bear Point site.

The data available concur in identifying and dating the mound and midden at Bear Point as of the Fort Walton Period.

Other sites in Baldwin County.—Moore (1901, pp. 432 and 433) lists another mound near Bear Point, lying at some distance from the first, and a mound at "Josephine Post Office." Both were small sand mounds. In the second Bear Point mound he found burials, artifacts, and pottery. The Josephine mound revealed no skeletal material or artifacts, and he assumed it to be a domiciliary tumulus.

ESCAMBIA COUNTY

East Pensacola Heights (Es-1).—On the southeastern point of the East Pensacola peninsula, where the land curves away to the west, is an old aboriginal occupation area (map 14). S. T. Walker, in his map of 1885 (p. 855), shows two sand burial mounds, but in 1940, during the Columbia University-National Park Service survey, no evidence of the mounds remained. Along the top of a steep, eroding cliff above Escambia Bay black midden stain can be observed for a depth of 10 to 30 centimeters below the humus. This occupation extends along the cliff for some 200 meters. The inland extent of the site could not be determined because of the vegetation. Sherds were not numerous along the exposed bank.

A surface collection from this site is classified as follows:

Fort Walton Complex	
Pensacola Series:	
Pensacola Incised	2
Pensacola Plain	15
Weeden Island Complex	
Wakulla Check Stamped	1
Miscellaneous	
Residual Plain	13
Unclassified	1
Total sherds	32

The site is reasonably identified with the Fort Walton Period, although the pottery sample is small.

Top bench mark (Es-2).—The long island of Santa Rosa is a part of Escambia County. During the 1940 survey 10 small archeological sites were located on the island. The largest of these was found about

5 miles east of the Pensacola Beach Casino at the foot of the highest dune on the island (map 14). On the crest of this dune is the U.S.G.S. bench mark, "Top." A fairly extensive area of oyster shells and eroded potsherds lies to the east of the dune. The midden is of very superficial depth.

A surface collection is classified as follows:

Fort Walton Complex	
Pensacola Series:	
Pensacola Plain	4
Weeden Island Complex	
Weeden Island Series:	
Weeden Island Plain	2
Wakulla Check Stamped	7
Miscellaneous	
Residual Plain	122
Total sherds	135

This site shows both Weeden Island II and Fort Walton Period occupations. The unusually large number of Residual Plain sherds is due to the erosion of the surface material by exposure to wind and shifting sands.

Site 5 miles west of Navarre (Es-3).—Near the sound shore, on Santa Rosa Island, opposite a point 5 miles west of Navarre on the mainland, is an area of oyster shells and scattered sherds (map 14). Unlike most of the other sites on the island this one is not located near a small bay or cove.

A surface collection is classified as follows:

Weeden Island Complex	
Weeden Island Series:	
Carrabelle Incised	8
Carrabelle Punctated	4
Weeden Island Plain	5
Wakulla Check Stamped	3
Complicated Stamped Series:	
Swift Creek Complicated Stamped	1
West Florida Cord-marked	6
Santa Rosa-Swift Creek Complex	
Santa Rosa Series:	
Basin Bayou Incised	11
Miscellaneous	
Residual Plain	146
Unclassified	4
Total sherds	188

This site may overlap from Santa Rosa-Swift Creek through the Weeden Island Periods. The collection lacks sufficient diagnostic sherds, and the great amount of Residual Plain is probably due to the extremely weathered nature of the sherds.

First site opposite Woodlawn (Es-4).—A short distance west of a point opposite Woodlawn is the first of four midden sites which are grouped close to each other on the Santa Rosa Island sound shore facing the mainland (map 14). Black, middenlike sand and shell is exposed in a number of shallow tidal pools which lie among the sand dunes. Sherds lie in the pools and in the sand and shells. An almost complete pot was one of the surface finds at this site.

A surface collection from the 1940 survey is classified as follows:

Weeden Island Complex	
Weeden Island Series:	
Weeden Island Incised	1
Carrabelle Incised	1
Wakulla Check Stamped	28
Miscellaneous	
Residual Plain	40
Unclassified	2
Total sherds	72

The quantity of Wakulla Check Stamped at this site, along with the few Weeden Island sherds, dates the midden as of the Weeden Island II Period.

Second site opposite Woodlawn (Es-5).—This midden area lies in a depression, at a narrow part of Santa Rosa Island (map 14), between the high dunes along the sound and the low ridge of dunes bordering the Gulf. Shells and sherds are found in tidal pools.

A surface collection from the 1940 survey is classified as follows:

Weeden Island Complex	
Weeden Island Series:	
Indian Pass Incised	1
Weeden Island Plain	3
Wakulla Check Stamped	6
Miscellaneous	
Residual Plain	40
Unclassified	1
Total sherds	51

This collection indicates a Weeden Island II dating.

Third site opposite Woodlawn (Es-6).—This site lies 150 meters east of Es-5 (map 14). It is south of a high dune which rises on the sound side of Santa Rosa Island. A few sherds were found scattered among shells.

A surface collection from the 1940 survey is classified as follows:

Santa Rosa-Swift Creek Complex	
Complicated Stamped Series:	
Swift Creek Complicated Stamped	15
(Most of these sherds appear to be of the Early Variety.)	
Miscellaneous	
Residual Plain	19
Unclassified	5
Total sherds	39

This site is placed in the Santa Rosa-Swift Creek Period.

Other sites in Escambia County.—During the 1940 survey five other midden sites were located on Santa Rosa Island in addition to those listed. These were all small, thin shell-midden areas with only a few sherds. Most of the sherds were badly eroded. The sites include a spot about one-quarter of a mile south of the United States Bureau of Fisheries station, another a mile to the east of the Pensacola Beach tower, a third opposite the little resort of Florosa, a fourth opposite a point 3½ miles west of Navarre, and a fifth opposite a point just east of Woodlawn. The few identifiable sherds from these sites indicate occupations dating from Fort Walton back to Santa Rosa-Swift Creek.

SANTA ROSA COUNTY

Santa Rosa Sound (Sa-1).—Moore (1901, p. 435) describes two sand mounds on the mainland facing Santa Rosa Sound at a point 12 miles from the western extremity of Santa Rosa Sound (map 14). The larger mound, which was 3.5 feet high, had a flat summit platform. Upon excavation it revealed no burials or artifacts and Moore was of the opinion that it had been built for domiciliary purposes. A smaller sand mound, built over a shell-refuse layer, showed both flexed and secondary burials, check stamped, complicated stamped, incised, and red painted pottery. Neither mound can be identified culturally from these descriptions.

In 1940 the much disturbed remains of these mounds were barely discernible in the midst of a series of shell heaps which covered an area about 200 meters in diameter. As there were no exposed cuts in the midden it was difficult to estimate the depth of the refuse. A large collection of sherds was made in the midden area. This is classified as follows:

Fort Walton Complex	
Fort Walton Incised	1
Pensacola Incised	1
Weeden Island Complex	
Weeden Island Series:	
Weeden Island Plain	10
Weeden Island Incised	6
Carrabelle Incised	4
Carrabelle Punctated	3
Tucker Ridge-pinched	1
Wakulla Check Stamped	8
Swift Creek Complicated Stamped	2
West Florida Cord-marked	2
Mound Field Net-marked	1
Santa Rosa-Swift Creek Complex	
Basin Bayou Incised	1
Franklin Plain	1
Miscellaneous	
Residual Plain	109
Smooth Plain	11
Unclassified	8
Total sherds	169

This particular collection dates principally from the Weeden Island I Period. Earlier and later occupations are represented by a very few sherds.

Maester Creek (*Sa-2*).—Maester Creek is a small stream emptying into East Bay near Escribano Point (map 14). S. T. Walker (1885, pp. 857-858) made some investigations near the point, to the south of the creek. He reports a very extensive Indian village site as indicated by shell refuse and potsherds. He also records an interesting mode of burial. At that time several graves had been casually discovered in the area, and all these were in pits 4 or 5 feet deep into which the body had been placed and covered with shells. The shells had then been covered with timber and the wood fired, slaking the lime in the shell and creating a thick, hard, cementlike slab cover over the bones. He describes the slabs as being found immediately under the surface and as being from 6 to 12 feet in diameter and 2 to 4 feet in thickness. The skeletons, which were surrounded with sand and cultural detritus, were, seemingly, primary and extended. Unfortunately, there is no way to identify culturally this interesting type of burial from present evidence.

In 1940 a sherd collection was made in this village site along the bay beach south of the creek. The following collection was recovered:

Fort Walton Complex	
Pensacola Plain	4
Santa Rosa-Swift Creek Complex	
Santa Rosa Series:	
Basin Bayou Incised	3
Alligator Bayou Stamped	1
Swift Creek Complicated Stamped	3
Miscellaneous	
Residual Plain	31
Unclassified	3
Total sherds	45

A small collection of sherds from the same site, which are now in the United States National Museum (Cat. No. 58202), is classified below:

Fort Walton Complex	
Fort Walton Incised	2
Pensacola Series:	
Pensacola Incised	8
Pensacola Three-line Incised	5
Pensacola Plain	4
Total sherds	19

These small collections indicate both Santa Rosa-Swift Creek and Fort Walton Period occupations.

About one-half mile north of Escribano Point, and to the north of Maester Creek, is the mound which Moore excavated in 1901 (pp. 433-434). This was apparently a circular, dome-shaped sand mound about 3 feet high and 30 feet in diameter. It contained 16 secondary single-skull and bundle burials. Some projectile points, a hone, some iron ore, masses of bitumen, and several pottery vessels were also found in the mound. Check stamped, plain, and incised and punctated types are described. Two vessels from the mound are illustrated by Moore (1901) as figures 11 and 12. These are classified as Weeden Island Incised, although neither is typical. From available evidence it is most likely that the mound dates from the Weeden Island II Period.

Graveyard Point (Sa-3).—This is the sand mound which Moore excavated and recorded under this name (Moore, 1901, p. 435) (see map 14). It is on the north shore of the eastern arm of East Bay. Moore listed the mound as a sand tumulus, circular in outline, 2.5

feet high and 75 feet in diameter. Although under cultivation in 1940, the dimensions were roughly the same. No shell refuse was discovered in the immediate vicinity, but Moore was of the opinion that the mound was domiciliary as no burials or artifact caches were found during his excavations. In 1940 several sherds were picked up on the plowed surface of the mound. These are classified below:

Weeden Island Complex	
Weeden Island Series:	
Weeden Island Plain	1
Carrabelle Incised	2
Carrabelle Punctated	2
Keith Incised	1
St. Petersburg Incised	1
Wakulla Check Stamped	4
Miscellaneous	
Residual Plain	7
Smooth Plain	1
Unclassified	2
Total sherds	21

This small collection is very definitely Weeden Island II Period.

Navarre (Sa-4).—A little more than 2 miles west of Navarre is a shell midden fronting on the sound beach. The shell deposits are situated on a sand ridge which is only 30 meters or so from the water's edge. The ridge is almost clear of vegetation, and it is the highest point of elevation in the immediate vicinity. It measures 130 meters east-west and 50 meters north-south. Although the surface is covered with shell, there are three small heaps or concentrations where the refuse is deeper. Oysters, scallops, and conchs are the common shells. Sherds were extremely plentiful, but unfortunately the site had recently been destroyed by commercial shell operations.

The following collection was made from the Navarre site in 1940:

Santa Rosa-Swift Creek Complex	
Santa Rosa Series:	
Basin Bayou Incised	4
Alligator Bayou Stamped	4
Santa Rosa Stamped	6
Complicated Stamped Series:	
Swift Creek Complicated Stamped	41
St. Andrews Complicated Stamped	2
Crooked River Complicated Stamped	3
Gulf Check Stamped	1
Franklin Plain	11
West Florida Cord-marked	1

Deptford Complex	
Deptford Bold Check Stamped	1
Deptford Simple Stamped	1
Miscellaneous	
Residual Plain	217
Smooth Plain	5
Unclassified	8
Total sherds	305

This midden site is clearly of the Santa Rosa-Swift Creek Period.

Hickory Shores (Sa-5).—This site has been designated as "Hickory Shores," the name of a real estate development lying just to the east of the midden. It is located on East Bay, approximately 10 miles east of the entrance of Pensacola Bay (map 14). The area of concentrated shell midden extends back south of the shore for 100 meters, and the east-west width of the site measures about the same. The occupation area sustains only scattered trees and undergrowth, but surrounding the shell, the woods are difficult to penetrate. Commercial shell excavation has torn up a part of the site, and the black midden and oyster shells are at least as deep as .50 meter. Sherds are not numerous.

A small surface collection made in 1940 is classified as follows:

Fort Walton Complex	
Pensacola Incised	6
Pensacola Plain	48
Weeden Island Complex	
Indian Pass Incised	4
Wakulla Check Stamped	2
Miscellaneous	
Residual Plain	2
Unclassified	1
Total sherds	63

This site is largely a Fort Walton Period occupation with a sprinkling of Weeden Island II.

First Gulf Breeze site (Sa-6).—On the mainland facing Santa Rosa Sound, 3 miles east of the entrance to Pensacola Bay, and on the east side of the bay, is the first of a series of four small shell-midden sites (map 14). The occupation can be seen from the beach where it is exposed along the low bank of the shore for a distance of about 100 meters. The Pensacola Boy Scout camp is located 400 meters to the west of the site.

The small 1940 surface collection is classified below:

Fort Walton Complex	
Pensacola Series:	
Pensacola Incised	7
Pensacola Plain	7
Santa Rosa-Swift Creek Complex	
Santa Rosa Stamped	1
Deptford Complex	
Deptford Bold Check Stamped	2
Miscellaneous	
Residual Plain	9
Unclassified	5
Total sherds	31

This is a Fort Walton site with a very few sherds of Santa Rosa-Swift Creek and Deptford Periods.

Second Gulf Breeze site (*Sa-7*).—Another midden along the shore of Santa Rosa Sound was located near the "Bald" U.S.G.S. bench mark (map 14). At this point the bank is considerably higher than either to the east or west, and this eminence was selected for habitation. There is little midden color to the soil as it is revealed along the exposed beach bank. Oyster and conch shells are found in gray sand for a few centimeters below the surface.

The following collection was made in 1940:

Fort Walton Complex	
Pensacola Series:	
Pensacola Incised	3
Pensacola Plain	17
Fort Walton Incised	2
Safety Harbor Incised	5
Weeden Island Complex	
Weeden Island Series:	
Weeden Island Incised	1
Weeden Island Plain	1
Tucker Ridge-pinched	1
Wakulla Check Stamped	17
Miscellaneous	
Twined Fabric-impressed (shell-tempered)	5
Residual Plain	73
Unclassified	6
Total sherds	131

This collection indicates Weeden Island II and Fort Walton Period occupations.

Third Gulf Breeze site (Sa-8).—See excavation account of Gulf Breeze site (Sa-8) under "Excavations on the Northwest Coast: 1940."

Fourth Gulf Breeze site (Sa-9).—This is a midden site on Santa Rosa Sound near the other Gulf Breeze sites (map 14). It stretches along the bluff back of the beach for a distance of about 100 meters. In no place does it appear to be more than .50 meter deep.

The collection made in 1940 is classified as follows:

Fort Walton Complex	
Pensacola Series:	
Pensacola Incised	1
Pensacola Plain	10
Fort Walton Series:	
Fort Walton Incised	2
Lake Jackson Plain	1
Miscellaneous	
Residual Plain	14
Total sherds	28

Although the collection is small, it is purely and indisputably of the Fort Walton Period.

Eighteen-Mile Point on Santa Rosa Sound (Sa-10).—This site was not visited during the 1940 survey. It was located and excavated in 1930 by T. M. N. Lewis, who published a brief account in the Wisconsin Archaeologist (1931, pp. 123-129). Lewis states that the mound was on the south shore of the Santa Rosa peninsula, 18 miles up the sound from Pensacola. The location as indicated on map 14 is in accord with this and is only approximate.

The site was a mound of sand and black midden earth. Originally it had been about 70 feet in diameter and about 4 feet in height. Shortly before Lewis' visit the mound had been partially destroyed by a storm and was, in this manner, called to his attention. The top 18 inches of the mound was a layer of sand. Under this sand layer was a stratum of shell and black earth about 10 inches in thickness. Below the midden layer was another stratum of sand. Eleven primary, extended burials were found in the bottom sand layer on the floor of the mound. Numerous pottery vesesels had been placed as a mortuary offering in the black earth and shell layer. These vessels had been intentionally destroyed by a basal perforation or by complete breakage. In addition to the pottery, conch-shell beads and mushroom-shaped ear pins or plugs of shell were also found in the mound.

Through the courtesy of Mr. Lewis I have been permitted to review a series of photographs of the pottery taken from this mound. Reasonably reliable identifications of types have been made from these photographs. These are given in the tabulations below:

Fort Walton Complex	
Pensacola Series:	
Pensacola Incised	13
Pensacola Plain	2
Total specimens	15

It is impossible to tell in every instance, but the vessels appear, in the photographs studied, to be shell-tempered. If some are grit-tempered, they undoubtedly belong to the companion Fort Walton series of the Fort Walton Complex.

The site is clearly of the Fort Walton Period.

Other sites in Santa Rosa County.—Moore (1901, p. 454) excavated a small sand mound at Don's Bayou on Choctawhatchee Bay which he considered to be a domiciliary structure.

Walker (1885, pp. 858-859) mentions mounds on Santa Rosa Sound which were located in the same general area as Sa-1. He also mentions a shell-midden site on the Rotherford place. This last location is in the same general vicinity as sites Sa-6, 7, 8, and 9. A sherd collection from the Rotherford place, near the old Government live-oak plantation, is composed of Fort Walton Complex types (U.S.N.M. Nos. 58195-58208).

OKALOOSA COUNTY

Wynhaven (Ok-1).—One and one-half miles east of the Santa Rosa-Okaloosa county line, just east of Wynhaven, there is a small shell midden on the sound shore about 100 meters south of U.S. Highway 98 (map 14). Oyster and clam shells have been deposited upon a sand ridge which lies 15 meters back from the water's edge. The area of the site is open and free of growth, but pine and scrub-oak forest encloses it on three sides. Two small excavations had been made in the shell, showing the refuse to be about .50 meter deep.

The 1940 surface collection of sherds from this midden is classified as follows:

Weeden Island Complex	
Weeden Island Series:	
Weeden Island Incised	1
Weeden Island Plain	1

Santa Rosa-Swift Creek Complex

Santa Rosa Stamped	2
Complicated Stamped Series:	
Swift Creek Complicated Stamped	17
St. Andrews Complicated Stamped	1
Franklin Plain	4

Deptford Complex

Deptford Bold Check Stamped	1

Miscellaneous

Residual Plain	101
Unclassified	12
(Most of these are indeterminate complicated stamped sherds.)	
Total sherds	140

The collection is dominantly Santa Rosa-Swift Creek Period.

Rocky Bayou, east (*Ok-2*).—Moore (1901, p. 455) excavated a sand mound of irregular outline, 72 x 112 feet in basal diameters and 4 feet in height, which was located about 100 meters east of the eastern side of the mouth of Rocky Bayou (map 14). As he found nothing in the mound, he was of the opinion that it had served a domiciliary purpose. In 1940 a surface collection was made from a shell midden which lies between the remnants of Moore's mound and the beach. This midden measures about 50 x 30 meters in extent and the depth appears to be about .50 meter.

Very few sherds were recovered:

Weeden Island Complex

Weeden Island Series:	
Weeden Island Plain	2
Carrabelle Incised	1
Wakulla Check Stamped	1

Miscellanous

Smooth Plain	2
Residual Plain	2
Unclassified	1
Total sherds	9

The very limited evidence indicates the Weeden Island II Period.

Rocky Bayou, west (*Ok-3*).—Moore (1901, p. 455) describes a mound on the west side of this bayou about 1.5 miles up from the mouth (map 14). The area was visited in 1940. No shell midden was discovered anywhere in the immediate vicinity and no surface material was found.

The mound was a sand tumulus, circular in outline, 2 feet high, and 28 feet in diameter. Moore discovered three secondary burials of the single skull form and a mass deposit of intentionally destroyed pottery. Scattered pottery caches and other artifacts were found at various points in the mound. A stone equal-arm elbow pipe and a pointed-poll stone celt [42] were among the latter. Most of the pottery was perforated or "killed." A plain, gourd-shaped, flattened-globular bowl is illustrated by Moore (1901, fig. 47). This specimen is probably Weeden Island Plain. This identification would seem to be corroborated by two vessels in the Peabody Museum, Harvard University. These are cataloged as Rocky Bayou and are, respectively, Carrabelle Punctated (No. 56370) and Weeden Island Plain (red painted) (No. 56729).

It is most likely that the mound dates from the Weeden Island Period.

Black Point (*Ok-4*).—The Black Point mound excavated by Moore (1901, pp. 454-455) is one-quarter of a mile northwest of the point (map 14). This was a circular, flat-topped mound, over 80 feet in diameter. The height is not given. Trenching revealed check and complicated stamped and incised sherds in the sand fill but not burials or mortuary deposits. Moore considered the mound as domiciliary.

This mound was not relocated in the 1940 survey, but a sherd collection was made along the bay bluff about 1 mile west of Black Point. Sand-dune formations are developing on the beach in front of the cliff, and sherds and shells are found scattered over the dunes where they have eroded and blown out from the original midden deposit. Our collection from this site was augmented by another given to us by William Meigs, of Niceville, Fla., who also accompanied us to the site.

Surface collection from Black Point:

Weeden Island Complex	
Weeden Island Series:	
Weeden Island Incised	15
Carrabelle Incised	49
Carrabelle Punctated	15
Keith Incised	4
Tucker Ridge-pinched	5
Weeden Island Plain	5
Wakulla Check Stamped	146
St. Petersburg Incised	2
Complicated Stamped Series:	
Swift Creek Complicated Stamped	3
St. Andrews Complicated Stamped	1

[42] Apparently this celt was given to Peabody Museum, Harvard University, where it is cataloged as No. 18580.

Santa Rosa-Swift Creek Complex	
Franklin Plain	1
Miscellaneous	
Smooth Plain	6
Plain Red	1
Residual Plain	310
Indeterminate Stamped	20
Other unclassified	19
Total sherds	602

There is little doubt that this large collection fits the Weeden Island II Period.

Site between Florosa and Mary Esther (*Ok-5*).—This is a midden on the mainland shore of Santa Rosa Sound near the mouth of a little stream which empties into the sound (map 14). The exposed shell midden can be traced along the bank for approximately 200 meters east of the stream. In no place does the deposit appear to be very deep.

A small and inconclusive surface collection was gathered from the site:

Fort Walton Complex	
Lake Jackson Plain	1
Weeden Island Complex	
Wakulla Check Stamped	3
Miscellaneous	
Residual Plain	18
Unclassified	5
Total sherds	27

Fort Walton (*Ok-6*).—Our 1940 excavations at the Fort Walton site have been treated separately under the section, "Excavations on the Northwest Coast: 1940." A brief résumé of the operations of Walker and Moore at the Fort Walton site are also included with that treatment. The 1940 excavations were, however, concerned with the village midden at Fort Walton, not the large temple mound. The present review and analysis is based upon this mound and its contents, particularly as these were revealed by Moore.

The Fort Walton temple mound is rectangular, flat-topped, about 12 feet high, and has a graded approach. It has been built in layers or stages. Sixty-six burials were recovered by Moore from the summit and sides of the mound; none of these had penetrated to any great depth and all were, apparently, intrusive into the mound. Secondary (single skull and bunched) and primary burials (extended) were encountered. Pottery and other artifacts were found with individual burials. In some cases bowls were found inverted over crania. What appeared to be ceremonially destroyed caches of pottery were also found in the mound apart from burial associations.

Nonceramic artifacts include: Chipped-stone points and scrapers, stone hones, hammerstones, discoidal stones, stone chisels, stone and bone beads, shell beads, and shell ear pins. Occasional pottery vessels were "killed" by perforation. Loop handles, polished black ware, and shell temper are three general ceramic traits which held Moore's attention. The illustrated pottery (Moore, 1901, pp. 435-454) is classified as follows:

Fort Walton Complex

Fort Walton Series:

Fort Walton Incised.......Figs. 15, 16, 17, 22, 23, 24, 25, 29, 30, 31, 40, 41

Point Washington Incised..........................Fig. 18

Pensacola Series:[48]

Pensacola Incised ....Figs. 20, 21, 32, 34, 36, 37, 39

Pensacola Plain ....Fig. 27

Moundville Engraved ....Fig. 19 (?)

Fort Walton effigy handles...........................Fig. 42

Other

St. Andrews Complicated Stamped.......................Fig. 44

Sherd with "cat" design...............................Fig. 45

(A similar element occurs on a vase from a Weeden Island Period site at Strange's Landing. See Moore, 1902, fig. 117.)

The burials in the Fort Walton flat-topped mound are all undoubtedly of the Fort Walton Period, and the mound almost certainly dates from the same time. The pottery identifications, as these concern the Fort Walton and Pensacola Series, are open to some question, as it is difficult to recognize temper type from a photograph; however, some of the original specimens were checked, and it is certain that both the grit- and shell-tempered types occur at the site. The St. Andrews Complicated Stamped sherd is quite clearly from an earlier horizon and was probably an accidental inclusion in the mound fill. This, of course, is not unusual, as the surrounding midden area shows Deptford, Santa Rosa-Swift Creek, and Weeden Island types as well as those of the Fort Walton Period. The "cat-face" sherd is more difficult to place. It may be either Weeden Island or Fort Walton.

---

[48] U. S. National Museum collections Nos. 58789-58798, contributed by S. T. Walker, consist of nine Pensacola Series sherds. These came from the same mound.

WALTON COUNTY

Okaloosa-Walton county line (*Wl-1*).—A midden of clam shells is cut through by Florida Highway 10 at a point 2.2 miles east of the Okaloosa-Walton line (map 15). The location is on a cliff above the bay beach, and the total area of the shell is about 50 meters in diameter. The refuse does not appear to be either deep or to contain many sherds.

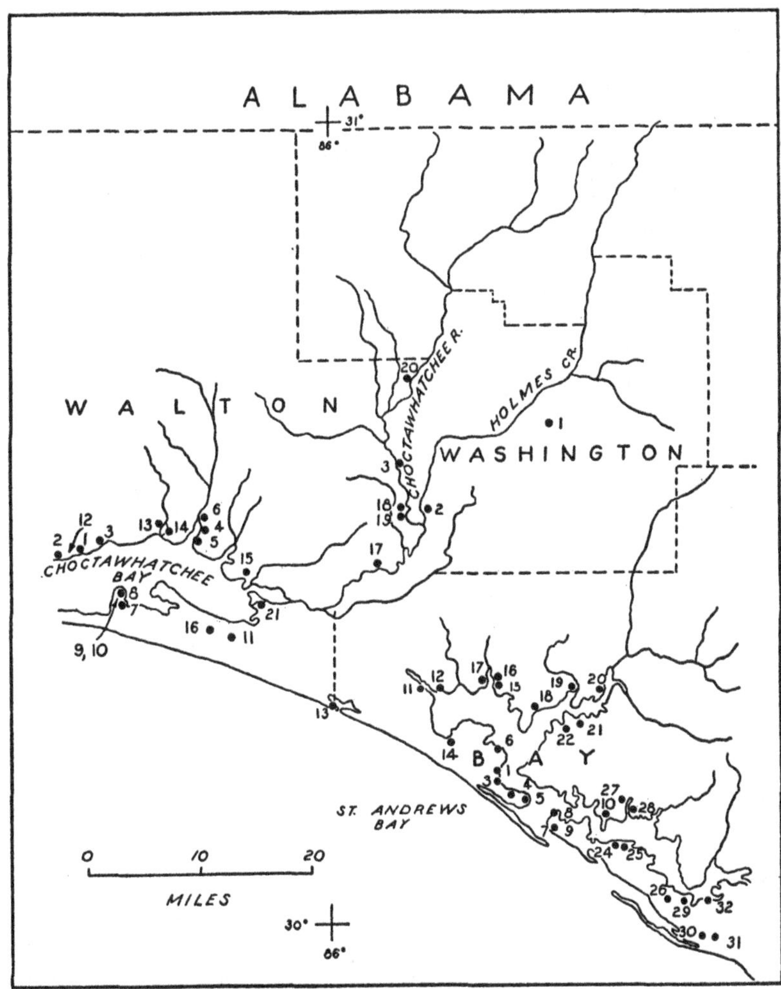

MAP 15.—Site map of Walton, Holmes, Washington, and Bay Counties. Sites indicated by numbers.

Surface collection:

Deptford Complex	
Deptford Bold Check Stamped	9
Deptford Simple Stamped	3
Miscellaneous	
Residual Plain	12
Total sherds	24

The small collection belongs to the Deptford Period.

Villa Tasso (*Wl-2*).—On the north shore of Choctawhatchee Bay, near the Okaloosa-Walton county line, is the small resort, Villa Tasso (map 15). An unevenly distributed shell midden extends for about 200 meters west of the main lodge of the resort. The deposits are in the form of small piles of clam shells, rising .25 to .50 meter above the surrounding sand. The bay beach is 40 to 80 meters distant.

Surface collection from Villa Tasso:

Fort Walton Complex	
Fort Walton Incised	2
Safety Harbor Incised	1
Weeden Island Complex	
Weeden Island Series:	
Weeden Island Plain	1
Carrabelle Incised	1
Carrabelle Punctated	4
Swift Creek Complicated Stamped	2
Miscellaneous	
Residual Plain	87
Total sherds	98

The collection indicates both Weeden Island and Fort Walton Periods.

Big Hammock (*Wl-3*).—Four miles east of the Okaloosa-Walton county line, on Florida Highway 10, is another midden of clam and oyster shells (map 15). This site is also cut through by the modern roadway, and the thin refuse deposit is revealed in cross section. The location is not more than 20 meters back from the bay bluff.

Somewhere in this same neighborhood Moore (1918, pp. 532-533) excavated four sand mounds. These were all low, circular mounds. One contained evidences of burials, the others simply an occasional sherd or artifact. From the descriptions none can be identified as to cultural period. They were not located during the 1940 survey.

A sherd collection made from the midden in 1940 is classified as:

Fort Walton Complex	
Pensacola Incised	2
Safety Harbor Incised	1
Weeden Island Complex	
Weeden Island Series:	
Keith Incised	2
Tucker Ridge-pinched	1
Wakulla Check Stamped	8
St. Petersburg Incised	1
Miscellaneous	
Residual Plain	42
Unclassified	7
Total sherds	64

Predominantly Weeden Island II but with some evidences of Fort Walton Period occupation.

McBee's mound (*Wl-4.*)—One mile northeast of Piney Point and .6 mile inland from the shore of Alaqua Bayou is a sand mound in the midst of a thick hammock (map 15). The property is owned by Alton McBee. The diameter of the mound is about 10 meters and the height about 1 meter. It had recently (1940) been excavated by unknown parties. A number of sherds were found in the fresh excavations. Mr. McBee is in possession of a stone celt which came from this mound. The artifact is 10 cm. long, 4 cm. thick, slightly flattened but with a pointed poll.

A surface collection from the McBee site is listed below:

Fort Walton Complex	
Fort Walton Series:	
Fort Walton Incised	9
Lake Jackson Plain	3
Pensacola Series:	
Pensacola Incised	6
Pensacola Plain	17
Miscellaneous	
Plain Red	1
Smooth Plain	2
Residual Plain	30
Total sherds	68

It is questionable whether the McBee site is a village area, a domiciliary mound of some sort, or a sand burial mound. No evidence of burials was seen or reported. At the same time, shell refuse, generally the indicator of a village or living area, was absent. The site is definitely of the Fort Walton Period.

Piney Point (*Wl-5*).—Alaqua Bayou is a small basin in the northeast of Choctawhatchee Bay, and Piney Point is a sandy, grass-grown peninsula, dotted with pine trees, which extends out into the mouth of Alaqua Bayou from the east (map 15). There are two extensive shell-midden areas near the point. The first and largest is north of the point. The second lies 300 meters away from the point to the southeast. Both front on the water's edge. A number of old excavations in the northernmost midden show oyster and clam shells and sherds. Depth of the refuse is probably about 1 meter. The 1940 collections from the two middens were combined and are given below:

Fort Walton Complex	
Fort Walton Series:	
Fort Walton Incised	7
Lake Jackson Plain	3
Pensacola Series:	
Pensacola Incised	2
Pensacola Plain	6
Weeden Island Complex	
Wakulla Check Stamped	1
Miscellaneous	
Smooth Plain	3
Residual Plain	22
Unclassified	1
Total sherds	45

The site belongs to the Fort Walton Period.

Hick's site (*Wl-6*).—The Hick's mound and village area lies a mile north of the McBee mound, near the head of Alaqua Bayou on the east bank (map 15). The mound is approximately 250 meters from the bayou bank. The mound is 25 meters in diameter, circular, and 1 meter high. It has been plowed over but not excavated. There were few sherds found on the mound. The village concentration, to judge from the distribution of surface sherds, is about 100 meters south and east of the mound away from the bayou.

The village surface collection from the Hick's site is given below:

Weeden Island Complex	
Weeden Island Series:	
Weeden Island Incised	1
Weeden Island Plain	8
Swift Creek Complicated Stamped	2
Wakulla Check Stamped	12
Miscellaneous	
Residual Plain	56
Unclassified	3
Total sherds	82

The site dates from the Weeden Island II Period.

G.F. Forrest site (Wl-7).—Hogtown Bayou is a part of Choctawhatchee Bay, formed by two small peninsulas jutting out from the south shore of that body of water. Two large shell middens on the western shore of Hogtown Bayou were examined during the 1940 survey. The most southern of these two was on the property of G.F. Forrest (map 15). It is a shell heap in a clearing near the farmhouse. North-south it measures 100 meters, and east-west it is 30 to 40 meters. The northern end has been cut away, exposing a profile of 1 meter of packed shell refuse. Aside from this, the site has never been excavated. A small collection was made from the surface and is given below:

Fort Walton Complex	
Fort Walton Series:	
Fort Walton Incised	6
Lake Jackson Plain	1
Pensacola Plain	4
Miscellaneous	
Residual Plain	11
Total sherds	22

These few sherds indicate a Fort Walton Period dating for the midden.

Mack Bayou midden site (Wl-8).—This site lies one-half mile north of the G.F. Forrest site, being farther out on the peninsula which forms the western shore of Hogtown Bayou. Shell refuse is found on both sides of Mack Bayou (map 15), a tributary of Hogtown Bayou. From the shore, shell extends for 100 meters or more back into the thick woods in all directions. Commercial shell operations have destroyed several of the best concentrations. Depth of the midden varies from .25 to 1.00 meter. The shells are mostly oysters and clams. For such a large site sherds were not abundant.

The surface collection from the Mack Bayou midden is classified below:

Fort Walton Complex	
Fort Walton Series:	
Fort Walton Incised	9
Lake Jackson Plain	5
Pensacola Series:	
Pensacola Incised	4
Pensacola Plain	21

Weeden Island Complex	
Weeden Island Series:	
Weeden Island Plain	3
Carrabelle Incised	1
Carrabelle Punctated	3
Indian Pass Incised	1
Wakulla Check Stamped	14
St. Petersburg Incised	1
Miscellaneous	
Plain Red	2
Indeterminate Stamped	11
Other unclassified	1
Total sherds	183

This midden seems fairly evenly divided between the Weeden Island II and Fort Walton Periods.

Cemetery on Hogtown Bayou (Wl-9).—Somewhere in the vicinity of the Mack Bayou shell midden Moore (1918, pp. 535-541) excavated an old Indian cemetery. (See map 15 for general location.) He describes the location (p. 536) thus:

> . . . . and on thick hammock land, near Mack Bayou, a part of Hogtown Bayou, on property the ownership of which we did not exactly determine, near but not immediately with the shell deposits, an aboriginal cemetery has been discovered and considerably dug into in a desultory way by residents and others.

Moore states that the cemetery was marked by low rises of sand and by pottery projecting above the surface of the ground.

Excavation revealed massed secondary burials, single skull and bunched interments, and skulls with vessels inverted over them. A total of over 100 burials was encountered. Pottery and other artifacts were found immediately associated with burials, and mass deposits of broken vessels and sherds were also found without immediate burial associations.

Projectile points, lance blades, knives, celts, hones, discoidals, and beads were among the stone artifacts found with the burials. Shell tools, ear pins, and beads, a copper pendant, and a variety of European objects were also found in the graves. These last include copper bells, glass beads, and various tools and weapons of iron. Pottery is described thoroughly though not illustrated, except for a small, stopper-like object which might be a pottery anvil (Moore, 1918, fig. 18). The trait of "killing" the vessels was present. Moore also refers to the use of a white filler-pigment in the incised lines of some of the vessels. There is little doubt that the vessels described belong to the Fort Walton Complex.

Mound near Mack Bayou (Wl-10).—Moore (1918, p. 541) locates this mound on the shore of Hogtown Bayou, one-eighth of a mile east of Mack Bayou (map 15). Apparently a low, circular mound, it measured 2.5 feet high and 28 feet in diameter. What may have been a very badly decomposed burial was accompanied by a pierced-stone plummet or pendant. Also in the mound was an object of stone described as a bar amulet (possibly a bar gorget). A flint knife and a sandstone hone made up the collection.

This little mound cannot be securely identified as to culture or sequence position, but the stone ornaments and the lack of pottery imply, in a general way, an early period.

Site west of Point Washington (Wl-11).—Almost 2 miles due west of the town of Point Washington is a shell midden in the middle of oak and palmetto country, which in 1940 had been cut through by a firebreak (map 15). The ground had been harrowed, and, consequently, sherds were easy to find. On either side of the break there were portions of the midden which were undisturbed and probably quite deep. Total area of the midden is about 100 meters by 50 meters. The location of the midden, with reference to Point Washington, checks closely with the location of a sand burial mound which Moore (1901, pp. 465-472) excavated. The remains of this mound were not found by the 1940 survey, although no serious attempt was made as the undergrowth was very heavy in the region.

The surface collection of this site is classified below:

Weeden Island Complex	
Weeden Island Series:	
Weeden Island Incised	6
Weeden Island Plain	21
Carrabelle Incised	7
Carrabelle Punctated	11
Swift Creek Complicated Stamped	5
Smooth Plain	5
Residual Plain	85
Unclassified	3
Total sherds	143

This collection is clearly Weeden Island I, showing, as it does, a sizable increment of Swift Creek and no Wakulla Check Stamped.

The mound which Moore excavated was described as being 2 miles in a westerly direction from Point Washington, near a spring. It was circular, 36 feet across the base, and 6 feet high, being composed of sand. Eleven burials were scattered through various parts of the mound. These were secondary bunched or single skull burials. A solitary, semiflexed burial, found at the center of the mound on mound base, was the only primary interment. There was a mass deposit of mortuary pottery as well as scattered caches of pottery. Nonceramic artifacts were found at random through the mound and also with specific burials. Projectile points, lump galena, sheet mica, and fragments of copper artifacts were present.

Moore mentions most of the common types of pottery although check stamped is notably omitted. The illustrated types (Moore, 1901) classified below are entirely Weeden Island and, more specifically, Weeden Island I. There are Weeden Island vessels which approach the type Basin Bayou Incised, a type usually grouped with the Santa Rosa-Swift Creek Complex. These are figures 67, 70, and 74. Basin Bayou Incised bears a close relationship to Weeden Island Incised, and it seems very probable that the Weeden Island type developed out of the Santa Rosa-Swift Creek one. That the midden site which we visited in 1940 was the village connected with the burial mound excavated by Moore seems even more likely in view of the fact that both belong to the Weeden Island I Period.

Pottery types from mound near Point Washington illustrated in Moore (1901):

Weeden Island Complex
- Weeden Island Series:
  - Weeden Island Incised.........Figs. 62, 63, 64, 67, 68, 70, 74, 75
  - Carrabelle Punctated ....Figs. 66, 72
  - Tucker Ridge-pinched ....Fig. 65
- Swift Creek Complicated Stamped....................Figs. 69, 73 (Late Variety.)

In addition to the specimens illustrated by Moore, three additional vessels from the same mound were examined in the Peabody Museum, Harvard University. These are all Weeden Island Period types, two being Weeden Island Plain (Nos. 56738, 56725) and one Carrabelle Punctated (No. 56726).

Pippen's Lake (Wl-12).—This sand mound was excavated by Moore (1918, pp. 531-532). It is situated near a small lake not far from the Choctawhatchee Bay shore just across the line from Okaloosa County (map 15). In 1940 we were unable to relocate the site.[43a]

[43a] J. W. Griffin and R. P. Bullen inform me (April 1949) that the Pippen's Lake mound is on the Okaloosa side of the line, Moore to the contrary notwithstanding.

The mound was circular, 2.5 feet high and 35 feet in diameter. Burials may once have been made in it, but no trace of them could be found in Moore's digging. He found, however, a mass ceremonial-pottery deposit and several scattered pieces of sheet mica and hematite fragments. The pottery was intentionally perforated. Moore mentions no check or complicated stamped wares. He illustrates (1918) three vessels which are classified below:

Weeden Island Complex
Weeden Island Series:
Weeden Island Incised..........................Pl. XIII, 2
Weeden Island Plain..............................Fig. 13
Tucker Ridge-pinched ....Fig. 12

The mound apparently dates from the Weeden Island Period, although the data are too few to place it as either I or II.

Basin Bayou, west (*Wl-13*).—This site, excavated by Moore (1901, pp. 456-458), was not visited in the 1940 survey (map 15). The mound was over 6 feet high and had a diameter of 40 feet. Moore does not say if the mound had a flat summit, but he mentions a ramp or graded approach. Within the mound he found four secondary bunched burials, scattered pottery caches, and sheet mica. Incised, punctated, red painted, and complicated stamped pottery are reported. Vessels were "killed."

Two pottery specimens are illustrated by Moore (1901). These are:

Weeden Island Complex
Weeden Island Series:
Weeden Island Incised (or Basin Bayou Incised)......Fig. 48
Weeden Island Plain...............................Fig. 49

The mound is Weeden Island, and the absence of check stamped, plus the presence of a specimen which is a borderline piece between Weeden Island and the earlier Basin Bayou type, suggests a probable Weeden Island I dating.

Basin Bayou, east (*Wl-14*).—On the opposite side of Basin Bayou is the other mound excavated by Moore (1918, pp. 534-535) (map 15). Like the western mound this one was also situated in thick woods. It was not visited in 1940. The mound was about 40 feet in diameter and 2.5 feet high. Previous to Moore's visit other parties had excavated the mound, and Moore found no undisturbed burials. Pottery, placed in mortuary caches, was the only element discovered in the body of the mound. Most of it had been intentionally destroyed. Moore lists plain, complicated stamped, and incised ware. Two very interesting vessels are illustrated (Moore, 1918). These are classified as:

Santa Rosa-Swift Creek Complex
Santa Rosa Series:
Basin Bayou Incised....................................Fig. 14
Alligator Bayou Stamped............................Fig. 16

These vessels, the presence of complicated stamped, the absence of check stamped, and the absence of Weeden Island types date the mound as Santa Rosa-Swift Creek Period.

Jolly Bay (Wl-15).—This mound is about 1 mile inland on the north side of Jolly Bay, a little inlet at the eastern end of Choctawhatchee Bay (map 15). It was not located during the 1940 survey. Moore excavated there in 1901 (Moore, 1901, pp. 459-465). The mound was partly destroyed before the Moore excavations, and it was impossible for him to determine the size, shape, and general nature of the construction. He suggests, however, that it had been flat-topped. The dimensions Moore gives are 70 by 55 feet with a height of almost 4 feet.

The 27 burials which Moore found were single skulls or the secondary bunched type. Vessels were found inverted over skulls, and other artifacts were placed with burials. Separate pottery caches were also distributed through the mound. Lanceolate blades and projectile points and celts and chisels make up the stonework from the mound. Shell tools were also recovered. Pottery was "killed" by perforation. Incised, check stamped, plain, polished black, and shell-tempered ware are the general descriptive categories listed for Jolly Bay. Illustrations (Moore, 1901) are classified as:

Fort Walton Complex
Fort Walton Incised...................................Figs. 51, 58
Pensacola Incised ....Figs. 52, 57
Moundville Engraved ....Fig. 53
Pensacola Series adornos.............................Figs. 59, 60

At the Peabody Museum, Harvard University, there are two specimens from Jolly Bay, presumably from the Moore collections but not illustrated by him. These are a Pensacola Incised (No. 56731) and a Pensacola Plain (No. 56732) piece.

The total evidence is irrefutably Fort Walton Period. It is interesting to note the presence of a single check stamped piece in the mound (Moore, p. 461, vessel 7). This specimen might have been Wakulla or, possibly, Leon Check Stamped, a later check type.

Cemetery near Point Washington (Wl-16).—This cemetery was searched for but not located in 1940. Moore found the site in 1901 (pp. 472-496), guided by reports of local people who had seen pottery vessels protruding above the surface (map 15). Like the Hogtown Bayou cemetery it was characterized by numerous low (about 1 foot) mounds of sand.

The cemetery near Point Washington was not exactly level, there being a number of irregular rises in the ground with flat spaces between. These rises, which probably did not exceed a foot in height, in three cases contained large deposits of human bones, solid masses with outlying bones here and there, these bones not being enough apart to call them separate burials, nor yet so closely associated that they might be considered one interment. One of these deposits had 17 skulls, all of adults but one, as to which we had not sufficient data to judge. Numbers of long bones accompanied the skulls. In other parts of the cemetery were single skulls, others with long bones and, in a few cases, long bones without the crania, in addition to the burials found under earthenware vessels, which will be taken up later. (Moore, 1901, p. 473.)

Pottery and artifacts were found with burials, and pottery was also found where it had been placed in detached caches. Projectile points, stone hones, shell pendants, shell gorgets, and shell beads were in the graves. European contact was clearly established by glass and iron objects taken from immediate burial associations.[44]

As mentioned, pots were found inverted over skulls. Many of the vessels were "killed." The pottery is extensively illustrated in Moore (1901) and is classified as follows:

Fort Walton Complex
- Fort Walton Series:
  - Fort Walton Incised. Figs. 76, 77, 78, 85, 99, 100, 107, 110, 111, 121
  - Lake Jackson Plain .... Fig. 104
  - Point Washington Incised ..... Figs. 84, 87, 90, 94, 95, 96, 97, 98, 103, 105, 106, 112, 116
- Pensacola Series:
  - Pensacola Incised .... Figs. 102, 109
  - Pensacola Three-line Incised .... Figs. 80, 81, 82
  - Pensacola Plain .... Fig. 83
- Fort Walton Complex sherds .... Figs. 113, 114, 117, 120
- Unclassified .... Fig. 79

Identifications between Pensacola and Fort Walton Series types are not strictly reliable except where the actual specimen was examined, as I did with several of these that are in the Museum of the American Indian, Heye Foundation. In addition to the above, there is a vessel in the Museum of the R. S. Peabody Foundation, Andover,

[44] The number of burials recovered by Moore is not given, but one has the impression that it was fairly high.

which came from the Point Washington cemetery and was presented to the Museum by Moore. This is Lake Jackson Plain (No. 38938).

The site is clearly of the Fort Walton Period.

Wise Bluff (Wl-17).—This mound lies several miles up the Choctawhatchee River (Moore, 1918, pp. 521-522) (map 15). It was 2.5 feet high and 38 feet in diameter. It contained at least four secondary burials, a mass pottery deposit, and also pottery with individual burials. Pottery vessels were "killed." Pottery is described as complicated stamped, plain, incised, and pinched. A vessel of the type Carrabelle Incised is illustrated in figure 2 (Moore, 1918). This type, plus the description of "pinched" ware, which is almost sure to be the type Tucker Ridge-pinched, indicates the Weeden Island Period.

Dead River, north mound (Wl-18).—Moore (1918, pp. 523-525) describes a very low mound on Dead River some 33 miles up the Choctawhatchee (map 15). Scattered single skull and bundle burials were found in the mound and with one were evidences of fire. A mass pottery deposit was disclosed in the mound. Pottery types included check stamped, incised, and plain.

The mound probably belongs to the Weeden Island Period.

Dead River, south mound (Wl-19).—A second mound, to the south of the first, was excavated by Moore on Dead River (Moore, 1918, pp. 523-525) (map 15). This was low tumulus about 30 feet in diameter. It contained three bundle burials, various caches or deposits of "killed" pottery, and a lump of galena. Plain, incised, complicated stamped, and pinched pottery is described.

The mound probably belongs to the Weeden Island Period.

Douglas Bluff (Wl-20).—This site is 54 miles up the Choctawhatchee River (map 15). Moore (1918, pp. 526-528) measured it as 3.5 feet high and 42 feet in diameter. He found single skull and bundle burials totaling five in all, a mortuary deposit of "killed" pottery, sheet-mica fragments, and shell cups. Plain, incised, red painted, complicated stamped, and check stamped pottery is listed and four vessels are illustrated (Moore, 1918):

Weeden Island Complex
- Weeden Island Series:
  - Weeden Island Incised .... Figs. 6, 10
  - Weeden Island Punctated .... Fig. 8

Miscellaneous
- Unclassified .... Fig. 9
  (An atypical specimen which suggests both Weeden Island and Basin Bayou Incised.)

The mound belongs to the Weeden Island Period.

Bunker Cut-off (*Wl-21*).—This site is on one of the mouths of the Choctawhatchee River, about 3 miles upstream (map 15). The mound, excavated by Moore (1918, pp. 519-520), was circular, almost 4 feet high, and 43 feet in diameter. About six burials, all secondary and probably of the bundle type, were discovered. Some of these were in submound grave pits, but it is not clear whether these pits were excavated after the mound was constructed or before. A truncated conical discoidal stone was found with one of the burials; what Moore calls a "bi-conical" pipe of pottery was with another burial. Miscellaneous mound finds include a pitted hammerstone, sherds, an iron spike, and some flint tools, probably knives.

The pottery is described as being very similar to that taken from "cemeteries" between Perdido Bay and the Choctawhatchee River. This implies the Fort Walton and Pensacola Series of types, and a single line drawing (Moore, 1918, fig. 1) would verify this. Check stamped ware was also present.

From limited evidence we date the mound as Fort Walton Period.

Other sites in Walton County.—Inland from a location known as "Euchee Valley," Walton County, there is a site collection now in the Florida State Museum at Gainesville (72822-72831). Consisting of about 40 sherds, this collection is predominantly of the Fort Walton Complex.[45]

WASHINGTON COUNTY

Midden northwest of Crystal Lake (*Wg-1*).—There is a shell midden of undisclosed extent in section 29, Township 2 N., Range 14 W. (map 15). This site was not visited during the 1940 survey, but a collection was made here shortly after that time by Dr. Robert O. Vernon (1942) in connection with a geological survey of Holmes and Washington Counties. This collection was submitted to me for classification in 1941:

Weeden Island Complex	
Weeden Island Series:	
Weeden Island Incised	1
Carrabelle Punctated	2
Wakulla Check Stamped	12
Miscellaneous	
Residual Plain	20
Indeterminate Stamped	6
Other unclassified	2
Total sherds	43

This collection is dated as Weeden Island II.

[45] This material was classified by Dr. John M. Goggin.

Spring Hill Landing (Wg-2).—This mound, 5 feet high and 33 feet in diameter, was excavated by Moore (1918, pp. 522-523). It is located on Holmes River, an affluent of the Choctawhatchee (map 15). Moore describes its shape as a truncated cone. The mound contained six secondary burials of the single skull or bundle types. Cultural materials included the mortuary deposit of pottery, sheet-mica fragments, and shell cups. Pottery was "killed." Moore mentions neither check nor complicated stamped types. Two illustrations are classified as Weeden Island Incised (Moore, 1918, figs. 3 and 4), and the mound is dated as of the Weeden Island Period.

Miller Field Landing (Wg-3).—This low mound, 2 feet high and about 30 feet in diameter, was excavated by Moore (1918, pp. 525-526) on the Choctawhatchee River (map 15). It contained a mortuary deposit of broken pottery which he describes as complicated stamped and incised. In a marginal part of the mound was a grave pit which contained a primary extended burial together with three single skull interments. A single complicated stamped sherd of the Swift Creek type is illustrated (Moore, 1918, fig. 5). The evidence here is extremely scanty but indicates a Weeden Island dating.

BAY COUNTY

Holley site (By-1).—The site is located on St. Andrews Bay, on the west bank, 1 mile south of the West Bay bridge (map 15). The shell midden which we surveyed in 1940 stretches for 100 meters along the bay shore. The sand burial mound, excavated by Moore (1901, pp. 164-167) lies 200 meters from the midden to the south-southwest. A surface collection from the midden is classified as follows:

Weeden Island Complex	
Weeden Island Series:	
Weeden Island Incised	1
Weeden Island Plain	14
Carrabelle Punctated	1
Wakulla Check Stamped	17
Complicated Stamped Series:	
Swift Creek Complicated Stamped	25
Crooked River Complicated Stamped	1
Santa Rosa-Swift Creek Complex	
Basin Bayou Incised	1
Deptford Complex	
Deptford Bold Check Stamped	1

Miscellaneous	
Smooth Plain	6
Residual Plain	131
Indeterminate Stamped	11
Other unclassified	1
Total sherds	210

The site collection is both Weeden Island I and II Periods.

Another small collection was made from this same site by Richard Stearns. This material, now in Peabody Museum, Yale University (no catalog No.), was classified for me by Dr. John M. Goggin as follows:

Weeden Island Complex	
Weeden Island Series:	
Weeden Island Incised	2
Weeden Island Plain	17
Wakulla Check Stamped	4
Swift Creek Complicated Stamped	14
Ruskin Dentate Stamped	1
Miscellaneous	
Residual and Smooth Plain	20
Total sherds	58

This collection, too, dates as both Weeden Island I and II.

The Holley sand mound dug by Moore was 2.5 feet high and 50 feet in diameter. It had seven scattered single skull and bundle burials, a mortuary deposit of pottery, and nonceramic artifacts both with and separate from burials. These last were sheet-mica fragments and shell drinking cups. Moore lists complicated stamped pottery but not check stamped. The illustrated vessels from Moore (1902) are classified below:

Weeden Island Complex	
Weeden Island Series:	
Weeden Island Incised	Figs. 60, 62
Weeden Island Plain	Fig. 61
Swift Creek Complicated Stamped (Late Variety.)	Figs. 64, 65
Swift Creek Complicated Stamped	Fig. 66

This illustrated material is augmented by two Weeden Island Plain vessels (Nos. 39084, 39092) and an unclassified plain miniature vessel (No. 39158) from the R. S. Peabody Foundation and by a Swift Creek, Early Variety (No. 17/4889) from the Heye Foundation Annex.

A consideration of the evidence presented from the mound, including the presumed absence of Wakulla Check Stamped, leads to the conclusion that it was built during the Weeden Island I Period.

West St. Andrews (*By-2*).—Along U.S. Highway 98, 1.4 miles east of the West Bay bridge, the roadbed cuts through an extensive shell midden (map 15). The midden is mainly oyster, and it is probably at least 1 meter deep in several places. A number of modern houses and an auto court have been built upon the shell. There are two circular, dome-shaped mounds on the north side of the highway. One of these is 1 meter high and the other 1.5 meters high. Small excavations which had been made sometime in the past show the mounds to be composed of sand, shell, and midden. Just south of the highway is an impressive mound about 3 meters in height. Its present appearance suggests that it was an unusually high conical sand mound. Moore (1902, p. 176) makes a very brief mention of a mound in this vicinity which he excavated. Apparently he found nothing in the mound. A surface collection gathered from all sections of the village area in 1940 is classified below:

Weeden Island Complex	
Weeden Island Series:	
Weeden Island Incised	3
Weeden Island Plain	32
Carrabelle Incised	1
Carrabelle Punctated	4
Tucker Ridge-pinched	2
Wakulla Check Stamped	2
Swift Creek Complicated Stamped	26
Miscellaneous	
Plain Red	7
Smooth Plain	16
Residual Plain	159
Indeterminate Stamped	5
Other unclassified	6
Total sherds	263

This collection is overwhelmingly of Weeden Island I Period.[46]

[46] There is a collection of 41 sherds in the Peabody Museum, Yale University, from a site recorded as Dyer's Point. A map accompanying this collection indicates the Dyer's Point site to be in the immediate vicinity of By-2. The material, however, is mixed Fort Walton and Weeden Island. Presumably another part of the extensive shell midden was occupied during the Fort Walton Period. This collection was made a number of years ago by Richard Stearns. The classification afforded me was made by Dr. John M. Goggin.

Sowell site (By-3).—The 1940 excavations, in the village midden at Sowell, have been treated separately under the section, "Excavations on the Northwest Coast: 1940." The present review and analysis is based upon the Sowell burial mound and its contents as these have been published by Moore (1902, pp. 167-174.)

The Sowell mound was made of sand and was 4.5 feet high and 50 feet in diameter (map 15). Burials in the mound were found in a massed heap and also scattered. Secondary bundle or single skull types and primary flexed burials were all recorded. Two burials were found on mound base. Probably 25 or so individuals were represented in all. Pottery was found in a mass mortuary deposit, with individual burials, and also in small caches at various places throughout the mound. Nonceramic goods, such as shell cups, shell beads, a stone plummet or pendant, and steatite pipe of undisclosed form were found either unassociated or with burials. Pottery was "killed," and plain, incised, check stamped, and complicated stamped types are all listed. Many of the human crania from the mound showed frontooccipital flattening.

The pottery illustrated by Moore (1902) is classified below:

Weeden Island Complex
- Weeden Island Series:
  - Weeeden Island Incised.......................Figs. 69, 72, 75
  - Weeden Island Plain.................................Fig. 77
  - Weeden Island Punctated....................Figs. 68, 71, 73
  - Carrabelle Incised ....Fig. 70
- Tampa Complicated Stamped...........................Fig. 79
- St. Petersburg Incised................................Fig. 78

Miscellaneous
- Unclassified ....Fig. 76

Additional Moore vessels from this mound are in the R. S. Peabody Foundation. These are: Weeden Island Plain, three specimens (Nos. 39145, 39002, 39003); Weeden Island Incised, three specimens (Nos. 39254, 39294, 39094); and Carrabelle Punctated (No. 39060).

The mound is definitely Weeden Island, possibly only Weeden Island II.

Drummond site (By-4).—The Drummond site, like the Sowell site, is on the bay-shore side of what is locally known as the "West Peninsula" of St. Andrews Bay (map 15). It is a mile southeast of Sowell where the land curves eastward forming a north shore on which the midden is situated. There are actually two shell beds, a larger one to the east and a smaller to the west. They are on small sand ridges and are separated by a little stream. A number of little pits have been dug into both. Shells are oyster, scallop, and conch. The refuse is not deep, but a moderately large surface collection was made from the two middens combined. Fifty meters west of the smaller, westernmost midden is a small sand mound which has an old central excavation. This mound does not seem to be one of those excavated by Moore, and the older local inhabitants, who remember Moore's expeditions, say that he did not dig the mound.

The 1940 surface collection from the two Drummond middens is classified as:

Fort Walton Complex	
Fort Walton Incised	2
Pensacola Plain	1
Weeden Island Complex	
Wakulla Check Stamped	2
Santa Rosa-Swift Creek Complex	
Swift Creek Complicated Stamped (Mostly Early Variety.)	31
Deptford Complex	
Deptford Bold Check Stamped	1
Miscellaneous	
Smooth Plain	4
Residual Plain	81
Indeterminate Stamped	2
Total sherds	124

Although all Gulf Coast complexes seem to be represented here by a sherd or two, the site is dominantly of the Santa Rosa-Swift Creek Period.

Bear Point (*By-5*).—Bear Point, or Strickland Point, as it is usually called today, was visited by Moore in 1902 (pp. 174-175) and again in 1918 (p. 545). The site is on the southeastern extremity of the West Peninsula of St. Andrews Bay (map 15). Almost 50 years ago Moore stated that great irregular ridges of shell and a shell enclosure could be seen at the site, but today the midden is a thin, largely destroyed, oyster-shell deposit covering an area about 150 x 150 meters on the bay shore. A surface collection made in 1940 is classified below:

Fort Walton Complex	
Fort Walton Series:	
Fort Walton Incised	44
Lake Jackson Plain	14

Weeden Island Complex	
Weeden Island Series:	
Weeden Island Plain	3
Carrabelle Punctated	2
Keith Incised	2
Wakulla Check Stamped	4
St. Petersburg Incised	2
Miscellaneous	
Residual Plain	119
Indeterminate Stamped	4
Total sherds	194

The collection belongs to the Fort Walton and Weeden Island II Periods. Two Spanish olive-jar fragments were also found on the site.

Moore cut into a small sand mound at Bear Point and discovered a total of 12 primary flexed and secondary bundle burials. These had oyster-shell association. Stone celts were also found with burials, and a cache of mortuary pottery was uncovered on one side of the mound. Plain, check stamped, and complicated stamped types are listed. He mentions that one of the plain vessels was gourd-shaped. Vessels were "killed" with a perforation. It seems most likely that the mound belonged to the Weeden Island Period.

Somewhere to the westward of the first mound Moore located three others which he describes as "flat." All proved to be domiciliary or, at least, they contained no burials or cultural materials of any note.

West Bay bridge site (By-6).—West Bay bridge crosses the narrow neck of the bay at the juncture of West Bay, North Bay, and St. Andrews Bay proper. It is on U.S. Highway 98. On the west shore there is a shell midden 350 meters north of the bridge. This is in a low-lying area, relatively free from heavy growth. The midden extends along the shore for 100 meters and inland for only 20 meters. Shells are principally oyster. Commercial excavations have cut the deposit to pieces but sherds are plentiful in the loose shell. The following collection was made in 1940:

Fort Walton Complex	
Fort Walton Series:	
Fort Walton Incised	9
Lake Jackson Plain	4
Weeden Island Complex	
Weeden Island Series:	
Weeden Island Incised	1
Weeden Island Plain	1
Wakulla Check Stamped	18
Swift Creek Complicated Stamped	2

Miscellaneous	
Residual Plain	60
Total sherds	95

The collection dates from Weeden Island II and Fort Walton Periods.

Davis Point, west (*By-7*).—Opposite the West Peninsula there is a comparable extension of land which helps form St. Andrews Bay. The little hamlets of Cromanton and San Blas are situated on this peninsula. On its northern end, facing outward toward the Gulf, is Davis Point. The burial mound at this site was the one which Moore excavated in 1902 (pp. 176-182); the mound excavated under the same name in 1918 (Moore, 1918, pp. 546-548) lies about a mile distant on the inner or bay shore (map 15).

In 1940 Woodbury and the writer relocated the burial mound of Moore's 1902 season and also explored a very extensive shell midden which is situated on the shore at a distance of a few hundred meters from the mound. The trees and undergrowth are heavy on the point, and the inland extent of the midden could not be accurately determined; but along the low bank back of the beach sherds and shell are found for several hundred meters. Although the midden did not appear to be very deep at any one spot, the site is one of the largest on the northwest Gulf coast. A surface collection is classified as follows:

Weeden Island Complex	
Weeden Island Series:	
Weeden Island Incised	1
Weeden Island Plain	12
Carrabelle Incised	1
Santa Rosa-Swift Creek Complex	
Alligator Bayou Stamped	1
Complicated Stamped Series:	
Swift Creek Complicated Stamped	28
St. Andrews Complicated Stamped	2
Deptford Simple Stamped	1
Miscellaneous	
Plain Red	1
Residual Plain	91
Unclassified	3
Total sherds	141

This collection is both Santa Rosa-Swift Creek and Weeden Island I.

The Davis Point mound excavated by Moore in 1902 was about 3 feet high and 45 feet in diameter. Numerous burials were found, both in a massed secondary deposit and as scattered individual interments. Some of the latter were of the secondary bundle or bunched type; others were primary and tightly flexed. Oyster shells and evidences of fire were noted with burials. Pottery was found in a mass mortuary deposit. Nonceramic artifacts were placed with burials and were also found separately in the mound. Stone celts, pitted stones, lump galena, fragments of copper objects, and pointed conch columellae were the mound artifacts. Pottery was "killed," and Moore mentions plain, incised, and check stamped types.

Frontooccipital flattening was noted on some of the skulls.

The illustrated material (Moore, 1902) is classified as follows:

Weeden Island Complex

Weeden Island Series:

Weeden Island Incised..............Figs. 81, 84, 86, 87, 89, 94
Weeden Island Plain..............................Fig. 88
Carrabelle Incised ....Fig. 85
Keith Incised ....Fig. 92
Wakulla Check Stamped.......................Fig. 91 (?)

Miscellaneous

Unclassified ....Fig. 83

This illustrated collection is verified as to type range by two vessels of Moore's from the same mound which were given to the R. S. Peabody Foundation. One is Wakulla Check Stamped (No. 39287) and the other Weeden Island Plain (No. 39153). Another specimen in the Heye Foundation Annex is Carrabelle Incised (No. 17/4951). The mound seems to be Weeden Island II Period, dating later than the midden collection.

Davis Point, east (*By-8*).—According to Moore's account (1918, pp. 546-548), this mound is located on East Bay, an arm of St. Andrews (map 15). It is about a mile from Davis Point in an easterly direction. The mound was circular, 3 feet high and 45 feet in diameter. Seven burials were scattered secondary single skull and bundle types. They were sometimes accompanied by masses of shell. Pottery had been placed in a mortuary deposit, but stone celts and hammerstones were found with specific burials or at random through the mound. Pottery was "killed." Moore lists check stamped, complicated stamped, plain, and incised. The illustrated vessels, figures 22 and 23 (Moore, 1918) are both Weeden Island Plain.

The dating of the mound is undoubtedly Weeden Island.

Midden in Davis Point area (By-9).—There is another collection from the Davis Point region which is worth analysis. This is a series of 276 sherds which were gathered in 1932 by Frank M. Setzler of the United States National Museum during a brief survey trip of the northwest coast (U.S.N.M. No. 373169). The exact location of this collection with references to sites By-7 and By-8 is not clear (map 15). The datum is simply "a shell heap across St. Andrews Bay, opposite Panama City." This is undoubtedly in the Davis Point section, and it may be from the large By-7 midden or, possibly from an unreported midden near the By-8 mound. The collection is presented below:

Fort Walton Complex	
Fort Walton Series:	
Fort Walton Incised	2
Lake Jackson Plain	1
Weeden Island Complex	
Weeden Island Series:	
Weeden Island Incised	3
Weeden Island Zoned Red	2
Weeden Island Plain	63
Carrabelle Incised	7
Carrabelle Punctated	37
Indian Pass Incised	3
Keith Incised	3
Tucker Ridge-pinched	19
Wakulla Check Stamped	27
Swift Creek Complicated Stamped (Late Variety.)	27
Mound Field Net-marked	1
Santa Rosa-Swift Creek Complex	
Franklin Plain	2
Miscellaneous	
Plain Red	7
Residual Plain	36
Indeterminate Stamped	6
Other unclassified (Virtually all these are very small fragments of the Weeden Island Series.)	40
Total sherds	286

This collection, in spite of the very small numbers of Fort Walton and Santa Rosa-Swift Creek sherds, dates primarily from the Weeden Island I and II Periods.

Parker's Branch (By-10).—Parker's Branch is on the northern or mainland side of St. Andrews Bay 5 miles southeast of Panama City and less than 1 mile southeast of the village of Parker (map 15). The site is an oyster- and conch-shell midden located in flat hammock land on a small stream branch which drains into the bay. The midden is thin and extends along the branch for 100 meters and back from the branch for 60 meters. A sand mound is reported somewhere in the immediate neighborhood of the branch, but a search failed to reveal it during the 1940 survey.

Two collections are available from this site. One was made during the 1940 survey and is given below:

Santa Rosa-Swift Creek Complex	
Swift Creek Complicated Stamped	31
(Mostly Early Variety.)	
Miscellaneous	
Plain Red	1
Residual Plain	106
Indeterminate Stamped	8
Total sherds	146

The other collection was made by Setzler[47] in 1932 (U.S.N.M. No. 373168), and from the description of the location of the site there is little doubt that it is the same one. It is classified below:

Santa Rosa-Swift Creek Complex	
Alligator Bayou Stamped	2
Complicated Stamped Series:	
Swift Creek Complicated Stamped	70
(Early Variety.)	
Crooked River Complicated Stamped	1
(Early Variety.)	
St. Andrews Complicated Stamped	2
(Early Variety.)	
New River Complicated Stamped	1
Franklin Plain	4
Miscellaneous	
Smooth Plain	7
Residual Plain	47
Indeterminate Stamped	2
Total sherds	136

The site is clearly of the Santa Rosa-Swift Creek Period.

[47] Setzler also collected sherds from a site known as "Sheepshead Bayou," somewhere to the north of Panama City. All the sherds from this site (U.S.N.M. No. 373170) are Fort Walton Period. I have not included it in the discussion for lack of more adequate location data.

West Bay Post Office (By-11).—Moore excavated a sand mound on a small western arm of St. Andrews Bay (Moore, 1902, pp. 130-140) (map 15). He described it as being over 50 feet in diameter, 8 feet high, and of truncated conical shape. We visited the site in 1940, relocating the mound which is now much smaller as a result of excavation and erosion. No shell midden was encountered nearby, but in the vicinity of the mound we observed a few Weeden Island Period sherds.

A few burials, presumably secondary, were found during Moore's work. There was a mass deposit of intentionally destroyed pottery, but other artifacts, including chipped-stone projectiles, stone celts, hones, and sheet-mica fragments were found with burials and at random through the mound. With some burials was evidence of former fires or charcoal deposits.

Pottery was "killed" by perforation. Moore mentions plain, incised, red painted, and complicated stamped, but does not include the check stamped type. His illustrations (1902) are classified as follows:

Weeden Island Complex
Weeden Island Series:
Weeden Island Incised....................Figs. 8, 13, 14, 15
Weeden Island Punctated..........................Fig. 10
Weeden Island Plain......................Figs. 1, 2, 3, 4, 6
Tucker Ridge-pinched ....Fig. 7

Santa Rosa-Swift Creek Complex
Santa Rosa Punctated..................................Fig. 11

Miscellaneous
Unclassified ....Figs. 5, 12
(Figure 5 is undoubtedly Weeden Island Series.)
Effigy lugs ....Figs. 16-19
(Probably Weeden Island adornos, but some are reminiscent of Fort Walton Period.)

Four vessels in the R. S. Peabody Foundation are also of the Weeden Island Period. These are: Indian Pass Incised (No. 39245); Carrabelle Incised (No. 96/R137); Carrabelle Punctated (No. 38934); and Keith Incised (No. 38972).

The mound is clearly Weeden Island and, judging from the presence of complicated stamped and the lack of check stamped types, of the Weeden Island I division.

West Bay Creek (By-12).—Moore (1918, pp. 542-543) excavated another mound on the opposite side of West Bay Creek (map 15) from the West Bay Post Office site.[48] This mound, not visited in 1940, was 2 feet high and 25 feet in diameter. No burials were found, although there was a destroyed cache of pottery. Plain, check stamped, complicated stamped, and incised types are mentioned in the text. A single illustrated vessel, with relief duck effigies, is the type Weeden Island Incised (Moore, 1918, fig. 19). The mound is Weeden Island Period.

Phillips Inlet (By-13).—Moore dug this mound in the 1918 season (1918, pp. 541-542). It is located on Phillips Inlet (map 15). The site could not be located in 1940. A sand mound, circular in outline, was estimated to have been about 4 feet high and was 45 feet in diameter. It contained two bunched or bundle-type secondary burials, a mass pottery deposit of destroyed vessels, and other artifacts both with and without burial associations. The latter are projectiles, celts, and sheet-mica fragments. No pottery is illustrated, but the descriptions suggest Weeden Island Incised types. Complicated stamped and check stamped are also listed. The mound is probably of the Weeden Island Period.

Brock Hammock (By-14).—This mound, also on St. Andrews Bay, several miles south of West Bay Post Office (map 15), was excavated by Moore in 1902 (p. 140).[49] It was not visited in 1940. It was 2.5 feet high and 38 feet in diameter. No burials were recovered, but these may have been taken out by excavators who preceded Moore. Plain, check stamped, and complicated stamped pottery was recovered. No material from this site is illustrated, but a vessel of the type Weeden Island Plain (No. 39139) is in the R. S. Peabody Foundation. The limited evidence implies a Weeden Island Period date for the mound.

Burnt Mill Creek, larger mound (By-15).—Located on the east bank of the creek, this mound was opened by Moore in 1902 (pp. 140-146) (map 15). The site was not visited in 1940. Moore lists the mound as truncated conical in shape, 4 feet high, and 50 feet in diameter. Eleven bundle and single skull burials were in the mound, and destroyed pottery was in a large cache, in smaller caches, and with burials. Sheet-mica fragments were present. Pottery was both "killed" with perforations and made with holes as a special mortuary ware. Plain and incised types are mentioned in the text.

---

48 In his 1902 report (p. 140) Moore makes a brief mention of a mound which is, apparently, in about the same location as this one. Presumably it was another mound, however, as he found nothing in it and considered it to be a domiciliary structure.

49 Moore (1918, p. 543) returned to the same vicinity and explored two very small mounds nearby. These seem to have been midden hummocks.

A classification of illustrations (Moore, 1902) is given below:

Weeden Island Complex
Weeden Island Series:
Weeden Island Incised........................Figs. 21, 24, 26
Weeden Island Punctated............................Fig. 20
Weeden Island Plain..........................Figs. 22, 23, 25

In the R. S. Peabody Foundation there is another vessel from the Moore excavations at this mound which falls in line with the above. It is Weeden Island Plain (No. 39349).

The mound dates from the Weeden Island Period.

Burnt Mill Creek, smaller mound (By-16).—Also on Burnt Mill Creek (map 15), this mound, 2.5 feet high and 28 feet in diameter, was excavated by Moore in the 1902 season (Moore, 1902, pp. 146-149). It was not visited in 1940. No burials were found, but a mass pottery deposit and a projectile point were encountered. Pottery was "killed." No check stamped is reported from the mound but complicated stamped was present. Illustrated (Moore, 1902) pottery is classified below:

Weeden Island Complex
Weeden Island Series:
Weeden Island Incised...........................Figs. 29, 33
Tucker Ridge-pinched ....Fig. 30
Swift Creek Complicated Stamped.........................Fig. 31
(Late Variety.)

Santa Rosa-Swift Creek Complex
Basin Bayou Incised......................................Fig. 28

Two vessels were classified in the R. S. Peabody Foundation. These were Weeden Island Plain (No. 39124) and Swift Creek Complicated Stamped (Late Variety) (No. 38930). The mound is Weeden Island I Period.

Burnt Mill Creek, west (By-17).—This site is on the west side of the creek about 1 mile from the mouth (map 15). It was not visited in 1940. Moore (1918, pp. 543-545) lists the measurements as about 3 feet high and 45 feet in diameter. Three or four single skull and bundle burials were found at various points in the mound, and there were evidences of old fires in the mound and near burials. Besides a mass pottery deposit there were also stone celts, sheet-mica fragments, and pieces of copper artifacts both with burials and placed singly. Only plain and incised pottery are mentioned in addition to the material illustrated. "Killing" of vessels by perforation is recorded, and one vessel (Moore's vessel 2) was a mortuary piece manufactured with holes. The two illustrated vessels from the mound, plate XIV and figure 21 (Moore, 1918), are both incised and are obviously related. They are difficult to classify as are the three specimens discussed from the "Site West of Point Washington" (see Moore, 1901, figs. 67, 70, 74). The breadth of line of the incisions is like Basin Bayou Incised, but the design arrangement, carrying out the bird idea, is more Weeden Island. As stated before, these types intergrade, and it seems certain that the bold-line Weeden Island Incised is a development out of Basin Bayou Incised.

This mound is probably Weeden Island I Period.

Alligator Bayou (By-18).—This is a mound site on the north side of St. Andrews Bay (map 15). It was not visited in 1940. Moore excavated here in 1902 (Moore, 1902, pp. 150-152). At that time the mound was of oblong shape, being 76 by 50 feet and a little over 6 feet high. It was composed of sand. No human bones were met with in Moore's excavations, but he attributes this to their decay in the moist soil of the mound. A projectile point, hematite ore, a mica spear-point form, a copper-covered wooden object, and a conch-shell drinking cup were the only nonceramic artifacts. Pottery had been ceremonially "killed" and placed in a mortuary deposit in the mound. The following ceramic features of a general nature were noted: plain ware, complicated stamped, red painted ware, incised types, scalloped rims, and tetrapodal supports. Illustrated (Moore, 1902) pottery is classified as:

Santa Rosa-Swift Creek Complex
- Alligator Bayou Stamped.......................... Figs. 34, 35
- Complicated Stamped Series:
  - Swift Creek Complicated Stamped.............. Figs. 39, 40
  - St. Andrews Complicated Stamped.................. Fig. 37
    (Early Variety.)
  - Crooked River Complicated Stamped................ Fig. 38

In addition, from this site there is a complete vessel of the type Crooked River Complicated Stamped (No. 38923) at the R. S. Peabody Foundation, and three Swift Creek specimens (Nos. 17/4900 and 18/246) in the Heye Foundation Annex. One of this last group is definitely of the Early Variety of the Swift Creek type.

The mound is of the Santa Rosa-Swift Creek Period.

Fannings Bayou (By-19).—This site in North Bay, an arm of St. Andrews, was not seen in the 1940 survey (map 15). Moore (1902, pp. 152-159) excavated a burial mound here in 1902. This mound was then 3 feet high and 40 feet in basal diameter. Nineteen secondary single skull and bundle burials were found, often with charcoal or evidences of fire above them. The burials were at various points throughout the mound. Pottery was in a mass deposit on one side of the mound; other artifacts were both with burials and distributed at random. These include a shell cup, a projectile point, and two spear forms cut from sheet mica. Both check and complicated stamped types of pottery were in the mound in addition to plain and incised vessels. Pots were "killed" with perforations. Illustrated (Moore, 1902) pottery is given below:

Weeden Island Complex
- Weeden Island Series:
  - Weeden Island Incised..............................Fig. 42
  - Weeden Island Punctated........................Figs. 44, 51
  - Weeden Island Plain...............................Figs. 43, 53
  - Tucker Ridge-pinched ....Fig. 47
- Wakulla Check Stamped...............................Fig. 52
- Swift Creek Complicated Stamped.......................Fig. 41
  (Late Variety.)

Miscellaneous
- Unclassified ....Figs. 46, 48
  (Figure 46 appears to be degenerate Weeden Island; figure 48 is suggestive of Crystal River Incised.)

At the R. S. Peabody Foundation there are five vessels of the type Weeden Island Plain from this site (Nos. 39040, 39038, 39812, 39040, 39334), and at Heye Foundation Annex there is a single specimen of Late Variety Swift Creek Complicated Stamped (No. 17/4893).

The site is definitely Weeden Island. The presence of both Wakulla Check Stamped and the Swift Creek Complicated Stamped, Late Variety, suggest both Weeden Island I and II.

North Bay (By-20).—This small mound on the North Bay arm of St. Andrews Bay was not seen during the 1940 survey but was excavated by Moore (1902, pp. 159-160) (map 15). It was 2 feet high and 38 feet in diameter. Sixteen burials were scattered through the mound and were single skulls or bundle forms. A cache of pottery was on one side of the mound, and a flint projectile point and a lump of lead sulphide were also found. Perforated or "killed" vessels were the rule. Many of these were check stamped but no complicated stamped is reported. No material is illustrated, but three vessels in the R. S. Peabody Foundation from this site are Wakulla Check Stamped (No. 39167), Weeden Island Incised (No. 39311), and unclassified Incised and Punctated (No. 39159).

The mound is Weeden Island II Period.

Anderson's Bayou (By-21).—Also on upper St. Andrews Bay, this mound was not relocated in 1940 (map 15). Moore (1902, pp. 160-162) gives the size of the mound as about 2 feet high and 55 feet in diameter. Moore found only four burials, representing at least six individuals, all secondaries of the single skull or bundle types. Decay of bone material was extremely marked, and the excavator was of the opinion that more burials had been placed in the mound. Besides a deposit of pottery on one side of the mound, hones, smoothing stones, hammerstones, sheet mica, stone beads, and sheet copper were recovered from mound fill. Both complicated and check stamped pottery types are reported.

The illustrated (Moore, 1902) pottery is classified as:

Santa Rosa-Swift Creek Complex
- Santa Rosa Series:
  - Alligator Bayou Stamped.............................Fig. 54
  - Basin Bayou Incised.................................Fig. 55
- Swift Creek Complicated Stamped................Figs. 59, 56, 58
  (Figure 59 is excellent example of the Early Variety.)

Miscellaneous
- Indeterminate Stamped ....Fig. 57

The R. S. Peabody Foundation collections from this site include a Swift Creek Complicated Stamped, Early Variety (No. 38945) and two plain vessels which may be Weeden Island Plain (Nos. 39179, 39159).

With the exception of the two check stamped sherds (Moore, 1902, p. 161), which might be the Wakulla type, and the possible Weeden Island Plain pots, the mound is clearly of the Santa Rosa-Swift Creek Period.

Large Bayou (By-22).—This mound is on the northern side of St. Andrews Bay (map 15). It was excavated by Moore (1902, pp. 163-164) but was not examined in the 1940 survey. The mound measured 4 feet high and 50 feet in diameter in Moore's time. Ten bunched or bundle-type burials were encountered. In several instances it appears as though pottery vessels had been placed as offerings with specific burials. A large cache of vessels was found in the mound, many of which were "killed." A hammerstone, a smoothing stone, and some mica were the only nonpottery objects mentioned. Moore lists check stamped, complicated stamped, miniature vessels, and compartment vessels in the general discussion. He illustrates no pottery, but the R.S. Peabody Foundation collections from the site include three Weeden Island Plain (Nos. 39121, 39316, 39172) and one Swift Creek Complicated Stamped, Late Variety (No. 39266) vessels.

The site is of the Weeden Island Period.

Cemetery at St. Andrews (By-23).—This site, originally surrounded by a shell ridge or embankment, no longer displayed this surface feature in 1940 (map 15). Moore (1902, pp. 175-176) found this embankment 2 to 4 feet high and encircling an area about 170 feet in diameter. Many vessels and burials were reported having been taken from the site prior to Moore's visit, but he found only a single vessel at a depth of 3 feet below the surface. Moore was of the opinion that the vessel, a bowl, had originally covered a burial which had disappeared through decay. The vessel in question, illustrated as figure 80 (Moore, 1902), is Fort Walton Incised. Presumably this cemetery belonged to that period.

Pearl Bayou midden (By-24).—Pearl Bayou or Craney Bayou is on the bay side of the eastern peninsula of St. Andrews Bay (map 15). It lies about 1 mile east-northeast of the hamlet of San Blas. The midden is on the sloping bank of the bay. In area it is 100 by 50 meters with additional patches and extensions of shell farther back from the water's edge in the woods. The refuse is extremely black organic material mixed with shell, and sherds were the most abundant of any site of this same size encountered during the 1940 survey. Several old excavations show that the rubbish is a meter or more in depth.

The 1940 collection from the site is classified below:

Weeden Island Complex	
Weeden Island Series:	
Weeden Island Incised	13
Weeden Island Plain	49
Carrabelle Incised	5
Carrabelle Punctated	20
Indian Pass Incised	3
Keith Incised	9
Tucker Ridge-pinched	7
Wakulla Check Stamped	275
Swift Creek Complicated Stamped	7
Miscellaneous	
Plain Red	2
Smooth Plain	28
Residual Plain	293
Indeterminate Stamped	11
Unclassified	9
Total sherds	731

This midden is clearly in the Weeden Island II Period.

Mound near Pearl Bayou (By-25).—This mound was situated about 1 mile east of Pearl Bayou proper, at some distance from the water's edge (map 15). We were unable to locate it during the summer of 1940. Moore (1902, pp. 183-188) says that the mound was 3.5 feet high and 40 feet in diameter. Burials were numerous, including a large mass interment of remains, some of which were flexed, some possibly secondary. In addition to the mass burial were a number of individual flexed burials found at various places in the mound. Near the mound margin some flexed burials were also found in shallow submound pits. In one instance, such a pit had a single flexed burial in the bottom and this burial was covered with oyster shells. Over the oyster shells were a number of other skeletons (Moore, 1902, fig. 95).

Pottery was in a large mortuary cache and in smaller, scattered caches. Other artifacts, projectile points, a lanceolate blade, a hammerstone, several celts, shell cups, and fragments of sheet mica, were both with and unassociated with the burials. Pottery was "killed" by perforation, and both check and complicated stamped types are recorded in the text as well as plain and incised wares.

Cranial deformation, probably frontooccipital, was noted on some of the skulls.

Illustrated (Moore, 1902) pottery is classified below:

Weeden Island Complex

Weeden Island Series:

Weeden Island Incised....................Figs. 100, 102, 104

Weeden Island Plain......................Figs. 103, 105, 106

Indian Pass Incised..................................Fig. 99

Swift Creek Complicated Stamped...................Figs. 97, 98

Miscellaneous

Unclassified ....Fig. 101

Additional data from this site, in the form of specimens in the R. S. Peabody Foundation, include three Weeden Island Plain pots (Nos. 39286, 39337, 39134) and a miniature vessel (No. 39171). A beaker of the type Basin Bayou Incised is in the Heye Foundation (No. 17/4038).

The mound is of the Weeden Island Period.

Strange's Landing (By-26).—This mound, on East Bay of St. Andrews Bay, was excavated by Moore (1902, pp. 192-196) (map 15). It was not visited in 1940. The mound was 4 feet high and 38 feet in diameter before Moore's excavation. Burials were both primary flexed and secondary bundle, numbering five in all. Flexed burials were found in shallow submound pits in some instances. These were usually covered with oyster or conch shells. Pottery was in a large mortuary deposit. A stone celt was placed near one of the burials. Pottery was "killed" by perforation and breaking. Both check and complicated stamped types are mentioned.

One skull from the Strange's Landing mound was flattened, probably frontooccipitally.

Illustrated (Moore, 1902) pottery is classified below:

Weeden Island Complex
Weeden Island Incised.....................Figs. 112, 114, 115, 117

Miscellaneous
Unclassified ....Fig. 116
(This vessel is strongly reminiscent of the type Crystal River Incised.)

Vessels in the R. S. Peabody Foundation confirm the above Weeden Island Period material. These are: two Weeden Island Incised (Nos. 39295, 38969); Weeden Island Plain (39122); and Carrabelle Punctated (39258).

The mound is Weeden Island Period.

Laughton's Bayou, mound A (By-27).—This mound is on the north side of the East Bay tributary of St. Andrews (map 15). It measured 3.5 feet high and 45 feet in diameter when Moore excavated it in 1902 (Moore, 1902, pp. 188-189). We did not find the mound in 1940. Moore also describes shell middens in the same field with the sand mound and mentions a circular shell enclosure.

The seven or eight burials in the mound were single skull and bundle interments found near mound center but not in a mass deposit. Sheets of mica, found near the mortuary cache of pottery, were the only nonceramic objects of the mound. Vessels in the cache were broken or "killed" by perforation. Plain, incised, and complicated stamped types were found, but no check stamped appeared.

Illustrated (Moore, 1902) pottery has been classified as given below:

Weeden Island Complex
Weeden Island Plain.....................................Fig. 107

Santa Rosa-Swift Creek Complex
Swift Creek Complicated Stamped.......................Fig. 108
(Early Variety.)

Material in the R. S. Peabody Foundation includes one vessel from this site which is Indian Pass Incised (No. 39105); specimens at Heye Foundation Annex include two Swift Creek Complicated Stamped, one Late Variety and one which is questionable as to phase (No. 17/4899).

This material suggests a Weeden Island dating of the earlier or Period I half.

Laughton's Bayou, mound B (By-28).—This mound is on the eastern side of the creek, opposite Laughton's mound A (map 15). Moore (1902, pp. 189-192) excavated it when its height was 7 feet and its diameter was over 40 feet. Even at that time the mound had been previously explored. The site was not located during the 1940 survey. Both secondary bundle and primary flexed burials were encountered in the mound, numbering nine in all. Oyster shells often covered burials, and there were also evidences of fires having been made beside the bones before they were enclosed in the sand. One instance of a subfloor grave pit with a single burial covered with shells is also noted. Pottery was recovered from a large mortuary cache at one side of the mound, and stone celts and pierced *Marginella* shell beads came from the immediate location of a burial.

Pottery was "killed" by perforation, and a vessel with prefired mortuary holes was also encountered. No complicated or check stamped pottery is mentioned in the account. The illustrated (Moore, 1902) pottery is classified as:

Weeden Island Complex
Weeden Island Series:
Weeden Island Incised....................Figs. 110, 111 (?)
Weeden Island Plain..............................Fig. 109

The mound is dated as of the Weeden Island Period.

Baker's Landing (By-29).—This site, also on East Bay (map 15), was not found by us in 1940 but was excavated by Moore (1902, pp. 196-197). In 1902 the mound had been much dug over, and its original shape was not determinable. Its approximate size was about 5 feet in height and 70 feet in diameter. Near the mound were shell midden and evidences of a circular shell enclosure. The nine burials in the mound were both secondary and primary. The former is represented by only one single skull burial; the latter by semiflexed, flexed, and extended forms. Most of the skeletons were covered with masses of oyster shell. Pottery, mostly broken, was found in a large deposit. No check stamped or incised types were associated. Two sherds (Moore, 1902, figs. 119, 120) are illustrated. These are Swift Creek Complicated Stamped (Early Variety). Two vessels, both St. Andrews Complicated Stamped (Early Variety), which came from Baker's Landing mound are in the Peabody Museum, Harvard (uncataloged). Three Swift Creek Complicated Stamped specimens were examined at Heye Foundation Annex (No. 17/4901).

The available evidence indicates a Santa Rosa-Swift Creek Period date.

Hare Hammock, larger mound (By-30).—The Hare Hammock mounds are situated near the base of the Crooked Island peninsula in the southeastern corner of Bay County (map 15). They were not relocated in 1940, and, like many others, may have entirely disappeared by now. When Moore visited the larger Hare Hammock mound (Moore, 1902, pp. 197-207) it had a height of 7.5 feet, a diameter of 56 feet, and was a perfect truncated cone in form. The 31 burials in the mound were both secondary and primary, including single skull, bundle, and flexed types. Many were covered with conch shells. Pottery was placed in the mound in a mass deposit and nonceramic artifacts were sometimes with burials, sometimes unassociated. These last were stone celts, a stone gorget, a fossil shark tooth, sheet mica, a lance or projectile point of chipped stone, and shell cups.

Both check and complicated stamped pottery is reported from the mound in addition to plain and incised types. Pottery was "killed" by perforations. The following is a classification of illustrated (Moore, 1902) material:

Weeden Island Complex
Weeden Island Series:
Weeden Island Incised....Figs. 122, 124, 127, 129, 131, 135, 136
Weeden Island Plain..........................Figs. 126, 134

This is supplemented by a single Weeden Island Plain vessel (No. 39033) from the R. S. Peabody Foundation which had been taken from the mound by Moore but not illustrated by him.

The site is of the Weeden Island Period.

Hare Hammock, smaller mound (By-31).—This mound was excavated by Moore in 1902 (Moore, 1902, pp. 207-210) and again in 1918 (Moore, 1918, pp. 549-553) (map 15). The second time he referred to it as "Mound near Crooked Island." We did not visit the site in 1940.

The mound was made of sand and measured about 45 feet in diameter and 3 feet high.

On the second visit Moore referred to a nearby village or midden area some 200 yards from the mound proper. His excavations, however, pertained only to the burial mound. Both secondary bundle and primary flexed burials were in the mound, totaling 13. Most of these seem to have been on mound base, and some of them were covered with layers of conch shell. Pottery was found in a major cache, in scattered subsidiary caches, and with individual burials. Lance points, celts, and a sheet-mica spear-point form were taken from the mound. Check stamped pottery is not reported, but complicated stamped was present in addition to incised and plain types. Vessels were "killed." Material which Moore (1902 and 1918) illustrated is classified below:

Weeden Island Complex
Weeden Island Series:
Weeden Island Incised....................Figs. 26, 28 (1918)
Hare Hammock Surface Indented............Fig. 138 (1902)
Tucker Ridge-pinched ....Fig. 25 (1918)
Swift Creek Complicated Stamped................Fig. 138 (1902)

There are also two vessels in the R. S. Peabody Foundation from this mound. One is Keith Incised (No. 38983); the other Weeden Island Plain (No. 39315).

The mound is Weeden Island, probably Weeden Island I.

Farmdale (By-32).—This burial mound, encountered by Moore (1918, pp. 548-549) but not by the 1940 survey, is located near the eastern end of East Bay not far from the hamlet of Farmdale (map 15). The mound was 2 feet high and 35 feet in diameter before Moore's excavations. Burials were secondary, fragmentary, and, in at least one instance, partially cremated. Evidence was found of only two individuals. Fires had been placed near to or upon the skeletal remains. Pottery was found in various small caches through the mound. Other artifacts, such as lance or projectile points of chipped stone, were taken from the immediate proximity of burials. Shell drinking cups were also present.

Only plain and incised ware is reported with the exception of one sherd showing relief modeling. Vessels were "killed." The only illustrated specimen, figure 24 (Moore, 1918), is the type Indian Pass Incised.

This mound is Weeden Island.

JACKSON COUNTY

Sampson's Landing (Ja-1).—This mound, about one-half mile from the Apalachicola River, was reported on by Moore in 1903 (pp. 489-491) (map 16). It was not visited in the 1940 survey. It was made of sand with an admixture of clay and gravel. The mound measured 4.5 feet in height and had a basal diameter of 45 feet. There were 47 burials in the mound. Both single skull and bundle burials were found, in some cases associated with remains of fire. Flexed burials were also present and in three instances were covered with limerock slabs. Pottery appeared as a mass deposit and in scattered caches. Nonceramic artifacts include stone celts, sheet-mica fragments, and shell cups.

Pottery vessels were "killed," and plain, incised, check, and complicated stamped types are reported. Two vessels are illustrated (Moore, 1903): Figure 155 is Swift Creek Complicated Stamped,

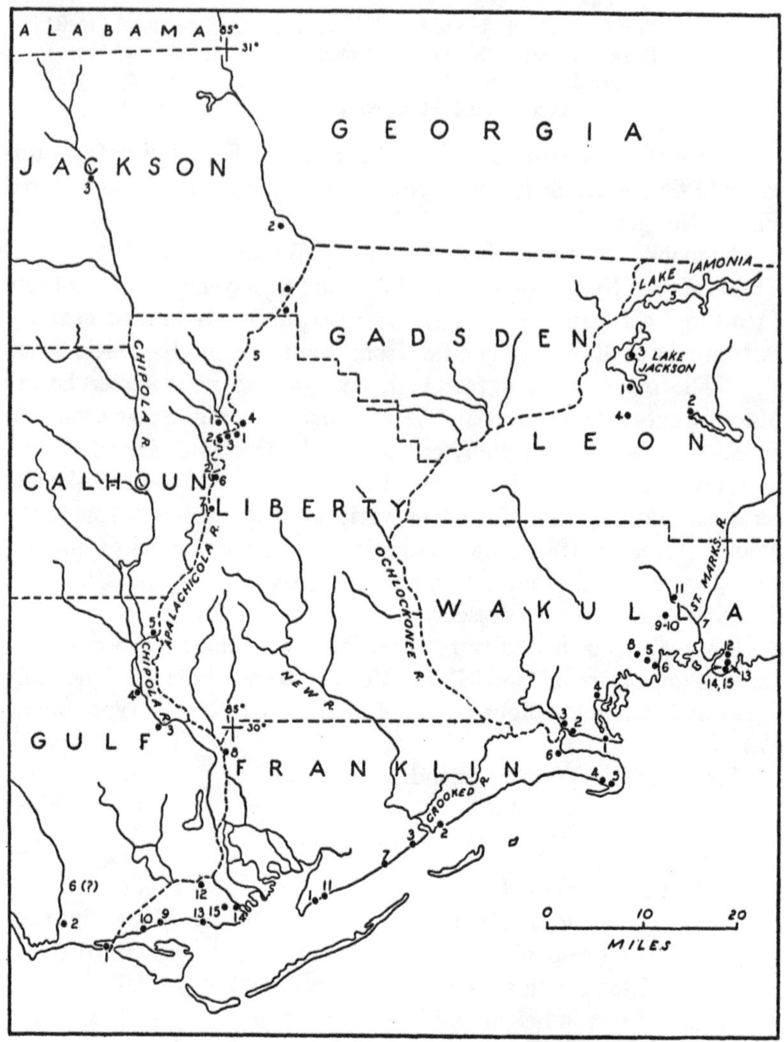

MAP 16.—Site map of Jackson, Calhoun, Gulf, Gadsden, Liberty, Franklin, Leon, and Wakulla Counties. Sites indicated by numbers.

Late Variety; figure 156 is an unclassified incised piece of a curious design and somewhat divergent technique. Additional material from Sampson's Landing in the R. S. Peabody Foundation (No. 6298) and the Heye Foundation Annex (No. 17/4987) are two Swift Creek

Complicated Stamped specimens, questionable as to Early or Late Variety identification.

The available evidence indicates the Weeden Island Period, although there is a possibility that the site may be earlier.

Kemp's Landing (*Ja-2*).—This location is about 1 mile from the Apalachicola River (map 16). It was reported upon by Moore in 1907 (pp. 428-429) but not visited during the 1940 survey. The mound was 4.5 feet high, 33 feet in diameter, and made of clay rather than sand. Only one single skull burial and a large deposit of mortuary pottery were recovered from the mound. Pottery was "killed," and incised, plain, check, and complicated stamped types are listed. Moore (1907) illustrates only one vessel, figure 1 (p. 429), an Indian Pass Incised specimen, but two other vessels of the Moore collection from the mound are in the R. S. Peabody Foundation. These last are both Swift Creek Complicated Stamped, Late Variety (Nos. 41800, 41798).

The mound is dated as of the Weeden Island Period.

Florida Caverns State Park (*Ja-3*).—This site (map 16) was not visited in the 1940 survey, but was examined in that year and in 1941 by Charles H. Fairbanks, of the National Park Service, and J. Clarence Simpson, Florida Geological Survey. I am indebted to Mr. Fairbanks for a synopsis of the situation and for the opportunity to examine sherd collections from the site.

Three site units are listed. These are "Cave No. 10," "Rock Shelter No. 1," and "The Parking Area." All three sites were relatively superficial occupation middens. Potsherds and projectile points were recovered from the surface. Sherd counts were not made of these collections, but all were predominantly of the Fort Walton Period.

CALHOUN COUNTY

Davis' Field (*Ca-1*).—The site is about 1 mile northeast of Blountstown on a tributary stream of the Apalachicola River (map 16). It was excavated by Moore (1903, pp. 468-473) but not visited in 1940. The mound was made of clay, circular in outline, about 4.5 feet high, and 70 feet in diameter. An outstanding feature was a smaller interior mound which covered a subfloor pit. The 26 burials recovered were secondary single skull and bundle types and also primary flexed interments. Some of the latter were in shallow pits below mound base. There were evidences of fire having been placed with burials, and in one spot it appeared as though a mass of logs had been placed over a skeleton and then fired. The small interior mound, made of clay and charcoal, contained no burials but had been built over a shallow pit which held the remains of a fire. A cache of pottery vessels had been placed on its top.

Pottery, except for the cache mentioned above, was all found in a large mortuary deposit of "killed" and broken vessels. Vessels were made with perforations as well as perforated after firing. Conch-shell cups and sheet-mica fragments were in the mound. Plain, incised, red painted, and complicated stamped pottery types are mentioned, but check stamped was absent. The illustrated (Moore, 1903) vessels are classified below:

Weeden Island Complex
- Weeden Island Series:
  - Weeden Island Incised.............................Fig. 131
  - Weeden Island Plain.....................Figs. 133, 134, 136

Two specimens in the Heye Foundation Annex from this site are classified as Swift Creek Complicated Stamped, Late Variety (No. 7/5166).

Both the illustrated and the Heye Foundation specimens indicate that this site is Weeden Island—probably, in view of the absence of check stamped, Weeden Island I.

OK Landing (Ca-2).—The exact location of this mound is not given by Moore (1918, p. 554), and it was not located in the 1940 survey (map 16). Presumably, it is somewhere above the Davis' Field site on the Apalachicola River. It was a small mound 3.5 feet high and 35 feet in diameter. It contained two unidentified secondary burials, a mass deposit of pottery, and a lump of galena. Plain, incised, check, and complicated stamped pottery are mentioned by Moore. Pottery was perforated to effect "killing." From the brief description of some of the vessels found it seems indubitable that this was a Weeden Island Period site.

Other sites in Calhoun County.—Moore (1903, pp. 467-468) tells of a rectangular, flat-topped pyramidal mound with a ramp approach about 1 mile northeast of Blountstown Landing. He was unable to excavate at the site, however.

At Atkin's Landing, about 6 miles above Blountstown, a small, low mound was excavated by Moore (1903, p. 480). He found nothing, as the mound had been riddled by previous digging.

GULF COUNTY

Indian Pass Point (Gu-1).—Indian Pass is the narrow entrance to St. Vincent's Sound between Indian Pass Point and St. Vincent's

Island. Located near the end of Indian Pass Point, one-quarter of a mile west of the pass, is the remnant of a small sand burial mound (map 16). This mound was excavated by Moore in his 1902 survey (Moore, 1902, pp. 211-214). The mound, composed of sand and shell, lies in the midst of sand dunes and stunted pine and oak trees in semigrown dune country. In 1940 we were unable to find any evidence of occupation near the mound. A few Weeden Island Plain sherds were found in the old craterlike excavation in the center of the mound.

The mound, in Moore's time, irregular in shape, was approximately 3 feet high and 50 feet in diameter. It contained numerous secondary burials of the bunched or bundle type. Pottery was found in a large, principal cache and in smaller deposits, and projectiles, celts, smoothing pebbles, hones, shell cups, hematite ore, and a shell chisel were also recovered.

Many of the skulls from this mound showed marked frontooccipital flattening.

Pottery was "killed." The listed pottery types include plain, incised, and check stamped. Complicated stamped is not mentioned. Illustrated (Moore, 1902) pottery is classified below:

Weeden Island Complex
Weeden Island Series:
Weeden Island Incised............................Fig. 145
Indian Pass Incised................................Fig. 144

Miscellaneous
Unclassified ....Fig. 143

This mound dates as Weeden Island II.

Gotier Hammock (Gu-2).—This site lies on the Gulf in St. Joseph's Bay (map 16). It was not located in 1940, but in 1902 Moore (1902, pp. 210-211) reported it as a much dug-over mound about 5 feet high and 60 feet in diameter. Moore found a few scattered bundle burials in the mound; some of these were in shallow pits below mound base. From his statements it is obvious that the mortuary deposit, or deposits, of pottery had largely been removed. Some of the few vessels found were "killed" by perforations. Plain, incised, complicated stamped, and red painted wares are remarked upon. One of the vessels he describes was a necked jar with complicated stamped decoration around the rim portion only. This is most likely to have been a Late Swift Creek Complicated Stamped piece. Two sherds are illustrated (Moore, 1902). These are: Figure 140, Weeden Island Incised; and figure 141, Swift Creek Complicated Stamped.

From the evidence, the mound appears to have been a Weeden Island Period burial place, probably Weeden Island I.

Burgess Landing (Gu-3).—This site is on a small tributary of the Chipola River which is, in turn, a tributary of the Apalachicola (map 16). It was excavated by Moore in his field trip of 1903 (Moore, 1903, pp. 443-445), but was not relocated in the 1940 survey. The mound, made of clayey sand, was about 5 feet high and almost 50 feet in diameter. The 12 burials within the mound were secondary and of the single skull and bundle types. Pottery in the mound formed a special mortuary cache, but nonceramic artifacts were found at random without particular associations. These last include projectiles, celts, hones, and sheet mica. Pottery vessels were "killed," and all principal types such as plain, incised, check stamped, complicated stamped, and red painted are listed. Only one vessel, a Weeden Island Plain specimen (Moore, 1903, fig. 93), is illustrated.

The mound is dated as Weeden Island.

Isabel Landing (Gu-4).—This mound site is also on the Chipola and was not visited in 1940 (map 16). Moore (1903, p. 445) excavated the mound, a tumulus almost 5 feet high and 50 feet in diameter, and found evidences of two secondary burials. Pottery was, for the most part, grouped in a cache. Vessels were "killed" by perforation. Moore lists check stamped, complicated stamped, plain ware, and punctated decoration. One of the vessels he describes may have been the type St. Andrews Complicated Stamped. In addition to the pottery, some sheet mica was found in the mound.

The lack of illustrated material makes identification difficult in this case, but the description best fits the Weeden Island Period.

Chipola Cut-off (Gu-5).—This mound is located near the canal which joins the Chipola and Apalachicola Rivers some miles above their natural junction (map 16). The mound, excavated by Moore (1903, pp. 445-466), was not visited in the 1940 survey. Moore described it as being 5 feet high and 45 feet in diameter and composed of sand with some clay admixture. Previous to Moore's operations the mound had been disturbed by miscellaneous and unrecorded digging.

Burials were found by Moore at 42 points throughout the mound but with a tendency toward massing along the southern margins. Bundle, single skull, and flexed or semiflexed forms were noted. Most burials were on mound base or in the mound fill but some, unfortunately not well identified as to form but probably secondary, were in submound pits. Pottery was found principally in a large cache but also in smaller caches and in some instances immediately associated with specific burials. There was one example of a vessel being inverted over a skull. For the most part, vessels were "killed" by breaking or perforation, although at least one example of prefired "killing," or mortuary ware with specially made holes, was recorded. This specimen was of the type Weeden Island Plain in contrast to most of the pottery from the mound which is of the Fort Walton Period.

Nonceramic artifacts, usually found associated with individual burials, include: Hematite ore, stone celts (some of which occurred in a cache below mound base), stone hones, shell tools (gouges and chisels), shell beads and hairpins, and bone awls and fishhooks. In addition, there is a toadstool-shaped pottery object (Moore, 1903, fig. 129) which may be a pottery anvil. European artifacts frequently associated with burials were brass disks, presumably gorgets. Glass beads were also found.

Pottery from the site was abundant and is well illustrated. Moore also made general observations as to the similarity to wares found farther to the west, near Pensacola (Fort Walton types), and as to the presence of polished black ware (probably shell-tempered). Loop handles and one interesting stirrup-spout fragment are worth special mention. Below is a classification of the Moore (1903) illustrations:

Fort Walton Complex
- Fort Walton Series:
  - Fort Walton Incised.....Figs. 96, 97, 98, 100, 101, 105, 109, 115, 122, 123, 124, 126, 127
    (Figure 109 is atypical in that design filler appears to be dentate-stamped rather than punctated.)
  - Point Washington Incised..........Figs. 106, 116, 117, 118, 121
  - Lake Jackson Plain..........................Figs. 114, 128
- Pensacola Incised ....Fig. 108

Weeden Island Complex
- Weeden Island Series:
  - Weeden Island Incised.....................Figs. 102, 112 (?)
  - Weeden Island Plain..............................Fig. 104
- Swift Creek Complicated Stamped.......................Fig. 120
  (Late Variety.)

The R. S. Peabody Foundation has additional material from the Moore excavations at Chipola Cut-off. This lot includes one Lake Jackson Plain vessel (No. 39267), one Fort Walton Incised vessel (No. 39313), and one St. Petersburg Incised jar (No. 39053). Nonceramic specimens from the same site are a shell spoon, a *Busycon* celt, a *Fasciolaria* chisel, and a single-grooved columella pendant or plummet.

This mixture of both Fort Walton and Weeden Island specimens in the same mound is almost without parallel in Moore's excavations. His excavation data do not, unfortunately, give sufficient detail to be of much help in explaining this situation. Two possibilities suggest themselves. One is that of intrusion, the assumption being that Fort Walton Period peoples utilized a Weeden Island Period burial mound for a cemetery. If this is so, the intrusive burials must have been made at considerable depths, as some of the skeletons accompanied by brass ornaments of European origin were found in submound pits. Furthermore, the intrusive diggings must have been very extensive in order to have placed a large cache of Fort Walton Period pottery in the mound in addition to the many graves. The second possibility is that a Fort Walton community had retained a number of Weeden Island pottery vessels in a mound of their construction. One objection to a continuity of this sort is that Wakulla Check Stamped, the marker type of the Weeden Island II Period, is absent from the mound, implying that the Weeden Island component belongs to the earlier or Weeden Island I Period. It would be more reasonable to expect continuity between Weeden Island II and Fort Walton than from Weeden Island I to Fort Walton.

Both hypotheses are possible, but neither is provable from the available data. The only conclusion we can be certain of is that the mound represents both Weeden Island and Fort Walton Periods.

St. Josephs Bay (*Gu-6*).—This site is not located but only listed on map 16. In 1893-94 C. H. B. Floyd sent a collection of vessels, some stone celts, and shell artifacts to the United States National Museum (Nos. 155318-155329) from a mound which he located as about 25 miles from Apalachicola on St. Josephs Bay. At that time it was identified as "Franklin County," but today a St. Josephs Bay location would be in Gulf County.

There is the possibility that this might be the Gotier Hammock (Gu-2) mound which Moore found so thoroughly dug over on his 1902 expedition. The collection is, however, a fine one and a distinct period lot. It is also illustrated and well known from the literature (Holmes, 1903, pl. LXXVIII). Late Variety Swift Creek, Weeden Island Plain, and Weeden Island Incised are all represented in the photograph. The presence of the heavy rim reinforcement which extends down over the vessel walls, as seen in the vessel in the upper left corner of the Holmes illustration, is reminiscent of Oklawaha

Plain, a Weeden Island I horizon marker from north-central and northeast Florida. This similar treatment is also noted on the incised vase or globed jar, lower row, third from right (Holmes illustration). These features and the Late Swift Creek specimens place the collection as Weeden Island I.

GADSDEN COUNTY

Aspalaga (Gd-1).—The Aspalaga site is on high ground back from the river landing of that name in the western corner of Gadsden County (map 16). It was excavated by Moore (1903, pp. 481-488) but not visited by the 1940 survey. The site consisted of a shell midden and three sand mounds. Two of these mounds, both low and inconspicuous, were found, according to Moore, to be domiciliary in character. That is, no burials or special caches of pottery were found within them. The third mound, which is the basis of Moore's report, was 6 to 9 feet in height and about 90 feet in diameter. In outline, the mound was slightly oblong rather than round.

Fifty-four burials were found in the mound, and these were single skull, bundle, and flexed types. Charcoal was in association with several. Most pottery was in a mass cache, but some specimens were with individual burials. Nonceramic artifacts were also with and apart from specific burials. Lance points, projectiles, celts, hammerstones, sheet-mica fragments, a mica spear-point form, hematite ore, a truncated stone disk, shell cups, shell tools, and shell beads make up this group.

Pottery is listed as plain, incised, red painted, and complicated stamped. Tetrapodal supports and notched rims are other common features which are given special mention. The illustrated pottery (Moore, 1903) is classified below:

Weeden Island Complex
Weeden Island Plain.......Figs. 146, 150, and probably 152 and 153

Santa Rosa-Swift Creek Complex
Swift Creek Complicated Stamped......................Fig. 151
(Early Variety.)
Crystal River Incised............................Figs. 147, 148

The additional panel of sherds shown in Moore, 1903, figure 154, consists of four Swift Creek Complicated Stamped (top, and left side), one of which (lower, left) is definitely of the Early Variety; one St. Andrews Complicated Stamped (bottom, center); one Weeden Island sherd (bottom, right); and one sherd of Fort Walton Incised (center, right).

The R. S. Peabody collections from Aspalaga show a single vessel which is four-lobed and of the type Basin Bayou Incised (No. 39131).

The ceramic evidence from this site points to a Santa Rosa-Swift Creek dating overlapping into Weeden Island I.

Other sites in Gadsden County.—Moore (1903, pp. 491-492) also investigated a group of mounds near Chattahoochee Landing on the Apalachicola River. There were seven mounds in all. Some of them appear to have been substructure or temple-type mounds. Others, which were low, rounded mounds, were excavated, and as nothing was found in them they were considered as domiciliary.

HOUSTON COUNTY, ALA.

McLaney place (Hn-1).—This site is located in the extreme western tip of Houston County, Ala., on the Choctawhatchee River. It was visited and excavated by Moore during his 1918 survey (Moore, 1918, pp. 528-530) but was not relocated in 1940. The site consists of a burial mound on a bluff above the river. The mound measured about 5 feet in height and over 30 feet in diameter. Five burials were discovered but are not described as to form. They lay upon or near mound base and apart from a mortuary cache of pottery. A chipped-stone celt or ax was the only artifact other than pottery. Only plain and red painted wares are mentioned. A gourd-shaped bowl of the type Weeden Island Zoned Red is illustrated (Moore, 1918, pl. XIII, fig. L).

The mound is placed as Weeden Island.

Fullmore's Upper Landing (Hn-2).—This mound is in the northeastern corner of Houston County, Ala., and was excavated during Moore's 1907 excursion up the Chattahoochee and Flint Rivers. The site was not visited in 1940. Moore (1907, pp. 438-444) describes the mound as about 3 feet high and as located on a slope. A few burials were in the mound, but these were too decomposed to determine burial form. Apparently masses of stones had been used for burial coverings.

Plain, incised, and red painted pottery are the only types listed. Vessels were "killed" and had been placed in a mortuary deposit in the mound. Illustrated (Moore, 1907) pottery is classified below:

Weeden Island Complex
Weeden Island Incised........................Figs. 18, 20, 22, 24

Miscellaneous
Unclassified ....Fig. 17
(This specimen is related to the Weeden Island Series.)

This site is of the Weeden Island Period.

DECATUR COUNTY, GA.

Hare's Landing (*Dr-1*).—This mound is located a mile or so inland from the Chattahoochee River. It is described by Moore (1907, pp. 429-437) as being 5 feet high and 48 feet in diameter. The site was not visited in the 1940 survey. Forty-three bundle and flexed burials were found in the mound. Both masses of phosphate rock and charcoal were found near many of the skeletons. Possibly the rocks had been used to construct a crude sort of cover for the burials. Pottery was in a major mortuary deposit and also in caches distributed through the mound. Other artifacts were found at random in the sandy-clay mound fill. Celts, hammerstones, lump galena, sheet-mica fragments, and conch-shell cups are all listed.

Moore mentions plain, incised, check stamped, complicated stamped, and red painted pottery. Vessels were either perforated or were made with holes as special mortuary ware. Moore (1907, pp. 429 ff.) illustrates the following pottery which is classified below:

Weeden Island Complex
Weeden Island Series:
Weeden Island Incised..........................Figs. 3, 5, 7
Weeden Island Punctated............................Fig. 2
Weeden Island Plain....................Figs. 7, 8, 9, 10, 12
Carrabelle Punctated ....Fig. 11

This site is of the Weeden Island Period.

Munnerlyn's Landing (*Dr-2*).—This mound, on the lower Flint River, was excavated by Moore (1907, p. 451) but not visited by us during the 1940 survey. The mound, about 3 feet high and 50 feet in diameter, was located in a field one-quarter of a mile from the river bank. The 16 burials discovered in the mound were badly preserved, but some were definitely typed as flexed. Charcoal was found near two of the burials. Pottery, for the most part, was in the large mortuary cache or small, scattered caches, but there was one case of a vessel in immediate association with a burial. A soapstone sherd was also found accompanying another burial. A stone celt was the only other artifact in the mound. The trait of "killing" was noted on pottery vessels, and check stamped, complicated stamped, and plain wares are listed as is the feature of tetrapodal supports. Moore (1907) illustrates two large sherds (figs. 25, 26). These are Swift Creek Complicated Stamped and, from such features as the folded rim and the undecorated margin below the rim, can be classed as the Late Variety of the type.

Absence from Munnerlyn's Landing of incised types makes it difficult to identify the site as to culture period. The complicated stamped types illustrated are Late Variety Swift Creek of the Weeden Island I horizon, yet the mention of tetrapods suggests the Early Swift Creek horizon, equivalent to the Santa Rosa-Swift Creek Period. Check stamped, if it is the Wakulla type, indicates a Weeden Island Period dating. On the other hand, if this check stamped is the Gulf Check Stamped type, or the Deptford type, a Santa Rosa-Swift Creek equation would be more consistent. The data are too few and too contradictory in this case to allow for a reasonable estimate comparable to those given for most of the other sites treated in this review. The best we can say is that the mound was made sometime between the beginnings of the Santa Rosa-Swift Creek Period and the close of the Weeden Island Period.

Kerr's Landing (Dr-3).—The Kerr's Landing mound was circular in outline, 5 feet high and 62 feet in diameter when Moore visited it (Moore, 1907, pp. 452-456). The location is on the Flint River about 5 miles below Bainbridge, Ga. We did not visit the mound in 1940. On mound base, near the center, were the remains of a fire. Burials were both secondary bundles and primary flexed, numbering 25. Pottery was massed in a large deposit, but other artifacts were occasionally found with burials or scattered separately in the mound. Nonceramic materials were a celt, projectile points of chipped stone, lump galena, and hematite ore.

Pottery vessels were "killed." The pottery types mentioned in the text are incised and punctated, plain, check stamped, complicated stamped, red painted, and cord-marked. The illustrated material (Moore, 1907) is classified below:

Weeden Island Complex
Weeden Island Series:
Weeden Island Incised..............................Fig. 28
Weeden Island Punctated.................Figs. 27, 30, 31, 32

The mound is clearly Weeden Island Period.

Hardnut Landing (Dr-4).—This mound, also on the Flint River, is located by Moore (1918, pp. 555-557) as being on the right-hand side of the river (going upstream), about one-half mile southwest of Hardnut Landing. It was not visited in the 1940 survey. The mound, as found by Moore, measured a little over 2 feet in height and 65 feet in diameter. The 21 burials were both bundle and flexed types and were, in some instances, accompanied by charcoal deposits. Pottery was found in a mass mortuary deposit, but sheet-mica fragments and shell drinking cups were at random through the mound or with burials.

Pottery was both "killed" by postfiring perforation, and specially made with holes. Most general pottery categories are mentioned in the account, including both complicated and check stamped types. Only a single vessel is illustrated (Moore, 1918, fig. 29). This specimen is a collared jar, made with holes in the walls, supported on tetrapodal feet, and bearing an incised and punctated decoration. It is vaguely suggestive of both the Weeden Island and Crystal River Incised types but differs from both. On the basis of descriptions of other vessels taken from the mound (p. 557), which include bird-effigy forms, it seems most likely that the mound dates as Weeden Island.

EARLY COUNTY, GA.

Shoemake Landing (Ey-1).—The mound was excavated by Moore (1907, pp. 437-438) but was not relocated in the 1940 survey. It is situated on the Chattahoochee River in the southwestern corner of Early County, Ga. Moore found it to be 2 feet high and 45 feet in diameter. It was constructed of sand and had been much plowed over. Decayed human bones were spotted in the mound but were too far decomposed to allow determination of burial form. A mortuary deposit of pottery came from one side of the mound. Pottery had been "killed" by breakage or mortuary perforation. Plain, incised and punctated, check stamped, and complicated stamped sherds are listed from the mound findings. Moore (1907) illustrates a vessel, figure 14, which is Weeden Island Incised, and a complicated stamped sherd, figure 13, which is related to the Swift Creek genre but is a distinct type.

On limited evidence the mound is placed as Weeden Island Period.

LIBERTY COUNTY

West Bristol midden (Li-1).—This site was the only one visited in 1940 at such a distance inland except for the survey work in Leon and Jefferson Counties. Bristol is a town located near the east bank of the Apalachicola about 50 miles from the mouth of that river (map 16). The site is a refuse area on the brow of a ravine on the western outskirts of Bristol. Sherds are found within a radius of some 30 meters. The "mound at Bristol" (Li-4), which Moore excavated in 1903, was reported by local inhabitants to be some little distance away and nearer the Apalachicola River.

A surface collection made at the West Bristol midden is classified below:

Weeden Island Complex	
Weeden Island Series:	
Weeden Island Incised	1
Weeden Island Plain	5
Carrabelle Incised	1
Wakulla Check Stamped	39
Miscellaneous	
Residual Plain	49
Unclassified	2
Total sherds	97

The site dates as of the Weeden Island II Period.

Yon mound (Li-2).—Moore (1903, p. 473) visited this mound and describes it as a large, squarish structure with rounded corners and a flat summit plateau. The location is given as 2 miles below Bristol (map 16). The basal diameter of the mound was given by Moore as 157 feet, and he estimated the height at about 29 feet. The mound had no ramp approach and the sides were steep. The flat top measured 68 feet across. The mound was trenched by Moore, though he does not state the depth or extent of the trenches. Presumably they were relatively superficial and confined to the summit. He uncovered only one small deposit of burned human bones.

Although the 1940 survey party did not visit this site, Dr. M. W. Stirling made a brief reconnaissance trip in this region in 1936. He located and photographed a mound of similar description at approximately the same location given by Moore. From the surrounding village area he collected the following lot of sherds which are now in the United States National Museum (No. 378423):

Fort Walton Complex	
Fort Walton Series:	
Fort Walton Incised	57
Lake Jackson Plain	96
Marsh Island Incised	20
Santa Rosa-Swift Creek Complex	
Alligator Bayou Stamped	1
Miscellaneous	
Cob-marked sherd	1
Total sherds	175

This collection obviously dates from the Fort Walton Period. It is highly probable that the mound dates from the same period.

Mound below Bristol (Li-3).—The location is listed by Moore (1903, pp. 473-474) as being about 1 mile west-southwest of Bristol (map 16). It was a circular sand mound, 3 feet high and 50 feet in diameter. The site was not found in 1940. Human remains were too decayed for identification of burial forms, but in a pit below mound base a pottery pipe (form undescribed but probably monitor) and three shell gouges were recovered. It is likely that this was a submound burial in which the bones had completely disintegrated. Pottery was found in a large mortuary deposit at one side of the mound, and a shell drinking cup, a pitted stone, and a chipped knife or projectile made up the total contents of the tumulus.

Pottery was "killed" by perforation. Check stamped, complicated stamped, plain ware, and the feature of notched or scalloped rims are given special mention. No incised or punctated types were found. No material is illustrated by Moore.

The mound is extremely difficult to place, owing to lack of illustrated specimens. Both complicated stamped and scalloped rim features suggest the Santa Rosa-Swift Creek horizon and this is offered as a tentative placement. The presence of check stamped raises questions as to the particular type of this check stamped as it did at the Munnerlyn's Landing mound (Dr-2). Wakulla Check Stamped would conflict with the Santa Rosa-Swift Creek assignment; on the other hand, Gulf Check Stamped or a Deptford Check Stamped would be in line with this early dating.

Mound at Bristol (Li-4).—Moore (1903, pp. 474-480) gives the location of this mound as about 300 yards northwest of the town of Bristol (map 16). It was a sand mound on a ridge, circular in outline, 2.5 feet high, and 56 feet in diameter. We did not relocate the mound in the 1940 survey. Fourteen bunched and single skull burials were found at various places in the mound, and a mass pottery deposit is reported. Other vessels were found here and there in the mound, and nonceramic artifacts were discovered both with and apart from burials. A hammerstone, a sheet-mica spear-point form, conch-shell cups, and shell beads had been placed in the mound. Pottery was both "killed" by perforations and made with holes. Check stamped, complicated stamped, plain, incised, and red painted types are all mentioned. Check stamped is reported as particularly common. Moore (1903) illustrates the following specimens:

Weeden Island Complex
- Weeden Island Series:
  - Weeden Island Punctated.........................Fig. 138
  - Weeden Island Plain.................Figs. 140, 141, 142, 144
- Wakulla Check Stamped.........................Figs. 137, 139

Miscellaneous

Unclassified complicated stamped........................Fig. 143

(This specimen resembles Late Swift Creek in form and decoration distribution, but the stamped designs and their application are more like the late period Georgia type, Lamar Complicated Stamped.)

The site is Weeden Island—probably Weeden Island II in view of the predominance of Wakulla Check Stamped and the presence of a complicated stamped vessel which verges on the Lamar Complicated Stamped type.

Rock Bluff Landing (*Li-5*).—This mound was located by Moore (1918, pp. 554-555) somewhere on the Apalachicola River in northwestern Liberty County (map 16). We did not visit it in 1940. The exact location is not given although it was situated about a mile inland from the river. Size was 4 feet high by 45 feet in diameter. The 13 burials recorded were too decayed for identification. They lay with the mass deposit of mortuary ware, and one burial was accompanied by a pot. A projectile point, a stone celt, and some shell beads were recovered, the latter being with a burial. Pottery was both "killed" by perforation and specially made with holes. Plain, incised, check, and complicated stamped types are listed.

Moore (1918) illustrates a vessel of mortuary ware that is classified as Weeden Island Plain (pl. XV).

The site is dated as Weeden Island.

Michaux Log Landing (*Li-6*).—Moore (1918, pp. 553-554) locates this site about 4 airline miles north of Estiffanulga (map 16). The location was not visited in 1940. The site is a mound 3.5 feet high and about 40 feet in diameter. Evidences of old fires were found in the mound to the extent of the entire nucleus of the tumulus being composed of burned sand. Some calcined human bones were in one deposit. The three or four other burials were secondary types, badly decayed. Pottery was in a mass deposit, and a projectile point was the only nonceramic artifact recovered. The vessels had been "killed." Plain ware, one crude incised piece, check stamped, and complicated stamped are listed as being present. No material is illustrated.

Data are insufficient to place the mound in the Gulf Coast chronology. Apparently it falls somewhere in the Weeden Island or Santa Rosa-Swift Creek range.

Estiffanulga (*Li-7*).—Moore (1903, pp. 466-467) found a mound about 1 mile northeast of Estiffanulga near the Apalachicola River (map 16). We did not visit the site in 1940. He describes the mound as being 3 feet high, 38 feet in diameter, and made of yellow clayey sand. The single find of human skeletal remains were too decayed for identification of burial type. Pottery vessels were found at several locations in the mound, as were sherds. Stone celts and projectile points made up the mound inventory. Pottery vessels were "killed" by perforation, and check stamped, complicated stamped, and plain types are described.

Data are too few for identification of the site.

Other sites in Liberty County.—There is a small sherd collection in the Peabody Museum, Yale University (uncataloged) which came from Torreya State Park. These were collected near a large mound. The collection is of the Weeden Island Period.

FRANKLIN COUNTY

Porter's Bar (Fr-1).—Porter's Bar is on St. George's Sound 3 miles east of East Point (map 16). The sand mound, which Moore (1902, pp. 238-249) excavated, lies 400 meters back from the beach. The associated shell midden begins about 200 meters from the mound and extends almost to the water's edge. Its east-west axis measures approximately 200 meters. U.S. Highway 319 cuts through the southern side of the midden. Depth of the refuse is probably not over 1 meter.

The surface collection from the Porter's Bar midden made during the 1940 survey is classified below:

Fort Walton Complex	
Fort Walton Incised	2
Pensacola Plain	1
Weeden Island Complex	
Weeden Island Plain	5
Santa Rosa-Swift Creek Complex	
Complicated Stamped Series:	
Swift Creek Complicated Stamped	31
Crooked River Complicated Stamped	1
Franklin Plain	2
Gulf Check Stamped	10
West Florida Cord-marked	1
Deptford Complex	
Deptford Bold Check Stamped	2
Deptford Simple Stamped	3
Miscellaneous	
Smooth Plain	1
Plain Red	2
Residual Plain	108
Unclassified	9
Total sherds	178

Four periods are represented in this collection in which Santa Rosa-Swift Creek sherds predominated. The count on Swift Creek Complicated Stamped may, however, be a little misleading in this regard as many of these sherds cannot be placed successfully as either Early or Late Variety.

The burial mound, which still remains in a partly destroyed condition, was measured by Moore (1902) as being 10 to 11 feet in height and having basal diameters of 60 by 78 feet. The mound was found to have been constructed of irregular layers of white, yellow, and blackened sand which had been built up over a primary layer of oyster shells. Primary flexed and semiflexed burials and secondary bundle and single skull types were all present, numbering 68 in all. One deposit of calcined human bone is mentioned. Burials were found on or near mound base as a rule. Some were in the basal shell stratum. Pottery was found in a mass cache and in smaller, scattered caches. In some instances vessels were with individual skeletons. The nonpottery artifacts were encountered both with and apart from individual burials. Stonework included projectiles, celts, hammerstones, and a plummet or pendant. Hematite ore, galena, sheet mica, bitumen, a carved kaolin "baton," copper work, cut animal jaws, shell pendants, shell cups, and shell tools are additional traits. A simple elbow-form pottery pipe from the mound is illustrated by Moore (1902, fig. 178).

Pottery vessels were "killed" by perforation. Moore discussed plain, incised, check stamped (scarce), complicated stamped, and red painted pottery. He also makes special mention of a human-effigy vessel form which he does not illustrate. The material which he pictures (1902) is classified below:

Weeden Island Complex
- Weeden Island Series:
  - Weeden Island Incised....Figs. 180, 183, 185, 188, 190, 191, 195
    (All these specimens, except figure 185, are of the bold incised and punctated division of the Weeden Island Incised type which is close in decoration technique to the Santa Rosa-Swift Creek Period type, Basin Bayou Incised.)
  - Weeden Island Plain..............Figs. 182, 187, 192, 198, 200
- Swift Creek Complicated Stamped..................Figs. 201, 203
  (Late Variety.)

Santa Rosa-Swift Creek Complex
- Swift Creek Complicated Stamped..................Figs. 196, 202
  (Early Variety (?).)
- Alligator Bayou Stamped..............................Fig. 194

Miscellaneous
- Unclassified ....Figs. 197, 199

Additional material from the Moore collections from this mound are in the R. S. Peabody Foundation collections. These include four Swift Creek Complicated Stamped, Late Variety (Nos. 39255, 38940, 39223, 39049), four Weeden Island Plain (Nos. 39157, 38920, 39262, 39310), and a plain miniature vessel (No. 39136). The Heye Foundation Annex collections supplement this with one Swift Creek, Late Variety, one Swift Creek unplaced as to Early or Late, and two Weeden Island Plain (No. 17/49997).

Total materials seem to divide between Weeden Island and Santa Rosa-Swift Creek Periods. The heaviness of the incised lines and punctations in the Weeden Island specimens, suggesting the boldness of both Basin Bayou Incised and Crystal River Incised, imply that it is an early Weeden Island or Weeden Island I. The check stamped piece which Moore mentions is most likely the Santa Rosa-Swift Creek type Gulf Check Stamped as this type was found in the Porter's Bar midden while Wakulla Check Stamped was not.

Carrabelle (*Fr-2*).—The 1940 excavations at this site have been discussed in detail under "Excavations on the Northwest Coast: 1940," "the Carrabelle site" (see maps 9 and 16). The location of Moore's (1918, pp. 557-560) excavations at the site and a brief mention of his findings are given in that section. As has been stated, we cannot be sure whether or not this burial site was formerly an artificial mound which had disappeared through previous digging, cultivation, or erosion, or whether it was simply a cemetery area. Lack of evidence for the former makes the latter interpretation the more probable.

Pottery was found in the sandy soil of the burial ground or cemetery at superficial depths (about 20 inches). Vessels, usually broken into piles of sherds, were grouped in small caches. A single exception was a complete vessel, broken only by "kill-hole" perforations. In addition to the illustrated pottery, Moore lists the check stamped type as being present. Two burials were found in the area. Both were deposits of thoroughly calcined human bone, placed near the pottery caches but not in immediate association.

Illustrated pottery (Moore, 1918) includes the complete vessel referred to which is a double but inner-connected jar of simple shape, supported by tetrapods. It is sand-tempered, decorated with simple stamping and a row of single dot punctations around the rim (Moore, 1918, fig. 30). Both it and the two top sherds in the sherd panel (Moore, 1918, fig. 31) are the type Deptford Simple Stamped. The sherd in the lower left corner (Moore, 1918, fig. 31) appears to be Alexander Incised. The lower right corner sherd (Moore, 1918, fig. 31) is decorated with carefully placed simple stamped lines running horizontally on the vessel.[50] Over this stamped decoration a linear-punctated design has been superimposed. This design is a series of "key-shaped" elements, highly reminiscent of design units of the Alexander Incised type. The sherd is from a sand-tempered vessel which, curiously enough, is of a rectangulate boat shape.

It is clear that the Carrabelle cemetery material excavated by Moore is distinct and different from any of the more commonly recognized ceramic complexes. Its closest affiliations seem to be with the Deptford Complex as indicated by the Deptford Simple Stamped sherds. It will be remembered that the Deptford Period was well represented at the site in the midden excavations so the presence of Deptford Period burials is not completely unexpected. The appearance of the Alexander-like sherds fits this time horizon satisfactorily, being in line with the chronological position of the Alexander Series in other localities of the southeastern United States.

Midden west of Carrabelle (Fr-3).—Two miles west of the town of Carrabelle on St. George's Sound there is a sand hill which extends for about 25 meters along the north side of U.S. Highway 319 (map 16). The roadway excavations have cut through a side of the hill, showing an oyster-shell midden, a little less than 1 meter deep, along the top. On the hill, back of the shell deposit among some trees, there is a hummock which may be an artificial mound. It does not appear to have been excavated.

The 1940 surface collection from the midden is classified below:

Weeden Island Complex	
Weeden Island Series:	
Weeden Island Incised	1
Weeden Island Plain	1
Wakulla Check Stamped	11
Swift Creek Complicated Stamped	2
West Florida Cord-marked	2
Deptford Complex	
Deptford Simple Stamped	1
Miscellaneous	
Smooth Plain	2
Residual Plain	16
Indeterminate Stamped	5
Other unclassified	1
Total sherds	42

This small collection is predominantly Weeden Island II.

50 This material was examined in the Heye Foundation Annex.

Tucker (Fr-4).—St. James Island is the land mass which makes up the southeastern corner of Franklin County. It is bounded on the west by the New River, on the north by the Crooked and Ocklockonee Rivers, on the east by Ocklockonee Bay, and on the south by St. George's Sound and the Gulf. On its southeastern tip there is a small peninsula which doubles back to the west forming Alligator Harbor. The Tucker site is situated on Alligator Harbor between that body of water and Tucker's Lake (map 16). There is an extensive shell midden at the site, several hundred meters long and over 100 meters wide. Near the western end of the midden is the burial mound excavated by Moore in 1902 (pp. 257-265). Heavy scrub growth has been cleared from a large central strip running through the midden site, either for the purpose of a firebreak or a right-of-way for a road (pl. 10, top). The shell had been superficially disturbed in this strip and sherds were easily obtained from the surface in 1940. Most of the shell is oyster although there are some conchs. It is difficult to estimate depth, but in undisturbed areas just off the cleared strip there are places which are probably 1 meter deep.

The 1940 collection from the Tucker midden is classified below:

Weeden Island Complex	
Weeden Island Series:	
Weeden Island Incised	16
Weeden Island Plain	61
Carrabelle Incised	12
Carrabelle Punctated	5
Keith Incised	4
St. Petersburg Incised	1
Wakulla Check Stamped	225
Santa Rosa-Swift Creek Complex	
Complicated Stamped Series:	
Swift Creek Complicated Stamped	45
Crooked River Complicated Stamped	4
St. Andrews Complicated Stamped	1
(Some of these complicated stamped sherds may belong to the Late Variety and as such are more properly grouped with Weeden Island than with the Santa Rosa-Swift Creek Complex.)	
Franklin Plain	6
Deptford Complex	
Deptford Linear Check Stamped	5
Deptford Bold Check Stamped	17
Deptford Simple Stamped	10

Miscellaneous

Plain Red	4
Smooth Plain	28
Residual Plain	253
Indeterminate Stamped	27
Unclassified	10
Total sherds....	734

Deptford, Santa Rosa-Swift Creek, and Weeden Island I and II Periods are all represented at this site, with Weeden Island predominating.

The Tucker burial mound is described by Moore (1902) as being 80 by 86 feet in basal diameters and about 9 feet high. The slope of the east side of the mound was more gentle than the other sides and appears to have been a ramp approach or graded way to the top of the mound. Evidences of the borrow pits could be seen nearby. Burial forms encountered were bundle, single skull, and primary flexed. Most of the 79 interments were grouped together on one side of the mound. Occasional flexed burials were found in pits in mound base. Two instances of oyster shells piled over burials and one of charcoal accompanying a burial were noted. Pottery was found largely in a mass cache deposit and also in smaller caches. Nonceramic artifacts were sometimes with burials, sometimes not. These included a flint scraper, polished celts, galena beads, sheet mica, copper fragments, shell cups, shell beads, and shell tools.

A few skulls showed frontooccipital deformation.

Tucker mound pottery was made with mortuary "kill" holes and also, in some cases, had been perforated after firing. Plain, incised, complicated stamped, check stamped, red painted, and pinched wares are all mentioned. The illustrated (Moore, 1902) pottery is classified as below:

Weeden Island Complex

Weeden Island Series:

- Weeden Island Incised...........Figs. 215, 221, 225, 227 (?)
- Weeden Island Plain.............Figs. 214, 216, 217, 220, 226
- Tucker Ridge-pinched ....Fig. 219

Swift Creek Complicated Stamped.................Figs. 223, 224
(Late Variety. These are very good examples.)

Santa Rosa-Swift Creek Complex

Basin Bayou Incised..................................Fig. 228
(This is a borderline specimen, verging toward Weeden Island Incised.)

This material is augmented by some of the Moore specimens from this mound which are in the R. S. Peabody Foundation. These include: One Carrabelle Punctated (No. 38939); six Swift Creek Complicated Stamped, Late Variety (Nos. 39014, 39031, 39107, 39101, 39025, 38951); and three Weeden Island Plain (Nos. 39076, 39120, 39083).

The abundance of Late Variety Swift Creek and the boldness of the Weeden Island Incised specimens represented in the illustrations place the mound in the Weeden Island I Period.

Yent mound (Fr-5).—The Yent mound was located by Moore (1902, pp. 265-274) as being one-half mile southeast of the Tucker mound (map 16). We were unable to locate it during the 1940 survey. This mound was 106 by 74 feet at the base. It sloped upward at a gentle angle on one side and had a small level top. Height was about 7.5 feet. Burials, totaling 74, were taken from the lower part of the body of the mound, from mound base, and from graves below mound base. Flexed, single skull, and bundle types were all present, and it was customary for the skeleton to be covered or surrounded with clam and conch shells. Pottery was found in a large cache and in smaller scattered caches of one or two vessels. Nonceramic artifacts occurred both with and apart from individual burials. Projectile points, celts, hammerstones, hones, plummets, and a soapstone monitor-type pipe were among the chipped- and ground-stone artifacts in the Yent mound. In addition, there was an object which from the description (Moore, 1902, p. 271) may be bar gorget. Also present were a sheet-mica spear point, worked sections of petrified wood, canine and fossil shark teeth, perforated porpoise teeth, imitation teeth of bone also perforated, a turtle-shell rattle, shell cups, shell beads, shell columellae pendants or plummets, a gorget of shell in form of a fish, worked tools of columellae and clam shells, imitation animal teeth of shell, and sheet-copper fragments.

Pottery was "killed" by perforation only; no ready-made mortuary ware, with holes, was encountered. Moore lists only plain, incised, and complicated stamped types. The illustrated (Moore, 1902) pottery is classified below:

Santa Rosa-Swift Creek Complex

Santa Rosa Stamped........Fig. 236
Crystal River Incised........Fig. 237
Swift Creek Complicated Stamped........Fig. 240
(Early Variety.)
West Florida Cord-marked........Fig. 238
(Early Variety.)

Miscellaneous

Unclassified Incised ....Figs. 234, 239
(Figure 234 may be Basin Bayou Incised; figure 239 is a very unique piece.)
Unclassified punctated ....Fig. 233
(Form of punctations like that of Santa Rosa Punctated.)
Plain, miniature vessel..............................Fig. 235

The Yent collection illustrated by Moore is supplemented by his gifts to the R. S. Peabody Foundation which include two Franklin Plain (Nos. 39325, 39103), one Carrabelle Punctated which is atypical in that it has the tetrapod base of the Santa Rosa-Swift Creek Complex, and five more of the plain, miniature vessels (Nos. 39175, 39176, 39178, 39174, 39166). These last are all under 5 cm. in height and are, proportionately, tall, narrow vase forms or flat-based pots.

This burial mound, in spite of the number of unusual vessels which cannot, at the present time, be classified satisfactorily, must date from the Santa Rosa-Swift Creek Period.

Ocklockonee Bay midden (Fr-6).—Approximately 1½ miles south of the mouth of the Ocklockonee River, in the southwest corner of Ocklockonee Bay, is a large clam-shell midden (map 16). The midden is distributed along a sand ridge which parallels the bay shore for a distance of 400 meters. An abandoned railroad cut exposes a cross section, revealing the depth of the deposit at .50 meter. In 1902 Moore (p. 282) located a low sand mound in this general area which he described under the title, "Mound near Ocklockonee Bay, Wakulla County." Although he locates the site in Wakulla County he indicates a Franklin County location for it on his site map (1902, frontispiece). The mound, like the midden discovered in the 1940 survey, was situated upon a sand ridge. As it had been thoroughly looted, Moore made no attempt to excavate but mentions bits of human bone and pottery scattered in the disturbed sand.

The surface collection gathered from the midden site in 1940 is classified below:

Weeden Island Complex	
Weeden Island Incised	1
Wakulla Check Stamped	9
Swift Creek Complicated Stamped	2
Miscellaneous	
Residual Plain	46
Indeterminate Stamped	5
Other unclassified	1
Total sherds....	64

This small collection places the midden as Weeden Island II.

Topsail Bluff (Fr-7).—Topsail Bluff is on St. George's Sound a trifle over 10 miles east of East Point (map 16). The shell midden is found along the top of a relatively high bluff or bank of the beach. The midden is thin, composed of oyster and conch shells, and stretches along the coast for 200 meters. Inland it has no extent of any consequence. The Topsail Bluff collection of 1940 is classified below:

Fort Walton Complex	
Pensacola Plain	1
Weeden Island Complex	
Weeden Island Series:	
Weeden Island Plain	2
Indian Pass Incised	1
Keith Incised	1
Wakulla Check Stamped	44
Swift Creek Complicated Stamped	10
Deptford Complex	
St. Simons Fiber-tempered Plain	2
Miscellaneous	
Smooth Plain	1
Residual Plain	55
Unclassified	6
Total sherds	123

This collection is predominantly Weeden Island II.

Brickyard Creek (Fr-8).—This site was worked by Moore (1903, pp. 441-443) but was not visited during the 1940 survey. The location is near the Apalachicola River in the northwestern corner of Franklin County (map 16). The mound, previously disturbed before Moore's visit, was 4 feet high and 35 feet in basal diameter. Only a few scrappy human-bone samples were found, and it appears as though most of the skeletal remains had decayed. Pottery was found in a mass deposit and in small caches. Other artifacts at random in the mound were projectiles, scrapers, hammerstones, hones, sheet-mica fragments, bone awls, and conch columella tools. Pottery vessels were "killed" by perforation. All the principal categories of pottery wares were present including both check and complicated stamped. The incised, punctated, and complicated stamped vessels described are most certainly Weeden Island and Late Swift Creek types. Figure 91 (Moore, 1903) is a Swift Creek fragment, and figure 92 (Moore, 1903) is an effigy lug, either Weeden Island or Fort Walton in style. The R. S. Peabody collection from this site contains two Weeden Island Plain vessels (Nos. 39268, 39089).

The mound is Weeden Island Period.

Nine-Mile Point (*Fr-9*).—Nine-Mile Point is 9 miles west of Apalachicola and 2 miles east of the Eleven-Mile Point site on St. Vincents Sound (map 16). It is a shell midden on the low bank back of the beach. The point is a slight projection into the sound dotted with a few palm trees (pl. 9, bottom). Behind and on each side of the point, palms, pines, scrub oak, and undergrowth form a heavy covering. Shells and sherds are found along the edge of the bank for 500 meters. The deposit extends back into the undergrowth for an unknown distance. At no point along the bank did the midden appear to be over .50 meter in depth.

The 1940 survey collection is classified below:

Weeden Island Complex	
Weeden Island Series:	
Weeden Island Incised	3
Weeden Island Plain	7
Carrabelle Punctated	1
Wakulla Check Stamped	13
Santa Rosa-Swift Creek Complex	
Alligator Bayou Stamped	1
Swift Creek Complicated Stamped	7
Deptford Complex	
Deptford Bold Check Stamped	1
St. Simons Fiber-tempered Plain	2
Miscellaneous	
Residual Plain	66
Unclassified	5
Total sherds	106

The Weeden Island Period predominates, probably both I and II, but Santa Rosa-Swift Creek and Deptford occupations are also indicated.

Eleven-Mile Point (*Fr-10*).—The most westerly site in Franklin County visited during the 1940 survey is Eleven-Mile Point, a midden on St. Vincents Sound 11 miles west of the city of Apalachicola (map 16). Here, in 1902 (pp. 214-216), Moore excavated a burial mound somewhere back inland from the shore. He recorded numerous shell middens along the sound shore, but excavated none of these. Eleven-Mile Point is a very slight projection extending out into St. Vincents Sound. There is little or no bank behind the beach on the point, and the shell midden lies 15 meters from the water's edge at high-tide level. Vegetation is thick surrounding the midden, but on the shell itself there are only a few palm trees. Shells of all types are found for 100 meters east-west along the beach front and for 40 meters back of the beach. Most of the midden has been excavated, presumably commercially, but a few remaining portions show the shell refuse to have been over 1 meter in depth.

The 1940 survey collection is classified below:

Fort Walton Complex	
Pensacola Plain	1
Weeden Island Complex	
Carrabelle Punctated	1
Wakulla Check Stamped	27
Swift Creek Complicated Stamped	3
Deptford Complex	
Deptford Simple Stamped	1
Miscellaneous	
Residual Plain	46
Unclassified	1
Total sherds	80

The collection is predominantly Weeden Island II, although the midden gives slight evidence of period mixture inasmuch as a Fort Walton sherd and a Deptford sherd are present.

The mound which Moore excavated at Eleven-Mile Point was situated some few hundred meters in from the shore and was not relocated by us in the 1940 survey. It was undoubtedly the burial place of the former inhabitants of one of the many middens which dot the coast in this neighborhood. As their contents differ it was probably not immediately related to the Eleven-Mile Point midden just discussed, at least not to the section sampled in the recent survey.

Moore (1902, pp. 214 ff.) described the mound as 50 feet in diameter and 3 feet high. Burials are mentioned as being present, but there is no description of numbers or types. Pottery was found in a mass mortuary deposit and also in smaller caches. Vessels were "killed" by perforation. No nonceramic artifacts are mentioned. Incised, complicated stamped, and plain pottery types are referred to, and there is a description of a compartment tray which is probably the type Weeden Island Plain. This specimen may very well be the one now in the R. S. Peabody Foundation (No. 57194). This bowl is the only piece from Eleven-Mile Point in the collections of that institution.

The illustrated pottery (Moore, 1902) is classified below:

Weeden Island Complex
Weeden Island Plain..............................Figs. 151, 152

Santa Rosa-Swift Creek Complex
Alligator Bayou Stamped..............................Fig. 150
Swift Creek Complicated Stamped.................Figs. 148, 149
(Figure 149 is definitely Early Variety.)

The mound is dated as Santa Rosa-Swift Creek. The Weeden Island Plain specimens are not sufficiently diagnostic to postulate a significant overlap with the Weeden Island Period. A wide range of vessel forms are included in the Weeden Island Plain type, and it may eventually be shown that a number of these forms are more characteristically found in Santa Rosa-Swift Creek Period contexts than in Weeden Island ones. At least several vessel forms may be characteristic of both the Weeden Island and Santa Rosa-Swift Creek Periods.

Green Point (Fr-11).—Moore (1902, pp. 249-256) located this mound just a short distance east of Porter's Bar (Fr-1). We searched the locality (map 16) but were unable to find the remains of the mound or a nearby midden. Quite probably the mound had disappeared by 1940. In 1902 it was 62 feet in basal diameter and between 2 and 5 feet in height, although even then the body of the mound had been considerably pulled down and spread by cultivation. The mound was of sand, occasionally blackened by organic material, and also contained pockets of shells. Most of the 80 burials in the mound were flexed or semiflexed, but single skull and bundle secondary burials were present as well. In some cases oyster shells may have been placed with or near burials as an intentional covering. Pottery was largely grouped in a special cache but was also found at various points in the mound and with individual burials. Other artifacts were associated with burials in some cases.

Moore records lance and projectile points, celts, hones, smoothing stones, hammerstones, shell cups, numerous shell gouges, grooved shell pendants, shell disks, a monitor pipe (stone or pottery?) with a basal perforation (Moore, 1902, fig. 213), and an "earthenware smoking pipe" of undisclosed form. Pottery vessels were "killed" by perforation. Plain, incised, complicated stamped, red painted, and fabric-marked wares are all mentioned. Moore also makes special note of the numerous vessels with tetrapodal supports and with notched or scalloped rims. A classification of the illustrated (Moore, 1902) material follows:

Santa Rosa-Swift Creek Complex
Crystal River Zoned Red....................Fig. 209
Swift Creek Complicated Stamped....................Figs. 205, 206, 208
(Early Variety.)
Franklin Plain....................Fig. 211

Miscellaneous
Unclassified complicated stamped....................Fig. 207
Plain (probably Weeden Island)....................Fig. 212

This collection is augmented by the R. S. Peabody Foundation material from the same mound. It includes three Swift Creek Complicated Stamped, Early Variety (Nos. 38924, 39075, 39248); one Franklin Plain (No. 39714); one bowl of the rare type Crystal River Negative Painted (No. 39147); and one Weeden Island Plain (No. 39205). In addition to the pottery, there are, as well, a stone monitor pipe, stone plummets, shell disks or *Busycon* saucers, shell spoons, shell chisels, pendants, and *Busycon* (or concave surface) celts.

The three pottery specimens in the Heye Foundation Annex collections are all of the type Swift Creek Complicated Stamped, Early Variety (No. 18/247).

This mound is clearly Santa Rosa-Swift Creek and shows a number of elements similar to those found at both Pierce mound A and Crystal River.

Huckleberry Landing (Fr-12).—This mound was not relocated in the 1940 survey. Moore (1902, pp. 234-238) discovered it about 5 miles up the Apalachicola River on the Jackson River tributary (map 16). The mound was made of sand with occasional pockets of clay or shell, 5 feet high, and had basal diameters of 38 by 52 feet. Nearby were extensive shell middens. Burials were in all parts of the mound, some being on or even below mound base, while others were very superficial. About two-thirds of the 34 skeletons were secondarily treated, being either single skulls or bundle interments; the remaining third were flexed primary burials. Moore noted pathology of the bone on two burials. Pottery vessels and nonceramic artifacts were found at various places in the mound, sometimes with burials. Celts, hones, pebble hammers, sheet mica, stone pendants, composite ear spools of pottery and copper, and turtle-shell rattles were all in the mound. Two pottery pipes were also recovered. One, a monitor style, was unassociated; the second, an equal-arm elbow form, came from a burial lying near the surface. Because of the location of the latter Moore admits the possibility that the burial and the accompanying pipe might be intrusive.

Pottery vessels were "killed" by perforation. Plain, complicated stamped, and a few sherds of check stamped pottery are described. The features of tetrapodal supports and scalloped rims are given special mention. Three illustrated sherds (Moore, 1902, figs. 173, 174, 175) are all Swift Creek Complicated Stamped, Early Variety. Two small bowls (Moore, 1902, figs. 171, 176) appear to be Weeden Island Plain. These illustrations of Moore's are bolstered by two Swift Creek Complicated Stamped Early Variety specimens from this same mound, which are in the R. S. Peabody Foundation (Nos. 39226, 39284) and three Early Variety Swift Creek in the Heye Foundation Annex (Nos. 18/250).

The mound is Santa Rosa-Swift Creek Period.

Five-Mile Point (*Fr-13*).—This shell midden is just west of Five-Mile Point, a small promontory on St. Vincents Sound, 5 miles west of Apalachicola (map 16). The bank behind the beach is about 2 meters high, and a thin shell midden extends for 100 meters along this bank. Undergrowth made it difficult to determine the inland scope of the site. Fragments of burned clay with stick and grass impressions were found in the midden, apparently house debris. A moderately large collection was obtained in 1940 and is given below:

Fort Walton Complex	
Fort Walton Series:	
Fort Walton Incised	20
Lake Jackson Plain	2
Pensacola Series:	
Pensacola Incised	4
Pensacola Plain	8
Weeden Island Complex	
Wakulla Check Stamped	3
Miscellaneous	
Smooth Plain	1
Residual Plain	124
Unclassified	1
Total sherds	163

The midden dates from the Fort Walton Period.

Pierce mounds and middens (*Fr-14*).—Moore (1902, pp. 217-229) located the Pierce group of mounds as being between 1 and 1.5 miles west of Apalachicola (map 16). The 1940 survey recorded two mounds and a considerable midden area at about this distance from the heart of the city. There are not five mounds, such as Moore describes, in the section 1 to 1.5 miles westward from the city. This may be because some of the mounds were completely excavated and leveled by Moore or by others who followed him. To the best of our knowledge, however, the site examined by us was the old Pierce site, as distinct from a number of other mounds which Moore worked in this same general vicinity.

The delta country of the Apalachicola was undoubtedly one of the most favorable and most densely populated areas for prehistoric peoples. In and surrounding the town there are numerous midden areas. Surface sherd collections were made in three places in the zone of the Pierce site. These various sublocations are discussed below, and the pottery from each is classified.

About a mile west of Apalachicola, touching on the railroad, and on the edge of the high land which lies south of the Apalachicola River swamps, there is an open field lying to the east of the modern cemetery. The field measures approximately 50 meters north-south and 75 meters east-west. The remains of what must once have been a great shell midden are clustered around a few palm trees (pl. 11, top). Judging from these small blocks around the trees, the depth of the shell was originally over 2 meters in some places. If there were any mounds in the field, they too have been destroyed. The 1940 collection from this area is tabulated below:

Fort Walton Complex	
Lake Jackson Plain	1
Pensacola Plain	1
Weeden Island Complex	
Weeden Island Series:	
Weeden Island Incised	3
Weeden Island Plain	9
Carrabelle Punctated	6
Keith Incised	2
Wakulla Check Stamped	13
Swift Creek Complicated Stamped	8
West Florida Cord-marked	1
Deptford Complex	
Deptford Simple Stamped	1
Miscellaneous	
Smooth Plain	4
Plain Red	1
Residual Plain	79
Unclassified	6
Total sherds	135

This collection is Weeden Island I and II.

Following the railroad one-quarter of a mile west of the first area there is a second refuse area and mound lying on the west side of the modern cemetery. The mound is a flat-topped pyramid, 2.50 meters in height, approximately 15 meters square at the summit, and 30 meters square at the base. Its measurements correspond roughly with those given by Moore (1902, p. 228) for Pierce mound C.

The north side of the mound has been sliced away by the railroad cut, exposing a sand and midden fill covered over with a shell mantle (pl. 11, bottom).

A shell-scattered village area of 3 or 4 acres lies to the south of the mound, and beyond this, on the south, as well as the north and west, are dense swamplands.

The collection from this section, both the mound top and surrounding midden, is classified below:

Fort Walton Complex	
Fort Walton Incised	11
Pensacola Incised	7
Safety Harbor Incised	1
Weeden Island Complex	
Weeden Island Series:	
Weeden Island Plain	1
Carrabelle Incised	1
Wakulla Check Stamped	15
Miscellaneous	
Smooth Plain	2
Residual Plain	52
Unclassified	2
Total sherds	92

This collection unit is divided between the Weeden Island II and Fort Walton Periods.

On a small rise of ground just west of the second area there is another mound [51] and shell-refuse area. The distance betwen the two locations is some 20 meters, and the two are separated by a sluggish stream and swamp-filled ravine. The mound is small, steep, 3 meters high, and is situated very near the railroad cut. The shape of the mound is somewhat indeterminate, but on the south side there is a sloping projection which may be a ramp. Sherds and shells are found on a patch of high ground extending some 75 meters south of the

[51] It is difficult to identify this mound with those listed by Moore at the Pierce site. The most likely is mound B (Moore, 1902, p. 228), although this mound was considerably higher than 3 meters (approximately 10 feet). Possibly subsequent digging and erosion have reduced its size.

mound. A collection of sherds from this village area, as well as the mound summit, is given below:

Fort Walton Complex	
Fort Walton Incised	1
Weeden Island Complex	
Wakulla Check Stamped	13
Swift Creek Complicated Stamped	3
West Florida Cord-marked	1
Miscellaneous	
Residual Plain	16
Unclassified	4
Total sherds	38

This third collection is largely Weeden Island Period.

Considered as a whole, the three Pierce surface collections, which represent a sampling from only a relatively small area of the total shell refuse in the vicinity, indicate occupation for the Weeden Island I and II and the Fort Walton Periods. Earlier Santa Rosa-Swift Creek occupation is not well represented.

Of the Pierce mounds excavated by Moore (1902, pp. 217-228), only the first, Pierce mound A, yielded results of any consequence. This mound must have been rectanguloid and flat-topped, as the measurements given are basal diameters, 96 by 76 feet, and summit diameters of the same axes, 40 by 34 feet. Height of the mound was 8 feet. No mention was made of a ramp approach; apparently none existed. The mound was composed of yellow sand except near the base and in occasional irregular lenses in the body; here oyster shells were common. On or near mound base were many evidences of fire. Of the 99 burials the greater part were primary and flexed although there were a few examples of extended burials and of secondary types.[52] The latter were single skulls, miscellaneous bone piles, and at least one mass burial of a secondary nature. Evidences of fires having been placed over or near burials were common although no true cremations were found.

Pottery was found in small caches in various parts of the mound, usually near the base where most of the burials had also been placed. Some instances of pottery with specific burials were noted. Other artifacts were both at random in the body of the mound and with individual burials. The nonceramic artifacts included chipped projectiles and chisels, stone celts, stone plummets, pearls (fresh-water), a copper tube, copper ear ornaments with hammered-silver plating, shell

[52] Moore notes that this number represented a great many more individuals.

beads, shell drinking cups, gougelike tools of shell columellae, a large bone gorget (identified as bison bone), and canine teeth.

Pottery vessels were "killed" by perforation. Such pottery traits or types as plain, incised, complicated stamped, and red painted wares are mentioned or illustrated. Miniature vessels, tetrapodal supports, notched or scalloped rims, and cord-marking were also noted by Moore. A pottery pipe of the monitor type was recovered. Illustrated pottery is classified below:

Santa Rosa-Swift Creek Complex
Crystal River Series:
Crystal River Zoned Red....................Figs. 158, 163
Pierce Zoned Red..............................Fig. 155
Santa Rosa Stamped..............................Fig. 162
Swift Creek Complicated Stamped......................Fig. 165

Miscellaneous
Unclassified ....Figs. 156, 160, 164

In the R. S. Peabody Foundation collections there are two specimens from the Pierce mound A. One is Pierce Zoned Red (No. 39301); the other is a monitor clay pipe (No. 39182). This last may, or may not, be the one to which Moore refers.

The mound is dated as Santa Rosa-Swift Creek. A number of interesting ceramic elements occur, particularly the types of the Crystal River Series and the unusual plain-ware forms such as a multiple-orifice vessel and a "grubworm" effigy.

Of the other mounds of the Pierce group, there is little to aid in cultural identification. Mound C, probably the mound of the second 1940 collection, was trenched and found to be constructed over a basal shell layer. Flexed burials and sherds of the check and complicated stamped types were encountered. Mound D proved, according to Moore, to be domiciliary in that it was composed chiefly of refuse. Mound E he also defined as domiciliary, but in this last case the mound was of clean sand rather than refuse.

Jackson mound (Fr-15).—Moore (1902, pp. 229-234) found this mound 2.5 miles west-northwest of Apalachicola (map 16). He describes it as 9 feet high with a basal diameter of 72 by 66 feet. No other comments are made as to mound shape. The data on the 26 burials are none too sound, as skeletal material was badly decayed; however, one cremation was definitely recorded. Other bone remains were centrally located in the mound. Bundle and single skull types of secondary burials were met with, but other identifications were uncertain. Pottery was, for the most part, concentrated on one edge of the mound in a special cache. Other artifacts, such as pipes, were found with burials. Projectile points, hematite ore, celts, hones, smoothing stones, hammerstones, galena, stone beads, plummets or pendants of stone, a plummet of quartz crystal, and a sheet-copper fragment were also present.

The pottery pipes from the Jackson mound come with a burial which was only 18 inches from the surface. This is a notable provenience, as all other burials were found on or near mound base. Also, the bones of this particular burial are reported to have been in a much better state of preservation than the others in the mound. Because of these facts Moore was of the opinion that the burial and the pipes might be later than the mound proper and its contents (see also the Huckleberry Landing site, Fr-12). The pipes in question are of the elbow variety (Moore, 1902, figs. 166, 167) made for the insertion of a stem or mouthpiece of wood or reed. One has a slightly flaring bowl and crimped or scalloped rim suggestive of the vessel rim treatment of the Santa Rosa-Swift Creek pottery type Franklin Plain. The edge of the bowl is also ticked with fine incised notches in a manner similar to a stone pipe from Crystal River, Ci-1 (Moore, 1903, fig. 38). Another pipe, found in the marginal fill of the Jackson mound, was made of steatite and is described as being of the "common rectangular block pattern" (Moore, 1902, p. 232).

Pottery vessels from the Jackson Mound were "killed" by perforation. Plain, incised, and complicated stamped are the only major ware categories mentioned. Illustrated (Moore, 1902) material is classified below:

Weeden Island Complex
Swift Creek Complicated Stamped......................Fig. 168
(Late Variety.)

Santa Rosa-Swift Creek Complex
Alligator Bayou Stamped..............................Fig. 170
Swift Creek Complicated Stamped......................Fig. 169
(Early Variety.)

A single vessel from the Jackson Mound in the R. S. Peabody Foundation collections is a plain piece, possibly Weeden Island Plain (No. 39108).

The Alligator Stamped type decoration on the multiple-orifice vessel at this site is interesting and further substantiates the dating of Pierce mound A where a multiple-orifice vessel was found in a context believed to be Santa Rosa-Swift Creek. The Jackson mound may be verging toward Weeden Island I, as suggested by the very definite Late Variety Swift Creek bowl; however, Santa Rosa-Swift Creek elements are dominant.

Other sites in Franklin County.—In the 1940 survey we visited a large shell midden on East Point peninsula, across the mouth of the bay from the city of Apalachicola. There are two middens at this site, both semilunar in form and composed of oyster shells (pl. 2, top). They are about 25 meters from the water's edge on a flat, sandy point. Both are as much as 3 meters in height. Only a single plain, sand-tempered sherd was found at the site after a diligent search. There is little doubt that these shell piles are artificial and of human origin. Their size, their undisturbed condition (as of 1940), and the scarcity of artifactual material combine to make the site extremely attractive as a place for future work pointed toward the problem of the earlier horizons.

Additional sites excavated by Moore in the Apalachicola vicinity but not included in the present analyses for lack of data are the Cool Spring mound, the mound near Apalachicola, the Cemetery mound, and the Singer mound (Moore, 1902, pp. 216-217 and p. 229). The mound near Apalachicola seems to have been a sterile sand structure and was considered domiciliary, but the others were burial mounds, probably of the Weeden Island or Santa Rosa-Swift Creek Periods. A possible exception to this last is the Cool Spring mound which might have been a Fort Walton Period temple mound used as a burial place. Farther east, near Carrabelle, Moore (1902, p. 257) mentions a mound on the west bank of the Carrabelle River about 1.5 miles inland. This was a burial mound but contained little.

In the Florida State Museum at Gainesville there is a collection taken from a mound near Apalachicola. The collection was presented to the museum by H. L. Grady. It consists of Fort Walton Period vessels, an elbow pipe of the Georgia Lamar Period type, shell pins, a *Busycon,* shell celts, and stone celts. Possibly this mound was one of the above which were excavated by Moore (1902).

LEON COUNTY

Lake Jackson (Le-1).—See excavation account of Lake Jackson, Leon County (Le-1), under the section, "Excavations on the Northwest Coast: 1940."

Lake Lafayette (Le-2).—Lake Lafayette lies less than 10 miles southeast of Lake Jackson.[53] About 1 mile northwest of the northwest tip of Lake Lafayette there is a flat-topped pyramidal mound of clay surrounded by fields which bear evidence of having been an old village site (map 16). The mound is oriented north-northeast by south-

[53] See Boyd, 1939, p. 272, for mention of this site.

southwest and is 36 meters on a side at the base. Estimated height is 4.50 meters. The only visible excavation is a hole made in the top. In 1940 a sherd collection was gathered from the surrounding village area. This collection is classified below:

Fort Walton Complex	
Fort Walton Series:	
Fort Walton Incised	4
Lake Jackson Plain	6
Pensacola Plain	1
Leon Check Stamped	2
Lamar Complicated Stamped	7
Weeden Island Complex	
Carrabelle Punctated	1
Wakulla Check Stamped	1
Miscellaneous	
Residual Plain	128
(Most of these were body fragments from Fort Walton Series vessels.)	
Indeterminate Stamped	9
Other unclassified	4
Total sherds	163

This village site and mound must date from the Fort Walton Period.

Rollins site (Le-3).—At a centrally located point on the eastern shore of Lake Jackson there is a small peninsula that protrudes very noticeably into the lake.[54] The Rollins mound and site are located on this peninsula (map 16). The mound is situated on the top of the high bluffs that overlook the lake valley. It is a flat-topped pyramidal structure which has no longer retained its full rectangular form. The base measures 27 meters north-south and 25 meters east-west. Estimated height is approximately 2 meters. There is a large, irregular excavation in the top. In the adjoining cultivated fields 5 Fort Walton Incised and 13 plain (probable Fort Walton Series) sherds were found in the red loamy soil. The site dates from the Fort Walton Period.

San Luis Mission site (Le-4).—The old San Luis Spanish Mission site is located at the James Messer Place, 2½ miles west of Tallahassee[55] (map 16). Along the crest of an eroded hill slope, in back of the Messer house, a number of aboriginal sherds and some Spanish olive-jar fragments were recovered in the small washes and

[54] See Boyd, 1939, p. 272, for mention of this site.

[55] Boyd, 1939, pp. 264 ff.

ravines. More pottery fragments were also picked up in the roadway to the west of the house. Three of the aboriginal sherds were of a faint complicated stamped type, suggestive of the Lamar style; the remainder were all plain. In addition to the 1940 survey material there are a few sherds in the United States National Museum (No. 148125) from this same site. One of these is a folded and crimped rim of the Lake Jackson or Lamar type; one is of the type Aucilla Incised; and three are unclassified plain.

The San Luis site is well documented in the historic sources. Excavations in the site, by Dr. M. F. Boyd, have revealed Spanish Colonial features. The limited aboriginal ceramic evidence places the site as post-Fort Walton. This late contact period in northwest Florida has been referred to as the Leon-Jefferson Complex (H. G. Smith, 1948).

Lake Iamonia (Le-5).—The exact location of this site is not known, so that its indication on map 16 is given only as the lake. The collection, which is in the Peabody Museum, Harvard University (Nos. 12-11/81200-81202), is apparently from a site unit, however. It is classified and described below:

Fort Walton Complex	
Fort Walton Series:	
Fort Walton Incised	17
Lake Jackson Plain	12
"Chunky" sherd (Lake Jackson Plain)	1
Miscellaneous	
Indeterminate Stamped	1
Baked-clay ball with simple stamped decoration, diameter 4 cm.	1
Total sherds and artifacts	32

The collection is clearly Fort Walton Period.

WAKULLA COUNTY

Marsh Island (Wa-1).—Marsh Island, on Ocklockonee Bay, was not visited on the 1940 survey (map 16). Moore (1902, pp. 274-281) describes the mound as oblong with rounded corners, being 98 by 68 feet at the base with a height of 7 feet. It is not clear as to whether or not the top was a flattened platform. About one-half of the burials encountered were of the bundle type, another one-quarter were single skulls, and a final quarter were primary flexed burials. These burials were found in two groups within the mound. Seven burials, some containing more than one individual, came from the upper 2 or 3 feet, as near as can be judged. The remainder were found on, near, or below mound base. This distinction is of real importance as it represents a cultural stratification. By position in the mound, and by accompanying artifacts, Moore demonstrates the seven upper burials to be later and intrusive. In view of this distinction, the two components from Marsh Island are discussed separately.

The Marsh Island Intrusive graves (Moore, 1902, pp. 275-277, Burial Nos. 61, 70, 85, 92, 104, 105, and 91) contained, in five cases, more than one individual. Interment was secondary, of either massed skulls and long bones or simply skulls. Another burial had only a single skull, and the remaining burial was an urn interment of an infant. One of the group secondary burials showed partial calcination of the bones, implying either actual cremation or partial burning of the bone in situ. Shell pins, shell beads, and, in the case of the urn burial, pottery vessels were the only completely native artifacts found with the upper level or Intrusive burials. European artifacts, or objects fashioned by the Indians from European goods, were more numerous. These included scissors, iron tools or weapons, sleigh bells, tubular brass beads, glass beads, and brass bracelets. The two pottery vessels with the urn burial, one as a container and one as a cover, were not "killed" by perforation. These vessels (Moore, 1902, fig. 241) are of the type Marsh Island Incised.

Loose in the mound was a single discoidal stone with two concave surfaces. The cultural associations of this object in the mound are not known; however, as the discoidal stone is so commonly found on the Middle Mississippian horizon throughout the southeastern states it is likely that it is a part of the Intrusive component at Marsh Island.

Most of the Intrusive grave skulls showed frontooccipital deformation.

There is no doubt that the Intrusive component at this site is late, extending well into the historic contact period. The Marsh Island Incised type differs from typical Fort Walton Period types, but I am inclined to believe it about contemporaneous; thus, secondary burials and the urn burial equate more closely with the Fort Walton Period than they do with the somewhat later Leon-Jefferson Period of the missionized Indians.

The lower component of the Marsh Island mound, presumably the component to be identified with the builders of the mound, is characterized by masses of shell placed over some of the approximately 100 skeletons, by undeformed crania, by the large mortuary cache of "killed" pottery buried on one side of the mound, by scattered pottery caches, and by nonceramic artifacts both with and apart from individual burials. Celts, smoothing stones, hones, plummets, hematite and plumbago ore, and sheet-mica fragments were present. Plain, incised, complicated stamped, and red painted pottery categories are listed. Illustrated (Moore, 1902) ware is classified below:

Weeden Island Complex	
Weeden Island Series:	
Weeden Island Incised	Fig. 242
Weeden Island Plain	Figs. 243, 244, 246
Swift Creek Complicated Stamped	Fig. 248
Miscellaneous	
Unclassified	Fig. 247

Three vessels in the R. S. Peabody Foundation undoubtedly belong with the lower component. These are a Swift Creek Complicated Stamped, Late Variety (No. 39922) and two Weeden Island Plain (Nos. 39143, 39170).

The lower mound component is Weeden Island I Period.

Surf (Wa-2).—Surf is a small settlement on the north shore of Ocklockonee Bay, 2 miles west of the Ocklockonee Bay bridge (map 16). There is a low shell midden in the midst of the settlement at a distance of about 25 meters from the bay. In all, the shell covers an area approximately 100 meters square. The refuse is a mixture of black midden and clam shells which has been thoroughly dug over and disturbed. A small collection was made here in 1940:

Weeden Island Complex	
Weeden Island Plain	3
Wakulla Check Stamped	20
Miscellaneous	
Residual Plain	27
Unclassified	1
Total sherds	51

The midden is clearly Weeden Island II.

Nichols (Wa-3).—On the north side of Ocklockonee Bay, near the mouth of the Sopchoppy, are the Nichols Old Fields (map 16). The distance from Surf is a little less than 1 mile. Moore (1902, pp. 281-282) investigated three artificial tumuli at this site and also described clam-shell middens. A midden, 25 meters in diameter with additional scatterings of shell, was located by our survey. A sand mound was noted 150 meters to the west of the midden area, presumably one of those excavated by Moore; the other two which he mentioned were not located. The 1940 surface collection from the midden is classified below:

Weeden Island Complex	
Weeden Island Series:	
Weeden Island Incised	2
Weeden Island Plain	5
Wakulla Check Stamped	6
Swift Creek Complicated Stamped	1
Miscellaneous	
Smooth Plain	5
Residual Plain	24
Unclassified	4
Total sherds	47

This midden dates as Weeden Island II.

The mound at Nichols which Moore excavated was at that time 5.5 feet high, 100 feet in diameter at the base, flat-topped, and with a ramp approach to the summit. It was made largely of sand but with basal and secondary layers of shell, suggesting its construction in stages. The 33 burials were all superficial in the top or sides of the mound. Most burials were flexed but a few were extended. Celts, shell beads, pebble hammers, and chert flakes accompanied some burials. Lump galena and a finger ring carved from a palm seed (?) were found loose in the mound.

Frontooccipital cranial deformation was noted on most of the skulls from the mound.

The only pottery in the mound was in the form of sherds, undoubtedly midden refuse. This included complicated stamped, check stamped, red painted, and punctated types. A loop handle is also mentioned.

Lack of associated pottery with the burials makes it impossible to date the mound. The mode of burial in the mound summit and flanks and the shape of the mound suggest the Fort Walton Period, but the sherds in the mound fill, except for the loop handle, sound more like Weeden Island.

Neither of the other two mounds described by Moore can be satisfactorily characterized. One of them may have been a midden heap; the other possibly was of the domiciliary type.

Hall site (Wa-4).—The Hall site is on Dickson's Bay, 1.5 miles northeast of the town of Panacea (map 16). The midden, composed of oyster and conch shells and black organic refuse, is exceedingly rich in cultural material, and as the site has been excavated recently, probably by commercial shell diggers, sherds cover the surface in great profusion (pl. 10, bottom). The area of occupation is about 250 by 100 meters at the widest point. The 1940 sherd collection is tabulated below:

Weeden Island Complex	
Weeden Island Series:	
Weeden Island Incised	3
Weeden Island Plain	72
Carrabelle Incised	3
Carrabelle Punctated	8
Keith Incised	2
Tucker Ridge-pinched	1
Wakulla Check Stamped	21
Swift Creek Complicated Stamped (Mostly Late Variety.)	34
Miscellaneous	
Smooth Plain	6
Residual Plain	204
Indeterminate Stamped	10
Other unclassified	7
Total sherds	371

The midden collection can be placed at Weeden Island I and II Periods.

The mound which was said by Moore (1902, pp. 282-303) to be very near the shell midden was not relocated in 1940. In Moore's time it was of circular outline, 60 feet in diameter at the base and 8 feet high. It may have had a flat summit platform, although there is some question about this as a previous excavator had dug a hole 10 feet in diameter in the top of the mound, possibly flattening what might have been a conical top. A causeway was attached to the mound on the west side. It was graded at its extremity but leveled off at a height of 5 feet, at which elevation it was conjoined with the mound. This may have served as a ramp approach to the mound summit, but the discrepancy in the elevation between causeway and mound makes this seem doubtful.

A bundle burial and some single skulls were found in the causeway. The first was accompanied by grooved-stone plummets. A shell cup and some pitted masses of plumbago were also discovered in the causeway fill. In the mound proper 31 burials were massed at one side. These were divided among the single skull, bundle, and flexed types. Oyster shells were only occasionally found placed over skeletons. Pottery was mostly confined to a large cache, and nonpottery artifacts, although sometimes with individual burials, were usually found apart from immediate burial associations. Celts, hammerstones, smoothing stones, hematite ore, lump galena, and shell beads were all taken from the mound. Pottery was "killed" with perforations and also made with holes as ceremonial mortuary ware. No check stamped pottery is mentioned, but other categories, including complicated stamped, were encountered. The pottery illustrated by Moore (1902) is classified below:

Weeden Island Complex

Weeden Island Series:

Weeden Island Incised....Figs. 249, 251, 254, 257, 262, 265, 273, 277, 281

Weeden Island Plain.....Figs. 253, 256, 260, 268, 269, 274, 275

Carrabelle Incised ....Figs. 264, 267

(Figure 264 also has elements of type Keith Incised in the rim border.)

Indian Pass Incised...............................Fig. 252

Weeden Island Series adornos..........Figs. 278, 279, 280, 283

Rattlesnake element ....Fig. 282

Swift Creek Complicated Stamped.............Figs. 271, 276 (?)
(Late variety.)

Santa Rosa-Swift Creek Complex

Crystal River Incised................................Fig. 255

Pierce Zoned Red....................................Fig. 270

Swift Creek Complicated Stamped.......................Fig. 272
(Early Variety.)

Miscellaneous

Unclassified incised ....Fig. 258

(Very unusual vessel decorated in a champlévé incision technique. Designs reminiscent of Weeden Island, Crystal River, and Hopewellian (as expressed in Ohio Valley bone-carving).)

The R. S. Peabody collections contain two specimens from this mound. The first of these (No. 39124) is a Swift Creek Late Variety vessel; the second (No. 39119) is a Weeden Island Plain compartment tray. In the Heye Foundation Annex there is a small collection of sherds from the Moore excavations at "Panacea Springs" (No. 16/3357). As Moore found nothing in the Panacea mound proper (Moore, 1902, p. 304), it seems more likely that this lot of material came from the nearby Hall mound diggings. Most of these sherds are Weeden Island types or Swift Creek, Late Variety, but there is one fragment of greater interest. This is a bowl piece, the interior of which has been covered with a black paint that is now quite eroded. Almost assuredly this is a Crystal River Negative Painted specimen.

The totality of evidence from the Hall mound dates the site as Weeden Island I. There is also some evidence to suggest a slight overlap with the earlier Santa Rosa-Swift Creek Period.

Spring Creek (Wa-5).—This site was visited in the 1940 survey, but we were unable to locate any midden area in the immediate vicinity of the mound which Moore (1902, pp. 304-305) excavated in 1902. The site is on the Spring Creek which drains into Apalachee Bay (map 16). The mound was curiously ridge-shaped in that it sloped gradually upward on an east-west line for 104 feet. Maximum height at the west end was 8 feet. The western slope of the mound was a steep descent. The transverse diameter of the mound was 68 feet at the base. Nothing is said of the summit. Quite possibly this was a mound similar to the Hall mound in that the mound nucleus had an elongation, causeway, or ramp attached to it. Nine burials were met with in the mound but these were almost completely decayed and indeterminable as to burial form. No major cache of pottery was discovered, but several perforated pots were uncovered at various locations. Nonceramic artifacts occurred with burials on occasion. Projectile or lance points, a celt, hammerstones, plummets, a gorget, a shell drinking cup, sheet-mica fragments, composite copper and bone ear ornaments, a shark tooth, and two stone pipes make up the mound inventory of nonpottery goods. One of the pipes is not described; the other is referred to as being of soapstone and of "the usual shape."

Only plain and incised pottery is mentioned. The only vessel illustrated is of the type Crystal River Incised.

On the basis of the single vessel the mound is dated as Santa Rosa-Swift Creek.

West Goose Creek (Wa-6).—The West Goose Creek Fishery site is about 1 mile southeast of Spring Creek. The site faces the waters of Apalachee Bay (map 16) on the east. The midden was located on a very slight rise of ground in the marshlands bordering the bay. In extent, it was 250 meters north-south and 50 to 100 meters east-west. Unexcavated portions around the edges are .75 meter deep. It is quite probable that the central area was 1.50 meters deep. The site has been completely gutted by commercial operations. A large surface collection was made in 1940:

Weeden Island Complex	
Wakulla Check Stamped	46
Santa Rosa-Swift Creek Complex	
Santa Rosa Series:	
Basin Bayou Incised	1
Santa Rosa Stamped	1
Franklin Plain	2
Swift Creek Complicated Stamped	9
West Florida Cord-marked	1
Deptford Complex	
Deptford Series:	
Deptford Linear Check Stamped	4
Deptford Bold Check Stamped	14
Deptford Simple Stamped	7
St. Simons Fiber-tempered Plain	3
St. Marks Plain	23
Miscellaneous	
Smooth Plain	1
Residual Plain	53
Indeterminate Stamped	1
Other unclassified	3
Total sherds	178

The midden dates from the Deptford, Santa Rosa-Swift Creek, and Weeden Island II Periods.

Near St. Marks (Wa-7).—A small collection was donated to Peabody Museum, Yale University, by A. B. Mason in 1883 (Cat. No. 3837). It is a group of sherds which were found in the bank of a small creek, along with an "Indian skeleton," near St. Marks. The location is not known more exactly and is indicated on map 16 only in a general fashion. This material is classified below:

Santa Rosa-Swift Creek Complex	
Swift Creek Complicated Stamped	61
Deptford Complex	
Deptford Series:	
Deptford Linear Check Stamped	1
Deptford Simple Stamped	1
Alexander Incised	1
St. Simons Fiber-tempered Plain	3
Miscellaneous	
Steatite sherds	1
Total sherds	68

The site is essentially Santa Rosa-Swift Creek but with a small scattering of Deptford and, possibly, earlier materials.

Mound Field (*Wa-8*).—The 1940 excavations in the Mound Field midden site (see maps 9 and 16) have been treated under the section "Excavations on the Northwest Coast: 1940." The nearby mound which Moore excavated (Moore, 1902, pp. 306-320) was between 9 and 11 feet high, 61 feet in diameter at the base, and 15 feet in diameter across the summit plateau. A graded approach joined the mound on the west side. The 21 burials were all secondary in as far as determinations could be made on the badly decayed skeletal material. Bundle and single skull were the common forms. All were superficial in the mound except two which were found near the base. The mortuary pottery was massed on one side of the mound, but nonceramic artifacts were found at random through the mound. These were projectile and lance points, hones, and sheet-mica fragments. Pottery vessels were "killed" by perforation and were also made with holes as special mortuary ware. All the principal categories of pottery were present in the mound except check stamped. The illustrated pottery in Moore (1902) is classified below:

Weeden Island Complex
- Weeden Island Series:
  - Weeden Island Incised............Figs. 285, 288, 292, 294, 300
  - Weeden Island Plain......Figs. 287, 289, 290, 291, 297, 298, 299
  - Weeden Island Punctated..........................Fig. 286
- Swift Creek Complicated Stamped.........Figs. 295, 296, 302, 303 (Late Variety.)
- Weeden Island rim effigies........................Figs. 304, 305

Santa Rosa-Swift Creek Complex
- Swift Creek Complicated Stamped......................Fig. 301 (Early Variety?)

This mound is clearly Weeden Island I.

Bird Hammock, mound A (*Wa-9*).—This mound lies 2 or 3 miles inland from the coast near St. Marks (map 16). Moore (1918, pp. 561-564) excavated two mounds in Bird Hammock in 1918. He describes them as A and B, situated at a distance of some 300 meters apart. We visited the mounds in 1940, but no midden area was observed near mound A and no collection was made. In Moore's time the mound was 8.5 feet high and 66 feet in basal diameter. The base was circular but nothing else was said of the mound conformation. Fourteen burials were found in the upper part of the mound and one on mound base. All were too decayed to determine burial positions. There was also a single deposit of calcined human bones. Pottery was in a mass deposit, composed largely of broken vessels. Sheet-mica fragments were the only nonceramic goods recovered. There was no definite evidence of "killing" by perforation, but two vessels were made with holes. The two specimens which Moore illustrates are Weeden Island Incised (Moore, 1918, fig. 32) and Weeden Island Plain (Moore, 1918, fig. 34). Sherds from the mound attest the presence also of check stamped and complicated stamped wares.

The limited evidence places the mound as Weeden Island Period.

Bird Hammock, mound B (Wa-10).—Moore (1918, pp. 563-564) located Bird Hammock mound B in a southerly direction from mound A. We also located a mound in this vicinity in 1940 (map 16). The mound that we saw had been excavated at some time in the past, presumably by Moore, and again more recently. Several sherds were picked up in the fresh excavations. Surrounding the mound were a number of low hummocks covered with shell refuse. These may have been aboriginal house sites. Moore investigated these humps and found them filled with kitchen refuse. The height of the burial mound in Moore's time was almost 6 feet and the basal diameters were 56 and 75 feet. From this, one deduces that the mound was either oval or rectanguloid. Two ramps, one on the southeast side and one on the southwest, did not lead to the mound top but joined the mound at about half its height (3 feet). One of these ramps was still visible in 1940. Moore said nothing about the conformation of the top of the mound.

Burials, 15 in number, were found at various places in the mound but except for a group of four skulls, obviously indicating secondary interment, nothing could be determined as to burial position in view of the advanced decay of the bones. Pottery was not in a mass deposit but in a number of smaller caches. Lances, projectile points, and sandstone hones were taken from burial associations. Pottery vessels from this mound were "killed" with a basal perforation, but there is little description given for the pottery. A single piece is mentioned as being decorated with red and white pigment, a rather curious combination in this area and context. A classification of the sherds picked out of the fresh excavations is given below:

Weeden Island Complex	
Weeden Island Plain	6
Swift Creek Complicated Stamped	7
Santa Rosa-Swift Creek Complex	
Franklin Plain	1
Miscellaneous	
Residual Plain	27
Total sherds	41

The probabilities favor a Weeden Island I dating.

Work place (Wa-11).—There is an old occupation area, marked by sherds but very little shell, on the A. L. Work place, 3 miles above the junction of the St. Marks and Wakulla Rivers on the east bank of the Wakulla. The country is flat river-bottom land of very sandy clay. Sherds have been upturned by cultivation over an area of several acres. The 1940 collection is classified below:

Fort Walton Complex	
Fort Walton Series:	
Fort Walton Incised	4
Lake Jackson Plain	6
Lamar Complicated Stamped	2
Miscellaneous	
Residual Plain	42
Fragment of European-made vessel	1
Total sherds	55

This midden is Fort Walton Period.

St. Marks mound (Wa-12).—We were unable to find this site during 1940, but Moore (1902, pp. 320-325) located it as being 2 miles northwest of the St. Marks Lighthouse (map 16). The mound was situated in the neighborhood of a number of shell-midden deposits. It measured 3 feet in height and 40 feet across the base. A single bundle burial was the only one encountered. Perhaps others had disappeared through decay. Pottery was found both in the group deposit and in scattered caches. Celts, hematite ore, sheet-mica fragments, and shell cups complete the nonceramic inventory. Pottery vessels were found "killed" by perforation. All the common categories of pottery are listed except for complicated stamped. Illustrated material (Moore, 1902) is classified below:

Weeden Island Complex	
Weeden Island Series:	
Weeden Island Incised	Figs. 309, 310, 311
Weeden Island Punctated	Figs. 306, 307, 308
Miscellaneous	
Unclassified	Fig. 312
(Probably Weeden Island Series but decoration is not typical.)	

There is a single specimen from this mound in the R. S. Peabody Foundation. It is Weeden Island Plain (No. 39273).

The mound is obviously Weeden Island and, probably, Weeden Island II.

Refuge headquarters (Wa-13).—This midden takes its name from the present headquarters of the National Wildlife Migratory Bird Refuge which is located on the site (map 16). The general location is some 3 miles southeast of the mouth of the St. Marks River and in the same section where Moore excavated the burial mound in 1902 (site Wa-12). The midden is on a hillock which is the western end of a series of sand ridges rising about 5 meters above the surrounding swampy regions. All the ridges show trifling evidences of occupation, but the principal concentration is within a 5-acre area around the headquarters buildings. This concentration is marked by dark organic stain, broken conch shells, and sherds. Depth of the deposit is nowhere disclosed by excavations; however, it is probably less than 1 meter deep. The 1940 collection is tabulated below:

Weeden Island Complex	
Weeden Island Series:	
Weeden Island Incised	10
Weeden Island Plain	11
Carrabelle Punctated	1
Wakulla Check Stamped	80
Swift Creek Complicated Stamped	1
Miscellaneous	
Plain Red	1
Smooth Plain	1
Residual Plain	100
Indeterminate stamped	5
Total sherds	210

The site falls into the Weeden Island II Period.

Refuge tower (Wa-14).—This midden is named for the lookout tower on the same National Wildlife Refuge range as the previous site. It is situated about one-half mile south-southwest of the headquarters site (Wa-13) (map 16). The location is a sand ridge, covered with black midden and soil, some 200 by 100 meters in extent. Depth of the midden could not be determined in 1940 but is probably under 1 meter. In addition to sherds there are numerous flint chips and cores on the ridge. This site was revisited in 1946 and 1947 by John W. Griffin, Hale G. Smith, and Dr. John M. Goggin and has been reported upon, briefly, by them. (See references given for site Wa-15, below.) The 1940 sherd collection is classified below:

Fort Walton Complex	
Fort Walton Incised	1
Weeden Island Complex	
Wakulla Check Stamped	3
Swift Creek Complicated Stamped	1
(Not determinable as to Early or Late Variety.)	
Miscellaneous	
Residual Plain	40
Complicated Stamped (shell-tempered)	1
Unclassified	3
Total sherds	49

Collections made by J. W. Griffin (1947) at the site also include Swift Creek, Crooked River Complicated Stamped, and what is probably Deptford Linear Check Stamped.

A consideration of both collections indicates a Santa Rosa-Swift Creek to Weeden Island date with scatterings of Fort Walton and Deptford materials.

Wildlife Refuge cemetery (*Wa-15*).—This site is located very near or contiguous with the tower site (map 16). Goggin (1947a, p. 273) lists it as a "few hundred feet east of its lookout tower." To the best of our knowledge Woodbury and I did not find the spot in 1940, though we had been informed of it by Nick Fallier, of Tallahassee. Published references to this cemetery are those of Goggin (1947a) and J. W. Griffin (1947). Because of the unusual objects of European provenience that have been found there, it has attracted a good deal of attention in the last few years.

The burial place was discovered by amateur archeologists, one of whom, Bill Kary of Tallahassee, obtained a rather remarkable collection. These objects were taken from graves found in a sand ridge similar to the one upon which the tower site is situated. They included a circular gold ornament, a copper crested bird ornament, a decorated copper plate, an embossed copper gorget, a plain copper gorget, a silver and a copper bead, a European mordaunt, glass beads, and trade bells. Another interested amateur, Montague Tallant, of Manatee, also obtained artifacts from the same site. These were a gold disk with embossed rosette design, a copper tablet, and a stone celt. These objects have been dispersed, but the accounts of Goggin and Griffin suffice for the record. Goggin has pointed out that the crested copper bird ornament, fashioned in a shape sometimes referred to as a "sweat-scraper," and the copper tablet are both objects which are duplicated in the Glades area of south Florida where they seem to represent a widely diffused cult. Both the bird ornament and the tablet, together with most of the other metal objects from the cemetery site, were made by the Indians but made from metals taken from the wrecks of European ships in the sixteenth century, probably in south Florida. Some of the artifacts, such as the mordaunt and the glass beads, are obviously European-made. One article deserves special mention. This is a copper plate which has been decorated by an incised technique. Griffin figures it in his short note (J. W. Griffin, 1947, p. 182). The design, which unfortunately has been partially destroyed by a later reworking of the plate, shows a man's legs dressed in European pantaloons opposing a stag which is depicted with a human phallus. This plate may well be the earliest Indian artistic representation of a European in the southeast, for, presumably, it was done by an Indian. The later reworking, also aboriginal, has cut the plate down to a celt-shaped gorget and added embossed dots.

A manuscript of Kary's indicates that the burials with which these ornaments were found were both extended and flexed. A Fort Walton Incised vessel, check stamped sherds, celts, polished-stone discoidals, stone pendants, an incised elbow pipe, shell objects, and finely made projectile points all came from the same graves. The Fort Walton vessel and the discoidals clearly date the graves as of the Fort Walton Period, and the presence of check stamped pottery, probably Wakulla, is not out of line, as Wakulla Check Stamped is known to continue over into the Fort Walton Period.

Other sites in Wakulla County.—Moore (1918, p. 560) excavated the Old Creek mound which was located near the coast between Ocklockonee Bay and St. Marks. This was a low circular mound of sand some of whose contents suggest Weeden Island, although the presence of a loop-handle sherd with nodes on the handle is suspiciously like Fort Walton.

On Live Oak Point, a peninsula projecting into Apalachee Bay between Panacea and St. Marks, we canvassed a scattered shell midden in the 1940 survey. Very few sherds were found and these were largely Weeden Island.

There is a mound at the juncture of the St. Marks and Wakulla Rivers, one-quarter of a mile from the modern landings at the town of St. Marks. The mound, which is conical and steep-sided, is constructed of sand and lies back 100 meters from the convergence of the two rivers. The present height is 3 to 4 meters and the basal diameter 30 meters. It is surrounded with a circular sand and shell embankment which is about 1 meter high. Another sand embankment leads from this circular enclosure down to the Wakulla River. To the south of this embankment a stone wall has been built leading from the mound to the Wakulla, paralleling the sand embankment. Trees and undergrowth cover the mound and the surrounding area. There is no visible midden nearby. Six sherds were found on the mound. Five of these were Residual Plain, and one was an incised fragment similar to the late seventeenth-century central Georgia type, Ocmulgee Fields Incised.

Local people of St. Marks maintain that the earthwork is a fortification of the early nineteenth century. It is obvious that the stone wall, and perhaps the sand embankment leading to the river, are European. The mound, though, judging from its appearance, may be aboriginal.

JEFFERSON COUNTY

Pine Tuft (Je-1)—Pine Tuft is the name given to a little grove of trees on a hilltop 16 miles east of Tallahassee on U.S. Highway 19 (map 17). The hill is 1.1 miles south and .7 mile west of the junction of U.S. Highway 19 and Florida Highway 43. The site

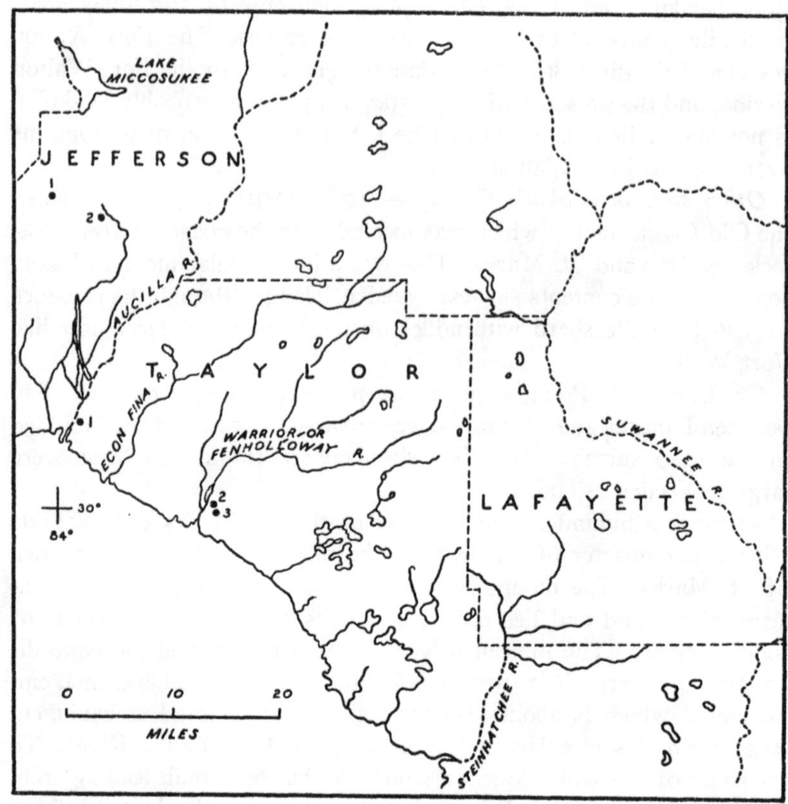

MAP 17.—Site map of Jefferson and Taylor Counties. Sites indicated by numbers.

was visited in the company of J. Clarence Simpson in 1940. On the hill, within a radius of 30 meters, there is evidence of clay flooring and plaster, together with old nails, European chinaware, Spanish olive-jar fragments, and a gun flint. The site may be a Spanish fort or mission settlement (Boyd, 1939, p. 273, site K). The aboriginal pottery from the site includes four complicated stamped and a number of unidentified plain sherds. The complicated stamped pottery is classified as Jefferson Ware.

This site must date from the Spanish Mission or Leon-Jefferson Period of the late seventeenth and early eighteenth centuries.

Scott Miller place (Je-2).—The Scott Miller place is 2.1 miles south and 1.1 miles east of the junction of U.S. Highway 19 and Florida Highway 96 (map 17). The site is on a hilltop now under cultivation. Wall and plaster fragments, evidences of old wall alignments, European sherds, iron spikes, olive-jar sherds, and aboriginal pottery fragments mark the site. This site is believed to be a Spanish fort or mission settlement (Boyd, 1939, p. 272, site J). The 1940 collection includes two Fort Walton Incised, two Lake Jackson Plain, three Jefferson Ware Complicated Stamped, and several plain sherds.

This site similarly dates from the Leon-Jefferson Period. Recent work of the Florida Park Service at the Scott Miller place has expanded our knowledge of the horizon and definitely verified this dating for the site (H. G. Smith, 1948).

TAYLOR COUNTY

Aucilla River mound (Ta-1).—The mound is on the east side of the Aucilla River about 2.5 miles from the mouth (map 17). Moore (1902, pp. 325-330) found it to be about 6 feet high and 64 feet in basal diameter, but it had been used as a livestock sanctuary for many years previous to his visit and it is likely that it had been trampled down considerably. The mound was made mostly of clay, but large limestone slabs were imbedded in the surface at all parts. Moore again visited the mound and completed his excavations on a second trip (1918, pp. 564-567, "The Lewis Place"). The following account summarizes both explorations.

Sixty-nine burials were recovered in all. These seem to have been both superficial and deep. Moore mentions three adults, all flexed, found lying near mound base. A child's skeleton, found under masses of limestone, was in a basal and central position in the mound as though it had been the nuclear burial. Both secondary (single skull and bundle) and primary flexed burials were often found surrounded or covered by cairns of large limestone rocks. One burial had evidences of fire in association but the bones were not calcined. Pottery was found in a mass cache and in several smaller caches; the other artifacts were, rarely, in accompaniment with burials.

Besides the burials in the mound others were found in low hummocks or rises of earth and refuse surrounding the mound. These were all flexed burials, usually without special mortuary goods. Apparently the entire area surrounding the burial mound had been an extensive village occupation zone.

Chipped-stone lances and points, a fragment of a polished bannerstone, hematite ore, sheet-mica fragments, a bone awl, and shell drinking cups were in the mound as grave goods. Pottery was "killed" by perforation. The ware categories complicated and check stamped were recorded, although the latter was rare.

The illustrated pottery (Moore, 1902 and 1918) is given below:

Weeden Island Complex

Weeden Island Series:

Weeden Island Incised..................Figs. 215, 317 (1902)
Weeden Island Punctated....................Fig. 314 (1902)
Weeden Island Plain....................Figs. 316, 319 (1902)
Weeden Island effigy.........................Fig. 38 (1918)
Weeden Island adorno......................Fig. 313 (1902)
Swift Creek Complicated Stamped................Fig. 37 (1918)
(Late Variety.)

The mound dates as Weeden Island I.

Warrior River, mound A (Ta-2).—Moore (1902, p. 337) locates this mound as 2.5 miles in an easterly direction from the mouth of the Warrior River (map 17). The mound was circular, 65 feet in diameter and about 9.5 feet high. The shape of the summit is not given. The mound was of sand but had been crudely plated with water-worn limestone slabs of large size. Similar boulders or slabs were also occasionally found inside the mound. Burials were badly decayed, but 29 were noted. Bundle or bunch, single skull, and flexed forms are all mentioned. Burials over which stone cairns had been made were found at more or less superficial depths. Both secondary and primary forms were so covered. Some burials were on mound base, but these, apparently, were not covered with limestone slabs. Pottery came mostly from a mass cache but was also found as individual vessels here and there in the mound. Projectiles, a celt, a rectangular stone gorget, and perforated conch cups came from the mound, the celt and gorget from burial associations.

Pottery vessels with holes made during their manufacture as well as perforations after firing were found. All principal categories of pottery decoration except check stamped were observed. Moore noted that complicated stamped and plain pottery was found nearer the interior center of the mound, while the incised styles came from the peripheries. This, he states, had been noticed in most of the mounds of the region. The illustrated material (Moore, 1902) is classified below:

Weeden Island Complex
Weeden Island Series:
Weeden Island Incised.........................Figs. 323, 324
Weeden Island Plain..............Figs. 320, 321, 322, 326, 327
Weeden Island adorno.............................Fig. 328

Santa Rosa-Swift Creek Complex
Swift Creek Complicated Stamped..................Figs. 325, 329
(Early Variety.)

Some additional material from the R. S. Peabody Foundation is of help in dating the mound. These specimens include one Tucker Ridge-pinched (No. 39299), three Swift Creek, Late Variety (Nos. 38988, 39334, 39296), and one Weeden Island Plain (No. 39318).

The mound is Weeden Island I. The absence of check stamped and the presence of two Early Variety Swift Creek pieces argue for an early Weeden Island date.

Warrior River, mound B (Ta-3).—Moore (1902, pp. 337-344) found this mound about 200 yards south of Warrior River mound A (map 17). It was of irregular outline, measuring 76 by 54 feet at the base and 7 feet high. Borrow pits near the mound were very obvious. All burials recorded, a total of 35, were secondary, being either bundle or single skull types. In only two cases were limerock slabs utilized as a burial covering; oyster shells also occasionally served this purpose. In general, limerock slabs were much less common than in Warrior mound A, although a few were found on the mound surface.

Pottery, besides being in a major cache and smaller caches, was found with individual burials. Other artifacts in the mound include a fossil shark tooth, chipped points, lance blades, knives, mica fragments, hematite ore, and a curious baton-shaped object of kaolin which has incised decorations reminiscent of the Basin Bayou Incised pottery type. Pottery vessels were "killed" by perforation. No check stamped pottery was found, but other principal ware groups were present including pinched decorated, probably the type Tucker Ridge-pinched. The illustrated (Moore, 1902) ware is classified below:

Weeden Island Complex
Weeden Island Series:
Weeden Island Incised............................Fig. 336
Weeden Island Plain.....................Figs. 331, 335, 337

Santa Rosa-Swift Creek Complex
Swift Creek Complicated Stamped.....................Fig. 334
(Probably Early Variety.)

Miscellaneous

Unclassified .... Fig. 332
(Interesting incised vessel which bears resemblance to vessel from the Yent mound (Moore, 1902) in three-line incision and vessel form.)

The R. S. Peabody Foundation has a single Weeden Island Plain vessel from this mound (No. 39164). In the Heye Foundation Annex are the sherds of a very interesting vessel of the Crystal River Negative Painted style (No. 18/251). Moore (1902, p. 341, vessel 14) describes this piece but not as negative ware. The specimen has a flanged and scalloped rim.

The mound is predominantly Weeden Island I but overlaps with Santa Rosa-Swift Creek.

Other sites in Taylor County.—Moore (1902, pp. 330-331) worked two small mounds on the Econfenee or Econfina River. One was a burial mound; the other contained nothing but masses of limerock. Neither can be identified. On his second visit (1918, pp. 567-568) he dug a third mound in the vicinity of the lower Warrior River. This proved to be a burial mound, and contained a compartment vessel and some sheet mica. Most likely the mound was of the Weeden Island Period.

DIXIE COUNTY

Horseshoe Point (Di-1).—Moore (1902, pp. 346-348) located a group of three mounds on the edge of a marsh a little to the north of Horseshoe Point (map 18). This was apparently a prehistoric population concentration as several large shell-refuse deposits were noted near the mounds. The first of the mounds which Moore excavated was partially situated upon such an old shell midden. This mound, circular in outline, was 40 feet in diameter and 6 feet high. Several burials were encountered in the sand of the mound but these are not enumerated or described. Pottery vessels were found singly in the mound. Some of the vessels were "killed" by perforation. Complicated stamped but not check stamped pottery was present as were incised and red painted types. Illustrated (Moore, 1902) pottery is classified below:

Weeden Island Complex

Weeden Island Plain .... Figs. 338, 340, 341
Swift Creek Complicated Stamped .... Fig. 339
(Late Variety.)

The mound dates as Weeden Island I.

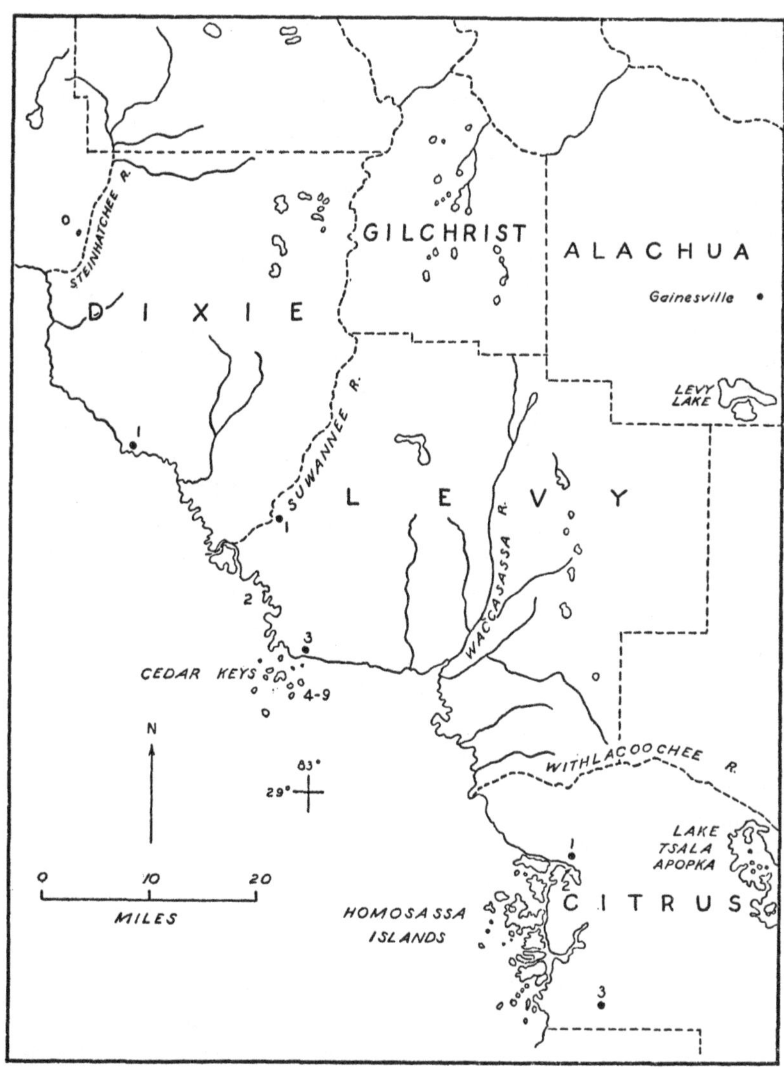

MAP 18.—Site map of Dixie, Levy, and Citrus Counties. Sites indicated by numbers.

The two other mounds of the Horseshoe Point group were tested. One was a long ridge-shaped tumulus which contained burials, celts, and plain "killed" pottery; the other was a circular mound in which he found nothing and, therefore, considered it as a domiciliary mound of sand.

Other sites in Dixie County.—Mound and midden sites are numerous along the Gulf Coast of Dixie County, but the data available are too scant to identify most of these as to cultural period. Moore (1902, pp. 344-346) describes some of these. A sand mound about 4 miles up the Steinhatchee River yielded bits of human bone, an occasional sherd, and some red paint. Near Goodson's Fishcamp, 2 miles down the coast from the mouth of the Steinhatchee, was another sand mound which contained secondary burials, punctated pottery, an ax, and a discoidal stone. Continuing down the coast to a point 3 miles from the mouth of the Steinhatchee is the Bear Hammock mound. This one failed to reveal anything during Moore's excavations. However, Montague Tallant reports that he made excavations in a mound at about the same location (personal communication, June 1948). Mr. Tallant refers to his site as the "Smith Mound." He found secondary and primary burials, stone celts, plain pottery, probably of the Weeden Island Period, perforated conch-shell cups, some conch-shell pins or tools, and what appeared to be a copper cup perforated with a "killing" hole. In addition to the Smith mound, Mr. Tallant also reports other sand mounds along the Dixie County coast between Horseshoe Point and the Steinhatchee. In one of them he found Weeden Island pottery. About 2 miles north of Horseshoe Point is a location known as Murphy Landing. A sand mound here, which Moore (1902, pp. 345-346) excavated, contained both primary and secondary burials, celts, and punctated, check stamped, and pinched pottery. It is possible that this was a Weeden Island site.

Late in the year 1948 Dr. John M. Goggin visited the coast in Dixie County and located three sites at a distance of 1 to 1½ miles southeast of Horseshoe Point. The sites lie just inland from an extensive salt marsh. They are designated as the Garden Patch 1, Garden Patch 2, and Garden Patch 3 sites. Garden Patch 1 is a natural sand ridge on which are the refuse remains of a midden. There is a sand mound on one end of the site. Garden Patch 2, situated in a hammock about 200 meters east-southeast of Garden Patch 1, is a sand mound. This mound measures about 70 by 125 feet and is 5 feet high. Garden Patch 3 is only a few yards from the Garden Patch 2 mound. Presumably it is the village associated with the former. It is a fairly deep and extensive shell midden. Goggin's analyses of the collections from these three sites would indicate that Garden Patch 1 was occupied in Weeden Island II times and Garden Patch 2 in the slightly earlier Weeden Island I Period. Garden Patch 2 site is, according to Goggin, the same location from which J. C. Simpson, of the Florida State Geological Survey, recovered a collection that is divided between Santa Rosa-Swift Creek and Weeden Island I elements. The dating on Garden Patch 3 site is not given owing to the scantiness of the sherd sample from the site.

The principal river in the Dixie and Levy Counties region is the Suwannee. In 1903 Moore's steamer made a side excursion up this river and a number of mounds were tested in what was then Lafayette (now Dixie) County. The results of this trip (Moore, 1903, p. 373) can briefly be summarized by saying that the low sand burial mounds were found to extend inland for at least 50 miles, that they contained secondary burials, and that the mortuary pottery found in some of them was probably of the Weeden Island style. No detailed accounts of these excavations are given by Moore.

LEVY COUNTY

Fowler's Landing, larger mound (Lv-1).—This landing is less than 10 airline miles inland from the Gulf Coast (map 18). By the river it is some 16 miles. The mound (Moore, 1903, pp. 364-371) was on the south bank of the Suwannee. It was made of sand, was circular, 7 feet high, and 50 feet in diameter. None of the 47 burials recovered were on mound base, all being in the upper fill of the mound. All were bundle burials. Pottery was found in a large cache and in a smaller deposit. Stone celts were in the sand fill of the mound. Vessels were "killed" by perforation. Incised, plain, and complicated stamped pottery is noted by Moore. His (Moore, 1903) illustrated specimens are classified below:

Weeden Island Complex
Weeden Island Series:
Weeden Island Incised....................Figs. 1, 3, 6, 7, 8
Weeden Island Plain..............................Fig. 5

The mound dates as of Weeden Island I.

At a distance of about 75 yards was another sand mound which had been riddled by previous digging although no bone scrap and very little pottery was exposed in the old cuts. Moore considered the mound to be of the domiciliary class.

Seven miles north of Cedar Keys (*Lv-2*).—The information from this site was provided by Montague Tallant who has excavated there. He describes the site as being a sand mound on an island which is one-quarter of a mile off shore at a distance of some 7 miles north of Cedar Keys (map 18). Opposite the island on the mainland there is a place known as Shell Point. An aboriginal midden is situated on Shell Point.

According to Mr. Tallant, Moore and others had preceded him at this site. It may very well be that Moore's "Mound on Pine Key, Levy County" (1902, p. 348) is the same site. Moore found a few burials and artifacts in the mound which, from the description, seem to be Weeden Island.

Tallant records secondary burials in the marginal fill of the mound, these being accompanied by caches of pottery vessels. He also reports skulls inside of large bowls. Extended and semiflexed burials were also in the mound. Some of the latter were in a submound pit. Stone celts, pendants, a copper gorget, and lump galena accompanied the pit burials.

In describing the pottery Mr. Tallant emphasizes duck-head adornos. The photographs of pottery from this mound which I have seen show Weeden Island and Santa Rosa-Swift Creek types. The latter include a very interesting gourd-shaped vessel of the type Alligator Bayou Stamped and a double-globed jar of Basin Bayou Incised. Both ovate and rectangulate boat-shaped plain-ware bowls were also present.

This mound was, apparently, in use from Santa Rosa-Swift Creek through Weeden Island I times. Tallant's description of what might be urn burials would also indicate a late period usage.

Gigger Point (*Lv-3*).—This mound is about 3 miles northeast of Cedar Keys, on the mainland (map 18). Moore (1903, pp. 374-377) says that the mound, which was made of sand and shell, was originally about 7 feet high but had been lessened by miscellaneous diggings prior to his arrival. It measured 46 feet across the base and was circular in outline. Moore counted approximately 90 burials but estimated that several more must have been disturbed or destroyed by the earlier diggers. The flexed form predominated, but a few extended burials, single skulls, and bundle types were noticed. Two graves were observed below mound base, and oyster shells were immediately associated with three other skeletons.

Pottery vessels were taken from immediate association with a burial. Besides these, there were a number of sherds in the mound.

Other artifacts came from burial associations and from the general mound fill. These include projectile and lance points, hammerstones, hones, smoothing pebbles, stone plummets or pendants, hematite ore, mica fragments, mica spear-point forms, a pendant coated with bitumen, a turtle-shell rattle, a bone awl, shell cups, a pierced clam shell, a shell chisel, shell pendants or plummets, and a gorgetlike shell ornament.

Pottery vessels were "killed" by perforation. Moore describes a five-compartmented tray which must certainly be a Weeden Island piece. Check stamped, complicated stamped, incised, red painted, and plain sherds were all met with. The only illustrated specimen is Carrabelle Punctated (1903, fig. 14). A fragment of limestone-tempered pottery, undoubtedly of the Pasco Series, is described in some detail by Moore.

The mound is dated as Weeden Island Period.

Note on Cedar Keys.—The small group of islands which cluster off the coast of Levy County are known as Cedar Keys. From the very beginnings of archeological work in Florida these keys attracted attention for their large shell-midden deposits. Sand burial mounds also dot these several islands. Several museum collections have been made at Cedar Keys in the past half century or more. Most of these are without detailed data, but in some cases it is possible to distinguish collections as specific site units apart from other collections. As such, they serve our purpose of site review and site dating and are so treated below. Other collections have insufficient data for this and are discussed only incidentally.

None of the sites is located specifically on map 18.

Aboriginal cemetery in Cedar Keys (Lv-4).—Moore (1918, pp. 569-571) visited this site and did some digging but found little aside from flexed and extended burials. The site, which was located in the city of Cedar Keys, had, however, been excavated previously. The previous investigator made certain data available to Moore, and a photograph of one pottery specimen was published with Moore's account (1918, fig. 39). This piece is typical Weeden Island Incised. Besides the pottery, a carved-stone duck-head effigy pendant had also been found in the same site.

The available data imply a Weeden Island Period identification. If this is correct, it is the only cemetery of the Weeden Island Period of which we have any knowledge. It seems quite possible that the site was originally a mound, most of which had been dug away by the time of Moore's visit, and that the Weeden Island pottery was taken from the mound by the earlier excavator.

Culpepper site (*Lv-5*).—We have no information on either the exact location or the nature of this burial-mound site. The collection, which is in the Peabody Museum, Harvard University (Nos. 74-26/12773-6) is classified below:

Weeden Island Complex	
Weeden Island Series:	
Weeden Island Incised	4
Carrabelle Incised	1
Carrabelle Punctated	11
Keith Incised	5
Tucker Ridge-pinched	1
Wakulla Check Stamped	6
Swift Creek Complicated Stamped (Late Variety.)	7
West Florida Cord-marked	1
Ruskin Dentate Stamped	5
Biscayne Check Stamped	1
Miscellaneous	
Alachua Cob-marked	1
Crystal River Incised (?)	1
Total sherds	44

This site collection dates as Weeden Island.

Way Key (*Lv-6*).—This collection, also at Peabody Museum, Harvard University (Nos. 74-26/12781-4), is said to have come from a burial mound on the key of the same name.

It is classified below:

Weeden Island Complex	
Weeden Island Series:	
Weeden Island Plain	5
Carrabelle Punctated	2
Wakulla Check Stamped	10
Swift Creek Complicated Stamped	6
Ruskin Dentate Stamped	9
Papys Bayou Punctated	1
Biscayne Plain	3
Glades Complex	
Glades Plain	2
Miscellaneous	
Residual Plain	14
Unclassified	3
Total sherds	55

On the basis of this collection the mound dates in the Weeden Island Period.

Palmetto Island (*Lv-7*).—This collection was made by Decatur Pittman in the 1880's. It was classified in the Florida State Museum at Gainesville (No. 542) by Dr. John M. Goggin in July 1947. The classification sheets were subsequently checked over and revised in consultation with Goggin.

Safety Harbor Complex	
Pinellas Incised	1
Weeden Island Complex	
Weeden Island Series:	
Weeden Island Incised	143
Weeden Island Punctated	627
Weeden Island Zoned Red	139
Weeden Island Plain	1,009
Carrabelle Incised	384
Carrabelle Punctated	477
Indian Pass Incised	56
Keith Incised	104
Tucker Ridge-pinched	25
Hare Hammock Surface-indented	8
Weeden Island Punctated with incised serpent head	1
Wakulla Check Stamped	1,313
Combination Weeden Island Incised and Wakulla Check Stamped	1
Combination Weeden Island Punctated and Wakulla Check Stamped	1
Ruskin Dentate Stamped	96
Complicated Stamped Series:	
Swift Creek Complicated Stamped (Late Variety.)	473
Crooked River Complicated Stamped (Late Variety.)	5
Tampa Complicated Stamped	59
Sun City Complicated Stamped	1
Old Bay Complicated Stamped	21
Thomas Simple Stamped	22
West Florida Cord-marked (Late Variety.)	16
Papys Bayou Series:	
Papys Bayou Incised	2
Papys Bayou Punctated	42
Papys Bayou Plain	2
St. Johns (or Biscayne) Series:	
St. Johns Check Stamped	24
St. Johns Plain	207
Dunns Creek Red	309
Pasco Series:	
Pasco Check Stamped	22
Pasco Plain	157
Pasco Red	3
Miscellaneous incised and punctated	11

Shell stamped	1
Complicated stamped	1
Loop handle	1
Santa Rosa-Swift Creek Complex	
Basin Bayou Incised (?)	1
Glades Complex	
Glades Plain (?)	1
Miscellaneous	
Plain Red (probably Weeden Island Series)	246
Residual Plain	738
Prairie Cord-marked	2
Fabric-impressed	2
Champlévé technique	2
(Reminiscent of Crystal River and of Lemon Bay Incised types.)	
Indeterminate Stamped	15
Other unclassified	161
(Mostly semi-obliterated punctated type.)	
Total sherds....	6,932

This is a burial-mound collection and in spite of the lack of data it is of real importance because of its size. The presence of significant numbers of St. Johns or Biscayne types, of the Papys Bayou Series, and the Pasco Series in association with Weeden Island is noted for the first time in this site review. The site is overwhelmingly Weeden Island. The great abundance of check stamped suggests Weeden Island II, but the presence of over 500 complicated stamped sherds argues for the Weeden Island I Period. Perhaps the collection represents a continuity over both periods of Weeden Island.

Hodgeson's Hill (*Lv-8*).—In July 1947 Dr. John M. Goggin made a small collection from this midden site in Cedar Keys. I had the opportunity to examine this collection in the Peabody Museum, Yale University.

Weeden Island Complex	
Wakulla Check Stamped	7
Ruskin Dentate Stamped	17
St. Johns (or Biscayne) Series:	
St. Johns Check Stamped	8
St. Johns Plain	5
Pasco Series:	
Pasco Check Stamped	19
Pasco Plain	8
Miscellaneous	
Residual Plain	72
Total sherds....	136

The collection dates as Weeden Island II.

In April 1949 I accompanied Dr. Goggin and a group of University of Florida students to the Hodgeson's Hill site. A fairly large collection, numbering over 200 sherds, was made at that time. The bulk of this collection, which was classified by Dr. Goggin, substantiates the Weeden Island II dating offered on the basis of the inspection of the previous collection. However, additional periods of occupation seem to be indicated although these are not well represented. A very few (3) Pinellas Plain sherds were recovered, suggesting a possible Safety Harbor occupation, and a few Deptford and Swift Creek sherds were also picked up. These last would imply a pre-Weeden Island habitation.

Piney Point (Lv-9).—There are two collections from this Cedar Keys midden which have been combined in this classification. The first and larger was made by T. Van Hyning in 1916 and is cataloged in the Florida State Museum, Gainesville, as No. 352. The second, at Peabody Museum, Yale University, was collected by Dr. J. M. Goggin in 1947.

Safety Harbor Complex	
Safety Harbor Incised	1
Weeden Island Complex	
Weeden Island Punctated	1
Wakulla Check Stamped	3
Complicated Stamped Series:	
Swift Creek Complicated Stamped (Late Variety.)	9
Tampa Complicated Stamped	1
Ruskin Dentate Stamped	4
Thomas Simple Stamped	1
West Florida Cord-marked (Late Variety.)	4
St. Johns (or Biscayne) Series:	
St. Johns Check Stamped	3
St. Johns Plain	5
Dunns Creek Red	1
Pasco Plain	74
Sarasota Incised	1
Gainesville Linear Punctated	2
Santa Rosa-Swift Creek Complex	
Franklin Plain	2
Miscellaneous	
Prairie Cord-marked	2
Cob-marked (?)	3
Residual Plain	38
Indeterminate Stamped	4
Other unclassified	4
Total sherds	163

This site dates as Weeden Island. A very small collection made in April 1949 is consistent with this dating.

Other sites in Cedar Keys.—In 1918 Moore (1918, pp. 568-569) excavated a mound in the city of Cedar Keys. This was a burial mound of sand and shell, but we are unable to identify it from the account.

One of the most interesting accounts of excavations at Cedar Keys is S. T. Walker's version of stratigraphy in one of the great shell refuse heaps. The heap, which was cut by a road-building operation, revealed a four-strata story of cultural deposition. At the bottom, in 3 feet of shell, there was only rude, heavy, sand-tempered pottery, undecorated, without rim modifications, and occurring only as sherds from large-size vessels. A second shell stratum, 4 feet in thickness, showed a gradual shift in pottery types with the earlier coarse ware being replaced by pottery decorated with incisions, punctations, and thickened or folded rims. Check stamped pottery was also in this level. Walker states that sand and gravel temper were abandoned in this second stage, but he does not indicate what new tempering material replaced these. A third stratum was marked by 2 feet of soil. There was very little material in the soil, but immediately below it were sherds with curvilinear incised decorations and rim projections or "ears." The fourth stratum, above the soil zone and again in shell, had a variety of new pottery designs. Bone and shell implements were frequent and game stones or discoidals appeared. At the very top of this fourth and final period were the first handled vessels in the sequence and numerous effigy rim adornos. From the account we cannot satisfactorily identify the four "periods." Possibly the earliest is comparable to an early phase of the Glades culture, such as Glades I, or Perico Island, although there is no substantiatory evidence to show that a Glades-like culture ever extended this far north. The second phase could have been Santa Rosa-Swift Creek or Weeden Island, and the third Weeden Island. The fourth stratum, at least for the uppermost part of the midden, suggests Fort Walton influence in the appearance of pottery handles.

The several collections from Cedar Keys, locations unidentified, are largely of the Weeden Island Period. Jeffries Wyman gave a collection to Peabody Museum, Harvard (No. 74-26/12771) which appears to be Weeden Island II. St. Johns and Pasco Series sherds are represented. The Florida State Museum has a large collection (No. 1395) which was made by Decatur Pittman either on Palmetto Island or on Lone Cabbage Island. It supplements the Pittman collection classified under Palmetto Island (Lv-6) in this report in that it is both Weeden Island I and II. Several other very small sherd collections, from unlocated Cedar Key proveniences, are largely Weeden Island Period. In the United States National Museum there is a small collection of sherds (Nos. 42481-42486) which were gathered from an unidentified earth or sand mound on Cedar Keys by H. T. Woodman. This collection is mixed between the Weeden Island and Safety Harbor Complexes. There is also a Weeden Island I collection which was given to the National Museum in 1869 by H. Clark (Nos. 8258-8274). A Franklin Plain tetrapod sherd was found in a small collection made by Dr. John M. Goggin at Goose Creek, Cedar Keys.

Other sites in Levy County.—There are a considerable number of other mound and midden sites in Levy County. Some of these were excavated by Moore; others have been investigated by amateurs or by unknown parties. There are the Hog Island mounds which Moore explored at the mouth of the Suwannee (Moore, 1902, p. 348; 1918, p. 568). One of these proved to be a shell heap, while another was made of shell and contained burials. The third Hog Island mound showed the type of limerock slab capping noted on mounds farther north. Moore (1902, p. 349) also worked a site described as "Mound near the Shell-heap, Levy County," but found little of consequence. A sand mound 3 miles northeast of Cedar Keys, on the mainland, was believed to have been of the domiciliary class (Moore, 1903, pp. 373-374). Below Cedar Keys, also on the mainland coast, were a series of mounds at Dry Creek, Burns Landing, and Bear Landing (Moore, 1903, pp. 377-378). Some of these were burial mounds; others may have been of the domiciliary type. None can be adequately dated from the descriptions.[56]

In a recent survey of the Cedar Keys area and the adjacent mainland (April 1949), Dr. Goggin and I located three midden dumps on the mainland coast of Levy County not far from the turn-off to the Cedar Keys causeway. (The exact locations of these sites and the corresponding collections are in the archeological laboratory at the University of Florida, Gainesville.) At site number 1 of this group of three, a small collection was obtained which included Deptford Bold Check Stamped, Deptford Simple Stamped, and a grit- or sand-tempered cord-marked pottery, presumably similar to what I have called West Florida Cord-marked. Site number 2 yielded a much larger collection, and out of about 150 sherds, 27 were Deptford

[56] John K. Small (1924) mentions sites at the Withlacoochee delta and the mouth of the Suwannee River.

Bold Check Stamped, 12 were Deptford Simple Stamped, and 2 Deptford Linear Check Stamped. Additional types included a majority of plain residual sand-tempered pottery, a few St. Johns Plain, a Swift Creek Complicated Stamped, and some Pasco Plain. Both of these sites I would consider to be late Deptford. The lateness seems indicated by the absence or scarcity of the marker type Deptford Linear Check Stamped, a type which, in the northwest, has the earliest frequency within the Deptford Complex. The third midden site of the group showed a mixture of Deptford (including 18 Deptford Linear Check Stamped), Swift Creek, and Weeden Island I and II types. Presumably, this collection represents a continuity of occupation throughout all three of these periods.

The importance of these finds is that they extend the geographical distribution of the Deptford Period and Complex farther south than we had as yet been able to do on the basis of previous data. Unfortunately, this information has been received too late to incorporate it in the various site tabulations.

CITRUS COUNTY

Crystal River (*Ci-1*).—This famous site is located on the Crystal River some 4.5 miles from the mouth (map 18). It was remarked upon by Brinton as early as 1867. F. L. Dancy, State Geologist of Florida, described it as being a truncated cone, purposefully built and not a mere refuse heap. Since then it has been the scene of three separate excavations carried out by C. B. Moore (1903, pp. 379-413; 1907, pp. 406-425; 1918, pp. 571-573). Although most of the digging and interest has focused upon the burial mound unit, the site is a complex of sand and shell works. Fronting on the river is the "great shell heap" which, from the map (Moore, 1903, fig. 16), would appear to be a high (28 feet) rectangular platform mound with a ramp approach. A lower, irregular shell deposit extends from the mound to the east. This looks very much like a midden accumulation. At the north end of the site are two more shell works. One may be no more than another midden concentration, but the other appears to be a second rectangular flat-topped temple mound with a graded approach. The burial mound is centrally located in the site. It consists of three distinct parts. At its outer perimeter is a circular embankment of sand, 75 feet wide and about 6 feet in height. The diameter across the circle is about 270 feet. Within the circular enclosure is an irregularly shaped platform of sand about 5 feet high but sloping off to the floor of the enclosure in all directions.

This platform averaged about 130 feet in diameter. Rising by an additional 5 feet above the platform is the mound proper. The basal diameter of the mound proper was about 70 feet and its summit was a circular flat top some 20 feet across.

During Moore's 1903 season he concentrated upon the mound proper but also carried out considerable digging in the surrounding platform. Both platform and mound were made of sand although layers or lenses of shell extended through each. In the mound proper there was a 2-foot-thick basal shell layer on the eastern side which ran in toward the center of the mound. In the platform, or "elevated ground" as Moore usually referred to it, a shell layer was continuous just below the surface on the southern and southeastern sides. No other major strata were observed. In the platform, burials were nearly always covered or surrounded with oyster shells and this trait was also met with in the mound proper although not so frequently. Ocher and limonite streaks and lenses were noted in the sand of the mound and platform but these, too, were localized burial deposits. Limerock slabs were encountered in at least one instance as a burial cover. Moore's most important statement concerning the structure of the mound and the platform, or "elevation," is given at the close of his 1907 summary when he says:

> The mound itself, as we have said, differed in composition from the sloping ground (platform) in that the mound contained much less shell and to a large extent was made up of clean sand. This sand continued to the very base of the mound on the general level of the surrounding surface, so that it seems clear that the mound was built first, and later surrounded, as to its lower part, by the sloping ground (platform). (Moore, 1907, p. 425.)

If correct, this establishes the mound proper as antecedent to the surrounding platform. In other words, the platform was not a base upon which the mound was built but a later "skirt" or annex to the mound.

In the mound and the platform 411 burials were tabulated by Moore during his combined 1902 (1903) and 1906 (1907) visits. In actual number of deceased human beings this probably represents between 500 and 600. During the 1902 season both secondary burials, including the bundle and single skull types, and primary flexed and extended burials were encountered. The primary forms outnumbered the secondary at a ratio of about 5 to 3. It will be remembered that this season's digging was in both mound proper and platform. In the 1906 season nearly all the burials recovered were primary, and the majority of these were extended at full length upon the back. Work of this season was confined solely to the section of the platform which had not been previously excavated, and the mound proper was not included except for minor peripheral portions that had not been destroyed during the earlier trip. In view of Moore's observation that the platform was built after the mound proper, as an adjunct to it, the burial data suggest a time trend in mortuary customs marked by the abandonment of secondary treatment and burial. This should be viewed with caution, however, as Moore also says, concerning the mound-proper burials:

> While burials in the mound were not unusually numerous, the height of the mound and the extreme dryness of the sand of which it was built, caused much caving and consequent disarrangement of burials. (Moore, 1903, p. 382.)

The "disarrangement" of which he speaks could have transformed primary into what appeared to be secondary burials.

Concerning the skeletons, Moore noted no cranial deformation, but he does speak of frequent bone pathology (1903, p. 383).

There is little information concerning the locations of burials within either mound or platform, although the implications are that they were found at all depths. In the platform there was evidence of some burials having been put in so as to disturb earlier graves and jumble the bones. For the most part artifacts, both ceramic and nonceramic, were found with individual burials rather than in common caches. There was, for instance, no large mass cache of broken or "killed" pottery as is found in most Weeden Island Period mounds. On his second visit Moore did, however, make the statement that there was some evidence in the platform for common burial deposits or caches as apart from individual offerings. This, in addition to burial form, is another feature differentiating the platform from the mound proper.

A third characteristic which distinguishes mound from platform is that the former contained the finest and most exotic pottery and nonpottery specimens. Virtually all the copper artifacts, all the complete smoking pipes, the best stone celts, the best shell ornaments, and most of the whole pottery vessels were taken from the mound proper and not the platform. Because of these differences between mound and platform the materials found in each will be discussed separately. There is some difficulty in segregating these, as Moore is not explicit in every case, but for the most part we can say that the artifacts recovered during the 1903 excavations belong to the mound proper and those of the 1906 diggings to the platform. One important exception to this is the pottery vessel shown as figure 21 in Moore's 1903 report. This piece is reported specifically as having come from the platform.

In the mound proper were a great abundance of nonceramic grave goods. Chipped-stone artifacts included numerous points, knives, lances (some ceremonially broken), and chert hammers. Ground-stone tools, weapons, and ornaments consisted of pebble hammers, hones, celts (some ceremonially broken), "cigar-shaped" stones, bar amulets, imitation animal teeth, sheet mica, stone beads, and a variety of stone pendants or plummets. These last were both elongated and spheroid and single- and double-grooved. Quartz crystals were also grooved as pendants. Stone material used in the manufacture of these objects ranges from igneous rocks and quartz through banded slate, catlinite, and limestone.

Shell materials were even more numerous than stone. Chisels and gouges were made from conch columellae, and drinking cups of *Busycon, Fasciolaria,* and *Melongena corona* are all reported, usually "killed" with a basal perforation. *Strombus* (or flat-surface variety) celts, perforated cardium shells, worked clam shells, *Busycon* hafted hammers, *Busycon* saucers or disks, and circular, scoop-shaped, semi-lunar, and rosette-form gorgets were recovered in addition to over 100 shell pendants or plummets similar in style to those made of stone. Shell beads were found only in a few cases.

A few perforated canine teeth, cut animal jaws, both modern and fossil shark teeth, what must be bone projectiles of the bipointed type, and a bone fishhook are listed.

Metal artifacts were relatively plentiful, and Moore describes copper plummets, bicymbal-type ear ornaments of copper which were sometimes plated with silver or meteoric iron, sheet-copper tablets decorated in repoussé technique, tubular beads, and conjoined copper tubes.

The use of bitumen on most of the shell and stone pendants or plummets is a feature of the site. Presumably this material was used as an adhesive for the suspension attachment. A large lump of bitumen came from the mound proper. Hematite ore was liberally sprinkled over and around many of the burials and artifacts.

Smoking pipes, which are both ceramic and stone, all came from the mound proper and include three soapstone elbow forms, one large limestone elbow type, two pottery elbow types, a pottery monitor, and a pottery tubular form (Moore, 1903, fig. 39). The soapstone and limestone pipes are all of the equal-arm rectangular block shape (see Moore, 1903, fig. 38). One of the pottery elbow pipes is described as having a flaring bowl.

The general description of pottery from the mound proper speaks of the abundance of podal supports. These were usually four in number but sometimes may have been three or more than four. Flanged rims, scalloped and notched rims, and miniature vessels were also common. The "killing" or basal perforation of vessels was the rule. Illustrated pottery, all in the 1903 report, is classified below:

Weeden Island Complex

Weeden Island Plain................Figs. 20 (bottom, 2d), 25, 33
Oklawaha Plain ....Fig. 20 (top, 2d)
Oklawaha Incised ....Figs. 20 (center, above; bottom, left); bottom, 3d), 37
(Also resemble Basin Bayou Incised.)
Ruskin Linear Punctated....................Fig. 20 (center, 2d)

Santa Rosa-Swift Creek Complex

Crystal River Series:
Crystal River Incised..........Figs. 20 (bottom, right), 21, 35
Crystal River Negative Painted...............Figs. 27, 28, 31
Combination Crystal River Incised and Negative Painted..... Fig. 20 (center, left)
Crystal River Zoned Red..................Fig. 20 (top, 3d)
Pierce Zoned Red.................................Fig. 24
Swift Creek Complicated Stamped[57]..........Fig. 20 (center, 3d)
Franklin Plain ....Figs. 26, 29, 30, 32, 36
West Florida Cord-marked...................Fig. 20 (top, left)
(Early Variety.)

Miscellaneous

Human effigy adorno (probably Santa Rosa-Swift Creek)..Fig. 19
Cord-marked or dentate-stamped.............Fig. 20 (top, right)
Unclassified incised ....Fig. 20 (center, right)
Check Stamped (may be Gulf or Deptford Bold).........Fig. 34

Besides the illustrated material, Moore's descriptions of individual vessels are given in some detail (Moore, 1903). Reasonably valid identifications of types from these may be added to the above. Weeden Island Plain is represented by nine vessels, Franklin Plain by one, Pierce Zoned Red by one, and there is also described a curious multiple-orifice form similar to the one from Pierce mound A (Fr-14).

The dating of the mound proper seems conclusively Santa Rosa-Swift Creek. The Crystal River Series and the abundance of Franklin Plain are definitive. The presence of Weeden Island Plain and what appears to be Oklawaha Plain and Oklawaha Incised does not seriously conflict with this assignment. The plain vessels from Crystal

[57] This sherd cannot be placed as either Early or Late Variety, but an examination of Moore's sherd collections from Crystal River, now in the Heye Foundation Annex, has revealed two Early Variety Swift Creek sherds.

River have been so classified except for those typed as Franklin Plain. The Crystal River Plain vessels are not, however, typical of Weeden Island Plain, and the same problem is raised here that we have been met with in discussing ceramics from some of the other Santa Rosa-Swift Creek burial mounds.[58] This problem raises the point of the desirability of splitting the Weeden Island Plain type, as it has been defined, so as to detach that range of material which we are coming to recognize as the plain ware associated with Santa Rosa-Swift Creek mounds.[59] Owing to a certain amount of overlap in plain wares between the two periods this is not being attempted at this time, but it is a factor to be kept in mind in the study of this report and in further Gulf Coast research. Oklawaha Plain and Incised types also seem to appear very early in Weeden Island I times or even in the Santa Rosa-Swift Creek Period. Oklawaha Plain has close parallels with some Weeden Island Plain vessels, differing only in paste and temper characteristics.[60] Oklawaha Incised has its closest parallels with the Santa Rosa-Swift Creek type, Basin Bayou Incised.

The descriptions of artifacts from the Crystal River mound platform parallel, in many respects, those of the mound proper (Moore, 1907). Stone pendants were abundant, and lance points, celts, a bar amulet, and sheet mica were all present. Bone points and sting-ray spine points, cut animal jaws, fossil shark teeth, and turtle shells were found as grave goods in the platform, while shell artifacts from platform proveniences were much the same and in similar frequencies as those in the mound proper. Illustrated pottery (Moore, 1903, 1907), which seems to have come from the platform includes:[61]

Weeden Island Complex

Weeden Island Series:

Weeden Island Incised................Fig. 2 (2d row, right)
Weeden Island Punctated...............Fig. 2 (3d row, left)
Weeden Island Plain..............................Fig. 8
Carrabelle Punctated ....Fig. 2 (top, left)
Keith Incised ....Fig. 2 (top, right)

Oklawaha Plain ....Fig. 1 (bottom, right)
Oklawaha Incised ....Fig. 2 (2d row, left)
(This may be Basin Bayou Incised.)

---

[58] See discussion of Eleven-Mile Point (Fr-10), pp. 274-276.

[59] In addition to Franklin Plain.

[60] Goggin has pointed out the close similarity in rim ornamentation between Oklawaha Plain and certain Weeden Island I vessels (Goggin, n.d. 2).

[61] All are from Moore, 1907, except the one example indicated from Moore, 1903.

Santa Rosa-Swift Creek Complex

Crystal River Incised.....Figs. 1 (bottom, left), 2 (3d row, center; bottom, left), 3, 9, 11; and fig. 18 (1903)

Santa Rosa Series:

Basin Bayou Incised........................Figs. 4 (?), 5, 7

Alligator Bayou Stamped..............Fig. 2 (3d row, right)

Swift Creek Complicated Stamped................Fig. 1 (center)

Deptford Complex

Deptford Simple Stamped..................Fig. 2 (bottom, right)

Miscellaneous

Unclassified incised ....Fig. 1 (top)

A text description of vessels not illustrated (Moore, 1907) indicates three Franklin Plain and five Weeden Island Plain. The latter are of the group of vessel forms which seem to be as common to Santa Rosa-Swift Creek contexts as Weeden Island.

The Crystal River platform seems to me to date, primarily, from the Santa Rosa-Swift Creek Period as does the mound proper. That some time difference does exist between the two is certainly implied by the absence of metal work, of pipes, of some pottery types, and by the presence in the platform and absence in the mound of typical Weeden Island Period sherds such as the Weeden Island Incised and Punctated, the Carrabelle, and the Keith pieces. It may be that burials were made in the platform in both Santa Rosa-Swift Creek and Weeden Island I times.[62]

On Moore's (1918) last visit to Crystal River he sank a series of test pits into the circular embankment which encloses both the platform and the mound. The embankment proved to be made mainly of midden refuse rather than clean sand. Twenty-four burials, all primary flexed or extended, were encountered. Shell tools, shell cups, shell pendants and gorgets, stone pendants, and stone points were found with the skeletons. These objects are very similar to those from the mound and platform. Potsherds were numerous but no whole vessels were associated with the dead. Probably these burials were made at about the same time as those in the mound and platform, but they cannot be satisfactorily dated.

No excavations of consequence were made in the other units of the site such as the rectangular, flat-topped mounds or the extensive shell middens. It is probable that the rectangular mounds date from a later period.

Before leaving Crystal River an additional word should be said about the problem of dating and correlations. Moore was the first to note Hopewellian similarities in the artifacts from the mound, par-

[62] Goggin (n.d. 2) has dated the platform as entirely Weeden Island I.

ticularly the metal work. A good many years later Greenman (1938) reaffirmed this connection. In 1944 Philip Phillips and I presented a paper which had as its central theme the occurrence of negative painted pottery at the site (Willey and Phillips, 1944). It was our contention at that time that the contents of the mound and platform dated from a late or slightly post-Weeden Island Period and that the unique copper specimens, although Hopewellian in type, were survivals from an earlier epoch. This was not a comfortable solution to the problem, but the baffling appearance of the negative painted specimens, a technique known elsewhere in the southeast from only the late Middle Mississippian horizon, seemed to justify the late dating. Furthermore, the Crystal River Incised type had its closest resemblances to Fort Walton Incised rather than Weeden Island or the Santa Rosa-Swift Creek types, or so I thought at the time. In the absence of the marker types Early Swift Creek or Alligator Bayou Stamped, except as sherds in the mound fill, a Santa Rosa-Swift Creek position seemed dubious. Since then, as a result of more intensive study of the problem, I have revised my earlier opinions.[63] I now feel that there is little doubt that Crystal River (Ci-1), Yent (Fr-5), and Pierce mound A (Fr-14) are all part of the Santa Rosa-Swift Creek Period.

Buzzard's Island (*Ci-2*).—This site is described as being 1 mile below the town of Crystal River on an island, presumably in the river (map 18). The island is low and marshy and at its highest point is an old burial ground. This cemetery was investigated by Rainey (1935) who found burials within an area about 40 feet in diameter. Near the center of the area was a great mass secondary burial. Rainey also found single burials which were secondary bundles or single skulls and a few primary flexed and extended skeletons. In some cases partial calcination of the bones and marks of fire in the soil near the burials gave indication of in situ burning or semi-cremation.

In 1947 I had the opportunity to examine the Rainey collection from this site in the Peabody Museum, Yale University (Nos. 22766-22781). The projectiles are small fish-tail triangulars, large ovate-triangulars with small nub stems and slight barbs, medium-size triangulars with straight stems, and a large ovate blade with a tapered stem and a single notch on the shoulder. There are chipped axes or celts, long ground-stone celts, rectanguloid ground-stone celts, and stone pendants. The pottery is largely Pinellas Incised and Pinellas

[63] This is treated in detail in Willey, 1948b.

Plain although there is a cob-marked vessel and a single St. Johns Plain sherd in the collection.

I would place the cemetery in either the Fort Walton or Safety Harbor Period. The absence of any Safety Harbor Incised suggests the northern complex, but the incised pottery present is definitely Pinellas rather than Fort Walton.

Chassahowitzka River (Ci-3).—Moore (1903, pp. 413-414) dug this mound which is situated near the source of the river some 8 miles inland (map 18). The mound was 4 feet high, although it had probably been higher, and 75 feet in diameter. He found 18 burials, probably all secondary bundles or single skulls. Pottery either accompanied individual burials or was found at random in the mound. Some vessels were "killed" by perforation. A small ax, some flint rejects, and a grooved stone pendant or plummet were the only artifacts other than the pottery. Pottery is described as plain, check stamped, or punctated. A single effigy adorno or handle is shown (Moore, 1903, fig. 63). This may be either a Fort Walton or Weeden Island sherd. No complicated stamped pottery was found.

The mound is probably Weeden Island II.

Other sites in Citrus County.—There are a great many other sites in the county, both along the coast and inland as far as Lake Tsala Apopka. An interesting small collection of one Swift Creek, one Deptford Simple Stamped, and one Perico Incised sherd was made on Johns Island at the mouth of the Chassahowitzka River by Walker (U.S.N.M. No. 59368). This would indicate a Santa Rosa-Swift Creek or earlier occupation. A series of collections in the Yale Peabody Museum and the Florida State Museum have been classified by Dr. John Goggin. One of these, from Duval Lake near Floral City, shows an occupation beginning in Santa Rosa-Swift Creek or Deptford times; another at nearby Dampier's Island is a Weeden Island Period collection; a third, from a site on Lake Tsala Apopka belongs to the Safety Harbor Period; a Weeden Island II collection of Pasco Plain and Pasco Check Stamped comes from the Swindel site in the northeast corner of the county; and another Pasco Series collection was made at Drake 2 site which Goggin (n.d.2) places as Weeden Island I.

Besides these, S. T. Walker obtained a big collection of European trade beads from a mound somewhere on Chassahowitzka Bay (U.S.N.M. No. 59376). Moore (1903, p. 379) excavated a sterile mound at Rock Landing on the Crystal not far from the great site; another (1903, p. 413) near the town of Crystal River; and a third mound on the Greenleaf place (1918, pp. 573-574) about 3.5 miles south of the town. The last was a burial mound with secondary burials but it cannot be dated for lack of artifacts.[64]

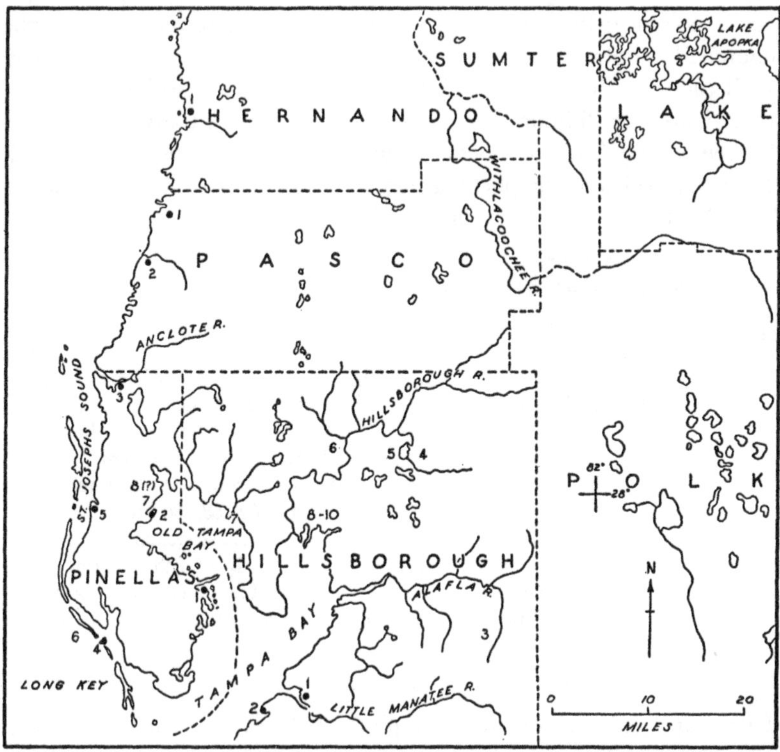

MAP 19.—Site map of Hernando, Pasco, Pinellas, and Hillsborough Counties. Sites indicated by numbers.

HERNANDO COUNTY

Bayport (He-1).—This is a mound about 1 mile north of the town of Bayport (Moore, 1903, pp. 415-424) (map 19). It was between 3 and 4 feet high and had a basal diameter of approximately 80 feet, although it was oblong rather than circular. About 40 burials were found, but these may represent a slightly higher number of skeletons. Bundles or bunched burials were the most common and

---

[64] John K. Small (1927) located mounds and shell middens in the vicinity of Crystal River; others have also been reported from Black Point, Coney Creek, Chair Island, Boggy Bay, Salt River, and near the mouth of the Homosassa River.

were discovered in all parts of the mound; a few instances of cremation or partial cremation were also met with. Shell tools, pottery, hematite ore, and a celt were associated with burials. A large vessel fragment with a loop handle had been placed over one burial. Projectile points, celts, and copper fragments were found loose in the mound fill. Pottery, besides that placed directly with burials, was in small caches. Most of it was broken or "killed" by perforation. The trait of prefired "killing," or the making of holes in the vessels before they were baked, is also noted. Plain, incised, punctated, red painted, check stamped, and complicated stamped categories are listed. Moore's (1903) illustrated pottery is classified below:

Safety Harbor Complex
Safety Harbor Incised.............Figs. 66 (3d row, 2d sherd), 71

Weeden Island Complex
Weeden Island Series:[65]
Weeden Island Incised....Figs. 66 (top, left; top, 2d sherd), 74
Weeden Island Punctated....Figs. 66 (top, 3d sherd; top, right; center, left; 2d row, 3d sherd; 2d row, right; 3d row, 1st sherd; bottom, left; bottom, 2d sherd), 67, 68, 69, 70
Weeden Island Plain......................Figs. 76, 77, 78, 79
Carrabelle Incised ....Fig. 66 (3d row, right)
Keith Incised ....Fig. 66 (bottom, right)
Swift Creek Complicated Stamped......Fig. 66 (2d row, 1st sherd)

Miscellaneous
Unclassified incised ....Fig. 72

This collection is augmented by a piece in the R. S. Peabody Foundation. This is Pasco Check Stamped (No. 38946).

The mound was obviously built in Weeden Island times and was probably used through both Weeden Island I and II Periods. The few Safety Harbor sherds, and the description of the loop-handled bowl as a burial cover indicate the mound's reuse as a Safety Harbor burial place.

Other sites in Hernando County.—Moore's other two excavations in this county cannot be satisfactorily placed as to period. Indian Bend, near the Chassahowitzka River (Moore, 1903, pp. 414-415), was a burial mound with both secondary and primary burials. Check stamped pottery was found in the mound as was a sherd of the type St. Petersburg Incised (Moore, 1903, fig. 65). This type is usually found in Weeden Island Period contexts but seems to be a very late Weeden Island II type. The Indian Creek mound is 5 miles south

[65] Some of these may be Papys Bayou Series sherds.

of Bayport. It was a burial mound (Moore, 1903, p. 424), but contained no artifacts.

Recent important discoveries in Hernando County were brought to my attention during the month of August 1948 by Dr. A. J. Waring, Jr. Dr. Waring excavated a midden site on a marsh island at the mouth of the Chassahowitzka River. The excavation (a 5- by 10-foot test pit) revealed an upper stratum composed mainly of oyster shells and salt-water mollusks. This upper stratum contained potsherds, principally of the Weeden Island Period. At a depth of 2.5 feet Waring encountered a lower midden stratum of fresh-water gastropods, fine fish bone, and ash. This lower stratum was solidified into a hard, rocklike mass. Flint artifacts were found imbedded in the stratum, but there was no pottery.

To quote Waring directly (letter of August 19, 1948):

> The flint forms consisted of scrapers as well as very interesting massive forms. These last are large crude hand axes, very much like the *coup-de-poing* form. They measure 10 to 12 inches in length. Other flint items are large hand choppers made of big, wedge-like flint flakes with edges battened round from use, and fragments of large ovate blades and knives.

Projectile points were found, but these are not described. Waring also took a longitudinally grooved stone from the lower stratum. This is a form which occurs in the Glades area on a late (Glades III) horizon, but, as far as I am aware, it is unknown in the later periods of the Gulf Coast.

From the description it would appear that this Chassahowitzka River site is the first prepottery station of the Gulf area to be reported. Waring continues:

> The finding of nothing but fresh-water molluscs (in the lower stratum) interested me considerably. The river is sufficiently salt at the site right now for oysters to grow, and river snails are about 3 miles inland. All this suggests a perceptible rise in ocean level since the time of the archaic site.

The replacement of fresh-water shells by salt- or brackish-water species strikes a familiar note as this is the sequence along the St. Johns and Atlantic Coast where the Archaic prepottery cultures were also associated with fresh-water mollusks. This change in shellfish has there been interpreted as a result of a prehistoric rise in ocean level at the close of the Archaic. Waring's findings and analysis would appear to parallel and verify the east coast phenomena.

However, even more recent excavations at the same site cast doubt upon the preceramic interpretation. R. P. Bullen, of the Florida Park

Service, in a letter dated May 23, 1949, writes concerning the same Chassahowitzka site:

> You will remember that Waring reported an upper stratum of oyster shells containing pottery and a lower deposit of consolidated snail shells. Apparently he found no sherds in this lower zone but we did.
>
> We also found, in a trench about 50-60 feet from his, the large, coarse, scraper-like blades closely associated with pottery. In fact pottery was found at substantial depths below the concentration of these large tools. Here the lower zone consisted of black dirt and oyster shells but no snail shells (incidentally there were a few oysters in the snail shell breccia of the other trench).

Obviously a thorough analysis of all materials and data from the Chassahowitzka River site, by both Waring and Bullen, is in order. Perhaps this will clarify the question of the possible preceramic layer, the position of the large flint blades or choppers, and the succession of fresh-water and marine shells. For the present we can only point to this newly discovered site as important if somewhat confusing.

PASCO COUNTY

Wekiwachee River (Pa-1).—Moore locates this mound as 2 miles south-southeast of the mouth of the river (Moore, 1903, pp. 425-426) (map 19). The mound was of oblong shape, being 86 by 64 feet and about 4 feet in height. The original summit shape is unknown, as the top had been trampled flat by cattle. In the middle of the mound was a virtual layer of human bones made up of secondary burials. Numerous bundle burials were found at other places in the mound as were a few flexed burials. A total of 145 burials, including a pocket of calcined human bone, make up the total, and this probably represents almost 200 persons. Shell drinking cups and stone celts were found with burials, and hammerstones, lance points, and a grooved-stone pendant were loose in the mound. A small deposit of sherds was at one side of the mound, and others were scattered about at random. A "killed" vessel accompanied the great mass burial in the center of the mound.

Besides perforation "killing" of vessels, one example of prefired "killing" of a pot was recorded. Check stamped, complicated stamped, and punctated ware are specifically mentioned. An illustrated panel (Moore, 1903) is classified below:

Weeden Island Complex

Weeden Island Incised..............Fig. 80 (top and bottom, left)
Ruskin Linear Punctated..................Fig. 80 (bottom, right)

Miscellaneous

Unclassified punctated ....Fig. 80 (top, right)

A vessel of Dunns Creek or Biscayne Red is in the R. S. Peabody Foundation (No. 38933).

The mound is Weeden Island, probably Weeden Island II.

Pithlochascootie River (*Pa-2*).—S. T. Walker (1880a, pp. 393-394) located and excavated two mounds near the mouth of this river on its south bank (map 19). One of these was a large flat-topped temple mound, made of alternate layers of sand and shell, oblong in shape, and measuring 168 by 55 feet and 5 feet in height.[66] Excavations in this mound revealed nothing. The second mound that Walker dug was 100 yards distant from the first. It was made of sand; an irregular oval shape; and had either a ramp approach or a projecting wing on one side. Walker records its size as 175 by 50 feet at its maximum diameters and 7 feet high.[67] Walker found burials, arrow points, pottery, and an iron spike in this mound. He makes a dubious claim of having found the skeletons arranged radially in the mound with heads toward a common center.

Moore found 62 burials in the same mound, but one of his burial units contained the remains of 57 individuals while others were composed of more than one person. Perhaps 150 individuals had been buried in the mound. Secondary burials were more common than primary. The single skull, bundle, and mass bone pile were all represented. There were also a few extended and flexed burials. With a big mass secondary burial were three deposits of calcined bones. As a rule the primary burials were found on mound base, while the secondary types of treatment were in the upper part of the mound.

Pottery was found with individual burials and in small scattered caches. Nonceramic artifacts were both scattered through the mound or with specific burials. Lance and drill points, quartz crystals, stone pendants, celts, pebble hammers, shell tools, shell cups, shell pendants, and bone tools were in the mound. Pottery was "killed" by perforation, and incised, check stamped, plain, complicated stamped, and painted categories are listed. The illustrated material (Moore, 1903, pp. 426-433) is classified below:

Englewood Complex

Englewood or Sarasota Incised..........................Fig. 83

Weeden Island Complex

Weeden Island Incised or Punctated.....................Fig. 87

Miscellaneous

Unclassified incised ....Fig. 84

---

[66] Moore's (1903, p. 427) measurements for the same mound are 142 x 70 feet and 9 feet in height.

[67] Moore (1903, p. 427) corrects this to 123 feet in length and only 4 feet in height.

The Walker collection (U.S.N.M. No. 35854-56) substantiates a Weeden Island dating. It is classified below:

Weeden Island Complex	
Weeden Island Series:	
Weeden Island Incised	14
Weeden Island Punctated	5
Weeden Island Plain	8
Carrabelle Incised	2
Wakulla Check Stamped	6
Complicated Stamped Series:	
Swift Creek Complicated Stamped (Late Variety.)	1
Sun City Complicated Stamped	1
Tampa Complicated Stamped	4
Ruskin Dentate Stamped	2
St. Petersburg Incised	1
Pasco Series:	
Pasco Check Stamped	3
Pasco Plain	3
Papys Bayou Series:	
Papys Bayou Incised	1
Papys Bayou Punctated	1
Biscayne Series:	
Biscayne Check Stamped	5
Biscayne Plain	2
Biscayne Red	5
Miscellaneous	
Plain Red	1
Smooth Plain	1
Residual Plain	3
Total sherds	69

The mound dates as Weeden Island II.

Other sites in Pasco County.—Walker (1880a, p. 394) mentions a flint workshop site about 5 miles south of the Pithlochascootie and 2 miles above the mouth of the Anclote River. Another site which must be in Pasco County is the Hope or Finley Hammock mound which Cushing (1897) excavated. This mound was 9 miles northwest of Tarpon Springs. Cushing stated the materials from this mound to be very similar to those from the Tarpon Springs or Safford mound of Pinellas County.

In the 1930's Dr. M. W. Stirling made test excavations in a small circular sand mound about 1 mile northwest from the town of Lacoochee. This is in the northeastern corner of the county on the Withlacoochee River. A few badly decayed burials and some plain potsherds were all that were recovered (personal communication, M. W. Stirling, June 1947).

PINELLAS COUNTY

Weeden Island (*Pi-1*).—This site is described under the section "Excavations on the West Coast: 1923-1936."

Safety Harbor (*Pi-2*).—This site is described under the section "Excavations on the West Coast: 1923-1936."

Tarpon Springs or Safford mound (*Pi-3*).—This is one of the most famous of the Gulf Coast mounds (map 19). In his survey of the 1870's Walker visited the Anclote River country and excavated a mound known then as the Ormond site (Walker, 1880a, pp. 396-399). He describes it as 95 feet in diameter and 5 feet in height, although even at that time it had been partially excavated. Moore (1903, p. 433) identified this mound as the Safford mound which Cushing later reexcavated (Cushing, 1897, pp. 352-354).

Walker found a few burials and illustrates one of the bundle forms (1880a, pl. III, fig. 2). He noted sherds and human bones in great profusion in all parts of the tumulus.

Cushing's explorations were much more productive. He took out over 600 human skeletons. Most of these seem to have been secondary bundles or single skull interments, but he does refer to a few primary extended burials being found in wooden cists or sherd-lined graves within the mound. Stone, bone, and shell artifacts were in accompaniment. Pottery vessels and sherds were extremely numerous. This material has, in part, been considered by W. H. Holmes (1903, pp. 125-128). The following classification refers to the Holmes (1903) illustrations:

Weeden Island Complex

Weeden Island Series:

Weeden Island Incised............................Pl. CV, a

Weeden Island (or Papys Bayou) Punctated................ Pls. CI, a, b; CII, a, b; CIII, a, b; CV, b, c

Weeden Island Plain......................Pls. CII, c; CV, d

Weeden Island Zoned Red........................Pl. CVI, a

Complicated Stamped Series:

Swift Creek Complicated Stamped.................Pl. CVIII

Tampa Complicated Stamped......................Pl. CVIII

Santa Rosa-Swift Creek Complex

Crystal River Incised................................Pl. CVI, d

Alligator Bayou Stamped..........................Pl. CVI, b,c

Miscellaneous

Unclassified incised ....Pl. CVI, e

(This design is reminiscent of a Weeden Island vessel from Strange's Landing, Moore, 1902, fig. 117, and a sherd from Fort Walton, Moore, 1901, fig. 45.)

Check stamped ....Pl. CIX

(This is not typical Wakulla or Gulf Check Stamped.)

Additional specimens, not illustrated by Moore, are in the University Museum, Philadelphia. These include one Basin Bayou Incised (No. 29-124-149) and two Crystal River Incised (Nos. 29-124-139 and 29-124-137).

The mound is divided between the Weeden Island I and Santa Rosa-Swift Creek Periods.

Johns Pass (*Pi-4*).—Walker (1880a, pp. 401-403) and Moore (1903, pp. 434-436) both visited this mound which is located on a small key just inside of the pass (map 19). Walker observed an abundance of potsherds, skeletal material, and a few European trinkets, all of which had washed out of the base of the mound. Moore describes the mound as circular, about 35 feet in diameter and 2 feet high. Walker's dimensions are only slightly larger, but he classifies the mound as oval in shape. Walker noted extended burials; Moore's excavations revealed a few flexed burials. It is also likely that there were many secondary burials in the mound although this cannot be certified from the descriptions. Probably 100 or more skeletons had been placed in the mound.

Hematite ore was found with some burials but artifacts were placed in the mound only as general mortuary offerings. These were unperforated conch-shell cups. The only pottery was in the form of sherds. Moore mentions check stamped, shell-tempered wares, and loop handles. A panel of sherds (Moore, 1903, fig. 88) is composed of two Pinellas Incised (lower left and upper right) and six Safety Harbor Incised.

The Safety Harbor material, the loop handles, and the shell-tempered ware clearly date the mound as Safety Harbor Period.

Clearwater (*Pi-5*).—There is a collection of potsherds and a *Busycon* pick in the United States National Museum (Nos. 4310, 43098, 35638, and 88409) which Walker obtained at Clearwater. As the site nearest Clearwater which he visited was a large shell midden 1 mile north of the town (Walker, 1880b, p. 419), we presume this to be the site (map 19). Sherds are classified below:

Safety Harbor Complex	
Safety Harbor Series:	
Safety Harbor Incised	2
Pinellas Incised	3
Pinellas Plain	5
Englewood Complex	
Sarasota Incised	1

Weeden Island Complex	
Weeden Island Punctated	1
Wakulla Check Stamped	2
St. Petersburg Incised	1
Biscayne (or St. Johns) Series:	
Biscayne Check Stamped	1
Biscayne Plain	1
Glades Complex	
Glades Plain	23
Miscellaneous	
Smooth Plain	1
Unclassified plain (may be Pinellas)	2
Unclassified cord-marked	1
Total sherds	44

The site indicates Weeden Island II, Englewood, and Safety Harbor Period occupations. The presence of Glades Plain is consistent with the excavated sites in this region (see "Excavations on the West Coast: 1923-1936," this report) in that this type appears coevally with the later Gulf Coast periods.

Boca Ciega Island (*Pi-6*).—This collection is from one of the islands forming Boca Ciega Bay (map 19). It was collected by Mrs. Pearl Cole, of Washington, D. C., and presented to the United States National Museum (No. 36066). Presumably it is from a midden site. It is classified below:

Safety Harbor Complex	
Safety Harbor Incised	1
Pensacola Plain	2
Weeden Island Complex	
Tucker Ridge-pinched	1
Wakulla Check Stamped	8
Biscayne (or St. Johns) Series:	
Biscayne Check Stamped	18
Biscayne Cord-marked	1
Glades Complex	
Glades Plain	8
Belle Glade Plain	1
Total sherds	40

The collection dates from Weeden Island II into Safety Harbor times.

Bayview (*Pi-7*).—There is some confusion about the location of this mound (map 19). Walker (1880a, p. 410) places it as about 1 mile north of Bayview Post Office, on the south bank of Alligator Creek. According to his map (1880a, p. 412) this would place it somewhere near Safety Harbor, although Walker (same map) seems to have Safety Harbor too far north. From the description of the Bayview mound it does not seem likely that it is the Safety Harbor or Phillippi Hammock mound.

He describes it as circular, 46 feet in diameter and less than 3 feet high. He found human burials in three distinct strata. Nothing is said about burial form other than it "differs slightly" from what he had previously indicated as a bundle-type burial. In the bottom layer no artifacts were found with burials. In the middle and top layers he found glass beads, brass and copper ornaments, scissors, looking-glass ornaments, crockery, and other trinkets of European provenience. The collection of pottery from the site, which is now in the United States National Museum (Nos. 35315-35326), numbers only four aboriginal sherds. These all belong to the Safety Harbor Complex.

Seven Oaks (Pi-8).—This is a sand burial mound located about one-half mile west of Seven Oaks (map 19). There is a collection of material from the mound in the Florida State Museum at Gainesville which has been classified by Dr. J. M. Goggin.

Safety Harbor Complex	
Safety Harbor Series:	
Safety Harbor Incised	39
Pinellas Incised	26
Pinellas Plain	19
Leon Check Stamped	31
Lamar-like complicated stamped (May be Jefferson ware.)	12
Weeden Island Complex	
Weeden Island Incised (?)	1
Wakulla Check Stamped	8
Thomas Simple Stamped	6
St. Johns Series:	
St. Johns Check Stamped	65
St. Johns Plain	10
Pasco Plain	1
Glades Complex	
Belle Glade Plain	1
Miscellaneous	
Residual Plain	42
Unclassified	10
Total sherds	271

In addition to the aboriginal pottery, the collection contained Spanish ware, sheet and coin silver beads, glass beads, a gold-plated clay bead, and an amber bead.

The diagnostic pottery from this mound argues for a Safety Harbor Period dating, and the early European trade material confirms this. The Wakulla Check Stamped, Thomas Simple Stamped, and St. Johns types are not sufficiently diagnostic of Weeden Island to predicate an earlier stage for the mound. Both Wakulla and the St. Johns types are known to continue over into the Safety Harbor Period.

Other sites in Pinellas County.—There were a great many mound and midden sites along both shores of Pinellas Peninsula. Both Walker (1880a, b) and Moore (1900, 1903) saw, excavated, and described several of these. Circular burial mounds, flat-topped temple mounds, midden heaps, and complex shell works are represented. The burial or temple mounds were made of sand or sand and shell, and they are carefully distinguished from the shell-midden sites. Burial and temple mounds which they list are at Anclote River,[68] the Myers site, Dunedin, Saxe's mound or the "Mound near Clearwater," Hog Island, Long Key, Four Mile Bayou, Pine Key, Point Pinellos, and Bethel's Camp. A flat-topped mound with a complex of shell embankments attached to it is described from Maximo Point. Great shell middens were noted at Dwight's Orange Grove near Clearwater (probably Pi-5), Indian Pass Church, Four Mile Bayou, Bear Creek, Boca Ciega Bay (possibly Pi-6), the vicinity of Point Pinellos, Big Bayou, Cox property, and Booker Creek. These midden sites appear to be the village areas which are related to the temple and burial mounds. In some cases, however, the lower levels of these middens may date back to an early Glades culture horizon (Perico Island Period) which antedates the later Gulf Coast cultures. The mound and embankment complex at Maximo Point is very similar in configuration to some of the Glades area sites of the Glades III Period.

HILLSBOROUGH COUNTY

Thomas (Hi-1).—This site is described under the section on "Excavations on the West Coast: 1923-1936."

Cockroach (Hi-2).—This site is described under the section on "Excavations on the West Coast: 1923-1936."

Picknick (Hi-3).—Sometimes referred to as the Thatcher mound, this site is on the south prong of the Alafia River near the town of Picknick (see map 19 for approximate location). The site was

[68] A small collection of Wakulla and Biscayne Check Stamped sherds comes from one of these sites known as "Spanish Wells." The collection is in the U. S. National Museum (No. 149358).

excavated by J. Clarence Simpson during the Florida State Archeological Survey of 1937 (Anon., 1937). It is described as a mound 60 by 70 feet at the base and 4 feet high. Burials were taken from the lowest mound levels. These were loosely flexed. A pottery vessel of the Safety Harbor Period accompanied one burial. Glass beads of European provenience and small "bird" points of flint were screened from the sand of the upper level of the mound.

Simpson describes narrow-necked pottery jars, use of effigy rim lugs or adornos, a frog-effigy bowl, and the trait of vessel "killing" by perforation. Copper-covered ear ornaments of wood were found with a skeleton near mound base.

A collection from the mound is now in the Florida State Museum at Gainesville. Dr. John M. Goggin has provided me with the following classification:

Safety Harbor Complex	
Safety Harbor Series:	
Safety Harbor Incised	23
Pinellas Incised	43
Pinellas Plain	7
Fort Walton frog-effigy vessel	1
Weeden Island Complex	
Weeden Island Series:	
Weeden Island Incised	2
Weeden Island Punctated	2
Weeden Island Plain	2
Little Manatee Zoned Stamped	1
St. Johns (or Biscayne) Series:	
St. Johns Check Stamped	2
St. Johns Plain	1
Glades Complex	
Belle Glade Plain	9
Miscellaneous	
Residual Plain	9
Unclassified complicated stamped	1
Red bottle form (probably Safety Harbor)	1
Total sherds	104

The collection is divided between Safety Harbor and Weeden Island II Complexes. The probabilities that the mound, or its lower levels, were built in pre-Safety Harbor times are strengthened by the fact that a burial with copper-covered ear plugs was found near mound base. The European contact seems superficial.

Jones (*Hi-4*).—This mound, on the east bank of Pemberton Creek near Thonotosassa, was also investigated by Simpson (Anon., 1939a) (map 19). It was a sand mound 75 feet in diameter by 3 feet in height. It was partially surrounded by a horseshoe-shaped ridge of sand which opened on the east.

Most of the 174 burials were in or on the old basal or premound layer. The common burial form was semiflexure. Some artifacts were in direct association with the dead. Evidences of house floors are reported at 12 inches below the surface of the mound; however, there were no post molds in association.

Most of the mound pottery was found in caches where it had been placed after being destroyed. Red ocher, "killed" shell cups, stone and shell pendants, including some carved animal forms, stone celts, and shell tools were found in addition to the pottery.

A Florida State Museum collection from the mound has been classified by Goggin:

Safety Harbor Complex	
Safety Harbor Series:	
Safety Harbor Incised	3
Pinellas Incised	6
Weeden Island Complex	
Weeden Island Punctated	17
Wakulla Check Stamped	1
St. Johns (or Biscayne) Series:	
St. Johns Check Stamped	1
St. Johns Plain	4
Miscellaneous	
Residual Plain	8
Total sherds	40

The mound dates from the Weeden Island II and Safety Harbor Periods.

Snavely (*Hi-5*).—This burial mound, near Thonotosassa (see map 19), was excavated by Simpson during the Florida 1937 survey (Anon., 1937). Goggin has examined collections from the site and dates the material as of the Safety Harbor Period.

Buck Island (*Hi-6*).—This mound is located near the junction of Cypress Creek and Hillsborough River, 12 miles northeast of Tampa (map 19). It was excavated by Simpson, and a collection in the Florida State Museum at Gainesville has been classified by Goggin:

Safety Harbor Complex	
Safety Harbor Series:	
Safety Harbor Incised	11
Pinellas Incised	9
Pinellas Plain	13
Weeden Island Complex	
Weeden Island Series:	
Weeden Island Punctated	17
Carrabelle Punctated	1
Tampa Complicated Stamped	1
Wakulla Check Stamped	1
Combination Carrabelle Incised and Wakulla Check Stamped	1
St. Johns (Biscayne) Plain	2
Papys Bayou Punctated	5
Glades Complex	
Belle Glade Plain	1
Miscellaneous	
Residual Plain	21
Total sherds	83

This mound is also divided between a Weeden Island II and a Safety Harbor dating.

Rocky Point (*Hi-7*).—The site is mentioned as a big shell heap 5 or 6 miles west of Tampa (Shepard, 1886) (map 19). Earlier, Stearns had given it a brief note (Stearns, 1870). There is a collection in the United States National Museum (Nos. 3246632-3246663) which is classified below:

Safety Harbor Complex	
Safety Harbor Series:	
Pinellas Incised	1
Pinellas Plain	6
Weeden Island Complex	
Papys Bayou Series:	
Papys Bayou Punctated	1
Papys Bayou Plain	1
Hillsborough Shell Stamped	1
Biscayne (or St. Johns) Series:	
Biscayne Check Stamped	1
Biscayne Plain	2
West Florida Cord-marked (Probably Late Variety.)	2

Miscellaneous

Limestone-tempered cord-marked	1
(Related to Pasco Series.)	
Unclassified	1
Total sherds....	17

Both Weeden Island II and Safety Harbor Periods are represented.

Other sites in Hillsborough County.—There are numerous other sites, both mounds and middens, in Hillsborough County. One of the first to attract attention was the old Fort Brooker mound near Tampa. This was investigated and described by Lt. A. W. Vogdes in the 1870's, but the best account and appraisal is given in Walker (1880a, pp. 411-413). This was probably a platform or temple mound, and it is described as being constructed of alternate sand and shell layers. At least one burial was found in addition to some check stamped pottery.

Another large and well-known site is the Bullfrog mound on Bullfrog Creek, a tributary of the Alafia River. Shepard (1886) and Walker (1880b, pp. 421-422) describe it, and Moore (1900, pp. 357-358) gives it brief mention. Long destroyed, the site appears to have been a complex of high shell mounds, shell ridges, and shell refuse piles. A similar site, at least in outward appearance, is Mill Point on the Alafia River (Moore, 1900, pp. 356-357). The Alafia River is also known for archeological objects taken from the phosphate beds in its immediate vicinity.

Among the more recent mound excavations that have been carried out by J. C. Simpson are those at the Spender, Cagnini, Branch, and Lykes mounds (Anon., 1937). Another mound in the vicinity of Tampa was excavated by J. J. Hall. This site, judging by a collection examined by Goggin in the University of Michigan Museum, was probably of the Safety Harbor Period.

Two excellent collections, but both lacking location data, probably came from Hillsborough County. They are listed only as "Tampa Bay." One is at Peabody Museum, Harvard University, and was obtained by F. W. Putnam in 1899. It is pure Safety Harbor but with a large increment of Lamar-like complicated stamped. The other was donated to the United States National Museum (No. 35373) by J. W. Milner. It is divided between types of the Safety Harbor and Weeden Island Complexes.

MANATEE COUNTY

Parrish mounds 1-5 (*Ma-1, 2, 3, 4, 5*).—These sites are described under "Excavations on the West Coast: 1923-1936."

Perico Island (*Ma-6*).—This site is described under "Excavations on the West Coast: 1923-1936."

Shaws Point (*Ma-7*).—This is one of the best-known sites on the Gulf Coast (map 20). Walker (1880b, pp. 416-422) described it as

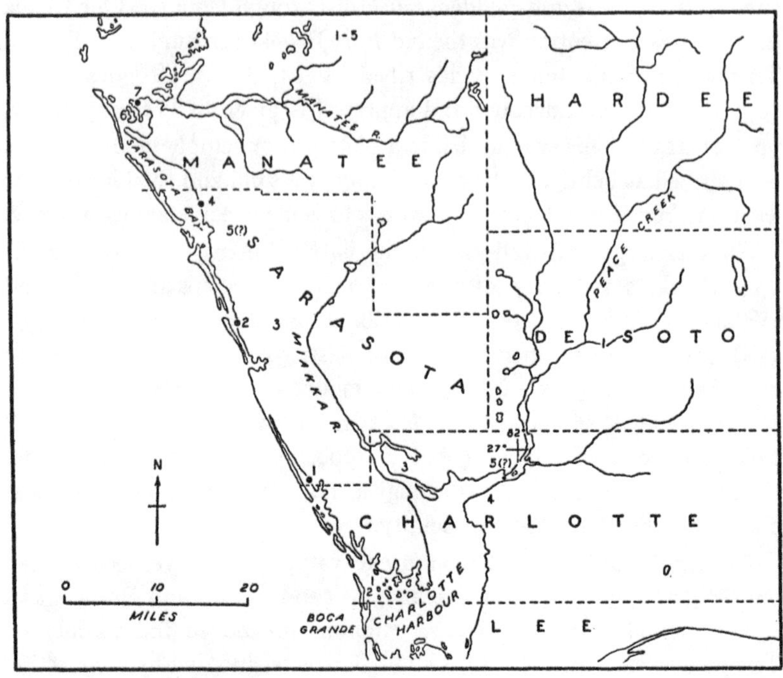

MAP 20.—Site map of Manatee, Sarasota, Charlotte, and DeSoto Counties. Sites indicated by numbers.

a series of shell tumuli stretching along the water front for over 150 yards with some of the hillocks being as much as 20 feet in height. The location has also been considered the landing place of the DeSoto expedition. In spite of its general notoriety, little is actually known of the archeology of the site. It was Walker's opinion that the site represented a great refuse heap or series of such heaps. Animal and fish bones, evidences of old fires, and potsherds were observed on the surface as well as in occasional cross sections.

There is a collection of pottery and artifacts from this site in the United States National Museum (Nos. 317078-317432, 329771-

329774, 341237-341244) which was presented by Charles T. Earle. It is given below:

Safety Harbor Complex	
Safety Harbor Series:	
Safety Harbor Incised	1
Pinellas Incised	10
Pinellas Plain	4
Leon Check Stamped	5
Pensacola Plain	10
Twined Fabric-impressed (Shell-tempered.)	2
Weeden Island Complex	
Weeden Island Series:	
Weeden Island Incised	1
Weeden Island Punctated	2
Weeden Island Plain	3
Wakulla Check Stamped	8
Complicated Stamped Series:	
Swift Creek Complicated Stamped	3
Sun City Complicated Stamped	1
Hillsborough Shell Stamped	4
Papys Bayou Punctated	2
Little Manatee Zoned Stamped	1
Biscayne (or St. Johns) Series:	
Biscayne Check Stamped	14
Biscayne Plain	3
Biscayne Red	3
Simple Stamped, Biscayne paste	5
Santa Rosa-Swift Creek Complex	
Alligator Bayou Stamped	1
Franklin Plain	1
Deptford Complex	
Deptford Bold Check Stamped	1
Glades Complex	
Glades Plain	34
Perico Plain	3
Belle Glade Plain	3
Miscellaneous	
Smooth Plain	1
Residual Plain	2
Unclassified	4
Total sherds	132

Besides the sherds there is a flanged pendant made of pottery.

Chipped stone in the collection includes large and medium-size stemmed projectiles, unstemmed projectiles, blades, blanks, a celt, and a rectangular European gun flint. Single-grooved plummets, a stone weight (?) with an encircling groove, and a stone pestle make up the ground-stone inventory. A bone dagger, bone pins, bipointed bone projectiles, tubular shell beads, *Busycon* picks or hammers, *Strombus* hammers, perforated *Venus* shells, *Strombus* celts, *Fasciolaria* hammers, columellae chisels and hammers, *Busycon* saucers or disks, shell gorges (?), single-grooved columellae pendants, and a two-hole circular shell gorget complete the list.

The collection contains pottery dating as Safety Harbor, Weeden Island, Santa Rosa-Swift Creek, and Deptford, although the two earlier periods are not well represented. Glades influence is seen in the pottery and particularly in the shell tools.

Other sites in Manatee County.—These are numerous, both along the coast and inland. Moore (1900, pp. 360-362) lists several sites, both sand burial mounds and shell middens. None of these can be identified from the brief descriptions.

SARASOTA COUNTY

Englewood (So-1).—This site is described under "Excavations on the West Coast: 1923-1936."

Osprey (So-2).—There are a number of shell middens along Sarasota Bay, one of which is at Osprey (map 20). Hrdlička made a collection here for the United States National Museum (Nos. 238493-2386502) which is analyzed below:

Safety Harbor Complex	
Safety Harbor Series:	
Safety Harbor Incised	10
Pinellas Incised	17
Pinellas Plain	14
Englewood Complex	
Englewood Series:	
Englewood Incised	1
Englewood Plain	3
Weeden Island Complex	
Weeden Island Series:	
Weeden Island Incised	4
Weeden Island Punctated	4
Weeden Island Plain	4
Weeden Island Zoned Red	1
St. Petersburg Incised	4
Papys Bayou Punctated	5
Biscayne (or St. Johns) Series:	
Biscayne Check Stamped	4
Biscayne Red	2
Biscayne Plain	9

Glades Complex	
Glades Plain	37
Belle Glade Plain	1
Miscellaneous	
Smooth Plain	2
Residual Plain	8
Cord-marked	2
Unclassified	8
Total sherds....	140

Busycon picks and hammers, *Busycon* celts, grooved-shell pendants, perforated *Arca* shells, *Strombus* hammers, a limestone hammerstone, and a flat-topped bone pin make up the Osprey collection.

In addition to the Hrdlička collection there is another in the National Museum which was contributed by J. G. Webb. It is marked simply as "Sarasota Bay," but the chances are it is also an Osprey collection. It shows approximately the same range of shell materials, a few Weeden Island Period sherds, and differs only in that it contains Spanish olive-jar fragments.

The Osprey midden shows occupation from Safety Harbor, Englewood, and Weeden Island II times. The Safety Harbor occupation probably continued into the historic period.

Pool Hammock (So-3).—The information on this site comes from H. L. Schoff, the excavator (letter of January 1933, Bureau of American Ethnology files). The location is on the Thompson property northeast of the town of Laurel (map 20). Mr. Schoff describes the site as a village some 2 acres in extent and with an average refuse depth of 18 inches. Burials were found at the eastern end of the area at superficial depths.

The Schoff collection (U.S.N.M. Nos. 367994-368000) is classified below:

Safety Harbor Complex	
Pinellas Incised	2
Weeden Island Complex	
Weeden Island Series:	
Weeden Island Incised	1
Weeden Island Punctated	1
Wakulla Check Stamped	1
Biscayne Plain	2
Glades Complex	
Glades Plain	2
Miscellaneous	
Complicated stamped on Biscayne paste	1
Total sherds....	10

The Schoff collection also includes stemmed and stemless projectile points of large to medium size, a grinding slab, bipointed bone projectiles, *Strombus* hammers, and columellae chisels.

The site was occupied in both Safety Harbor and Weeden Island II times.

Whittaker or Whitfield estate (So-4).—This is a mound site located 2 miles north of Sarasota near the shore (map 20). The mound measures 60 feet in diameter and 10 feet in height. It was investigated by Mr. Schoff who has provided the National Museum (No. 364695) with a small collection of sherds which are given below:

Safety Harbor Complex	
Safety Harbor Series:	
Safety Harbor Incised	1
Pinellas Incised	3
Pinellas Plain	11
Biscayne Check Stamped	1
Total sherds	16

The mound dates from the Safety Harbor Period.

True Site (So-5).—I have assigned a name to this site after the owner of the collection, David O. True, of Miami, Fla. According to Mr. True, the materials which he has or had in his possession came from a mound somewhere in Sarasota County. The location is not known, but is said to be somewhere to the northeast of the Tamiami Highway at a distance of about 6 miles (map 20).

The site was a sand burial mound about 8 feet high. Burials were found in all parts of the mound, but the available data also indicate that there was one "central" burial on mound base. About 50 skeletons were found. Burial treatment or position is not known. Pottery vessels of the Safety Harbor Incised type were found in the mound. In addition, Mr. True has a conical copper ornament which measures about 3 cm. in diameter, a multicolored chevron glass bead, and other miscellaneous European trade artifacts.

The mound dates from the Safety Harbor Period.

Other sites in Sarasota County.—There are numerous other burial-mound and midden sites in the county, but location and specimen data are too scant to be of help in adequate identifications. Moore (1900, pp. 360-362) mentions some of these along the coast.

CHARLOTTE COUNTY

Cayo Palu (Ch-1).—This is a burial-mound site on a small key just inside Boca Grande Pass (map 20). It was excavated by Montague Tallant, and a sherd collection has been donated to the United States National Museum (Nos. 378302-378310). The material has been classified as:

Weeden Island Complex	
Oklawaha Plain	1
Biscayne (or St. Johns) Series:	
Biscayne Plain	29
Biscayne Red	21
Miscellaneous	
Unclassified incised	1
Unclassified plain	8
Total sherds..	60

This collection is augmented by some photographs of restored vessels from the site which include three more Oklawaha Plain specimens. In addition, Goggin has reviewed scattered specimens from this mound and has identified them as Weeden Island. This includes one Weeden Island Punctated sherd (Goggin, n.d.2).

The presence of the Oklawaha type and the absence of any check stamped, either Biscayne or Wakulla, implies a Weeden Island I dating. The site has significance as the southernmost Weeden Island burial mound yet brought to our attention.

Gasparilla Sound (Ch-2).—Moore (1905, p. 302) dug this mound which is situated on Boca Grande Key (map 20). Its exact location is not known, and as the key lies half within Charlotte and half within Lee Counties it is possible that the mound may be in Lee.

The mound which was almost destroyed before Moore's excavations was a sand burial tumulus. About 15 skeletons were recorded, all apparently flexed primaries. Shell cups, some perforated, were with the burials. A few sherds were found in the mound fill. Moore (1905, figs. 4, 5) shows two of these, both of which are Pinellas Incised.

The mound, on this evidence, dates from the Safety Harbor Period.

Widder Creek (Ch-3).—This site, apparently a midden, was excavated near El Jobean (map 20). The collection is now in the Heye Foundation (Cat. No. 20/1177). It is composed of 35 Glades Plain and 2 Belle Glade Plain sherds. A stemmed flint point, a *Busycon* pick, and some miscellaneous shell artifacts were found in addition to the pottery (Nos. 20/1179-1183).

The site appears to be purely of the Glades Complex and may date from the Perico Island Period.

Punta Gorda (Ch-4).—This site near or at Punta Gorda (map 20) was excavated by Mr. Turbeyfill of the Heye Foundation in the

1930's. It was a shell midden and contained Glades and Belle Glade Plain pottery. The sample collection (Heye No. 19/7361-7367) shows the two types in about equal portions. Bone tools, shell artifacts, and a European white pipestem fragment make up the collection.

The site appears to be purely of the Glades Complex and may date from the Perico Island Period except for the European trade pipe.

Hickory Bluff (*Ch-5*).—This is one of Moore's sites (Moore, 1905, p. 302) on which we have no exact location data. At the time of his excavations it was in DeSoto County. At the present, the location is probably in Charlotte County (map 20).

It was a mound, probably a sand burial mound, in which he found a few sherds. Three of these are shown. Figure 1 is Safety Harbor Incised; figures 2 and 3 are Pinellas Incised (Moore, 1905, p. 303).

The data indicate a Safety Harbor date.

DE SOTO COUNTY

Arcadia site (*De-1*).—This site was a sand burial mound located a few miles south of Arcadia (map 20). In 1935 a selection of vessels from this mound were in the possession of Clarke Brown, of Arcadia. All these specimens are bottle forms with basal perforations. They have been classified as Safety Harbor Incised, and they bear a close resemblance to that type as it is found at Safety Harbor proper and other Tampa Bay sites. The bottle form is a good Safety Harbor shape. Also, the decoration is similar. An important difference is that the Arcadia site specimens are decorated with much greater skill and care than that usually seen in Safety Harbor pottery. Designs are balanced and well executed. Stirling (1936, p. 353) referred to this Arcadia variant as "Arcadia Ware," setting it apart from Safety Harbor but recognizing their relationship.

In this report I am including the Arcadia variant with Safety Harbor Incised, as I feel I would not be able to segregate them as separate types with consistency. The degree of difference is called to attention, however; and it may be that the Arcadia mound represents a slightly earlier phase of the Safety Harbor Period than that more commonly seen in the other sites.

CONCLUSIONS

From this review of available data on Gulf Florida mound, midden, and cemetery sites it is possible to equate, with complete assurance, the culture sequences that have been established for the northwest coast and the Manatee region. It is demonstrated that similar culture periods are to be found in the intervening central coast region and that these serve to complete the linkage. Certain periods may be extended for the entire Gulf Coast area, and others, while more re-

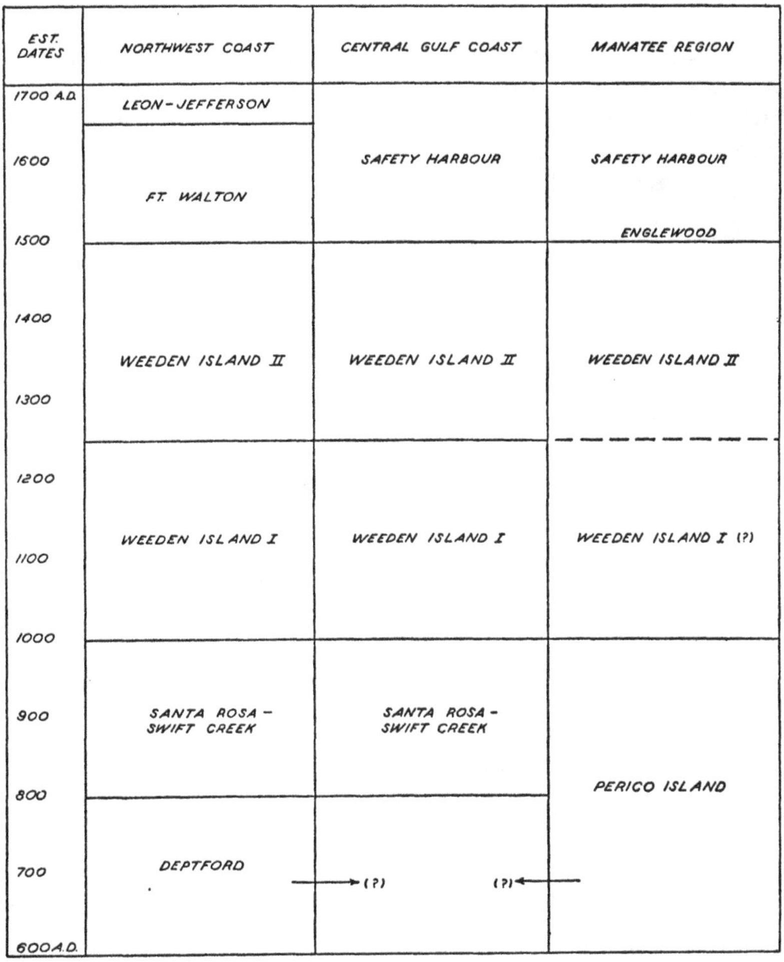

EST. DATES	NORTHWEST COAST	CENTRAL GULF COAST	MANATEE REGION
1700 A.D.	LEON-JEFFERSON		
1600	FT. WALTON	SAFETY HARBOUR	SAFETY HARBOUR
1500			ENGLEWOOD
1400			
	WEEDEN ISLAND II	WEEDEN ISLAND II	WEEDEN ISLAND II
1300			
1200			
	WEEDEN ISLAND I	WEEDEN ISLAND I	WEEDEN ISLAND I (?)
1100			
1000			
900	SANTA ROSA - SWIFT CREEK	SANTA ROSA - SWIFT CREEK	
800			PERICO ISLAND
700	DEPTFORD	→ (?) (?) ←	
600 A.D.			

Fig. 20.—Combined chart of culture sequences for the three regions of the Florida Gulf Coast area.

stricted in their distributions, may, nevertheless, be related to each other in a horizonal fashion. The chart on figure 20 depicts these regional variations, similarities, and their time relationships.

The cultural dating of the sites in this review and the subsequent grouping of these sites into culture periods is the intermediate step antecedent to the descriptions of Florida Gulf Coast culture periods. The listings below summarize the number of sites and the types of sites which are grouped in each period or multiple-period category. Site datings have been made throughout on the preponderance of evidence from a site. In those cases where a site is dated as of more than one period, pottery types of two or more complexes have been proportionately well represented in the site collection. In referring back to the individual site discussions it will be noted that there are instances where one or two sherds of a complex occur at a site but have not been considered sufficient to be represented in the dating.

Leon Jefferson Period
3 midden or village sites

Fort Walton Period
8 midden or village sites
3 temple-mound sites
6 temple-mound and village sites
2 burial-mound sites
4 cemetery sites

Safety Harbor Period
2 temple-mound and village sites
13 burial-mound sites
1 cemetery site

Weeden Island II Period
16 midden or village sites
1 domiciliary-mound (?) site
12 burial-mound sites

Weeden Island I Period
3 midden or village sites
18 burial-mound sites

Weeden Island Periods (combined or undifferentiated)
4 midden or village sites
37 burial-mound sites
1 cemetery or burial-mound (?) site

Santa Rosa-Swift Creek Period
5 midden or village sites
12 burial-mound sites

Deptford Period
1 midden or village site
1 cemetery site

Perico Island Period
2 midden or village sites (questionable)
2 burial-mound, cemetery, and midden sites

The following are all of two or more period components:

Fort Walton and Weeden Island II Periods
7 midden or village sites

Fort Walton, Weeden Island I and II Periods
2 midden or village sites

Fort Walton and Weeden Island I Periods
1 midden or village site
2 burial-mound sites

Fort Walton and Santa Rosa-Swift Creek Periods
2 midden or village sites

Safety Harbor, Englewood, and Weeden Island II Periods
2 midden or village sites
1 burial-mound site

Safety Harbor and Weeden Island II Periods
2 midden or village sites
4 burial-mound sites
1 village and cemetery site

Safety Harbor, Weeden Island I and II Periods
1 burial-mound site

Safety Harbor, Weeden Island, and Santa Rosa-Swift Creek Periods
1 midden or village site

Weeden Island I and Santa Rosa-Swift Creek Periods
3 midden or village sites
7 burial-mound sites

Weeden Island I and II and Santa Rosa-Swift Creek Periods
1 midden or village site

Santa Rosa-Swift Creek and Deptford Periods
1 midden and cemetery site

Weeden Island II and Perico Island Periods
1 burial-mound site

Weeden Island II, Santa Rosa-Swift Creek, and Deptford Periods
1 midden or village site

Fort Walton, Weeden Island I and II, and Santa Rosa-Swift Creek Periods
2 midden or village sites

Fort Walton, Weeden Island I and II, and Santa Rosa-Swift Creek Periods
1 midden or village site

Weeden Island I and II, Santa Rosa-Swift Creek, and Deptford Periods
2 midden or village sites

Weeden Island or Santa Rosa-Swift Creek Periods (questionable)
3 burial-mound sites

Santa Rosa-Swift Creek or Deptford Periods (questionable)
1 burial-mound site

Fort Walton Period (questionable)
2 temple-mound sites

VI. THE CULTURE PERIODS

THE EARLIEST INHABITANTS

There is very little evidence concerning the earliest inhabitants of the Florida Gulf Coast.[69] Presumably these were preagricultural, preceramic groups of American Indians who subsisted upon fish, shellfish, and game. The lower levels of some of the great shell heaps on the St. Johns River in eastern Florida contain the refuse remains of a people who followed this type of life.[70] Elsewhere in the southeastern United States, particularly along the banks of some of the major rivers, there are fresh-water mussel heaps which represent the dwelling places of early hunting and gathering groups. As some of these sites are of considerable size and depth it appears that the populations at this time were not small and that they were concentrated, at least in some instances, in stable communities. There is little likelihood that sites of the preceramic period comparable in size to those of the St. Johns or the Tennessee River ever existed in Gulf Florida. Possibly the lower levels of some of the big Tampa, Cedar Keys, Suwannee and Withlacoochee River shell mounds will show this preceramic horizon. It is also possible that careful excavation in some of the smaller shell heaps along the Gulf will reveal prepottery layers.

In many areas of the eastern United States, including the aforementioned St. Johns and Tennessee River basins, this preceramic stage of culture was marked, toward its close, by the appearance of the first pottery. This first pottery is a crude fiber-tempered ware. Although characterized by some local peculiarities it is, on the whole, amazingly uniform and easily recognizable. Its chronological position is equally uniform in that in almost every instance where stratig-

---

69 Evidences of an even earlier Paleo-Indian occupation in Florida are seen in the Folsom-like points from central Florida and in the controversial Vero finds of the Florida east coast.

70 Excavations at the mouth of the Chassahowitzka River, Hernando County, by Dr. A. J. Waring, Jr., have revealed what may be a preceramic site, the first to be reported from the Gulf Coast area. According to Waring the preceramic levels at the site are characterized by heavy flint choppers and by refuse that is predominantly fresh-water shell. Later ceramic-bearing refuse consists of oyster shells.

More recent (May 1949) excavations at the same site, by R. P. Bullen, cast some doubt on the preceramic interpretation. (See pp. 327-328.)

raphy obtains, the fiber-tempered pottery has appeared at the bottom of the ceramic sequence. On the Georgia coast fiber ware has been referred to as St. Simons Plain (Caldwell and McCann, 1941, pp. 50-51); in the Savannah basin and in South Carolina as Stallings Plain (J. B. Griffin, 1943, pp. 159-160); in northern Alabama as Wheeler Plain (Haag, *in* Webb and De Jarnette, 1942, pp. 513-514); and on the St. Johns as Orange Plain (J. B. Griffin, 1945, pp. 219-221). In view of this chronological position and geographical distribution the appearance of fiber-tempered pottery on the Gulf Coast assumes significance in considering the problem of the earliest inhabitants of the area.

Up to the present time only a very few sherds of the fiber-tempered pottery (St. Simons Plain) have been found in Gulf Coast sites. These have all been midden sites, and, in most cases, sites which showed other early period pottery types. Goggin (n.d.2) has recently established a tentative Orange Period for the Gulf Coast, inferring an extension of the cultural period of the same name from northeast Florida. At Carrabelle (Fr-2), the only Gulf site at which we have stratigraphic coordinates for the type, a very few sherds were taken from the lowest levels of test pits in association with Deptford Period sherds. Farther south, at Perico Island, fiber ware is associated with the Perico Series types on what is probably a time level comparable to the Deptford. In interior Georgia the situation is something the same in that the fiber-tempered types have not been satisfactorily isolated but always appear with early sand-tempered types such as the Deptford. As the situation now stands we can only say that there may have been a fiber-tempered pottery or Orange Period in the archeology of Gulf Florida, but there is also a possibility that the fiber types occurred there peripheral to their own centers of development and as minority types associated with a later horizon.

Of the sites which I have covered, a few fiber-tempered sherds appeared from the following. All are in the northwest except Perico Island.

Carrabelle (Fr-2)
Topsail Bluff (Fr-7)
Nine-Mile Point (Fr-9)
West Goose Creek (Wa-6)
Near St. Marks (Wa-7)
Perico Island (Ma-6)

Goggin (n.d.2) also reports a fiber-tempered sherd (Stallings Linear Punctated) from Cedar Keys and another (Orange Plain) from the Wacissa River.

THE DEPTFORD PERIOD

Period definition.—The Deptford Period is defined by the appearance and numerical predominance of the pottery types Deptford Linear Check Stamped and Deptford Bold Check stamped. These types are often accompanied by Deptford Simple Stamped. Deptford is the earliest established period for the northwest coast region of the Gulf Coast area and in Florida is known only for this region (fig. 20).

The sites.—Eight, or possibly nine, sites exist for this period.

Pure sites
- Middens:
  - Okaloosa-Walton County Line (Wl-1)
- Cemeteries:
  - Carrabelle (Fr-2)

Mixed sites
- Middens:
  - Porter's Bar (Fr-1)
  - Carrabelle (Fr-2)
  - Tucker (Fr-4)
  - Nine-Mile Point (Fr-9)
  - West Goose Creek (Wa-6)
  - Near St. Marks (Wa-7)

Questionable
- Burial mound:
  - Mound near Mack Bayou (Wl-10)

All these sites are in the northwest, in Walton, Franklin, and Wakulla Counties.[70a]

Settlement pattern.—All the sites except two are villages situated on or near the Gulf or tributary bays. All are marked by shell refuse. The only pure Deptford site is a thin midden about 50 meters in diameter. The other midden sites at which the complex occurs are larger, but it is impossible to tell just how much of the village areas was occupied in Deptford times.

Economy.—Based upon marine foods and, probably, wild game and plants. These should have been sufficiently plentiful for sedentary communities of small size.

Organization of society.—Probably small, autonomous bands based upon kinship affiliations. It is unlikely that religious expression had achieved formal organization.

[70a] Since this was written Goggin and I located three shell middens in Levy County, opposite Cedar Keys, which show Deptford Period occupations (April 1949). (See pp. 315-316.)

Disposal of the dead.—There is reliable evidence from only one site (Fr-2). Here, two cremated burials were found at shallow depths within, or on the margin of, the village midden area. Artifacts were not placed with the burials, but caches of purposefully destroyed pottery were found in the ground nearby.

The evidence for burial mounds during this period is exceedingly weak. At one site, Mound near Mack Bayou (Wl-10), there is a burial mound which might possibly qualify. This was a low, circular sand mound which contained only a single burial of unidentifiable burial type. A stone plummet and a bar gorget were the only distinctive artifacts in the mound.

Ceramic arts.—Pottery of the period is simple but reasonably well made and well fired. Forms are few. Decoration is plastic and by impression except for a very few examples which may be trade pieces. Judging from excavation and surface collections pottery was not as abundant as in the later periods. This might, however, be directly correlated with smaller populations.

There are few types for the period, with only one major series, the Deptford. Deptford Linear Check Stamped is the most distinctive and diagnostic type. Because of the questionable status of the fiber-tempered pottery in Gulf Florida the type St. Simons Plain is described with the Deptford Complex. St. Marks Plain probably, although not assuredly, dates from this period. Alexander Incised is also included although it appears only infrequently, probably as trade.

The Deptford Complex of pottery types in the order in which they are described:

- Deptford Series:
  - Deptford Linear Check Stamped
  - Deptford Bold Check Stamped
  - Deptford Simple Stamped
- St. Marks Plain
- St. Simons Plain
- Alexander Incised

Type Descriptions

Type name.—DEPTFORD LINEAR CHECK STAMPED.

Definition as a type.—From the Georgia coast by Caldwell and Waring (1939). The following description is based upon a collection of sherds from the Carrabelle site in northwest Florida.

Ware characteristics:

Method of manufacture: Coiling or annular method.

Temper: Fine sand.

Paste texture and color: Compact, slightly contorted, but quite even. Large particles of sand or quartz are very rare. Paste is often buff throughout, although sometimes only the surfaces, or only the exterior surface, has been fired buff while the core has been reduced to a gray color.

Surface texture, color, and finish: The exterior surface is covered with stamped decoration, except, perhaps, for the base. Interior surfaces are smoothed (show striations of smoothing) and sometimes have a low polish. Exterior surfaces are nearly always buff but often with gray or black fire-mottling. Interiors are buff or gray-black.

Hardness: 2.5 to 3.5.[71]

Thickness: Ranges from 5 to 8 mm.

Decoration:

Technique: The design was impressed upon the soft, unfired clay of the vessel with a carved wooden or bone instrument. The instrument may have been either cylindrical or flat. It was repeatedly pressed or rolled on the vessel surface.

Design: The design is distinguished from other check stamped pottery by the large, pronounced, parallel lands of one direction and the smaller transverse lands of the other. The large, pronounced lands are usually placed parallel with the horizontal plane of the vessel mouth, but sometimes they are arranged diagonally on the vessel. The pronounced lands are much wider and raised much higher on the vessel surfaces than are the transverse lands. The pronounced lands are 2 to 3 mm. wide; the small transverse lands are often less than 1 mm. The pronounced lands may be from 2 to 6 mm. apart; the transverse lands are nearly always closer together than the pronounced lands. The unit of decoration appears in some cases to be the single row of checks or a series of small transverse lands bounded by two heavy lands. There are indications that the unit of stamped decoration sometimes consisted of more than a single row. There is considerable overlapping of the rows of stamping. (See pl. 12.)

Distribution: Probably all exterior vessel surface.

Form:

Total vessel: Estimated as pot forms with slightly flared or slightly converged orifices and conoidal or subconoidal bases.

Rim: Slightly incurved or inslanting rims, some of which also have a slight eversion at the mouth. Also slightly outslanting or flared rims. (See fig. 21, top.)

Lip: Some are flat; others slightly rounded. A few come to a rounded point.

Base: Probably conoidal or subconoidal, but may be small and flattened.

Appendages: None recorded. Tetrapod supports are the only very good possibility.

Geographical range of type: Caldwell and Waring report the type from the St. John's River in Florida northward into South Carolina. It is known well inland on the Savannah River and the Altamaha River system in Georgia. A few pieces have turned up in east Tennessee. In northwest Florida I have noted it between St. Andrews Bay and Apalachee Bay on the coast.

---

[71] Moh's scale of relative hardness is used here and throughout this report.

Chronological position of type: Represents earliest known ceramic type found in any large quantity in northwest Florida. Precedes the Santa Rosa-Swift Creek Period types. In the lower Savannah basin, at Stallings Island, Ga., and on the Georgia coast this type has early associations, following the early Stallings Island and St. Simons complexes of plain and decorated fiber-tempered pottery and preceding the early complicated stamped pottery of the Swift Creek series.

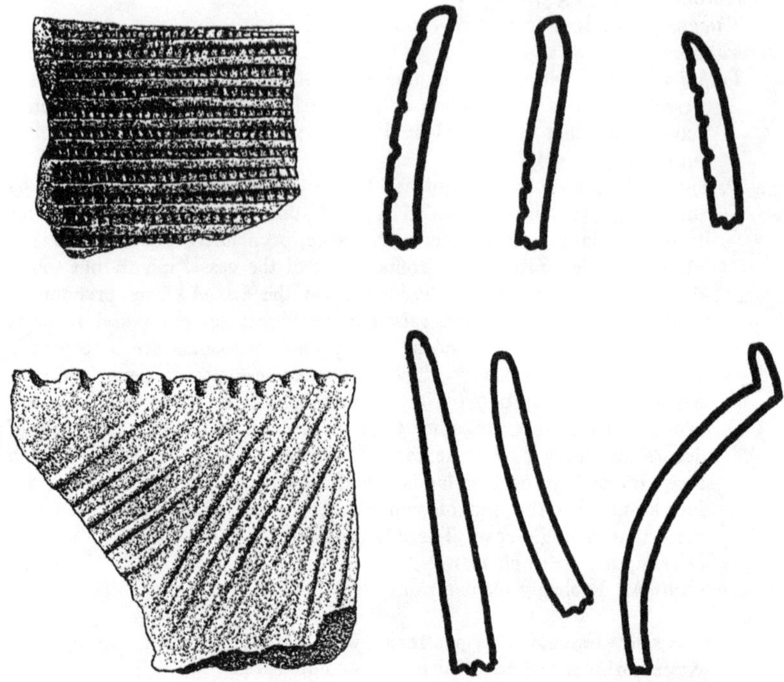

FIG. 21.—Deptford Period rim forms. *Top:* Deptford Linear Check Stamped; *bottom:* Deptford Simple Stamped. (Interiors to right.)

Relationships of type: The northwest Florida and south Atlantic representations of Deptford Linear Check Stamped resemble each other closely enough to be considered as the same type. The type has no other known close relatives. Later check stamped types of the Florida-Georgia region, and the Southeast at large, may be later developments of the Deptford Check Stamped idea. In any event, Deptford Linear Check Stamped is the earliest appearance of check stamped pottery in the Southeast.

Bibliography: Caldwell and Waring (1939); Willey and Woodbury (1942, p. 240); Caldwell and McCann (1941, pp. 50-51); Lewis and Kneberg (1946, pl. 47).

Type name.—DEPTFORD BOLD CHECK STAMPED.

Definition as a type: From the Georgia Coast by Caldwell and Waring (1939). The following description is based upon a collection from northwest Florida. Not as valuable a period marker as the Deptford Linear type. Lacking the peculiar linear design, it is more difficult to distinguish from other types of check stamped pottery.

Ware characteristics: Same as Deptford Linear Check Stamped except for greater thickness which ranges from .6 to 1.2 cm. (This greater thickness may be due to a greater proportion of base sherds in the collection under consideration.)

Decoration: Technique of application and distribution of decoration are the same as Deptford Linear Check Stamped.

Design: Check stamped units of undetermined size. Individual rectangles usually square and the lands of both directions are the same size. Considerable variability in the size of rectangles, ranging from 3 to 7 mm. Squares are deep, and lands are bold and wide. (Pl. 13, *a-c.*)

Form:

Total vessel: Probably pot form with subconoidal or truncated conoidal base.

Rim: Simple, unmodified, slightly outcurving. (Evidence weak.)

Base: Much thicker than upper walls. Some are flattened cones with footed supports.

Appendages: Teat-shaped supports. One measures 2 cm. high and 3 cm. in diameter at base.

Geographical range of type: Same as Deptford Linear Check Stamped.

Chronological position of type: Part of the Deptford Complex and Period. A slightly later time range, overlapping with Santa Rosa-Swift Creek Period types, is indicated for northwest Florida.

Relationships of type: Immediate relationships are obviously with Deptford Linear Check Stamped and, possibly, with Gulf Check Stamped.

Bibliography: Caldwell and Waring (1939); Caldwell and McCann (1941, pp. 50-51); Willey and Woodbury (1942, p. 240); Kelly (1938, pl. 10).

Type name.—DEPTFORD SIMPLE STAMPED.

Definition as a type: From the Georgia coast by Caldwell and Waring (1939). This present description is based upon a collection from the northwest Florida coast. The type is not a good period marker in northwest Florida. It occurs only as a minority type, and it has a very long life span.

Ware characteristics:

Method of manufacture: Coiling or an annular technique.

Temper: Sand. Fine and medium-grained. Seems slightly coarser, on the average, than the tempering of Deptford Linear Check Stamped.

Paste texture and color: Fine, compact, and slightly contorted. May be light buff, reddish buff, or gray-black. Also may have dark core with one or two buff-fired surfaces.

Surface texture, color, and finish: Various shades of buff or gray-black. Buff surfaces are often mottled with gray fire-clouding. Interior surfaces range from smooth to abrasive. Smoothing marks visible.

Hardness: 2.5 to 3.5.

Thickness: Range from 9 to 3 mm. with average about 6 or 7 mm.

Decoration:

Technique: Impression of grooved wooden paddle or thong-wrapped paddle upon unfired surface of vessel.

Design: Arrangements of parallel, linear grooves. Appear to have been three, four, or more grooves or thongs to the stamping unit. These series or units of parallel lines were applied roughly parallel to each other as a rule, but there is a good deal of diagonal and transverse overlapping. The grooves vary from 2 to 5 mm. in width. They are placed vertically, horizontally, and diagonally on the vessel. They vary in length from 1.5 to 5 cm. or over. (Pl. 13, *d-f.*)

Distribution: Apparently complete exterior surface of vessel. (There are a few examples of where the stamping stops just short of the lip.)

Form:

Total vessel: Pot form, deep bowl, flattened-globular bowl suggested by sherds. Moore (1918, fig. 30) shows a small double vessel (pl. 41, *d*).

Rim: Direct, outstanding or outflaring, and incurving. Slight eversion at orifice noted in one instance (see fig. 21, bottom).

Lip: Rounded or a round point. Some specimens marked by deep notches or small scallops. These were made with a cylindrical stick, or similar object, impressed directly on top of the lip.

Base: No evidence. Perhaps subconoidal or round.

Appendages: Tetrapods noted for type on the Georgia coast, and the Moore specimen referred to above has tetrapodal supports.

Geographical range of type: Caldwell and Waring define the south Atlantic range as from St. Simons Island, Ga., to an unknown distance into South Carolina. In northwest Florida it is probably in greatest density between Apalachee and St. Andrews Bays. It is occasionally found on the west coast of the peninsula.

Chronological position of type: This is not clear-cut in Florida, although Deptford Simple Stamped is coexistent with Deptford Linear Check Stamped in its first occurrence on the northwest coast. It continues upward in the sequence and is found with Santa Rosa-Swift Creek Period types quite consistently. There are also indications that it is occasionally found in Weeden Island Period contexts.

Relationships of type: Undoubtedly related to other simple stamped pottery throughout the southeastern United States. Mossy Oak Simple Stamped of central Georgia and Bluff Creek Simple Stamped of northern Alabama are two such examples. Probably it is the prototype for the later Gulf Coast type, Thomas Simple Stamped.

Bibliography: Caldwell and Waring (1939); Caldwell and McCann (1941, pp. 50-51); Haag (1939, type: Bluff Creek Simple Stamped); Jennings and Fairbanks (1939, type: Mossy Oak Simple Stamped); Willey and Woodbury (1942, p. 240).

Type name.—ST. MARKS PLAIN.

Definition as a type: Defined here from the northwest Florida coast.

Ware characteristics:

Method of manufacture: No coil fractures observed.

Temper: Seems to be clay; very little sand or grit. Some inclusion of very fine fibers.

Paste texture and color: Very lumpy, angular, and contorted. Gray core and light buff-fired surfaces.

Surface texture, color, and finish: Surfaces are smoothed but tend to be bumpy. Both surfaces, particularly the exterior, are characterized by large pockmarks where pieces have broken out. Interiors usually black, but exteriors are a chalky buff which is also very fire-mottled. Small fiber vermiculations on surface are common.

Hardness: 3 to 4.

Thickness: Varies from 1 to 1.5 cm.

Form: No exact data, although body sherds suggest large vessels.

Geographical range of type: Only from a single site in Wakulla County on the northwest Florida coast.

Chronological position of type: Surface associations and conditions at the site where this material was found suggest that it is either Deptford or Santa Rosa-Swift Creek in time.

Relationships of type: Similarities to St. Simons Plain (of which sherds were also found at site in question) and to Tchefuncte Plain of the Tchefuncte Period of the Lower Mississippi Valley (Ford and Quimby, 1945).

Type name.—ST. SIMONS PLAIN.

Definition as a type: Brief description under this name by Caldwell and McCann (1941, pp. 50-51) from the Georgia coast. Detailed descriptions of two other very similar types, Stallings Plain, from South Carolina (J. B. Griffin, 1943, pp. 159-160), and Orange Plain, from east Florida (J. B. Griffin, 1945, 219-221), have been published. It is possible that all three of these may eventually be grouped together as a single type. My own familiarity with the St. Simons type has led me to use this name in the present report. The collections which I have examined from northwest Florida and from west Florida are indistinguishable from the Georgia St. Simons type.

Ware characteristics:

Method of manufacture: No evidence of coiling fractures.

Temper: Characterized by cylindrical vesicles which are the result of carbonization of vegetal fibers with which ware was tempered. This fiber may have been Spanish moss. Some sherds show evidence of a much greater fiber content than others. Fine sand and coarse quartz sand is also seen in some of the sherds.

Paste texture and color: Paste core is laminated, contorted, and dotted with the vesicles left by the fibers. The exterior surface is fired buff to a depth of 2 or 3 mm. Remainder of sherd is gray or black.

Surface texture, color, and finish: Exterior and interior surfaces both show vermiculations left by carbonized fibers. Exterior is buff but fire-mottled; interior is gray or buff. Both surfaces are smoothed but bumpy and irregular, showing striations. (Pl. 13, *g*.)

Hardness: 2 to 2.5.

Thickness: 1 to 1.2 cm.

Form: Present collection inadequate. Stallings Plain along the Georgia coast is of simple bowl shape.

Geographical range of type: Comparable types found from Charleston, S. C., on the north, to lower St. Johns River, on the south. It is known from Stallings Island and from central Georgia. The few sherds in northwest Florida have been found within the range of the Deptford Complex.

Chronological position of type: In northwest Florida has been found in association with the Deptford Complex. At Carrabelle St. Simons Plain appeared in the lowest levels of a Deptford Period midden. Along the Atlantic seaboard it is the earliest pottery known, preceding the Deptford Period.

Relationships of type: A part of the lower, eastern-southeast distribution of fiber-tempered early pottery. Related to Wheeler Plain in the Wheeler and Pickwick basins of the Tennessee River.

Bibliography: Caldwell and McCann (1941, pp. 50-51); J. B. Griffin (1943, pp. 159-160; 1945, pp. 219-221); Wyman (1875, pp. 52-56); Moore (1894, pts. 1 and 2); Holmes (1894a; 1903, pp. 120-124, pl. 84, fig. 57); Kelly (1938, p. 30, pl. 10); Haag (*in* Webb and De Jarnette, 1942, pp. 513-514); Ford and Willey (1941, p. 334); Fairbanks (1942, pp. 223 ff.); Claflin (1931, pp. 13-17, pls. 11-20).

Type name.—ALEXANDER INCISED.

Description: This type was defined by Haag (1939). It is a sand-tempered ware decorated with thin incised lines that have been made while the vessel surface was quite soft so that the paste tends to pile up along the lines of incision. Rectilinear and simple curvirectilinear designs are typical, including the key design.

A sherd was noted from northwest Florida at the Carrabelle cemetery site (Moore, 1918, fig. 31, bottom, left).

Haag observed the chronological position of the type to be immediately after the fiber-tempered ware or approximately coeval with the Deptford horizon.

Other arts and technologies.—There is very little known of the arts and crafts of the Deptford Period other than their pottery making. It is most likely that their homes were simple affairs built of perishable materials. A few chipped-stone projectile points have been identified of this period inasmuch as they came from the Deptford levels at the Carrabelle (Fr-2) site. These are triangular-bladed points, some medium and some large (3.5 to 8 cm. in length). Some are deeply notched; others have small shoulders and stems which taper to a rounded base. Flaking varies from fine to rough. Pebble hammers and sandstone whetstones are the only other artifacts which can be placed in this period.

Speculations on population and period duration.—As yet, no huge, deep middens have been found which represent this period, and as very few small occupation sites are known it is not likely that the population was large. Comparatively speaking, it would appear to have been much smaller than the preceramic or fiber-tempered ceramic

(Orange) periods of the St. Johns River and east Florida. It was undoubtedly smaller than the Santa Rosa-Swift Creek or Weeden Island populations.

The absence of deep sites suggests brevity of duration for the period but by no means proves it as the simplicity of the culture, and its technology implies slowness of change and extended duration.

THE PERICO ISLAND PERIOD

Period definition.—This period is defined by preponderant percentages of the pottery types Glades Plain and Perico Plain. Shell and bone artifact types such as *Busycon* picks, *Busycon* (concave-surface) and *Strombus* (flat-surface) celts, and bipointed bone projectile points are often associated. Perico Island is the earliest period for the Manatee region of the Gulf Coast area where it seems to have its principal focus as an extension of the Glades culture. The period is also represented in the southern end of the Central region of the Gulf Coast area.

Compared to Deptford, Perico Island lacks clarity of definition as a period. It has a sequence position prior to the Weeden Island I Period and is, apparently, coeval with Deptford and Santa Rosa-Swift Creek (see chart, fig. 19). Glades Plain often occurs, however, in Weeden Island and even Safety Harbor contexts, and the same is true of some of the shell tools or weapons which are characteristic of the Perico Island Period.

The sites.—Three definite and two questionable sites of the period are recorded for this survey of the Gulf Coast area. This does not include the numerous Weeden Island and Safety Harbor Period sites at which Glades pottery types appear in association.

Pure sites

- Middens:
  - Widder Creek (Ch-3) (questionable)
  - Punta Gorda (Ch-4) (questionable)
- Burial mound, cemetery, and midden:
  - Cockroach (Hi-2)
  - Perico Island (Ma-6)

Mixed sites

- Burial mound (cemetery):
  - Weeden Island (Pi-1)

Settlement pattern.—Settlements are along the marshy shore, quite often on little islands, or near-islands, which were undoubtedly very favorable shellfishing stations. There are reliable data on two of the above-listed sites, and both of these are large shell-midden areas. The Perico site had two main midden concentrations, the larger about 300 by 40 yards in extent and at least 6 feet deep. Ridges of shell refuse extended out from the main midden masses for several hundred yards along the shore, and these ridges were dotted with refuse concentrations. A burial mound was situated at the end of one of the shorter ridges which joined the largest midden heap.

This pattern of mounds and associated ridges is found widely throughout the Glades area but usually on a later time horizon than Perico Island.[72] Similar sites are reported for the Tampa Bay section at Point Maximo and at the mouth of the Alafia River. It is not known if these last-named sites are of the Perico Island Period or later.

The functional nature of these shell embankments and mound arrangements is a matter for speculation. It has been thought that many such elaborate sand and shellwork sites in the Glades area were so constructed to provide canoe harbors or "courts" with the dwellings placed on the mounds or ridges. This may be the explanation for some of the sites, but Perico Island is neither so elaborate nor so situated as to make this likely. The ridge that joins the large midden and the burial mound at Perico may be an artificial construction to provide a causeway between the village area and the burial place. Such a causeway could have had a purely ceremonial significance or it could have been built because of the wet, marshy ground and frequent high water. The other ridges along the coast may have served as pathways between house groups.

Cockroach Key has a different arrangement. There are no causeways or ridges here, but the whole key, an area totaling about 240 by 160 yards, is covered by shell debris. In some places it is likely that the debris is as much as 30 feet thick. A burial mound had been built on a part of the rubbish.

To sum up, the community arrangement for the Perico Island Period is a living area concentrated upon a small eminence along a marshy shore or an offshore key. The eminences are sometimes supplemented by ridges or embankments connecting village or house concentrations with each other or with burial mounds. Burial mounds and cemeteries were made on or near the living sites.

Economy.—The economy of this period was probably wholly based upon marine foods or hunting and gathering on the nearby shore.

---

[72] Goggin (n.d. 2) identifies shellworks of this type as Glades III Period, a much later dating than Perico Island Period.

Horticulture would have been possible at certain places along the shore, but the close connection of the Perico Island culture with the nonhorticultural Glades tradition makes this unlikely.

The abundance of shell refuse and the community works such as the causeways and mounds imply a bountiful food supply and a margin of surplus in the economy.

Organization of society.—Probably autonomous village units, each with its own ceremonial functions. Some of these were fairly large.

Disposal of the dead.—In cemeteries and burial mounds. Primary inhumation in a flexed position was the rule. Grave pits were often lined with shells. Secondary burial appears to be a late trait in the Perico-Glades culture and is probably only associated with a post-Weeden Island continuation of it. Neither the Weeden Island site submound level nor Perico Island proper, both of which are pre-Weeden Island, show secondary burials. Burial offerings are either absent or extremely rare. Over 200 burials were found in mounds and cemeteries at both Perico Island and Cockroach Key.

Ceramic arts.—The pottery of the Perico Island Period is in the traditions of the Glades area rather than the Gulf Coast. Vessels are large, open, simple bowls. They are poorly and unevenly made as a rule although fairly well fired. Decoration is rare and when it occurs is plastic and by incision or incision-punctation. Rim modifications or appendages are absent. Pottery is abundant.

The two principal types are Glades Plain and Perico Plain. The Perico decorated types are associated with the Perico Island Period proper. Belle Glade Plain, Okeechobee Plain, and Miami Incised occur as a very few sherds only in those sites which appear to continue into post-Weeden Island times.

The Perico Island or Glades Complex of types in the order in which they are described:

- Glades Series:
  - Glades Plain
  - Miami Incised
- Perico Series:
  - Perico Plain
  - Perico Incised
  - Perico Linear Punctated
- Belle Glade Plain
- Okeechobee Plain

Type Descriptions

Type name.—GLADES PLAIN.

Definition as a type: By Goggin from south Florida (Goggin, 1939, 1940, 1944a, 1944b). The present description is a brief synopsis with particular reference to the type as it occurs in the Manatee region.

Description: A sand-tempered, gray-black ware. A few examples of buff- or red-fired surfaces noted. Thickness from 6 to 10 mm. or over. Hardness 3.0 or over. Deep and shallow bowls. Average diameter of bowl is about 30 cm. Most of these are simple open forms with straight, incurving, or slightly outslanting rims. When incurved, the inturn is usually high on vessel wall. A small cuplike bowl and a fragment of an unusually thick subconoidal base are two exceptions to the large bowl forms. Rims are unmodified. Lip may be flat as though executed by slashing off the upper margin of the vessel before firing. Some lips are rounded. Faint ticking on exterior edge of rim is not typical and probably is a feature of Glades Plain in post-Weeden Island times, as it is not found in sites of the Perico Island Period proper. (See pl. 14, *i;* pl. 53, *b, d, e.*)

Comment: The type is not a good period marker, and its presence does not denote the Perico Island Period. Glades Plain has an early inception on a Glades I and Perico Island Period level but continues much later.

Type name.—MIAMI INCISED.

Definition as a type: By Goggin (1944a) who states:

"A variety of Glades Gritty ware with diagonal incised lines running from near the rim to some distance down the side of the vessel. These lines are usually in groups of four separated from each other by a distance equal to the space the group covers." This is probably one of the earliest decorated types of the Glades area, falling early in the Glades II Period (Goggin, personal communication, 1948).

Type name.—PERICO PLAIN.

Definition as a type: From Perico Island site, present paper.

Ware characteristics:

Method of manufacture: Probably by coiling.

Temper: Sand and lumps of crushed limestone.

Paste texture and color: Black or gray core. Compact matrix but temper lumps abundant.

Surface texture, color, and finish: Usually black or gray although sometimes a whitish buff. Tooling marks are evident on both surfaces. In general, better made and smoother than Glades ware.

Hardness: 3 or over.

Thickness: 5 to 8 mm.

Form:

Large simple bowls with incurved rims. Rims are unmodified and lips are rounded or round-pointed with slight interior bevel.

Geographical range of type: Known only from Perico Island.

Chronological position of type: Dates from Pre-Weeden Island era and is probably coeval with Deptford and/or Santa Rosa-Swift Creek Periods of northwest Florida. May cross-date to south with Glades I, Glades II, or both.

Relationships of type: Form resemblances to Glades Plain suggest common ancestry. May be prototype of Pasco Series pottery which is found farther to the north.
Bibliography: Willey (1948a).

Type name.—PERICO INCISED.
Definition as a type: From the Perico Island site, present paper.
Ware characteristics: (Same as Perico Plain.)
Decoration: Sharp incised lines made with fine-edged tool on wet paste. Design arranged in border band below rim. Two motifs known. One of these has opposed series of parallel diagonal lines. The other has horizontal parallel lines with diamond-shaped insets. The insets are filled with triangular punctations. (Pl. 14, *a, d.*)
Form: Limited evidence shows bowl with incurved rim and bowl or jar with short collar.
Comment: Associations with Perico Plain. May be related to incised types of the Glades Series or to incised types of the St. Johns Series.
Bibliography: Willey (1948a).

Type name.—PERICO LINEAR PUNCTATED.
Definition as a type: Perico Island site, present paper.
Ware characteristics: (Same as Perico Plain.)
Decoration: Drag-and-jab punctation which is deeply impressed. Punctations are elongated in form. Rim band designs of opposed diagonal lines or sets of diagonal lines. Narrow bands filled with separate deep punctations. (Pl. 14, *b, c, e.*)
Form: Bowl with incurved rim.
Comment: (See Perico Incised.)
Bibliography: Willey (1948a).

Type name.—BELLE GLADE PLAIN
Definition as a type: By Willey (n.d.) from the Belle Glade site and Palm Beach County.
Description: A ware which is intermediate between Glades Plain and Biscayne Plain in amount of sand used as an aplastic and in resultant hardness. Forms are usually large simple bowls with slightly incurving rims. Specimens from the Manatee region of the Gulf Coast have a rounded or round-flat lip rather than the perfectly flat lip that is more common in the Glades area proper. Not a satisfactory time marker, as Belle Glade Plain is probably found in all three of the major Glades Periods. It is, however, more common to Glades II and III than Glades I.

Type name.—OKEECHOBEE PLAIN.
Definition as a type: By Willey (n.d.) from Palm Beach County.
Description: A gradation in the plain-ware gamut of the Glades area which is intermediate between Belle Glade Plain and Biscayne Plain and is characterized by a fairly hard polished surface. Difficult to recognize and not a good time marker.

Other arts and technologies.—The Perico Island Period is characterized by the utilization of shell for weapons, artifacts, and ornaments. These include *Busycon* hammers (pl. 15, *g, h*) or picks, the *Busycon* cup, both *Strombus* (pl. 15, *a;* pl. 16, *a, b*) and *Busycon* (pl. 15, *c, d;* pl. 16, *c*) celts, *Strombus* hammers, columella pendants of the plummet type (pl. 15, *b;* pl. 16, *g*) shell tools (pl. 15, *e, f*) and beads (pl. 16, *e*). Bone work was well developed as it is in the Glades area cultures. Bone points of the bipointed type, (pl. 16, *d*) bone awls (pl. 16, *h*) and bone daggers (pl. 15, *m*) are reported. Stonework is scarce (pl. 15, *i-l;* pl. 16, *f, j*) or completely absent.

Speculations on population and period duration.—Besides the few sites which we were able to list as belonging to the Perico Island Period there are probably others for which we have no data. It has been suggested that the Alafia River and Point Maximo sites may have belonged to this period, and a number of coastal middens in Pinellas, Hillsborough, Manatee, and Sarasota Counties reveal Glades Complex sherds. None of these sites can be dated securely in the Perico Island Period owing to the fact that Glades ceramic types are often found in late period contexts in the Manatee and southern central coast regions. This makes it impossible to determine from surface collections whether or not an earlier Perico Island horizon had been represented at the sites. It is probable that the lower levels of big midden sites, such as Shaws Point, were Perico Island Period occupations.

The Perico Island and Cockroach middens were large sites with deep refuse. A population of 200 people at any one time does not seem an excessive estimate for either. If there were 10 such sites in the Manatee region and along the southern edge of the central Gulf Coast, this would mean that the population of the Perico Island Period stood at about 2,000 persons.

The considerable refuse depth and the relative simplicity of the culture argues for a fairly long, stable period. If our estimates for the later periods approach any accuracy at all, then Perico Island must have extended over a 200- to 300-year period at the least.

THE SANTA ROSA-SWIFT CREEK PERIOD

Period definition.—The ceramic coefficients of this period are Swift Creek Complicated Stamped (Early Variety), the related early complicated stamped types, the Santa Rosa Series incised and rocker stamped potteries, Franklin Plain, and the types of the Crystal River Series.

The best diagnostics are Alligator Bayou Stamped (Santa Rosa Series), Santa Rosa Stamped, and rim and base sherds of the Swift Creek and Franklin types. The period is sharply defined.

The sites.—Seventeen pure sites, 21 mixed sites, and 4 doubtful sites are recorded.

Pure sites

Middens:

Third site opposite Woodlawn (Es-6)
Navarre (Sa-4)
Wynhaven (Ok-1)
Drummond (By-4)
Parker's Branch (By-10)

Burial mounds:

Basin Bayou, east (Wl-14)
Alligator Bayou (By-18)
Anderson's Bayou (By-21)
Baker's Landing (By-29)
Mound below Bristol (Li-3)
Yent mound (Fr-5)
Eleven-Mile Point (Fr-10)
Green Point (Fr-11)
Huckleberry Landing (Fr-12)
Pierce mound A (Fr-14)
Spring Creek (Wa-5)
Crystal River (Ci-1)

Mixed sites

Middens:

Five miles west of Navarre (Es-3)
Maester Creek (Sa-2)
Gulf Breeze (third site) (Sa-8)
Fort Walton (Ok-6)
Davis Point, west (By-7)
Porter's Bar (Fr-1)
Carrabelle (Fr-2)
Tucker (Fr-4)
Nine-Mile Point (Fr-9)
West Goose Creek (Wa-6)
Mound Field (Wa-8)
Refuge tower (Wa-14)
Shaws Point (Ma-7)

Midden and cemetery:

Near St. Marks (Wa-7)

Burial mounds:

Aspalaga (Gd-1)
Porter's Bar (Fr-1)
Jackson mound (Fr-15)
Hall site (Wa-4)
Warrior River, mound B (Ta-3)
Seven miles north of Cedar Keys (Lv-2)
Tarpon Springs (Pi-3)

Questionable:

Burial mounds:

Mound near Mack Bayou (Wl-10)
Sampson's Landing (Ja-1)
Michaux Log Landing (Li-6)
Munnerlyn's Landing (Dr-2)

Sites of this period extend from Escambia to Manatee Counties. The concentration appears to be in Franklin and Wakulla Counties, and there are more sites along the northwest coast than there are on the central coast or in the Manatee region. Survey of midden sites has been much less thorough, however, south of Jefferson County; and this may account for the relatively fewer Santa Rosa-Swift Creek sites in the southern counties.

Settlement pattern.—The midden sites of this period are, with a few exceptions, located on stream banks, along bays, or along the Gulf shore. All middens, even those which are located back a little distance from streams or Gulf, are marked by shell refuse. Most of these sites are smallish, ranging from 30 to 100 meters in diameter. There are some larger middens, such as the Tucker site, which occupy an area several hundred meters in extent, but these are mixed sites and the extent of the occupation in Santa Rosa-Swift Creek times alone has not been determined. Most of the middens are not deep, averaging between .50 and 1 meter. Besides shell, they are composed of black organic soil and animal and bird bones.

Burial mounds are often situated near a midden. Usually they are a few hundred meters distant, tending to be back inland when the midden sites front on the coast or a stream. In some instances the mounds may be within the area of occupation, but this is not commonly the case.

Economy.—It is obvious from the nature of the refuse that marine foods, particularly shellfish, were an important part of the diet. Animal and bird bones imply that a substantial part of the food economy was based upon hunting. We have no direct evidence for the practice of horticulture during this period, but indirect evidence suggests that it probably played a part in the subsistence pattern. The Santa Rosa-Swift Creek Period has extra-areal cross ties with the Hopewellian culture, and maize agriculture was known in other parts of the eastern United States at this time.

The general cultural level, as indicated by manufactures and by mortuary customs, implies a margin of surplus in the economy.

Organization of society.—The numerous small villages, many of which have a burial mound in association, probably maintained political and religious autonomy. In some instances two or more villages may have combined to use the same burial mound, forming a little political nucleus. The elaborate mortuary customs reflected in the burial mounds and their grave goods is indicative of a strong religious orientation and concern with a cult of the dead. It is likely that both secular and sacred powers were in the hands of the same individual or group of individuals in each community or small group of communities. Many of the pottery vessels found with the dead are esoteric, complex, nonutilitarian forms, probably made for the mortuary purpose alone. This shows that not only were considerable energies directed toward funerary and religious rites, but that there must have been some degree of craft specialization. Differentiation is noted in the number and quality of objects placed with the dead. Prestige and pomp obviously surrounded some individuals and not others. Those so honored were probably priest-chiefs, and it is not unlikely that a class of "nobles," comparable to those of Natchez social stratification, was beginning to emerge.

There are no "big centers" during this period which would indicate the dominance of certain communities over others. Pierce mound A (Fr-14) and Crystal River (Ci-1) are the two most elaborate funerary-mound sites of the time, but although they exceed other sites in quality and quantity of grave goods, this difference is not marked enough to set them apart as special "centers."

Disposal of the dead.—The burial mounds of the period were made of sand with occasional lenses, pockets, or partial layers of shell. Evenly superimposed, discernible strata are not characteristic. The question of mound shape cannot be answered satisfactorily, because many of the mounds had been partially destroyed before they were properly observed and recorded. Of the pure Santa Rosa-Swift Creek mounds, seven seem to have been circular; five were either oblong or rectanguloid. At least one of the oblong mounds had a flattened top. Another was formed so that one long, extended side may have served as a ramp or approach leading to the summit. One mound was surrounded by an embankment. That some of these mounds may have had ramps or were flat-topped, both features common to later temple-type mounds in the Southeast, is extremely interesting. Unfortunately, the data are too undependable to make a more positive statement about it at this time.

The circular mounds were about 50 to 60 feet in diameter and ranged from 2.5 to 10 feet in height. The oblong mounds ranged from about 50 to over 100 feet in length and were usually about two-thirds as wide as they were long. Height varied from 5 to 10 feet.

Among the mixed-period burial mounds, the oblong form was noted several times, and one mound had an extension which might possibly have served as a ramp. The size range of these mounds is about the same as that noted for the pure Santa Rosa-Swift Creek mounds. In every case these were mounds which overlapped with the succeeding Weeden Island I Period.

Although easily traceable layers or mantles implying mound building in stages are not reported for Santa Rosa-Swift Creek mounds, there are some things suggesting that the mounds were built up intermittently over a period of time rather than as single operations. There are cases of subfloor pits where burials were made before the mound was erected over them, and there are instances where it appears that burials were placed in the mound in small pits made at different levels during mound construction. There are also examples of one burial cutting through another. Frequently burials were found in groups at different horizontal and vertical mound locations, which may mean that at periodic funeral ceremonies the remains of a number of individuals were interred or incorporated in an addition to the mound. A very clear-cut example of an addition to a mound is the Crystal River (Ci-1) site where a large apron or platform was built around the base of the mound proper to accommodate more human remains and artifacts.

That these additions or successions of burials were not separated by appreciable time intervals is seen in the ceramic styles that are found with the burials. In most Santa Rosa-Swift Creek mounds there are no marked chronological differences in the pottery. In the mixed-period mounds it is possible that the accretional manner in which the mounds were probably built up is reflected in the mixture of Santa Rosa-Swift Creek and Weeden Island I styles.

There is great variation in the numbers of burials found in the mounds. Usually, but not in every case, the number of burials is in direct correlation with the size of the mound, the larger mounds having more individuals buried in them. The number of recorded burials, which is usually less than the number of actual skeletons or individuals, varies from 6 to 600. The median is somewhere around 60.

Both primary and secondary burials are characteristic, the two types usually being found in the same mound. At Crystal River there is a suggestion that primary interment tends to replace secondary owing to its more common occurrence in the mound platform or annex, but this trend is not present, or was not noted, in other mounds of the period. Secondary treatment includes bunched or bundle burial, in which the skull was placed together with a pile of long bones;

single skull burial in which lone skulls were interred; and mass burials, in which heaps of long bones and skulls were piled together. Primary burial includes extended (on back), flexed, and semiflexed forms.

The secondary burials must represent human remains which had been placed in a charnel house after death and left there to rot before disarticulation. Primary burials may, in some cases, have been so exposed but, by definition, they were placed in the mound in an articulated condition. Cremation is extremely rare in this period, an occasional deposit of calcined human bone being found in two or three of the mounds. Exposure of the bones or body to fire is more common. This appears to have been done in situ with a fire having been kindled in proximity to the body. Occasionally these fires affected some of the bones, but more often they merely left a deposit of charcoal and ash near the remains.

Placing of shells, usually oyster, over or around a burial was noted in several mounds. Nonceramic artifacts, such as ear ornaments, flint blades, or celts were often found with individual burials, particularly the primary burials. Pottery vessels were more rarely so placed. As a rule, pottery offerings were found in the mound in mass caches where many of them had been broken and others were simply destroyed by perforating the base. At Crystal River stone artifacts as well as pottery had been intentionally destroyed or "killed."

Cranial flattening was noted in only one mixed site of the period, Porter's Bar (Fr-1).

Ceramic arts.—Compared to the earlier Florida wares the pottery of this period is elaborate and complex. The ware is well made and well fired. It tends to be slightly thinner than earlier or later periods. Both interior and exterior surfaces are often polished. Decoration is largely plastic, including rocker stamping, deep incision, punctation, and stamping with a carved-block unit or paddle. Occasionally red pigment is used in zone painting. Negative or resist-dye painting is also recorded. Pottery is abundant.

Following the Deptford and Perico Island Periods, the pottery of Santa Rosa-Swift Creek demonstrates a marked divergence from many of the old traditions. Stamping, it is true, is retained, but the complicated designs differ greatly from the simple check patterns. The rocker stamping and deep incision and punctation are innovations. The sudden burst of a variety of exotic vessel forms, the stylized zoomorphic designs of the incised and rocker-stamped pottery, the occasional naturalistic representations, and the use of positive and negative pigments raise the ceramic industry of the area to a new level of achievement.

The high frequency of pottery in the burial mounds and the obviously ceremonial, nonutilitarian nature of some of this pottery, show that ceramics were a well-integrated part of ritual and religious practices.

Santa Rosa-Swift Creek pottery types in the order in which they are described:

- Santa Rosa Series:
  - Alligator Bayou Stamped
  - Basin Bayou Incised
  - Santa Rosa Stamped
  - Santa Rosa Punctated
- Complicated Stamped Series:
  - Swift Creek Complicated Stamped (Early Variety)
  - Crooked River Complicated Stamped (Early Variety)
  - St. Andrews Complicated Stamped (Early Variety)
  - New River Complicated Stamped
- Gulf Check Stamped
- West Florida Cord-marked (Early Variety)
- Crystal River Series:
  - Crystal River Incised
  - Crystal River Zoned Red
  - Crystal River Negative Painted
  - Pierce Zoned Red
- Franklin Plain
- Unusual forms (not a type)

Type Descriptions

Type name.—ALLIGATOR BAYOU STAMPED.

Definition as a type: From the northwest coast of Florida, present paper. In a previous summary (Willey and Woodbury, 1942, p. 242) the type was referred to as Marksville Stamped. It is felt, however, that the zoned stamped pottery of northwest Florida, while being similar to the Marksville and Troyville Zoned Stamped types of south Louisiana, differs sufficiently to be grouped under a separate type name. Eventually a revision in the typology of eastern ceramics may unite zoned stamped pottery into a single major style or type with variant subdivisions such as Hopewell, Marksville, Alligator Bayou, and others.

Ware characteristics:

Method of manufacture: Fractures indicate coiling or annular technique.

Temper: Appears to be ground clay (small, hard, angular pieces noted) or ground sherds in some cases. Some specimens tempered with fine to medium sand.

Paste texture and color: Varies from coarse, lumpy, and very contorted to fine-grained and slightly contorted. Color variation from chalky white, through buff and red-buff. Also gray-black. Core sometimes gray-black, or interior half of sherd gray-black with exterior half fired to a buff.

Surface texture, color, and finish: Clay-tempered sherds have soft, slightly chalky texture. Undecorated exterior surfaces smoothed to a low polish. Interior surfaces usually very irregularly smoothed and bumpy. Surface color most often a fire-mottled dull buff, although there are many variations in intensity and shade.

Hardness: 2.5 to 4.

Thickness: 2.5 to 7 mm.; average 5 mm.

Decoration:

Technique: Broad-lined incisions made in the semisoft clay of the vessel before firing and areas of notched or unnotched rocker or roulette stamping.

Design: Opposed plain and rocker-stamped areas. Incised figures are vaguely birdlike in several instances (fig. 22, *b, d*). More often they are unidentified curvilinear and rectilinear figures (fig. 22, *a, e*). In some cases the actual design or figure represented is left plain and the background is filled with stamping. The filling-in of the design with stamping, leaving the background plain, is also represented. Incised lines are usually from 3 to 5 mm. wide, are deep, and are round-bottomed. The stamping, if done with a rocker, may be the result of rocking the end or edge of a thin instrument back and forth on the vessel surface. The zigzag lines may be smooth or dentated. The same effect could have been produced by rouletting with a smooth or notched-edge disk. (Pl. 17; pl. 19, *c-e*.)

The general impression is one of boldly but surely executed designs. There is little detail. All figures are expressed by wide, flowing bands.

Distribution: Most of exterior vessel body except base.

Form:

Total vessel: Flattened-globular bowl, squared flattened-globular bowl, collared globular bowl, cylindrical beaker, squared beaker, and multiple-orifice vessel are all represented.

Rim: Incurved rims with exterior folds or with marginal thickening on the direct, unmodified outslanting rims. (See fig. 23, top.)

Lip: Flat, round-flat, and round-pointed.

Base: Round, flat and circular, and flat and squared.

Appendages: Bird's-head effigies affixed to rims.

Geographical range of type: Most common in northwest Florida, but found in village sites and in burial mounds as far south and east as Tarpon Springs (Pi-3) and Tampa Bay.

Chronological position of type: Marker of the Santa Rosa-Swift Creek Period. Vessels are occasionally found in mounds which show predominance of Weeden Island Period types, however.

Relationships of type: Closely related to Marksville Stamped and Troyville Stamped of the Marksville and Troyville Periods of the Lower Mississippi Valley. Also related to Hopewellian rocker-stamped pottery of the Ohio Valley and Middle West.

Bibliography: Willey and Woodbury (1942, p. 242); Setzler (1933); Ford and Willey (1939; 1940, pp. 65 ff).

FIG. 22.—Santa Rosa-Swift Creek Period vessels. *a, b, d, e,* Alligator Bayou Stamped; *f-i,* Basin Bayou Incised; *c,* Santa Rosa Stamped. (Redrawn from Moore. Year, figure number, and site: *a,* 1902: 54, Anderson's Bayou; *b,* 1902: 35, Alligator Bayou; *c,* 1902: 236, Yent; *d,* 1918: 16, Basin Bayou, east; *e,* 1902: 150, Eleven-Mile Point; *f,* 1918: 14, Basin Bayou, east; *g,* 1902: 228, Tucker; *h,* 1918: 21, Burnt Mill Creek, west; *i,* 1902: 55, Anderson's Bayou. All ¼ actual size.)

Type name.—BASIN BAYOU INCISED.

Definition as a type: From the northwest coast of Florida, present paper. In a previous summary of the archeology of northwest Florida the type was illustrated as Marksville Incised (Willey and Woodbury, 1942, fig. 2F). For the present it is believed that the Florida type differs sufficiently to warrant a separate type name.

Ware characteristics:

Method of manufacture: No good coiling fractures observed, but it seems likely that an annular process was employed.

Temper: Fine sand most common. Also what seems to be crushed clay, or possibly sherd temper.

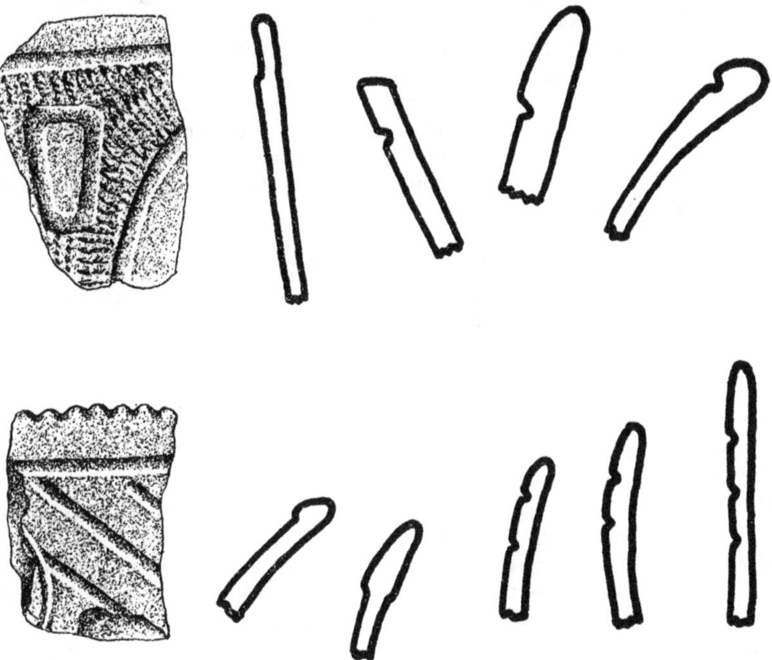

FIG. 23.—Santa Rosa-Swift Creek Period rim forms. *Top:* Alligator Bayou Stamped; *bottom:* Basin Bayou Incised. (Interiors to right.)

Paste texture and color: In some cases fine-granular compact, and slightly contorted. In others, coarser grained and more markedly contorted. Core often gray. Exterior surfaces frequently fired gray-buff, buff-white, or red. Sometimes sherds fired all the way through to a buff or red.

Surface texture, color, and finish: Exterior surfaces which are not decorated carefully smoothed to a low polish. Interiors are not well smoothed. Some sherds have a chalky feel; others are sandy and abrasive. Vessels with open mouths and easily visible interiors are more carefully smoothed on the interiors than small-mouthed vessels. Surface color ranges from gray through shades of buff into red. Mottling from firing common.

Hardness: 2.5 to 3.5.

Thickness: 3 to 6 or 7 mm.; average 4-5 mm.

Decoration:

Technique: Incised lines made in still soft, unfired clay. Lines made with end of rather large cylindrical stick or other instrument.

Design: Both rectilinear and curvilinear motif and combination of both on same vessel. Lines average 2 to 3 mm. in width and are deep and round-bottomed. Arrangements of parallel, diagonal lines, concentric rectangles, concentric triangles, meandering scrolls, and complex and highly stylized life figures make up the designs (fig. 22, *g, i*). "Bird" designs which utilize the entire exterior surface of the vessel are carried out by depicting wings, tail, head, and other parts on different sides of the vessel, leaving large undecorated spaces between them (fig. 22, *f, h*). Deep hemiconical terminal punctations or pits are a feature marking the ends or junctures of lines. (Pl. 18, *d-h.*)

Like Alligator Bayou Stamped, the designs are bold and flowing. Detail is found within limited, circumscribed areas only. (Pl. 41, *f.*)

Distribution: Vessel exterior except base. Rim nearly always set off from area of decoration by a single bordering incised line, a centimeter or so below orifice.

Form:

Total vessel: Sherds indicate flattened-globular bowls and straight-sided beakers. Moore illustrates flattened-globular bowls, long-collared jars, cylindrical and squared beakers.

Rim: Incurved with and without exterior marginal fold or thickening. Straight or slightly outslanted without marginal fold. (See fig. 23, bottom.)

Lip: Scalloped or notched, round-flat, round-pointed, and flat.

Base: Round, flat and circular, and flat and square.

Appendages: None recorded.

Geographical range of type: Common on the northwest coast of Florida, but also found along the west coast.

Chronological position of type: Santa Rosa-Swift Creek Period. Has longer upward life span than either Alligator Bayou or Santa Rosa Stamped and is more commonly found in Weeden Island Period contexts.

Relationships of type: Related to Marksville Incised of the Lower Mississippi Valley and also to the later Troyville Period type of the same area, Yokena Incised. Locally, Basin Bayou Incised is probably a prototype of such Weeden Island types as Weeden Island Incised and Indian Pass Incised.

Bibliography: Willey and Woodbury (1942); Ford and Willey (1939; 1940, pp. 75 ff).

Type name.—SANTA ROSA STAMPED.

Definition as a type: From northwest coast of Florida, present paper. In a previous summary (Willey and Woodbury, 1942, p. 242) the type was very briefly described under this name.

Ware characteristics:

Method of manufacture: Fractures indicate coiling or annular technique.

Temper: Ground clay or sherds and/or sand.

Paste texture and color: Same range of variation as Alligator Bayou Stamped. The thinner ware seems to have buff-fired surfaces more commonly than the thicker.

Surface texture, color, and finish: (See Alligator Bayou Stamped.)

Hardness: 2.5 to 4.

Thickness: 4 to 7 mm.

Decoration:

Technique: Rows of continuous rocker or roulette stamping before firing.

Design and distribution: Continuous or connected semilunar markings which vary in length from 1 to 2.5 cm. (fig. 22, *c*). The stamping tool was usually unnotched, although there are some examples of the use of a notched or dentate-edge implement. The arrangement of rows of stamping seems to have been both vertical and horizontal on the vessel exterior. The rows are close-spaced, frequently overlapping. There is no use of incision, punctation, or zoning of the decoration by any

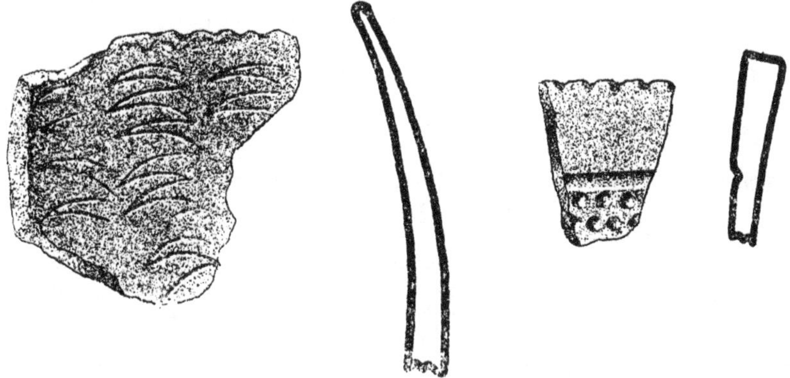

FIG. 24.—Santa Rosa-Swift Creek Period rim forms. *Left:* Santa Rosa Stamped; *right:* Santa Rosa Punctated. (Interiors to right.)

other technique. Sherds indicate that the stamping covered most of vessel exterior. (Pl. 18, *a-c*.)

Form:

Total vessel: The sherds possibly indicate the pot form with one sherd showing a definitely flared orifice. Moore illustrates a collared globular bowl (Moore, 1902, fig. 236).

Rim: Outflared or direct. (See fig. 24, left.)

Lip: Scalloped or notched. Some are simple and round-pointed in cross section.

Base: Flattened in some cases. (Data very limited.)

Appendages: Small teatlike tetrapodal supports.

Geographical range of type: Northwest coast of Florida. Seems to be concentrated mainly to the west of St. Andrews Bay, although occasional specimens found farther to east.

Chronological position of type: Marker of the Santa Rosa-Swift Creek Period.

Relationships of type: Related typologically and by association to other types of Santa Rosa Series. Decoration suggests similar stamped types of Tchefuncte Period of south Louisiana rather than the Marksville Period.

Bibliography: Willey and Woodbury (1942, p. 242); Ford and Quimby (1945, pp. 56-57).

Type name.—SANTA ROSA PUNCTATED.

Definition as a type: From the northwest coast of Florida, present paper.

Ware characteristics: (See Alligator Bayou Stamped.)

Decoration:

Technique: Broad, round-bottomed incised lines and hemiconical punctations made in the clay before firing.

Design: Broad zones or figures, apparently both rectilinear and curvilinear, traced in incised lines. These bands or zones are filled with close-spaced hemiconical punctations. (Pl. 18, *i, j.*)

Distribution: Vessel exterior.

Form: Short-collared jars. (Data very limited.) (See fig. 24, right.)

Geographical range, chronological position, and relationships of the type: Associations seem to be all with Santa Rosa Series types. Resemblances to Crystal River Incised are noted. There are definite similarities to the Louisiana Marksville-Troyville type, Churupa Punctated.

Bibliography: Ford and Willey (1939).

Type name.—SWIFT CREEK COMPLICATED STAMPED (Early Variety).

Definition as a type: From Swift Creek site near Macon, Ga., by A. R. Kelly (1938, pp. 25-31). Willey (1939) and Jennings and Fairbanks (1939) have also contributed to the definition of this important Southeastern type. As yet no major report has been issued on the Swift Creek site. This site was stratified and, according to Kelly, early, middle, and late divisions were detected in the complicated stamped type. The present description of Swift Creek Complicated Stamped (Early Variety) is not based upon comparisons made with Kelly's three subdivisions but upon a stratigraphic early and late breakdown of Swift Creek Complicated Stamped as it occurs in northwest Florida, particularly at the Carrabelle site. It will be noted, though, that the distinction made between the Early and Late Varieties of the type in Florida do correspond in several respects to the stylistic divisions made in the life of the type at Macon (see Kelly, 1938, pl. 11).

The separation of Florida Swift Creek pottery into Early and Late Varieties is a tentative mechanism set up to take into account recognizable changes in the history of the type. It would perhaps be advisable to designate the Late Variety as another type under a different name. It was thought, however, that this would conflict with the central Georgia definition of the type, and it was decided to group all the material in question as Swift Creek. Future analysis of the Macon Swift Creek pottery may make it clear as to just how much coincidence and difference exists between Florida and Georgia Swift Creek.

In the stratigraphic analyses of the present report both Early and Late Varieties of Swift Creek are listed together as Swift Creek Complicated Stamped. The decision to divide the type was not made until after the original classification of the sherds. In order to test the validity of the Early and Late Varieties a great many sherds from the Carrabelle test pits were reexamined by levels. A clear-cut distinction in vessel form and rim treatment between Early and Late was immediately perceived. More careful examination brought out differences in design motifs and elements, execution of stamping, and ware quality. It was finally found that classification of sherds into Early and Late Varieties was possible in all cases except those of some small body sherds where form, rim, and decoration were difficult to determine.

Ware characteristics:

Method of manufacture: Coiling or annular technique.

Temper: Fine sand and mica with occasional coarser particles.

Paste texture and color: Compact, fine-grained, and slightly contorted. Color usually gray-black at core. Both or exterior surfaces buff. Sometimes sherds are fired through to buff color. Rarely they are gray-black all the way through.

FIG. 25.—Santa Rosa-Swift Creek Period vessels. *Left:* St. Andrews Complicated Stamped, Early Variety; *right:* Swift Creek Complicated Stamped, Early Variety. (Redrawn from Moore. Year, figure number, and site: *left,* 1902: 37, Alligator Bayou; *right,* 1902: 59, Anderson's Bayou. *Left* is ¼ actual size; *right* is ½ actual size.)

Surface texture, color, and finish: Exterior covered with stamped decoration. Interior surfaces carefully smoothed, sometimes to a low polish. Surfaces various shades of buff or gray. Fire-mottled.

Hardness: 3 or slightly less to 4.5; average 3.5.

Thickness: 4 to 6 mm. with average nearer 4. Bases only slightly thicker than walls or rims.

Decoration:

Technique: Impression of a carved instrument, probably of wood, upon the soft, unfired clay of the vessel. Instrument may have been a flat paddle, a curved rocker, or cylindrical in form.

Design: Designs are predominantly curvilinear, although rectilinear elements are sometimes combined with curvilinear ones (pl. 20; pl. 22, *c, d, f, g*). Design units or motifs are usually made up of a number of elements, making a rather complicated whole. There is sufficient repetition of these design units on a vessel to show that the stamping unit (paddle, rocker, or cylinder) was repeatedly pressed onto the vessel until the surface was virtually covered (fig. 25, right). There is a good deal of overlapping of design motifs.

The designs described below are in terms of the raised, not the depressed, surfaces. These, of course, correspond to the carved-out portions of the stamping instrument. The following design units or motifs are noted: (1) "Stars" in a circle with 6 or 7 points (fig. 26, *a*). There is also a solid depressed dot in the middle of the "star." The "star" in circle element is apparently a part of a greater motif. (2) Concentric circles with center dot (fig. 26, *c*). They are arranged tangent to each other. Other elements are often combined. (3) "Figure 8" designs made up of several concentric lines (fig. 26, *b*). (4) Winged concentric circles (fig. 26, *a*). (5) Concentric circle with attached double-looped bar (fig. 26, *d*). (6) Circle and dot with four petals or attached loops surrounded by a series of concentric curved lines (fig. 26, *f*). The concentric curved lines are broken by four equidistant lobate elements which converge toward the central "flowerlike" figure. (7) Series of attached ovals nested into a similar series above and below (fig. 26, *g*). Ovals marked with simple hachure. (8) Concentric ovals or "eyes" set in a field of flowing curved lines (fig. 27, *a*). (9) Concentric sigmoid figures (fig. 27, *b*). (10) Various concentric "teardrops" are hatched, giving a "snowshoe" effect (fig. 27, *c, d*). (11) Nested lobate figures with central "eye," as in a peacock feather (fig. 27, *f*). (12) Use of concentric rectangles in conjunction with curvilinear figures (fig. 27, *h*). (13) Connected spirals, diamonds, and nested irregular curvilinear-rectilinear figures (fig. 27, *g, i*).

There are, in addition, a good many variants of the elements and motifs described, as well as other distinct motifs. In fact, the impression is one of almost numberless designs. Yet there is an over-all similarity of style.

Execution is fairly good. The impressions are generally clear except where there is overlapping. Depth of impressions averages about 1 mm., and the average width of the raised lines of the design is 1.5 mm.

Distribution: Exterior vessel surface except for base.

Form:

Total vessel: Pot form with slightly outflared orifice and rounded base.

Rim: Straight and vertical or slightly outslanted or outcurved at orifice. Occasionally the merest extrusion or thickening on exterior edge. (See fig. 28.)

Lip: Small, close-spaced, round-bottomed notches most common. Also wider scallops. Flat, round-flat, and round-pointed.

Base: Rounded.

Appendages: Small, solid tetrapodal supports.

Geographical range of type: Especially plentiful in northwest Florida and south and central Georgia. This last seems to be the region of its greatest developments and possible origin. Also found in north Georgia, adjacent portions of Alabama, South Carolina, and in eastern Tennessee. Distribution in other parts of Florida not clarified. It is probable that it occurs all though north-central Florida. It is found on the St. Johns as an important minority type. On the west coast Swift Creek and related complicated stamped types are found as far south as Tampa Bay.

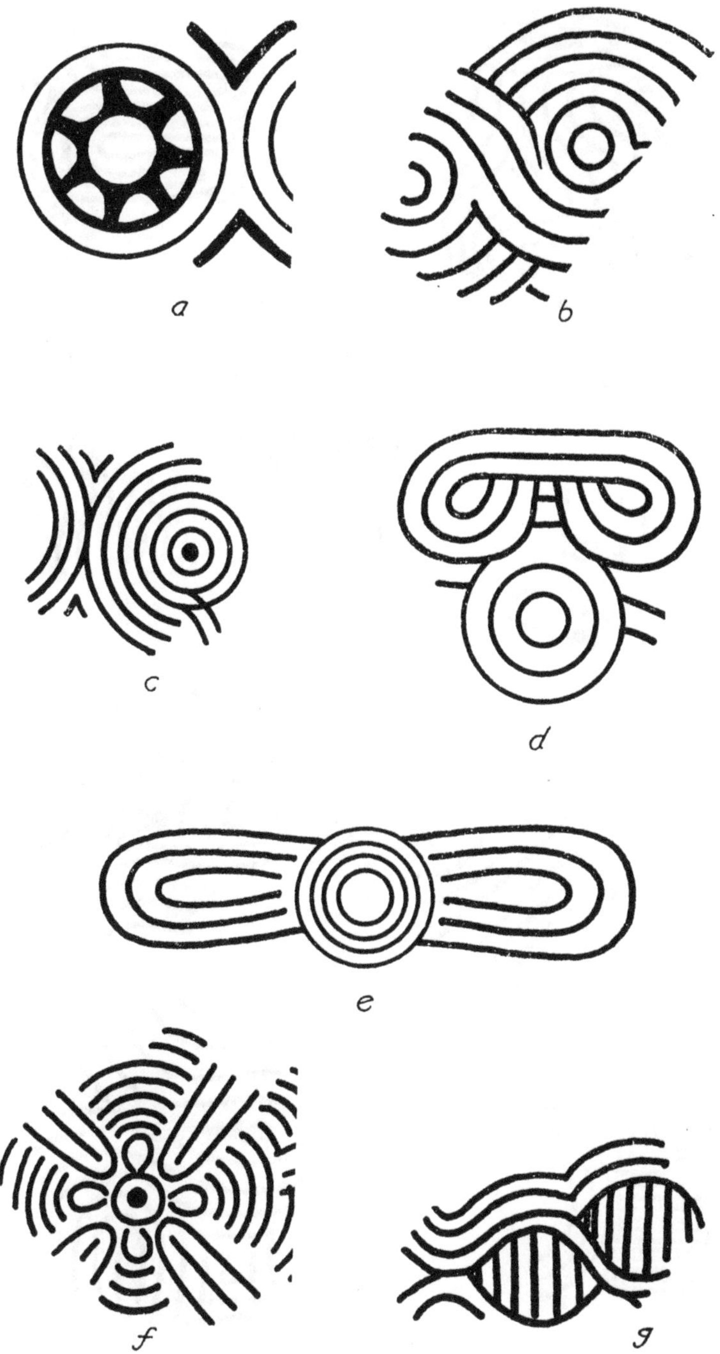

FIG. 26.—Swift Creek Complicated Stamped design units, Early Variety.

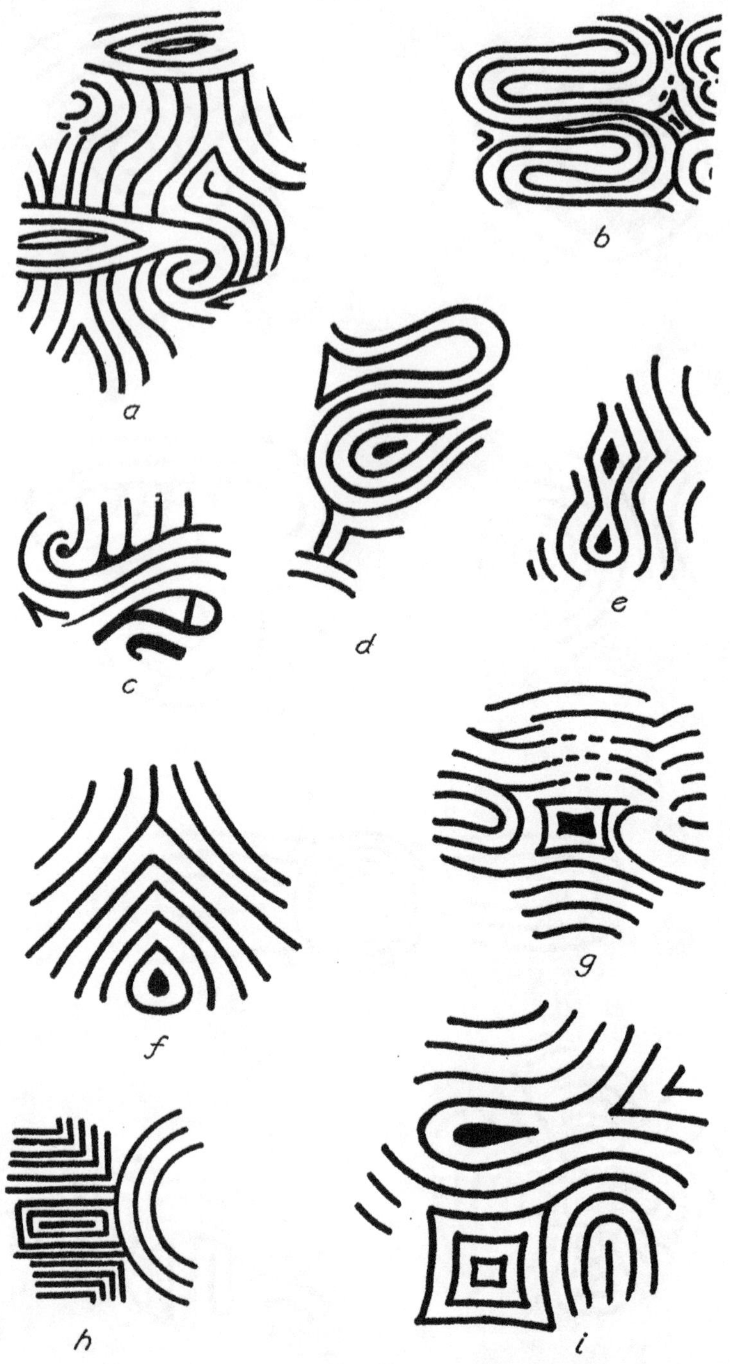

FIG. 27.—Swift Creek Complicated Stamped design units, Early Variety.

Chronological position of type: Santa Rosa-Swift Creek marker type. On the Georgia coast it precedes the predominantly cord-marked Wilmington Period, and in central Georgia it precedes early manifestations of Middle Mississippian. On the St. Johns River it is found in the latter half of the St. Johns I Period.

Relationship of type: Early Swift Creek seems to be the prototype of most of the similar complicated stamped pottery of the Southeast. Pickwick Complicated Stamped of northern Alabama and the complicated stamped types of the Candy Creek culture of the Chickamaugua Basin, in Tennessee, are clearly related to Swift Creek. Complicated stamped sherds found as far north as the Ohio Valley, in Hopewell associations, are of this same family.

Bibliography: Kelly (1938, pp. 25-31); Willey (1939, 1945); Jennings and Fairbanks (1939); Haag (1939); Lewis and Kneberg (1946, pls. 46, 47).

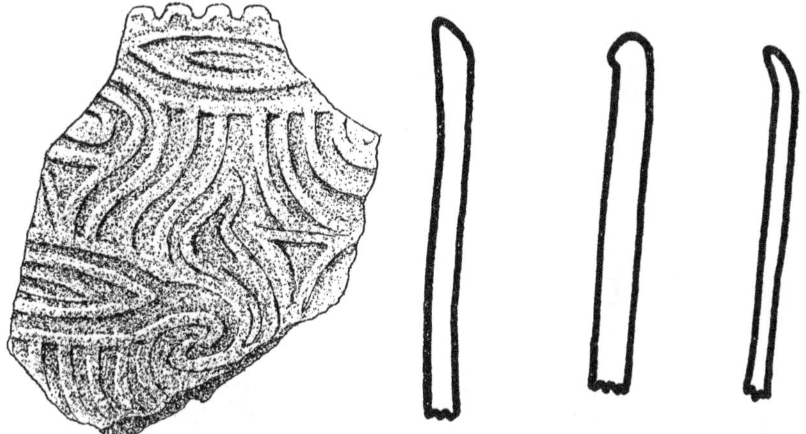

FIG. 28.—Santa Rosa-Swift Creek Period rim forms. Swift Creek Complicated Stamped, Early Variety. (Interiors to right.)

Type name.—CROOKED RIVER COMPLICATED STAMPED (Early Variety).

Definition as a type: From northwest Florida coast, present paper.

Ware characteristics:

Method of manufacture: Fractures indicate coiling or annular technique.

Temper: Fine sand and mica.

Paste texture, color, and finish: Interior surfaces smoothed, in some cases to a polish. Exterior surfaces decorated with stamping. Surfaces usually buff with fire-clouding. Occasionally surfaces are entirely gray-black.

Hardness: 3 to 3.5.

Thickness: Average 4 to 5 mm.

Decoration:

Technique: Carved wooden paddle or other similar instrument impressed on soft unfired surfaces of vessel.

Design: A pattern of rectilinear zigzag lines or chevrons (fig. 29, top). These chevrons are continuous down the sides or around the body of the vessel. They are very close-spaced (2 or 3 mm.). The design differs from a "herringbone" motif in that there are no lines connecting the angles of the nested chevrons. Angle of chevrons varies from slightly acute to very obtuse. Overlapping of the design is fairly common. Execution good. (Pl. 19, *a-b*.)

Distribution: Probably most of vessel exteriors.

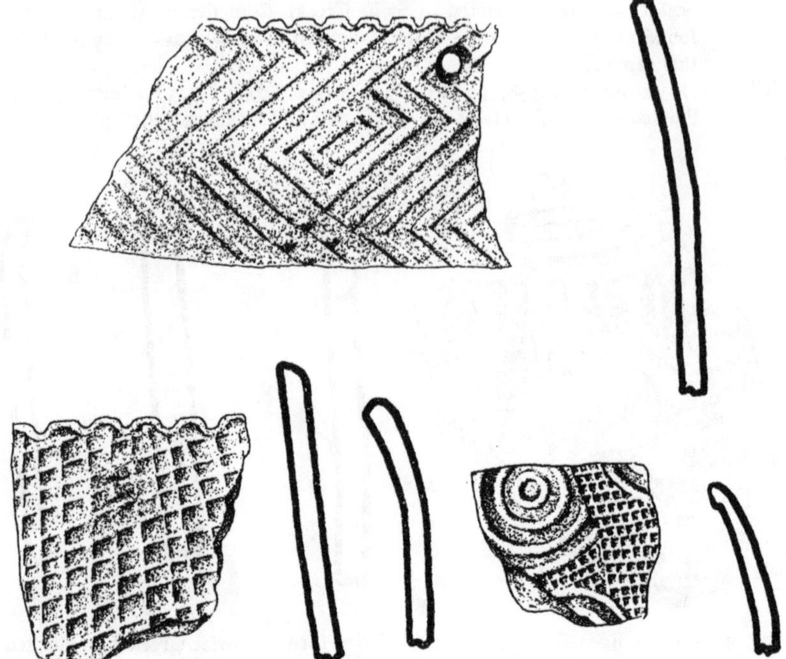

FIG. 29.—Santa Rosa-Swift Creek Period rim forms. *Top:* Crooked River Complicated Stamped; *bottom, left:* Gulf Check Stamped; *bottom, right:* New River Complicated Stamped. (Interiors to right.)

Form:

Total vessel: Sherds indicate pot form with slightly outflared orifice.

Rim: Slightly outflared (fig. 29, top).

Lip: All specimens examined have scalloped or notched lips.

Appendages: One sherd shows very small solid support.

Geographical range of type: Northwest coast of Florida, particularly around Carrabelle and to the east.

Chronological position of type: Early variety is found as a minor type in the Santa Rosa-Swift Creek Period.

Relationships of type: Clearly related to the complicated stamping tradition of the lower Southeast. The closest parallel is an as yet unpublished type, "St. Simons Herringbone Stamped," from St. Simons Island on the Georgia Coast (Preston Holder, personal communication, 1937).

Type name.—ST. ANDREWS COMPLICATED STAMPED (Early Variety).

Definition as a type: From the northwest Florida coast, present paper.

Ware characteristics:

Method of manufacture: Coiling or annular technique.

Temper: Fine sand and mica.

Paste texture and color: Compact, slightly contorted, but fine-grained and homogeneous. Buff throughout or gray-black core with one or both surfaces fired buff.

Surface texture, color, and finish: Well smoothed, even to a low polish on interiors. Orange-buff to dull buff. Sometimes black or gray depending upon firing. Buff surfaces often fire-clouded.

Hardness: 2.5 to 3.5.

Thickness: 4 to 6 mm.

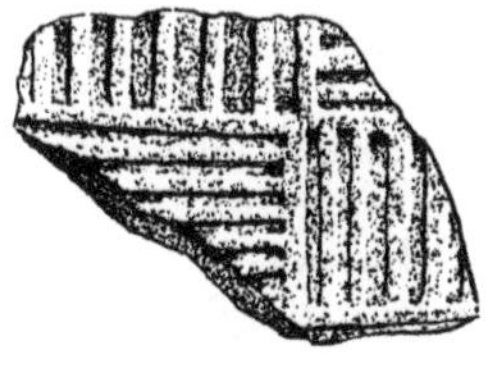

FIG. 30.—St. Andrews Complicated Stamped, Early Variety.

Decoration:

Technique: Application of carved wooden paddle or instrument to unfired, soft surfaces of vessel.

Design: Three principal motifs are noted. One is a field of simple hatched rectangles arranged in a checker fashion or with lines of hachure of each rectangle running at right angles to the lines of hachure of the rectangle next to it (fig. 30, center). There are 4 to 10 lines within a rectangle or square. Squares measure from 2 to 3 cm. Another motif is made up of a field of diagonally bisected rectangles with each triangular half filled with hachure running at right angles to its complementary triangle (figs. 25, left; 30, left). A third motif is less definite. It is characterized by concentric rectangles or triangles. The lines are usually more widely spaced than is the case for the other two motifs (fig. 30, right).

Distribution: Most of the vessel, except base in some instances.

Form:

Total vessel: Sherds suggest pot form. Moore shows one pot with slightly flared orifice.

Rim: Inslanted or slightly outflared. Moore shows specimen with wide scallops.

Lip: Flat-round or flat.
Base: One sherd shows subconoidal base.
Appendages: None known.

Geographical range of type: Pensacola to Apalachee Bay, northwest Florida. More common at eastern end of this range.

Chronological position of type: Santa Rosa-Swift Creek Period. Related to other rectilinear complicated stamped types of lower Southeast. Napier Complicated Stamped of central Georgia is an example of a similar type.

Bibliography: Jennings and Fairbanks (1939, type: Napier Complicated Stamped); Kelly (1938, p. 45 and pl. 10).

Type name.—NEW RIVER COMPLICATED STAMPED.

Definition as a type: Northwest coast of Florida, present paper.

Ware characteristics:

Method of manufacture: Coiling or some annular technique.
Temper: Fine sand and mica.
Paste texture and color: Compact, granular, and slightly contorted. Buff cross section or gray core with buff-fired surfaces.
Surface texture, color, and finish: Interior surfaces smoothed to a low polish. Pale dull buff to orange-red buff. Black fire mottling.
Hardness: 2.5 to 3.5.
Thickness: Average of 5 mm.

Decoration:

Technique: Carved wooden paddle or other similar instrument impressed upon soft clay.
Design: Combination of curvilinear and rectilinear elements. Background area done in check stamping which most clearly resembles the small clear check of Gulf Check Stamped. Concentric circles, lobate figures, interlocked whorls, and "rayed" elements or stars are the foreground features. In some instances these circles, etc., seem to be a part of the same design unit as the check stamping, as if the combination design had been carved onto the stamping medium (fig. 29, bottom, right); in other instances the circles, lobate forms, stars, etc. are separately superimposed upon the check background. (Pl. 21, *a-e.*)
Distribution: All sherds observed have decoration covering entire exterior surface.

Form:

Rim: Slightly outflared (fig. 29, bottom, right).
Lip: Round-pointed and flat-round.

Geographical range of type: The northwest coast of Florida in the vicinity of Carrabelle.

Chronological position of type: Santa Rosa-Swift Creek Period.

Relationships of type: Related to both check and complicated stamped series, most specifically to Gulf Check Stamped and Swift Creek Complicated Stamped. Does this type mark the appearance of the first curvilinear and complicated designs stamped on pottery? It occurs stratigraphically at about the proper time, at the point of transition from Deptford into Swift Creek.

Type name.—GULF CHECK STAMPED.

Definition as a type: From the northwest coast of Florida, present paper. This type is not well established at the present time.

Ware characteristics:

Method of manufacture: Fractures indicate coiling or an annular technique.

Temper: Fine sand and mica with very few exceptions.

Paste texture and color: Compact and slightly contorted, but homogeneous. Large particles of sand, grit, and clay (?). Paste is buff throughout in some cases; is gray-black but rarely; and is occasionally gray-black at the core with buff-fired surfaces.

Surface texture, color, and finish: Exterior surface covered with stamped decoration. Interior surfaces are well smoothed and sometimes have low polish. The buff surface color varies from a bright reddish buff to a very pale yellow-gray. Fire clouding is common.

Hardness: 2.5 to 3.5.

Thickness: Ranges from 6 to 3 mm. with an average slightly under 5 mm.

Decoration:

Technique: Impressed upon surface of an unfired vessel with a carved wooden paddle or instrument upon which a considerable area of the surface was carved with lines arranged in a grid-bar fashion.

Design: Check stamped units of undetermined size. Individual rectangles usually oblong and sometimes diamond-shaped. Lands of one direction slightly higher, broader, more pronounced than those of the other. Rectangles are deep, clearly made, and do not vary much in size (3 by 5 mm. is a good average). Pronounced lands a little over 1 mm. wide and lesser lands a little under 1 mm. wide. There is very little overlapping of the design. To sum up, the check stamping for this type is neater, more carefully done, both as to design and execution, than any other check stamped type from Gulf Florida. (Pl. 21, *f, g*.)

Distribution: Exterior surface. Extends up to lip. Distance downward on vessel undetermined.

Form:

Total vessel: Probably pot form.

Rim: Outslanting and slightly outflared rims. Some of the latter suggest that pot was constricted just below orifice (fig. 29, bottom, left).

Lips: Round-flat and unmodified except for a trifling extrusion of paste on exterior surface; or scallops or notches made by pressing a cylindrical tool onto the top of the lip. These scallops or notches vary from 1 cm. to 5 mm. in spacing.

Base and appendages: No data.

Geographical range of type: Northwest Florida coast between St. Andrews and Apalachee Bays.

Chronological position of type: In northwest Florida the type appears during the Deptford Period and continues up into the Santa Rosa-Swift Creek Period. It is not a good marker type for either period owing to its scarcity and the difficulty sometimes experienced in distinguishing it from other check stamped types when dealing with small body sherds. The scalloped or notched rim is, however, a good horizon marker in this area, commonly found as a feature of Santa Rosa-Swift Creek.

Relationships of type: Undoubtedly related to all types of the generic division of southeastern stamped potteries listed as "checked." Its chronological position in Florida suggests that it is a continuation of the check stamped tradition begun in the Deptford Period.

Type name.—WEST FLORIDA CORD-MARKED (Early Variety).

Definition as a type: Tentatively described in present paper. The specimens from northwest Florida appear to be another expression of cord-wrapped paddle marking found in the Lower Mississippi Valley and the lower Southeast. Its resemblance to other cord-marked types from the Southeast, and its relative scarcity in Florida, indicate that the type should be merged eventually with other cord-marked types found in the interior.

In the stratigraphic analyses of this report West Florida Cord-marked of both the Early and Late Varieties are listed as a single type. Most of the sherds studied were of the Early Variety. The Late Variety of the type was set up to take care of those few sherds appearing in a Weeden Island context and distinguished by the characteristic Weeden Island folded rim.

Ware characteristics:

Method of manufacture: Fractures indicate coiling or annular technique.

Temper: Mostly with fine sand. There are several sherds from a single vessel which was tempered with what appear to be lumps of clay and huge angular pieces of grit.

Paste texture and color: Granular except in the clay-grit specimens mentioned above. Usually black or gray paste core and sometimes blackish surfaces. Buff-fired surfaces and also red or buff throughout.

Surface texture, color, and finish: Exterior surfaces completely roughened. Interior surfaces fairly well smoothed. Color varies as noted under paste description.

Hardness: 2.5 to 4.

Thickness: Ranges from 4 mm. to 1 cm.; average 6 mm.

Decoration:

Technique: Impressions of cord-wrapped paddle or stamping tool on wet clay of vessel exterior.

Design: Close-spaced cord marking except in few cases. Cord impressions are deep and clear. Cords used were probably coarsely twined. (Pl. 21, *h*.)

Distribution: Apparently entire vessel exterior. Cord impressions run vertically, diagonally, and horizontally on the vessel with vertical placement the most common. One specimen has diagonal arrangement of cord impressions on body with vertical impressions (4 cm. long) around rim.

Form:

Total vessel: Pots with both slightly flared and slightly converged orifices indicated.

Rim: Direct and slightly inslanting or slightly outflared. Thickened a little below orifice.

Lip: Round-pointed with slight exterior eversion and rounding in some cases. Some are notched or scalloped.

Base: Conoidal(?) or subconoidal(?).

Appendages: None observed.

Geographical range of type: The northwest and central-west Florida Gulf coast.

Chronological position of type: The Santa Rosa-Swift Creek Period. Owing to its scarcity and lack of stratigraphic data for the type, this period placement is very tentative.

Relationships of type: To the various Southeastern cord-marked wares. Deasonville Cord-marked of Louisiana and Wilmington Cord-marked of the Georgia coast are good examples.

Bibliography: Ford and Willey (1939: Deasonville type); Caldwell and Waring (1939: Wilmington Heavy Cord-marked type).

Type name.—CRYSTAL RIVER INCISED.

Definition as a type: From west Florida in the present paper.

Ware characteristics: Probably a coiled ware. Tempered with fine sand and mica. The paste is homogeneous and granular, resembling Swift Creek Complicated Stamped of the Early Variety. Buff-fired surfaces. Both interior and exterior surfaces are smoothed, occasionally polished.

Decoration:

Technique: Deep, medium-wide incised lines and large, round-dot punctations. Incision sometimes displays "fractured" edges showing that lines were made after complete sun drying.

Design: Combination lobate forms and circles (fig. 31, *a*), recticurvilinear flags (fig. 31, *b, d*), cruciform arrangements, starlike points attached to lobate or circular elements (fig. 31, *g*), and pendant loops (fig. 31, *c*). These elements are often filled with fields of large dot punctations. The various elements are combined into complicated designs. These may or may not be highly conventionalized life forms. Some pieces show obvious naturalism, including a hand design, human face, bird, etc.

Distribution: Vessel exterior. Usually pendant from rim but sometimes covers entire vessel.

Form: Flattened-globular bowls, cylindrical beakers, double-globed vessels, collared jars, composite-silhouette jars. Rims are unmodified or have a fold or slight flange.

Geographical range of type: Known from Franklin to Citrus Counties along the Gulf Coast. May have even greater extent.

Chronological position of type: Santa Rosa-Swift Creek Period. May extend into Weeden Island I.

Relationships of type: Some similarities to Santa Rosa Punctated. May be prototype of Weeden Island Incised.

Bibliography: Willey and Phillips (1944); Willey (1948b, 1948c).

Type name: CRYSTAL RIVER ZONED RED.

Definition as a type: Gulf Coast of Florida, present paper.

Ware characteristics: Adequate data are lacking, but the few sherds examined are very close to Crystal River Incised.

Decoration: Combines the deep line incision and large dot punctation with use of red pigment. Pigment is carmine to crimson and is applied, as a rule, in zones which are not filled with fields of punctation. Designs are horizontal bands, curvilinear rosettes (fig. 31, *f*), and, in one case, a naturalistic hand (fig. 31, *e*).

Form: Beaker and composite-silhouette jar known.

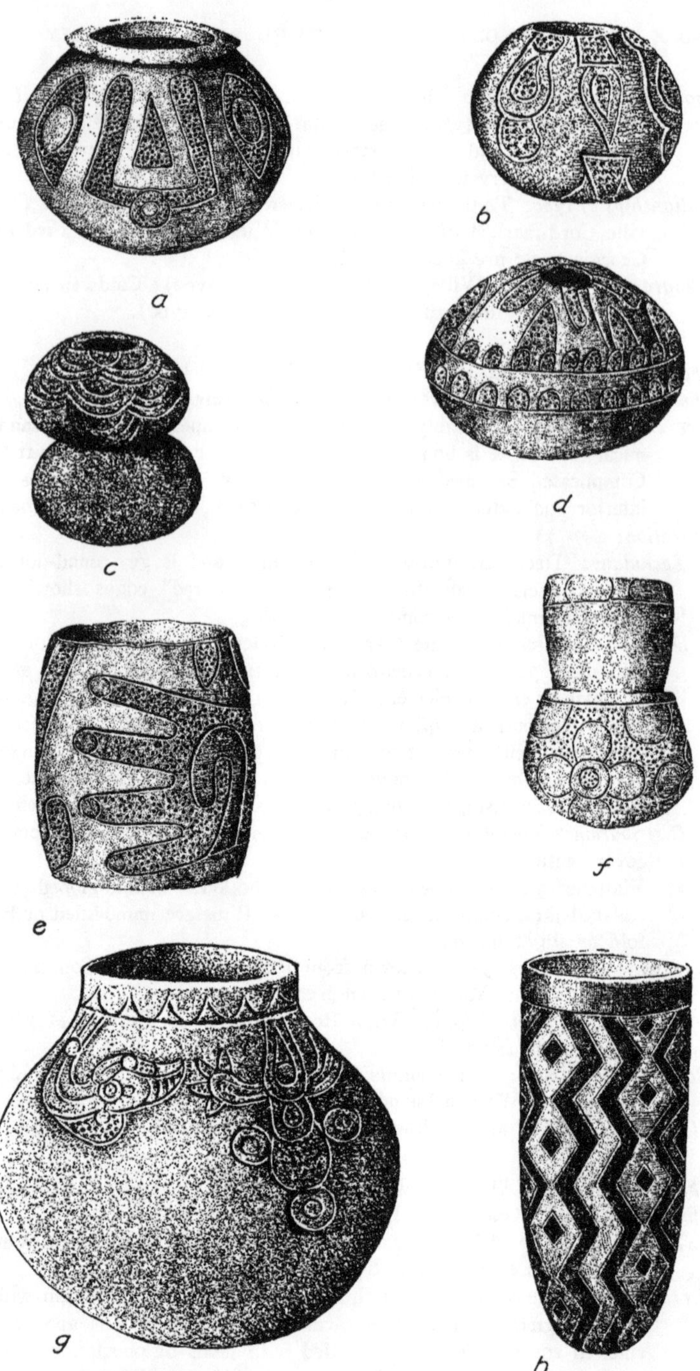

FIG. 31.—Santa Rosa-Swift Creek Period vessels. *a-d, g,* Crystal River Incised; *e, f,* Crystal River Zoned Red; *h,* Pierce Zoned Red. (Redrawn from Moore. Year, figure number, and site: *a,* 1907:9, Crystal River; *b,* 1903:21, Crystal River; *c,* 1902:284, Spring Creek; *d,* 1902:255, Hall; *e,* 1902:158, Pierce Mound A; *f,* 1902:163, Pierce Mound A; *g,* 1903:148, Aspalaga; *h,* 1902:270, Hall. All ¼ actual size.)

Geographical range of type: (Same as Crystal River Incised.)
Chronological position of type: (Same as Crystal River Incised.)
Relationships of type: To Crystal River Incised. May also be a prototype for later Weeden Island types.

Type name.—CRYSTAL RIVER NEGATIVE PAINTED.
Definition as a type: Gulf Coast of Florida, this paper. Previously mentioned by Willey and Phillips (1944) and Willey (1948b).
Ware characteristics: Much the same as Crystal River Incised except that the ware is thinner and better polished.
Decoration:
Technique: Resist-dye process whereby design is brought out in the natural buff color of the vessel by the application of a black dye which fills in the background. Has sometimes been referred to as "lost-color" process.
Design: Only five specimens of the type are known. Three of these are from Crystal River (Ci-1); one is from Warrior River, mound B (Ta-3); and one is from Green Point (Fr-11). A bold running scroll with interspaced dots, a running volute with interspaced dots and a dotted border band, nested triangles and chevrons, and a series of separate horizontal U-shaped elements are the known designs. (Pl. 23.)
Distribution: Apparently most of exterior vessel body.
Form:
Total vessel: Small flattened-globular bowls, large flattened-globular bowls, and globular bowls with flared collars.
Rim: Small and large flanges. In one case the flange is scalloped. Also scalloped rims and unmodified rims.
Base: Rounded.
Appendages: None known.
Geographical range of type: From Franklin to Citrus Counties along the Gulf Coast.
Chronological position of type: Santa Rosa-Swift Creek Period.
Relationships of type: Has general ware series relationships to the other Crystal River types and to the subsequent Weeden Island Period types. May be an ancient prototype of the late Middle Mississippian negative painted pottery found in other parts of the Southeast.
Bibliography: Willey and Phillips (1944); Willey (1948b).

Type name.—PIERCE ZONED RED.
Definition as a type: Gulf Coast of Florida, present paper. Few data are available.
Ware characteristics: About the same as Crystal River Negative Painted.
Decoration:
Technique: Combination of line incision and enclosed red zones. Lines have been made when paste has been extremely dry but before firing. Lines are medium broad and deep. Red pigment is carmine to crimson.
Design: Very simple rectangular panels, horizontal bands, vertical zigzag bands (fig. 31, *h*), diagonal bands, diamonds, and pendant loops. (Pl. 22, *a*.)
Distribution: Exterior vessel walls.
Form: Eccentric U-shaped double vessel and a cylindrical beaker.

Geographical range of type: (Same as Crystal River Series.)
Chronological position of type: (Same as Crystal River Series.)
Relationships of type: Obvious prototype of Weeden Island Zoned Red although designs are much more simple.

Type name.—FRANKLIN PLAIN.
Definition as a type: From the northwest coast of Florida, present paper. Type based upon substantial number of plain rim and distinctive basal sherds. Associated plain body sherds, which may in many cases come from the same vessels, were not classified as Franklin Plain owing to the difficulties in distinguishing it from Weeden Island Period plain ware.
Ware characteristics: Very similar to Swift Creek Complicated Stamped (Early Variety). Both surfaces are smoothed and the smoothing marks are often evident. No evidence of polish.

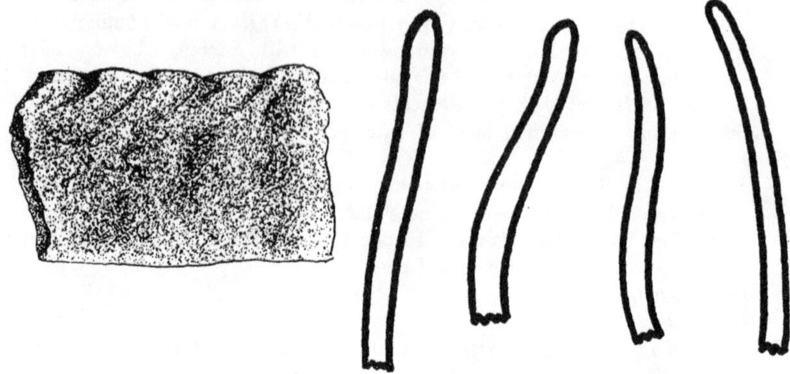

FIG. 32.—Santa Rosa-Swift Creek Period rim forms. Franklin Plain. (Interiors to right.)

Form:
Total vessel: No very good evidence. Sherds suggest pots with slightly converged or flared orifices, and, possibly, jars with short, flared collars (pl. 22, *e*). There are some vessels illustrated by Moore which may belong to this type. These include: a long-collared jar; a pot with slightly flared orifice; a composite-silhouette inset jar-bowl; and a short-collared jar with lobes.
Rims: Rims are inslanted, inturned with a slight recurve, and outflared. Many are thinned near the orifice (fig. 32).
Lip: The general conformation of the lip is either round-pointed or flat. The distinguishing feature of the type is the scalloping or notching on the top of the lip. This varies from widely spaced smooth scallops, whose crests are separated by 1 to 2 cm., to narrow deep notches, measuring as little as 5 mm. from crest to crest.
Bases and appendages: Subconoidal to flattened round bases. Tetrapodal supports are identical with those found on Swift Creek Complicated Stamped (Early Variety). Supports are arranged in a square and are teat-shaped and solid. They range in height from 1.5 cm. to barely

visible nodes; in diameter they range from 1 to 3 cm. Spacing varies from over 6 cm. to less than 3 cm. When supports occur on a vessel of markedly subconoidal form a little rectangular platform is formed on the base. (Pl. 21, *i*.)

Geographical range of type: All along the northwest Florida coast. Extends southward to Tampa Bay.

Chronological position of type: Santa Rosa-Swift Creek Period.

Relationships of type: Related to the decorated wares of the Santa Rosa-Swift Creek Period.

Residual group: UNUSUAL FORMS.

Description: Not a type. There are a few examples of unusual plain ware forms which almost certainly belong to the Santa Rosa-Swift Creek Period. One of these is the multiple-orifice vessel (Moore, 1902, fig. 164, Pierce mound A (Fr-14), is a good example). This shape also occurs in the type Alligator Bayou Stamped. Another is the unusual complete effigy form (Moore, 1902, fig. 156, Pierce mound A (Fr-14)). Such specimens have not been classified as Weeden Island Plain or with any type, but are described separately under the site discussions.

Other arts and technologies.—The stone industry seems to have been moderately well developed in this period. Projectiles and large lance points were met with in many of the burial mounds. Some of these were large, beautifully chipped ceremonial blades. These could have been made from native flint. There is little information on point forms. In our stratigraphic work on the northwest coast few projectiles (see pl. 24, *c, d*) were found in the pit levels of this period, and Moore offers few illustrations or descriptions of chipped-stone material. Polished-stone celts were fairly common. These were of medium length, averaging about 10 inches, and of the pointed-poll variety (pl. 42, *h*). The stone of which the celts were made is imported material. The celts may have been made locally or they may have been traded from the north. Miscellaneous hones, smoothing stones, and pebble hammers were found in most of the burial mounds. Stone beads, bar amulets, plummet-type pendants, and rock-crystal pendants were occasionally present in the burial mounds. In addition to stone, other minerals were utilized in the manufacture of artifacts or were found as raw materials in the mounds. These include galena, mica, bitumen, kaolin, and hematite. There are two instances of spear-point forms cut from mica. There are also two batonlike objects of kaolin. These last have been decorated with incised designs.

Shellwork included, besides the conch cups, chisels and adzes made from columellae of the conch, *Busycon* hammers, *Strombus* celts, plummet-type pendants (pl. 24, *a*), gorgets (pl. 24, *f*), and beads. Bone was used for projectiles (pl. 24, *b*), fishhooks, and gorgets.

Turtle-shell rattles, perforated canine teeth, shark teeth, and cut animal jaws are additional miscellaneous items.

The smoking complex for this period is better represented than it is in either earlier or later periods. More pipes and a greater variety of pipes are found. Pottery monitors (pl. 24, *e, g, h*) and stone monitors both occur, with the first being more common. A single tubular pipe is known; this is from Crystal River (Ci-1) and is of pottery. Both stone and pottery elbow pipes occur. Sometimes these are equal-arm types; others have flaring bowls and are ornamented with incision. The Huckleberry Landing (Fr-12) and Jackson (Fr-15) mounds offered some doubt as to whether or not the elbow pipes found there were or were not intrusive. The fact that similar pipes are present in other mounds of the Santa Rosa-Swift Creek Period argues for their inclusive presence.

The metalwork of the Santa Rosa-Swift Creek Period is better done and more plentiful than in later periods. Metals are unknown from the earlier horizons. Copper is the usual metal and is obviously an import. It is also probable that the actual artifacts themselves were made elsewhere and imported, as the forms are identical with those found as far north as the Ohio Valley. Copper-covered ear spools of wood and bone are reported as are all-metal bicymbal-type ear ornaments. Some of the latter have hammered silver (pl. 24, *i, j*) or meteoric iron plating. Conjoined copper tubes are known from the Crystal River site as are sheet-copper ornaments decorated by a repoussé technique. Miscellaneous copper fragments are listed for several of the mounds.

Although no examples are extant, it is almost certain that wood carving was an accomplished art for the period. The designs on the complicated stamped pottery are intricate and well conceived. This means that such designs were first carved upon the stamping medium; and, lacking evidences of such stamps in imperishable materials, it is believed that they were carved from wood. It is very likely that other articles of wood were similarly decorated. Unfortunately for the archeologist what may have been the most splendid artistic expression of their culture, ornamented woodwork, has perished completely.

In summation it can be said that most of the handicrafts of the Santa Rosa-Swift Creek Period Indians do not come up to their pottery, where they display an unusual virtuosity. Stone chipping shows average skill; stone grinding and polishing, if indigeneous, is equally able; metalwork is probably not local. Shell carving, on the other hand, is undoubtedly local and well adapted. Ornaments, such as a fish-effigy gorget, exceed shell carving as it was known in the

Glades area but are not products of consumate skill. Plummets, *Busycon* hammers, and *Strombus* celts are identical with those from the Glades area, and the ideas for these artifacts probably were borrowed from the south. Wood carving was well developed.

The various artifacts found in the mounds give us a skeletonized idea of some of the activities of the Santa Rosa-Swift Creek People. Stone and shell tools and weapons were obviously used in work, war, fishing, and hunting. The functions of specific objects is speculative. Stone and shell celts and shell hammers could have been effective as cutting, digging, or fighting implements. The rather large number of ornamental or ceremonial objects is noteworthy. It is believed that the stone or shell plummets or pendants were used as dress ornaments. Gorgets, beads, amulets, teeth, animal jaws, and copper ear spools are clearly ornamental. Smoking may have had a ritualistic, a nonritualistic, or a dual function in the society. The placing of hunting and fighting weapons in the mounds shows a regard for the importance of these activities. Purposeful breakage of celts and flint points which accompany the dead, in much the same way that pottery vessels were purposefully destroyed, reflects an animistic concern for the destruction and "release" of the object to accompany the spirit of the dead.

Speculations on population and period duration.—There are 19 midden and 19 burial-mound sites of this period. Twelve of the burial mounds are pure sites, while seven are mixed with a later period. As mounds are more noticeable, have attracted more interest, and have been explored more often than village sites, I believe it likely that the 19 burial mounds which we have identified as Santa Rosa-Swift Creek represent a greater proportion of the total burial mounds of this period than the 19 midden sites represent in relation to the total number of villages. This would mean that not every Santa Rosa-Swift Creek village site had in association its own burial mound. Although our data are insufficient to make a conclusive determination of this important point, there is considerable evidence to indicate that some midden sites were without special places of burial. The 19 mound and 19 village sites which we are analyzing are not all, as is evident from the site lists, combined village-mound units. For example, several of the Santa Rosa-Swift Creek middens which were explored during the 1940 survey had no burial mound in association. From this it would appear that several of the village sites, probably those clustered within a radius of a few miles, banded together to build a mound for common use.

As a trial estimate we will say that middens are three times as numerous as mounds. If there were once four times as many Santa Rosa-Swift Creek mounds in the Gulf Coast area as we have accounted for in our review, say approximately 80, the number of village communities, as represented by middens, would then total 240. I realize that these figures are little better than guesses, given whatever approach to validity that they may have by my first-hand impressions of the country and its archeological sites. I believe, though, that the figures which I have set represent a maximum rather than a minimum number of sites.

We move even farther away from controlled data and evidence in trying to estimate population figures. Multiplying the estimated number of living communities (240) by the figure of 30 persons per average community we arrive at a total population, at any one time during the period, of 7,200. It is, of course, likely that these small, thin sites were not all occupied at the same time. To arrive at a living mean, the 7,200 might be shaved to 5,000 or less.

An estimated duration of 200 years is set for the Santa Rosa-Swift Creek Period. Santa Rosa-Swift Creek ceramics and other artifacts show a much greater degree of specialization, a greater intricacy of detail, and an over-all superiority to those of the Deptford or Perico Island Periods. Although stylistically different they stand on the same level of skill as Weeden Island. The inner stylistic changes of Santa Rosa-Swift Creek are less marked than those which characterize the growth of Weeden Island. This does not necessarily mean that less time was involved for the Santa Rosa-Swift Creek development than for Weeden Island, but taking into consideration as well the several cross-datings of the Gulf Coast sequence with other sequences outside of the area, I am inclined to allow only half as much time for Santa Rosa-Swift Creek as I do for the full chronological span of Weeden Island.

THE WEEDEN ISLAND PERIODS

Period definition.—Two periods, Weeden Island I and II, follow in that order after Santa Rosa-Swift Creek. Weeden Island I is denoted by the first appearance of the Weeden Island Series of pottery types. The only exception to this is the type Weeden Island Plain. As now defined, Weeden Island Plain covers a great range of vessel forms, some of which first appear in the Santa Rosa-Swift Creek Period. Further refining of the Gulf Coast sequences and typology will probably result in a separation of this type into two parts, an early and a late.

The decorated types of the Weeden Island Series are Weeden Island Incised, Carrabelle Incised, Carrabelle Punctated, and a number of others which usually appear in minor percentages. Swift Creek Complicated Stamped (Late Variety) is also a marker type for the Weeden Island I Period.

The ceramic indicator for Weeden Island II is the type Wakulla Check Stamped. Weeden Island Series types also continue. Some types, such as Weeden Island Punctated, are more common in this period than in Weeden Island I. A distinctive feature of Weeden Island II in the northwest is the virtual disappearance of Swift Creek Complicated Stamped (Late Variety) and other related complicated types.

There are also minor temporal and regional variations in the Weeden Island Periods. Weeden Island Incised of the Weeden Island I Period tends to be characterized by deeper, bolder incised lines and a greater variety of vessel forms than in the II Period. Weeden Island Plain of the I Period is often seen in such forms as compartment trays and flattened-globular bowls with the heavy, cut-out rim fold so typical of the central and east Florida type, Oklawaha Plain. These forms and features apparently disappear in Weeden Island II. Around Tampa Bay, at the southern end of the central coast region and southward into the Manatee region, a group of types appear that are either absent or rare in the Weeden Island Complex of the northwest. Among these are the Papys Bayou Series, the Little Manatee Series, the Hillsborough Series, and a variant complicated stamped series. Most of these seem to be Weeden Island II types.

The sites.—The site review shows 21 pure sites of the Weeden Island I Period and 12 sites in which Weeden Island I is mixed with other period components. Most of these mixed sites, it will be noted, are the same burial mounds which were noted as mixed under the Santa Rosa-Swift Creek Period.

Pure sites
- Middens:
  - Santa Rosa Sound (Sa-1)
  - Site west of Point Washington (Wl-11)
  - West St. Andrews (By-2)
- Burial mounds:
  - Site west of Point Washington (Wl-11)
  - Basin Bayou, west (Wl-13)
  - Holley (By-1)
  - West Bay Post Office (By-11)
  - Burnt Mill Creek, smaller mound (By-16)
  - Burnt Mill Creek, west (By-17)

Laughton's Bayou, mound A (By-27)
Hare Hammock, smaller mound (By-31)
Davis' Field (Ca-1)
Gotier Hammock (Gu-2)
St. Joseph's Bay (Gu-6)
Tucker (Fr-4)
Bird Hammock, mound B (Wa-10)
Aucilla River mound (Ta-1)
Warrior River, mound A (Ta-2)
Horseshoe Point (Di-1)
Fowler's Landing, larger mound (Lv-1)
Cayo Palu (Ch-1)

Mixed sites

Middens:

Villa Tasso (Wl-2)
Davis Point, west (By-7)
Mound Field (Wa-8)

Burial mounds:

Aspalaga (Gd-1)
Chipola Cut-off (Gu-5)
Porter's Bar (Fr-1)
Jackson mound (Fr-15)
Marsh Island (Wa-1)
Hall site (Wa-4)
Warrior River, mound B (Ta-3)
Seven miles north of Cedar Keys (Lv-2)
Tarpon Springs (Pi-3)

There are 29 pure sites and 19 mixed sites of the Weeden Island II Period.

Pure sites

Middens:

First site opposite Woodlawn (Es-4)
Second site opposite Woodlawn (Es-5)
Rocky Bayou, east (Ok-2)
Black Point (Ok-4)
Hicks site (Wl-6)
Midden northwest of Crystal Lake (Wg-1)
Pearl Bayou midden (By-24)
West Bristol midden (Li-1)
Midden west of Carrabelle (Fr-3)
Ocklockonee Bay midden (Fr-6)
Topsail Bluff (Fr-7)
Eleven Mile Point (Fr-10)
Surf (Wa-2)
Nichols (Wa-3)
Refuge headquarters (Wa-13)
Hodgeson's Hill (Lv-8)

Domiciliary mounds:
- Graveyard Point (Sa-3)

Burial mounds:
- Maester Creek (Sa-2)
- Rocky Bayou, west (Ok-3)
- Sowell (By-3)
- Davis Point, west (By-7)
- North Bay (By-20)
- Indian Pass Point (Gu-1)
- Mound at Bristol (Li-4)
- St. Marks mound (Wa-12)
- Chassahowitzka River (Ci-3)
- Wekiwachee River (Pa-1)
- Pithlochascootie River (Pa-2)
- Parrish mound 5 (Ma-5)

Mixed sites

Middens:
- Top bench mark (Es-2)
- Hickory Shores (Sa-5)
- Second Gulf Breeze site (Sa-7)
- Big Hammock (Wl-3)
- Mack Bayou (Wl-8)
- Bear Point (By-5)
- West Bay bridge (By-6)
- West Goose Creek (Wa-6)
- Clearwater (Pi-5)
- Boca Ciega Island (Pi-6)
- Rocky Point (Hi-7)
- Osprey (So-2)

Midden and cemetery:
- Pool Hammock (So-3)
  (Cemetery features at this site probably relate to later Safety Harbor occupation.)

Burial mounds:
- Weeden Island (Pi-1)
  (Underlain by Perico Island Period cemetery.)
- Thomas (Hi-1)
- Picknick (Hi-3)
- Jones (Hi-4)
- Buck Island (Hi-6)
- Englewood (So-1)

A number of sites either could not be differentiated as Weeden Island I or II or they combined characteristics of both of these periods to indicate that use or occupation had lasted over both periods. Most of these are burial mounds, but some are village locations. There are 42 such combined or undifferentiated sites which are purely Weeden

Island. Eleven more sites show combined or undifferentiated Weeden Island features mixed with other periods.

Pure sites

Middens:

Holley (By-1)
Midden in Davis Point area (By-9)
Hall site (Wa-4)
Piney Point (Lv-9)

Burial mounds:

Pippen's Lake (Wl-12)
Wise Bluff (Wl-17)
Dead River, north (Wl-18)
Dead River, south (Wl-19)
Douglas Bluff (Wl-20)
Spring Hill Landing (Wg-2)
Miller Field Landing (Wg-3)
Bear Point (By-5)
Davis Point, east (By-8)
West Bay Creek (By-12)
Phillips Inlet (By-13)
Brock Hammock (By-14)
Burnt Mill Creek, larger mound (By-15)
Fannings Bayou (By-19)
Large Bayou (By-22)
Mound near Pearl Bayou (By-25)
Strange's Landing (By-26)
Laughton's Bayou, mound B (By-28)
Hare Hammock, larger mound (By-30)
Farmdale (By-32)
McLaney place (Hn-1)
Fullmore's Upper Landing (Hn-2)
Kemp's Landing (Ja-2)
OK Landing (Ca-2)
Burgess Landing (Gu-3)
Isabel Landing (Gu-4)
Hare's Landing (Dr-1)
Kerr's Landing (Dr-3)
Hardnut Landing (Dr-4)
Shoemake Landing (Ey-1)
Rock Bluff Landing (Li-5)
Brickyard Creek (Fr-8)
Bird Hammock, mound A (Wa-9)
Gigger Point (Lv-3)
Culpepper (Lv-5)
Way Key (Lv-6)
Palmetto Island (Lv-7)

Cemetery or burial mound (?):

Aboriginal cemetery in Cedar Keys (Lv-4)

Mixed sites
- Middens:
  - Five miles west of Navarre (Es-3)
  - Fort Walton (Ok-6)
  - Sowell (By-3)
  - Porter's Bar (Fr-1)
  - Carrabelle (Fr-2)
  - Tucker (Fr-4)
  - Nine-Mile Point (Fr-9)
  - Pierce midden (Fr-14)
  - Refuge tower (Wa-14)
  - Shaws Point (Ma-7)
- Burial mounds:
  - Bayport (He-1)

There are also the three sites questionable as to period but which may be Weeden Island or Santa Rosa-Swift Creek.

Questionable
- Burial mounds:
  - Sampson's Landing (Ja-1)
  - Michaux Log Landing (Li-6)
  - Munnerlyn's Landing (Dr-2)

The following totals summarize the numbers of sites of various kinds for the Weeden Island Periods.

Weeden Island I			33
Pure		21	
Middens	3		
Burial mounds	18		
Mixed		12	
Middens	3		
Burial mounds	9		
Weeden Island II			48
Pure		29	
Middens	16		
Domiciliary mounds	1		
Burial mounds	12		
Mixed		19	
Middens	12		
Middens and cemetery	1		
Burial mounds	6		
Weeden Island (combined and undifferentiated)			53
Pure		42	
Middens	4		
Burial mounds	37		
Cemetery or burial mound	1		
Mixed		11	
Middens	10		
Burial mounds	1		

Sites of the Weeden Island I Period, on the basis of our review, are more common in the northwest coast region than the central coastal or Manatee regions. Definite Weeden Island I sites do occur in the central coastal section, however. Only one site, Cayo Palu (Ch-1), about which we know very little, is recorded as a Weeden Island I site for the Manatee region. Proportionately, Weeden Island II sites are a little more common in the south than Weeden Island I. In general, the Weeden Island culture can be said to be characteristic of the entire area of the Florida Gulf Coast but with the greater density along the northwest and upper central west coasts.

Settlement pattern.—The topographic location of Weeden Island sites is the same as that noted for Santa Rosa-Swift Creek Period sites in that both are found along the coast, on bay shores, or on streams. Occupation sites are small in extent, averaging less than 100 meters in diameter and about .50 meter in depth. Larger, deeper sites that contain Weeden Island Period materials usually show evidences of occupations during other periods as well. Nearly all Weeden Island Period sites are marked by shell refuse.

Burial mounds are situated near but usually not within or upon the midden areas. Mounds accompany many but not all of the village sites. As with Santa Rosa-Swift Creek it is likely that a single mound served more than one small community.

The question of domiciliary or temple mounds, artificial mounds built primarily as bases for houses or other buildings, is very puzzling. Three Weeden Island I burial mounds may have been used as temple or house substructures in that there is some evidence to the effect that they had ramp-type or graded approaches leading up to the summits. These are the Basin Bayou, west (Wl-13), the Hall (Wa-4), and the Mound Field (Wa-8) sites.[73] All three mounds contained typical Weeden Island inclusive burials and mortuary artifacts. Other possible domiciliary mounds are the various sand mounds which Moore excavated and found to be sterile or nearly so. These mounds were artificial, and most of them were low and amorphous as to shape. Their lack of cultural materials makes it impossible to date most of them accurately in the time scale, but as they are often found near Weeden Island burial mounds or Weeden Island middens it is possible that they were Weeden Island Period structures. Several such mounds were tested by Fewkes at Weeden Island proper (Pi-1). These were a part of the mound group along with midden accumulations and the

[73] I have not included the mound at the Nichols site (Wa-3) which has a ramp. This mound cannot be dated successfully but may have been built during the Fort Walton Period.

Weeden Island burial mound. Another apparent temple mound was excavated by both Moore and Walker on the Pithlochascootie River. Near this tumulus was a second one which proved to be a Weeden Island II burial mound. One of the few apparent domiciliary mounds that can be dated with reasonable assurance is the small sand mound at Graveyard Point (Sa-3). A collection from here was classified as Weeden Island II.

Summing up the case for the temple- or domiciliary-type mound in the Weeden Island Periods, we can state that if mounds of this sort did occur they were rare. It is possible in some cases that they may have served both temple and mortuary functions.

One other feature should be mentioned before we leave the examination of Weeden Island settlement patterns. This is the circular shell enclosure. At Laughton's Bayou, mound A (By-27), a Weeden Island I burial mound, a circular shell enclosure was noted in a nearby field. Another such enclosure was observed at Bear Point (By-5), also a Weeden Island site. These enclosures have not, of course, been definitely dated, but it is probable that they belong to the Weeden Island Period. They may be the remains of old village fortifications or they may have had only a ceremonial significance.

Economy.—It is presumed that the subsistence economy of the Weeden Island Periods was divided among marine foods, land animals, and horticultural products. For the first two there is abundant evidence in the middens. Concerning domesticated food plants, the situation is about the same as for the Santa Rosa-Swift Creek Period. The time position of Weeden Island makes it reasonable to believe that the Weeden Islanders were agriculturists, but, as yet, there is no direct proof of this. A hint of dietary change is seen in the Carrabelle (Fr-2) and Mound Field (Wa-8) midden excavations. At both sites the lower Santa Rosa-Swift Creek Period levels contain much more shell than the upper Weeden Island Period levels. This shift in midden content may signal a change from a diet predominantly made up of shellfish to one in which plant foods played a greater part.

Organization of society.—Few changes can be inferred between the Weeden Island Periods and the preceding Santa Rosa-Swift Creek Period as regards the organization of society. The small villages, or groups of two or three villages, were probably autonomous in political and religious matters. There is still the same strong orientation toward a cult of the dead, and it is likely that mundane and sacred powers were closely related. Funerary goods were manufactured in large numbers, especially pottery vessels. There is less differentiation, however, in the quantity and quality of goods placed with the dead. During the Santa Rosa-Swift Creek Period both mass deposits of mortuary goods and individual offerings were found in the burial mounds. In Weeden Island nearly all gifts to the dead were placed in a common mass deposit. This may mark a decline in prestige accorded priests or other leaders. Special treatment of bodies or skeletons does continue, though. In several of the Weeden Island mounds one or two individuals were found centrally in the mound, often below mound base in a specially prepared pit grave as if to signify their importance as persons of distinctive station in the society.

There are no outstanding ceremonial sites of the period which would rank above the others. This equality is even more marked than in the Santa Rosa-Swift Creek Period where one or two sites stood out slightly above the others in size and richness.

Disposal of the dead.—Burial of the Weeden Island Periods was in mounds of sand made expressly for the purpose. Only one instance of cemetery burial is recorded in this review (Cedar Keys (Lv-4)) and that is questionable. Most of the mounds of the Weeden Island I Period were circular in outline. Two of the largest were oblong (Hall (Wa-4) and Mound Field (Wa-8)), and both of these have sloping extensions which may be ramp approaches. Another extension or ramp approach is recorded for Basin Bayou, west (Wl-13), a circular mound. It will be remembered that the oblong mound form and the mound extensions or ramps were fairly common features of the Santa Rosa-Swift Creek Period; they are also found among some of the mixed Santa Rosa-Swift Creek and Weeden Island I burial mounds. The Weeden Island I occurrences of these features would appear to be a carry-over from the earlier period. As with Santa Rosa-Swift Creek, it is very questionable whether or not the mound extensions were actually ramps; data are insufficient to decide this point.

The Weeden Island I mounds range in height from 2.5 to 9 feet and in diameter from less than 30 to over 80 feet. Most were dome-shaped or truncated-conical. They were made of gray, white, or tan sands. Dark humus-stained areas, masses of charcoal or decayed wood, layers or lenses of shell, red ocher, masses of clay, and limestone rocks were sometimes present in addition to the pure sand. Evenly bedded strata showing a layered structure were rarely found. Only in one case (Davis Field (Ca-1)) is there evidence for an interior mound. In this instance the inner mound covered a subfloor pit, the bottom of which was lined with charcoal. Burned timbers and charcoal in some of the mounds suggest that fires were made near the burials and that the sand and earth were sometimes piled over wooden structures which had been destroyed by fire. Decayed but unburned logs on mound base also suggest structures, perhaps tombs. Limerock slabs were sometimes used as platings for mound surfaces and as coverings for individual burials within the mounds. More often, oyster or conch shells were heaped over burials as though to form protective mantles for individual skeletons.

Both secondary and primary burials were found in mounds with the secondary bundle and single skull inhumations tending to be more common than the flexed primary type. In general, the primary burials are found in the lower parts of the mound, on mound base, or below base in subfloor pits. Exposure of bodies in "houses of the dead," scraping of the bones, and the storage of bones after fleshing but prior to burial are all suggested by the Weeden Island types of secondary burial. The storing up of the disarticulated skeletal remains of the dead for periodic burial ceremonies is probably the explanation for the mass deposits of secondary burials. Such periodic funeral rites were very likely the occasions for building or adding to the mounds.

What appear to be primary burials may, in some cases, have been subjected to secondary treatment. After exposure and fleshing the still articulated or partially articulated skeleton could have been placed in the mound in a flexed, semiflexed, or extended (rare) position as desired. It was Moore's opinion that this practice had been followed in some instances. It is also likely that regular primary inhumation was carried out.

As in Santa Rosa-Swift Creek, very occasional cremated remains were found. These are definite cremations and must be considered apart from bones which were only partially or slightly calcined as though by in situ fires. This custom of placing a fire near the human remains after burial was a fairly common one during the Weeden Island Periods.

In Weeden Island I mounds the number of burials ranged from 3 or 4 to about 80. These were accompanied by a profusion of artifacts. Mass deposits of pottery rather than individual offerings were the rule. These were more often found on the east side of the mound, usually extending from the margin in toward mound center in a sort of pathway. This pathway was literally paved with potsherds which represented vessels that had, clearly, been purposefully broken for the deposition ceremony. Complete, or nearly complete, vessels were also in the deposit. Many of these had been destroyed by breaking a small hole through the base as though to "kill" or release the spirit of the vessel. This animistic belief may also be reflected in strange nonutilitarian vessels found in these deposits. These had been made and fired with holes already cut into base and walls. Smaller caches of pottery were often found at various locations in the mounds. Only rarely was an isolated vessel found sufficiently near a primary or secondary burial to attribute it to the burial as a specially placed offering.

Nonceramic artifacts of stone, shell, bone, or various minerals were found in the mounds both as general mortuary offerings and as offerings to specific individuals. The latter practice, that of placing them with individuals, was not as common in the Weeden Island Period as it was in Santa Rosa-Swift Creek; however nonpottery objects were found with individual skeletons much more frequently than pottery.

The above discussion of burials and burial mounds refers primarily to Weeden Island I but can, for the most part, be applied to Weeden Island II as well as to the list of Weeden Island burial mounds which we were unable to differentiate as either Period I or Period II. Weeden Island II mounds have almost the same size range as Weeden Island I. Height of mound is from 2 to 7 feet and diameter from 30 to 80 feet. They are constructed in the same manner. Most of them are circular and dome-shaped, although two mounds are oblong or rectanguloid. The extension or ramp-approach features are, however, missing. The number of individuals found in Weeden Island II mounds seems to be, generally, about the same as Weeden Island I, although in two sites, Weeden Island proper (Pi-1) and Thomas (Hi-1), 300 to 400 burials were recovered.

Cranial flattening is noted in three Weeden Island II sites, two undifferentiated Weeden Island sites, and in the mixed Santa Rosa-Swift Creek site at Porter's Bar (Fr-1).

Ceramic arts.—Weeden Island pottery is the most outstanding of the Gulf Coast and, in many respects, of the entire aboriginal eastern United States. This relative excellence pertains to quality of ware, vessel form, and surface decoration. Most of it is sand-tempered, even, and homogeneous. Generally, it is buff-colored; sometimes gray; and rarely slipped. It is reasonably hard, and well fired by eastern United States standards, and very well shaped and smoothed. Much of it is polished.

Vessel forms are exceedingly numerous. Variations on the flattened-globular bowl and the collared jar predominate. Vessels tend to be small, as in the Santa Rosa-Swift Creek Period. Most of the forms do not appear to have been used for cooking but rather for storage, drinking, eating, or ceremonial purposes. Cooking vessels did, of course, exist. Most of them are represented only in sherd collections and were large open bowls or deep, round-bottomed pots. Unusual forms occur, such as compartmented trays and composite-silhouette vessels; however even these show less variation than in the previous Santa Rosa-Swift Creek Period.

There is a great variety of decoration. Incision and punctation are two of the principal techniques. A light red pigment is used frequently as a zone filler in connection with incision techniques, and sometimes as a complete vessel slip. Stamping, including check, complicated, and simple varieties, is another major decorative technique of the period. Only rarely are incision or punctation and stamping techniques combined upon the same vessel. Design among the incised and punctated types is quite stylized. Curvilinear geometric forms and highly conventionalized life depictions (probably bird drawings) are most common. Rectilinear geometric motifs and more naturalistic curvilinear designs are also known. A third major technique is modeling, which is often used in expressing effigy or semieffigy forms. In such forms, usually birds, the wings, head, etc., are often embellished with incision-punctation techniques to give a more naturalistic effect. Modeling is also used for small adorno effigy figures which are attached to noneffigy-form vessels. While commonly combined with incision-punctation, modeling is only rarely used in conjunction with the stamping techniques.

Although Weeden Island has much in common with the preceding Santa Rosa-Swift Creek Period, it has progressed farther toward stabilization and is less experimental both in vessel form and decoration. In general, the differences between Weeden Island I and II seem to be these: Weeden Island II is more stabilized and more conventionalized than Weeden Island I; in this it appears to carry the trend noted between Santa Rosa-Swift Creek and Weeden Island I to its logical conclusion. Weeden Island II is by no means a degenerate style, but the freshness, the originality, the great number of exotic forms and designs seen in Weeden Island I are lacking.

Even more than in Santa Rosa-Swift Creek the pottery manufactures of the Weeden Island Period were closely bound up with ritual observances for the dead.

The Weeden Island pottery types in the order in which they are described:

Weeden Island Series:
- Weeden Island Plain
- Weeden Island Incised
- Weeden Island Punctated
- Weeden Island Zoned Red

Carrabelle Incised
Carrabelle Punctated
Indian Pass Incised
Keith Incised
Tucker Ridge-pinched
Hare Hammock Surface-indented

Complicated Stamped Series:
Swift Creek Complicated Stamped (Late Variety)
Crooked River Complicated Stamped (Late Variety)
St. Andrews Complicated Stamped (Late Variety)
Tampa Complicated Stamped
Sun City Complicated Stamped
Old Bay Complicated Stamped

Wakulla Check Stamped
Thomas Simple Stamped
West Florida Cord-marked (Late Variety)
Mound Field Net-marked

Hillsborough Series:
Hillsborough Shell Stamped
Ruskin Dentate Stamped
Ruskin Linear Punctated

St. Petersburg Incised

Papys Bayou Series:
Papys Bayou Plain
Papys Bayou Incised
Papys Bayou Punctated
Papys Bayou Diagonal-incised

Little Manatee Series:
Little Manatee Zoned Stamped
Little Manatee Shell Stamped
Little Manatee Complicated Stamped

The remaining types are not primarily of the Weeden Island Complex, but as they occur in Weeden Island Period contexts in the Gulf Coast area they are described here.

Biscayne or St. Johns Series: [74]
Biscayne (St. Johns) Plain
Biscayne (St. Johns) Check Stamped
Biscayne (Dunn's Creek) Red
Biscayne Roughened
Biscayne Cord-marked

---

[74] In northeast Florida pottery of this series has been referred to under the name of St. Johns, in southwest Florida and south Florida the name Biscayne has been applied. There is apparently no difference. In this paper I have used the Biscayne name in dealing with southern sites and the St. Johns Series names farther north. This is inconsistent with recognized procedures of pottery nomenclature and is a concession to previous usage and literature. The two series should eventually be combined as one, preferably under the St. Johns name as this seems to be the area of origin for the ware.

Pasco Series:
- Pasco Plain
- Pasco Check Stamped
- Pasco Red

Gainesville Linear Punctated

Residual Group:
- Residual Plain
- Smooth Plain
- Plain Red

Type Descriptions

Type name.—WEEDEN ISLAND PLAIN.

Definition as a type: From Gulf Coast Florida, present paper. Plain ware of the Weeden Island type has been informally recognized for some years. In order to make the classification of sherds from the stratigraphic excavations as objectively verifiable as possible, only rim sherds were listed as Weeden Island Plain. It is probable that the residual group "Smooth Plain" is almost wholly composed of body sherds of Weeden Island Plain vessels. In addition, other less well-finished Weeden Island Plain body sherds were undoubtedly thrown into the other category, "Residual Plain."

Ware characteristics:

Method of manufacture: Coiling or annular technique.

Temper: Fine sand with only rare coarser particles in the form of grit or lumps of clay. Mica is observed in most sherds.

Paste texture and color: Granular. Some tendency, occasionally observed, toward lamination and contortion of paste, although this does not affect the hard, compact quality of the paste. May be oxidized to buff color throughout; may have buff surfaces and gray core; may have only an exterior buff surface; or may be gray-black throughout.

Surface texture, color, and finish: Surface color varies according to the firing. Light buff, red-buff, gray, and mottled black are the most common. Fire clouding is frequent. Both surfaces well smoothed to polished. Red paint of a carmine shade has been used as a slip on many specimens. Those so painted were nearly all of natural buff surface. Paint has the appearance of a "fugitive" red as it is much worn and, in some cases, almost completely obliterated. Nevertheless, it does not rub off and appears to have been fixed by firing, so the term "fugitive" does not properly apply. In some cases the paint was applied only to the interiors of open bowls; in others the interiors and the lip and vessel rim fold were painted red with vessel exterior left unpainted; rarely was red paint applied completely to both surfaces. Vessels with red paint are virtually all of the open bowl form. (Pl. 39, *e-f*.)

Hardness: 2.5 to 4.

Thickness: Vessel walls average 6 to 7 mm. with rims appreciably thicker.

Form:

Total vessel: Includes medium-deep, hemispherical and shallow open bowls. Bowls with incurving sides vary from those which are only slightly incurved to others which are flattened-globular. Some flattened-globular

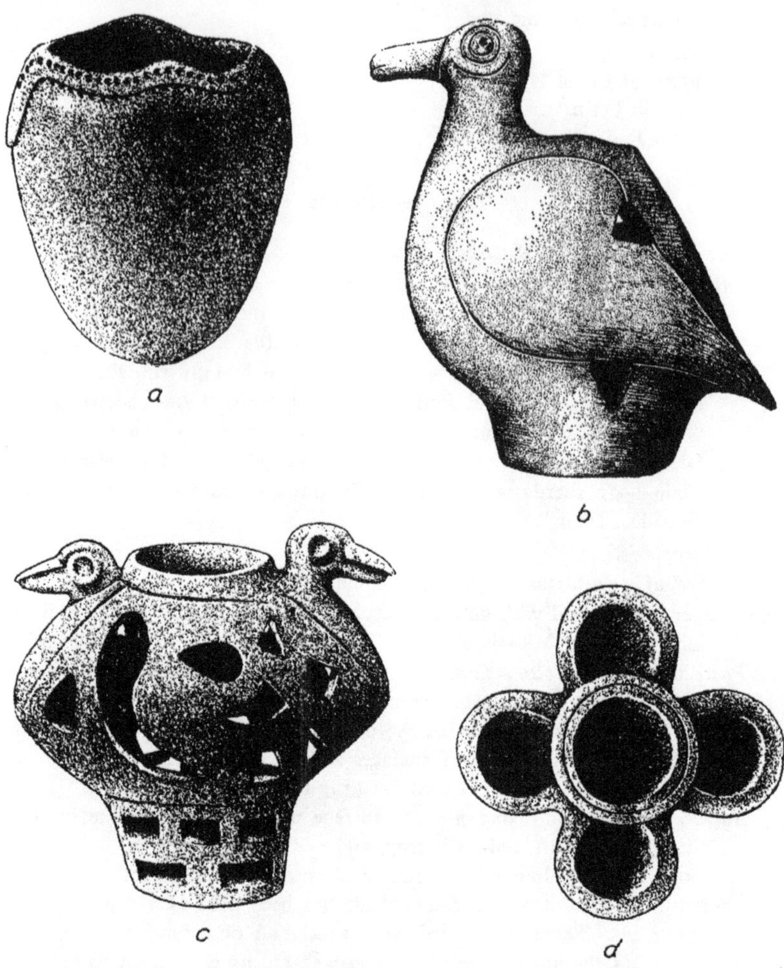

FIG. 33.—Weeden Island Period vessels. All Weeden Island Plain. (Redrawn from Moore. Year, figure number, and site: *a*, 1903: 78, Bayport; *b*, 1902: 256, Hall; *c*, 1902: 23, Burnt Mill Creek, larger mound; *d*, 1902: 268, Hall. All ¼ actual size.)

bowls are collared. There are also jars, simple (fig. 33, *a*) and short-collared, long-collared, and with squared collars. There are, in addition, a number of unusual-shaped vessels. These are nearly always found as mortuary ware, some of which was manufactured with holes and was obviously for ceremonial purposes only. These forms include multiple-compartment trays (fig. 33, *d;* pl. 41, *e*), double bowls, single-globed jars, double-globed jars, gourd-effigy bowls with single lateral handle, various forms of bowls and jars with affixed effigy figures or adornos (fig. 33, *c*), semieffigy bowls and jars (fig. 33, *b*) human-figure vessels (pl. 41, *b, c*), globular bowls with multiple body lobes, and miscellaneous eccentric shapes.

Rim: Rims are commonly thickened at or near the vessel orifice. This thickening is accomplished by both exterior, and, occasionally, interior folds. Sometimes there is no fold but the rim is, nevertheless, thickened. On the conventional shapes, rims are incurved (globular bowls) and outslanted (open bowls). Occasionally globular bowl rims are sharply recurved. Rim folds are rounded, rectanguloid, and trianguloid. The fold, or thickened margin, is often underlined with a single incised line. Occasionally, there are two incised lines with one encircling the side of the fold. (See fig. 34.)

Lip: Both flat and rounded. Many of the folded or thickened rims are bevelled either to the inside or outside. Incised or linear punctate lines on top of the lip may occur.

Base: Both rounded and flat.

Appendages: Rim projections, of which there are usually four to a vessel. These may be triangular or ovate-triangular. Sometimes they extend out horizontally; in other instances they are slanted upward at a 45-degree angle from the plane of the vessel mouth. They vary greatly as to size, some extending only a centimeter or so from the vessel rim while others project 3 or 4 cm.

Geographical range of type: The entire Florida Gulf Coast area.

Chronological position of type: Weeden Island I and II Periods.

Relationships of type: Related to the plain wares of both the Troyville and Coles Creek Periods of the Lower Mississippi Valley (see Ford and Willey, 1939).

Bibliography: Willey and Woodbury (1942); Willey (1945).

Type name.—WEEDEN ISLAND INCISED.

Definition as a type: From the Florida Gulf Coast area, this paper. This distinctive decoration type has been recognized for many years. Holmes (1903, pp. 110 ff.) referred to some of it as "Appalachicola ware"; Cushing (1897) recognized it at Tarpon Springs, and Stirling (1936) referred to the entire Weeden Island Series as "Weeden Island ware." The latter name has had current usage in the past two decades and has been selected as the type name. In an earlier paper (Willey and Woodbury, 1942, pp. 242-243), the type Weeden Island Incised was defined to include what has been here divided into Weeden Island Incised and Weeden Island Punctated. The two types are similar and obviously closely related. In the stratigraphic classifications and tabulations for northwest Florida they were lumped together as Weeden Island Incised; however, in the classifications of mound materials from the Florida west coast they were treated as separate types and are so described here.

Ware characteristics: (See Weeden Island Plain.) There are some examples of the use of red paint in Weeden Island Incised. Often bowl interiors will be red-slipped, or rim folds will be painted red. Less often the complete exterior was red-slipped.

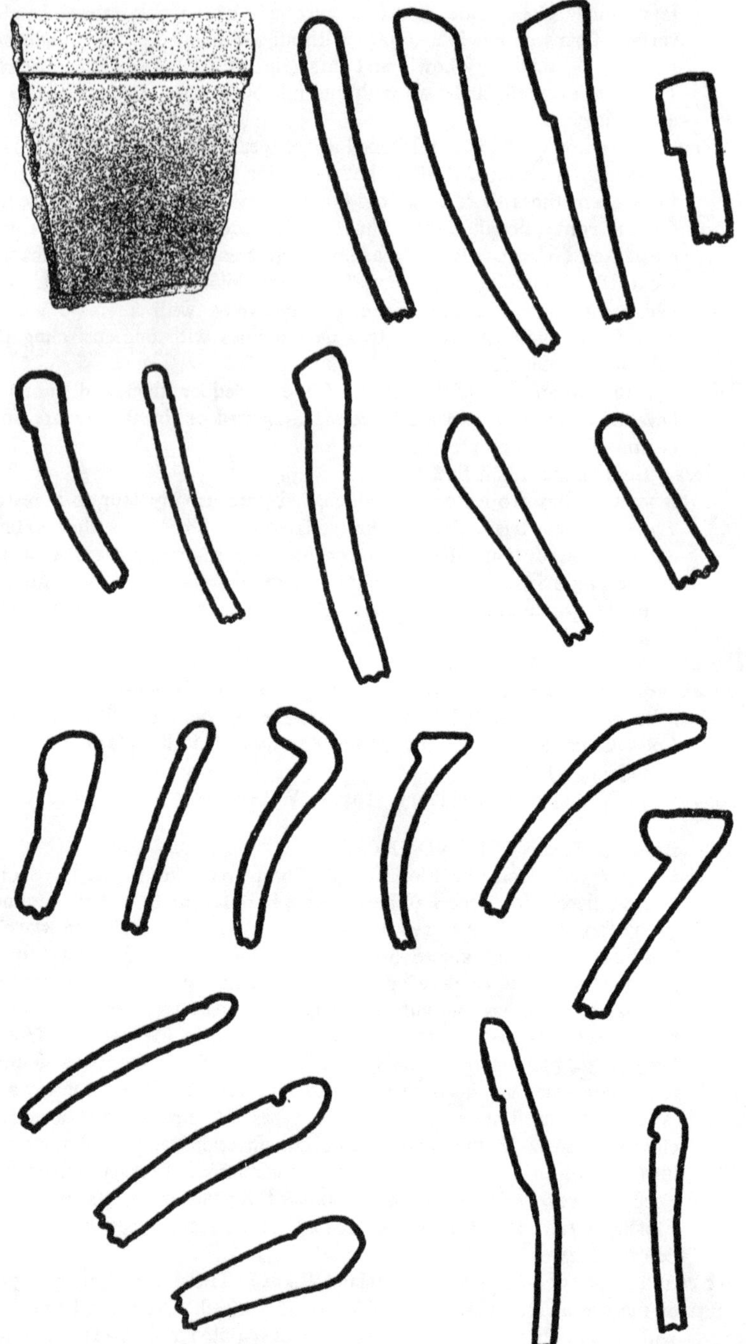

Fig. 34.—Weeden Island Period rim forms. Weeden Island Plain. (Interiors to right.)

Decoration:

Technique: Combination of incised lines, of varying depths and widths, made with a pointed instrument, and small dot, hollow-reed, and triangular punctations. All decorations made before firing.

Design: Basic design principle is one of contrasting areas with the featured design expressed in the negative, or in undecorated areas (figs. 35, 36, 37, 38). Hachure, cross hachure, and fields or rows of punctations are used as backgrounds. Background areas and plain areas are separated by an incised line. Design is essentially curvilinear and includes continuous meanders and simple and compound lobate forms. In the negative-meander design a single incised line often runs through the middle of the plain area. This line may be dotted and/or terminated by large, deep triangular or hollow-reed punctations (fig. 36, *a, e*). Moore and others have stated that the underlying motif of many of the Weeden Island designs is a bird representation. There are examples where this is undoubtedly true, and the modeling of the vessel form, plus small effigy adornos, further express the bird idea. However, the treatment is extremely stylized (fig. 35, *a, c;* 36, *d;* 38, *a-c*), and in most specimens the bird is not easily recognized. It should be said that the artist's conception was usually that of a single bird represented on each vessel, often resulting in a nonrealistic disposal of design units to express his total idea. (Pl. 25, *a-f;* pl. 26, *a-e.*)

Distribution: Decoration is often confined to a zone encircling the upper half of the vessel exterior; however, the decorating of the entire exterior surface, with the exception of the base, is often noted. Interior decoration is frequent on the laterally projecting rim appendages of the shallow open bowls.

In general, the conception of the design is excellent, stylized, and symbolic; its execution is competent, or even masterly. The craftsman's control over his medium is not excelled anywhere, or at any time, in the pottery of the eastern United States.

Form:

Total vessel: In the middens, sherds indicate a number of minor variations on a few basic shapes. These are: open bowls, bowls with slightly incurved rims, flattened-globular bowls, and simple jar forms. In the burial mounds these forms are repeated, but a number of others are found in addition. These include: Squared flattened-globular bowls, collared globular bowls, square and cylindrical beakers, beaker bowls, double- and single-globed jars both plain and in semieffigy form, gourd-effigy bowls with single lateral projecting handle, lobed or melon bowls, and miscellaneous forms. (See figs. 35, 36, 37, 38 for examples of some of these.)

Rim: Rims include a variety of incurving forms, some of which are abruptly recurved near the margin. Outslanting rims of open bowls or beakers are less common. Folding or thickening of the rim is very common. Exterior folding or thickening are more common than interior folding. Folds are both simple and compound, averaging 1 cm. in height. As a rule they are not as thick or massive as those of the Weeden Island Plain type. Incised or linear punctated lines often encircle the fold on

Fig. 35.—Weeden Island Period vessels. Weeden Island Incised. (Redrawn from Moore. Year, figure number, and site: *a*, 1918: 26, Hare Hammock, smaller mound; *b*, 1902: 122, Hare Hammock, larger mound; *c*, 1903: 3, Fowler's Landing. All about ⅓ actual size.)

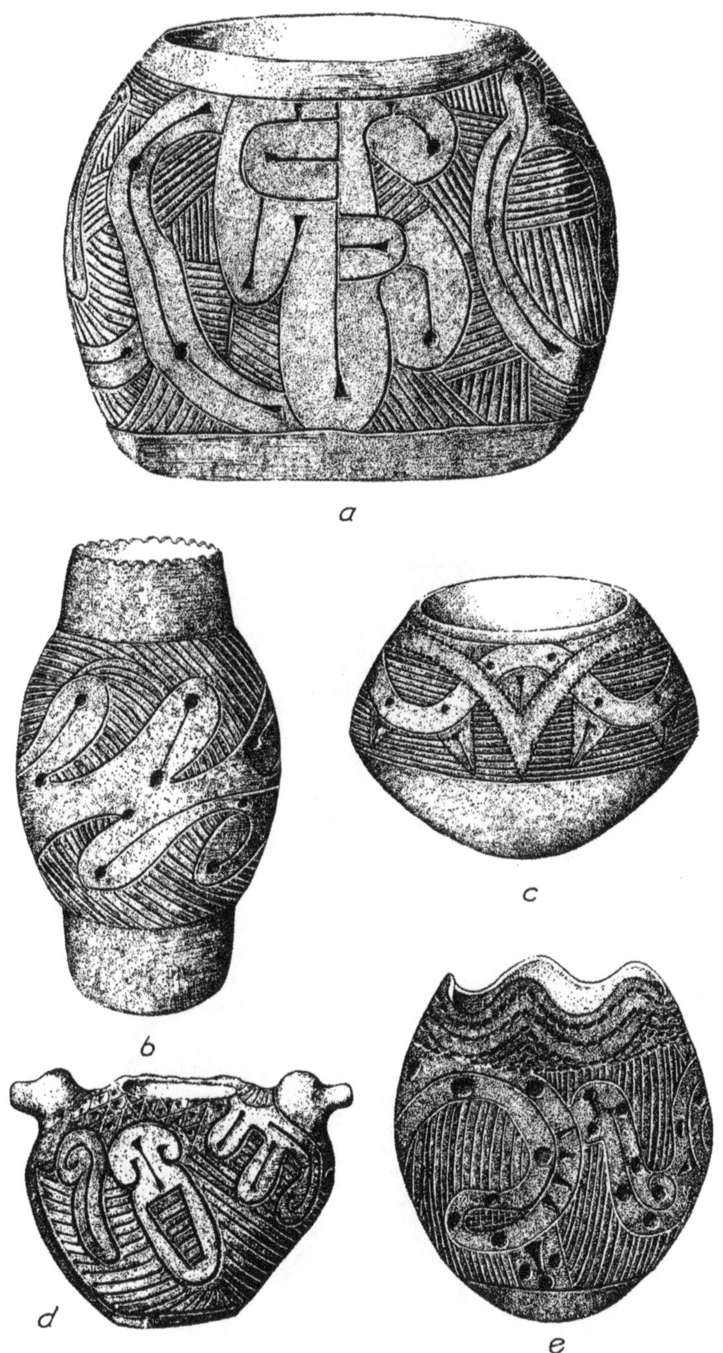

FIG. 36.—Weeden Island Period vessels. Weeden Island Incised. (Redrawn from Moore. Year, figure number, and site: *a*, 1918: 39, cemetery, Cedar Keys; *b*, 1907: 3, Hare's Landing; *c*, 1902: 75, Sowell; *d*, 1918: XIII, Pippen's Lake; *e*, 1902: 49, Fannings Bayou. All about ⅓ actual size except *c*, which is ¼.)

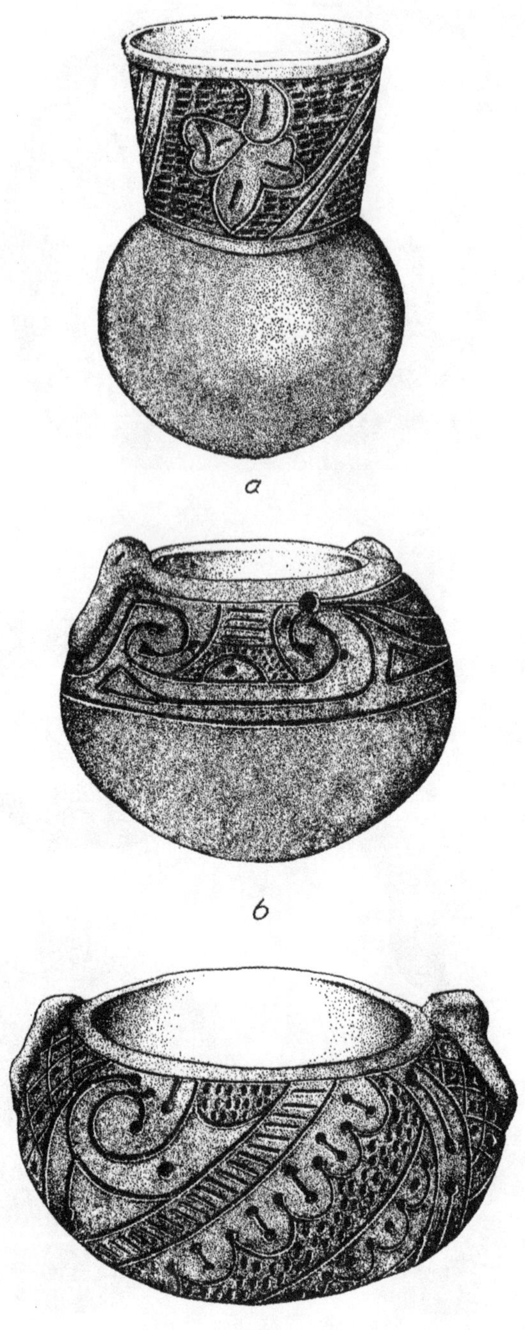

FIG. 37.—Weeden Island Period vessels. Weeden Island Incised. (Redrawn from Moore. Year, figure number, and site: *a*, 1902: 221, Tucker; *b*, 1903: 74, Bayport; *c*, 1902: 14, West Bay Post Office. All ⅓ actual size.)

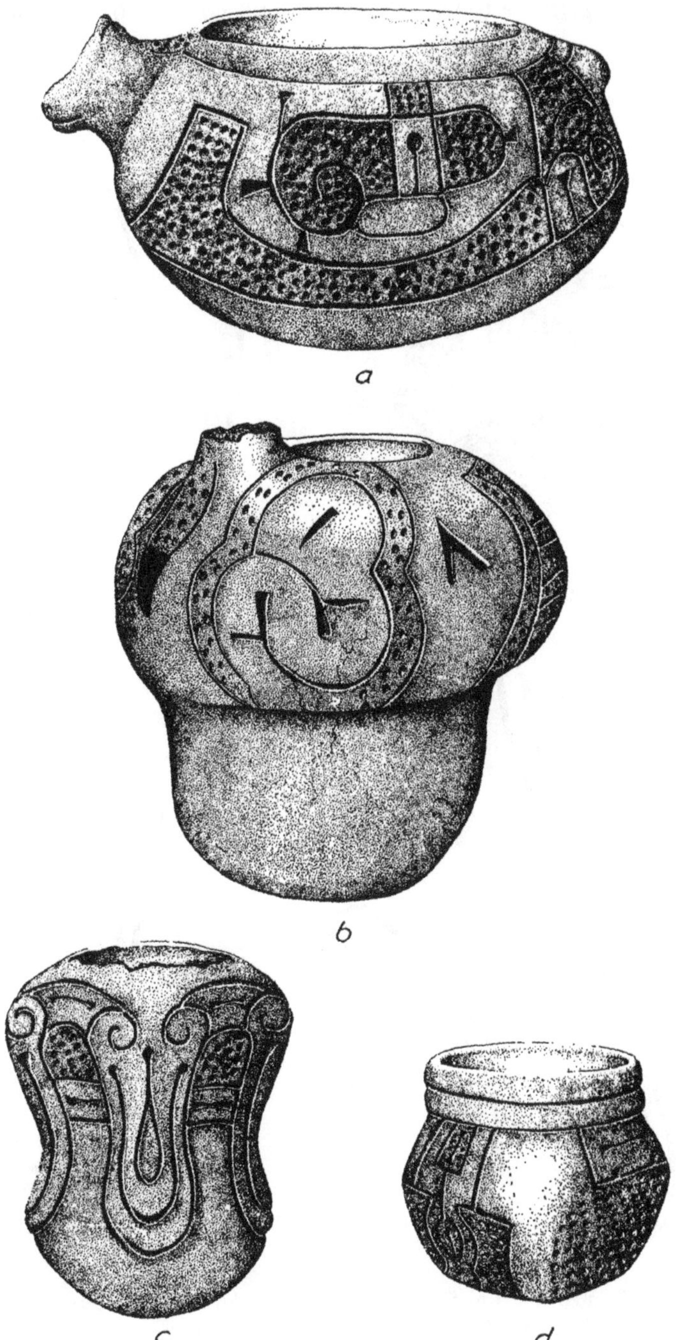

FIG. 38.—Weeden Island Period vessels. Weeden Island Incised. (Redrawn from Moore. Year, figure number, and site: *a*, 1902: 13, West Bay Post Office; *b*, 1903: 131, Davis Field; *c*, 1918: 19, West Bay Creek; *d*, 1901: 64, site west of Point Washington. All ⅓ actual size.)

the side. Folds are usually underscored by an incised line. Unmodified rims are also set off from the rest of the vessel by an incised line 5 mm. to 1.5 cm. below the lip. (See fig. 39.)

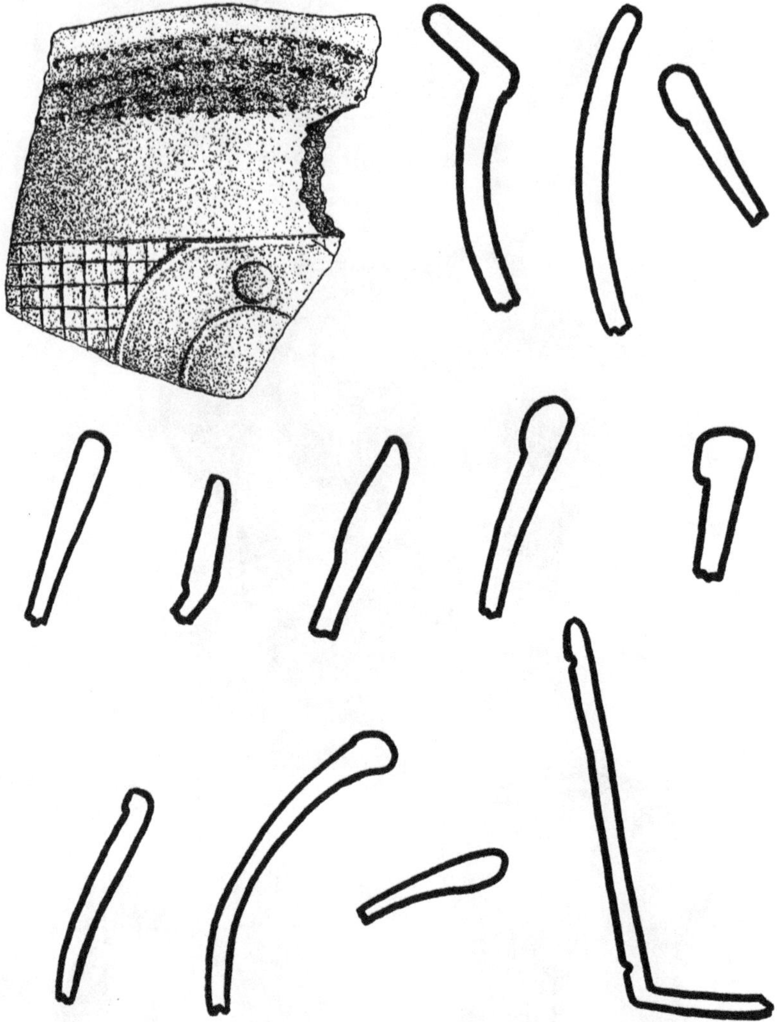

Fig. 39.—Weeden Island Period rim forms. Weeden Island Incised. (Interiors to right.)

Lip: Pointed-round to flat-round. Also flat. An incised or linear-punctated line often encircles the vessel on top of the lip.

Base: Bases are round, flat-circular, and flat-rectangular.

Appendages: Triangulate lateral rim projections, often bearing decoration on their interior surfaces, arranged four to an open bowl. These are much like those mentioned for the Weeden Island Plain type. Solid effigy adornos affixed to the exterior vessel wall at and just below the rim. Occasionally they project slightly above the rim. There may be one or two to a vessel. Bird's heads are most common, especially the duck. Animals and humans are less common.

Geographical range of type: The Florida Gulf Coast area from Pensacola to the Little Manatee. Probably extends west of Pensacola for an unknown distance. Occasional pieces are found in the St. Johns area of Florida, but these appear to be trade specimens.

Chronological position of type: The Weeden Island I and II Periods. Incised and punctated decoration tends to be bolder and heavier in the earlier period.

Relationships of type: Closest to French Fork Incised of southern Louisiana Troyville and Coles Creek Periods (Ford and Willey, 1939). Presumably the types of the Weeden Island Series merge with those of the Troyville-Coles Creek Series somewhere among the Alabama-Mississippi coast.

Bibliography: Cushing (1897); Holmes (1903); Stirling (1936); Willey and Woodbury (1942); Willey (1945).

Type name.—WEEDEN ISLAND PUNCTATED.

Definition as a type: From the Florida Gulf Coast area, this paper. Formerly included within the type Weeden Island Incised (Willey and Woodbury, 1942).

Ware characteristics: (See Weeden Island Plain.)

Decoration:

Technique: Fine dot or small triangular punctations impressed into the soft clay of vessel before firing. Use of deep, rounded punctations, large triangular punctations, and hollow-reed punctations for the termination or segmentation of lines. Occasional use of fine incision but only as subsidiary elements in the punctated designs.

Design: Basically curvilinear and tends to emphasize contrasting areas of plain polished surface versus punctated fields. Design often brought out negatively by punctating only the backgrounds. Continuous meanders, scrolls, lobate forms, leaflike forms, circles, and triangles are usual elements. These elements are outlined with lines of close-spaced punctations and are often filled with close or wide-spaced punctations. The various geometrical elements are usually connected by lines of fine punctations, integrating all parts of the design into an over-all composition. As in Weeden Island Incised, the bird idea may be expressed in a highly stylized and conventionalized form. Relief modeling and applique techniques are used to delineate effigy features, usually bird heads. (Pl. 25, *g, h;* pl. 27, *a, d, e, g, h;* pl. 28, *a, c-h.*)

Conception of design is excellent and seems well confined within the limits of a clearly understood style. Execution is sure and displays a graceful lightness of touch. (See fig. 40.)

Distribution: Often confined to upper portions of exterior vessel surface but sometimes extends over most of vessel exterior except base. Also applied to upper sides of triangular rim projections on bowl forms.

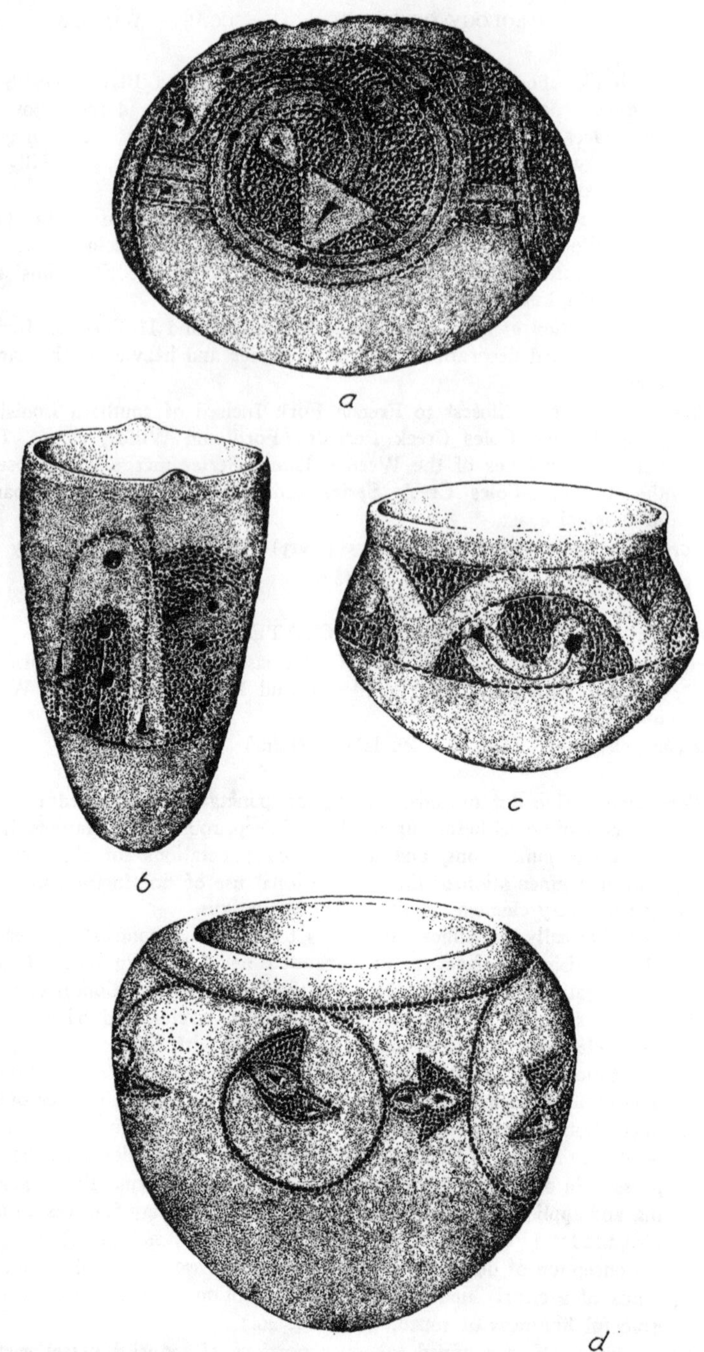

FIG. 40.—Weeden Island Period vessels. Weeden Island Punctated. (*a-c*, redrawn from Moore; *d*, from Holmes, 1903, pl. CIII, Tarpon Springs. Moore year, figure number, and site: *a*, 1907: 27, Kern's Landing; *b*, 1902: 44, Fannings Bayou; *c*, 1902: 51, Fannings Bayou. Vessels *a*, *b*, *c*, are actual size; *d*, ⅓ actual size.)

Form:

Total vessel: Flattened-globular bowl most common. Simple jars, open bowls, short-collared jars, cylindrical beakers.

Rim: Commonly thickened at orifice. Incurved, outslanted, straight walls, depending upon vessel shape. Frequent use of exterior folds which may be underlined or encircled with a row or two of punctations (fig. 41).

Lip: Both flat and rounded. Use of encircling row of punctations.

Base: Rounded or flat.

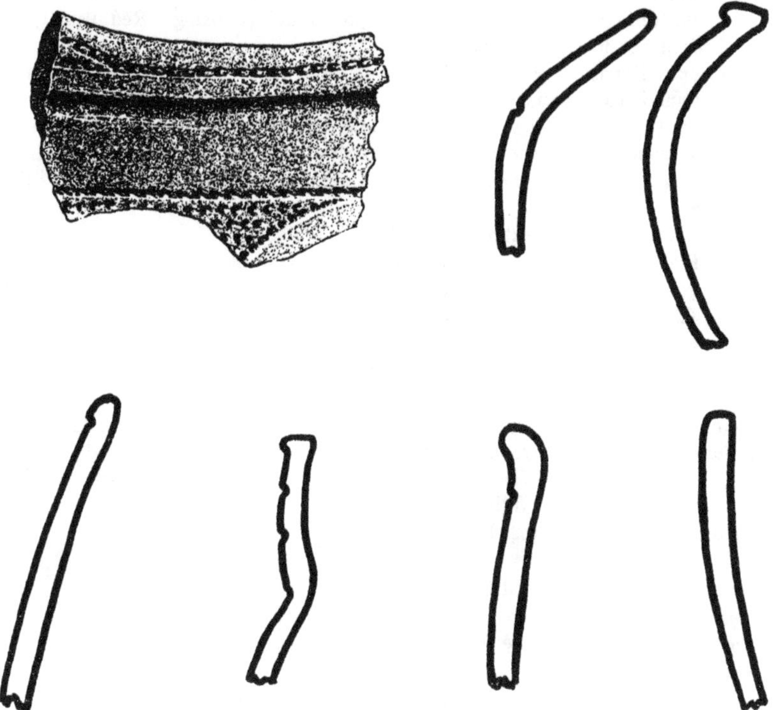

FIG. 41.—Weeden Island Period rim forms. Weeden Island Punctated. (Interiors to right.)

Appendages: Large triangular rim projections or "ears" are used on open bowls.

Geographical range of type: The Florida Gulf Coast but with greater frequency of occurrence in the central coast and Manatee regions than in the northwest.

Chronological position of type: Is largely a Weeden Island II type, although it occurs in Weeden Island I.

Relationships of type: Related to Weeden Island Series types and to such types as Ruskin Dentate Stamped and Ruskin Linear Punctated. May be related to Perico Linear Punctated (which is probably earlier) and to Gainesville Linear Punctated (which is apparently coeval). Has relationships to the type French Fork Incised of southern Louisiana (Ford and Willey, 1939).

Bibliography: Willey (1945).

Type name.—WEEDEN ISLAND ZONED RED.

Definition as a type: From Gulf Coast Florida, this paper.

Ware characteristics: (See Weeden Island Plain.) Weeden Island Zoned Red is virtually always buff-fired and well polished.

Decoration:

Technique: Incisions and large triangular punctations made in sun-dried but unfired clay. Red pigment applied before firing. Red usually a light red to carmine shade.

Design: Bands or zones outlined with fine incised lines. The lines are sometimes ornamented with deep triangular punctations much as in the types Weeden Island Incised and Weeden Island Punctated. Bands or zones may form chevrons, triangles, loops, lobate forms, or circles. Zones or backgrounds to the zones are colored with red pigment. (Pl. 26, *f-h;* pl. 29, *a.*)

Distribution: Vessel exteriors.

Form: Flattened-globular bowl, cylindrical beaker, human-effigy vessel, and gourd-effigy vessel (fig. 42, *g*) all noted. Rims seem to be unmodified (fig. 43, left), lips rounded. Bases round or flat. No appendages observed.

Geographical range of type: Not a common type but seems to be found from the northwest as far south as Hillsborough County.

Chronological position of type: Probably both Weeden Island I and II.

Relationships of type: Probably the descendant of Pierce Zoned Red. Shows relationship to Woodville Red Filmed, a Louisiana Troyville Period type (Ford and Willey, 1939).

Bibliography: Willey (1945).

Type name.—CARRABELLE INCISED.

Definition as a type: From the northwest coast of Florida, this paper.

Ware characteristics: (See Weeden Island Plain.)

Decoration:

Technique: Medium and fine incised lines on soft, unfired surfaces.

Design: Parallel incised lines placed vertically or diagonally on vessel (fig. 42, *f*). Arrangement in simple row, herringbone fashion, or nested triangles. There is a variation of the latter where alternate triangles are filled with horizontally placed lines. Decoration is often set off, above and below, by an incised line. Execution often less expert than with Weeden Island Incised. (Pl. 29, *b-f;* pl. 33, *a-e.*)

Distribution: Usually is confined to a band beneath rim (upper one-third of the vessel) on exterior surface. Sometimes, on beaker forms, extends from rim to base.

Form:

Total vessel: Flattened-globular bowls, collared globular bowls, simple and collared jars, beakers.

Rim: Incurving, direct, and outslanting. Exterior folds. When not folded, rims may be slightly thickened (fig. 44).

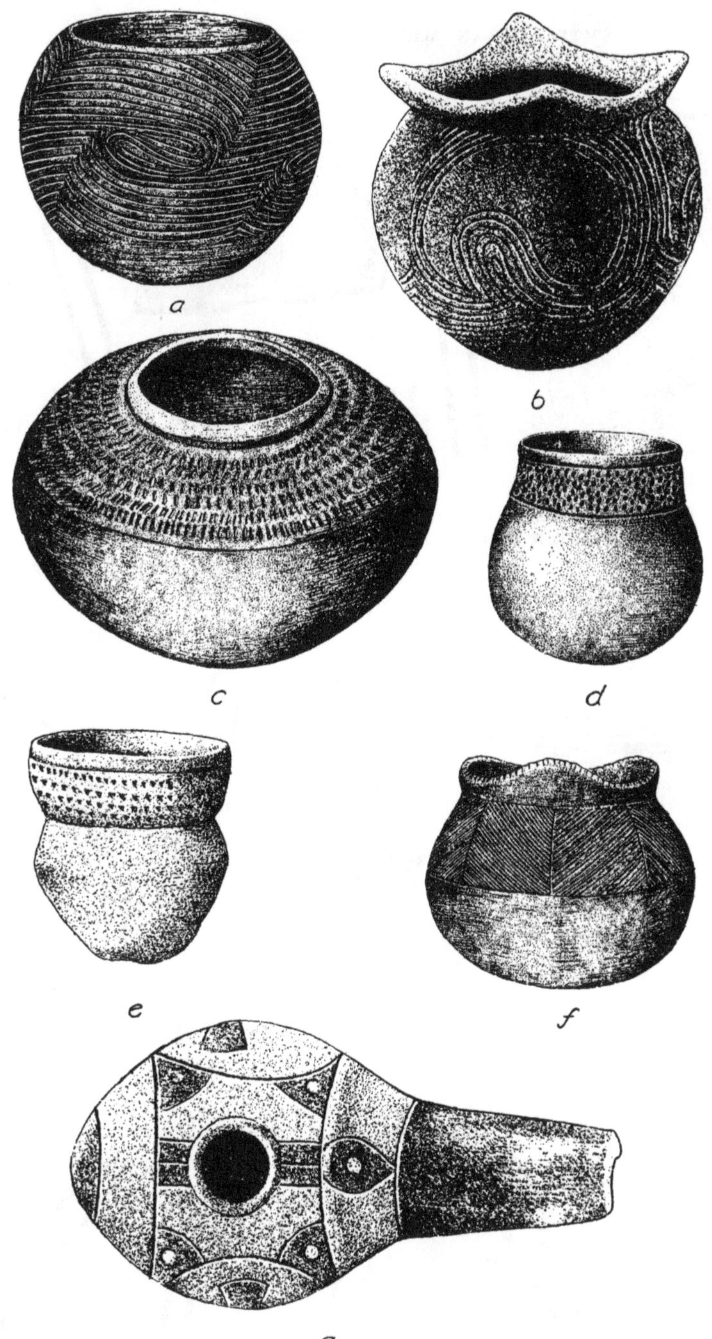

FIG. 42.—Weeden Island Period vessels. *a, b,* Indian Pass Incised; *c-e,* Carrabelle Punctated; *f,* Carrabelle Incised; *g,* Weeden Island Zoned Red. (Redrawn from Moore. Year, figure number, and site: *a,* 1902: 144, Indian Pass Point; *b,* 1918: 24, Farmdale; *c,* 1903: 14, Gigger Point; *d,* 1907: 11, Hare's Landing; *e,* 1901: 66, site west of Point Washington; *f,* 1918: 2, Wise Bluff; *g,* 1918: XIII, McLaney place. Vessels *a, c-f,* ¼ actual size; *b,* about ⅓ actual size; *g,* ½.)

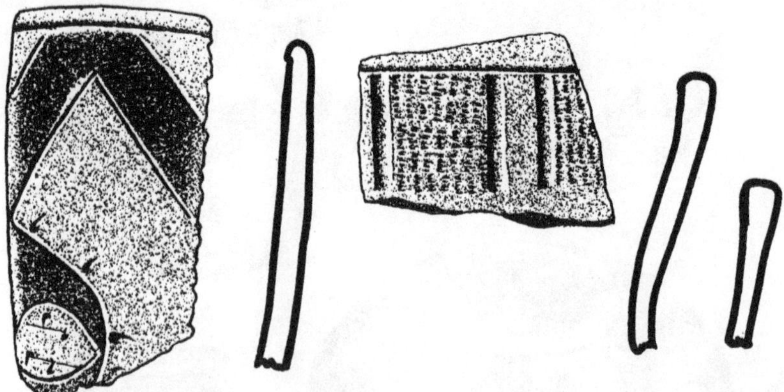

Fig. 43.—Weeden Island Period rim forms. *Left:* Weeden Island Zoned Red; *right:* Little Manatee Zoned Stamped. (Interiors to right.)

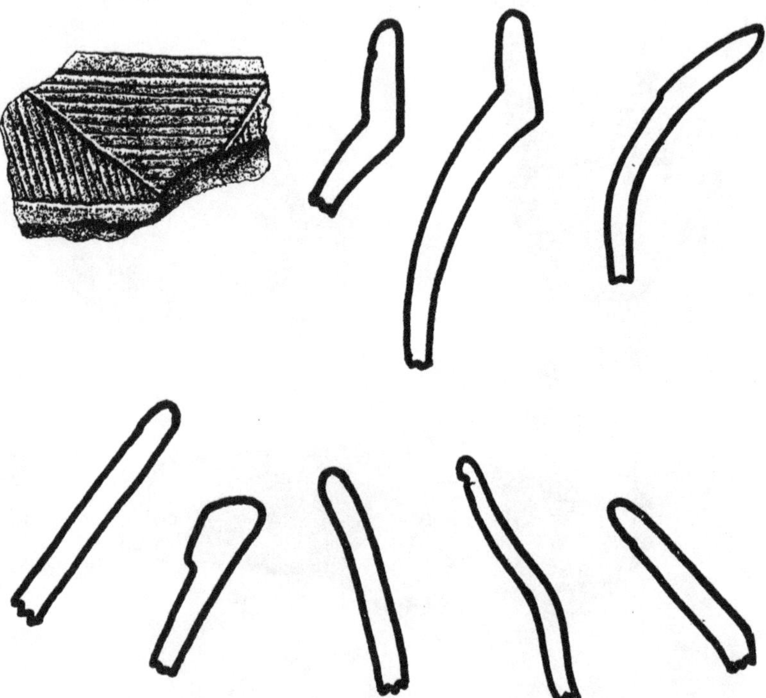

Fig. 44.—Weeden Island Period rim forms. Carrabelle Incised. (Interiors to right.)

Lip: Flattened-round to pointed-round. Occasionally there is an incised line encircling vessel on top of lip.

Appendages: Triangular, horizontal, or upslanting projections from rim. Four to a vessel.

Geographical range of type: Florida Gulf Coast.

Chronological position of type: Weeden Island I and Weeden Island II Periods.

Relationships of type: Similar to type Mazique Incised from the Lower Mississippi Valley Troyville and Coles Creek Periods (Ford and Willey, 1939). Also similar to and may be prototype of Marsh Island Incised type of the Fort Walton Period.

Bibliography: Willey (1945).

Type name.—CARRABELLE PUNCTATED.

Definition as a type: Northwest coast of Florida, this paper.

Ware characteristics: (See Weeden Island Plain. Some Carrabelle Punctated is coarser in texture and temper size than other Weeden Island Period types.)

Decoration:

Technique: Punctations in unfired clay.

Design: Arranged in a field around the upper portion of the vessel below the rim (fig. 42, *c-e*). A good deal of variation as to kinds of punctations used. These variations tend to grade into each other. They are: Fingernail punctations placed longitudinally or parallel to the vertical axis of the vessel; stick-made punctations, rectanguloid and trianguloid with considerable size range; round-bottomed dents or shallow stick punctations; hollow-reed punctations; and double-rowed fingernail punctations with paste slightly pinched and piled up near punctation. Field of punctation may be underlined with an incised line. (Pl. 30; pl. 31, *a, b*.)

Form:

Total vessel: Globular bowl with flared orifice, flattened-globular bowl, short-collared jar, and a jar with cambered rim.

Rim: Direct and slightly incurving. Slightly thickened near margin. Thin, flat exterior fold common (fig. 45).

Lip: Flat-round to pointed-round.

Geographical range of type: Gulf Coast Area. Seems to be most common between Apalachicola River and Cedar Keys.

Chronological position of type: Weeden Island I and II Periods. There is, however, a suggestion that Carrabelle Punctated is the first of the incised or punctated types of the Weeden Island Series to be introduced.

Relationships of type: The type Alexander Pinched, of north Alabama (Haag, 1939), resembles Carrabelle Punctated as does the type Rhinehardt Punctated, of the Troyville and Coles Creek Periods of southern Louisiana (Ford and Willey, 1939).

Bibliography: Willey (1945).

Type name.—INDIAN PASS INCISED.

Definition as a type: Northwest coast of Florida, this paper.

Ware characteristics: (See Weeden Island Plain.)

Decoration:

Technique: Fine to medium incised lines made with sharp instrument on soft unfired clay.

Design: Close-spaced arrangement of lines giving almost a "combed" appearance in some cases (fig. 42, *a, b*). Designs are sweeping curvilinear loops, whorls, and straight-line herringbone arrangements. In the latter case the design is made up of a great many lines as opposed to the type Carrabelle Incised. (Pl. 31, *c-f.*)

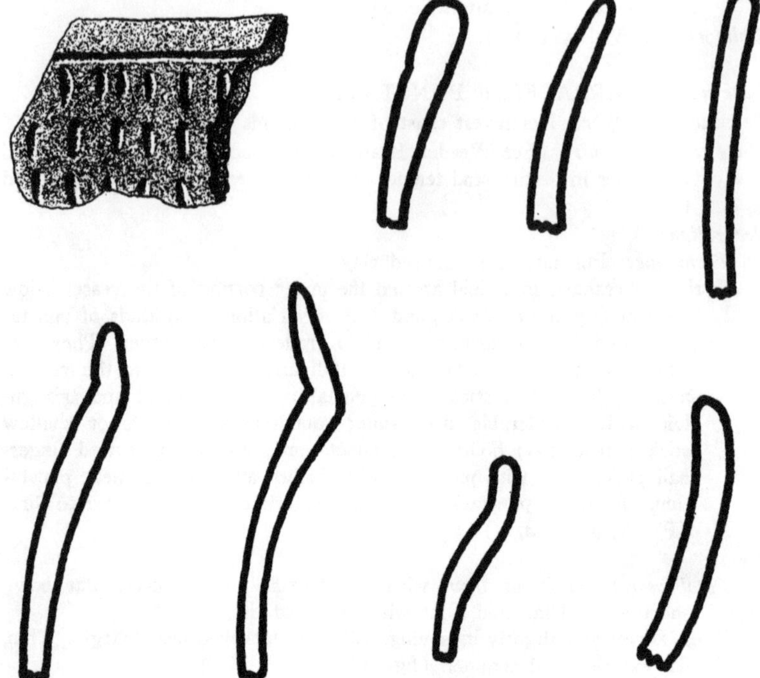

FIG. 45.—Weeden Island Period rim forms. Carrabelle Punctated. (Interiors to right.)

Distribution: Usually placed in a band around upper two-thirds of vessel exterior; sometimes entire exterior except base; and sometimes small band below neck.

Form:

Total vessel: Flattened-globular bowls, short-collared jars, and trilobed jar all noted.

Rim: Plain direct or slightly incurving. Similar profiles with exterior folds. Incised line often encircles rim just below lip, with or without the fold (fig. 46, bottom).

Lip: Rounded and flattened-round. Incised and linear-punctated line noted in top of lip on some specimens.

Appendages: Rim projections, trianguloid in form, which extend upward and outward.

Geographical range of type: Florida Gulf Coast.

Chronological position of type: Weeden Island I and II Periods.

Relationships of type: Design arrangement suggests some varieties of type Yokena Incised (Ford and Willey, 1939) of the Troyville Period of the Lower Mississippi Valley. Undoubtedly a part of the Weeden Island Series.

Bibliography: Willey (1945).

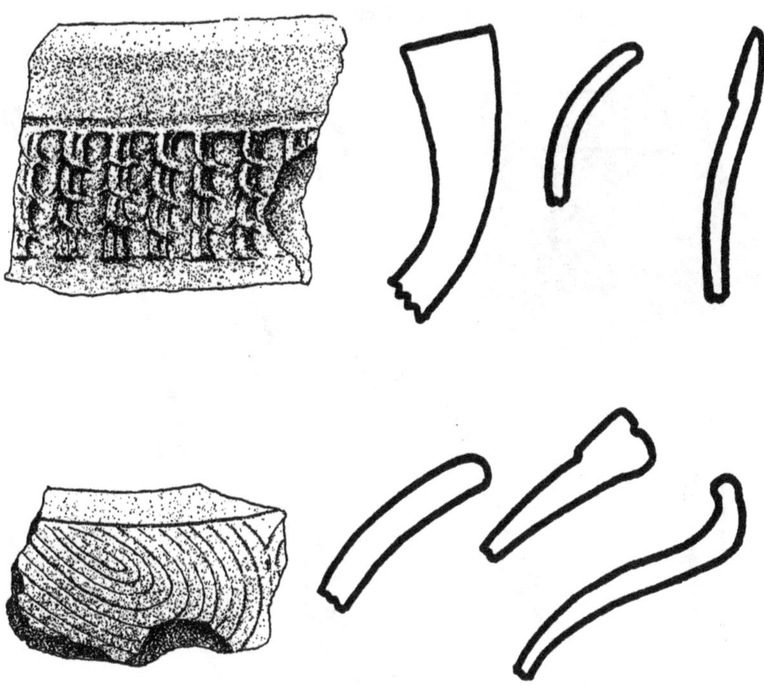

FIG. 46.—Weeden Island Period rim forms. *Top:* Tucker Ridge-pinched; *bottom:* Indian Pass Incised. (Interiors to right.)

Type name.—KEITH INCISED.

Definition as a type: Northwest coast of Florida, this paper.

Ware characteristics: (See Weeden Island Plain.)

Decoration:

Technique: Incised lines occasionally in conjunction with punctations.

Design: A band of diagonal cross hatching with diamonds ranging from 5 to 3 mm. in length. Dot punctations are sometimes placed at all or some of the intersections of the incised lines. (Pl. 32, *a-d;* pl. 33, *f, i.*)

Distribution: Zone below lip on exterior of vessel. An incised line usually separates decorated zone from the rim and from the undecorated portion below.

Form:

Total vessel: Probably flattened-globular bowls and collared jars.

Rim: Incurving and outflaring rims, often thickened below lip. Round and flat exterior folds below rim. These folds range from 5 mm. to 2 cm. in width and may or may not be separated from the design by an undecorated area (fig. 47).

Lip: Rounded with variations toward both flat and pointed.

Base: Probably rounded, and, possibly, flat in some cases.

Appendages: Triangular rim projections.

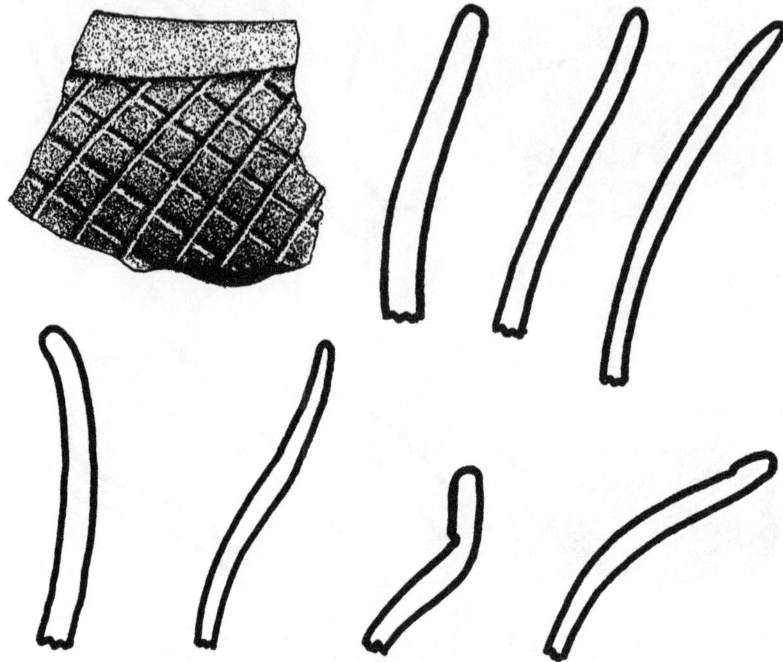

FIG. 47.—Weeden Island Period rim forms. Keith Incised. (Interiors to right.)

Geographical range of type: Florida Gulf Coast, following general distribution of more characteristic Weeden Island types.

Chronological position of type: Weeden Island I and II Periods.

Relationships of type: Definitely a part of Weeden Island Series. Quite similar decoration seen in Beldeau Incised, a Coles Creek Period type from Louisiana (Ford and Willey, 1939).

Bibliography: Willey (1945).

Type name.—TUCKER RIDGE-PINCHED.

Definition as a type: Northwest Florida coast, present paper.

Ware characteristics: (See Weeden Island Plain.)

Decoration:

Technique: Ridges made by pinching up the vessel surface before firing.

Design: Rows or ridges of pinched-up or piled-up surfaces (fig. 48, *a-d*). These may vary from rows of pinching, where each individual fingernail marking and accompanying pile are distinguishable as separate units, to continuous ridges. Ridges are spaced by 1 cm. or less and vary in depth from 1 to 4 mm. (Pl. 32, *e-f*.)

Distribution: Decoration is in a band below the vessel rim with the rim border left plain. The rows are arranged parallel to the vertical axis of the vessel.

Form:

Total vessel: Flattened-globular bowls, globular bowls with flared orifice, short-collared jars, long-collared jars, and cylindrical beakers.

Rim: Incurved, and incurved with short recurve at orifice. Small exterior flat folds. Massive rectanguloid and trianguloid (in cross section) folds (fig. 46, top).

Lip: Round-pointed. Flat. The latter have incised line, marked with triangular punctations, on the top.

Base: Both rounded and flat.

Appendages: Triangular "ears" or projections extending out from rim flush with lip. These are found on the massive folded rims. They are about 1.5 to 2 cm. long and more or less equilateral. They are marked with a large, deep, triangular punctation on the top.

Geographical range of type: All along Florida Gulf Coast.

Chronological position of type: Weeden Island, especially Period II.

Relationships of type: Suggestive of Coles Creek Ridge-pinched of the Coles Creek Period, southern Louisiana.

Bibliography: Willey (1945).

Type name: HARE HAMMOCK SURFACE-INDENTED.

Definition as a type: Florida Gulf Coast, this paper. A rare type.

Ware characteristics: (See Weeden Island Plain.)

Decoration:

Technique: Deep, smooth-bottomed indentations. These are of oval form, about 2 cm. long, 1 cm. wide, and 5 mm. deep. Possibly made with finger in wet or soft clay.

Design and distribution: Random arrangement over vessel exterior (fig. 48, *e*).

Form: Very few data. Moore shows one vessel of this type which may be a plant effigy.

Georgraphical range of type: Has been found in both northwest coast and central coast regions.

Chronological position of type: Probably both Weeden Island I and II.

Relationships of type: None obvious.

Bibliography: Willey (1945).

Type name.—SWIFT CREEK COMPLICATED STAMPED (Late Variety).

Definition as a type: Northwest coast of Florida, present paper.

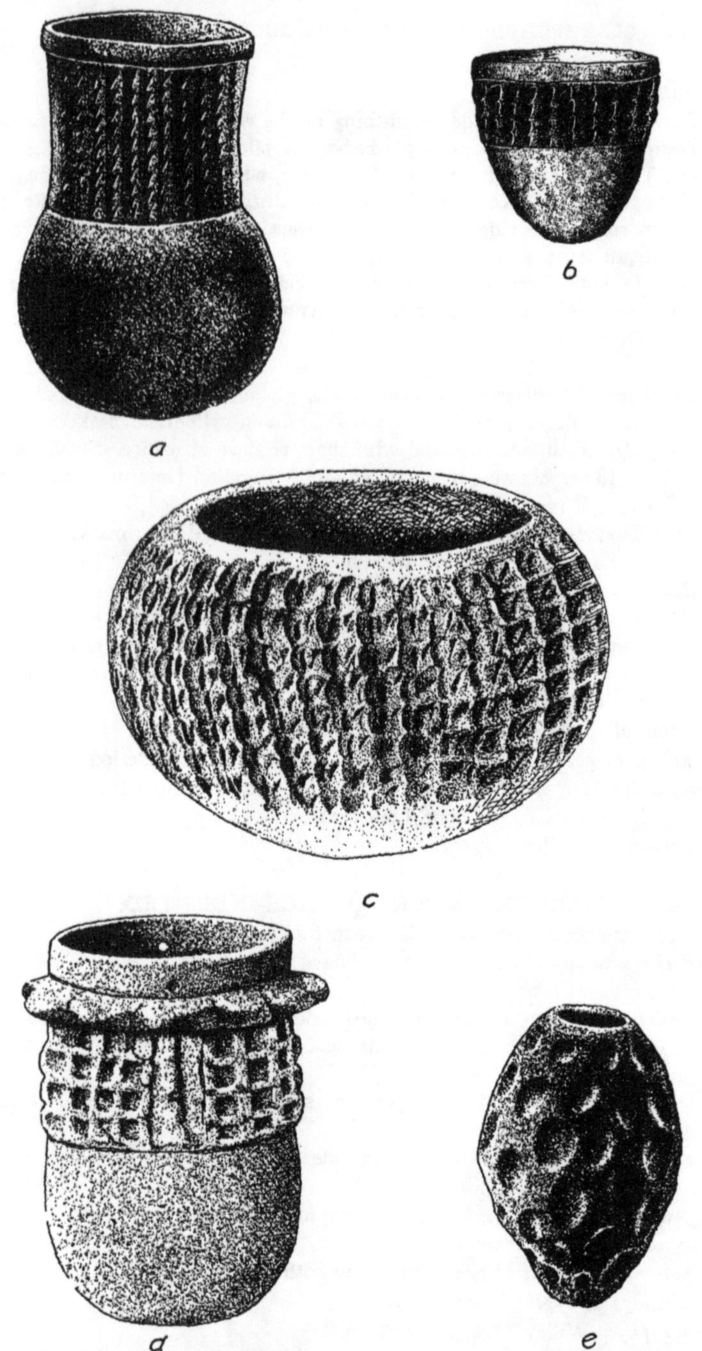

FIG. 48.—Weeden Island Period vessels. *a-d*, Tucker Ridge-pinched; *e*, Hare Hammock Surface-indented. (Redrawn from Moore. Year, figure number, and site: *a*, 1918: 25, Hare Hammock, smaller mound; *b*, 1901: 65, Site West of Point Washington; *c*, 1902: 7, West Bay Post Office; *d*, 1918: 12, Pippen's Lake; *e*, 1902: 138, Hare Hammock, smaller mound. Vessels *a, b, d,* about $\frac{1}{3}$ actual size; *c*, $\frac{1}{2}$ actual size; *e*, $\frac{1}{4}$ actual size.)

Ware characteristics:

Method of manufacture: Coiling or other annular technique.

Temper: Fine and coarse sand. On the average, the aplastic is coarser than for the Early Variety of Swift Creek Complicated Stamped.

Paste texture and color: Compact, fine or coarse-grained and slightly contorted. Usually gray core and buff surfaces. Sometimes gray-black throughout.

Surface texture, color, and finish: Areas of exterior vessel surfaces which are not covered with stamping are well smoothed. Interior smoothing is very good in some cases but rough and careless in many others. Surfaces are various shades of buff, much fire-clouded, and, occasionally, completely gray-black.

Hardness: 3, or slightly less, to 5.

Thickness: Range from 4 to 9 mm.; average about 6 mm.

Decoration:

Technique: Impression of a carved instrument, probably of wood, upon soft unfired clay.

Design: Complicated, predominantly curvilinear designs. In many respects they are very close to the designs of the Early Variety of the type. In general, motifs are less intricate in the Late Variety, and there is not so great a range of variation. The following are common designs: (1) hatched "teardrop" or "snowshoe" elements (fig. 49, *a, b, c*); (2) concentric spirals (fig. 49, *e*); (3) concentric circles as a part of a greater design (fig. 49, *d*); (4) interlocking scrolls and rectilinear elements (fig. 49, *f*); (5) intertwined meander; (6) simple, concentric curved lines.

Execution is more boldly and carelessly done than in the Early Variety of the type. This results in either deeper impressions than is common in the Early Variety, or what appear to be hastily applied, faint impressions. Usually the design appears to have been smoothed over while the clay was still soft. This results in flattening the raised areas of the decoration, giving the designs of the Late Variety a ragged, semiobliterated appearance, and making the raised areas very broad. (See figs. 50, 51; pl. 34; pl. 35, *a-f;* pl. 36, *a.*)

Distribution: Usually confined to an area encircling the upper portion of the vessel, such as the shoulders or collar of a bowl or jar. Decoration usually separated from orifice by an undecorated rim strip. Sometimes a wide, undecorated band is left above the zone of decoration and under the rim strip or folded rim.

Form:

Total vessel: Long- and short-collared jars and simple jars. Flattened-globular bowls and collared globular bowls also occur as do some pot forms.

Rim: Incurved, and incurved and recurved. Also inslanted and outslanted. A characteristic feature is an exterior fold or thickening. In some cases this has been formed by folding the clay over the edge of the orifice; in other cases a strip of clay has been added. Folds vary from a few mm. to 2 cm. in width. It often looks as though the rim had been folded down over the stamped decoration. In cross section, the

FIG. 49.—Swift Creek Complicated Stamped design units, Late Variety.

FIG. 50.—Weeden Island Period vessel. Swift Creek Complicated Stamped, Late Variety. (Redrawn from Moore, 1902: 224, Tucker. Shown at ⅜ actual size.)

FIG. 51.—Weeden Island Period vessels. Swift Creek Complicated Stamped, Late Variety. (Redrawn from Moore. Year, figure number, and site: *a,* 1901: 69, site west of Point Washington; *b,* 1903: 155, Sampson's Landing; *c,* 1902: 296, Mound Field; *d,* 1902: 223, Tucker; *e,* 1918: 37, Aucilla River. Vessels *c, d* are $\frac{1}{2}$ actual size; *a,* $\frac{3}{8}$; *b,* $\frac{1}{4}$; *e,* about $\frac{2}{5}$.)

rims may be thick and round or long and flat. A few are thick, heavy, and rectangulate. An occasional rim thickening has been pinched up into nodes which project in a horizontal plane. (See fig. 52.)

Lip: Most are flat-round or round; some are round-pointed, some flat.

Base: Round. Sometimes flat and circular or flat and squared.

Appendages: None known.

Geographical range of type: Gulf Coast of Florida. Inland into Georgia. Northwest Florida coast seems to be the center for this Late Variety of Swift Creek. Intensity of spread into north-central Florida and St. Johns region is not determined.

Chronological position of type: Mainly Weeden Island I Period.

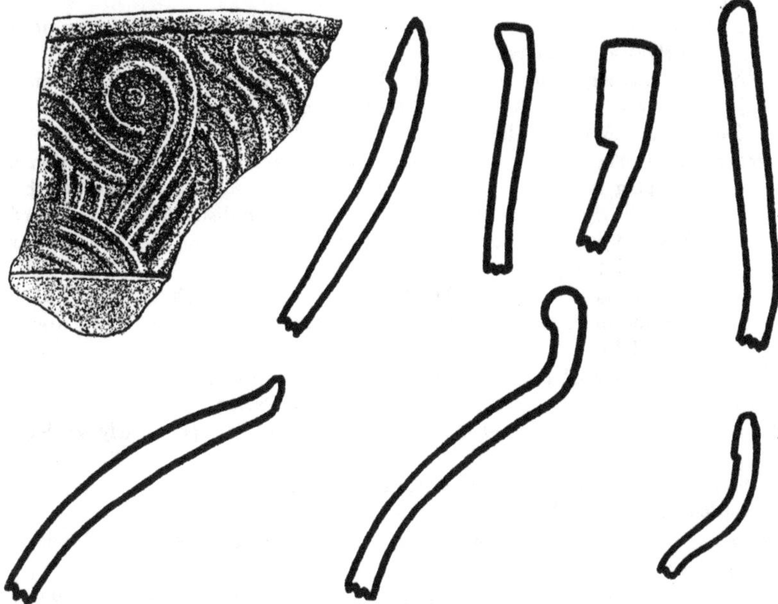

FIG. 52.—Weeden Island Period rim forms. Swift Creek Complicated Stamped, Late Variety. (Interiors to right.)

Relationships of type: Obviously a development out of the Early Variety of the type. Has resemblances to middle and late Swift Creek pottery of central Georgia (Kelly, 1938) and coastal Georgia. Has Florida parallels in the Late Varieties of St. Andrews and Crooked River Complicated Stamped. Also shows influences of Weeden Island ceramic tradition in rim and vessel shapes.

Type name: CROOKED RIVER COMPLICATED STAMPED (Late Variety).

Definition as a type: From northwest Florida, present paper.

Ware characteristics: Differs from Early Variety of the type by being tempered with coarse sand and uncrushed grit, in being coarse and contorted in paste cross section, and in presenting rough and granular surfaces. Hardness is at 3.5 to 4.5, and thickness averages 7 mm.

Decoration: Same as Early Variety of the type except for slovenly execution of the stamping.

Form: (Not sufficient data.)

Geographical range of type: Northwest coast of Florida.

Chronological position of type: Appears in Weeden Island I Period.

Relationships of type: (See Crooked River Complicated Stamped, Early Variety.)

Type name.—ST. ANDREWS COMPLICATED STAMPED (Late Variety).

Definition as a type: Northwest coast of Florida, present paper.

Ware characteristics:

Temper: Coarse sand and uncrushed grit.

Paste texture and color: Coarse and somewhat contorted. Color same as Early Variety of type.

Surface texture, color, and finish: Interior surfaces smoothed but bumpy. Heavy grit particles extrude through on both surfaces.

Thickness: Average about 7 mm.

Decoration: Concentric rectangle motif is most common design. Execution of stamping is careless, and, as a rule, designs are larger and bolder than in the Early Variety of the type. In decoration distribution some sherds show only a band of stamping just below the rim with lower part of vessel left plain.

Form: Sherds suggest short-collared jar and flattened-globular bowl. Rims straight or incurved with small flat or round exterior fold. Round-pointed lip.

Geographical range of type: Northwest coast of Florida.

Chronological position of type: Weeden Island I Period.

Relationships of type: (See St. Andrews Complicated Stamped, Early Variety.)

Type name.—TAMPA COMPLICATED STAMPED.

Definition as a type: This paper, Tampa Bay section.

Ware characteristics: (See Swift Creek Complicated Stamped, Late Variety.)

Decoration:

Technique: Impression of carved wooden paddle or stamping medium on soft, unfired clay of vessel.

Design: Medium-deep to faint impressions of a spiral, concentric circle, or dot-in-circle, design unit. Unit varies in diameter from 2 to 6 cm. Application is haphazard and sloppy with considerable overlapping of the unit. (Pl. 35, *g-j*.)

Distribution: May cover vessel exterior or may be restricted only to upper portion of vessel.

Form:

Total vessel: Simple jars, pots, or deep bowls, and flattened-globular bowls.

Rim: Outslanting or incurved. Exterior folds. Lips rounded and usually unmodified.

Geographical range of type: Is most common around Tampa Bay and south into the Manatee region. Also found sporadically farther north.

Chronological position of type: Largely Weeden Island II. It appears that late complicated stamped types continue into Weeden Island II in the Tampa Bay vicinity and the Manatee region.

Relationships of type: Clearly related to Swift Creek, particularly Swift Creek of the Late Variety.
Bibliography: Willey (1948a).

Type name.—SUN CITY COMPLICATED STAMPED.
Definition as a type: This paper, from the Tampa vicinity and the Manatee region.
Ware characteristics: (See Swift Creek Complicated Stamped, Late Variety.)
Decoration:
Technique: Impression of a carved wooden paddle or stamping medium on soft, unfired clay of vessel surface.
Design: Concentric diamond figure with dot in center, concentric diamond with solid diamond figure in center, or concentric rectangle unit. Units are about 3 cm. long and 1.5 cm. wide. Sloppily executed with considerable overlapping of unit impressions. Lines of the design unit tend to be narrow and the impression faint. Applied to vessel exterior. (Pl. 36, *d-e.*)
Form: Flattened-globular bowl with unmodified rim.
Geographical range of type: Largely from Tampa Bay and the Manatee region.
Chronological position of type: Mostly Weeden Island II.
Relationships of type: Related to St. Andrews Complicated Stamped.
Bibliography: Willey (1948a).

Type name.—OLD BAY COMPLICATED STAMPED.
Definition as a type: From the Tampa Bay vicinity, this paper.
Ware characteristics: (See Swift Creek Complicated Stamped, Late Variety.)
Decoration:
Technique: Impression of carved paddle or stamping medium on the soft, unfired vessel surface.
Design: A small check stamped background, reminiscent of Wakulla Check Stamped, over which has been impressed a secondary set of design units. These last may be spirals, dot-in-circles, ovals, lozenge-shaped elements, and even criss-crossed simple stamping. (Pl. 35, *k;* pl. 36, *b, c.*)
Distribution: Exterior surface, probably all except base.
Form: Bowls with incurved rims, long-collared jars, beakers. Possibly pot forms. Rim projections of triangular form, arranged four to a vessel.
Geographical range of type: Largely Tampa Bay and the Manatee region but also found sporadically to the north.
Chronological position of type: Probably confined to Weeden Island II.
Relationships of type: May be descendant of New River Complicated Stamped.
Bibliography: Willey (1948a).

Type name.—WAKULLA CHECK STAMPED.
Definition as a type: Gulf Coast of Florida, present paper.
Ware characteristics:
Method of manufacture: Coiled or annular technique.
Temper: There is a greater range of tempering materials in Wakulla Check Stamped than in the pottery of the Weeden Island Series. There appear to be three divisions which intergrade from one to the other. The intermediate division in tempering is the use of fine sand as in the Weeden Island Series types. Another division uses much coarser

sand, including fairly large pieces of quartz. At the opposite end of the scale is a tempering division which is characterized by only a very small amount of fine sand. Specimens of this division tend to grade off toward the temperless Biscayne ware.

Paste texture and color: Varies from granular to laminated, but is always hard and compact. Cores are usually gray or black, although some pieces have been fired buff all through. Buff-fired surfaces are common on either or both sides of the specimen.

Surface texture, color, and finish: Interiors not as well smoothed, on the average, as in pottery of the Weeden Island Series. Exteriors seem to have been completely covered with check stamping. Buff, mottled buff, or gray-black in color.

Hardness: 2.5 to 4.

Thickness: Walls from 5 to 8 mm. Bases, rims sometimes thicker.

Decoration:

Technique: Stamping wet vessel surface with cross-grooved or checked implement.

Design: Solid field of fine to medium-size checks. Squares from 1 to 5 mm. Lands of both directions of equal size. Clear but light impressions. Rather carefully applied as a rule with little overlapping. (Pl. 39, *a, b;* pl. 40, *a-f.*)

Distribution: Vessel exterior nearly, or wholly, covered.

Form:

Total vessel: Flattened-globular bowls, bowls with incurved rims, deep bowls with outslanting rims, pots, and jars with long and short collars.

Rim: Incurved, both marked and slight, outslanted, direct, slightly everted at orifice, and slightly outflared. Both unmodified and folded. Small, round exterior folds are undecorated; but the long folds have check impressions extending over fold up to lip. (See fig. 53.)

Lip: Varies from pointed to flat, although the latter are rare.

Base: Rounded in most cases.

Appendages: Triangular rim projections or "ears."

Geographical range of type: Gulf Coast of Florida. Possibly has extensions inland to the east.

Chronological position of type: Weeden Island II. Slight overlap into Fort Walton Period.

Relationships of type: Probably related to all the small-check stamped pottery of the Southeast of this approximate time level, including Pontchartrain Check Stamped of the Louisiana Coles Creek Period (Ford and Willey, 1939), Wheeler and Wright Check Stamped types of north Alabama (Haag, 1939), the Savannah Period Check Stamped pottery of the Georgia coast (Caldwell and Waring, 1939), and Biscayne Check Stamped of east Florida. May be a development out of a Deptford and Gulf Check Stamped continuity.

Bibliography: Willey and Woodbury (1942); Willey (1945).

Type name.—THOMAS SIMPLE STAMPED.

Definition as a type: From Tampa Bay vicinity, this paper.

Ware characteristics: Probably coiled. Compact and sand-tempered with a gray or buff core. Surfaces gray or buff. Thickness varies from 5 to 11 mm. with average at 8 mm.

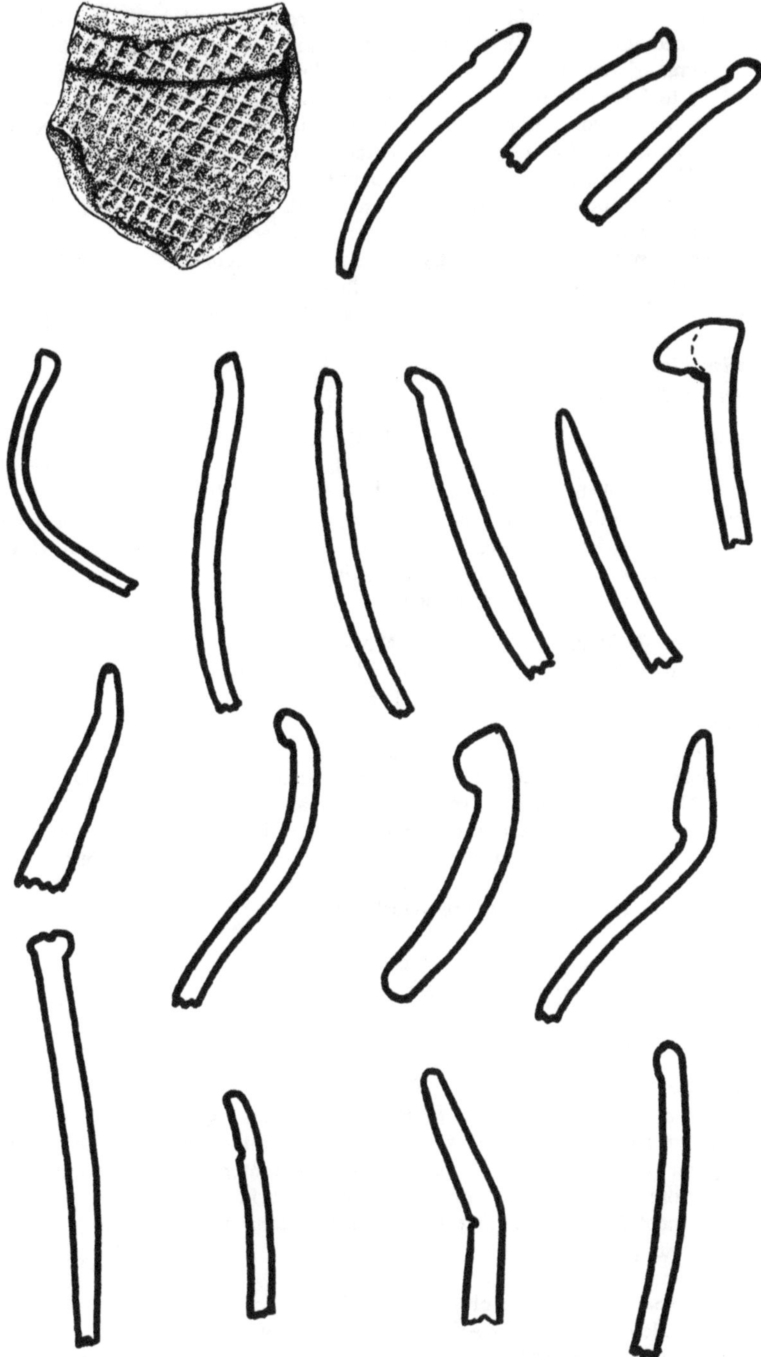

FIG. 53.—Weeden Island Period rim forms. Wakulla Check Stamped. (Interiors to right.)

Decoration: Unfired surface of vessel has been stamped with a straight-lined stamping tool. This may have been a carved paddle. Individual unit of the stamp is short (1.5 cm. long) and is composed of from 3 to 6 parallel bars. The bars of the stamp are close-spaced and about 2 mm. wide. Application is overlapping and orientation on vessel irregular. Most of the vessel exterior is covered. (Pl. 37, *c, d.*)

Form: Medium-deep bowls with outcurved sides and bowls or jars with slightly incurved sides. Rims unmodified. Lips round-pointed. A few rather crudely formed triangular rim projections noted.

Geographical range of type: Mostly in the Manatee region and around Tampa Bay. Does extend farther north, however.

Chronological position of type: Weeden Island II. May also appear in Weeden Island I.

Relationships of type: Related to Deptford Simple Stamped.

Bibliography: Willey (1948a).

Type name.—WEST FLORIDA CORD-MARKED (Late Variety).

Definition as a type: From northwest Florida. Based upon a few cord-marked sherds whch have exterior folded rims of the Weeden Island type.

Description: Similar in ware qualities to the Early Variety of the same type. Cord-marked surfaces tend to be semiobliterated rather than clear. There is a deep line underscoring the rim fold.

Associations: Weeden Island Period.

Type name.—MOUND FIELD NET-MARKED.

Definition as a type: Northwest coast of Florida, present paper.

Ware characteristics: (See Weeden Island Plain.)

Decoration:

Technique: Net impressions in clay before firing.

Design: Net-impressed decoration of diamond-shaped mesh. Diamonds about 1 cm. long. There is a deep pit at each intersection of the cord impressions suggestive of a knot. Decoration may have been effected with a net-wrapped paddle. Impressions usually semiobliterated or blurred.

Distribution: Probably entire vessel exterior.

Form:

Total vessel and rim: Jars or collared jars. Rims slightly outflared or incurved and recurved. Exterior folds present.

Lip: Flat and rounded.

Associations: Weeden Island I and II Periods on the northwest Florida coast.

Type name.—HILLSBOROUGH SHELL STAMPED.

Definition as a type: From Tampa Bay vicinity, this paper.

Ware characteristics: Probably a coiled ware. Sand-tempered. Usually granular and compact with only occasional contortions and laminations. Core is black, gray, or dark brown. Surfaces often buff. Interior smoothing excells exterior surface treatment. Thickness averages 8 to 9 mm.

Decoration:

Technique: Impression of the edge of a scallop shell or the back of a scallop shell onto the soft, unfired surface of vessel.

Design: Wide-spaced application of back of shell. Each unit application has 3 or 4 bars, each bar being about 1 mm. wide and 8 mm. long.

Between bars are rows of tiny dots which are a part of the same impression. When edge of scallop shell is used, the applications are close-spaced, giving the effect of rows of small, round dots, comma-shaped dots, or triangular dots. There is considerable overlapping of these rows of dots, and the rows have no particular orientation on the vessel. (Pl. 38, *b-g*.)

Distribution: Covers most or all of exterior vessel.

Form: Deep, open bowls and jars or bowls with incurved walls. Very small, rounded exterior rim folds are sometimes used. Lips are round-pointed. There are some triangular rim projections.

Geographical range of type: Mostly from Tampa Bay vicinity.

Chronological position of type: Probably confined to Weeden Island II.

Relationships of type: Similarities noted to Ruskin Dentate Stamped, a companion type. Vaguely reminiscent of Crooks Stamped, a shell-stamped type of the Marksville Period of southern Louisiana (Ford and Willey, 1940).

Bibliography: Willey (1948a).

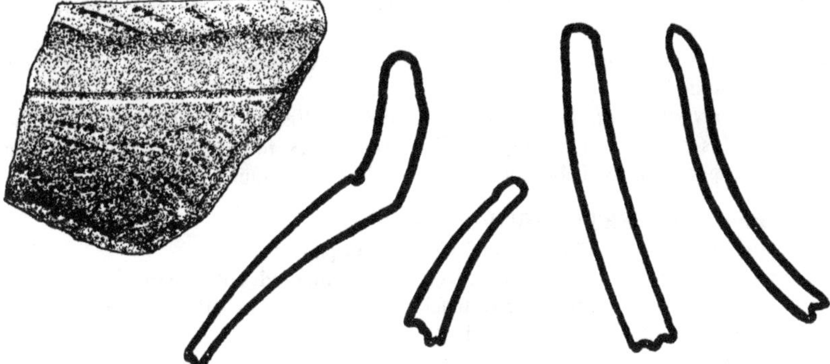

FIG. 54.—Weeden Island Period rim forms. Ruskin Dentate Stamped. (Interiors to right.)

Type name.—RUSKIN DENTATE STAMPED.

Definition as a type: From the Florida Gulf Coast, this paper.

Ware characteristics: (See Hillsborough Shell Stamped.)

Decoration:

Technique: Impressions of a small tooth-edge implement in the unfired clay.

Design: Rows of small dentations arranged in an irregular fashion. Most specimens appear to have been stamped with a small unit stamp with four or five teeth. The pits of the individual impressions are about 1 mm. across. Some are rectangular, others semilunar. Some specimens appear to have been decorated with a single-track roulette or, possibly, a single-pointed punctating instrument. All are characterized by rows of small pit impressions, and the rows are oriented in all directions. (Pl. 36, *i*; pl. 37, *a*, *b*.)

Distribution: Vessel exterior. Possibly most of surface.

Form: Globular bowls, jars with short collars, and open bowls. Rims are sometimes thickened at the margin with suggestions of exterior folds (fig. 54.) Triangular rim projections or "ears." Incised line below rim in some cases. Lip rounded but varies from pointed to flattened.

Associations: Florida Gulf Coast. Most common around Tampa Bay and in the Manatee region. Weeden Island Period context, probably Weeden Island II.

Type name.—RUSKIN LINEAR PUNCTATED.
Definition as a type: From vicinity of Tampa Bay, this paper.
Ware characteristics: (See Hillsborough Shell Stamped.)
Decoration:
Technique: Linear or drag-and-jab punctations made in soft, unfired clay of vessel. Lines of punctations vary from deep to shallow but are alike in that they are composed of a series of punctations, quite often triangular in shape.
Design: Rectilinear chevron arrangements. Usually close-spaced. (Pl. 37, *g*.)
Distribution: Vessel exterior. Usually separated from orifice by an undecorated border. Extent down sides of vessel unknown.
Form: Beaker-bowls and flattened-globular bowls. Folded rims. Triangular rim projections.
Geographical range of type: Seems to center around Tampa Bay but is also found in central Gulf Coast region.
Chronological position of type: Definitely Weeden Island II and may be Weeden Island I.
Relationships of type: Shows relationships to Weeden Island Punctated and Ruskin Dentate Stamped. Has similarities to earlier linear-punctated types such as Tchefuncte Incised (Ford and Quimby, 1945, p. 58).

Type name.—ST. PETERSBURG INCISED.
Definition as a type: Florida Gulf Coast, this paper.
Ware characteristics: A coiled ware. Sand-tempered with compact, granular paste core. Core is gray-black; surfaces are usually buff-fired. Very much like Weeden Island Plain.
Decoration:
Technique: Incised lines made in soft clay before firing.
Design: Lines arranged horizontally on vessel, encircling neck or body below rim. Lines vary from faint and sharp to deep and broad. Spacing of lines ranges from 5 mm. to 1 cm. Quite often the incised lines have an "overhanging" or "clapboard" appearance when viewed in profile. (Pl. 32, *g, h;* pl. 33, *j, k;* pl. 46, *f*.)
Distribution: Exterior. Upper portion of vessel.
Form: Mostly collared jars. Rims unmodified.
Geographical range of type: All of Florida Gulf Coast but seems to be more common around Tampa Bay. The type appears as a minority one in all regions and contexts.
Chronological position of type: Weeden Island II and probably Englewood. May extend into Fort Walton Period.
Relationships of type: Closest parallel is Coles Creek Incised, marker type of the Coles Creek Period in southern Louisiana (Ford and Willey, 1939).

Type name.—PAPYS BAYOU PLAIN.
Definition as a type: Central Gulf Coast and Manatee regions, this paper.
Ware characteristics: Indistinguishable from the soft gray or buff Biscayne or St. Johns ware. It is temperless, scratches with fingernail, and is 7 to 8 mm. thick. Surfaces usually polished.

Form: Flattened-globular bowls, deep open bowls, cylindrical beakers. Rims have exterior fold. Ovate and triangular rim projections. Lip usually rounded with occasional use of triangular punctations on lip or rim projections.

Geographical range of type: Central Coast and Manatee regions. Also extends eastward into peninsular Florida as a minority type.

Chronological position of type: Probably both Weeden Island I and II, but more common in the later period.

Relationships of type: Shows a blending of Weeden Island and St. Johns or Biscayne traditions.

Bibliography: Willey (1948a).

Type name.—PAPYS BAYOU INCISED.

Definition as a type: (Same as Papys Bayou Plain.)

Ware characteristics: (Same as Papys Bayou Plain.)

Decoration: Much like Weeden Island Incised, but the range of design is not so great. Tends to utilize fine-line incision. Emphasizes conventionalization of design as seen in the Weeden Island Incised of the Weeden Island II Period.

Form: Much like Weeden Island Incised except more limited. There are fewer unique or effigy forms. Flattened-globular bowl and jar shapes most common.

Geographical range and chronological position: (Same as Papys Bayou Plain.)

Type name.—PAPYS BAYOU PUNCTATED.

Definition as a type: (See Papys Bayou Plain.)

Ware characteristics: (See Papys Bayou Plain.)

Decoration: (See Weeden Island Punctated.) (Pl. 27, *b*, *c*, *f*; pl. 28, *b*.)

Form: (See Weeden Island Punctated.)

Geographical range and chronological position: (Same as Papys Bayou Plain.)

Type name.—PAPYS BAYOU DIAGONAL-INCISED.

Definition as a type: (See Papys Bayou Plain.)

Ware characteristics: (See Papys Bayou Plain.)

Decoration: (See Carrabelle Incised.)

Form: Large jar with folded rim only definite shape evidence.

Geographical range and chronological position: (Same as Papys Bayou Plain.)

Type name.—LITTLE MANATEE ZONED STAMPED.

Definition as a type: Southern part of central Gulf Coast and the Manatee region, this paper.

Ware characteristics: Soft temperless ware of the St. Johns or Biscayne variety. Identical with Papys Bayou and St. Johns or Biscayne Series.

Decoration:

Technique: Incision and dentate stamping on soft, unfired clay of vessel. Incised lines are round-bottomed and 2 to 3 mm. wide. The dentate stamp is applied direct and not in rocker fashion. Unit of stamp would appear to be a single row of four or five teeth. The dentate unit was impressed in close-spaced arrangement, giving the treated surface the appearance of being filled with close-spaced punctations or dots.

Design: Rectangular zones 2 to 4 cm. in width which are made by outlining with incision. They are arranged checkerboard fashion and alternate as plain rectangles and rectangles filled with dentate stamping. (Pl. 36, *g*, *h*; pl. 37, *e*, *f*.).

Distribution: Probably confined to upper one-half or two-thirds of exterior vessel walls.

Form: Large vessels suggested. Deep bowl or pot form. Slightly outslanting or incurving walls and rims which thicken to exterior (fig. 43, right). Lips almost flat.

Geographical range of type: Tampa Bay and Manatee region. Occasionally found farther north and sometimes eastward to the St. Johns area.

Chonological position of type: Weeden Island II and possibly earlier.

Relationships of type: Probably related to Alligator Bayou Stamped of the Santa Rosa-Swift Creek Period.

Type name.—LITTLE MANATEE SHELL STAMPED.

Definition as a type: From southern central Gulf Coast and the Manatee region.

Ware characteristics: (See Little Manatee Zoned Stamped.)

Decoration:

Technique: Incision and shell-edge stamping in soft, unfired clay of vessel.

Design: Rows of shell-edge stamping spaced about 2 to 3 mm. apart. Each shell-edge impression (probably scallop shell) is about 8 mm. long. (Pl. 38, *a.*)

Distribution: In a border below vessel rim. Border is underlined with incised line.

Form: Simple open bowl with unmodified rim.

Geographical range and chronological position of type: Central Gulf Coast and Manatee region. Weeden Island II Period and, possibly, earlier.

Relationships of type: Similar to Hillsborough Shell Stamped.

Type name.—LITTLE MANATEE COMPLICATED STAMPED.

Definition as a type: Vicinity of Tampa Bay.

Description: (See Little Manatee Zoned Stamped.) Decorated with complicated stamped designs. These designs are concentric circles and also concentric circles as a part of a larger and more intricate design. Execution is poor with overlapping of impressions.

Comments: Associations seem to be with other Little Manatee types. It is not a common type. Obviously represents a blending of complicated stamped tradition with temperless ware of St. Johns and Biscayne Series.

Type name.—BISCAYNE PLAIN.

Definition as a type: First described by Goggin (1940, 1944a). Willey (n.d.) has also described the type under this name. It is identical with St. Johns Plain. The Biscayne Series types were first described from south Florida and the Tampa Bay section; the St. Johns types from northeast Florida.

Ware characteristics: A soft, chalky pottery. Core is dark gray or black and the surfaces buff. Fire mottling is common. Surfaces may be rough or smooth. Hardness 2.5 or less.

Form: Bowls with incurved rims, large, deep, open bowls, collared globular bowls, boat-shaped bowls, and flattened-globular bowls. Rims usually unmodified. Lip rounded, flat-round, flat.

Geographical range of type: Most of peninsular Florida. Seems to center on St. Johns drainage.

Chronological position of type: In the central coastal and Manatee regions of the Gulf Coast it is most abundant during Weeden Island II but probably appears first in Weeden Island I. It is at least this early, if not earlier, on the St. Johns. On the Gulf Coast it continues into Englewood and Safety Harbor Periods.

Bibliography: Goggin (1940, 1944a); Willey (n.d.).

Type name.—BISCAYNE CHECK STAMPED.

Definition as a type: Defined by Goggin (1940, 1944a); Willey (n. d.) has brief descriptions. Is identical with type St. Johns Check Stamped described by Masius (n.d.).

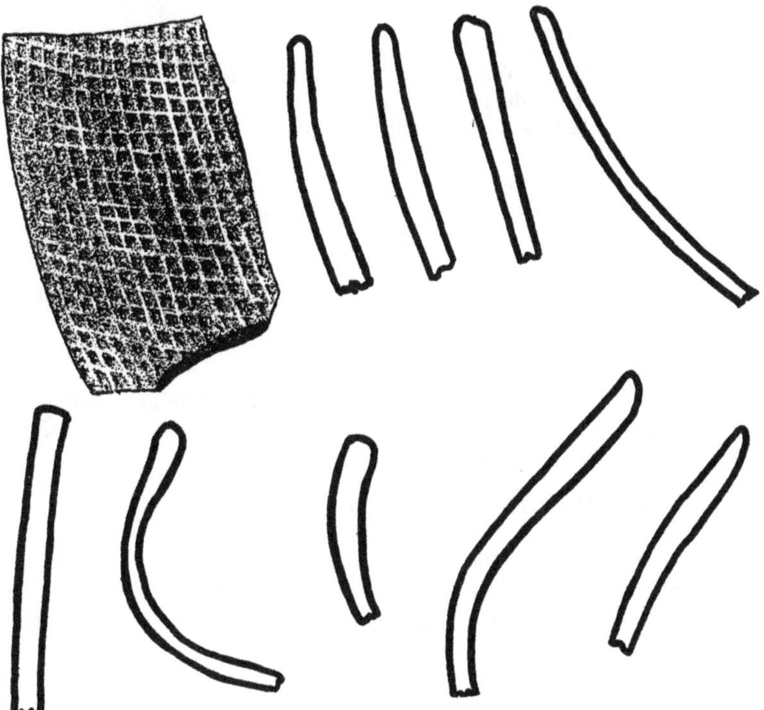

FIG. 55.—Weeden Island Period rim forms. Biscayne or St. Johns Check Stamped. (Interiors to right.)

Ware characteristics: (See Biscayne Plain.)

Decoration: Check-stamp or grid-bar unit impressed on soft clay of vessel exterior. The size of the rectangles of the checking and the width of the lands forming the rectangles varies from 5 mm. to 1 cm. Both oblong and square checks occur. Impressions are usually deep and clear but sometimes blurred by overlapping. Covers most of vessel exterior. Sometimes a band below the rim is left plain. (Pl. 40, *g;* pl. 50, *e.*)

Form: Large, deep, open bowls or pots, with straight or slightly outslanting walls, flattened-globular bowls, and simple jars. Rims usually unmodified, although an occasional exterior fold is seen (fig. 55). Occasional triangular rim projections.

Geographical distribution of type: Principal distribution is east Floridian but occurs in abundance along Gulf Coast as well. Virtually absent in northwest Gulf region, however.

Chronological position of type: Throughout Florida it first appears on the Weeden Island II horizon. Along the Gulf Coast it continues on into Englewood and Safety Harbor Periods.

Relationships of type: Undoubtedly has early prototypes, probably of the Deptford level. Bears closest resemblance to contemporary Wakulla Check Stamped type.

Bibliography: Goggin (1940, 1944a); Willey (n.d.); Massuis (n.d.)

Type name.—BISCAYNE RED.

Definition as a type: By Willey (n.d.) from south Florida. The type Dunns Creek Red from the St. Johns drainage seems identical. This type was first described by J. B. Griffin (not published) and later by Goggin (1948a).

Ware characteristics: (See Biscayne Plain.) Surfaces well smoothed, often polished over paint. One or both surfaces are covered with a red slip which ranges from light red to red-brown. Paint tends to rub off easily but appears to have been fired on.

Form: Open shallow bowls and flattened-globular bowls are most common. Rim unmodified; lip round or flat-round.

Geographical range of type: Throughout Florida peninsula. Seems to center in northern St. Johns and east-central Florida.

Chronological position of type: Goggin (1948a) reports it as diagnostic of Weeden Island I and St. Johns I. It also occurs later on the Gulf Coast.

Bibliography: Goggin (1948a); Willey (n.d.).

Type name.—BISCAYNE ROUGHENED.

Definition as a type: From Englewood site, this paper.

Ware characteristics: (See Biscayne Plain.)

Decoration: Scoring or striating the soft, unfired exterior surface of the vessel. Striations are shallow and 2 to 3 mm. in width. Random application. (Pl. 46, *g*.)

Form: Deep pot with outflared walls.

Geographical range and chronological position of type: Very few data. Occurs in Manatee region, and a few sherds have been found farther north. Probably dates from Weeden Island and Englewood Periods.

Type name.—BISCAYNE CORD-MARKED.

Description: A few specimens from Englewood site. This type is a Biscayne ware with fine close-spaced cord marking applied to exterior surface of vessel. No form data. Probably a Weeden Island and Englewood Period type.

Type name.—PASCO PLAIN.

Definition as a type: By Goggin (1948a) from central Florida. The following description is a condensation of his account.

Ware characteristics: Probably coiled. Heavily tempered with fine to large limestone lumps. These often leach out leaving large holes in surface.

Paste texture is coarse. Color ranges from gray to tan to black. Fire-clouded. Surfaces poorly smoothed and uneven.

Form: Open and slightly constricted bowls with unmodified rims.

Geographical range of type: The southwestern part of the central Florida area may be the hearth of the type, but it also extends out to the central Gulf Coast.

Chronological position of type: Weeden Island I and II. Possibly has an even greater time range.

Relationships of type: May be related to Perico Plain, a crushed-limestone-tempered type of the Manatee region which is, apparently, earlier.

Bibliography: Goggin (1948a).

Type name.—PASCO CHECK STAMPED.

Description: After Goggin (1948a). Temper particles are somewhat smaller than in Pasco Plain. Check stamping applied with paddle or comparable instrument. Small checks of 3 to 4 mm. and large checks of 6 to 10 mm. Bowl forms with incurved walls and unmodified rims. Range in southwestern part of central Florida and the adjacent Gulf Coast. Probably confined to Weeden Island II Period.

Type name.—PASCO RED.

Description: Very similar to Pasco Plain ware but slipped with a medium-dark red film on exterior vessel surface. Probably Weeden Island II Period, but extends later. (Pl. 54A, *d.*)

Type name.—GAINESVILLE LINEAR PUNCTATED.

Definition as a type: By Goggin (1948a) from Gainesville section. This description is based directly upon his.

Ware characteristics: Probably coiled. Two temper variants. One is a chalky, temperless ware comparable to the Biscayne Series pottery; the other is medium to fine quartz sand. Medium to fine paste texture. Tan to black in color. Surfaces well smoothed.

Decoration:

Technique: Lines of broad, shallow, linear punctates, touching or slightly apart.

Design: Series of parallel horizontal and vertical punctated lines. The horizontal lines apparently completely encircle the vessel; and the vertical lines may radiate from the bottom of the vessel.

Distribution: In some cases rim and upper body of the vessel; in other cases the punctation apparently covers the whole vessel. All rims seem to have a clear space about 2 cm. wide below lip.

Form: Simple hemispherical bowls with unmodified rims.

Geographical range of type: Gainesville and west to Cedar Keys (?), south to Lake Tsala Apopka.

Chronological position of type: Uncertain, but probably Weeden Island II.

Bibliography: Goggin (1948a).

Residual group.—RESIDUAL PLAIN.

Definition: Not a type but a residual category for all the plain sand or grit-tempered body sherds, or nondistinctive rim sherds, of Deptford, Santa

Rosa-Swift Creek, and Weeden Island Period sites. The great bulk of the residual sand-tempered plain comes from the latter two periods.

Some Fort Walton Period plain pottery may also be included, but if so it is at a minimum. Because of the more distinctive nature of Fort Walton plain body sherds, an attempt was made to classify them under the type Lake Jackson Plain.

Ware characteristics:

Method of manufacture: Coiled or annular technique.

Temper: Mainly fine sand. Coarse grit also included. Also what may be particles of crushed clay or potsherds.

Paste texture and color: Compact, both fine- and coarse-grained. Sometimes contorted. Core sometimes completely red or buff but more often gray or black.

Surface texture, color, and finish: Surfaces even but not well smoothed. Surfaces usually buff-fired, although some sherds are fired gray-black throughout.

Hardness: 2 to 4, with an average toward the higher figure.

Thickness: Considerable variation but average thickness is greater than with decorated wares. 8 mm. a good mean.

Form:

Total vessel: Basic shapes most commonly represented or suggested from shape of sherds are: Open bowls, flattened-globular bowls, and large jars with or without short collars. In general, the sherds suggest that these plain, often coarse, vessels were larger than the decorated vessels.

Rim and lip: Rims or lips with characteristic modifications were classified as Weeden Island Plain or as Franklin Plain.

Associations: Most of this coarse residual sand-tempered pottery is probably associated with the Weeden Island Period. In both the Deptford and Santa Rosa-Swift Creek Periods many vessels tended to be more or less covered with stamped decoration, resulting in fewer plain body sherds. In the Weeden Island Period, decoration was commonly restricted to the upper portions of the vessels.

Residual group.—SMOOTH PLAIN.

Definition: Not a type but a residual category for all the plain sand- or grit-tempered body sherds, or nondistinctive rim sherds, which have a definite surface smoothing. Refers mostly to Weeden Island Periods, but also includes earlier and later materials.

Description: Probably all coiled pottery. Usually homogeneous and even as to paste texture. Surfaces smoothed or polished. Usually buff-fired surfaces. Thickness averages 6 to 7 mm. Hardness 2 to 4, with average nearer higher figure.

Form: General range of Weeden Island shapes.

Residual group.—PLAIN RED.

Definition: Not a type but a residual category for all plain sand- or grit-tempered sherds, or nondistinctive rim sherds, which have a definite surface smoothing and a red slip on one or both surfaces. Refers almost entirely to the Weeden Island Periods.

Form: General range of Weeden Island shapes.

Other arts and technologies.—Other craft technologies of the Weeden Island Periods were not as highly developed as pottery making. Projectiles and lance points were found in many of the burial mounds although not in large numbers. Knives, chisels, scrapers, and other articles of chipped stone were less common. In the Weeden Island middens, stemmed triangular-bladed points (pl. 42, *a, b*), some with deep notches and barbs (pl. 42, *e*) or with fish-tail bases, occurred, as did a leaf-shaped point with a slightly rounded stem (pl. 42, *b, d*). All these are medium-size points. Occasionally small triangular points are also associated with Weeden Island (pl. 42, *c*). The lance points in the mounds are medium to large size, well chipped, and may be ceremonial blades. Workmanship on the midden points is average. Scrapers, drills, and chert hammerstones were also recovered from Weeden Island Period midden levels. Polished-stone celts, mostly of the medium-length, pointed-poll variety (pl. 42, *i*), were common to the burial mounds as were pebble hammers, smoothing stones (probably used in pottery making), and sandstone hones. These utility stones along with mica fragments, pieces of quartz crystal, and bits of broken stone celts, were also recovered as midden debris. Stone pendants, both single-tapered and double-tapered, were only moderately common, being found mostly at the southern end of the Gulf Coast area. Stone gorgets were rare. Sheet mica and lumps of galena were characteristic burial-mound materials. Spear-point forms cut from the mica are a frequently met burial object. Galena, on the other hand, seldom seemed to have been used for artifacts, a single bead being the only specimen known. Hematite was found in a great number of mounds; bitumen and plumbago were much less common. Bitumen appears to have been used as an adhesive on other artifacts.

Perforated teeth were rare. In general, all bone objects were infrequently met with. This includes such items as the cut animal jaws and turtle-shell rattles reported in the Santa Rosa-Swift Creek mounds. Shell drinking cups, often perforated, were common to the mounds, but shell plummets were not. Shell beads, and shell punches and chisels came from a half dozen mounds.

The smoking complex, judging from the remains, was less well developed than in the Santa Rosa-Swift Creek Period. No monitor-style pipes are definitely known. Two stone pipes are reported, presumably of the elbow form. Two other pottery elbow pipes came from burial mounds, although one of these was from a mixed Weeden Island I-Santa Rosa-Swift Creek mound. A single bowl fragment of a pottery pipe, representing a bird effigy, came from a Weeden Island midden excavation. (Pl. 42, *g*.)

Copper was discovered in six burial mounds only. In every case it was represented only by a small, unidentifiable fragment, possibly the remains of an ornament.

Weeden Island activities, as these can be estimated from artifacts and their mortuary implications, differ somewhat from those of the Santa Rosa-Swift Creek Period. Stone tools and weapons for work, hunting, and war are a little less fine and there is less emphasis upon their ceremonial significance. Possibly the old cults and magical beliefs surrounding hunting were becoming less important, and, consequently, fewer caches of fine blades or celts were placed with the dead. The disappearance of the cut animal jaws and the perforated animal teeth in the Weeden Island Periods seems to substantiate this hypothesis. The Weeden Island mounds also have fewer stone objects of probable ritualistic or ornamental types, such as plummets and gorgets, than did the Santa Rosa-Swift Creek burial places, and Weeden Island shellwork is less common and less ambitious than that of the earlier period. Copper ornaments and objects become rare in Weeden Island. This scarcity of metal may have been due to ritualistic changes in the culture, but it also suggests a partial discontinuation of the extensive trade by means of which such copper articles passed from one area to another through the eastern United States. That such trade did not completely break down during Weeden Island times is indicated by the relative abundance of mica and galena, both raw materials brought from well beyond the borders of Florida.

The smoking custom seems to have diminished in Weeden Island as pipes are uncommon and the monitor and tubular forms are not reported at all.

Wood carving obviously continued over from Santa Rosa-Swift Creek times. The complicated stamped pottery of the Weeden Island I Period is not as well stamped or decorated as that of the previous period. This, together with its virtual disappearance in Weeden Island II, may represent a decline in the wood-carver's craft. On the other hand, some of the incision-punctation pottery techniques of Weeden Island look like modes of decoration that originated on wood, suggesting that a parallel development in wood ornamentation may have continued.

Speculations on population and period duration.—There are a total of 83 burial mounds recorded in our Gulf Coast review which were built or used during the Weeden Island Periods. The same survey shows 50 midden or other habitation sites for the same periods. Both of these totals include both pure and mixed sites. It was stated in our speculations concerning Santa Rosa-Swift Creek Period population that the burial mound total probably represents a larger proportion of the actual total number of burial mounds for the period than the midden total did for the actual number of living sites. The same assumption holds for the Weeden Island Periods. Midden sites are small, difficult to find, and are virtually unreported in the literature. Mound excavation, on the other hand, makes up virtually all of the Gulf Florida archeological literature. For these reasons, here as with the Santa Rosa-Swift Creek Period, the burial-mound figure is taken as the starting point for our computations.

Assuming there were once four times as many Weeden Island mounds as we have accounted for would bring the 83 figure up to 332. Following the same formula as before, we add the further assumption that there were three times as many middens as mounds for the period. This gives us an estimate of almost 1,000 living sites. Multiplied by 30 persons per site the population totals 30,000 as opposed to the 7,200 for Santa Rosa-Swift Creek, an almost quadrupled figure.

This Weeden Island estimate is a combined period total, however. If the 30,000 were halved between Weeden Island I and II, the figure of 15,000 persons for each period would be more comparable to the 7,200 for Santa Rosa-Swift Creek. As the 7,200 figure was reduced to 5,000 to allow for the fact that not all the middens sites may have been occupied at the same time, the 15,000 total for each of the Weeden Island Periods could be similarly cut down to about 10,000 as a final speculation on the living mean per Weeden Island period.

These guess-computations show a marked increase between Santa Rosa-Swift Creek and the Weeden Island Periods. According to them the population doubled during the change from Santa Rosa-Swift Creek to Weeden Island I.

Concerning possible population differences between Weeden Island I and II, the evidence does not indicate clearly in favor of either. The site review showed 27 burial mounds which could be dated as Weeden Island I, alone. This is opposed to only 18 dated as Weeden Island II. But in addition to these, there were 38 burial mounds of Weeden Island affiliations classified as undifferentiated or combined. I think that the majority of these were probably Weeden Island II rather than I, so that the totals between the two periods would actually be more balanced than they appear from the separate period datings. Our midden samples, on the other hand, show that Weeden Island II sites predominate over those of Weeden Island I by a ratio of 30 to 6. Fourteen additional middens are combined or undifferentiated. In view of all these considerations I would estimate the population to have been about equal for the two periods.

An estimated 500 years is set on the chronology chart as being the time span covered by the two Weeden Island Periods. That the Weeden Island Periods are assigned over double the time accorded to Santa Rosa-Swift Creek is largely the result of comparisons with other chronologies outside the Florida area and an acceptance of their relative scales, plus an interpretation of the ceramic changes that occurred during the Weeden Island Periods as being indicative of a longer lapse of time than that encompassed by Santa Rosa-Swift Creek. Relative midden depth, as observed in the excavated sites, tends to substantiate this.

THE FORT WALTON PERIOD

Period definition.—The diagnostic pottery types for the Fort Walton Period are Fort Walton Incised and Pensacola Incised. Related types of both the Fort Walton and Pensacola Series are confined to this period. There seems to be no continuity of Weeden Island types as such except for Wakulla Check Stamped which appears in small quantities in some Fort Walton Period middens.

There is one regional or subregional variable. Types of the Pensacola Series, which are shell-tempered, occur more frequently at the western end of the northwest coast region, diminishing toward the east.

The sites.—There are 23 pure and 16 mixed sites of the Fort Walton Period.

Pure sites

Middens:

- East Pensacola Heights (Es-1)
- First Gulf Breeze site (Sa-6)
- Fourth Gulf Breeze site (Sa-9)
- Piney Point (Wl-5)
- G. F. Forrest site (Wl-7)
- Florida Caverns State Park (Ja-3)
- Five-Mile Point (Fr-13)
- Work place (Wa-11)
- Lake Iamonia (Le-5)

Temple mounds (and villages):

- Bear Point (Ba-1)
- Fort Walton (Ok-6)
- McBee's mound (Wl-4) (may be a burial mound)
- Jolly Bay (Wl-15)
- Yon mound (Li-2)
- Lake Jackson (Le-1)
- Lake Lafayette (Le-2)
- Rollins site (Le-3)

Burial mounds:
- Eighteen-Mile Point on Santa Rosa Sound (Sa-10)
- Bunker Cut-off (Wl-21)

Cemeteries:
- Cemetery on Hogtown Bayou (Wl-9)
- Cemetery near Point Washington (Wl-16)
- Cemetery at St. Andrews (By-23)
- Wildlife Refuge cemetery (Wa-15)

Mixed sites

Middens:
- Top bench mark (Es-2)
- Maester Creek (Sa-2)
- Hickory Shores (Sa-5)
- Second Gulf Breeze site (Sa-7)
- Third Gulf Breeze site (Sa-8)
- Villa Tasso (Wl-2)
- Big Hammock (Wl-3)
- Mack Bayou (Wl-8)
- Sowell (By-3)
- Bear Point (By-5)
- West Bay Bridge (By-6)
- Porter's Bar (Fr-1)
- Carrabelle (Fr-2)
- Pierce middens (Fr-14)

Burial mounds:
- Chipola Cut-off (Gu-5)
- Marsh Island (Wa-1)

Questionable

Temple mounds:
- Pierce mound C (part of Fr-14)
- Nichols (Wa-3)

All the Fort Walton Period sites are in the northwest coast region.[75] Midden sites of the period are evenly distributed along this coast. Fewer cemeteries are known, but these, too, are found in all parts of the region. Burial mounds are rare. Temple mounds are known throughout the region but are most common near Tallahassee. They also occur inland on the Apalachicola River.

Settlement pattern.—The coastal villages of the Fort Walton Period are much the same as those of preceding periods. Most of the sites are located along coasts, bays, or waterways. They are characterized by shell-midden refuse, and vary in extent from 25 to 100 meters in diameter. Most of the larger Fort Walton midden sites are mixed

[75] This distribution of Fort Walton sites was, of course, one of the reasons for establishing the northwest coast region as apart from the other subdivisions of the Gulf Coast area.

sites. Fort Walton Period middens seem to have less depth than those of the preceding periods. This was observed by excavations in mixed sites where Fort Walton Period refuse was found to be very superficial.

The inland villages of the Fort Walton Period are larger than most of those found on the coast and contain only scant amounts of shell refuse. It is not known if Fort Walton sites are more numerous in the interior than sites of other periods; this impression that they might be is undoubtedly strengthened by the fact that many of the inland Fort Walton sites are marked by large mounds, and these have attracted more attention than would be accorded small middens or small mounds and are, consequently, better known. Several of the inland Fort Walton sites have large flat-topped temple mounds and rather extensive surrounding village areas. One such site in the vicinity of Tallahassee (Lake Jackson (Le-1)) is a group of six temple mounds. Temple mounds also occur at the larger Fort Walton sites of the coast, but these coastal mounds do not compare in size with the big mounds of the Tallahassee section or the upper Apalachicola River.

A review of the Fort Walton temple mounds reveals the following with regard to shape and size. Of the eight definite mounds, six are rectangular and two circular. Two mounds, questionable as to a Fort Walton Period dating (Pierce mound C (Fr-14) and Nichols (Wa-3)), are also rectangular. The rectangular mounds vary in height from 4 to 30 feet. Basal measurements are as much as 195 by 145 feet in one case and 150 by 150 feet in another. All the rectangular mounds tapered upward to a rectangular flat top or platform which was usually about one-half as large as the basal area. Shape outline was both square and oblong, and sloping earth ramps were observed leading to the tops of some but not all of the mounds.

The two circular mounds are 3 and 7 feet high, respectively. These are mounds which had been excavated (Bear Point (Ba-1) and McBee's Mound (Wl-4)) previous to any reported observations. It is possible that their outlines had been modified by such excavations.

Two burial mounds of the period are reported and, in addition, there are two examples of Fort Walton Period reuse of Weeden Island Period mounds. Four Fort Walton cemeteries are known.

Economy.—On the coast marine foods continued to play some part in the Fort Walton diet, although this seems to have been a diminishing one. Interior sites, such as Lake Jackson (Le-1), show very little shell refuse, the debris on these sites being mostly decayed organic matter. Animal and fish bones still occur in middens, but the impression is that they, like shell, compose a smaller proportion of the rubbish than in former periods. These observations concur with what we would expect for the period. The Fort Walton culture is essentially Mississippian in type and equates with the late Middle Mississippian time horizon in the Southeast. As other Mississippian cultures possessed a well-developed agricultural economy at this time, there is little doubt that agriculture was known to the Fort Walton peoples, although we lack the definite finds to prove it. The suggested shift of the bulk of the population at this period, from the coast to the more fertile interior, fits in with the assumption that native agriculture became more important and widely practiced during the Fort Walton Period than previously.

Organization of society.—There are archeological implications for change in the political and social organization of the Fort Walton Period as opposed to the Weeden Island. In the first place, the ratio between the number of temple mounds and the number of midden sites during Fort Walton shows fewer mounds than comparable ratios between Weeden Island or Santa Rosa-Swift Creek burial mounds and middens. This reduction in the number of ceremonial sites or centers, with relation to the numbers of middens or villages, indicates a trend toward politico-religious cohesion in the Fort Walton Period. It is doubtful that this trend resulted in the entire northwest coast region becoming a single political unit in the Fort Walton Period, but it suggests that there were only several rather than a great multitude of autonomous units. There is support for this in the ethnohistorical accounts of the sixteenth century which describe what seem to be political assemblages or federations that include several communities, a considerable area, and a capital town.

Secondly, the temple mounds themselves imply a different social orientation than the burial mound. The latter is solely a place of burial while the former is a means of lending prestige and impressiveness to a political or religious building and its occupants. Burials are sometimes found in the temple mounds, but these are clearly later additions incidental to its principal function. The shift from the Weeden Island burial mound to the Fort Walton temple mound suggests a decline in the importance of the death cult and a concomitant rise in the significance of tribal leaders. Together with the presumed larger political units of the Fort Walton Period, this would mean that secular powers and functions of the leaders had been increased over previous periods.

The nature and distribution of grave goods conforms to this interpretation. Specially made mortuary ceramics disappear and, in general, grave goods are less abundant and elaborate than they were for either Santa Rosa-Swift Creek or the Weeden Island Periods. However, grave artifacts, especially pottery, are more often found with individuals than placed as group offerings, and there is a greater variation in the amount and quality of objects placed with individual burials than during the Weeden Island Periods.

Disposal of the dead.—The burial customs of the Fort Walton Culture, as compared with Santa Rosa-Swift Creek or Weeden Island, are neither as distinctive nor as standardized. Fort Walton dead were buried in cemeteries, in the floors of temple mounds, and in burial mounds. Among the latter there are instances where earlier mounds of the Weeden Island Periods were used as repositories for Fort Walton burials.

The records of burials in three temple mounds, Bear Point (Ba-1), Fort Walton (Ok-6), and Jolly Bay (Wl-15), all state that the graves were intrusive into the tops and flanks of the mounds. At Bear Point and Jolly Bay burials were of the secondary types. The burials found in the big Fort Walton (Ok-6) mound were both secondary and primary extended. The other Fort Walton Period temple mounds have not been thoroughly explored for burials. The burials in one of the Fort Walton burial mounds were primary extended, and in the other they were all secondary. In the two Weeden Island mounds, into which Fort Walton Period burials had been intruded, the Fort Walton burials were secondary in one case (Marsh Island (Wa-1)) and both secondary and primary flexed in the other (Chipola Cut-off (Gu-5)). The cemeteries contained both massed and scattered secondary burials in two instances, Hogtown Bayou (Wl-9) and Point Washington (Wl-16), and extended and flexed primaries in the other, Wildlife Refuge (Wa-15). The Hogtown Bayou and Point Washington cemeteries were characterized by low rises of sand, not over a foot in height and a few feet in diameter. These small hummocks marked areas of mass burials. Burials in the temple mounds ranged from 27 to 66 in number, although I think it likely that some of the big mounds actually yielded more than were tabulated. Approximately 100 individuals were found in each of the two cemeteries with the massed secondary burials.

Large destroyed caches of pottery vessels were found in both the Fort Walton Period temple mounds and in the cemeteries. These were also found in the burial mounds, although in the case of the Chipola Cut-off (Gu-5) mixed-period mound it is not clear from Moore's account (1903, pp. 445-466) whether these caches consisted of Fort Walton as well as Weeden Island Period vessels. As mentioned, pottery deposition for the Fort Walton Period often differed from Weeden Island in that vessels were frequently found with individual skeletons. In fact, a distinctive Fort Walton trait was the inversion of a large pottery vessel over the skull of a dead individual. This was noted both in temple-mound and cemetery burials of single skulls. There is also one instance of urn burial at Marsh Island (Wa-1). Nonceramic artifacts were commonly placed with individual skeletons and were also found unassociated in cemeteries and mounds.

Cranial deformation was noted for Marsh Island (Wa-1) and Point Washington (Wl-16).

The sum total of impressions concerning Fort Walton disposal of the dead is that the period was a time of change in mortuary customs. The old burial-mound idea competes with the newer modes of interment in temple-mound floors or in cemeteries. The fact that burials were placed in the earlier Weeden Island mounds suggests some continuity of the burial-mound practice, but the custom had waned to such an extent that the desire was lacking to build a mound for the purpose. Burial in the temple mounds may, to a degree, represent a continuity of the mound-burial idea although in a different form. Treatment of the bodies of the dead was much the same as in the earlier periods. Charnel houses and bone cleaning must have remained in vogue. Primary burial, more often extended than flexed, also was practiced. Old ideas concerning mortuary goods were retained to the extent that vessels were still intentionally "killed" or destroyed and sometimes mass caches of pottery were buried near the dead as common offerings. New elements are seen, however, in the vessels placed specially with individuals, and the greater emphasis on individual grave artifact arrangements.

Ceramic arts.—Fort Walton pottery is technically competent and abundant, but it lacks the esthetic excellence that characterized Weeden Island. As a ware it is somewhat coarser than the previous periods with either a heavy grit or crushed shell being used as temper. The appearance of shell temper is one of the diagnostic traits of the period. Surface decoration, except for some check stamping, is executed mainly in heavy incision and punctation. Red pigment is occasionally used, and engraving appears so infrequently that it is considered a foreign element. Modeled ornamentation is fairly common and takes the form of zoomorphic and anthropomorphic rim adornos. These adornos represent the Fort Walton ceramic art at its best. There is a tendency for vessels to be larger than in the preceding periods, and the casuela bowl and the bottle are the most distinctive and the most common of the new forms. As opposed to the earlier periods, there is a strong tendency for conformacy in both design and vessel shape. The exotic effigy forms of the Santa Rosa-Swift Creek and Weeden Island Periods are missing. Design elements and arrangement are more standardized and predictable than before. Except for the quite realistic adornos there is little detectable life naturalism in the decoration. Designs are both curvilinear and rectilinear and highly conventionalized. The drawing lacks the grace, lightness of touch, and flowing quality of the Weeden Island style.

Fort Walton ceramics represent a break with the older Gulf Coast traditions in that new influences of a Middle Mississippian origin have been strong factors in the formation of the style. Some resemblances to the incised and punctated types of Weeden Island are suggested, although it is not clear if this is the result of a local Gulf Coast continuity or some more indirect relationship. An obvious local carry-over is the type Wakulla Check Stamped which lasts on into the Fort Walton Period as a minority type and probably serves as the basis for the development of the later type, Leon Check Stamped. Moundville Engraved, an obvious inland Alabama type, occurs on the Gulf Coast during the Fort Walton Period, probably as trade.

The Fort Walton pottery types in the order in which they are described:

- Fort Walton Series:
  - Lake Jackson Plain
  - Fort Walton Incised
  - Point Washington Incised
- Pensacola Series:
  - Pensacola Plain
  - Pensacola Incised
  - Pensacola Three-line Incised.
  - Pensacola Red
- Marsh Island Incised
- Moundville Engraved

Type Descriptions

Type name.—LAKE JACKSON PLAIN.

Definition as a type: From the Florida northwest coast, present paper. Brief synoptic description in Willey and Woodbury (1942). Based upon rim and appendage sherds. Associated body sherds were grouped in the Residual Plain category, although the plain ware of the Fort Walton Period can be sorted out from Weeden Island and Santa Rosa-Swift Creek unidentified sherds with about 80 percent accuracy.

Ware characteristics:

Method of manufacture: Coil fractures observed.

Temper: Sand and medium-size grit particles and what appears to be crushed clay. In general, tempering material coarser than in previous periods.

Paste texture and color: Paste is sometimes fine and compact but more often it is coarse, lumpy and contorted. Paste cores are usually gray; fired surfaces are often whitish buff, buff, or reddish buff.

Surface texture, color, and finish: Surfaces are smoothed but never achieve a polish. They are distinguished by temper particles, usually pieces of quartz, which extrude through onto the surface. In the case of the predominantly clay-tempered specimens hard clay particles give the surface a coarse texture. Surfaces are commonly mottled, and vary in color, depending upon the degree of firing. (See pl. 44.)

Hardness: 3 to 4.

Thickness: 6 to 9 mm., with average about 8.

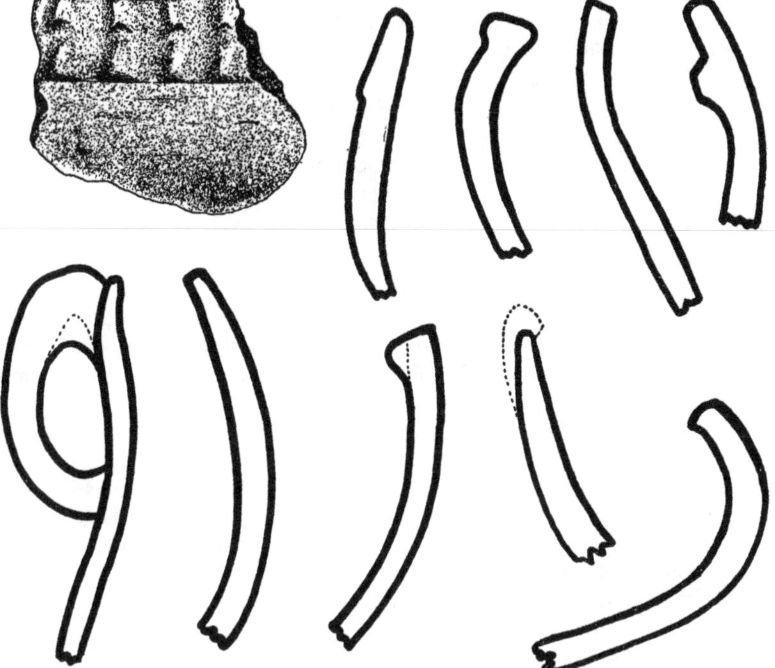

FIG. 56.—Fort Walton Period rim forms. Lake Jackson Plain. (Interiors to right.)

Form:

Total vessel: Vessels tend to be larger than in earlier Gulf Coast periods. The casuela bowl, collared globular bowl, globular bowl with flared orifice, open bowl and complete frog-effigy bowl are all recorded.

Rim: Casuela rims are inturned. Collared ollas have straight, inslanting or outflared rims. Rims often thickened near or at margin. Some rims are unmodified. Exterior rim folds, when they occur, are thin and flat but wide. They are often pinched or fluted. Sometimes a strap of clay was added to the exterior wall just below the rim, and this strip is pinched or fluted. Small applique nodes often added along rim exterior in place of fluting. Fingernail or long punctations, placed in row beneath rim, or on rim exterior, are another variation. (See fig. 56.)

Lip: Sometimes pointed or round-pointed, sometimes flat or squared. Most characteristic feature is a row of close-spaced notches which are always placed diagonally on the exterior edge of lip.

Base: Rounded.

Appendages: Small vertically oriented lugs placed on the rim exterior. These may or may not have a projection above the lip. Both vertically placed loop and thick strap handles occur. The large ones are 6 to 8 cm. long and over 2 cm. wide. Small loop handles are 3 to 4 cm. long and about 1 cm. wide. Some handles have single, double, or triple nodes.

Geographical range of type: Most common in the northwest from Pensacola to St. Marks and inland as far as the Tallahassee section and well up the Apalachicola River system. Rarely found in central coast or Manatee regions where it is replaced by Pinellas Plain.

Chronological position of type: Fort Walton Period. Continues into Leon-Jefferson Period.

Relationships of type: Related to late Mississippian pottery of south and central Alabama and Georgia. Lamar Series types have similar rim treatment and shapes. Related to Pinellas Series of Safety Harbor Period and to types of the Leon-Jefferson Period.

Bibliography: Willey and Woodbury (1942, pp. 245-246).

Type name.—FORT WALTON INCISED.

Definition as a type: From the northwest coast of Florida, this paper. Briefly described by Willey and Woodbury (1942, p. 244). Has been revised since that time to include only "substyles 1 and 2" as they were defined in that paper.

Ware characteristics: (See Lake Jackson Plain.)

Decoration:

Technique: Lines and punctations incised into soft surface of vessel. Lines are deep, wide, and usually rectangular in cross section. Large round dot or square punctations most common. Hollow-reed punctations sometimes used.

Design: Elements are volutes, interlocked scrolls, running scrolls, circles, trifoil figures, crescentic forms, S-shaped and reverse-S figures, rectilinear stepped figures, pendant loops, and triangles. Elements are usually repeated around vessel in a connected design pattern. Dot punctations used as filler for both backgrounds and for design proper. Incised lines sometimes used as filler. (See fig. 57, *a-d;* pl. 43; pl. 45, *f, g.*)

Distribution: Around upper part of bowl, as a rule, and on vessel exterior. Interior decoration occurs on upper surfaces of rim appendages or projections to large, open bowls.

Form:

Total vessel: Shallow bowls with lateral expansions, casuela bowls, collared globular bowls, short-collared jars, beaker-bowls, bottles, gourd-effigy forms, flattened-globular bowls with effigies affixed.

Rim: Usually inslanting or incurving but depends on vessel form. Most rims thickened except for a perceptible thinning at the lip edge. Long,

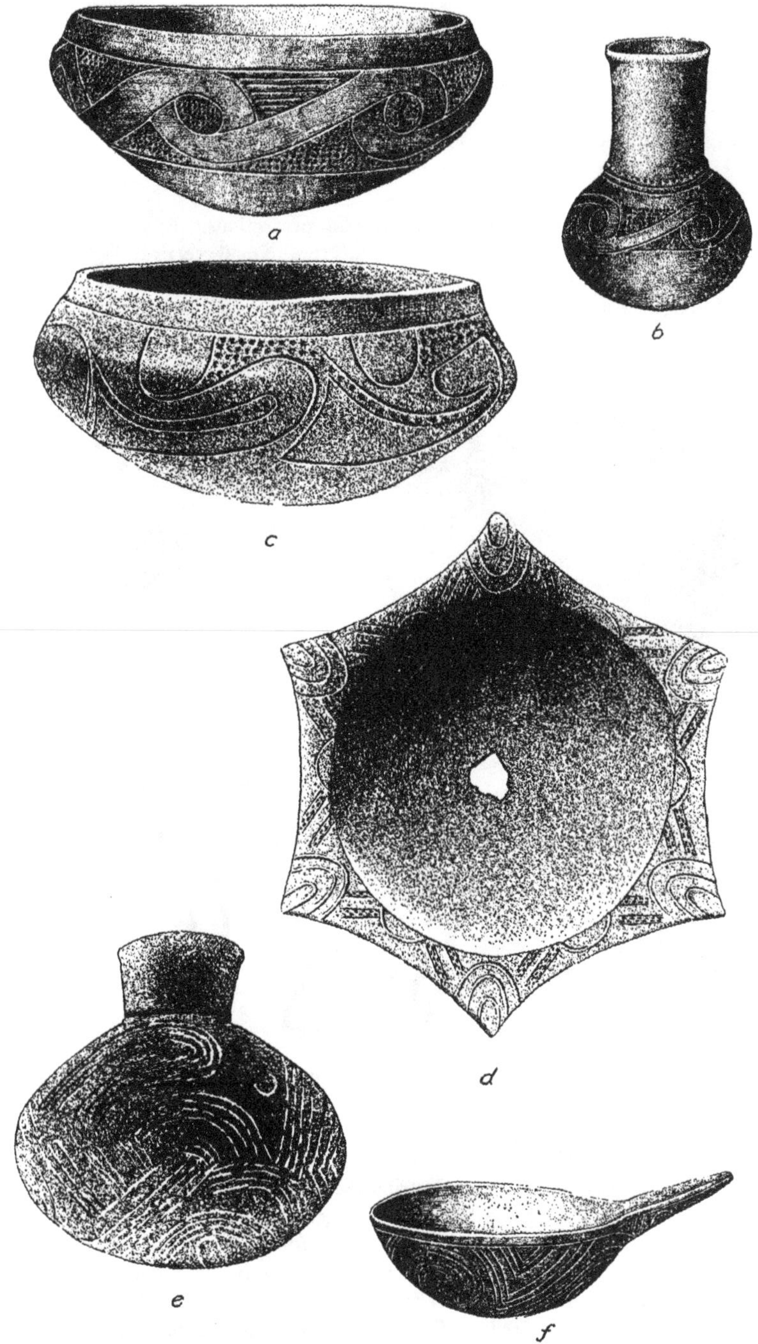

FIG. 57.—Fort Walton Period vessels. *a-d,* Fort Walton Incised; *e,* Pensacola Three-line Incised; *f,* Point Washington Incised. (Redrawn from Moore. Year, figure number, and site: *a,* 1901:24, Fort Walton; *b,* 1903:105, Chipola Cut-Off; *c,* 1901:17, Fort Walton; *d,* 1901:22, Fort Walton; *e,* 1901:81, Point Washington; *f,* 1901:96, Point Washington. Vessels *a, b, d, f* are ¼ actual size; *c, e,* ½ actual size.)

thin folds are common. These are usually underlined with an incised line. (See fig. 58.)

Lip: Rounded or round-pointed. Rather close-spaced notches are placed diagonally on the exterior margin of the lip.

Base: Rounded.

Appendages: Lateral or horizontal rim projections. Bird head-and-tail effigies placed on opposing sides of rim. Small vertical lugs, usually four to a vessel, placed just below the lip on exterior. These lugs may be flush with lip or may project above it.

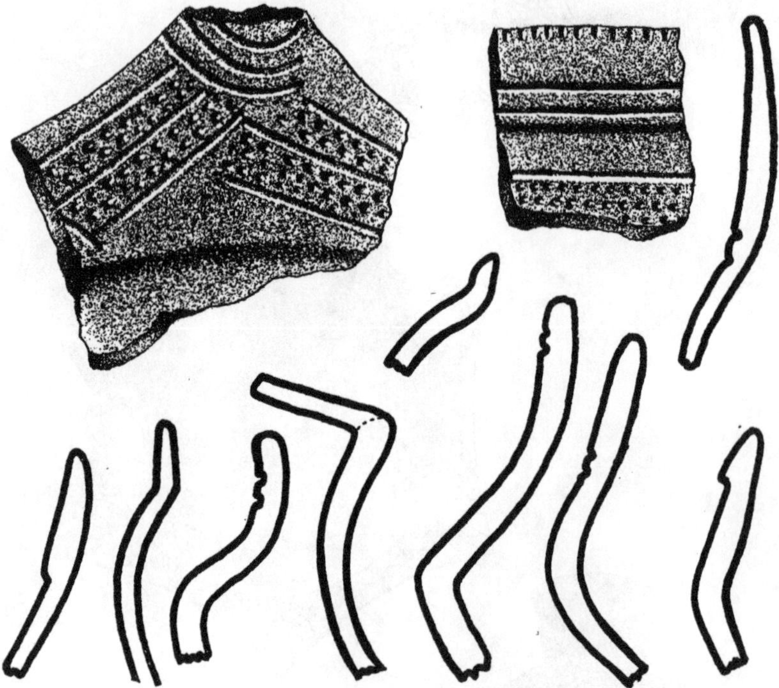

Fig. 58.—Fort Walton Period rim forms. Fort Walton Incised. (Interiors to right.)

Geographical range of type: Northwest coast of Florida with inland extension for at least 100 miles. Distribution unrecorded along Alabama coast and interior Alabama but probably occurs in these areas.

Chronological position of type: Marker type for Fort Walton Period.

Relationships of type: General similarity to many late Middle Mississippian incised types of both grit- and shell-tempered wares. Rather close to Lamar Bold Incised of Georgia. Undoubtedly is prototype and contemporary of Pinellas Incised of Safety Harbor Period of the central Gulf Coast.

Bibliography: Willey and Woodbury (1942, p. 244).

Type name.—POINT WASHINGTON INCISED.

Definition as a type: Northwest coast of Florida, this paper. Previously included in a very brief description of Fort Walton Incised (Willey and Woodbury, 1942, p. 244: see "substyle 3").

Ware characteristics: (See Lake Jackson Plain.)

Decoration:

Technique: By incision in soft vessel surface. Use of series of two, three, or four lines to carry out all designs (fig. 57, *f*).

Design: Loop figures in isolation, complicated scroll patterns, running scrolls, ovals intersected with cross bars, diamonds and V-shaped figures, and combinations of curvilinear and rectilinear elements into composite patterns are the principal design motifs. (Pl. 45, *a-e.*)

Distribution: Most often confined to upper portion of vessel exteriors but there are examples of designs extending to and over the base.

Form:

Total vessel: Shallow bowl or dish, flattened-globular bowl, casuela bowl (most common), collared globular bowl, short-collared jars, bottles (common), double bowl, jar with cambered rim, simple bowl with effigies affixed, gourd-effigy form.

Rim: (See Fort Walton Incised.)

Lip: (See Fort Walton Incised.)

Base: Usually rounded.

Appendages: Animal or bird head-and-tail effigies on bowls.

Geographical range of type: Northwest Florida coast. Seems more common to the western end of this range. Probably extends into coastal Alabama and interior Alabama.

Chronological position of type: Fort Walton Period.

Relationships of type: Closest similarities of design are seen in Fatherland Incised, a Natchezan type of southern Mississippi (Quimby, 1942) which utilizes the parallel three- or four-line element in the formation of various scroll and other curvilinear designs. Also has close affinities with Fort Walton Incised in ware, shape, and decoration.

Bibliography: Willey and Woodbury (1942, p. 244: "substyle 3" under Fort Walton Incised); Moore (1901, Point Washington cemetery site, pp. 472-496); Quimby (1942, pp. 263-264).

Type name.—PENSACOLA PLAIN.

Definition as a type: Northwest Florida, this paper.

Ware characteristics:

Method of manufacture: Some fractures suggest coiling method, although this is not as definite as in the other types or series.

Temper: Crushed live shell. There is also a little sand and grit.

Paste texture and color: Sometimes compact; sometimes laminated and contorted. Paste core usually is gray and surfaces usually buff or red-buff. In some cases pottery was fired gray-black throughout.

Surface texture, color, and finish: Surfaces were probably smoothed and polished before erosion. Most specimens are pitted as a result of the temper particles leaching out. Several of the black or gray-black sherds have retained a polished, unpitted surface. Color varies according to firing.

Hardness: 2.5 to 3.5.

Thickness: Ranges from 5 to 11 mm., with average closer to lower figure.

Form:

Total vessel: Forms undoubtedly comparable to those of the Fort Walton Series.

Rims: Usually unmodified except for an occasional heavy, round exterior fold.

Lip: From flat to round-pointed.

Base: Probably rounded.

Appendages: Small vertical loop handles and ornamental nodes beneath the rim.

Geographical range of type: Most common in extreme western end of northwest Florida, but it is found in small quantities as far east and south as Tampa Bay. Probably very common in south Alabama.

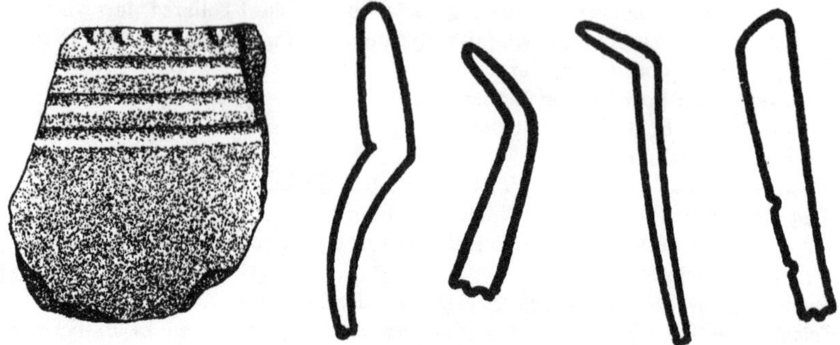

FIG. 59.—Fort Walton Period rim forms. Pensacola Incised. (Interiors to right.)

Chronological position of type: The Fort Walton Period. Also found as a minority type in Safety Harbor sites.

Relationships of type: Related to shell-tempered ware of late Middle Mississippian horizon throughout the Southeast. Has more specific relationships to types in south and central Alabama. Resembles Lake Jackson Plain in vessel forms.

Type name.—PENSACOLA INCISED.

Definition as a type: This paper, northwest Florida.

Description: Ware same as Pensacola Plain. Vessel forms comparable to those described for Fort Walton Incised. (See fig. 59.) Decoration about the same as Fort Walton Incised except there seems to be a little more emphasis on incision with less punctation. (See fig. 60.) Some designs suggestive of highly stylized "death's-head" motif.

Geographical range and chronological position: Found mainly in western northwest Florida but extends to the east and south as a minority type. Belongs to the Fort Walton Period.

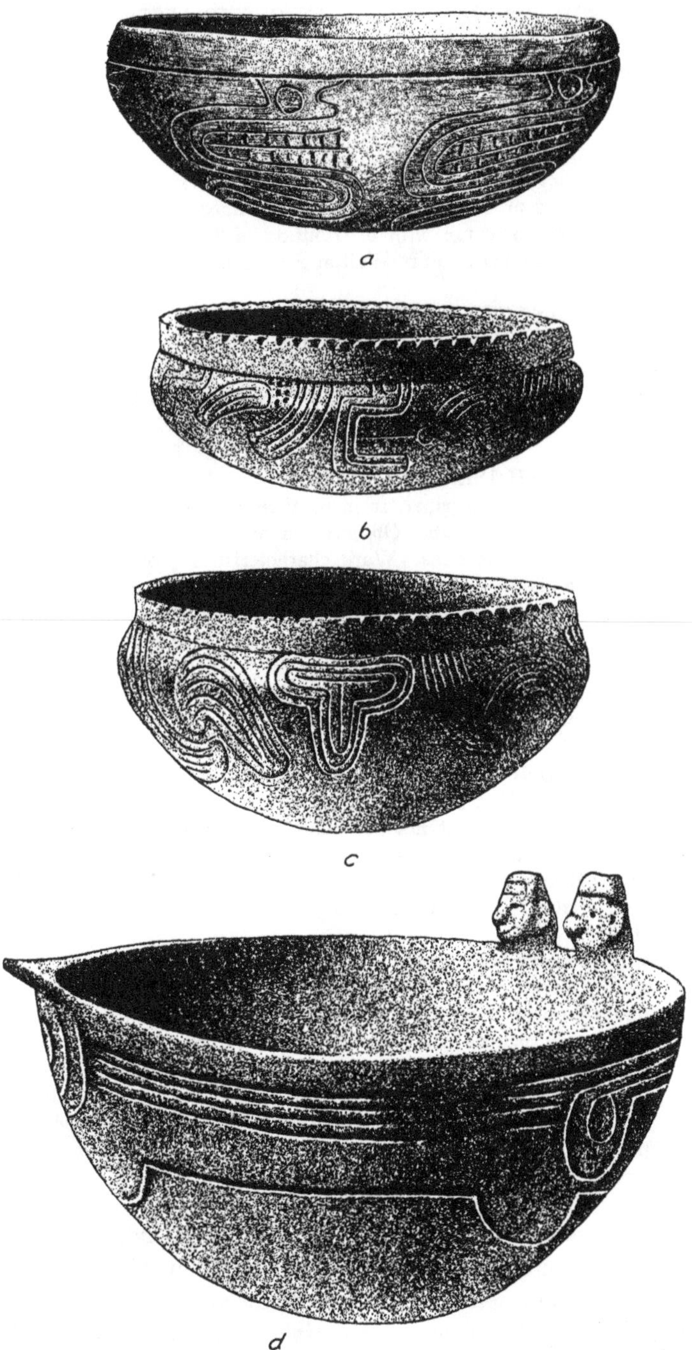

FIG. 60.—Fort Walton Period vessels. All Pensacola Incised. (Redrawn from Moore. Year, figure number, and site: *a*, 1901:21, Fort Walton; *b*, 1901:2, Bear Point, Alabama; *c*, 1901:5, Bear Point, Alabama; *d*, 1901:37, Fort Walton. Vessels *a-c* are ¼ actual size; *d*, ½.)

Type name.—PENSACOLA THREE-LINE INCISED.

Definition as a type: This paper, northwest Florida.

Description: Parallels the type Point Washington Incised except that the ware is shell-tempered (fig. 57, *e*).

Geographical range and chronological position: Western end of northwest Florida and probably south and central Alabama. May extend to south Mississippi to merge with distribution of Natchezan type, Fatherland Incised. Belongs to Fort Walton Period in Florida.

Type name.—PENSACOLA RED.

Definition as a type: This paper, northwest Florida.

Description: A Pensacola Series shell-tempered ware which has been slipped with a medium to dark red pigment. Not common but very distinctive owing to temper and color.

Type name.—MARSH ISLAND INCISED.

Definition as a type: This paper, from northwest Florida.

Description: Very limited data. Observed in Moore (1902, fig. 241) and in a few surface collections. Ware characteristics probably parallel those of Lake Jackson Plain. Decoration by medium-bold line incision. Design in band around vessel below rim. Consists of opposed triangles which are filled with parallel incised lines. Also chevron arrangements made up of diagonally placed series of parallel incised lines below rim, and parallel vertical lines below rim. Open-bowl form. May be related to the earlier type, Carrabelle Incised.

Type name.—MOUNDVILLE ENGRAVED.

Definition as a type: Has been informally recognized by Southeastern workers for several years but not yet published as a type. Very brief sketch offered here is based upon a vessel in the Moore collection from Jolly Bay (Moore, 1901, figs. 53, 55).

Ware characteristics: A black polished pottery tempered with finely crushed shell.

Decoration: Employs both incision and engraving. Major outlines of designs usually done in broad-line incision. Background work done in fine-line engraved hachure or cross hachure. Designs usually consist of life forms such as eagles, men with eagle masks, human skulls, etc. These design elements are a part of the Southern Cult (see Waring and Holder, 1945). A collared globular bowl is shown by Moore. This specimen appears in a Fort Walton Period context which is approximately coeval with, or only slightly later than, other similar examples of cult art in Alabama and Georgia.

Other arts and technologies.—As in Weeden Island, ceramics were the outstanding craft products of the Fort Walton Period or, at least, the outstanding examples still available to the archeologist. The virtual absence of stamped pottery may signify a decline in wood carving, although this is by no means certain. Chipped-stone work seems less well developed than in the earlier periods. The large, fine blades found in

Santa Rosa-Swift Creek and Weeden Island burial mounds are not as common as formerly. Some projectile points and knives do occur in middens and as burial goods. Medium-size triangular-bladed stemmed and barbed points and large triangular points with tapered stems were found in midden-site excavation along with chipped-stone scrapers. The small triangular points, so common to other late Mississipian cultures in the southeast, may be a feature of the Fort Walton Complex, but our data are insufficient to make a definite statement of this. Stone celts, hones, pebble hammers, discoidal stones, and beads are the reported ground-stone products. The celts of the period are of two forms. The medium to large pointed-poll celt (pl. 42, *j*), also found in Weeden Island, is present, as is a smaller, thinner, rectangulate celt (pl. 42, *k*) which is more diagnostic of the Fort Walton Period. The only ores or minerals found in Fort Walton burial sites are hematite and limonite.

Shell cups are rare, but shell tools, beads, and long spike-form ear pins are frequent. Shell plummet-type pendants and shell gorgets are occasionally found. Bone awls, bone fishhooks, and bone beads are recorded from one or two sites. In general, except for shell ear pins and shell beads, the shell and bone industries have declined from earlier standards. Native metalwork is exceedingly rare. At one site, two copper spear-form objects were found, but it is not certain if these were made from aboriginal copper. Curiously, no pipes of either stone or pottery were reported from any of the sites reviewed. At two sites toadstool-shaped objects of pottery were recovered. These may have been pottery trowels or, possibly, as Moore suggested, bottle stoppers.

Objects made by the Indians from European importations include sheet-silver, copper, and brass ornaments and tablets. European manufactures are iron tools, nails, and weapons, silver buttons, coins, glass beads, and a glass ring. These materials indicate either casual or trade contacts, and, with the exception of metalwork, they probably had little effect upon native crafts either as a deterrent or as a stimulant.

In general, Fort Walton manufactures reflect little change in stonework other than a probable slight decrease in stone-chipping skills. Stone tools and artifacts are otherwise about the same as in Weeden Island except for the appearance of discoidals which probably heralds the introduction of the "chunkee" game. Shell ornaments are more common than in Weeden Island and the shell ear pin is a new type for the Gulf Coast area. Otherwise, work in shell is even less popular than before. The shell drinking cup as an element of burial furniture is rare. Virtually all native metalwork is gone. Trade contacts in copper or copper artifacts, vigorous in Santa Rosa-Swift Creek but faint in Weeden Island, seemed to have now disappeared altogether. Galena and mica, two trade minerals from the north, have also disappeared. The smoking custom has either disappeared, weakened, or changed its form of appliances. European metals and metal objects were reworked by the Indians during the period, and this may possibly account for diminished trade with and interest in sources of northern native copper. European manufactured items were, apparently, rare and highly prized as tools, weapons, and ornaments.

Speculations on population and period duration.—The guess-computation formula which we employed in estimating population totals for the Weeden Island and Santa Rosa-Swift Creek Periods is not equally applicable to the Fort Walton Period. In Fort Walton times the Indian settlement pattern had changed. Temple-mound sites were the ceremonial and political centers and the population nuclei. For Santa Rosa-Swift Creek and Weeden Island periods we used the number of burial mounds as the basis for our population computation; for Fort Walton this is not feasible as it is certain that we have nowhere near a representative record of the number of burial sites for the period. Cemeteries, being unmarked by mounds, are difficult to locate, and the four of which we have note probably represent but a very small proportion of the total, while burial mounds had virtually disappeared. For Fort Walton our best possibilities for reasonable estimates lie in a consideration of the middens and temple mounds.

There are a total of 23, pure and mixed, Fort Walton habitation sites. These are simple middens without mounds. This number compares favorably with the 50 Weeden Island Period middens which we recorded, and with the Santa Rosa-Swift Creek midden total of 19. Both Santa Rosa-Swift Creek and Weeden Island counts pertained to the entire Gulf Coast area. The Fort Walton count, as opposed to this, pertains only to the northwest coast region. Hence, a total of 23 middens for the Fort Walton Period would indicate a population density in northwest Florida, during this period, considerably greater than Santa Rosa-Swift Creek and at least as great as that of the Weeden Island Period. This probability is further strengthened if we add the temple-mound sites to the simple midden total. Most of the temple mounds are surrounded with big middens. Although these temple-mound centers may have been supported in part by outlying villages, they were also sustained by their own immediate inhabitants who, to judge from the amount of refuse around the mounds, were fairly numerous. Thus we are, I believe, on firm footing when we say that the population of the Fort Walton Period in northwest Florida was the equivalent of Weeden Island for the same area. Weeden Island population for the whole Gulf Coast has been estimated at from 15,000 to 10,000 persons per period (Weeden Island I and Weeden Island II). For the northwest coast alone we might halve this, or 7,500 to 5,000.

There is, however, another important consideration in this problem of Fort Walton Period population estimates. Our surveys and site reviews have been largely confined to the immediate coast and the major rivers. In the Fort Walton Period we note, though, that some of the biggest sites are located inland on lakes or small streams. This implies proportionately greater population concentrations in the interior than on the coast, and tends to raise the population estimates for the Fort Walton culture area as a whole. Mooney and Kroeber (see Kroeber, 1939, p. 138) have estimated a total population of 12,000 persons for the combined Apalachee, Apalachicola, Sawokli, Chatot, and Pensacola tribes. These were the tribal groups occupying the Fort Walton culture area in the sixteenth and seventeenth centuries. The Mooney-Kroeber figure is considerably in excess of the 7,500 to 5,000 computed here; however, by giving additional weight to the big interior sites, our figures could reasonably be boosted to the 12,000 estimate.

We have not in this discussion considered historic or ethnographic evidence. The Mooney-Kroeber estimates are based upon ethnohistoric rather than archeological data, and it is interesting to note that the Narvaez and De Soto chronicles of the sixteenth century both indicate that the large population centers were inland rather than on the Gulf shore. For a consideration of the sixteenth-century population of northwest Florida (presumably identical with the Fort Walton culture and period) from the standpoint of history and ethnography see pages 533-535.

The Fort Walton Period is estimated as being of relatively short duration, from A. D. 1500 to 1650. The terminal date is established upon the basis of the entrance and influence of the Spanish missions. After 1650 the Indian culture of the region was profoundly changed and enters the final or Leon-Jefferson Period. We feel quite sure that the Apalachee Indians encountered by De Soto on his journey possessed the Fort Walton rather than the earlier Weeden Island culture. The trade goods of the Fort Walton Period graves are those of sixteenth-century Europeans. It will be remembered that a Spanish-Mexican coin dating between 1521 and 1550 was found in a Fort Walton cemetery at Bear Point (Ba-1), Ala. The date and the locality suggest that the Indians may have obtained the coin from the De Luna expedition of 1559. As to how far back of the Spanish entradas we should place the beginning of the Fort Walton Period is more perplexing. Fort Walton is a Middle Mississippian-influenced culture. Furthermore, it is late Middle Mississippian, having close links with such cultures as the Georgia Lamar. In view of this, I hesitate to push the beginning date back of the year A. D. 1500. It should be mentioned that the relative brevity of the period is indicated by depth in refuse deposits. Whereas Santa Rosa-Swift Creek and Weeden Island deposits were 1 to 1.40 meters in depth at the Fort Walton (Ok-6) midden site, Fort Walton Period types were confined to the upper 10 to 30 cm. This superficiality of Fort Walton Period refuse was also noted at other midden sites.

THE ENGLEWOOD PERIOD

Period definition.—The diagnostic pottery types of the Englewood Period are Englewood Incised and Sarasota Incised. Associated types, such as Englewood Plain and Lemon Bay Incised, have little or no diagnostic value at our present stage of knowledge. Biscayne Series pottery and Glades Plain, also found in association, are not marker types for the period. In general, the period is little known and the evidence scant.

The sites.—The present review records only three sites at which sufficient materials of the Englewood Complex were found to enable us to designate them as stations of the period. All, including the type site, are mixed sites.

Mixed sites
- Middens:
  - Clearwater (Pi-5)
  - Osprey (So-2)
- Burial mounds:
  - Englewood (So-1)

The Osprey and Englewood sites are in the Manatee region and the Clearwater site is near the southern margin of the central coast region. Occasional Englewood types are found at other Manatee and central Gulf Coast sites.[76] To my knowledge, none are known from the northwest coast.

---

[76] Moore illustrates very little Englewood pottery; however, the vessel shown on page 430, figure 83 (Moore, 1903) is either Englewood Incised or Sarasota Incised. This specimen came from the Pithlochascootie River mound (Pa-2). The site dates as Weeden Island II.

Settlement pattern.—Shell-midden villages with nearby burial mounds along the Gulf Coast and bay shores. Probably very comparable to Weeden Island patterns.

Economy.—Marine foods played an important part in the subsistence. By analogy with Weeden Island and Safety Harbor, it is presumed that agriculture was practiced.

Organization of society.—Probably similar to Weeden Island with autonomous villages, or small group of villages, each maintaining their own ceremonial mound for burial purposes.

Disposal of the dead.—The only known burial site is the sand burial mound at the type site. The burial mound at the Englewood site was one of two. It was 110 feet in diameter and 13 feet high. Conical in form, the tumulus was composed of sand, and its interior structure was revealed as a smaller interior mound over which the larger outer mound, or mound layer, had been heaped. Under the inner or primary mound was a shallow burial pit. This had been covered with sand mixed with red ocher before the construction of the primary mound. The absence of any sod line or weathered surface on the primary mound implies that little time had elapsed after its completion before the secondary mound was put down.

Over 100 burials in the burial pit underlying the primary mound were bundle or single skull interments. Scattered at various depths in the body of the primary and secondary mounds were over 100 others. Most of these were bundle burials, although a few primary flexed burials were among them.

The bulk of the pottery from the Englewood mound was in a great mortuary deposit on the mound base. This pottery had either been broken or intentionally perforated.

Ceramic arts.—Englewood pottery seems to offer a partial transition between Weeden Island II and Safety Harbor. The Englewood mound (So-1) is a case in point for such a transition, containing, as it does, ceramics of all three complexes. Nevertheless, Englewood is sufficiently distinctive to be considered as a separate pottery group. On the whole, it shows less imagination and variety than Weeden Island and is less well done both as to form and decoration. As compared to Safety Harbor it is better made, fired, shaped, and decorated although there is probably less range of variation in decoration than in Safety Harbor.

In addition to the characteristically Englewood types, others are noted, and some of these, undoubtedly, were also made by the Englewood potters. The Biscayne Series types are the most important of these. Glades Series types may also have been made locally as a result of Glades area influence.

The Englewood pottery types in the order in which they are described:

Englewood Series:
  Englewood Incised
  Englewood Plain
Sarasota Incised
Lemon Bay Incised

Type Descriptions

Type name.—ENGLEWOOD INCISED.
Definition as a type: This paper, from the Englewood site, Sarasota County.
Ware characteristics:
Method of manufacture: Apparently coiled.
Temper: Fine sand.
Paste texture and color: Fairly even and granular. Buff, gray, and black.
Surface texture, color, and finish: Usually buff-colored.
Hardness: 3 or harder.
Thickness: Averages 6 to 7 mm.
Decoration:
Technique: Medium-deep incisions and punctations.
Design: Usually rectilinear designs but with simple curvilinear elements sometimes combined. Interlocking rectilinear elements in which incised bands are alternately filled with teardrop-shaped punctations. Continuous crisscross or diamond elements in which band zones are left plain and background filled with teardrop or dot punctations. Zigzag incised bands or connected chevrons in which background is filled with punctations and chevrons are left plain. Rectangular panels with diagonal incised bands and backgrounds filled with punctations. Continuous curvilinear plain bands arranged S-fashion with punctated backgrounds. Vertical and diagonal bands alternately filled with punctations. (See fig. 61; pl. 46, *a, b;* pl. 47.)
Distribution: Covers either upper shoulder or most of exterior walls. Plain band at rim usually set off from decoration by one or more horizontal incised lines.
Form:
Total vessel: Cylindrical beakers, short-collared jars, simple jars, deep bowls or beaker-bowls, open bowls.
Rim: Direct and unmodified. May be outslanted or incurved. (See fig. 62.)
Lip: Flat or flat-round. One example of ticking on outer edge.
Base: Flat-circular most common.
Appendages: None known.
Geographical range of type: Known only from Sarasota County and immediately surrounding regions.
Chronological position of type: Probably occupies a position between Weeden Island II and Safety Harbor Periods, to some extent overlapping with both.
Relationships of type: Has resemblances to both Weeden Island Incised and Safety Harbor Incised. Also vague design resemblances to early types.
Bibliography: Willey (1948a).

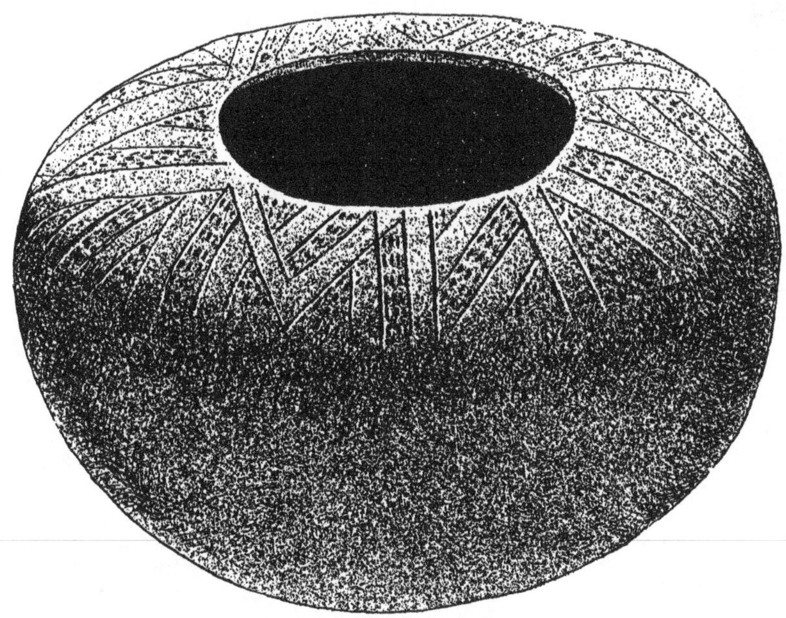

FIG. 61.—Englewood Period vessel. Englewood or Sarasota Incised. (Redrawn from Moore, 1903, fig. 83. Pithlochascootie. About ¼ actual size.)

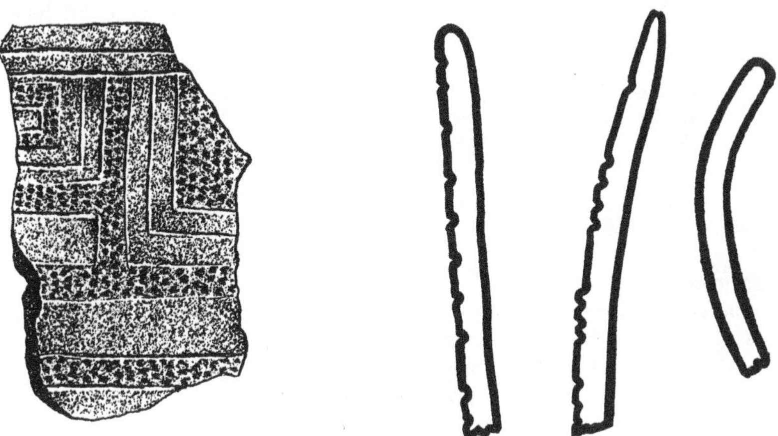

FIG. 62.—Englewood Period rim forms. Englewood Incised. (Interiors to right.)

Type name.—ENGLEWOOD PLAIN.

Definition as a type: From Englewood site, this paper.

Ware characteristics: (See Englewood Incised.)

Form: Boat-shaped bowls with small vertical rim projections at ends of long axis, simple bowls with slightly incurved rims, simple open bowls, and ollas or jars with short outflared collars. Rims are direct and unmodified or have slight marginal thickening. (Pl. 46, *d, e.*)

Range, period, and relationships: Parallels Englewood Incised.

Bibliography: Willey (1948a).

Type name.—SARASOTA INCISED.

Definition as a type: From Englewood site, Manatee region, and Tampa Bay, this paper.

Ware characteristics: This is a Biscayne or St. Johns type paste, soft and temperless. Core is gray-black and surfaces are buff. It is well smoothed, both in and out. Thickness averages 5 to 6 mm.

Decoration:

Technique: Medium to fine line incision and triangular-shaped or teardrop punctations made in soft vessel surface.

Design: Bands arranged diagonally to vertical axis of vessel and filled with punctations (fig. 61), interlocking rectilinear bands and chevron arrangements alternating plain and punctate-filled, triangles pendant from rim filled with punctations, and series of triangles point-to-point or nested and filled with punctations are the principal motives. (Pl. 46, *c;* pl. 48, *g, h.*)

Distribution: Vessel exterior. Tendency to restrict to upper part of vessel.

Form: Flattened-globular bowls, open bowls with slightly incurved rims, and pot forms. Rims unmodified. Lips flat to round-pointed.

Geographical distribution of type: Manatee region. Also north to Tampa Bay and beyond as a minority type. Occasionally has turned up in St. Johns area.

Chronological position of type: Weeden Island II, Englewood, and Safety Harbor Periods. May have a little greater time span, extending both earlier and later than Englewood Incised.

Relationships of type: Related to Biscayne-St. Johns and similar wares. Related to Englewood Incised. May have some relationship with St. Johns incised and punctated types.

Bibliography: Willey (1948a).

Type name.—LEMON BAY INCISED.

Definition as a type: Manatee region, this paper.

Ware characteristics: Sand-tempered ware averaging 3.5 to 4 on hardness scale. Well smoothed and often polished. Surface color from reddish buff to gray; core is sometimes gray-black.

Decoration:

Technique: Thin to medium wide and deep incised lines that have been made in vessel after clay had dried but before firing. Occasionally, lines look as though they are engraved, as they display fine fractured edges. Triangles and rectangles of paste are also cut out in champlévé fashion. (Pl. 48, *c-f.*)

Design: Composed of series of parallel lines about 5 to 10 mm. apart. May be arranged vertically, diagonally, or horizontally to rim. Elements essentially rectilinear, although some curvilinear segments are noted on some sherds. Data for over-all design patterns are lacking.

Form: Beakers. No rim modifications. Lip rounded.

Geographical range of type: Rare type. Found in Manatee region in small quantities. Occasional sherds occur on coast farther north.

Chronological position of type: Uncertain. Englewood Period and, possibly, Weeden Island II.

Relationships of type: Uncertain. Possibly to Weeden Island types such as St. Petersburg Incised.

Other arts and technologies.—Data are very few. In the Englewood mound were a few perforated conch-shell cups, a single *Busycon contrarium* hoe, some flint scrap, and a few pieces of red ocher.

Speculations on population and period duration.—Data are too limited to make any population estimates for this period. Apparently, sites of the period are not numerous, although this impression might be due to insufficient field survey. As a period, I have placed Englewood intermediate between Weeden Island II and Safety Harbor in the Manatee region. No attempt has been made to indicate the duration of the period, except that it was brief, probably lasting for a few decades after A. D. 1500. It is also possible that it continued for a time coeval with Safety Harbor.

THE SAFETY HARBOR PERIOD

Period definition.—The key types for the period are Safety Harbor Incised and Pinellas Incised. The Pinellas Series shows close relationship to Fort Walton Incised and Lake Jackson Plain of the Fort Walton Period, and there are also connections with the Leon-Jefferson Period of the northwest. Occasional Pensacola Series sherds occur in Safety Harbor contexts.

The sites.—There are a total of 25 sites of the period. Sixteen of these are pure sites; 9 are mixed.

Pure sites

- Temple mounds (and villages)
  - Safety Harbor (Pi-2)
  - Parrish mound 2 (Ma-2)
- Burial mounds:
  - Safety Harbor (Pi-2)
  - Johns Pass (Pi-4)
  - Bayview (Pi-7)
  - Seven Oaks (Pi-8)
  - Snavely (Hi-5)
  - Parrish mound 1 (Ma-1)

Parrish mound 2 (Ma-2)
Parrish mound 3 (Ma-3)
Whittaker site (So-4)
True site (So-5)
Gasparilla Sound (Ch-2)
Hickory Bluff (Ch-5)
Arcadia site (De-1)

Cemeteries:
Buzzard's Island (Ci-2)

Mixed sites

Middens:
Boca Ciega Island (Pi-6)
Rocky Point (Hi-7)
Shaws Point (Ma-7)

Burial mounds:
Bayport (He-1)
Thomas (Hi-1)
Picknick (Hi-3)
Jones (Hi-4)
Buck Island (Hi-6)

Cemeteries (and middens):
Pool Hammock (So-3)

Safety Harbor sites are found largely in the Manatee region but also extend north into the central coastal region. The areal demarcation between Fort Walton and Safety Harbor is not determined, but, presumably, it must fall somewhere near the Aucilla River boundary which separates the central from the northwest coasts. Buzzard's Island, the northernmost Safety Harbor site listed by this review, is atypical in that the marker type Safety Harbor Incised is not found and in that the burials are in a cemetery and not a mound. The diagnostic pottery at the site is, however, Pinellas Incised.

The disproportionately large number of burial mounds as compared with middens which the review shows is, undoubtedly, the result of sampling rather than a reflection of a cultural situation. Systematic midden-heap survey has not been conducted along the central or Manatee coasts.

Settlement pattern.—Safety Harbor village sites are middens, composed largely of shell, which are situated along the coast, bays, and rivers. The ecological picture is much the same as that observed for Weeden Island. There is little information on the size of Safety Harbor Period middens. Some of the midden sites around Tampa Bay and to the south are extensive although many of these were also occupied in other periods and the extent of the Safety Harbor occupation has not been determined. At Safety Harbor proper (Pi-2), a site which is reportedly of only the one period, the area of occupation is several hundred yards in range. This site is probably larger than most of those of the Safety Harbor Period, however.

Burial mounds are found near some of the middens. In other instances burial mounds have been described as being isolated from any evidences of habitation, but it is likely that a search would have revealed nearby middens. Usually the burial mounds are located singly, although in a few cases two or more mounds were found close together. These additional mounds may have been other burial tumuli or they may have been domiciliary mounds. The frequency and importance of house or temple mounds during the Safety Harbor Period are not fully known. That they did exist, however, is certain. The best example is the combined burial and temple mound at Parrish mound 2 (Ma-2). Another, which is quite probably Safety Harbor Period, but has not been explored, is the big flat-topped mound at Safety Harbor proper. The temple or house mound is not, judging from our reviewed sample of Safety Harbor sites, as numerous in Safety Harbor as in Fort Walton.

For the present, the Safety Harbor settlement-pattern data can best be summarized by saying that most communities were small. A village, or a little group of villages, maintained its own burial mound much as in the old Santa Rosa-Swift Creek or Weeden Island Periods. The temple-mound idea was known, and there is one large village site (Safety Harbor (Pi-2)) which has such a mound in addition to a burial mound. This site seems to have been much bigger than other villages of the period, being more comparable to a Fort Walton Period site. At another site (Parrish mound 2 (Ma-2)) is a mound which seems to have functioned both as a burial tumulus and as a temple substructure.

Economy.—Marine foods continued to be a major dietary item in this period. There is little doubt that the period was also agricultural.

Organization of society.—The trend toward political and religious cohesion estimated for the Fort Walton Period could also be said to extend to Safety Harbor but to a less marked degree. The large sites with temple mounds were known, but the pattern was not as common as it was farther to the north.

Disposal of the dead.—Most Safety Harbor burials were made in burial mounds. Such mounds were built by the Safety Harbor people for this purpose; also mounds of the earlier Weeden Island Period were utilized a second time by the Safety Harbor Indians. In form and structure, the burial mounds of the period were much like those of Weeden Island, being circular in outline, conical or dome-shaped in form, and ranging from 2 to 10 feet in height. Mound diameter varied from about 35 to 80 feet. Two mounds, Jones (Hi-4) and Parrish mound 3 (Ma-3) were partially surrounded with crescent-shaped sand embankments. Besides the mound burials, two cemetery sites are also reported. There is also one instance of burials in a mound which also served as a temple substructure (Parrish mound 2 (Ma-2)).

Secondary burial was the most common form of treatment. These were bundle, single skull, and mass burials. Some of the burial mounds contained only secondary burials; others had mixtures of secondary and primary burials, the latter being both extended and flexed types. In two mounds only primary burials are described. In most mounds, cremation, either complete or partial, was very rare; however, in the Parrish mound 2 (Ma-2), the combined temple and burial mound, masses of semicremated human bones were found in a submound pit as well as in the body of the mound. Two in situ cremations of primary burials were discovered in this same site. At the only cemetery site from which burials are described, Buzzard's Island (Ci-2), massed and scattered secondaries, and primary flexed and extended types are all listed.

The numbers of burials in the mounds and cemeteries ranged from as few as 15 to over 200.

Funerary artifacts consisted of pottery, nonceramic aboriginal artifacts, and articles of European provenience. Pottery vessels found in the mounds were usually "killed" by intentional perforation. In some cases they were arranged in special caches or deposits on mound base; in other instances they were placed with or inverted over individual skeletal remains. In most mounds, other artifacts, of shell or stone or of European manufacture, had been placed with individuals.

Cranial deformation does not seem to have been practiced during this period.

In general, we can say that Safety Harbor burial practices conform with Weeden Island more closely than do those of Fort Walton. Mound burial was customary with cemetery burial being rare. The best-known cemetery of the period is well to the north in Citrus County, approaching the Fort Walton region. Secondary treatment of the dead and the charnel house or bone-cleaning complex continued, and some primary inhumation was also followed. In the placement of a pottery vessel with or over the individual dead, Safety Harbor seems to be pursuing the same trend noted in Fort Walton.

Ceramic arts.—Safety Harbor pottery is generally poorly made, fired, and decorated. Shapes tend to be badly formed and designs vaguely conceived and executed with carelessness. Although there is quite a range of excellence or lack of excellence in Safety Harbor types, the best are usually below Weeden Island, Fort Walton, or Englewood standards and the worst are absurdly handled. The total feeling is one of break-down in the ceramic art, carrying with it the implications of an impoverishment of the cultural forces and traditions that served as an incentive and guide to the aboriginal pottery maker.

Two streams of influence are clearly seen. The one, represented in the type Safety Harbor Incised, follows out of old Weeden Island vessel form and decorative concepts; the other, seen best in the Pinellas types, is an offshoot of the Fort Walton style traditions and the Middle Mississippian impetus behind them. A minority representation of Lamar, or Lamar-like, Complicated Stamped pottery shows connections with the late Georgia period.

Biscayne types, particularly Biscayne Check Stamped, are also found in Safety Harbor Period sites and probably represent a continuation from Weeden Island II through the Englewood Period. Glades types, which may also have been made locally, are associated with the Safety Harbor Complex; but, like the Biscayne ware, are not diagnostic markers for the period.

The Safety Harbor types in the order in which they are described:

- Safety Harbor Series:
  - Safety Harbor Incised
  - Pinellas Plain
  - Pinellas Incised
- Lamar Complicated Stamped

Type Descriptions

Type name.—SAFETY HARBOR INCISED.

Definition as a type: From Tampa Bay and the Manatee region, this paper. Stirling (1936) gave this name to a general ware group, covering the entire Safety Harbor Series. Willey and Woodbury (1942, pp. 244-245) presented a synoptic description in which both Safety Harbor Incised and what is now Pinellas Incised were covered.

Ware characteristics:

Method of manufacture: Probably coiled.

Temper: Ranges from fine sand through medium-coarse sand to a clayey, possibly temperless paste.

Paste texture and color: Depending upon aplastic, paste ranges from granular and compact to coarse, contorted and laminated. The latter is crumbly and friable. Although lacking in temper particles there is no resemblance to the smooth, soft, even Biscayne ware. Paste color is usually brown.

Surface texture, color, and finish: Surface is rough and often crackles easily. Lumps of clay may extrude. Color is gray to brown to buff. Poorly smoothed on both surfaces with tooling marks in evidence.

Hardness: 2.5 to 3.

Thickness: 5 to 8 mm.

Fig. 63.—Safety Harbor Period vessels. All Safety Harbor Incised. (Drawn from photographs and sketches. Vessel *c*, from True Site; others from Arcadia site. Actual heights as follows: *a*, about 19 cm.; *b*, about 26 cm.; *c*, ?; *d*, about 26 cm.; *e*, ?; *f*, about 14 cm.)

Decoration:

Technique: Incised line and dot punctations made in soft or wet surface of vessel before firing.

Design: Crude and poorly drawn rectilinear and curvilinear designs which are essentially geometric. Volutes pendant from rim, concentric diamond elements (fig. 63, *e*), parallel lines in curvilinear formations, encircling wavy or zigzag bands (fig. 63, *b, f*), X-shaped elements with scroll ends (fig. 63, *c*), continuous intertwined bands, and filfot-cross elements (fig. 63, *a*). Punctations used as filler for designs or backgrounds. Punctations are also used to follow or outline incised line designs (fig. 63, *c*). Indentation or fluting and low-relief modeling are sometimes seen as decorative features (fig. 63, *e, f*). Portrayal of naturalistic designs is occasionally attempted but is always highly stylized. A serpent design, suggested by a highly conventionalized

FIG. 64.—Incised and punctated design from a Safety Harbor Period vessel. (From Parrish mound 3. Compare with pl. 54A.)

snake's rattle (fig. 63, *c*), is observed on one vessel, and serpent or feather symbolism is seen on another (fig. 64). (See pl. 49; pl. 52, *c-h;* pl. 54A, *a, b, e.*)

Distribution: Vessel exteriors. Usually neck and upper half of body. Sometimes most of body.

Form:

Total vessel: Bowls with slightly incurved rims, flattened-globular bowls, deep bowls with curious recurved rim and flat base, beaker-bowls, short-collared jars, long-collared jars, bottles.

Rim: Unmodified or slightly thickened.

Lip: Quite often flat, sometimes rounded.

Base: Usually rounded, but some are flat and circular.

Appendages: None.

Geographical range of type: Manatee region, Tampa Bay, and for an undisclosed distance north of Tampa Bay.

Chronological position of type: Safety Harbor Period.

Relationships of type: Descendant of Weeden Island Incised and, probably, Englewood Incised. Also has some relationship to Fort Walton in such features as bottle forms.

Bibliography: Stirling (1936); Willey and Woodbury (1942); Willey (1948a).

Type name.—PINELLAS PLAIN.

Definition as a type: Central Gulf Coast and Manatee regions, this paper.

Ware characteristics: (See Safety Harbor Incised.) As a rule, however, tends to be harder, more compact than Safety Harbor Incised.

Form:

Total vessel: Large open bowls with slightly incurved rims, casuela bowls (fig. 65, *a, b;* fig. 66, *d*), collared globular ollas, and pot forms (fig. 67).

Rim: Sometimes folded on exterior. Use of nodes and pinched punctations on or below rim (fig. 67). (See pl. 50, *a-d, f;* pl. 52, *b.*)

Lip: Characteristically has deep to slight indentations, crimping, or ticking on exterior edge.

Base: Probably rounded.

Appendages: Small, vertically placed loop handles with nodes at top, crude effigy (?) handles with nodes, large, ovate horizontal rim projections.

Geographical range of type: Manatee and central coast regions. May extend farther north than Safety Harbor Incised.

Chronological position of type: Safety Harbor Period.

Relationships of type: Closest relative is Lake Jackson Plain.

Type name.—PINELLAS INCISED.

Definition as a type: From central coast and Manatee regions, this paper.

Ware characteristics: (See Safety Harbor Incised.) Also tends to be harder, more compact than Safety Harbor Incised.

Decoration:

Technique: Medium to broad line incision and small to large dot punctations made in soft or wet paste of vessel before firing.

Design: Much more limited in range than Safety Harbor Incised. Single line arcade encircling vessel below rim with a row of heavy, often rectangular, punctations above is a common motif. Rectilinear-curvilinear guilloche or meander with background sometimes filled by punctations (fig. 65, *b, c;* fig. 66, *b*) (this motif is quite similar to Fort Walton Incised), parallel incised lines and volutes, and running scrolls or wavy bands (fig. 66, *a, c*) composed of two or three lines are other designs. In general, execution is slovenly. (Pl. 51; pl. 52, *a;* pl. 53, *a.*)

Distribution: Almost always confined to upper exterior portion of vessel.

Form:

Total vessel: Big collared ollas or bowls, simple open bowls with slightly incurved or straight rims, and casuela bowls.

Rim: Unmodified or slightly thickened.

Lip: Indentations or pinchings on exterior rim edge.

Base: Rounded.

Appendages: Vertical loop handles with nodes at top.

Geographical range of type: Central Gulf Coast and Manatee regions.

Chronological position of type: Safety Harbor Period.

Relationships of type: Closest relative is Fort Walton Incised.

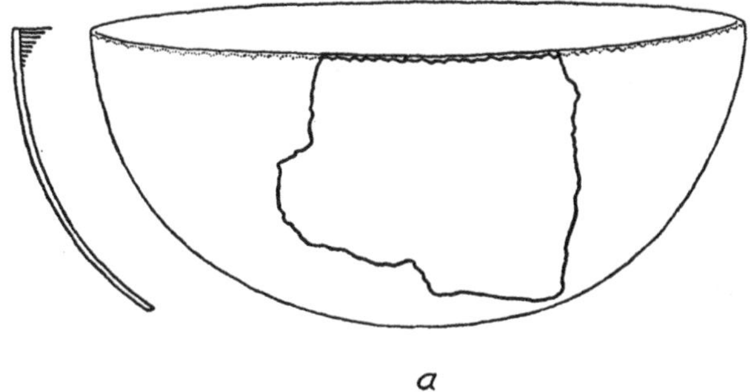

a

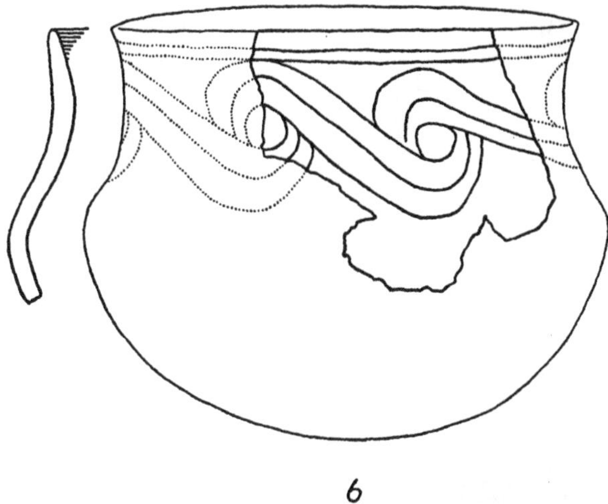

b

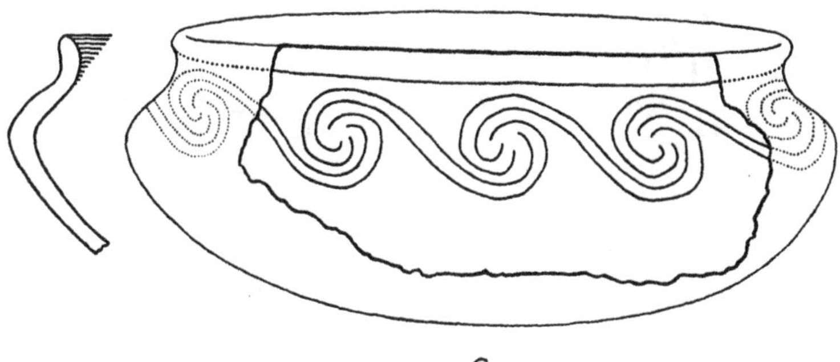

c

Fig. 65.—Safety Harbor Period rims and vessel forms. *a*, Pinellas Plain; *b*, *c*, Pinellas Incised.

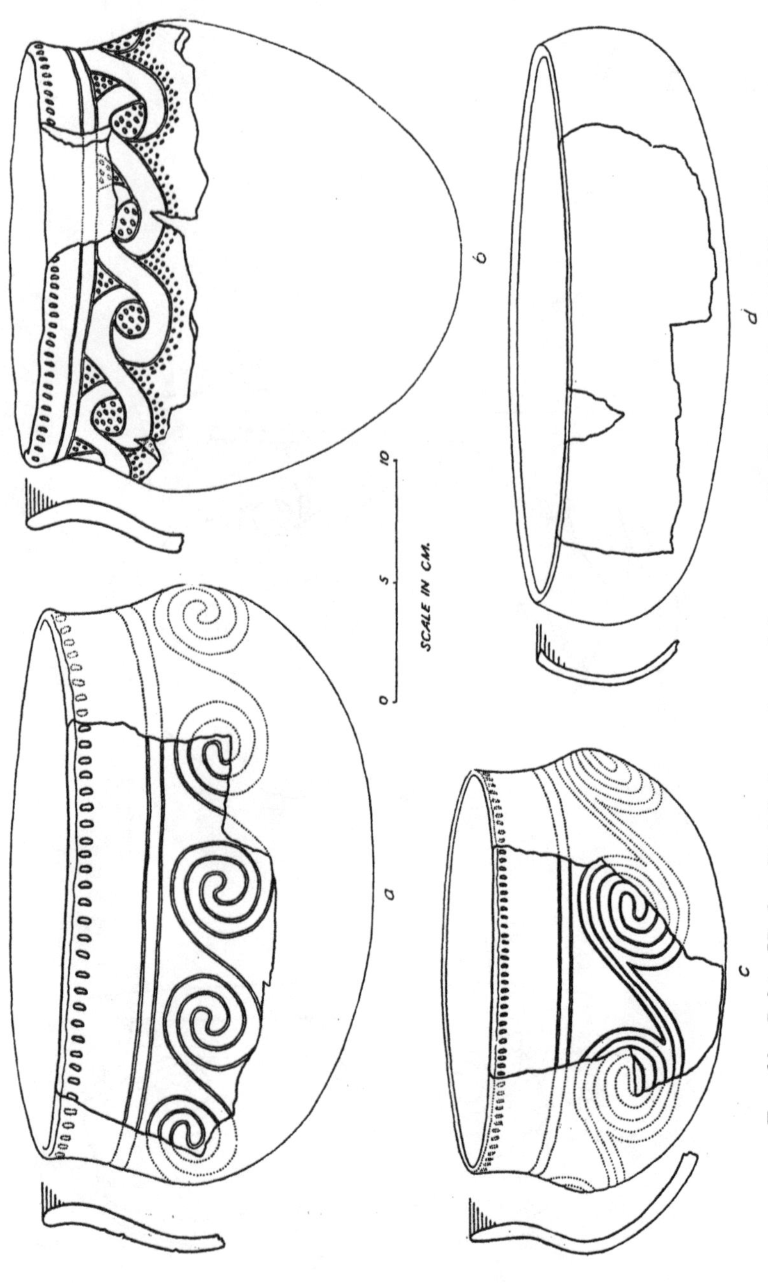

FIG. 66.—Safety Harbor Period rims and vessel forms. *a–c*, Pinellas Incised; *d*, Pinellas Plain.

Type name.—LAMAR COMPLICATED STAMPED.

Definition as a type: From central Georgia by Kelly (1938, pp. 46-47). Described in detail by Jennings and Fairbanks (1939) and briefly by Willey (1939, p. 144). A similar type has been described from the Georgia Coast by Caldwell and Waring (1939: type Irene Filfot

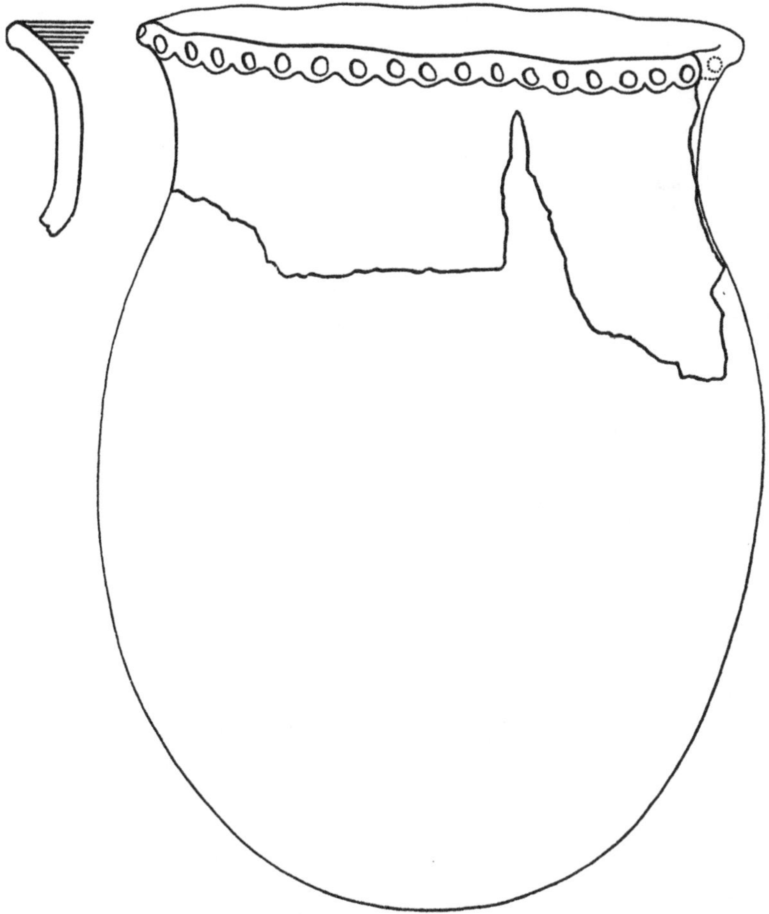

FIG. 67.—Safety Harbor Period rim and vessel reconstruction. Pinellas Plain.

Stamped). Brief description in this report is based upon these earlier descriptions and upon a few vessels and sherds from Tampa Bay and the Manatee region.

Ware characteristics: A coiled, sand- and grit-tempered ware. Varying in hardness from 3 to 5. Thickness of body about 8 mm., with rims and bases thicker.

Decoration: Impressions of carved-paddle or stamping unit. Designs are complicated and composed of curvilinear and rectilinear elements. The

Florida specimens from the Parrish Mounds (Ma-1 and Ma-3) show a circle-and-dot and a complicated connected-rectangle design. (Pl. 53, *c;* pl. 54A, *c.*)

Form: Pot forms slightly constricted below orifice but with outflaring rims. Bases rounded. Rim is folded and then pinched or crimped. (Applies to Florida specimens under discussion.)

Geographical range of type: Lamar Complicated Stamped is found throughout most of Georgia and into adjacent Alabama and South Carolina. Similar types are seen in North Carolina and eastern Tennessee. In Florida it occurs as far south as Tampa Bay, but these occurrences may be only the result of trade. Eastern extension in Florida not well known but probably occurs there only as trade if at all.

Chronological position of type: In Georgia it is the marker type for the Lamar Period in central Georgia, a period believed to be about contemporaneous with Fort Walton. On the Georgia coast Lamar Complicated Stamped or closely related types continue later than this. Florida Gulf Coast occurrences are in the Safety Harbor Period.

Relationships of type: Most likely a Georgia import and not a Floridian development out of Swift Creek Complicated Stamped. In Georgia the type probably developed out of the earlier complicated stamped types such as Swift Creek and Napier. The Lamar influence in Florida may be responsible for the very late Jefferson stamped types of the Leon-Jefferson Period.

Bibliography: Kelly (1938); Willey (1939); Jennings and Fairbanks (1939); Caldwell and Waring (1939).

Other arts and technologies.—The Safety Harbor peoples had no craft skills in which they excelled those of the other culture periods of the Gulf Coast. As stated, their ceramics were decidedly inferior to Weeden Island. Their techniques in stone chipping are about on a par with those of Weeden Island although they seem to have produced fewer large, fine blades. Smaller projectile points of several varieties were made in quantity, however. Large and medium-size stemmed points vary from triangular to ovate-triangular in form and may or may not have shoulder barbs. Small, stemless triangular points, the common late period point in many parts of the Southeast, are frequent. Larger stemless points are also present as are a variety of knives, scrapers, and drills. (See pl. 54B; pl. 55; pl. 56; pl. 57, *a-u;* pl. 59, *d, e.*) Stone plummets are found in the mounds but not in great numbers (pl. 59, *c*). Stone celts, on the other hand, are either absent or extremely rare. Minerals are scarce, red ocher and lump kaolin being the only ones recorded. Shell tools and weapons are more common than in previous periods except for Perico Island. *Busycon* picks and hammers and conch cups and dippers were found in most of the Safety Harbor mounds. Plummet-type pendants and beads (pl. 59, *g, h*) were made of shell.

The scarcity of complicated stamped pottery suggests a possible decline in woodworkers' arts, but in one of the Safety Harbor mounds a piece of charred, carved wood was found which, from the nature of its design, indicates the retention of carving skills (pl. 59, *i-l*). No aboriginal smoking pipes are known from the burial mounds or middens of the period, but one elbow-type pipe was found in the Buzzard's Island (Ci-2) cemetery in Citrus County. Native metalwork with indigeneous metals is not recorded, but European trade metals had been reworked to form various ornaments (pl. 58, *g*). Imported European objects taken from wrecked Spanish ships, or traded south from early settlements, were common to many of the mounds. These include actual manufactures such as iron axes, swords, knives, guns, olive jars, glass seed beads, larger glass beads (pl. 58, *e*), glass pendants (pl. 58, *f*), copper and brass ornaments (pl. 59, *b*), and clay pipes (pl. 57, *v-x*). Bone or tortoise-shell combs (pl. 58, *a, b;* pl. 59, *a*) are probably also of Spanish manufacture. Sheet silver rolled into tubular beads (pl. 58, *d*), sheet gold fashioned into cones (pl. 58, *c*), and miscellaneous sheet-metal ornaments are native reworkings of imported materials or objects.

The abundance of Safety Harbor artifacts of chipped stone may partly be explained by the natural sources of flint which the Indians had near at hand in the vicinity of Tampa Bay. It may also partly be explained by a greater continued dependence upon hunting as a means of livelihood than was the case in the northwest with the Fort Walton culture. However, neither of these explanations are fully satisfactory as the previous Weeden Island Periods in the Tampa Bay section do not produce an abundance of chipped-flint work. The absence of ground-stone axes may simply be due to the absence of suitable stone this far south. In the northwest the Indians were much closer to the sources of supply in the southern Appalachians. Stone celts were replaced in the south by the *Busycon* hammer and pick tool. This shell pick or hammer is a characteristic Glades area artifact and was common in the Manatee region during the Perico Island Period. Although not commonly used by the Weeden Island peoples it seems to have been taken up in the later Safety Harbor Period. European trade goods appear to have had a greater effect upon the Safety Harbor Indians than upon those of the Fort Walton Period. Foreign metals and glass beads replaced native craft ornaments to a very large extent, and the old smoking complex was continued almost entirely with European pipes.

Speculations on population and period duration.—Estimates on Safety Harbor Period population have been made much as those for Santa Rosa-Swift Creek or Weeden Island. Our site review shows 18 burial mounds built or used by the Safety Harbor people. Multiplying this by 4 gives us a total of 72 as a possible maximum number of mounds. Computing three villages to one burial mound brings us to a total of 216 village communities. This multiplied by 30 persons per community totals about 6,000. This figure refers principally to the Tampa Bay district and the Manatee region, as very few Safety Harbor Period sites are known north of Pinellas County.

The dating and duration of the Safety Harbor Period is conditioned by the dates assigned to the Fort Walton and Leon-Jefferson cultures. Archeological and ethnohistorical data indicate a range of from about A. D. 1500 to 1725.

THE LEON-JEFFERSON PERIOD

Period definition.—This period is just emerging as a result of very recent field work (see H. G. Smith, 1948). The diagnostic pottery types are Mission Red Filmed, Aucilla Incised, and a series of complicated stamped types referred to as Jefferson ware. Minority types indicate connections to other late periods in the Southeast. These are Ocmulgee Fields Incised, Lamar Complicated Stamped, and Alachua Cob-marked. There is continuity with the Fort Walton Period as seen in the presence of the types Fort Walton Incised and Leon Check Stamped.

European trade items are also a diagnostic of the period. Spanish olive-jar fragments, glass, and various metal objects are common. The sites of the Leon-Jefferson Period were Spanish-Indian settlements operated by the Franciscan monks between 1650 and 1725.[77]

The sites.—Three pure sites of the complex are known from the present review.

Pure sites
- Middens:
  - San Luis Mission (Le-4)
  - Pine Tuft (Je-1)
  - Scott Miller place (Je-2)

All these sites are in northwest Florida in Leon and Jefferson Counties.

[77] H. G. Smith (1948) notes that in 1633 the Franciscans began to establish a chain of missions from St. Augustine to the Apalachicola River. They were in full operation by at least 1650. In 1704 the Apalachee mission Indians were virtually destroyed by Col. James Moore of South Carolina. It is likely that within 20 years after this date all the Apalachee were gone and the missions abandoned.

Settlement pattern.—Settlements of this period were built around the nucleus of a Spanish mission, trading post, or fort. There are no outstanding aboriginal monuments such as mounds. The living communities of which we have knowledge are all located inland in fertile farm country. They are hilltop villages from which the natives worked the crops grown in the vicinity of each site. The average size of individual sites has not been determined fully, but the ones that I have observed appear to have included an area of perhaps 200 meters in diameter.

Concerning one site, the Scott Miller place (Je-2), Smith (1948, p. 316) writes:

> The excavated mission had buildings constructed by the wattle and daub technique with hewn and split log framework and roof construction. The woodwork was secured by wrought iron nails. The mission complex was made up of two buildings and a borrow-refuse pit. The larger of the two structures was composed of two rooms with a surrounding patio wall. This complex measured 58 x 39 feet. The smaller building was probably an aboriginal abode, a stable, or some other minor building. This building measured 19 x 16 feet and did not have heavy construction or very high wattle and daub walls. Presumably most of this building was thatched.

Economy.—Agriculture was probably practiced in the old way but under the eyes of the priests and other Europeans.

Organization of society.—The mission church undoubtedly was the focal point of the new society of this period. In a way, this provided a continuity, to which the Indians were undoubtedly accustomed, of secular and sacred control being held in the hands of the same authorities. The old war patterns were probably extinguished or suppressed. The easy defeat of these mission Indians at the hands of the Creeks under Moore may, in part, be attributed to this change of habits.

Disposal of the dead.—No data are available. One would surmise, however, that inhumation as primary extended burials in Christian cemeteries was the custom.

Ceramic arts.—Pottery making continued in this period, although the vigor and skill of Weeden Island, Fort Walton, or even Safety Harbor was lost. Technical standards of manufacture and firing seem to have suffered less than those of form or decoration. This is, of course, to be expected, as the latter were features more intimately tied up with aboriginal tribal lore and religion. Nevertheless, the decorative techniques and vessel forms that persist in Leon-Jefferson have roots in earlier periods and can be traced back to these. Incised pottery shows some similarity to Fort Walton types, with Fort Walton Incised continuing in small percentages. Plain pottery also shows a relationship to the Fort Walton Period, and check stamped and complicated stamped wares are known.

One interesting aspect of the ceramics of the period is in the effects of European pottery styles. This is seen, for example, in the ring-base plate form.

The Leon-Jefferson pottery types have been described briefly by Smith (1948), and the present descriptions, with a few noted exceptions, are based upon his work. The principal Leon-Jefferson types in the order in which they are described are:

Mission Red Filmed
Miller Plain
Aucilla Incised
Leon Check Stamped
Jefferson ware

In addition there are a number of types which appear to be trade influences, either from Georgia or from the east. These are, in order of their description:

Lamar Bold Incised
Ocmulgee Fields Incised
Alachua Series: [78]
  Alachua Plain
  Alachua Cob-marked
  Prairie Cord-marked

The type Fort Walton Incised which occurs in this complex has been described with the types of the Fort Walton Period. Smith (1948, p. 316) also lists a Gritty Plain ware which he does not describe. Presumably this is a type comparable to Residual Plain.

Type Descriptions

Type name:—MISSION RED FILMED.
Definition as a type: From Jefferson County, by H. G. Smith (1948).
Description: Apparently a hard, grit-tempered ware with smooth, highly polished surfaces. Plate forms have interior decoration in red-painted zones, and cups and small globular jars are completely red-slipped. These red surfaces are fired and highly burnished. The plate with an annular ring base is the most common form.

At the present, the type is known for Leon and Jefferson Counties and dates from the Leon-Jefferson Period. The type is related to other historic period types such as Kasita Red Filmed (Fairbanks, 1940) and red filmed types of the St. Augustine Period (Smith, 1948).
Bibliography: Smith (1948); Fairbanks (1940).

---

[78] Smith (1948, p. 316) lists only Alachua Cob-marked as appearing in Leon-Jefferson sites. Goggin (1948a) considers the other two Alachua types to be approximately coeval, at least in part.

Type name.—MILLER PLAIN.

Definition as a type: From Jefferson County, by H. G. Smith (1948).

Description: A sand- and grit-tempered ware with a compact paste and hard surfaces. Vessel forms are similar to those of the Ocmulgee Fields Complex of Georgia (Kelly, 1938, pp. 56-57; Jennings and Fairbanks, 1939; Fairbanks, 1940). The most common shape is a shallow bowl with incurved, straight, or flaring rim; flat or rounded lip; and a rounded, flat or annular base. Other forms are the plate, bottle, casuela bowl, lugged shallow bowl, and European-influenced pitcher shape.

The type is known for Leon and Jefferson Counties and dates from the Leon-Jefferson Period. Its affiliations are with the related types of the complex and with the plain wares of the Ocmulgee Fields Complex.

Bibliography: Smith (1948); Kelly (1938, pp. 56-57); Jennings and Fairbanks (1939; type Ocmulgee Fields Incised); Fairbanks (1940; various types of Ocmulgee Fields Complex).

Type name.—AUCILLA INCISED.

Definition as a type: From Jefferson County, by H. G. Smith (1948).

Description: Ware is apparently much the same as Miller Plain. The decoration is composed of two to five parallel incised lines, which may or may not dip to form a loop design encircling rim of vessel; chevron designs and various other rectilinear and curvilinear designs, which may or may not have the background filled by punctates, also occur. Punctates are usually placed below the lip. Shallow-bowl and casuela forms are represented. Rims are usually incurved with lip flat or rounded. Lip lugs noted. (See fig. 68, *a-d.*)

Leon and Jefferson Counties of northwest Florida. Type dates in the Leon-Jefferson Period. Has close resemblances to Ocmulgee Fields Incised (Jennings and Fairbanks, 1939); and to Lamar Bold Incised (Jennings and Fairbanks, 1939); and to Pinellas Incised.

Bibliography: Smith (1948); Jennings and Fairbanks (1939).

Type name.—LEON CHECK STAMPED.

Definition as a type: Northwest Florida, this paper.

Ware characteristics: Sand and coarse-grit temper. Black paste core and buff surfaces. Thickness ranges from 8 to 10 mm.

Decoration:

Technique: Impression of checked or grid-bar stamping medium into soft surface of vessel (fig. 68 *k*).

Design: Individual checks average about 1 cm. in diameter. The lands are sometimes low and faint, sometimes wide and heavy. Checks are diamond-shaped on some specimens. Some specimens appear to have been slightly smoothed after stamping which tends to blur and obscure the lands. Sometimes fingernail punctations occur on collar. (Pl. 60, *a-c.*)

Distribution: Vessel exterior. Extent unknown.

Form: Outflared rims, round-pointed lips.

Geographical range of type: Through northwest Florida but centering in Leon and Jefferson Counties. Occasionally found in central Gulf Coast region.

Chronological position of type: Leon-Jefferson Period but also found in Fort Walton and Safety Harbor contexts as a minority type.

Relationships of type: Probably a development out of Wakulla Check Stamped.

Bibliography: Mentioned by Smith (1948).

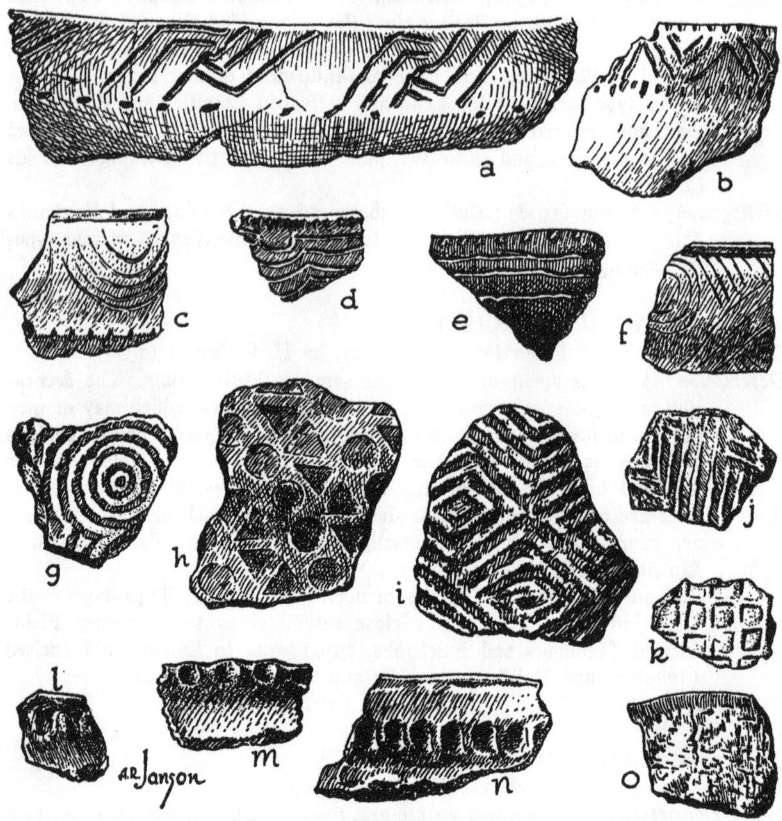

FIG. 68.—Leon-Jefferson Period and associated sherd types. *a-d,* Aucilla Incised; *e,* Fort Walton Incised; *f,* Ocmulgee Fields Incised; *g-j, l-n,* Jefferson ware; *k,* Leon Check Stamped; *o,* Alachua Cob-marked. From northwest Florida. (After Smith, 1948, pl. 32.)

Type name.—JEFFERSON WARE.

Definition: Not a type in the usual sense but a series of types as yet undifferentiated into separate type divisions. Defined by H. G. Smith (1948) from Jefferson County.

Ware characteristics: Paste compact with laminations occurring along vessel wall in some cases. Temper is grit and sand as a rule but occasionally coarse quartz or crushed sherds. Surfaces are smoothed. Core is gray, brown, or black. Hardness ranges from 3.5 to 5.

Decoration: There are one plain and four complicated stamped types within the ware group. These stamped types include the following motifs: (1) concentric rectilinear figures; (2) concentric circles with raised-dot centers; (3) a pattern of triangles and circles; and (4) herringbone figures. The plain type is characterized by a pinched or punctated rim which has sometimes been folded over before pinching treatment. (See fig. 68, *g-j, l-n;* pl. 60, *d-f.*)

General relationships: The complicated stamped types have strong similarities to the Lamar Complicated Stamped type of Georgia (Jennings and Fairbanks, 1939). There are also similarities to late Swift Creek Complicated Stamped and to the other complicated stamped types of the Swift Creek and Weeden Island Periods. The reappearance of a rather degenerate complicated stamped series in the Leon-Jefferson Period is something of a puzzle in terms of sequence continuity. For the most part, complicated stamped dies out in Gulf Florida, especially northwest Florida, during the Weeden Island II Period and is virtually absent in the Fort Walton Period. Complicated stamped pottery in the Leon-Jefferson Period would not, in view of this break in the sequence continuity, appear to be a local development out of Florida Late Swift Creek. It seems much more likely, in the light of present evidence, to have been a secondary introduction of the complicated stamping idea into Florida from Georgia at the end or close of the Fort Walton Period and the beginning of the Leon-Jefferson Period.

The plain ware of the Jefferson Series, represented by the pinched or punctated rims, has its closest parallels with Lake Jackson Plain of the Fort Walton Period, out of which it probably developed, and with Pinellas Plain of the Safety Harbor Period, which may have exerted an influence upon it during their parallel growth.

Bibliography: Smith (1948).

Type name.—LAMAR BOLD INCISED.

Definition as a type: From central Georgia, by Kelly (1938, pp. 47-48); and by Jennings and Fairbanks (1939).

Description: A grit-tempered ware decorated with broad incised lines, hollow-reed punctations, and, rarely, dot punctations. Curvilinear designs (scrolls) usually combined with rectilinear elements, particularly horizontal lines between scrolls. Some rectilinear elements stand alone. A row of hollow-reed punctates is usually placed at base of the incised decoration which is a border around upper portion of the vessel. The forms of casuela bowls, on which the incised designs occur, are often covered on the base with Lamar-type complicated stamping.

Geographical distribution of type: Georgia, eastern Alabama, and parts of the Carolinas. In northwest Florida only as occasional pieces.

Chronological position of type: The Lamar Period in Georgia, particularly the latter part of the period. In northwest Florida it occurs in the Leon-Jefferson Period.

Relationships of type: Is related to Fort Walton Incised. May be ancestral, in part, to Ocmulgee Fields Incised and Aucilla Incised.

Bibliography: Kelly (1938, pp. 47-48); Jennings and Fairbanks (1939); Willey (1939).

Type name.—OCMULGEE FIELDS INCISED.

Definition as a type: By Kelly (1938, p. 56), from central Georgia, and by Jennings and Fairbanks (1939).

Description: A grit-tempered ware in which, very rarely, crushed shell is used. Is orange-buff to light brown or brown on surfaces with darker paste core. Smoothed surfaces show tooling marks, and there is a possibility of a light clay wash. Decorated with narrow incised lines which appear to have been partially smoothed over. Designs are scrolls, guilloches, combined scrolls and straight lines, chevron elements, and horizontal lines parallel to lip. Decoration confined to rim area of casuela forms or the upper and interior surfaces of flaring rims on open bowls. Rims insloped or incurved on casuelas, outflared on open bowls. Lips rounded or flat-round and generally thickened on exterior edge by slight protruberance. (See fig. 68, *f*.)

Geographical range of type: Jennings and Fairbanks (1939) report type for most of Georgia. Its Florida diffusion seems rather limited, being mainly in north or northwest near Georgia boundaries.

Chronological position of type: Dates from Ocmulgee Fields Period at Macon (ca. 1650-1750 and later). In Leon and Jefferson Counties, Fla., it is a minority type of the Leon-Jefferson Period. This is approximately coeval with the Georgia dating.

Relationships of type: Related to Aucilla Incised which is contemporaneous. Probably a development out of Lamar Bold Incised.

Bibliography: Kelly (1938, p. 58); Jennings and Fairbanks (1939).

Type name.—ALACHUA PLAIN.

Definition as a type: By Goggin from vicinity of Gainesville in central Florida (Goggin, 1948a). This description follows his.

Ware characteristics: Coiled ware. Tempered with medium-grain quartz sand. Fairly uniform paste texture but with some lamination. Gray, buff, or dark brown color range. Poorly smoothed surface.

Form: Simple bowls with unmodified rims.

Geographical range of type: Around Gainesville.

Chronological position of type: May occur as early as Weeden Island and Fort Walton Periods, extending into Leon-Jefferson.

Type name.—ALACHUA COB-MARKED.

Description: After Goggin (1948a). An Alachua Series ware. Surface is poorly smoothed and marked with corncob. Pattern of corncob stamping may be rows of parallel marks (in pairs) up to 1.5 cm. apart, or they may be so close together as to be overlapping, or the marking may be haphazard. Treatment applied to all parts of vessel exterior. Found in vicinity of Gainesville and west to Jefferson County. A very late type, contemporaneous with Leon-Jefferson Period, but may occur earlier. (See fig. 68, *o*.)

Type name.—PRAIRIE CORD-MARKED.

Description: After Goggin (1948a). Ware same as Alachua Plain. Cord impressions usually formed by rows of medium to small cords impressed with a cord-wrapped paddle (?). They may be parallel, crisscrossed, or haphazardly applied. Apparently applied over all of vessel exterior. Simple bowl forms and globular bowls. Rims are unmodified. Found in vicinity of Gainesville. Probably coeval with Alachua Cob-marked and also may be somewhat earlier.

Other arts and technologies.—Native crafts of the missionized Indian culture of the Leon-Jefferson Period, in addition to pottery making, are reflected in the following types of artifacts which Smith (1948, p. 316) reports from the Scott Miller site (Je-3): Small and large triangular projectile points and large notched points; chipped-stone scrapers with blunt scraping edge; discoidal stones, which he says are not "chunkee" stones; grinding or smoothing stones; hones; corn pounders; and mauls. This rather small inventory reveals that some of the former pursuits, such as hunting and agriculture, were carried on in the ways of the past. Significantly, ceremonial objects of stone, shell, wood, mica, or native metals are absent. Smith lists such European ornamental or ceremonial items as a metal ring and a crucifix. Other Spanish artifacts, but of a utility nature, were olive jars, glazed pottery, glass bottles, a spur rowel, a flintlock striker, guns, an ax, and various household items. (See pl. 60, *g-i*, for comparable items.)

Speculations on population and period duration.—Estimates for the Leon-Jefferson period are much less speculative than those of the other culture periods. The archeological manifestations are well identified with the Spanish missions established among the Apalachee Indians. For the mid-seventeenth century, when the missions were at their peak, Swanton has estimated a total population of 5,000 Indians (Swanton, 1946, p. 91). By 1704, the year in which most of the missions were destroyed, this figure had dropped to 2,000. During the intervening period the Indians were clustered about nine mission stations (Swanton, 1922, p. 110).

Period duration for the Leon-Jefferson culture is relatively brief and accurate. We know that the missions were introduced into the Apalachee country in 1633 and largely destroyed in 1704. Allowing a few years for the transition from the essentially aboriginal Fort Walton Period culture to the European-Indian Leon-Jefferson culture, and a few more for the final subsidence of Leon-Jefferson, we have set the beginning date at 1650 and the terminal date at 1725.

APPENDIX A: CLASSIFICATION OF FLORIDA GULF COAST VESSEL FORMS

Vessels are described here under a series of descriptive headings and organized under various categories. There are three main categories: (1) basic forms; (2) composite forms; and (3) effigy forms. The basic forms include the bowl, jar, beaker, beaker-bowl, bottle, and pot. Under each of these are a number of subdivisions. Composite forms are those which, in various ways, combine the basic forms. These are defined as compartment vessels, multiple-orifice vessels, composite-silhouette vessels, and pedestal vessels. Under each are subdivisions. The effigy forms duplicate the basic and composite forms in most cases, but they are treated separately in order to emphasize their effigy quality. They include effigy-affixation, semi-effigy, complete-effigy, and lobed forms. Each is, in turn, subdivided.

These are the descriptive types, for vessel forms, used throughout the report. They apply to the ceramics of all periods. The classification is based principally upon the C. B. Moore collections.

Basic Forms

Bowls: Vessels whose maximum diameter is greater than their width but which have appreciable side walls. Orifice may be open or constricted. Bottoms are usually rounded but may be slightly flattened at the center of base.

Simple bowl.—A medium-deep bowl with maximum diameter at or near orifice. Walls are vertical or slightly incurved. Bottoms rounded or flat-round. Size range 10 to 22 cm. in diameter with average at 14 cm. Height approximately 3/5 of diameter. Common. (Fig. 69, *a.*)

Globular bowl with flared orifice.—A deep bowl with globular body and outslanted or outflared upper walls. There is considerable variation in the upper wall segment. Bottoms are rounded or flat-rounded. Size range 12 to 21 cm. in diameter with average about 16 cm. Height approximately $\frac{4}{5}$ to $\frac{5}{6}$ of diameter. Moderately common. (Fig. 69, *b.*)

Shallow bowl or dish.—A very shallow bowl with outslanted or slightly outcurved sides. Bottoms are flat-rounded. Size range 33 to 16.5 cm. in diameter. Height approximately $\frac{1}{4}$ or less of diameter. Rare. (Fig. 69, *c.*)

Shallow bowl with lateral expansions.—A shallow bowl with maximum diameter from tip to tip of lateral expansions around orifice. Midwalls curve outward. Lateral expansions or projections may turn slightly upward. Bottom flat-rounded. Size range 17 to 35 cm., with average 25 cm. Height $\frac{1}{4}$ of diameter or less. Common. (Fig. 69, *d.*)

Flattened-globular bowl.—A medium-deep to deep bowl with maximum diameter at about midpoint of vessel and with inturned sides and

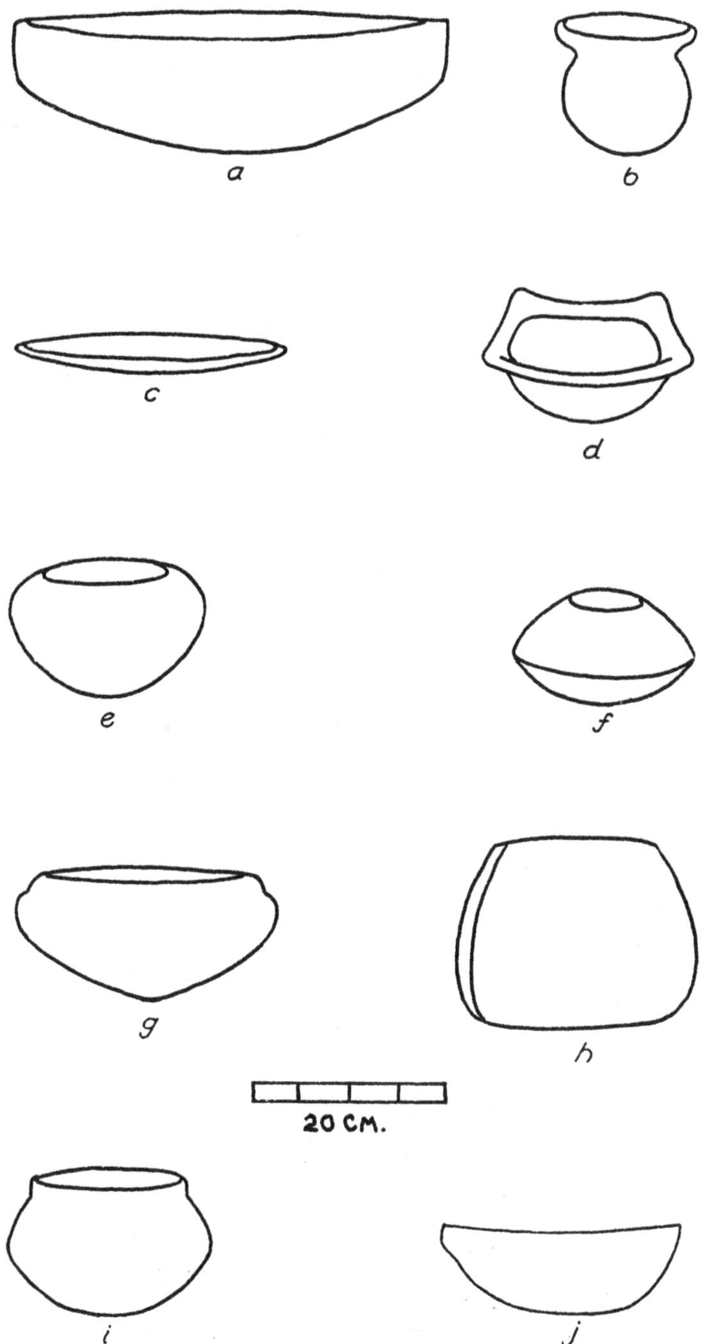

FIG. 69.—Florida Gulf Coast vessel form classification. Bowls. *a*, simple; *b*, globular bowl with flared orifice; *c*, shallow bowl or dish; *d*, shallow bowl with lateral expansion; *e*, *f*, flattened-globular bowl; *g*, casuela bowl; *h*, squared flattened-globular bowl; *i*, collared globular bowl; *j*, boat-shaped bowl.

constricted orifice. Walls curve inward with varying degrees of abruptness. Some bowls of this class have sharp-angled shoulder. Orifice modified, if at all, only by rim thickening or folding, not by collar or neck. Bottom usually rounded or flat-rounded, occasionally flat at center of base. Size range 9 to 35 cm. in diameter, with average about 18 cm. (Only a few specimens are over 25 cm. in diameter). Height varies from ½ to almost the equivalent of the diameter. Tends to grade into simple jar form. Common. (Fig. 69, *e, f.*)

Squared flattened-globular bowl.—Very similar to flattened-globular bowl form except for the distinguishing characteristic of squared base and body. The portion of the bowl above the point of maximum diameter is rarely as definitely squared as the base or lower part of the body although the corners may be marked. Bottom is flat. Size range 13 to 20 cm. in diameter, with average 16 cm. Height from ½ to ¾ of diameter. Moderately common. (Fig. 69, *h.*)

Casuela bowl.—A medium-deep bowl with maximum diameter somewhat above the midpoint. Upper walls are inturned less markedly than in the case of the flattened-globular bowl. In some cases there is a slight inset or indentation of the upper walls above the shoulder. The orifice is slightly constricted, but is, proportionately, much larger than in the case of the flattened-globular bowl. Bottom rounded or flat-rounded. Size range 13 to 48 cm. in diameter with average at 30 cm. Height ½ to ⅗ of diameter. Common. (Fig. 69, *g.*)

Collared globular bowl.—A deep globular bowl with incurving walls which constrict at the base of a short neck or collar. The collar may be outturned, inslanted, or straight. The maximum vessel diameter is at midpoint on body. Orifice varies from almost the equivalent of maximum diameter to ½ maximum diameter. Bottom rounded, flat-rounded, or occasionally flattened at center of base. Size range 9 to 26 cm. in diameter, with average of 18 cm. Height from ⅘ to equivalent of diameter. Moderately common. (Fig. 69, *i.*)

Boat-shaped bowl.—Medium-deep or shallow bowl which is oval or ovate-rectangular in form. Vessel walls usually outslanted or straight. Bases are usually flat-rounded. Both diameters considerably greater than height. Moderately common. (Fig. 69, *j.*)

Jars: Vessels whose total height is greater than maximum diameter and whose walls curve inward to a constricted orifice or to a constriction at the base of a collar or neck. They may or may not have a collar. Bottoms are rounded, flat-rounded, or flat.

Simple jar.—A jar without a collar. Maximum diameter may be at, above, or below the midpoint of the vessel. Walls incurve or inslant to a constricted orifice. There is considerable variation in the proportional size of the orifice. Bottoms are round, flat-rounded, or flat. Size range, 7 to 22 cm. in diameter, with average 13 cm. Height greater than diameter by ratio of 6-5 to 2-1. Common. (Fig. 70, *a.*)

Short-collared jar.—A jar with a short collar. Collar may be straight or outflaring so that the diameter of the orifice equals that of the maximum diameter of the body. Maximum diameter of body is usually about at midpoint. Collars are ¼ to ⅕ of the total vessel height. Bottoms are round, flat-round, and flat. Size range 11 to 16 cm. in diameter, with

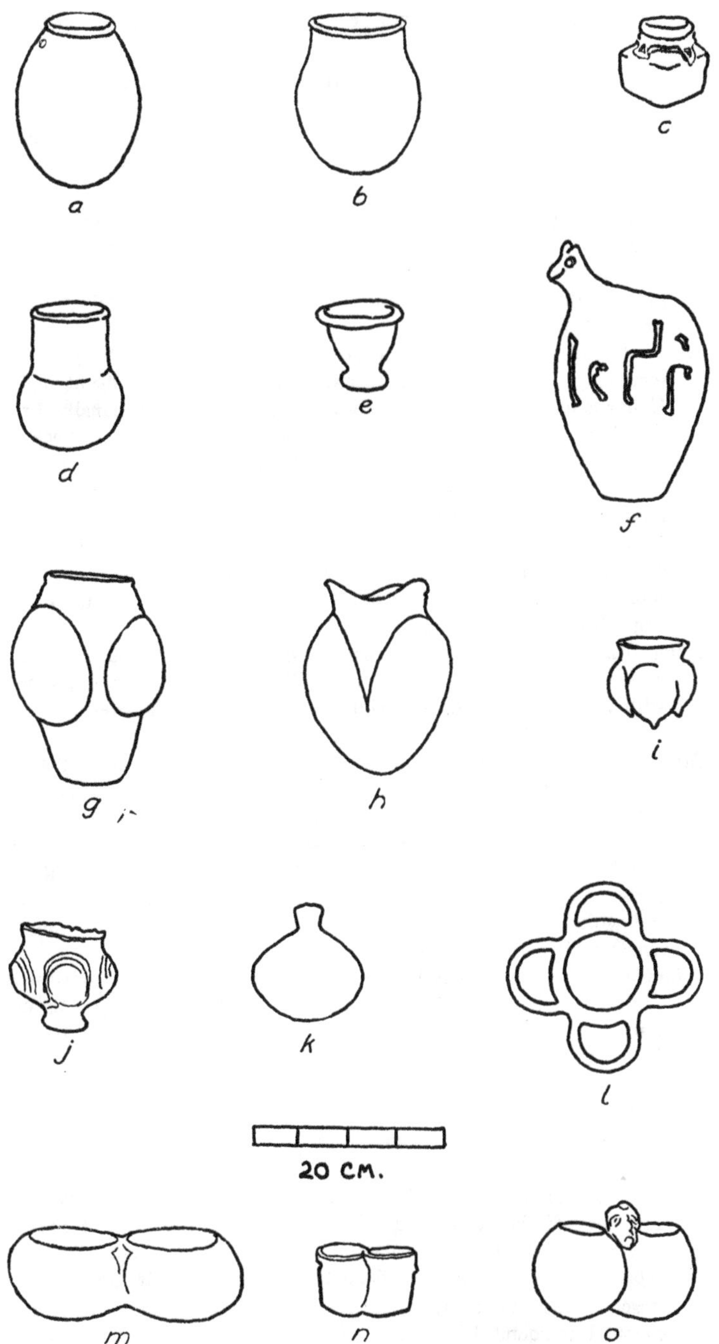

FIG. 70.—Florida Gulf Coast vessel form classification. Jars, bottles, composite forms, effigy forms. *a,* simple jar; *b,* short-collared jar; *c,* squared short-collared jar; *d,* long-collared jar; *e,* pedestal vessel; *f,* simple jar with effigy affixed; *g, h,* simple jar with lobes; *i,* short-collared jar with lobes; *j,* pedestal jar with lobes; *k,* bottle; *l,* multiple-compartment tray; *m,* double bowl; *n,* double beaker; *o,* double bowl with effigy affixed.

average 13 cm. Height greater than diameter by ratio of 4-3 to 5-4. Common. (Fig. 70, *b.*)

Squared short-collared jar.—A jar with body-collar proportions similar to the short-collared jar. Body of jar squared. Inturn at shoulder sharp with upper walls converging into base of collar. Walls below shoulder usually slope slightly inward to base. Maximum diameter is usually a little above midpoint of body of jar. Bottoms flat with squarish base. Size range 8 to 16 cm. in diameter with average of about 11 cm. Height greater than diameter by ratio of 5-4 to 5-3. Moderately common. (Fig. 70, *c.*)

Long-collared jar.—Jar with globular or flattened-globular body and walls incurving to base of collar. Maximum diameter of body at midpoint. Collar is long and straight or slightly outslanting. Occasionally diameter at orifice is equal to maximum diameter of body. Length of neck ⅓ to ⅔ of total vessel height. Bottoms are round and flat-rounded. Size range 5 to 22 cm. in diameter, with average about 12 to 15 cm. Height greater than diameter by 3-2 ratio. Common. (Fig. 70, *d.*)

Beakers: Vessels whose total height is considerably greater than their maximum diameter. Walls are straight, or very nearly so, and are vertical, outslanting, or a trifle inslanted. Bottoms are flattened with a definite angle between walls and base.

Cylindrical beaker.—A beaker that is cylindrical or round. Diameter varies but little from base to orifice. Size range 7 to 15 cm. in diameter, with average about 9 cm. Height greater than diameter by ratio of 2-1 to 1.5-1. Moderately common. (Fig. 71, *i.*)

Squared beaker.—Similar to round or cylindrical beaker except that vessel is square or rectangular at the base. Squareness with pronounced corners may, or may not, extend to rim. Walls are straight or outslanting. Size range 10 to 17 cm. in diameter, with average 13 to 14 cm. Height greater than diameter by ratio of 2-1 to 1.5-1. Rare. (Fig. 71, *h.*)

Beaker-bowls: Vessels whose maximum diameter is greater than total height and which have straight walls and flat bases with a definite angle between walls and base.

Cylindrical beaker-bowl.—A beaker-bowl with a round or cylindrical body. Walls may be vertical or outslanting. Size range 12 to 14 cm. in diameter. Diameter greater than height by ratio of about 7-5. Rare. (Fig. 71, *l.*)

Squared beaker-bowl.—A beaker-bowl with a squared body. Walls vertical or outslanting. Size range 9 to 12 cm. in diameter. Diameter greater than height by ratio of about 6-4. Rare. (Fig. 71, *k.*)

Bottles: Vessels with an elongated collar or neck and an orifice which is markedly smaller than the maximum diameter of the vessel body. The body of the vessel is usually globular. Bottoms flat or flat-round. Size range 9 to 11 cm. in diameter, with average 10 cm. Total height approximately equivalent to diameter. Common. (Fig. 70, *k.*)

Pots: Vessels whose total height is greater than maximum diameter with conoidal or rounded bases and with straight walls which may converge or outflare very slightly at the orifice.

Pot with slightly converged orifice.—Near the mouth the walls of the pot contract very slightly, but not enough to give the effect of a shoulder.

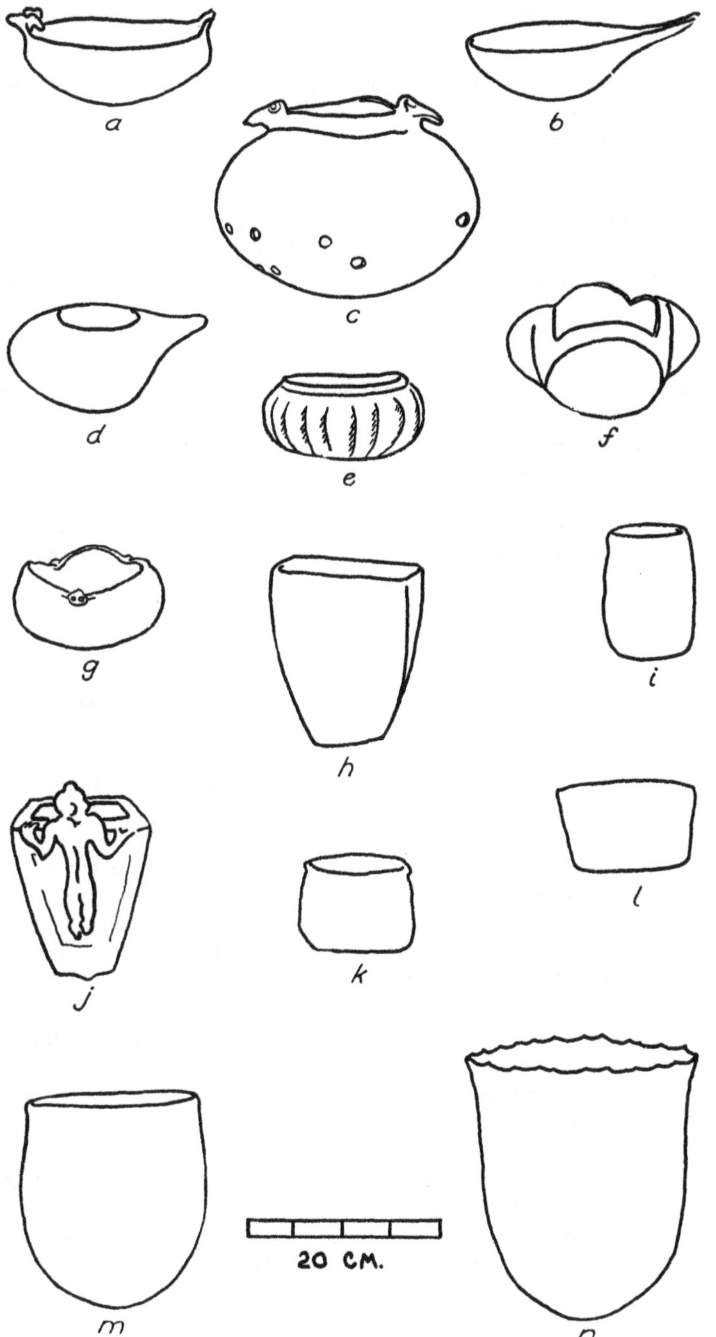

FIG. 71.—Florida Gulf Coast vessel form classification. Effigy forms, lobed forms, beakers, beaker-bowls, pots. *a*, simple bowl with effigies affixed; *b*, *d*, gourd forms; *c*, flattened-globular bowl with effigies affixed; *e*, *f*, *g*, flattened-globular bowl with lobes; *h*, squared beaker; *i*, cylindrical beaker; *j*, squared beaker with effigy affixed; *k*, squared beaker-bowl; *l*, cylindrical beaker-bowl; *m*, pot with slightly converged orifice; *n*, pot with slightly flared orifice.

Size range 12 to 20 cm. in diameter, with average about 16 cm. Height is greater than maximum diameter by ratio of from 2-1 to 8-7. Moderately common. (Fig. 71, *m.*)

Pot with slightly flared orifice.—Near the mouth the walls of the pot may contract slightly and then reflare or they may slant outward from base to orifice with a final outflare. Size range 9 to 25 cm. in diameter with an average at about 16 cm. Height is greater than maximum diameter by ratio of 3-2 to 6-5. Moderately common. (Fig. 71, *n.*)

Composite Forms

Compartment vessels: Vessels having two or more compartments or container sections.

Multiple-compartment tray.—Relatively flat trays having three or more container sections or conjoined bowls. The sections or bowl units are medium-deep with hemispherical interiors. They are separated from each other by thick compartment walls. The bowl units measure from 6 to 14 cm. in diameter with the average nearer the lower figure. A cruciform arrangement of five compartments is common with the central bowl often a little larger than the other four and sometimes elevated above them. Divisions of three and four compartments may be in a T-shaped arrangement or in a straight line. Compartments are rectangular, triangular, and crescentic as well as circular. Over-all diameters of trays range from 15 to 27 cm. Moderately common. (Fig. 70, *l.*)

Double bowl.—Double or conjoined hemispherical bowls. Bowls average about 8 to 9 cm. in diameter. Over-all length 15 to 27 cm. Rare. (Fig. 70, *m.*)

Double beaker.—Conjoined cylindrical beakers. Each unit about 4.5 cm. in diameter and 6.5 cm. in height. Rare. (Fig. 70, *n.*)

Conjoined pot.—Two pot forms joined together and partially separated by a partition which is open at the bottom. The vessel has small tetrapod feet. It is about 10 cm. high and 18 cm. long. Rare. (Fig. 72, *k.*)

Multiple-orifice vessels: Vessels having two or more openings.

Triple- and quadruple-orifice vessels.—A globular body with three (or four) spouts placed together on the top of the body. The spouts are short, wide-mouthed, and slightly flared. Diameter of vessel is about 20 cm. Rare. (Fig. 72, *i.*)

U-shaped double-orifice vessels.—Two mouths or spouts which are joined together by a connecting section. 10 to 12 cm. high and 17 and 24 cm. long. Rare. (Fig. 72, *j.*)

Composite-silhouette vessels: Vessels which have an abrupt differentiation in outline as of a beaker and bowl or two bowls, etc., joined together, one above the other.

Jar with cambered rim.—Small jar or pot forms which constrict at a point about one-third of their total height below the rim and then recurve and again constrict at the orifice. Diameters 12 to 18 cm. Height somewhat greater. Rare. (Fig. 72, *a.*)

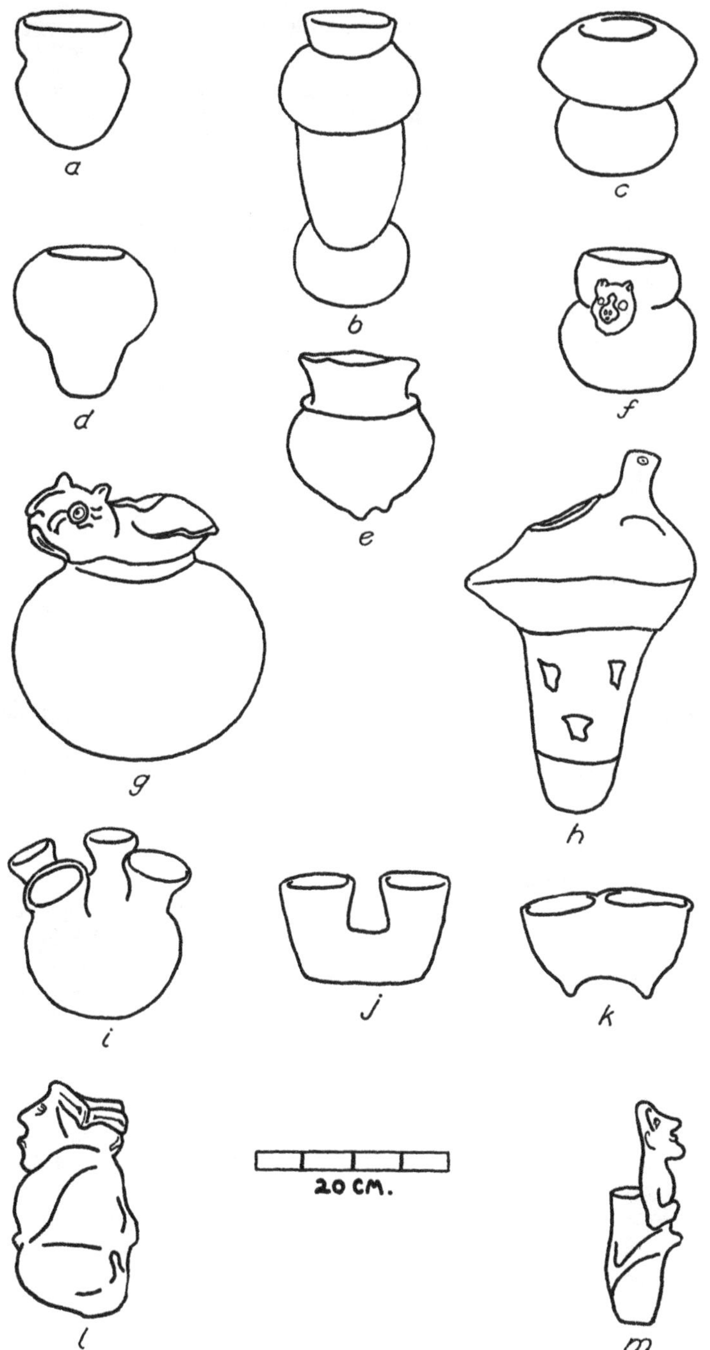

Fig. 72.—Florida Gulf Coast vessel form classification. Composite forms and effigy forms. *a,* jar with cambered rim; *b, c,* double-globed jar; *d,* single-globed jar; *e,* inset jar-bowl; *f,* jar with cambered rim and effigy affixed; *g,* double-globed jar in semieffigy form; *h,* single-globed jar in semieffigy form; *i,* quadruple-orifice vessel; *j,* U-shaped double-orifice vessel; *k,* conjoined pot; *l,* human-effigy vessel; *m,* human-figurine vessel.

Double-globed jar.—Jars which are characterized by two globular or flattened-globular sections, one above the other. These two globes may be contiguous or they may be separated by a section of the vessel of lesser diameter and parallel vertical walls. Some specimens may have cylindrical, flat-bottomed, beakerlike bases. Some have short collars. Size range 9 to 16 cm. in maximum diameter with an average of about 11 cm. Height greater than diameter by ratio of 2-1 to 8-7. Moderately common. (Fig. 72, *b*, *c*.)

Single-globed jar.—Jars which are characterized by a globelike upper portion and a narrower, cylindrical, flat-bottomed base. The orifice of the globe may or may not have a collar attachment. Size range of maximum diameter from 15 to 23 cm. In most instances this diameter is about the equivalent of the total height. Common. (Fig. 72, *d*.)

Inset jar-bowl.—These vessels have a globular bowl-like base into which has been set an elongated cylindrical upper portion. They differ from long-collared jars in that the inset is quite clear, with the rim of the bowl, or lower portion, showing plainly on the outside of the cylindrical inset. Diameter 10 to 16 cm. Height slightly greater. Rare. (Fig. 72, *e*.)

Pedestal vessels: Small jars with definite pedestal bases. Rare. (Fig. 70, *e*.)

Effigy Forms

Effigy affixation: These are vessels of various shapes which are distinguished by affixed effigy figures or adornos.

Simple bowl with effigies affixed.—These bowls have what appear to be bird head-and-tail projections on the rim on opposite sides of the vessel. Size range 15 to 31 cm. in diameter. Moderately common. (Fig. 71, *a*.)

Flattened-globular bowl with effigies affixed.—There are a number of variations in the nature and placement of the effigies or adornos in this type. A number of the bowls have two bird heads placed on opposite sides of the vessel rim; some have only a single bird head on the rim; others have a bird head-and-tail arrangement on opposite sides of the vessel. In the case of the latter the head and tail usually project out from the vessel a little below the plane of the rim. A dog, a fish, and a frog(?) are also utilized as effigies, but the bird is by far the most common. Size range 9 to 37 cm. in all-over diameter. Common. (Fig. 71, *c*.)

Collared globular bowl with effigies affixed.—A frog bowl with head, tail, and legs shown as affixations or in relief on the four sides of the bowl. 14 cm. in diameter. Rare.

Simple jar with effigies affixed.—Effigies include unidentified birds, owls, ducks, and unidentified animals. In most instances heads are placed on the rim, although some of the effigy faces are very large and an entire side of the jar is used for portrayal. Size range 10 to 22 cm. in diameter. Height is greater. (Fig. 70, *f*.)

Squared beaker with effigies affixed.—Has human figure affixed on one side of vessel. Diameter 14 cm. and height 18 cm. Rare (one specimen). (Fig. 71, *j*.)

Double bowl with effigies affixed.—A double bowl with a human effigy head placed at the junction of the rims. Diameter 16.5 cm. and height 11 cm. Rare. (Fig. 70, *o.*)

Jar with cambered rim and effigies affixed.—A cambered jar with an animal head placed on the side of the vessel at junction of body and cambered rim. Diameter 13 cm. and height 13.5 cm. Rare. (Fig. 72, *f.*)

Semieffigy: Vessels in which the form has been only partially modified and combined with adornos, modeling, and decorative techniques to give an effigy effect.

Single-globed jar in semieffigy form.—All are bird forms, including an unidentified bird with a small head and pointed beak, the owl, and the duck. Modeling often includes portrayal of head, back, and wings and clear delineation of the head with the rest of the body merely suggested. All vessels of this form type have flat, cylindrical, beaker bases. The upper portion of the jar varies from a slight expansion to a large bowl. Size range 15 to 33 cm. in diameter. Height may be slightly greater or less than diameter. Moderately common. (Fig. 72, *h.*)

Double-globed jar in semieffigy form.—These vessels approximate the double-globed contour described under the composite-silhouette vessels. Only two specimens were observed. One is a small jar in which the wings of the bird are suggested by the upper globe or bulge. The other is a large globular vessel with a completely modeled owl effigy nesting on the top of the globe. Respective diameters are 19 and 26 cm. Rare. (Fig. 72, *g.*)

Complete effigy: Vessels in which the form has been largely conditioned by the effigy effect desired rather than limiting the effigy by the vessel specifications.

Gourd form.—Simple and globular bowls with a single handle projecting out from the side of the vessel after the fashion of a gourd. Handles are sometimes halved or scooplike, sometimes cylindrical and solid. Over-all diameters range from 11 to 24 cm. Rare. (Fig. 71, *b, d.*)

Human-effigy vessel.—These are squat male figures of jar proportions. They are modeled in full-round. Head, facial features, arms, legs, and genitals are depicted in a semirealistic, semistylized fashion. Size range 6 to 19 cm. in diameter. Height is greater than diameter by ratio of 3-2. Moderately common. (Fig. 72, *l.*)

Human-figurine vessel.—This vessel is a small, narrow cylinder attached to the back of a standing male figure. The figure is similar to a large, solid figurine. It is 9 cm. at the shoulders (point of maximum breadth) and 21 cm. high. Only one specimen observed. Rare. (Fig. 72, *m.*)

Eccentric effigy vessel.—These are curious shapes. Seashells, plants or fruits, and shoe forms are represented. Rare.

Wedge-shaped vessel.—These are flattened cones or wedge shapes, having an oblong orifice and a pointed base. They have an average maximum diameter of 10 cm. and an average height of about 15 cm. Rare.

Lobed forms: Lobed vessels are those with bodies divided vertically into three or more bulbate sections.

Flattened-globular bowl with lobes.—Have four or more lobes and present a "melon" effect. Diameter range from 16 to 22 cm. Rare. (Fig. 71, *e, f, g.*)

Simple jar with lobes.—Tall jar with three lobes located midway between base and orifice. Only one specimen observed. Height 22 cm. (Fig. 70, *g*, *h*.)

Short-collared jar with lobes.—Four- and three-lobed specimens observed. The four-lobed vessel has tetrapodal supports, one to a lobe. Diameter from 6 to 16 cm. Rare. (Fig. 70, *i*.)

Pedestal jar with lobes.—Single specimen. Diameter 12.5 cm. (Fig. 70, *j*.)

Miscellaneous

Miniature vessels: Very small vessels, most of which are rather carelessly made. They conform, in general, to the forms observed in the larger vessels. The short-collared jar, single-globed jar, and pot forms are best represented. Moderately common.

APPENDIX B: TRAIT LIST OF FLORIDA GULF COAST CULTURES

Deptford

Settlements:
1. Small villages on rivers and bays.
2. Shell refuse.

Economy:
3. Hunting-fishing-gathering.

Organization of society:
4. Probably small autonomous bands.
5. Formal politico-religious organization unlikely.

Disposal of the dead: (Data very scanty, open to question.)
6. Burial in villages.
7. Cremation.
8. No grave goods with individual burials.
9. Caches of destroyed pottery in burial area.

Ceramics:
10. Deptford Linear Check Stamped.
11. Deptford Bold Check Stamped.
12. Deptford Simple Stamped.
13. St. Marks Plain.
14. St. Simons Plain.
15. Alexander Incised.

Artifacts:
16. Large to medium-size triangular-bladed chipped projectile points, notched or stemmed.
17. Pebble hammers.
18. Whetstones.

Perico Island

Settlements:
1. Large villages on marshy shores and offshore islands.
2. Shell refuse.
3. Shell embankments and mound arrangements.

Economy:
4. Hunting-fishing-gathering.

Organization of society:
5. Probably autonomous village units.
6. Formalized politico-religious functions with each village unit.

Disposal of the dead:
7. Cemeteries.
8. Burial mounds.
9. Primary flexed burials.
10. Burial offerings absent or rare.

Ceramics:
11. Glades Plain.
12. Miami Incised.

13. Perico Plain.
14. Perico Incised.
15. Perico Linear Punctated.
16. Belle Glade Plain.
17. Okeechobee Plain.

Artifacts:

18. *Busycon* hammers or picks.
19. *Busycon* cups or vessels.
20. *Strombus* celts.
21. *Busycon* celts.
22. Plummet-type shell pendants.
23. Shell tools.
24. Shell beads.
25. Bipointed bone projectile points.
26. Bone awls.
27. Bone daggers.

Santa Rosa-Swift Creek

Settlements:

1. Small villages on rivers and bays.
2. Shell refuse.
3. Burial mounds located near or on midden.

Economy:

4. Hunting-fishing-gathering.
5. Maize agriculture implied.

Organization of society:

6. Probably autonomous village units or small groups of villages.
7. Formalized politico-religious functions with each village unit or group unit.
8. Cult of the dead.
9. Social differentiation or stratification.
10. Craft specialization.

Disposal of the dead:

11. Burial mounds, both circular-conical and oblong-flattened.
12. Extensions on burial mounds.
13. Surrounding embankments with mounds (rare).
14. Mounds constructed intermittently over considerable period of time.
15. Subfloor burial pits.
16. Burial pits inclusive within mound.
17. Primary extended burials.
18. Primary flexed and semiflexed burials.
19. Secondary bundle burials.
20. Secondary single skull burials.
21. Full cremation (rare).
22. Partial in situ cremation.
23. Oyster and other shells with burials.
24. Nonceramic artifacts with individual burials.
25. Pottery with individual burials (rare).
26. Mass cache of ceremonially destroyed pottery.
27. Ceremonial destruction of nonceramic burial artifacts.
28. Cranial flattening (one case).

Ceramics:

29. Alligator Bayou Stamped.
30. Basin Bayou Incised.
31. Santa Rosa Stamped.
32. Santa Rosa Punctated.
33. Swift Creek Complicated Stamped (Early Variety).
34. Crooked River Complicated Stamped (Early Variety).
35. St. Andrews Complicated Stamped (Early Variety).
36. New River Complicated Stamped.
37. Gulf Check Stamped.
38. West Florida Cord-marked (Early Variety).
39. Crystal River Incised.
40. Crystal River Zoned Red.
41. Crystal River Negative Painted.
42. Pierce Zoned Red.
43. Franklin Plain.
44. Unusual vessel forms (see discussion).

Artifacts:

45. Large, well-chipped ceremonial blades.
46. Projectile points, probably large and medium-size stemmed forms.
47. Polished stone celts.
48. Hones.
49. Smoothing stones.
50. Pebble hammers.
51. Stone beads.
52. Bar amulets.
53. Plummet-type pendants of stone.
54. Rock-crystal pendants.
55. Galena.
56. Mica.
57. Mica spear-point forms.
58. Kaolin.
59. Batonlike objects of kaolin.
60. Hematite.
61. Bitumen.
62. *Busycon* cups or vessels.
63. *Busycon* hammers or picks.
64. Chisels and adzes of conch columellae.
65. *Strombus* celts.
66. Plummet-type pendants of shell.
67. Shell gorgets.
68. Shell beads.
69. Bone projectile points.
70. Bone fishhooks.
71. Bone beads.
72. Bone gorgets.
73. Turtle-shell rattles.
74. Perforated canine teeth.
75. Shark teeth.
76. Cut animal jaws.
77. Monitor pipes of stone.
78. Monitor pipes of pottery.

79. Tubular pottery pipes.
80. Equal-arm elbow pipes of pottery.
81. Flaring-bowl elbow pipes of pottery (?).
82. Elbow pipes of stone.
83. Copper-covered ear spools.
84. Copper bicymbal ear spools.
85. Copper ear spools plated with silver.
86. Copper ear spools plated with meteoric iron.
87. Conjoined copper tubes.
88. Sheet-copper ornaments.

Weeden Island

Settlements:

1. Small villages on rivers and bays.
2. Shell refuse.
3. Burial mounds located near or on midden (possibility of domiciliary or temple mounds?).

Economy:

4. Hunting-fishing-gathering.
5. Maize agriculture implied.

Organization of society:

6. Probably autonomous village units or small groups of villages.
7. Formalized politico-religious functions with each village unit or group unit.
8. Cult of the dead.
9. Social differentiation or stratification.
10. Craft specialization.

Disposal of the dead:

11. Burial mounds, both circular-conical and oblong-flattened.
12. Extensions on burial mounds (Weeden Island I only).
13. Mounds constructed intermittently over considerable period of time.
14. Small interior mound (rare, although record on this trait is not adequate).
15. Subfloor burial pits.
16. Log tombs on mound base (?).
17. Burial pits inclusive within mound.
18. Limerock slabs used within mound construction.
19. Primary extended burials (rare).
20. Primary flexed and semiflexed burials.
21. Secondary bundle burials.
22. Secondary single skull burials.
23. Mass secondary burials.
24. Full cremations (rare).
25. Partial in situ cremations.
26. Oyster and other shells with burials.
27. Limerock slabs covering burials.
28. Nonceramic artifacts with individual burials (uncommon).
29. Nonceramic artifacts as general mortuary offerings.
30. Pottery with individual burials (very rare).
31. Mass cache of ceremonially destroyed pottery.
32. Cranial flattening probably more common in Weeden Island II.

Ceramics:

33. Weeden Island Plain
34. Weeden Island Incised.
35. Weeden Island Punctated.
36. Weeden Island Zoned Red.
37. Carrabelle Incised.
38. Carrabelle Punctated.
39. Indian Pass Incised.
40. Keith Incised.
41. Tucker Ridge-pinched.
42. Hare Hammock Surface-indented.
43. Swift Creek Complicated Stamped (Late Variety).
44. Crooked River Complicated Stamped (Late Variety).
45. St. Andrews Complicated Stamped (Late Variety).
46. Tampa Complicated Stamped.
47. Sun City Complicated Stamped.
48. Old Bay Complicated Stamped.
49. Wakulla Check Stamped.
50. Thomas Simple Stamped.
51. West Florida Cord-marked (Late Variety).
52. Mound Field Net-marked.
53. Hillsborough Shell Stamped.
54. Ruskin Dentate Stamped.
55. Ruskin Linear Punctated.
56. St. Petersburg Incised.
57. Papys Bayou Plain.
58. Papys Bayou Incised.
59. Papys Bayou Punctated.
60. Papys Bayou Diagonal-incised.
61. Little Manatee Zoned Stamped.
62. Little Manatee Shell Stamped.
63. Little Manatee Complicated Stamped.
64. Biscayne (St. Johns) Plain.
65. Biscayne (St. Johns) Check Stamped.
66. Biscayne (Dunn's Creek) Red.
67. Biscayne Roughened.
68. Biscayne Cord-marked.
69. Pasco Plain.
70. Pasco Check Stamped.
71. Pasco Red.
72. Gainesville Linear Punctated.
73. Residual Plain.
74. Smooth Plain.
75. Plain Red.

(Types 43, 44, and 45 are principal markers for Weeden Island I; types 49, 65, 70 are principal markers for Weeden Island II. Types 64, 65, 66, 67, 68, 73, 74, 75 are also found in later periods.)

Artifacts:

76. Large well-chipped lance points.
77. Medium-size stemmed, triangular-bladed points, some with deep notches or barbs or with fishtail bases

78. Medium-size leaf-shaped points with rounded stems.
79. Small stemless triangular points.
80. Knives, chisels, scrapers, drills, flint hammerstones.
81. Polished stone celts.
82. Smoothing stones.
83. Hones.
84. Pebble hammers.
85. Plummet-type pendants of stone.
86. Stone gorgets (rare).
87. Galena.
88. Galena beads (rare).
89. Mica.
90. Mica spear-point forms.
91. Hematite.
92. Bitumen.
93. Plumbago.
94. Perforated teeth (rare).
95. Cut animal jaws (rare).
96. Turtle-shell rattles (rare).
97. *Busycon* cups or vessels.
98. Plummet-type pendants of shell (rare).
99. Shell beads.
100. Chisels and punches of conch columellae.
101. Elbow pipes of stone.
102. Elbow pipes of pottery.
103. Bird-effigy pipe of pottery.
104. Copper ornaments (unidentifiable).

Fort Walton

Settlements:

1. Small villages on rivers and bays.
2. Shell refuse.
3. Large villages in the interior.
4. Burial mounds located near or on village area (uncommon).
5. Rectangular and circular flat-topped substructure mounds within village area.

Economy:

6. Hunting-fishing-gathering.
7. Agriculture definitely known.

Organization of society (supplemented by ethnohistory):

8. Semiautonomous large villages with satellite villages.
9. Territorial federations with capital towns.
10. Formalized politico-religious functions with each large village and with capital towns on a higher level.
11. Importance of secular and military power.
12. Social differentiation and stratification.
13. Craft specialization.

Disposal of the dead:

14. Burial mounds, circular-conical.
15. Cemeteries.

16. Burials intrusive into earlier burial mounds (Weeden Island).
17. Burials intrusive into various levels of substructure mounds.
18. Primary extended burials.
19. Primary flexed and semiflexed burials.
20. Secondary bundle burials.
21. Mass secondary burials.
22. Secondary single skull burials.
23. Nonceramic artifacts with individual burials (common).
24. Nonceramic artifacts as general mortuary offerings.
25. Mass caches of ceremonially destroyed pottery.
26. Pottery with individual burials (common).
27. Pottery vessel inverted over skull.
28. Urn burial (rare).
29. Cranial deformation.

Ceramics:

30. Lake Jackson Plain.
31. Fort Walton Incised.
32. Point Washington Incised.
33. Pensacola Plain.
34. Pensacola Incised.
35. Pensacola Three-line Incised.
36. Pensacola Red.
37. Marsh Island Incised.
38. Moundville Engraved.

Artifacts:

39. Large well-chipped blades or lance points.
40. Medium-size triangular-bladed stemmed and barbed points.
41. Small stemless triangular points (?).
42. Polished stone celts.
43. Polished stone celts, thin rectangulate forms.
44. Hematite.
45. Limonite.
46. *Busycon* cups (rare).
47. Shell beads.
48. Spike-form ear pins of shell.
49. Plummet-type pendants of shell.
50. Shell gorgets.
51. Shell chisels and other columellae tools.
52. Bone awls.
53. Bone fishhooks.
54. Bone beads.
55. Copper spear-form objects (aboriginal copper ?).
56. Pottery trowels or anvils (?).
57. European materials (rare).

Englewood

Settlements:

1. Small villages on rivers and bays.
2. Shell refuse.
3. Burial mounds located near or on midden.

Economy:

4. Hunting-fishing-gathering.
5. Maize agriculture implied.

Organization of society:

6. Probably autonomous village units or small groups of villages.
7. Formalized politico-religious functions with each village unit or group unit.
8. Cult of the dead.
9. Social differentiation or stratification.
10. Craft specialization.

Disposal of the dead:

11. Burial mounds, circular-conical.
12. Small interior mound.
13. Subfloor burial pit.
14. Burial pits inclusive within mound.
15. Primary flexed burials.
16. Secondary bundle burials.
17. Secondary single skull burials.
18. Mass cache of ceremonially destroyed pottery.

Ceramics

19. Englewood Incised.
20. Englewood Plain.
21. Sarasota Incised.
22. Lemon Bay Incised.
23. Biscayne Series types in association.
24. Glades Series types in association.

Artifacts:

25. *Busycon* cups.
26. *Busycon* hoe.
27. Red ocher.

Safety Harbor

Settlements:

1. Small villages on rivers and bays.
2. Shell refuse.
3. Burial mounds located near or on midden.
4. Rectangular flat-topped structure mounds within village area.

Economy:

5. Hunting-fishing-gathering.
6. Maize agriculture.

Organization of society:

7. Large villages with satellite smaller villages.
8. Territorial federations with capital towns (?).
9. Formalized politico-religious functions within each village or group of villages (degree of centralization probably not as great as Fort Walton).
10. Importance of secular and military power.
11. Cult of the dead.
12. Social differentiation and stratification.
13. Craft specialization.

Disposal of the dead:

14. Burial mounds, circular-conical.
15. Cemeteries.
16. Burials intrusive into earlier burial mounds.
17. Burials intrusive and inclusive in substructure mound.
18. Subfloor burial pits (probably rare).
19. Burial pits inclusive within mound.
20. Primary extended burials.
21. Primary flexed and semiflexed burials.
22. Secondary bundle burials.
23. Secondary single skulls burials.
24. Mass secondary burials.
25. Full cremations (rare, except at one site).
26. Partial in situ cremations (rare, except at one site).
27. Nonceramic artifacts with individual burials (common).
28. Pottery with individual burials (common).
29. Pottery vessel inverted over skull.
30. Mass caches of ceremonially destroyed pottery.

Ceramics:

31. Safety Harbor Incised.
32. Pinellas Plain.
33. Pinellas Incised.
34. Lamar Complicated Stamped.
35. Biscayne Series types associated.
36. Glades Series types associated.

Artifacts:

37. Large and medium-size stemmed and barbed points.
38. Large stemless points.
39. Small triangular stemless points.
40. Knives, scrapers, drills.
41. Plummet-type pendants of stone.
42. Red ocher.
43. Kaolin.
44. *Busycon* picks and hammers.
45. *Busycon* cups.
46. Plummet-type pendants of shell.
47. Shell beads.
48. European metal artifacts reworked.
49. European artifacts (common).

Leon-Jefferson

Settlements:

1. Small to large villages.
2. Built around nucleus of Spanish mission-forts.

Economy:

3. Hunting-fishing-gathering (probably diminished).
4. Agriculture.

Organization of society:

5. Authority in hands of Europeans.
6. Village unit with politico-religious functions (mission and fort).

Disposal of dead:

(No data. Presumably Christian cemetery burial.)

Ceramics:

7. Mission Red Filmed.
8. Miller Plain.
9. Aucilla Incised.
10. Leon Check Stamped.
11. Jefferson ware.
12. Lamar Bold Incised.
13. Ocmulgee Fields Incised.
14. Alachua Series types associated.
15. Continuity of some Fort Walton types.

Artifacts:

16. Large triangular projectile points.
17. Large notched projectile points.
18. Small triangular projectile points.
19. Scrapers.
20. Discoidal stones (not chunkees).
21. Grinding or smoothing stones.
22. Hones.
23. Pounders.
24. Mauls.
25. European artifacts (common).

VII. A SUMMARY OF THE ETHNOHISTORY

HISTORY OF EUROPEAN EXPLORATIONS

The peninsula of Florida, owing to its proximity to the early Spanish bases established in the West Indies, was the first area of native North America to be subjected to European exploration and conquest. Many of these adventurous forays struck the Gulf Coast, and because of this the Indians were aroused against the white invaders very early in the sixteenth century and fought with ferocity to maintain their holdings and their way of life. Subsequently, during Spanish colonization, these Florida Gulf Coast Indians were among the first in the North American continent to suffer disruption, population decimation, and general cultural break-down. These events, dramatizing the impact of two worlds, took place between the years A. D. 1500 and 1700. At the beginning of the sixteenth century the Florida Gulf Coast cultures were thriving and vigorous; two centuries later they had all but vanished except for the archeological record which they left behind them.

It is difficult to say which of the Europeans was the first to reach the shores of Florida. We know, however, that the event must have taken place very shortly after the discovery of the New World and the implantation of the Spanish Colonies in the West Indies. To Ponce de Leon, in 1513, goes the official credit of Florida discovery, although it is almost certain that he was preceded by other less-heralded explorers. It is questionable as to just what section of Gulf Florida or with what Indian group De Leon touched. Swanton and others (Swanton, 1946, pp. 34 ff.) feel that it was most likely south Florida and among the Calusa rather than farther north. He was received with hostility in 1513 and again in 1521, the second voyage ending in his death.

Afterward, coasting vessels under the commands of Diego Miruelo, in 1516, and Alvarez de Pineda, in 1519, followed along the Gulf Coast shore, but their records tell us of little except the antagonistic attitudes of the aroused Indians. Pineda does, however, describe 40 villages, indicative of quite a population concentration, in the vicinity of what was probably Mobile Bay.

The Narvaez expedition of 1528 gave the Gulf Coast tribes their first taste of European soldiery in the mass. Narvaez is believed to have landed just north of Tampa Bay, whence he struck off inland afoot with 300 men. He crossed the Withlacoochee and Suwannee Rivers and eventually reached Apalachee towns where his men found corn and other food supplies. The party was driven out of the Apalachee country by the Indians, and they marched westward to Pensacola Bay, in which vicinity they reported long-haired aborgines who put up a battle with slings and darts.

On the other side of the peninsula other Spaniards, under Ayllon and Quexos, were busy laying the groundwork for bad relations between White and Indian as early as 1520-21. These explorers discovered the St. Johns River and carried off a group of Indians as slaves to the West Indies. Ayllon and Quexos also attempted unsuccessful colonies on the South Carolina and Georgia coasts.

In May of 1539 the famed De Soto expedition landed at the southern end of Tampa Bay. The party consisted of 600 men, their camp followers, horses, hogs, mules, dogs, and heavy provisions. It was Spain's first full-dress attempt to repeat in the North American woodlands what had been carried out so successfully in Mexico and Peru. De Soto and many of his followers were, in fact, veterans of the Peruvian venture. As it turned out, their stay in Gulf Florida was not an extended one, but the accounts of the expedition, together with those of the Narvaez party, give us our only descriptions of Indians and Indian culture in the area for the period. They landed near an Indian town called Ucita which is believed to be the present location of Shaw Point in Manatee County. This site, as is the case with many points or passages of the De Soto party, is disputed, but it seems fairly certain that the landfall was made somewhere in the Tampa Bay section. Ucita, or Ocita, is thought to have been a Timucuan town. From here they made contact with an inland chief who was said to dominate the tribes of the coast. This relationship among the tribes is interesting and may signify a general trend for the times. In the northwest as well, the more powerful centers and towns were in the interior, not immediately upon the coast. From Ucita, De Soto marched north and crossed the Alachua area which was occupied by a powerful Timucuan group, the Potano. Other Timucuan tribes were met with, and the Spanish had their first big fight with the Indians, probably the Uriutina, at a place called Two Lakes. They crossed the Suwannee River on September 25, after having left Ucita on July 15 of that year. The last Timucuan town encountered, after resuming their march northward, was called Agile or Aucilla and was located on that river. After crossing the Aucilla they found themselves in Apalachee territory, presumably meeting up with some of the same Indians that had known the Narvaez party of 1528. Their definiteness about the matter of the tribal boundary between the two groups is of interest as it shows that the Indians of the area had clear convictions concerning territorial or "national" divisions. Shortly after, on October 6, they arrived at Iniahica, the principal Apalachee town which was located in the vicinity of Tallahassee, possibly at the site of Lake Jackson (Le-1). (See pp. 95-98.) Throughout, the march had been an inland not a coastal one with the main body of the army passing along a route at least 30 to 50 miles from the Gulf.

The De Soto company spent the winter of 1539-40 at Iniahica while their unwilling hosts awaited their departure with unconcealed anticipation. Apparently, only the size and strength of the army kept it from being set upon and wiped out. During the wait, subsidiary parties of exploration were sent out to seek a harbor as a base for supplies for the coming year. This was done by selecting such a site to the westward at either Pensacola or Mobile. Except for these minor survey parties, the Florida Gulf Indians were spared further attentions of the De Soto party. In March of 1540 the main army set out to the northwest, crossing the Ocklockonee and, eventually, the Flint River. Hereafter, they encountered the Muskogean groups of Georgia who were, at least at first, much less hostile to the invaders than the Timucuans or Apalachees. De Soto's subsequent travels led inland and he never returned to the Gulf Coast.

After De Soto, there were sporadic contacts with the Indians of the Gulf Coast for the next several decades. Many of these were by way of wrecked treasure ships returning from Panama to Spain. From these the Indians salvaged gold and other articles. The boy Fontaneda was the victim of one of these wrecks in the sixteenth century and lived for years among the Indians of south Florida. Attempts at colonization and Christianization of the Indians were also made in the mid-sixteenth century. One of these, instigated by Menendez, was with the Tocobaga in Old Tampa Bay in 1567. This small expedition ended disastrously for the Spanish. A much larger venture was undertaken under the leadership of De Luna. This was farther to the north in the neighborhood of Mobile Bay. Probably the largest group of colonists yet to land in North America, the De Luna party comprised over 1,000 persons, including Mexican Indians. Working north from the Mobile-Pensacola region these colonists spent over a year in Alabama, but the project was finally abandoned and the survivors returned to Hispaniola.

The first successful Florida colony was founded on the east side of the Peninsula in 1565 at St. Augustine. Its settlement came about as a countermeasure to a French thrust of 1564. In that year Laudonniére had established a town on the lower St. Johns River, but the Spanish immediately retaliated by wiping out the settlement and setting up their own not far distant. The French interlude in Florida, though brief, is responsible for the best ethnological accounts of the Indians of the time. These accounts pertain to the Timucuan tribes that inhabited the northeastern part of the peninsula and were the linguistic kinsmen of the Timucuan groups encountered by Narvaez, De Soto, and others in Gulf Florida.

The Spanish mission system grew out of the St. Augustine base. In the north the Franciscans were quite successful, first founding missions among the Timucua and eventually reaching the Apalachee in 1633. Farther south the Indians were less amenable. We know that in 1612 a punitive expedition was sent against the Tocobaga by way of reprisal for attacks by those Indians against some of the missionized natives of the north. There was also trouble in the north as well. Revolt flared among the Apalachee in 1647, and in 1656 the Timucua rose in northeast Florida with the result that the trouble spread to the west involving the Apalachee. These revolts may mark the crucial breaking point of the old northwest Florida native cultures. The rebellions were put down with some bloodshed, and many of the Indians fled the area forever. Following the revolt of 1656, conditions in the Apalachee country and along the northwest coast seem to have been fairly stable and peaceable.

Forces were at work outside of the area, however, that were to bring about the destruction of the western missions and terminate the era of relative peace. As a result of sporadic border warfare between the Spanish and the lower Creeks on the Chattahoochee River in what is now south Georgia, many of the Creeks left their homeland, joining their relatives on the Ocmulgee River in central Georgia. Here they were consolidated into an effective fighting force by Col. James Moore who led the English-Creek raid upon the Apalachee-Spanish missions in 1704. The missions never recovered from this blow. Following more fighting in 1706-7, many of the Apalachee, Apalachicola, and Chatot were uprooted from northwest Florida and moved to the Savannah River where they settled under the watchful eye of the English in the Carolinas. Some fugitives from the removal fled west and took protection under the French at Mobile. The English and Creeks also carried their war against the Timucua missions, destroying many of them. The period was one of confusion and flux. In 1715 the Yamasee moved south out of Georgia and joined the Timucua in northeast Florida. At the same time some of the Apalachee and Apalachicola returned to their old homes in Florida. The tribal identities of the old northwest Florida tribes begin to disappear early in the eighteenth century. Some of the Indians merged with the Creeks who were moving south out of Georgia; others went west and joined the Apalachee and Apalachicola villages around Mobile and Pensacola, preserving for a while their tribal organizations. The old cultural traditions of the Gulf Coast were, however, lost or submerged in the confusion of war and change and never reappeared.

For our consideration of the development and history of native Indian cultures in Gulf Florida the early European explorations and colonizations may be divided conveniently into two periods. The earlier period begins at about 1500, the time at which the first Spaniard appeared in Florida. Although these strangers must have struck fear into the hearts of the natives, it is doubtful if these essentially casual adventurers had the effect of seriously upsetting the aboriginal patterns of life. Even the relatively huge De Soto party served to irritate rather than to destroy or profoundly change the Indian tribes.[79] One of the most important of the circumstances conditioning relations between Indians and Europeans during this early period of contact was the attitude of the Spaniards. The latter were at this time interested in a duplication of their Mexican or Peruvian triumphs which had been based upon quick material gain (gold) and rapid control of native governmental machinery (conquest of Aztec and Inca Empires). Neither proved possible in aboriginal eastern North America. Gold was rare or absent, and the political systems of the southeastern woodlands were not structured to permit a sudden coup d'etat type victory whereby a small group of outsiders could, as it were, decapitate the government and assume control of the body politic. In view of these interests of the invaders and the conditions surrounding the invaded, the outcome was inevitable: frustration and exhaustion for the former and only temporary alarm and disruption for the latter.

The second period of contact had an orientation significantly different from the first. The goals of the Spaniard were no longer quick plunder and glory but colonial establishment and religious conversion of the inhabitants. The effect of this second phase upon the

[79] The factor of disease is the one possible contradiction to this. We know that a century later European diseases did have disastrous effects upon native Florida populations. There is no record of what happened in 1539-43, or immediately afterward, but it is likely that conditions for contagion would not have been as great as they were later under colonization.

Indians was markedly greater than anything that had happened to them during the previous century of contact. In the Gulf area from 1633 onward native cultures underwent serious change. Some of it proceeded peacefully, although there were brief periods of revolt. Disease and the Indian death rate undoubtedly increased. This Spanish mission phase lasted until just after the close of the seventeenth century when it was brought to a violent end as the result of intertribal warfare stimulated by the competition of the European powers who were rivals for the lands and peoples of the New World.

The reality of these two periods of European contact in Gulf Florida, the first, purely exploratory and adventuristic, the second, colonial and systematic, is clearly reflected in the archeological cultures of the northwest coast. The earlier Fort Walton culture, though in occasional contact with the Spaniards, is thoroughly native and integrated; the later Leon-Jefferson culture, on the other hand, is one which has been turned from its old channels and is undergoing rapid acculturative change.

TRIBES

The Apalachee.—The Apalachee were probably the most powerful of the tribes living in the northwest Gulf Coast area of Florida. Linguistically, their affiliations are with the southern division of the Muskogean stock. The importance and stability of this tribe are attested by the numerous early historical accounts covering the 200-year period following the arrival of the first Europeans. At the time of the Narvaez (1528) and De Soto (1539-40) expeditions the Apalachee occupied a large part of northwest Florida. Swanton (1922, pp. 109-110) defines their territory as follows:

> The Apalachee proper occupied, when first discovered, a portion of what is now western Florida between the Ocilla (Aucilla) River on the east and the Ocklockonee and its branches on the west. They probably extended into what is now the State of Georgia for a short distance, but their center was in the region indicated, northward of Apalachee Bay. Tallahassee, the present capital of Florida, is nearly in the center of their ancient domain.

Later, he enlarges this territory slightly by placing their western boundary at the Apalachicola rather than the Ocklockonee River (Swanton, 1946, p. 89).

A number of Apalachee towns and communities are mentioned in the sixteenth-century chronicles. Some of these seem to be principal towns, separated from each other by several leagues. Of these, Iniahica was the most important and was located near the present site of Tallahassee. Other important Apalachee towns mentioned by the De Soto narrators are Calahuchi, Uzela, and Ochete. All these seem to have been in the interior. Another major town, Aute, visited by the Narvaez party, lay some 9 days' march to the southwest of the other Apalachee towns, being near the sea. It is also likely that there were Apalachee towns other than those of which we have record.

These principal towns seem to have been the various nuclei around which the settlement pattern of the Apalachee was structured. Unfortunately, we have no very good descriptions of these towns which would indicate the disposal of mounds, temples, public buildings, and dwellings. Cabeza de Vaca, in the narrative of the Narvaez expedition, states that one of the major Apalachee towns contained about 40 small houses. He describes the houses as being made of straw. The village area, as he pictures it, seems to have a clearing in a dense, swampy forest. He also mentions that houses were "scattered all over the country" (Swanton, 1922, p. 113). This last would imply smaller outlying settlements at some distance from the main centers. It seems confirmed by the De Soto chronicler, Elvas, who says, in speaking of the country around Iniahica:

> At the distance of a half a league to a league apart there were other towns which had much maize, pumpkins, beans, and dried plums of the country, whence were brought together at Anhayca (Iniahica) Apalache what appeared to be sufficient provision for the winter. (See Swanton, 1922, pp. 116-117, footnote p. 117.)

The storing of food supplies, taken from surrounding villages, in the principal town of Iniahica definitely suggests the pattern of the politico-religious center sustained by outlying farming communities.

The economy of the Apalachee was primarily agricultural. Corn, beans, and squash were the principal cultivated foods, and these were supplemented by native fruits. The fruit trees do not seem to have been cultivated in a strict sense but may have been tended in some fashion. Elvas states:

> These ameixas (persimmons) are better than those of Spain, and come from trees that grow in the fields without being planted.

Elvas refers to these as "dried plums," Ranjel mentions "dried venison" stored in the villages, and we know beans and corn were also stored. It would appear that the food preservation techniques of the Apalachee were quite adequate. Supplementary diet from hunting and fishing is reflected in the Ranjel statement:

> The Province of Apalache is very fertile and abundantly provided with supplies with much corn, kidney beans, pumpkins, various fruits, much venison, many

varieties of birds and excellent fishing near the sea; . . . . . (Swanton, 1922, p. 116.)

Political unity is implied for the Apalachee in all the early statements, but we do not know how this was effected or exactly what it meant. There was general agreement among the Indians that Iniahica was their principal town, but it certainly was not the only Apalachee town of importance. Elvas records that "the lord of all that country and Province (of the Apalachees) resided" at Iniahica (Swanton, 1922, p. 116). However, the nature of the authority this "lord" wielded, whether or not authority rested in the hands of one man or more, and the manner in which the authority was enforced are not revealed. It is most likely that the "Province of Apalachee" was a confederacy of closely related tribes or subtribes, each, perhaps, with its own principal town. The dominance of Iniahica, as the most populous and strongest unit, was recognized by the other groups within the confederacy, but there is no evidence of tribute by other towns to Iniahica other than the transporting of food supplies to the main town from nearby villages (apparently not principal towns). It is not clear as to whether or not there was warfare among the various Apalachee towns. In the Cabeza de Vaca account of the 1528 expedition there is an inference to what might be internecine enmity of this sort, but, for the most part, peace and unity seemed to have prevailed, at least in the sixteenth century.

Little cultural detail is afforded in the early Spanish descriptions. We know nothing concerning the burial customs of the Apalachee, and very little of their manufactures. Cabeza de Vaca mentions deer skins and "mantles made of thread." Over 100 years later Apalachee clothing is described as being made of bark, skins, and roots of trees. Feather headdresses and gold are listed in Cabeza's account as having been in the possession of Timucua Indians who claimed to have received them from the Apalachee. It is likely that the gold was from Spanish wrecks. Mortars for grinding corn are mentioned, but there is no description of them. Probably they were made of wood. The Apalachee are described as excellent archers by both of the early expeditions. Cabeza states:

Their bows are as thick as an arm, from eleven to twelve spans long, shooting an arrow at 200 paces with unerring aim. (Swanton, 1922, p. 114.)

Cabeza noted that Spaniards wearing armor were, nevertheless, killed by arrows shot with "force and precision." The nature of the projectile points is not disclosed, however. In connection with warfare, Garcilasso says that the Indians took the scalps of the Spaniards, which were much prized, and hung them upon the arms of their bows.

It is presumed that life must have continued much the same for the Apalachees until the seventeeth century. After the establishment of the mission systems we know that there were important changes in the old culture. Except indirectly, the historical sources of the seventeenth and eighteenth centuries give us little on the exact nature of the changes. These are seen best in the contrasting archeological patterns of the Apalachee area. It is a certainty that the Indian Mission culture of the archeologically defined Leon-Jefferson Period can be identified as Apalachee of the period of 1633 to 1704 or slightly later. From this it can be reasonably inferred that the almost wholly indigenous archeological culture of the Fort Walton Period, which immediately precedes the Leon-Jefferson, corresponds to the Apalachee as they were found by Narvaez and De Soto in the sixteenth century.

Other tribes of northwest Florida.—There are records of a number of other tribes occupying the area to the west of the Apalachee, but these accounts do not, for the most part, treat of these Indians during the sixteenth century. One of these groups was the Chatot. These people are classified as an independent linguistic group of the southern division of the Muskogean stock. Their original homeland probably was along the Apalachicola River, but they do not appear in the literature until 1639 at which time they were living somewhere to the west of the Apalachicola, probably near the middle course of the Chipola. Spanish missions were established among them in 1674. After this their history was more or less a common one with the Apalachee missionized Indians. (See Swanton, 1922, pp. 134-137; 1946, pp. 107-108.) The Sawokli are another group who seem to have had an old claim to a portion of northwest Florida. Linguistically, the Sawokli are classed as a subdivision of the Hitchiti group, southern division, Muskogean stock. Their original home is believed to have been somewhere along the Gulf Coast to the west of the Apalachicola River. By 1675 they were located on the Apalachicola River a few miles below the present Georgia-Florida line. They were missionized and, later, became involved in the Creek wars along with the Apalachee and their neighbors. (See Swanton, 1946, pp. 179-181.) The Apalachicola were a related Hitchiti-speaking tribe or small group of tribes. They were located on the river of the same name near the present site of River Junction in the late seventeenth century. They were attacked and scattered by the English and Creeks in 1706-7 (Swanton, 1946, pp. 92-93). Farther to the west, around Pensacola Bay, were the Pensacola. Apparently, these Indians were in that vicinity during the sixteenth century at the time of Narvaez' voyage. Cabeza de Vaca describes them as being tall and well built and living in permanent houses made of matting. The chief was lodged in a special house and was dressed in a cloak of "marten-ermine" skins. They had slings, darts, and bows and arrows for weapons. Some are described as wearing their hair long. Many years later, in 1686, the Spaniards recorded a tribe by the name of Pancocolos or Panzacola (Pensacola) at Pensacola Bay. These Pensacola were then at war with the neighboring Mobile. Shortly after this they seem to drop from history, although there are some later accounts which may refer to them. Linguistically they are Muskogean, being a subdivision of the Choctaw group (Swanton, 1922, pp. 143-150).

The remaining tribes that lived for a short time in northwest Florida appear to have been relatively late comers. Swanton (1946, map 11) locates these as the Yamasee, Yuchi, Tawasa, Pawokti, Tamathli, Mikasuki, and Osochi. Most were Muskogean or Yuchean peoples who moved into Florida from the north late in the seventeenth or in the eighteenth century. The Osochi may have been a Timucuan tribe from peninsular Florida.

Archeological identification of the tribes that lived on and west of the Apalachicola River can be made only in a very general way. It is likely that the ancestors of the Chatot, Apalachicola, Sawokli, and Pensacola were the bearers of the Fort Walton culture as it existed west of the Apalachee region. Probably these tribes made up small nations, each with its own territory, much as did the Apalachee. They had a common linguistic heritage and the cultural differences that existed among them, as reflected in the archeology of the Fort Walton Period throughout northwest Florida, were not great. After the Spanish mission period of the seventeenth century these tribes may have developed a culture very similar to that we have termed the Leon-Jefferson. Leon-Jefferson sites have not, as yet, been reported west of the Apalachee territory, although they may be disclosed in the future. On the basis of what we know of the history of the Spanish missions in north Florida it is to be expected that mission influence upon Indian cultures would have been less pronounced west of the Apalachicola River.

The Timucua.—South and east of the Aucilla River, extending over two-thirds of the way down the entire Florida peninsula, is the area once occupied by the Timucuan-speaking tribes. This relatively large region did not have the semblance of political unity that characterized the Apalachee nation. It seems, rather, to have been composed of a number of tribes or chieftainships, many of which were at war with each other. Further, the archeology reveals little cultural unity for the area. The Gulf Coastal strip, extending from the Aucilla River down to Charlotte Harbor (the central Gulf Coast and Manatee archeological regions) was fairly homogeneous in the later periods (Weeden Island and Safety Harbor); however, this cultural homogeneity cannot be extended across the peninsula to interior Central Florida or the St. Johns area where the Timucuan linguistic stock also prevailed.

It will be remembered that both Narvaez and De Soto landed in Timucuan territory and marched through that country before reaching the land of the Apalachees. Their routes lay back from the coast partly within the Gulf Coast area but mostly within central Florida. The principal early tribes in the country through which they passed, as located by Swanton (1946, map 11), are, from south to north: the Pohoy or Ocita (Ucita); the Mococo; the Tocobaga; the Acuera; the Ocale; the Potano; the Utina; the Onatheaqua; and the Yustaga.[80] As with the Apalachee, the cultural data on these Timucuans are rather scanty as far as the Spanish sources are concerned. There is, in fact, nothing on the tribes of the immediate coast north of Tampa Bay. What information we have comes largely from the tribes situated 30 to 50 miles in the interior. Data on the Timucua as a whole are, however, richly supplemented by the French accounts of 1564-65. These mainly refer to Timucuan tribes living on or near the St. Johns River. To just what extent can these eastern data be used to apply to Timucuan tribes farther west and south?

We have made the observation that there are differences existing between the archeology of the western and eastern Timucuan areas. These differences pertain largely to styles of manufactures. Many similarities between east and west do exist, and the similarities seem to be of a fundamental sort, applying to basic technologies, to burial customs, and to the construction of mounds, the latter reflecting something of the religious, social, and political mores of the people. In the light of such similarities it is reasonable to believe that the observations which the French made on the eastern Timucuans have at least partial relevance in a consideration of their western relatives.

The first description of a Timucua community is that of Ucita on Tampa Bay, the landing place of the De Soto expedition in 1539. This account from the De Soto narratives states:

> The town (of Ucita) was of seven or eight houses, built of timber, and covered with palm leaves. The chiefs's house stood near the beach, upon a very

[80] A complete list of Timucua provinces, tribes, towns, chiefs, and later missions, covering east Florida as well as the Gulf Coast, is given by Swanton (1922, pp. 322-330).

high mount, made by hand for defense; at the other end of the town was a temple, on the roof of which perched a wooden fowl with gilded eyes. (Swanton, 1922, p. 353.)

Significantly, we note substructure mounds at the site and a differentiation between the chief's house and the temple. It is not made clear whether or not the temple building also stood upon a mound. Farther north, in the Uriutina country, open courts or "town yards" were noted by the Spanish (Swanton, 1922, p. 353). Presumably, these "courts" were centers around which houses or other buildings were grouped.

In northeast Florida the French give more detailed descriptions of towns and houses, and these differ in some respects from what the Spanish saw at Ucita. These eastern Timucuan houses also were made of timbers and covered with reeds or palmettos, but Le Moyne describes the chief's house as being in the center of the village with the houses of the principal men grouped around it. According to him the dwelling of the chief was semisubterranean. The Le Moyne drawings show most of the Timucua houses as circular in form, but the squarish ground plan was also used by the Indians. These oblong houses were, apparently, both gabled and dome-roofed and often served as "town houses." Concerning the town house, Swanton (1922, p. 353) quotes from Spark:

Their houses are not many together, for in one house an hundred of them do lodge; they being made like a great barne . . . . hauing no place diuided, but one small roome for their king and queene.

The absence of mention of substructure mounds or mounds of any kind is curious, as the archeological record reveals temple-type mounds in northeast Florida in the late periods, contemporaneous with those of the Safety Harbor culture in the west.[81] The town house feature may be distinct from anything in the west or northwest; however, the records of Apalachee dwellings are not sufficiently detailed to enable us to compare this point. The Timucua often fortified their towns. Le Moyne describes this:

A position is selected near the channel of some swift stream. They level it as even as possible, and then dig a ditch in a circle around the site, in which they set thick round pales, close together, to twice the height of a man; and they carry this paling some ways past the beginning of it, spiralwise, to make a narrow entrance admitting not more than two persons abreast. The course of the stream is also diverted to this entrance; and at each end of it they are accustomed to erect a small round building, each full of cracks and holes, and

[81] The St. Johns II Period, estimated as terminating around 1650.

built, considering their means, with much elegance. In these they station as sentinels. . . . . (Swanton, 1922, p. 379.)

The French were very explicit concerning the food economy of the Timucua. Corn or maize was the main staple, and Laudonniére maintained that they planted twice a year, in March and again in June. According to Le Moyne they planted late in the fall and let the corn remain in the ground to ripen the following summer or spring. Pumpkins and beans are also mentioned as important crops. Land for planting was cleared by burning and tilled with mattocklike instruments made of wood. Agricultural labor was performed by both sexes and was directed as a group effort by the chief or "king." Common and probably private storehouses were provided for the agricultural produce. Both Laudonniére and Le Moyne state that the three winter months were spent in small, individual family huts in the woods, during which time the Indians subsisted largely upon fish and game. Fish and animal foods were also taken, prepared, and used within the larger community settlements. Le Moyne's famous drawing of the babracot, or wooden rack, placed upon forked stakes over a fire, shows fish, a deer, an alligator, and a snake, among other animals, being smoked and dried. Such prepared animal foods were then placed in storehouses. Besides the more nutritious plant foods it appears the Timucua also included various wild roots and fruits in their diet. Tobacco was used and, undoubtedly, cultivated.[82]

The principal Timucuan sociopolitical unit was the tribe, and the tribe was headed by a chief who wielded great authority. The dignity and rank of the chief was emphasized with a pomp that is surprising considering the relatively simple economic and technological levels of the culture. The larger tribes were composed of a great number of towns which had been combined into a domain. Apparently each town was a self-sustaining economic unit with its own chiefs or leaders, but these head men were, in turn, under the command of the principal town of the tribe and the tribal high chief. The French speak of five of these "supertribes" or confederacies. On the lower St. Johns were the Saturiwa; the Timucua proper, or Utina, were situated around Santa Fe Lake in Alachua County; the Potano were in the Alachua plains, and to the northwest of these eastern Timucua were the Onatheaqua and the Yustaga. It is probable that some of these tribal holdings were about as extensive as the territory claimed by the Apalachee in northwest Florida. South and west of

---

[82] Swanton (1922, pp. 357-362) gives considerable detail on Timucua foods, farming, hunting, and fishing.

the principal Timucua tribal states were others, perhaps less powerful, such as the Ocita and the Tocobaga of Tampa Bay.

Concerning social organization Swanton says:

Two different classifications seem to be represented here, of which the second is plainly along the line of clans, and the groups probably were in fact clans similar to those of the Creeks. The first, however, indicates a kind of aristocratic system which appears to have been based on male descent and recalls somewhat the special privileges accorded to children and grand children of "Suns" among the Natchez. Perhaps these "lineages" were actually associated with clans, ... (Swanton, 1922, p. 370.) [83]

The power and dignity of the chiefs was reflected in all phases of life. His special function as a religious leader, as distinct from the tribal shaman or sorcerer, is indicated by Le Moyne's description of sun worship. In these rites the chief leads the prayers and directs the offerings to the sun god. The chief's central position in cult life is further exemplified by Le Moyne in his description of human sacrifice:

Their custom is to offer up the first-born son to the chief. When the day for the sacrifice is notified to the chief, he proceeds to a place set apart for the purpose, where there is a bench for him, on which he takes his seat. . . . . The ceremonies being through, the sacrificer takes the child, and slays it in honor of the chief, before them all, upon the wooden stump. (Swanton, 1922, p. 382.)

Warfare was developed around the significance and prestige of the chief. It was highly ceremonialized and based upon raiding, capture, and ritualistic torture of prisoners.

In civil councils or ceremonies the chief's prerogatives were equally marked. A marriage ceremony for a great chief is described by Le Moyne:

When a king chooses to take a wife, he directs the tallest and handsomest of the daughters of the chief men to be selected. Then a seat is made on two stout poles and covered with the skin of some sort of rare animal, while it is set off with a structure of boughs, bending over forward so as to shade the head of the sitter. The queen elect having been placed on this, four strong men take up the poles and support them on their shoulders, each carrying in one hand a forked wooden stick to support the pole at halting. Two more walk at the sides, each carrying on a staff a round screen elegantly made, to protect the queen from the sun's rays. Others go before blowing upon trumpets made of bark, which are smaller above and larger at the farther end and having only the two orifices one at each end. They are hung with small oval balls of gold, silver, and brass, for the sake of a finer combination of sounds. Behind follow the most beautiful girls that can be found, elegantly decorated with necklaces and armlets of pearls, each carrying in her hand a basket full of choice fruits,

---

[83] Swanton (1922, pp. 362-371) considers social organization in detail.

belted below the navel and down to the thighs with the moss of certain trees, to cover their nakedness. After them come the bodyguards.

With this display the queen is brought to the king in a place arranged for the purpose, where a good-sized platform is built up of round logs, having on either side a long bench where the chief men are seated. The king sits on the platform on the right hand side. (Swanton, 1922, p. 372.)

The litter and throne are symbols of high status in a well-defined class or caste system.

Disposal of the dead among the eastern Timucua was, apparently, by simple burial. Le Moyne's drawing of ritual mourning for a dead chief shows a small hillock, beneath which the body has been buried. Around the hillock are a circle of arrows placed in the earth, and on top of the hillock is a shell drinking cup. The hillock itself is not described in Laudonniére's text (Swanton, 1922, p. 373), but possibly it represents a burial mound although the heap of earth is, to judge from the proportions of the drawing, very small. It is said that the house and belongings of the chief were burned after his death. Priests (sorcerers?) were buried in their houses which were afterwards burned. In the west burial customs were somewhat different. In 1528 the Narvaez party, somewhere in the central part of the peninsula, came upon an Indian village (apparently Timucuan) where they saw several human corpses, each in a box and each covered with a painted deer hide. This suggests the storage of the bodies of the dead, probably prior to secondary burial. Swanton (1922, p. 374) quotes from an early manuscript concerning burial among the Tocobaga:

When one of the principal caciques dies, they cut him to pieces and cook him in large pots during two days, when the flesh has entirely separated from the bones, and adjust to one another until they have formed the skeleton of a man, as he was in life. Then they carry it to a house which they call their temple. This operation lasts four days and during all this time they fast. At the end of the four days, when everything is ready, all the Indians of the town get together and come out with the skeleton in procession, and they bury it with the greatest show of reverence.

This is certainly secondary burial, a form of interment quite common among the Indians of the central Gulf Coast during both the Weeden Island and Safety Harbor Periods. At Safety Harbor proper (Pi-2), probably a Tocobaga site, secondary burials were found in a burial mound of sand (see pp. 135-142). It is not clear from the above description whether or not the bones were buried in a mound or a cemetery.

The manufactures of the Timucua included wooden benches, beds, and stools for the houses, pottery, baskets, wooden vessels, carrying baskets, woven sieves, fans, mats, painted gourds, dressed skins, stone axes, feather fans, shell tools, bows, and arrows. Pottery pictured by the French shows a variety of forms. Among these are strap-handled jars, a definitely late period form in the archeological sequences for Florida. The stone axes or celts are, of course, common to the archeological collections from all parts of the Timucua area, east as well as west, and in all the middle and late periods. Projectile points are described by the French as being made of the "teeth of fishes" (probably shark teeth), of stone, of metals (probably European trade metal), and of hardened wood. Arrows were carried in skin quivers.

Canoe travel, in square-ended dugout canoes, was the only method of transport other than walking. The Indians possessed the domesticated dog.

The Timucua themselves are described by Ribault as being "of good stature, well shaped of body as any people in the world; very gentle, courteous, and good-natured, of tawny color, hawked nose, and of pleasant countenance." The breechclout of painted deerskin was customary for adult males while women wore a skirt made of Spanish moss or of skin. Garments imported from the western Timucua, which came to the eyes of the French, were made of feathers and colored rushes. The eastern Timucua men wore their hair in a curious "upswept" hairknot as is seen in all the Le Moyne drawings. Feather and metal ornaments were worn in the hair or on the head, and woven hats are also depicted. Other ornaments for the person include ear plugs, fresh-water pearls, shell beads and gorgets, fish-tooth bracelets, and pendants, diadems, and gorgets of gold, silver, and copper. These last probably were made of metals taken from Spanish treasure ships, although some may have been wholly aboriginal. Tattooing of the skin and painting of the body and face seem to have been fairly common. (See Swanton, 1922, pp. 345-352.) Most of the artifacts and ornaments listed by the French explorers can be identified among the archeological collections from the Timucua area.

There is little question but that the Timucuan peoples around Tampa Bay were the bearers of the Safety Harbor type culture in the seventeenth century. In fact, the Safety Harbor site proper is generally conceded to be the Tocobaga capital. It is less certain if Safety Harbor type culture was in existence 50 to 100 years earlier at the time of the De Soto landings, although a correlation of the Ucita site with the Safety Harbor Period is the most likely possibility. The only other alternative would be that Weeden Island culture was still extant in 1539, a correlation that is less probable. We know that at Ucita De Soto observed the chief's house based upon a mound, undoubtedly a substructure or "temple"-type mound. Although substructure mounds may appear as early as the Weeden Island Period, they are much more securely identified with the Safety Harbor Period.

The Safety Harbor Period is, of course, the period of European contact in both the central Gulf Coast and Manatee regions; no other period in these regions incorporates European trade goods. Trade goods are found in the majority of Safety Harbor sites and more abundantly in some of these than in others. These sites remain, however, aboriginal rather than Europeanized. Mound burial, for example, continues throughout the Safety Harbor Period as far as we can determine. In other words, the Indian Mission culture, comparable to the Leon-Jefferson Period of the northwest, is lacking on the central Gulf Coast, although we are quite certain that some of the Safety Harbor sites were occupied contemporaneously with Leon-Jefferson. This accords with the historical records of the establishment and maintenance of the mission chain in Florida. While the northern tribes were brought successfully into the fold, the southern groups either resisted or were largely ignored by the Spanish during the sixteenth and seventeenth centuries. After 1700 some of the Tocobaga and Pohoy came north and settled near missons in the vicinity of St. Augustine where most of them died of pestilence in 1726. This removal, presumably, terminated the Safety Harbor culture.

Very little is known of Timucuan peoples of the Gulf Coast either north or south of Tampa Bay. Goggin (n.d.2) is of the opinion that the coastal strip to the south, in effect the largest part of the Manatee archeological region, was not occupied during the latter half of the Safety Harbor Period. He bases this upon absence of any historical accounts of peoples in this region plus the fact that most of the Safety Harbor sites south of Manatee County are without European trade materials and apparently represent only the earlier phases of the Safety Harbor Period (prior to A. D. 1600). To the north of Tampa Bay and environs our site surveys and reviews reveal only two late period sites, Bayport (He-1) and Buzzard's Island (Ci-2). The scarcity of late period sites from the central Gulf Coast north of Pinellas County and the absence of any early historical accounts of Indians in this region may mean that the region was deserted, or nearly so, during the sixteenth and seventeenth centuries.

POPULATION ESTIMATES

The best population estimates which can be made for the historic tribes of the Florida Gulf Coast are reckoned from census figures provided by soldiers, administrators, and missionaries in the seventeenth and early eighteenth centuries. There are almost no data of this sort from sixteenth-century exploration accounts. Estimates which I offer for the mid-sixteenth century are my own and are projections backward from seventeenth-century totals.

In northwest Florida many of the population figures given by the Spanish missionaries for the Apalachee during the seventeenth century were exaggeratedly high. Swanton questions these and offers a total of 5,000 persons for this tribe as of the year 1676 (Swanton, 1946, p. 91). Mooney, estimating for 1650, places the figure at 7,000 (Mooney, 1928, p. 8). At the time of the defeat of the Apalachee by the English and the Creeks in 1704, their population is believed to have declined to about 2,000 (Swanton, ibid.). The 5,000 to 7,000 estimate for the mid-seventeenth century should, I think, be increased somewhat for the mid-sixteenth century, although I doubt if the difference was great. The Indian cultures of 1650 were just beginning their transition from aboriginal to Europeanized, and the results of the white man's rule had not yet built up to their cumulative effect. I offer an estimate of from 6,000 to 8,000 Apalachee as of 1550.

The Chatot were, apparently, less numerous than the Apalachee. In 1674 there were probably about 500 persons in the tribe (Swanton, 1946, p. 108). One hundred years or more before, there may have been 1,000.

In 1750 the Sawokli numbered 50 men (Swanton, 1946, pp. 180-181). This figure probably stands for five times as many people in the tribe, or a total of 250. We know that by 1750 the northwest Florida tribes had all suffered population decimation. A mid-seventeenth-century estimate of 500 does not seem excessive, projected to a 1550 guess of 1,000 persons.

The Apalachicola, similarly, numbered about 200 Indians in 1715 (Swanton, 1946, pp. 92-93). In the mid-seventeenth century their population was probably in the neighborhood of 500, with a 1550 total of 1,000.

We have almost no data for the Pensacola. A sheer guess of 1,000 persons for 1550 is offered.

These figures total 10,000 to 12,000 Indians for northwest Florida at about the year 1550. The sum approximates that given on Kroeber's revision of Mooney's chart for the combined tribes of northwest Florida (Kroeber 1939, p. 138). If this is a 1650 rather than 1550 estimate, I am inclined to say that it is too high. If, however, Kroeber is offering a "climax" period population total his summary of 12,000 fits with that given here (see pp. 468-470).

On the Gulf Coast of the peninsula we are unable to do as well by way of estimates. The Timucua figures advanced by Mooney are based upon the eastern and northern Timucua. The Tocobaga, one of the few Timucuan groups of the Gulf Coast upon which we have any figures, were said to have been able to muster 1,500 warriors to meet the Spanish in 1567. This, if reliable, was probably the full military strength of the tribe which would give us a total population in the neighborhood of 7,500 persons. Swanton (1946, p. 196) casts some doubt on the 1,500 figure, and I am also of the opinion that it is excessive. Mooney estimated 1,000 Tocobaga for 1650. No figures of any kind are available for the Mococo, but there were said to be 300 Pohoy in the year 1680. I offer the archeological estimate of 5,000 for the Tampa Bay region as of 1550 with a subsequent decline in the seventeenth century (see pp. 487-488).

VIII. CONCLUSIONS

CULTURAL CONTINUITIES

Settlements.—The earliest communities of the Florida Gulf were shellfishing stations along the shore or the immediate tributary bays and streams. These are marked by shell-midden piles. Except for a single site of the preceramic period (see pp. 327-328), those of which we have knowledge can be divided into two groups. In the northwest are the small shell-refuse sites of the Deptford Period. These are without works such as artificial mounds, embankments, or fortifications. Around Tampa Bay and farther south are the shell-midden remains of the Perico Island Period. The Perico Island Period is thought to have been coeval, in its earlier phases, with Deptford. Perico Island sites are larger than those of the Deptford Period and often of great depth. The affiliations of Perico Island ceramics are with the Glades area, and the whole culture has ties with south Florida rather than the central west or northwest Gulf Coasts. At some of the Perico Island sites there are artificial mounds and embankments. A problem is raised as to whether these features can be considered as coeval with the Deptford Period or whether they are somewhat later in time and are the result of Santa Rosa-Swift Creek or Weeden Island influences upon Perico Island. I am inclined to believe that the latter interpretation is the correct one. This would mean that the Perico Island culture continued later than the Deptford Period, and, in doing so, underwent changes in settlement pattern that reflect those of the succeeding culture period of the northwest and central west coasts, the Santa Rosa-Swift Creek.

Santa Rosa-Swift Creek settlements are small coastal and riverine middens, probably only a little larger than those of the Deptford Period but not as large as those of Perico Island. Santa Rosa-Swift Creek sites are much more numerous than those of the preceding periods, however, and they are characterized by a new feature. It is during this period that the first burial mounds appear. These mounds are generally made of sand and are located near but not immediately upon the living sites. Not every Santa Rosa-Swift Creek midden was accompanied by a burial mound, and it is estimated that an average of three small villages combined to build a single mound.

Sites of the Weeden Island Periods are virtually identical with those of the preceding Santa Rosa-Swift Creek culture. They are small middens, usually less than 100 meters in diameter and about .50 meter in depth. They are more numerous than the Santa Rosa-Swift Creek sites and are found in all three subareas or regions of the Gulf Coast: the northwest, central coast, and Manatee. The sand burial mound, introduced in the Santa Rosa-Swift Creek Period, is common; and it is again estimated that a burial mound was maintained by approximately three villages.

The continuity of settlement pattern seen running through Santa Rosa-Swift Creek and Weeden Island is broken in the Fort Walton Period in northwest Florida. Small coastal village sites are much the same size and have much the same ecological relationships as in preceding periods. They are, also, about as numerous as Weeden Island village sites. The important difference is noted in the appearance of flat-topped temple mounds and temple-mound sites. If an average of three villages joined together to construct a burial mound in the Santa Rosa-Swift Creek and Weeden Island Periods, it is certain that several times this number converged to build a Fort Walton Period temple-mound site. These sites were undoubtedly central settlements or "capitals." This is inferred from the archeology and is supported by sixteenth-century accounts of the Indians in this region. In the Fort Walton Period the burial mound virtually disappeared, but southward, in central west Florida and the Manatee region, the old Weeden Island pattern of the burial mound as the nucleating ceremonial site continues in the Englewood and Safety Harbor Periods. Temple mounds appear in the south at this time, but are not common. Safety Harbor village middens are about the same size and have about the same type of locations as those of the Weeden Island Periods.

The final phase of aboriginal settlement is seen in the Leon-Jefferson Period of northwest Florida. By this time the Indian populations were grouped around Spanish missions and forts. In the southern part of the Gulf area the missions were not established with the same success as they were in the north.

To recapitulate the continuity of prehistoric Gulf Coast settlements we can begin by following the simple village site from earliest to latest times. This is the basic community and undoubtedly was the fundamental economic unit. These villages were probably small tribes or subtribes in which most of the individuals were held together by blood ties. In Gulf Florida these villages were usually located near the sea or on important rivers and were fishing stations. Around Tampa these sites were larger in the early periods than they were in the northwest, probably as the result of a greater abundance of shellfish in the south. In the Santa Rosa-Swift Creek and Weeden Island Periods the basic village community continues much the same except that communities begin to cooperate in small groups of two, three, or four for the purpose of building ceremonial sites or burial mounds. Still later, in Fort Walton times, the small village community continues, but social integration has reached a point where a considerable number of such communities band together to build and supply temple-mound capitals. These capitals were, in part, supported by the Indians who dwelt there permanently, but they were also sustained by other Indians of the greater tribe who lived at some distance from the temple-mound capital. This idea of the temple-mound capital had penetrated into the central Gulf Coast in the Safety Harbor Period, but it was not as well established there as it was in the Fort Walton Period of the northwest coast. Native settlement patterns organized out of small villages but around temple-mound centers collapsed with the founding of Spanish missions in northwest Florida during the Leon-Jefferson Period. The missions then became the nucleating centers.

Economy.—The very nature of village or living sites throughout the prehistoric sequence in Gulf Florida indicates that shellfish and other marine foods were an important part of the Indian diet at all periods. In the Deptford and Perico Island Periods the economy was oriented toward the sea plus the hunting and gathering of some land animals and plants. In Santa Rosa-Swift Creek times we have postulated the appearance of maize agriculture. This is purely inferential and follows out of more general interpretations of eastern United States prehistory. Even with maize, and perhaps squash and beans, hunting and fishing remained as important food-gathering techniques throughout Santa Rosa-Swift Creek. Economy in Weeden Island times was, presumably, about the same as Santa Rosa-Swift Creek. In the light of an increase in the number of sites it may be that agriculture was more widely practiced than previously; however, shellfishing, fishing, and hunting continued as supplementary modes of subsistence. The Fort Walton Period we know was agricultural. Sixteenth-century Spanish accounts tell of crops of maize, beans, and squash and of storehouses filled with such produce. The gathering of fruits and wild plants, fishing, and hunting were all practiced, but there are several things which suggest that agriculture became more important during this period than it had been before. First, there is the change in settlement pattern with the rise of the big towns or temple-mound centers. These new population concentrations, larger than those of the previous periods, could have been supported in the Gulf Florida environment only by intensive agriculture. Second, there seems to have been a population shift in Fort Walton times from coast to interior. The largest sites of the period are found inland in the better farm lands. This was attested by the sixteenth-century explorers and is also reflected in the archeology. Such a shift from littoral to interior might have been conditioned by other factors, but the rising importance of agriculture must have played a part. And third, the Fort Walton culture has extra-Floridian relationships with other prehistoric cultures which compose a late southeastern horizon characterized by an intensive agricultural economy.

Food economy for the Safety Harbor Period was probably somewhere intermediate between that of Weeden Island and Fort Walton, while Leon-Jefferson economy must have been much the same as Fort Walton.

Society.—The social organization of the early periods, Deptford and Perico Island, was probably coextensive with the village units. That is, each living community was politically and religiously, as well as economically, independent. At this time there seems to have been little group expression of a ceremonial nature. We are judging, of course, from the archeological record in which we see little in the way of advanced artistic or craft expression and no large monuments of any kind.

In the subsequent Santa Rosa-Swift Creek and Weeden Island Periods the burial mounds are evidence of an organizational structure over and above the simple village unit. Provided we are correct in our assumptions, intervillage cooperation was involved for the task of constructing and dedicating a mound. The religious or sacred quality of these burial mounds cannot be doubted. Considering the economic and technical level of the Santa Rosa-Swift Creek and Weeden Island Periods, the Indians were lavish and extravagant in their veneration of the dead. Their mortuary goods were among their finest craft products. Such emphasis suggests profound religious motives in the society. There are virtually no archeological clues as to the nature or prevalence of warfare. If common it is likely to have consisted of village raids and counterraids organized on a small scale. Although sixteenth-century accounts of north Florida Indians are replete in their descriptions of class differentiation, the archeological story covering the centuries previous does not point this up. Differences in burial treatment are noted in some of the mounds with certain individual skeletons being accorded a central position in the mound, a special grave, and somewhat richer burial furniture. This is more true of Santa Rosa-Swift Creek than the later Weeden Island Periods. Nearly all Weeden Island burial mounds contained mass deposits of grave goods, seemingly placed as a common offering to all the dead within the mound rather than for any individual. There is a continuity in the actual treatment of the body between Santa Rosa-Swift Creek and the Weeden Island Periods. Secondary inhumation was practiced in both but was probably more common in Weeden Island. We know very little of earlier burials except that the Perico Islanders practiced primary inhumation and that there are two instances of cremated cemetery burials in the Deptford Period. This latter practice was only rarely carried over into the later periods.

There are evidences of greater change in the organization of society between Weeden Island and Fort Walton than between Santa Rosa-Swift Creek and Weeden Island. The new settlement pattern, structured around the temple-mound sites, had a basis in larger political groupings than were known in previous periods. The Spanish explorers remark upon the concepts of nationality that the Indians of the Gulf Coast possessed, and these early travelers also describe the crossing of well-defined territorial boundaries of large tribes or nations. Groups of several small villages were clustered around each of the principal towns, and among the Apalachee we know that several of these towns were bound together by a supertribal government which had a recognized capital. Warfare, between tribes, was an established institution and governed by strict rules. Among the Timucua, religious prerogatives were closely bound up with military and civil privileges and duties, all centering in the hands of the chiefs. Government could, in this sense, be considered theocratic, but it is likely that the Fort Walton Period rulers exercised greater secular powers than their Weeden Island predecessors. Rites for the dead are, relatively, less elaborate for Fort Walton than in the preceding periods. Burials were often placed in cemeteries or in the floors or sides of the temple mounds. There is more individual emphasis on grave goods than in Santa Rosa-Swift Creek or Weeden Island Periods; but, with the disappearance of the burial mounds, one cannot help but feel that burial ceremonialism was less of a social integrative force than formerly.

The Safety Harbor Period probably represented a transitional stage between Weeden Island and Fort Walton societies.

Leon-Jefferson demonstrates great change on the social organizational level. It is likely that many forms of tribal and group allegiance dissolved when the Indians came under the spiritual and political overlordship of the Spanish. Chieftainship of a sort remained but without the religious sanctions that bolstered the position under aboriginal conditions.

Technology.—The appearance of maize agriculture at the beginning of the Santa Rosa-Swift Creek Period, if we are correct in placing it at this point in the culture sequence, was the single most revolutionary technological change for the Indians of Gulf Florida. It is paralleled by a number of cultural changes, but by only one other important technological innovation. This last is the ground- and polished-stone ax or celt. The ground-stone ax is the classic Neolithic type specimen in the Old World, generally considered the clearing and cultivating tool and virtual symbol of early agriculture. In the archeology of the eastern United States some forms of ground-stone axes, particularly grooved axes, are a part of the Archaic horizon which is generally thought to precede Eastern maize horticulture. We know, too, that stone grinding and polishing techniques were part of Archaic stage crafts in many parts of the eastern United States. Nevertheless, in most places in the East, and certainly in Florida, the polished-stone celt is not a part of the Archaic horizon. Its sudden appearance on the Santa Rosa-Swift Creek time level marks a definite technological advance.

Most of the elements of Gulf Coast aboriginal technology known in the middle and late periods were present at the inception of our sequence.[84] The "paleolithic" technology of stone chipping for the manufacture of points and knives, the "neolithic" art of pottery making, and the skills of working in shell, wood, and probably bone, were all Deptford or Perico Island Period accomplishments. From this time forward these technologies can be traced through their respective continuities of change and modification. These are changes which result from the artisan's more complete mastery of his craft, from the introduction and development of minor techniques, and through the media of varied stylistic expressions.

Continuity can be followed with relative ease in ceramic technology. In the quality of pottery ware the basic standards were established in the Deptford and Perico Island Periods. These standards resulted in the production of a coiled, sand-tempered, even and granular pottery which had been fired with erratic air control to a fairly hard consistency. The sand-tempered Deptford and Perico wares represent a definite break away from the old fiber-tempered ceramic of the Southeast which may have preceded Deptford and Perico Island on the Gulf Coast. From the Deptford Period on,

[84] Metals, worked by cold-hammering techniques, are an exception, as these do not appear until the Santa Rosa-Swift Creek Period. It is likely that the Florida metal specimens of this and the Weeden Island Period were imports, not local products.

pottery ware qualities remain constant until the Fort Walton horizon. Santa Rosa-Swift Creek pottery is a little finer and thinner than Deptford, but ware differences are generally slight, and Weeden Island presents no marked temper or paste contrasts to Santa Rosa-Swift Creek. Much of the Fort Walton Period pottery is also sand-tempered, but coarser grit temper makes its appearance in this period. The most noticeable innovation, however, is the use of crushed shell as temper. These changes characterize Fort Walton and Leon-Jefferson but not Englewood or Safety Harbor which continue in the Weeden Island ware traditions.

Vessel forms show more inclination to rapid change than the materials of manufacture and conditions of firing. Deptford vessels were virtually all simple pot forms with unmodified rims, and occasional tetrapodal supports,[85] and Perico Island vessels were open bowls with slightly incurved rims. Both of these forms are seen in all the later periods; however, during the succession of periods a great many new forms are introduced. For example, in Santa Rosa-Swift Creek the old Deptford pot form is quite common, but, in addition, we have a great number of new shapes including flattened-globular bowls, boat-shaped bowls, beakers, composite-silhouette vessels, and collared jars. There are many variations on these new basic forms such as vessels with squared bodies and bases. Besides the principal forms, the Santa Rosa-Swift Creek Period is noted for unusual or exotic vessel forms. Two of the most noticeable are the multiple-orifice vessels and the effigy forms. One feature which may be a carry-over from the Deptford Period is the use of tetrapodal supports. These were rare in Deptford but frequent in Santa Rosa-Swift Creek. In Weeden Island I the potters continued to create the strange, exotic nonutilitarian forms first noted in Santa Rosa-Swift Creek. By Weeden Island II Period there are fewer of these odd forms, but most vessels conform to the basic innovations of Santa Rosa-Swift Creek. There is one notable discontinuation, however; tetrapodal supports became extinct in the Weeden Island Periods. With the Fort Walton Period, forms are more limited in variety than was the case for Santa Rosa-Swift Creek or Weeden Island. The two new and characteristic Fort Walton forms are the bottle and the casuela or carinated bowl. It is not clear as to just what degree these two new forms have been influenced by and are a development out of previous Weeden Island vessel shapes. Certainly

---

[85] There is one boat-shaped bowl and one double vessel dating from the Deptford Period. See Carrabelle (Fr-2) site discussion (pp. 267-268).

the bottle bears some relationship to the collared jar and the casuela bowl to the flattened-globular bowl. At the same time, there is also reason to believe that both may be new introductions to Gulf Florida. Data are still insufficient to resolve the problem of ceramic continuities between Weeden Island and Fort Walton. One feature of the Fort Walton Period is, however, definitely new. This is the strap-handle attachment. Safety Harbor Period vessels conform to both Weeden Island and Fort Walton shape styles while Leon-Jefferson vessel shapes combine ideas seen in Fort Walton with others, like the annular-based plate, that appear for the first time in this very late period.

Pottery decoration presents some very interesting sequence continuities. In the Deptford Period the almost universal mode of decoration was by stamping. The stamped designs were simple linear arrangements or check patterns. There is one Deptford example of a design worked out in linear punctation (see Carrabelle site (Fr-2), pp. 267-268). In the southern part of the Gulf Coast area stamping seems to have been known only on trade pottery during the Perico Island Period. The little Perico Island pottery that is decorated has been treated with fine-line incisions or linear punctations similar to those noted on the single Deptford Period exception. In the succeeding Santa Rosa-Swift Creek Period check and simple stamping continue, with some modifications, from the Deptford Period; but the outstanding stamped type is of a complicated rectilinear or curvilinear design pattern. This is the pottery of the Swift Creek tradition, and this type of decoration is closely associated with the pot-form vessel. The other major element in Santa Rosa-Swift Creek Period ceramic decoration is the complex of incision, punctation, rocker stamping and occasional red painting. All appear to be new to the Gulf Coast area and not derived from the Perico Island incision or linear punctation. These modes of vessel decoration have a close association among themselves and are also associated with the new vessel forms which appear at this same time. Thus, in both vessel shapes and vessel decoration the Santa Rosa-Swift Creek Period was one of fusion of two rather strikingly different sets of ideas: on the one hand, the conoidal-based pots decorated with the stamping technique; and on the other, globular bowls, beakers, collared jars and unusual forms decorated with incision, punctation, rocker stamping or red zoned painting. One other element of pottery decoration which appears for the first time in this period, and which probably has antecedents separate from either the stamped or incised and rocker-stamped traditions, is negative painting. This is true negative color application involving the resist-dye process.

In the Weeden Island Period both the incision punctation and the complicated stamping continue. The first is predominant, and complicated stamped pottery lasts until the beginning of Weeden Island II. Both techniques are stylistically modified, but the developmental relationships to Santa Rosa-Swift Creek pottery are obvious. The typical Weeden Island ware is incised or punctated. Rocker stamping, as it was seen in the Santa Rosa-Swift Creek type, Alligator Bayou Stamped, has virtually disappeared, with only a semblance of the technique retained in the Weeden Island type, Little Manatee Zoned Stamped. Negative painting does not appear in the Weeden Island Periods or again in the Florida Gulf sequence. One prominent mode of decoration becomes popular in the Weeden Island Periods. This is modeling. Usually it takes the form of zoomorphic adornos attached to vessel rims or walls. More rarely, it is expressed in complete effigy shapes. A few of the latter were noted in Santa Rosa-Swift Creek, and it may be that modeling-type decoration had its beginnings in that period. Its great vogue, however, was in the Weeden Island Periods.

A consideration of the modeling technique leads us into the problem of continuity of design as well as decorative techniques. The common form of Weeden Island Period modeled adornos is the bird. Usually, there are bird heads affixed to the rim of a bowl or jar. Quite often, what appear to be the wings or tail of the bird are indicated on the vessel in incision or punctation techniques. Such designing is highly stylized and difficult to interpret in naturalistic terms. Similar designs, perhaps a little less stylized, also occur in the preceding Santa Rosa-Swift Creek Period, presumably as prototypes for the bird-motif designing that is so typical of Weeden Island. It is quite likely that the Weeden Island artist transposed the bird motif into the modeling technique. Besides the bird design another design idea was also transferred from Santa Rosa-Swift Creek to Weeden Island. This is the rendering of design in the negative. Often a Weeden Island design proper is left plain and only the background is filled in with incision or punctation. This is a method of design expression used in Santa Rosa-Swift Creek incised, rocker-stamped, and punctated types as well as the negative painting of that period.

By the dawn of the Fort Walton Period the stamped techniques of decoration had almost completely disappeared in northwest Florida. In central west Florida and the Manatee regions check stamping continued into the Safety Harbor Period, and occasional late complicated stamped types are also seen. Most Fort Walton pottery is, however, decorated by incision and punctation, modeling, or both. As with the vessel shapes, we are undecided as to whether this represents a continuity from the Weeden Island Period or is a new introduction from outside of the Gulf area. Probably both continuity and outside contact are involved. Some Fort Walton designs, such as the negative meander, suggest continuity from the earlier local periods. Bird-head rim effigies are also very similar to the Weeden Island ones. In the Leon-Jefferson Period incised and punctated techniques and designs carry over from Fort Walton, although these are reinforced by ideas impinging upon northwest Florida from the south Georgia area. A revival of the complicated stamped technique and complicated stamped designs reminiscent of those in Swift Creek and related types can best be explained as a reintroduction of pottery decorative ideas that previously had been extinguished in Florida. The sporadic appearance of these complicated stamped types in Safety Harbor Period sites, farther to the south, are accounted for in the same way.

Technology in stone offers a less clear developmental picture. Adequate period identification data on most projectile-point collections makes it difficult to give a concise summation. In chipped stone large and medium-size stemmed projectiles were made during Deptford times, and these continue in the later periods. In Santa Rosa-Swift Creek more and finer blades and points were manufactured. Some of the large lanceolate blades of the period are among the finest chipped-stone tools or weapons made at any time or place in Florida. Large fine blades are also found in Weeden Island Period mounds. Stemmed points, triangular and ovate-triangular bladed, belong to the Weeden Island horizon; small, triangular, unstemmed points appear for the first time; and scrapers, drills, and knives were also manufactured. Both large and small triangular points are present in Fort Walton and Safety Harbor sites. In Safety Harbor chipped-stone work is more common than in any of the other periods.

Ground-stone work of any consequence has its beginnings in the Santa Rosa-Swift Creek Period. The appearance of the stone celt has been mentioned as an important technological introduction. These celts, made of hard imported stone, were of the pointed-poll variety. The body of the celt is rounded or ovate in cross section. The pointed-poll celt carries on into the Weeden Island and Fort Walton Periods but is rare in Safety Harbor. In the Fort Walton Period a new celt form appears in addition to the pointed-poll type. This is a proportionately thinner, flatter, and more rectangulate shape. Stone plummet-type pendants, grooved for suspension at one or both ends, are very common to Santa Rosa-Swift Creek, somewhat less so to Weeden Island, infrequent in Safety Harbor, and absent in Fort Walton and Leon-Jefferson. In general, articles like stone beads, bar amulets, stone gorgets, stone pipes, and rock-crystal ornaments were more usual in Santa Rosa-Swift Creek than in Weeden Island. The presence of raw sheet mica in burial mounds is characteristic of both Santa Rosa-Swift Creek and Weeden Island, while the use of sheet mica for fashioning symbolic or ornamental objects is a Weeden Island trait. Mica is not found in Fort Walton, Safety Harbor, or Leon-Jefferson sites, nor is ground-stone work of any sort, except for the celts, typical of these later periods. One rare exception is the stone discoidal which occurs in Fort Walton for the first and only time in the sequence.

Shellwork has its inception in the Perico Island Period, but, as far as we know, was not characteristic of the contemporaneous Deptford Period in the northwest. Perico Island shell weapons or tools include the *Busycon* hammer or pick, *Strombus* hammers, and *Strombus* and *Busycon* celts.[86] Shell was also utilized during this period for the manufacture of plummet-type pendants and shell beads. All these artifacts are Glades area types. *Busycon* hammers, *Strombus* celts, and the plummet pendants appear in the Santa Rosa-Swift Creek Period. Besides these, Santa Rosa-Swift Creek sites also show chisels and adzes made from conch-shell columellae, shell gorgets, shell beads, and conch-shell drinking cups. All are Glades area artifact types although we have no specific record of them for the Perico Island Period. There is less shellwork in the Weeden Island Periods than in Santa Rosa-Swift Creek. Celts and hammers are absent, and shell beads, punches, and chisels were found in only a few sites. The shell cup is the only ubiquitous shell artifact of the period. In Fort Walton there are none of the larger shell tools, and the shell drinking cup is a rare item. Shell chisels or punches, spike-form ear pins, and beads are all present, however. Safety Harbor differs markedly in that *Busycon* picks and hammers, shell plummet-type pendants, shell beads, and cups of shell were found in most of the mounds of the period. In retrospect, this is a curious, broken continuity for shellwork. Apparently shell tools were very early in the

[86] It is likely that the *Strombus* celt was a Perico Island Period imitation of the stone celts of the north. This also suggests that the Perico Island Period lasted until Santa Rosa-Swift Creek times, the earliest appearance of the stone celt in the north.

south but did not appear in the northern part of the area until Santa Rosa-Swift Creek times. They are not important in Weeden Island or Fort Walton sites, but in the south they are revived in the Safety Harbor culture. This suggests a double diffusion from the south of shell implements or the techniques of making these implements, the first dating began from the Perico Island Period and a secondary late diffusion on the Safety Harbor level.

Craft work in bone, horn, or teeth does not, in general, characterize the Gulf Coast area. In other areas of the Southeast bone implements and decorated bone were noteworthy developments of the Archaic horizon. Possibly such finds will eventually be made in west Florida. What bonework is known now comes mainly from the Santa Rosa-Swift Creek and Perico Island Periods. This consists of bipointed projectiles, awls, and daggers, all made from mammal bones. Some bone projectiles, bone fishhooks, bone gorgets, turtle-shell rattles, perforated teeth, shark teeth, and cut animal jaws are associated with Santa Rosa-Swift Creek sites. There is only an occasional bead or fishhook found in the later periods.

Probably one of the most highly developed crafts of the Gulf Coast aborigines was wood carving. Our knowledge of it is limited to a secondary record, the impression of carved designs on pottery. Some wood carving was known in the Deptford Period for the checked and simple stamped pottery was, apparently, impressed with carved wooden stamps. No inferences can be made about Perico Island woodwork, but in the Santa Rosa-Swift Creek Period carving in wood may have enjoyed a sudden boom. Pottery of the period is decorated with intricate stamped designs produced with the aid of a carved wooden stamping unit. The carver's art may have declined in the Weeden Island, Fort Walton, and Safety Harbor Periods. At least, the intricate complicated stamped designs on pottery disappear at the close of Weeden Island I. Some carving was done, however, as we have direct evidence in a small fragment of gracefully carved charred wood taken from a Safety Harbor Period mound. Pottery decorated with inferior stamped designs appears in the Leon-Jefferson Period.

Metalwork makes its first appearance in the Santa Rosa-Swift Creek Period. This is cold-hammered copper, meteoric iron, and silver. Ear ornaments, copper tubes, embossed plates, and cut-out designs on plates comprise the metal artifacts. The metals from which they were made are, obviously, imports. It is questionable as to whether or not the actual objects were made in Gulf Florida or made elsewhere and imported. Their similarity to Ohio Valley forms suggest the latter.

Copper or metal objects are much less common in the Weeden Island Periods. European, or European-transported, metals come in during the Fort Walton and Safety Harbor Periods. Sometimes these have been reworked locally by hammering and engraving. Some of the reworked metal objects from these periods show considerable skill, and this argues that perhaps metal craftsmanship was known in Gulf Florida in the earlier periods. The argument, however, is weakened by the lack of a strong continuity in aboriginal metal products from the Santa Rosa-Swift Creek Period, through Weeden Island and into the late periods.

PEOPLES

(By Marshall T. Newman)

An analysis of Floridian Indian physical types in time and space is difficult with the present data. These data consist of Hrdlička's two reports (1922, 1940); Von Bonin and Morant's (1938) biometric analysis of Hrdlička's 1922 measurements; and our own hasty examination of several cranial series in the United States National Museum. Hrdlička's earlier study was based upon 173 (121 male, 52 female) undeformed Florida skulls and a few long bones, most of which came from the lower portion of the Central region and the upper portion of the Manatee region of the Gulf Coast. The total series for his later study was expanded to 426 (232 male, 194 female) undeformed skulls, with the bulk of them still from the middle Gulf Coast. Thus the Northwest, Central peninsular, Atlantic Coast, and Southern areas were meagerly represented. This spotty distribution, coupled with his almost complete disregard of chronological pegs upon which he might have hung his series in the 1940 report, lays open to question certain parts of Hrdlička's conclusions on the peopling of Florida.

It was Hrdlička's opinion that the native population of Florida was a robust Indian group in which two distinct, although intermixed, physical types could be discerned. The numerically predominant type, in terms of his series at least, was brachycephalic, extremely high-headed, of medium stature (males 165-168 cm. or 5 feet 5-6 inches; females 152-154 cm. or 5 feet), and possessing exceptionally rugged faces and lower jaws. Hrdlička identified this type with the Timucuans of the north half of the State. He considered these people as simply a southern extension of the Gulf or Centralid type of the southeastern States, but attributed the exceptional bony ruggedness of the Floridians to their marine diet which was undoubtedly extra rich in phosphates. The minority type was essentially mesocephalic and characteristically less massive. It occurred only as a rarity in Gulf Coast and St. Johns area series, but on the slim basis of three small series,[87] Hrdlička felt these mesocephals were more prevalent in the northwest and south of Florida. The lack of a "pure" mesocephalic series in his collections was explained by long-time intermixture between the two Floridian types, although he (Hrdlička, 1922, p. 89) showed some confidence that future excavations would reveal a "fairly pure" mesocephalic group. He related this mesocephalic type to Muskogean-speaking intruders, and specifies the Seminoles. The type was considered a modification of the Algonkin or Silvid group to the north.

Hrdlička believed that the brachycephalic group represented the indigenous population, and that the mesocephals entered the peninsula at a later time. He guarded himself, however, by offering two other explanations, which he thought less probable. The first was that the brachycephalic people invaded the lower southeastern States from Mexico, intermixed with the longer-headed Muskogean-speakers in Alabama and Georgia, and in that way brought the mesocephalic element into Florida. The second explanation considers the remarkable head height, and inferentially some of the other Floridian characteristics, a local development induced possibly by special environmental factors.

Von Bonin and Morant, in their reanalysis of Hrdlička's 1922 measurements, have added three points of interest to the present synthesis. In the first place, sensing the arbitrary nature of Hrdlička's two Floridian types, they compared his total Gulf Coast series with a pooled series of all others from Florida, including the Seminoles. None of the mean differences were found to be statistically significant. Secondly, they calculated standard deviations for the total Florida series, and found its variability to be quite unexceptional. From the data at hand, they saw no justification for subdividing the total series into types, although they felt that more abundant material might make it possible to distinguish regional and time differences. Thirdly, they used the Coefficient of Racial Likeness to compare the total Florida male series with the Central Californian (mostly Yokuts) series. This led them to note that both Central Californians and Floridians were placed by Von Eickstedt (1934) in his "gruppe Margide" or Marginal type. While there is an attractive neatness in having geographically and culturally marginal areas occupied by

[87] Of 8 skulls from Santa Rosa Island near Pensacola, 1 is dolichocephalic, with the rest showing indices over 80. Among 8 skulls from Canal Point east of Lake Okeechobee, 2 are dolichocephalic; 3 more have indices under 80. In a Seminole series of 13, only 1 shows an index over 80.

racially marginal peoples, it will take more than the pat "efficiency" of the Coefficient of Racial Likeness and the gross, sweeping coverage of Von Eickstedt to demonstrate such a proposition. One rather obvious objection is that while Central Californians were notably low-headed, Floridians were exceptionally high. Stewart (1940) has shown the considerable diagnostic value of head height as a racial determinant among Indians, pointing out that generally high-heads were early and low-heads late in the sequences of Indian physical types. Further researches may indicate other objections to a close racial affinity between so-called Marginal peoples, although such relationships are hard to deny on the basis of present knowledge.

Returning to Hrdlička and his two Floridian physical types, we must agree with Von Bonin and Morant on the arbitrary nature of the mesocephalic group. Without arguing against some separateness for his Seminole series, we feel that the other Florida mesocephals are more likely individuals on the lower end of the index range in the brachycephalic group than representatives of another type. Our reasons for doing so are twofold. First, Hrdlička made little attempt to document the distinctiveness in other ways of the few mesocephals he selected; and second, within a series showing a mean length-breadth index of 79-81—a good mean range for Florida—the individual variability would be from about 74-87. If the longer-headed individuals fail to show differences of a parallel nature in the face and other areas, their separation as a distinct type is hard to justify. All this is not to deny the very real possibility of several different physical types in Florida's racial prehistory. Rather we submit that Hrdlička's mesocephalic type requires validation beyond the "opinion of experience." In addition, the identification of the mesocephalic type with Muskogean-speakers may be questioned. Certainly bearers of the Fort Walton culture, the Apalachee, were the first quite definite Muskogean peoples in Florida. Culturally their influence extended south only to about the Aucilla River. For them to have directed mesocephalic genes to south Florida, without perceptibly influencing the central part of the State, stretches one's credulity. If we are correct in the foregoing, Hrdlička's mesocephalic type as well as his source for it are to be seriously questioned.

Hrdlička (1922, p. 89) stated that there was no evidence of any earlier Floridians than the brachycephalic population. The recent re-evaluation of the controversial Vero and Melbourne finds by Stewart (1946) raises the very good possibility of an early dolichocephalic population living on a Paleo-Indian or, at least, Archaic level. Even if a Pleistocene dating for Vero and Melbourne is questioned, they are probably entitled to greater antiquity than the earliest sites from which Hrdlička obtained his series. Now if there was a Paleo-Indian or Archaic population of dolichocephals in Florida, there is no apparent trace of it in Hrdlička's series, where only 4 percent are long-headed and in our opinion simply represent one morphological extreme of the brachycephalic range.

This brings us to a point where we can develop a hypothesis of our own, more in accord with the present cultural chronology in Florida, and with the sequence of physical types elsewhere in the Southeast. The Vero and Melbourne skulls suggest an early dolichocephalic population in Florida, just as has been amply substantiated in Alabama (Newman and Snow, 1943) and Kentucky (Snow, 1948). One of the most likely places to look for more skeletal remains of these people would be in the large Archaic prepottery middens in the St. Johns area. The time of entrance of the brachycephalic people into peninsular Florida is hard to gauge, but it probably begins on a Santa Rosa-Swift Creek or St. Johns I level. Certainly they had arrived in South Florida by the equivalent Glades I-II periods, judging by Hrdlička's measurements and our inspection of the sizeable Perico Island series. Hrdlička's measurements on the Belle Glade skulls (Glades II-III) also indicate brachycephals in the Glades area. Within the Central Gulf Coast region, the small and rather fragmentary Weeden Island series cannot be distinguished from the Perico Island skulls, either by Hrdlička's measurements or our own inspection. The same is true for the larger Safety Harbor series. Thus, as far as we can determine, there does not seem to be any change in physical type along the Central Gulf Coast and Manatee region from Perico Island to Safety Harbor times. The more exact racial position of these series—as well as the whole Florida brachycephalic group—is a problem we cannot solve at present. With little doubt, the similarities in conformation of the vault link the Florida brachycephals most closely with the Gulf or Centralid people of the Southeast. The differences in the facial skeleton, which are largely in the direction of greater massiveness in the Florida group, may be of racial or subracial proportions, or as suggested by Hrdlička (see p. 549) may be due to a diet especially rich in phosphates. Needed to settle this question is a detailed comparison of Florida series and those from the Muskogean-occupied portions of the Southeast. This comparison would contrast the early brachycephals in the Southeast, presumably as exemplified by the Florida series, and the later brachycephals.

Since cranial deformation is a culture trait recorded in bone, it has become part of the province of the physical anthropologist to observe it. Hrdlička's earlier (1922, pp. 83-85) summary observes that all Florida cranial deformation is of two types, intentional fronto-occipital or presumed intentional occipital. He also adds that both the frequency and degree of head flattening diminish on the Gulf Coast from northwest to southeast. To this we can add the chronological generalization that the trait seems to be late rather than early. Only one occurrence was noted in Moore for a Santa Rosa-Swift Creek-Weeden Island I burial mound; two come from Weeden Island mounds, undifferentiated as to period; three flattened skulls are reported from Weeden Island II mounds;[88] and two Fort Walton Period burial sites are known to show the trait. Cranial deformation was not recorded for Safety Harbor or Englewood Periods. It is not clear, however, how many of these instances are cases of frontooccipital (definite) deformation and how many are only of the simple occipital (probably accidental) types. A review of Hrdlička's later crania studies on Florida (1940) reveals no instances of frontooccipital flattening of an undisputed intentional nature. That true frontooccipital flattening did occur seems attested to, however, by an illustration of a skull from the Sowell Mound (Weeden Island Period) in Moore (1902, fig. 67).

As far as available data go it is, perhaps, most significant that cranial deformation never became a widespread trait in Florida in spite of its common occurrence in the middle and late horizons of the Southeast.

EXTRA-AREAL CONTACTS AND AFFILIATIONS

The south.—To the south of the Florida Gulf Coast area is the Glades archeological culture area. It comprises the southern end of the Florida peninsula from a point at Boca Grande Pass on the west to Fort Bassenger on the Kissimmee River and, thence, to St. Lucie Inlet on the east coast (Goggin, 1947b, p. 119). The Glades is a low-lying region of coastal mangrove swamps and interior grassy marshes. It was, and in some places remains today, a semitropical refuge wilderness. For early American maize horticulturists the Glades country was not a favorable environment; but for a people whose economy was based upon hunting and fishing it offered resources and advantages.

Most archeologists are of the opinion that the Glades area was a cultural cul de sac, receiving but not reciprocating in the diffusion of

[88] These counts do not include cases of slight, questionable flattening in the Weeden Island mound proper (Pi-1) or the Thomas site (Hi-1).

ideas among the prehistoric Indians of Florida and the Southeast. Continued research in the Glades and neighboring areas has demonstrated this to be largely true, although there are some exceptions.

Connections between the Glades area and the Gulf Coast probably go back to preceramic levels. Relationships between Gulf Coast and Glades at this early time, if such existed, must have been those of a general cultural homogeneity. We would expect that these early fishers, hunters, and shellfish gatherers were closely related peoples who migrated from north to south along the shore until a number of villages, each possessing a culture very similar to the next, were founded all along the Gulf Coast and well into the Glades area.

The earliest specific evidence we have for contact between Gulf Coast and Glades follows the preceramic and fiber-tempered pottery eras and manifests itself on a Deptford-Perico Island-Glades I horizonal equation (see fig. 76 for chronological alignments). On this time level it is presumed that all the culture periods involved were still prehorticultural. Regional differences were just beginning to emerge and stabilize out of the cultural homogeneity of the preceramic and fiber-pottery periods, and contact and interchange between Glades and Gulf Coast was probably by way of diffusion of ideas and trade rather than actual mass migrations of people. Glades culture at this time extended farther north than it did in later periods, overlapping into what we have defined as the Gulf Coast area. Perico Island is this northernmost extension and variant of the Glades culture and as such equates with the Glades I and Glades II Periods as they have been established farther south. The boundary line between the Perico Island or early northern Glades-like culture and the Deptford culture of northwest Florida is not definitely known, but Perico Island sites are found as far north as Pinellas County. A few Deptford sherds have been found in Perico Island sites, but no Perico Island sherds or Glades-type shell tools are known from the Deptford sites to the north. Cultural contact as it existed must have been from north to south to judge by the limited evidence available.

A little later the exchange of artifacts and ideas between Gulf Coast and Glades seems to have received stimulation. This is seen in contacts between the Perico Island culture, which evidently lasted on after the close of the Deptford Period, and the new period of the north, Santa Rosa-Swift Creek. The burial-mound idea probably was diffused south at this time, and a single complicated stamped sherd of the Santa Rosa-Swift Creek Period was also found at the Perico Island site. Going in the other direction we have, apparently, the strongest influences out of the Glades and into the Gulf Coast at any period in the sequence. Shell hammers or picks, shell celts, and other shell artifacts, typical of the Glades area, are found in Santa Rosa-Swift Creek burial mounds well up the Gulf Coast. Boundaries between Glades and northern cultures still are not well defined, but there is evidence for assuming that the Santa Rosa-Swift Creek culture was rapidly moving south and encroaching upon territory formerly dominated by the Perico Islanders.

Following the Santa Rosa-Swift Creek Period some contact between Glades and Gulf Coast was maintained during the Weeden Island and Englewood Periods. This is seen almost solely in the exchange of pottery between the southern Weeden Island sites and the Glades. Glades II and III Period pottery types are found in such Weeden Island sites as the Thomas mound (Hi-1) in southern Hillsborough County while occasional Weeden Island and Englewood sherds have shown up in Glades sites as distant as Belle Glade in Palm Beach County (Willey, n.d.). In the late periods Glades-Gulf Coast contacts again pick up. Not only is Glades pottery common in Safety Harbor Period middens and burial mounds, and Safety Harbor ceramic types frequently found in Glades sites, but *Busycon* and *Strombus* shell implements are also present in Safety Harbor sites. It is probably at about this time that many of the big flat-topped shell mounds and complex shell embankment sites were constructed along the southern shores of Tampa Bay and along the Glades area coast. It is likely that the idea of big flat-topped mounds of the temple type was a diffusion southward from Fort Walton via Safety Harbor. The big shellworks around Tampa Bay may have been built by Safety Harbor people, or they may represent a late movement of Glades tribes northward which brought a reintroduction of the temple-mound building complex modified by the addition of the complex embankment features that are so typical of the Glades area.

The east.—The culture areas or regions east of the Gulf Coast have been defined by Goggin (1947b) as: Central Florida, which lies immediately to the east of the central Gulf Coast; the Kissimmee region, lying immediately east of the southern portion of the central Gulf Coast and the Manatee region; the Northern St. Johns, along the Atlantic and the St. Johns River; and the Melbourne region, which lies between the Northern St. Johns and the Glades area. Of the four, the Northern St. Johns region is the most distinctive and the most divergent from the Gulf Coast. Central Florida is, essentially, a geographical transition between the St. Johns and Gulf Coast. The Melbourne region is very close to the Northern St. Johns, and serves as a traditional zone between it and the Glades area. The Kissimmee is a small region most closely related to the Glades area.

As with the Glades area, the earliest connections between the Gulf Coast and east Florida are obscure. It is quite likely that preceramic and Orange Period relationships existed, with a very similar culture in both areas. The first definite tie-ups come on a Santa Rosa-Swift Creek level. In Central Florida, our knowledge of which comes mostly from Alachua County, Goggin (n.d. 2) has defined a Pre-Cades Pond Period (see fig. 76) which equates with Santa Rosa-Swift Creek. Pottery of this period shows relationship to Franklin Plain and the Early Variety of Swift Creek.[89] The burial mound with primary burials is also a feature of the Pre-Cades Pond Period. In general, the drift of influence was probably from west to east at this time. Later, during the Cades Pond Period, connections with the Gulf Coast Weeden Island I culture are reflected in such Weeden Island ceramic traits as compartment vessels, Weeden Island Incised and Plain types, and Swift Creek Complicated Stamped, Late Variety. These wares may be actual trade pieces from the west. St. Johns I types are also present in Cades Pond sites, and the distinctive type, Oklawaha Plain (pl. 41, *a*), characteristic of Central Florida and the St. Johns area, shows close linkages with Weeden Island I Period ceramics. The burial mounds of the Cades Pond Period contain secondary burials.[90] The Central Florida Hickory Pond Period correlates with Weeden Island II of the Gulf Coast. This is a burial-mound period in which Weeden Island trade wares are present. Ceramic influence was, apparently, passing both ways at this time. St. Johns Check Stamped, a type developed on the St. Johns River, is found in both Hickory Pond and Weeden Island II sites, while local Central Florida types such as Gainesville Linear Punctated and Prairie Cord-marked turn up in Weeden Island II sites on the Gulf Coast as trade wares. Comparable cross ties have been established for the later Alachua and Fort Walton Periods.

---

[89] A mound excavated by James Bell (1883, pp. 635-637) in the southern part of Alachua County yielded pottery showing these Santa Rosa-Swift Creek affinities (U.S.N.M. No. 45802).

[90] Cades Pond Period sites were excavated by Bell (1883, pp. 635-637) near Gainesville, Alachua County. Mound 3 of this group was a 12-foot-high burial mound containing 1,000 or more secondary burials along with Weeden Island I and Cades Ponds sherds (U.S.N.M. No. 43176). Bell's mound 5, of the same group, also fits the Cades Pond-Weeden Island I time horizon (U.S.N.M. Nos. 43176-43177-43179). The Snowden mound, excavated by J. P. Rogan, also dates from this same period, judging by the collection (U.S.N.M. No. 88079). The Snowden mound was about 3 miles southeast of Gainesville.

South of Alachua and Marion Counties there is a small section of interior Florida centering upon Lake County and including part of the adjoining counties of Sumter and Orange. In his first consideration of Florida culture areas and subareas, Goggin (1947b) included this Lake County section in the Central Florida area; later (Goggin, n.d. 2) he related it as a subdivision of the Gulf Coast area. I have not, in this report, considered it as a part of the Gulf Coast. Like north-central Florida, it is transitional between the Gulf Coast and the St. Johns areas. However it is considered from a regional-taxonomic point of view, the Lake County section has significance in showing the eastward extent of Gulf Coast influences.

Data for the Lake County region come largely from Moore (1895a) and Featherstonhaugh (1899). Moore excavated several sites in the region, among them the Hopson, Tavares, Helena, and Old Okahumpka mounds. These were all low sand and earth mounds containing secondary burials. Polished-stone celts, stone projectiles, stone and shell pendants of various kinds, copper beads and decorated sheet-copper objects, sheet mica, and pottery were found in the mounds. The traits of "killing" vessels by perforation and of making vessels with holes for mortuary purposes were also noted. Pottery is not typical of either Weeden Island or Santa Rosa-Swift Creek. In the Hopson mound were a rather crude double bowl, on the order of a Weeden Island compartment tray, and a rectangular boxlike bowl. Both vessels were plain. More direct contact with the Gulf Coast is seen in a sherd from the Tavares site which is typical Weeden Island (or Papys Bayou) Incised (Moore, 1895a, pl. LXXXVI, fig. 4). Goggin (n.d.2) equates the Hopson mound with Santa Rosa-Swift Creek and the others with Weeden Island I. I agree that the mounds equate with the Gulf Coast burial-mound periods, either Weeden Island or Santa Rosa-Swift Creek, but hesitate to refine the dating on any of them beyond this identification.

Featherstonhaugh (1899) excavated near Lake Apopka, Orange County, at a group known as the Brooker mounds. He describes the site as four mounds which were grouped within a few hundred feet of each other. One was a burial mound; the others he believed to be house platforms. He found several hundred secondary burials in the burial mound along with polished celts, a duck-head stone pendant, shell plummet pendants, shell beads, shell pins, thin plates of copper, and great masses of broken pottery. Featherstonhaugh's collections from the site, now in the United States National Museum, contain, among other items, a single-cymbal copper ear spool (No. 173819) and a collection of sherds (Nos. 173821-173824). The latter includes

Biscayne and Papys Bayou Series types. Biscayne and Wakulla Check Stamped date the mound on the general Weeden Island II horizon, but it is possible that the mound has been used in a later period as well, as Featherstonhaugh describes Venetian glass beads and iron tools.

As stated, the preceramic and early ceramic levels of the St. Johns region have no well-defined counterparts on the Gulf Coast. It is possible, though, that certain pottery traits of the Orange, or fiber-tempered ceramic, Period do carry over into the later Gulf Coast periods. One indication of this is the linear-punctation technique that is so common in Weeden Island ceramics. This technique is not present in Deptford or Santa Rosa-Swift Creek but is a feature of the Orange Period. The transference of the linear-punctation feature from the Orange Period on the St. Johns to Weeden Island on the Gulf Coast is a possibility to be considered; however, intermediate stages of this transference and development have not yet been revealed.

It is with the subsequent St. Johns I Period that the specific connections between Gulf Coast and St. Johns areas appear in great numbers. This linkage is seen in burial mounds, secondary burials, stone celts, the use of copper, mica, galena, *Strombus* celts, *Busycon* cups, common mortuary deposits of pottery, the "killing" of vessels, and a variety of pottery traits. During the earlier part of the St. Johns I Period, the phase contemporaneous with Deptford and Santa Rosa-Swift Creek, Deptford pottery appears as trade in the St. Johns region along with the local St. Johns and Oklawaha types. Tetrapodal supports on pottery also come into the St. Johns at this same time. One of the distinctive features of the local St. Johns ware of the early St. Johns I is the boat-shaped or boxlike bowl form, and the probabilities favor the development of this trait in the St. Johns region. For it is here that the boat-shaped vessel form, an uncommon one in other parts of the Southeast, enjoys its greatest vogue. The boat-shaped bowl probably passed from east to west at this early period as it is known in at least one Deptford site in northwest Florida. Early Swift Creek Complicated Stamped pottery occurs as a minority type in the early phase of the St. Johns I Period, but, according to Goggin (n.d.2), it comes in slightly later than the Deptford types. Contemporaneous with the Swift Creek types we have the greatest clustering of Hopewellian traits of any period in the Northern St. Johns sequence. This is, of course, paralleled by the strong Hopewellian cast of the Santa Rosa-Swift Creek Period in west Florida. These influences are seen, particularly, in the relative abundance of ornamental metalwork in these periods. These Hopewellian influences probably passed to the St. Johns by way of the Gulf Coast Santa Rosa-Swift Creek culture, or they may possibly have come from the north. The isolated geographical position of the St. Johns region favors a western entry through the Gulf area.

In the latter phase of the St. Johns I Period the Gulf Coast influences are out of Weeden Island, and there are numerous examples of western trade wares in the east. It is at this time in the west (Weeden Island II) that the eastern type, Oklawaha Plain, is both accepted as a trade ware and imitated. The later St. Johns II Period is characterized, as is Weeden Island II, by the rise of the small check stamped pottery. On the Gulf this is Wakulla Check Stamped, and in east Florida it is the St. Johns or Biscayne Check Stamped. These widely popular types probably had their origins on the St. Johns River and spread from there to the Gulf and even farther west. Toward the end of the St. Johns II Period temple mounds with ramps and late ceramics of the Fort Walton and Englewood styles are seen on the northern St. Johns. The St. Johns sequence closes with a Spanish Mission-Indian culture, the St. Augustine Period, which is comparable and related to the Leon-Jefferson Period in northwest Florida.

South of the Northern St. Johns is the Melbourne region which is largely a pale reflection of happenings to the north. There are, apparently, no burial mounds in the Malabar I Period, which corresponds with St. Johns I. Burial mounds appear in Malabar II along with the small check stamped pottery and the stone celt (Goggin, n.d.2). This region, because of its geographical position and general backwardness had neither much effect upon, nor was it closely bound up with, the course of developments on the Gulf Coast.

The north.—We have seen how, following the preceramic and fiber-tempered pottery periods, the Gulf Coast and east Florida were similarly influenced. In some cases this was a matter of exchange between the Gulf area on the one hand and Central Florida and the St. Johns regions on the other. But it is also obvious certain other elements were probably derived from a third source. To attempt to explain some of these diffusions we look northward to the Georgia area. During the preceramic and fiber-tempered periods the Georgia coast and the lower Savannah River displayed many similarities to the comparable Mount Taylor (preceramic) and Orange (fiber-tempered ceramic) Periods of the St. Johns (see fig. 76). In the succeeding Deptford Period,[91] coastal Georgia seems to have been a

[91] A. J. Waring, Jr., has recently isolated a new chronological period between the Georgia Stallings Island and Deptford Periods. Pottery of this new period

center for certain ceramic ideas. These are expressed in the Deptford Complex which is best known from the Georgia coast and South Carolina. Deptford is, in effect, a South Atlantic complex, and everything points to its having diffused into Florida from the north and northeast. The geography of the situation suggests that Deptford influence probably reached the Northern St. Johns prior to its arrival on the northwest Gulf Coast. In view of this it is curious that Deptford has not yet been demonstrated to be full period in east Florida as it is in the west.

The feature of tetrapodal supports is associated with the Deptford Complex in northwest Florida and appears on this time horizon in east Florida. On the Georgia coast, the type Deptford Simple Stamped shows the podal appendages, although the Deptford check stamped types do not (Caldwell and Waring, 1939). It is possible although disputable that the tetrapodal-support idea made its way into Florida from the north, with the Deptford Complex. The origin and distribution of this ceramic feature in the southeastern and eastern United States is still a puzzle. It will be discussed further in the succeeding section on "The West and the North."

The problem of the first appearance of the burial mound in the Southeast is unsettled. This question, as it affects Gulf Florida, is involved with the origins of Swift Creek and related types of complicated stamped pottery. Swift Creek Complicated Stamped of the Early Variety is one of the diagnostics of the Santa Rosa-Swift Creek Period in Gulf Florida, and is also found in the early phase of the St. Johns I Period farther east. The area of intensity for the Swift Creek is south and central Georgia (fig. 73, *e-j*), overlapping into adjacent northwest Florida. In both the St. Johns and Gulf Coast areas complicated stamped pottery does not appear until after the advent of the first burial mounds. On the other hand, in central Georgia its earliest occurrences are thought to be unaccompanied by the burial-mound trait. In consideration of this I am inclined to believe that the burial-mound idea did not come into Florida from the immediate north or by way of Georgia; but complicated stamped pottery, which seems to have had an early history separate from the burial mound, apparently did spread from a hearth in Georgia southward into Florida.

After the Santa Rosa-Swift Creek Period, relationships between Gulf Florida and Georgia were maintained in the realm of trade in raw materials. Mica and stone for celts were two of the main im-

---

is sand-tempered ware, and, seemingly, represents an intermediate stage between the decorated fiber-tempered pottery and the Deptford types. (Waring, personal communication, 1947-48.)

FIG. 73.—Related pottery types from Louisiana and Georgia. *a, b,* Marksville Stamped; *c, d,* Marksville Incised; *e, j,* Swift Creek Complicated Stamped. (Redrawn from the following sources; *a, b, c,* after Setzler, 1933, pls. 1, 4, 3; *d,* after Ford and Willey, 1940, fig. 36; *e-j,* after Kelly, 1938, pl. 11.)

ports from the uplands, while Gulf shells were sent north in return. Weeden Island Period sites were established well up the major river systems into Georgia as the northernmost outposts of the culture. Such sites have been found in the Okefenokee Swamp in south Georgia,[92] and the big Kolomoki site in southwest Georgia was inhabited at least for a time by Weeden Islanders (personal communication, A. R. Kelly and W. Sears, July 1948). Farther to the north Weeden Island influences in vessel and rim forms are seen in late Swift Creek levels near Macon.

During the Fort Walton Period there are a number of similarities between the Gulf Coast and the contemporaneous Lamar Period of Georgia, but it is most likely that this is the result of both areas responding to a third major influence rather than the direct effects of one upon the other. Very late, in the Leon-Jefferson Period, ceramic influence attributable to Georgia is seen in northwest Florida. The appearance of late complicated stamped wares in Florida at this time is a part of such influence. There is historic corroboration of this in that Creek tribes are known to have moved into north Florida at the close of the seventeenth century.

The west and the north.—It was from the west and the northwest that the major cultural influences were exerted upon Gulf Florida. It has been seen how south and east Florida, especially in the later periods, were on the receiving rather than the giving end of the main currents of diffusion as these passed between the Gulf Coast and the remainder of Florida. To the immediate north, the cultures of Georgia were largely influential in forming the ceramic patterns of the Gulf Coast during the earlier periods after which their influence lessened. It was from the west along the Gulf and the Gulf Coastal Plain that an important series of new ideas and, possibly, peoples came that were to link the Florida Gulf Coast with the vigorous and rapidly changing culture centers of the Mississippi Valley. It is likely that these western influences began as early as the Deptford Period, and they were probably derived out of the Tchefuncte culture of Louisiana (see fig. 76) or from similar and equally early manifestations in Alabama (Wimberly and Tourtelot, 1941) and Mississippi (Jennings, 1941). The Tchefuncte culture is characterized by incised, punctated, linear-punctated, and rocker-stamped pottery, by small, collared jars with tetrapodal supports, the coiling principle in pottery making, the use of smoking pipes, and the burial mound with both

[92] Collections in the Peabody Museum, Yale University, from Bug-a-boo Island (Nos. 21579-21580) and Buzzard mound (No. 21575), both in the Okefenokee, are clearly Weeden Island.

primary and secondary burials. Pottery types of the north Alabama Alexander Series are found in association. (See Ford and Quimby, 1945.) It is from Tchefuncte that I am disposed to derive the tetrapodal vessel supports for Deptford and subsequent periods of the lower eastern Southeast. The podal support trait, as it appears in Deptford, is simple and rare. In the coeval Tchefuncte culture it is elaborated and common (see Ford and Quimby, 1945, fig. 18). In Tchefuncte supporting feet occur on vessel bases and with vessel shapes that are in a different tradition than either the subconoidal pots of Deptford and similar Woodland styles or the deep open bowls of the Archaic fiber-tempered pottery. The burial-mound idea may also have been transferred from west to east on the Tchefuncte-Deptford level. If so, it did not become popular on the Florida Gulf for some time as no Deptford Period burial mounds are recorded either there or in Georgia. It is reasonable to believe, however, that Deptford burial mounds will be found and, as such, should represent the inception of the mound idea in Georgia and Florida. Along with the burial mound, or at about the same time, the customs of secondary burial and ceremonial breakage of grave pottery probably were diffused into Gulf Florida from the west.

It must be emphasized that the question of the burial-mound complex in Gulf Florida is but one aspect of the larger historical problem of the origin and diffusion of mound burial in the eastern United States and that the interpretations given here are admittedly tentative. More finely calibrated sequence dating, either relative or absolute, must be developed in eastern archeology before such a complex problem and all its ramifications can be satisfactorily resolved. This applies to the widespread net of relationships linking Tchefuncte, Adena, and other burial-mound cultures as well as to the nature of the specific connections that existed between Tchefuncte and the cultures of Gulf Florida and south Georgia.

With the beginnings of the Santa Rosa-Swift Creek Period the affiliations of the Florida Gulf and Lower Mississippi Valley become very close. Tribal migrations from west to east may have taken place at this time. If the burial-mound complex was established in west Florida toward the close of the Deptford Period, and more or less simultaneously with the rise of the Swift Creek pottery styles, Marksvillian ceramic influences from the west were then intrusive into this early Swift Creek burial-mound culture. Or if the Marksvillian ceramic traits came into Gulf Florida as a part of the burial-mound complex, Swift Creek styles were added to this complex after its arrival and establishment. Data on this point are not sufficient to enable us to choose between the alternatives. The Marksvillian and Troyvillian (fig. 74) ceramic influences in Florida are very specific (fig. 73, *a-d*), although there are differences between the Santa Rosa Series and the Louisiana pottery types. The Santa Rosa pottery was definitely Florida-made, not imported ware. The cambered rim decorated with incised cross-hachure, which is typically Marksvillian and Hopewellian, is not, for example, found in Santa Rosa-Swift Creek; and there are other differences which suggest a parallel development in the two regions rather than a complete dependence of one upon the other. Some of these differences may hark back to earlier influences into Florida out of Tchefuncte. For instance, the type Santa Rosa Stamped is much closer in decorative features to Tchefuncte Stamped than it is to Marksville Stamped, and Crystal River Incised has a much greater resemblance to the Tchefuncte type, Orleans Punctated (Ford and Quimby, 1945, pp. 62-63, pl. 6) than it has to any Marksville type.

Monitor pipes of the Santa Rosa-Swift Creek Period can be related to similar pipes in the Marksville Period, and copper ear spools of the cymbal and bicymbal types are also both Marksvillian and Santa Rosa-Swift Creek. Other Gulf Florida copper forms, such as the conjoined tubes and the repoussé placques or ornaments are more Ohio Hopewellian than Marksvillian. At least copper has never been found in such abundance in the reported Marksville mounds. This may indicate channels of Hopewellian influence into Florida other than the Marksville. Possibly such copper artifacts were traded directly south out of the Ohio Valley through Alabama and Georgia rather than down the Mississippi River and then along the Gulf Coast to Florida.

One fascinating element in Santa Rosa-Swift Creek which has no parallel in Marksville, or in any Hopewellian culture, as far as we know, is the negative-painting or resist-dye process of decorating pottery. The Gulf Coast occurrences of negative-painted pottery are the earliest in the east, antedating by what must be several centuries the use of the negative technique in Middle Mississippian pottery design in the Cumberland area and other parts of the Southeast. The most reasonable explanation is that the resist-dye process was transferred from wood, textiles, or gourds to pottery in Gulf Florida. Knowledge of the technique in connection with perishable materials may have come into the Southeast from east Mexico. The Vera Cruz-Tamaulipas area is the nearest locality in which negative-painted pottery is found.

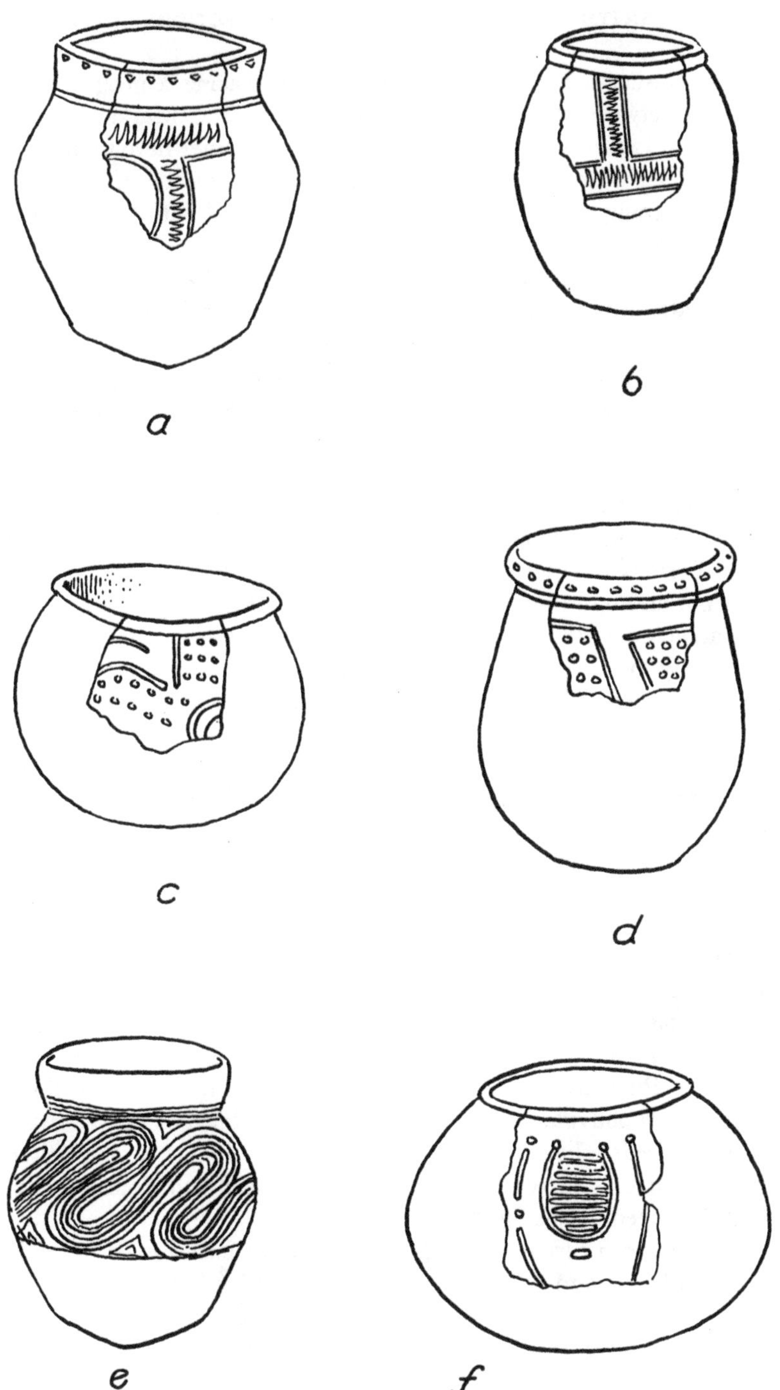

FIG. 74.—Related pottery types from Louisiana. *a, b,* Troyville Stamped; *c, d,* Churupa Punctated; *e, f,* Yokena Incised. (After Ford and Willey, 1939.)

In this discussion we have refrained from placing a geographical boundary between the Santa Rosa-Swift Creek and Marksville cultures, but it is almost certain that the two merge somewhere in the 150 miles that separate Pensacola Bay from the delta of the Mississippi. This intervening coastal strip should be investigated with the problem of such a contact in mind.

In the succeeding Weeden Island Periods the Santa Rosa-Swift Creek settlement pattern of the small villages and the associated burial mounds is retained; but, contemporaneously, a similar community type was undergoing profound changes in the Troyville and Coles Creek cultures of Louisiana. Large temple-mound sites were founded in the Troyville Period and became widespread during Coles Creek, while the burial mound either completely disappeared or is very rare for these periods. The extent to which the temple-mound complex became established in Gulf Florida during the Weeden Island Periods has not been fully determined, but it is certain that it was not an important feature. Possibly the idea was just beginning to be accepted as there are some Gulf Coast mounds of modest size which may be Weeden Island temple mounds, and in southwest Georgia the big Kolomoki temple mound may be a Weeden Island structure.

The strong ceramic affinities of the Gulf Coast and the Lower Mississippi Valley during the Weeden Island and Troyville-Coles Creek Periods are best seen in the types Weeden Island Incised and Weeden Island Punctated and the Louisiana type, French Fork Incised. In the Louisiana sequence the French Fork type has its inception in the Troyville Period, reaches its maximum occurrence just at the close of this period, and decreases and finally disappears during the Coles Creek Period. Other types further strengthen this Florida-Louisiana relationship. Mazique Incised and Rhinehardt Punctated in Louisiana have parallels in Carrabelle Incised and Carrabelle Punctated, and Weeden Island Zoned Red has a striking likeness to Woodville Red Filmed. Additional linkages can be made between Weeden Island Plain and Coles Creek Plain, Keith Incised and Beldeau Incised, and Wakulla Check Stamped and Pontchartrain Check Stamped. (See fig. 75.)

These western ceramic affiliations of Weeden Island exist not only between Florida and the Lower Mississippi Valley but extend up the drainage of the Red River in Louisiana into southwestern Arkansas. In the latter area the Weeden Island-like pottery, as found at the Crenshaw site (Dickinson, 1936), underlies late Caddoan pottery. Krieger (1946, fig. 26) has dated it as of about A.D. 1200-1300 (see Crenshaw, fig. 76).

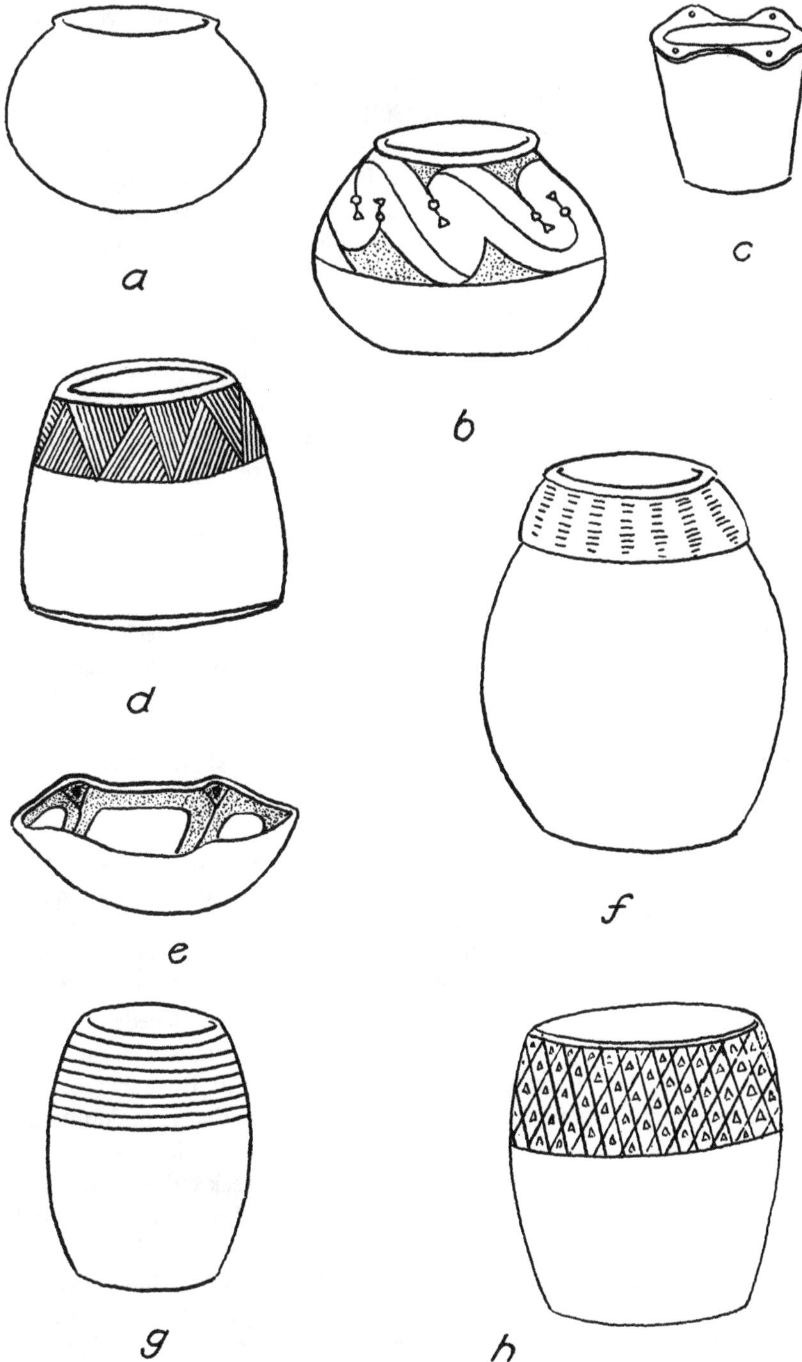

FIG. 75.—Related pottery types from Louisiana. *a, c,* Coles Creek Plain; *b,* French Fork Incised; *d,* Mazique Incised; *e,* Woodville Red Filmed; *f,* Rhinehardt Punctated; *g,* Coles Creek Incised; *h,* Beldeau Incised. (After Ford and Willey, 1939.)

That separate parallel developments of the Weeden Island or French Fork style took place in Gulf Florida, southern Louisiana, and southwestern Arkansas is not a plausible assumption. Although there are regional differences, there is too much of a unity in this Weeden Island-French Fork-pre-Caddo style group to account for it by parallel developments from a similar ancestry. Of the three areas where the Weeden Island-like wares occur, the greatest diversity and elaboration of what might be called the central stylistic themes are found in Gulf Florida. This suggests a Floridian origin and development with a subsequent westward diffusion. There are possible types for the Weeden Island or French Fork style in Marksville but those of Santa Rosa-Swift Creek are more convincing. For example, the type Crystal River Incised is a more logical ancestor to Weeden Island Incised than any of the Louisiana Marksville types.

If we are correct, and the principal flow of ceramic ideas during the Troyville and early Coles Creek Periods was from east to west, then this stream of influence and its direction certainly continued in late Coles Creek and Weeden Island II times. Small check stamped pottery appears in southern Louisiana at this period and seems to come from the east where similar types were extremely popular during the Weeden Island II. As opposed to this the marker type for Coles Creek, Coles Creek Incised, had only a slight effect upon Florida ceramic traditions. This is seen in St. Petersburg Incised, a rather rare type in late Weeden Island II.

The distribution of Weeden Island culture actually extends west of the boundaries of the Gulf Coast area as we have defined them. Continued archeological explorations in south Georgia and south Alabama are almost certain to reveal more sites of the type. On the lower Tombigbee River in Alabama, 50 to 75 miles from the Gulf Coast, Moore (1905, pp. 253-262) excavated three Weeden Island burial mounds—Payne's Woodyard, Carney's Bluff, and Kimbell's Field. Along the Alabama coast, De Jarnette and Bucker (ms. of 1937) explored a mound in lower Baldwin County that is undoubtedly Weeden Island. The westward continuation of Weeden Island and the eastward extension of the Troyville-Coles Creek cultures are still to be plotted, but the presence of Weeden Island as a burial-mound and ceramic complex in much of south Alabama is assured.

The possibility of a much wider range for Weeden Island ceramic ideas than we have outlined above should be kept in mind. Weeden Island is, essentially, a pre-Middle Mississippian culture. While there is undoubtedly some contemporaneity between Weeden Island II and the earlier phases of Middle Mississippi (Temple Mound I horizon) the artistic patterns of Weeden Island were formulated before this. They were, in fact, in formulation during the Santa Rosa-Swift Creek Period. One fact should be emphasized. *During the Santa Rosa-Swift Creek and Weeden Island I Periods no other area in the eastern United States produced such an elaboration of pottery vessel forms, decorative techniques and designs, and effigy modeling as did the Florida Gulf Coast.* Only the Middle Mississippian and Caddoan potteries rival the Weeden Island in elaborateness and skill, and these styles are clearly later in time. In Santa Rosa-Swift Creek and Weeden Island I we note the following techniques: incision, punctation, linear punctation, rocker stamping, direct painting, negative painting, effigy modeling, and complicated stamping. Several of these technical traits are found in late Middle Mississippian pottery; and two of them are particularly characteristic of much of it. These last are effigy adorno modeling and negative painting. It is suggested here that both of these techniques may have been derived from a culture with Weeden Island-type ceramics that preceded and influenced later Middle Mississippian wares in the Central Mississippi or Lower Ohio Valleys. Such a transition could have been taking place during the early Middle Mississippian periods in western Arkansas and eastern Tennessee and Mississippi or even farther north. A hint of contact is seen at Cahokia, Ill., where occasional sherds which are very much like Weeden Island Incised have been found in association with the earlier or Old Village occupation of that site (Willey, 1945, p. 243). All this is, of course, a hypothesis for which most of the evidence is lacking, but the striking similarity between Middle Mississippian bird and human-head rim effigies and those of Weeden Island prompts it when one realizes that the Weeden Island tradition for this sort of thing is considerably the older.[93]

Influence from the west and the north is plainly dominant in the Fort Walton Period of Gulf Coast prehistory, and these influences, though fainter, are registered in the south in the contemporaneous Safety Harbor Period. Although the idea for the temple mound may have reached west Florida in Weeden Island times, it did not become firmly established until Fort Walton. It is likely that during this later period the temple mound and the ceremonial complexes which surrounded it were introduced under different circumstances than previously. This was probably as part of an actual invasion of

[93] In this connection, another link between a Gulf Coast burial-mound culture and the late Middle Mississippian horizon is the suggestive prototypes for the Southern Cult in the ceramic designs found at Crystal River, a Santa Rosa-Swift Creek Period site (see Willey, 1948c).

the northwest Gulf region by a people whose culture was predominantly Middle Mississippian. Something of the possibilities of continuity between Weeden Island and Fort Walton ceramics has already been discussed. Design lay-outs and rim effigy forms may be local Florida transfers from Weeden Island to Fort Walton. Or the Fort Walton rim effigy could be a reintroducton of an old Weeden Island idea that had been integrated into and modified by a Middle Mississippian culture. Whichever was the case we can be fairly sure that some other new ceramic modes were being brought into west Florida during the Fort Walton Period. These new features of vessel form, vessel decoration, and of temper can be traced to south, central, and even northern Alabama. Large bowls used for burials covers, stylized death's-head (?) designs, shell temper, frog-effigy bowls, the bottle form, and black engraved ware are some of them.

It is in the Fort Walton Period that a very few evidences of the Southern Cult (Waring and Holder, 1945; Krieger, 1945) appear in west Florida. These are the engraved eagle and eagle-mask designs on a polished black pottery specimen from the Jolly Bay (Wl-15) site in Walton County. Occasional "Cult" pieces are found in the late sites of the St. Johns farther east, but "Cult" influence does not seem to have been strong in Gulf Florida.

The West Indies.—The problem of Florida-Antillean connections has been considered for many years. It is, I believe, a fair statement to say that the case for cultural influence in either direction has never been satisfactorily demonstrated. This does not deny the possibilities of such contact. It is, indeed, curious that more evidences of trade or intercommunication have not been found.[94] Fontaneda, the shipwrecked Spanish boy who spent several years with the Calusa Indians in the sixteenth century, reported that there was a colony of Arawaks living in southwest Florida for a time under the sovereignty of the Calusa leader Calos (Escalente Fontaneda, 1944). In spite of what seem to be the potentialities of the situation there is little in the archeology of either Florida or the Antilles that implies cultural affiliations of the same order which we have been discussing for Gulf Florida and other areas of the southeastern United States.

Osgood has approached the problem of Florida-West Indian connections on the time level of the Southeastern Archaic culture. He has taken the hypothesis (Osgood, 1942, p. 57), also advanced by others, that the first inhabitants of Cuba were a former North

[94] The only bona fide West Indian trade item found in Florida is a stone ax from a site in Alachua County (Goggin and Rouse, 1948). This ax is of the "eared" variety common to the Lesser Antilles.

American preagricultural, preceramic people who were gradually forced south in the Florida peninsula and eventually crossed over to Cuba where they ultimately evolved the Ciboney type culture. He dates this movement at about A.D. 500 which is only slightly earlier than the estimated beginnings of the agricultural and ceramic periods in Florida whose populations are presumed to have been responsible for displacing the Floridian Archaic tribes. The Archaic Southeastern emigrants apparently had the Greater Antilles to themselves until they were compressed into western Cuba by the expansion of the agricultural, pottery-making Arawaks who invaded the islands from South America.

This hypothesis is plausible and should be investigated further. The main difficulty has been in the tracing out of relationships between western Cuba and south Florida by comparisons of the shell tools found in the two areas. These are similar, but the environments are similar; and the shell implements in question are also so extremely simple that they fail to clinch the argument for a diffusion (Osgood, 1942, pp. 40-43). Even if true, the greater part of the story of Gulf Coast development, as presented here, is not affected by this theory. Only the postulated preceramic period would be involved.

Rouse has viewed the problem also from the point of view of Florida-to-the-Antilles diffusions (Rouse, 1940). He was primarily concerned with the origins of the Meillac pottery, a ceramic tradition that is found in the northern Greater Antilles and which is the earliest pottery in those islands where it follows the preceramic horizon. It was his thesis that the relatively simple incised and modeled Meillac ware had been influenced by North American decorative techniques. He drew his Southeastern comparisons not from Florida, alone, but from several areas as well as from different time levels. Rouse's methodology was not grounded on comparisons of types or styles but with the cross-matching of what he termed "modes." These modes are isolated elements such as "punctation," "curved incised lines," or "naturalistic design." By treating the data in this rather atomistic fashion, he was able to demonstrate that Meillac pottery had a greater over-all similarity to pottery of the southeastern United States than it did to wares in northeastern South America. This was the crux of his argument, and although it does have a bearing upon Southeastern-West Indian relationships, it does not aid us greatly in working out the time and place of specified diffusions. The frame of reference is too general to make his conclusions more than suggestive.

The most intriguing Florida-Antillean similarities are, I think, between Weeden Island pottery and the Carrier ceramic style of the

Indies. The Carrier style is the late, most widely distributed, best-known pottery type of the Greater Antilles. It has in the past usually been referred to as "Arawak pottery." [95] In mode-for-mode or element-for-element comparisons, using the Carrier modes described by Rouse (1940, pp. 59-60), an imposing case can be made for the relationship of Weeden Island and Carrier. Out of the 23 Carrier modes 21 are found in Weeden Island. While there is an annoying, elusive similarity between the two styles, this resemblance is nowhere near as strong as the mode analysis might lead one to believe. A close inspection of the modes or elements held in common weakens, rather than strengthens, the arguments for relationship between the two styles. For example, the modes of "naturalistic design" and "zoomorphic head lugs" are quite distinct as they are found in each style: Weeden Island emphasizes the bird motif; Carrier, the monkey or the bat. "Curved incised lines," "curvilinear incised design," "punctation," and "modeling" are designations so general that they have little meaning except for very broad contrasts or comparisons. At the same time, a few of the modes stand up fairly well under this scrutiny. "Line and dot incision," or terminal punctations in or at the ends of incised lines, in Carrier are deep, hemiconical gouges terminating a broad, round-bottomed incision or groove. This incision and punctation is a little bolder than seen in most Weeden Island Incised, but it compares very favorably with some of the Weeden Island Incised pottery of Weeden Island I or some of the bold line incision techniques of the preceding Santa Rosa-Swift Creek Period. Another mode, "inturned shoulders," producing the flattened-globular bowl form, is a fairly common New World pottery shape, but the fact that the Florida Gulf Coast seems to be an early Southeastern center for the trait cannot be ignored. In the same way, "ridge on outside rim," or folded rim, is a simple idea, but, like the flattened-globular bowl, its Southeastern center is the Florida Gulf. The "boat-shaped bowl" is another mode of this same kind. Florida is the center for the form. It is more common on the St. Johns than the Gulf Coast but does occur in the latter area in Weeden Island times and earlier.

We have then, a number of features in Carrier ceramics which are also typical or present in Weeden Island. Some of these, like the flattened-globular bowl, the folded rim, and the boat-shaped bowl are

[95] Rouse has established regional styles for the various geographical units of the West Indies. The late period styles or types in Puerto Rico (Esperanza and Capá), Dominican Republic (Boca Chica), and eastern Cuba (Pueblo Viejo) are all similar to the Carrier from Haiti and the Bahamas (Rouse, 1948).

very characteristic of the Florida or Florida Gulf Coast area; spread to other parts of the Southeast from there; and may have been introduced from the West Indies. These similarities and the distributional facts that accompany them are not sufficient to prove diffusion between Florida and the Antilles, but they are provocative enough to keep the door open to this possibility. Time equations between the two areas would not preclude such diffusions. The Carrier and related styles were flourishing in the West Indies at the time of Columbus or up until about A.D. 1500. The date line 1500 is also the estimated terminal date of the Weeden Island culture in Florida. Beginning dates for both Weeden Island and Carrier can only be estimated, and with less accuracy than the terminal dates. As such they do not serve as reliable data points for plotting the course of area-to-area connections. The best we can say is that if diffusion did take place it could have proceeded from north to south or vice versa. Such a contact would have bypassed both western Cuba and southern Florida which lack, respectively, the Carrier and Weeden Island types.

There is one other possibility of ceramic influence between the Antilles and the Southeast. Holmes suggested many years ago (Holmes, 1894b) that complicated stamped pottery in the southeastern States was the result of the introduction of West Indian art forms in wood carving onto the North American mainland. He had come upon this idea while examining a unique carved wooden stool or *duho* from Turk's Island in the Bahamas. In his opinion the carved designs on the stool were strikingly like those found on Southeastern complicated stamped pottery, and he inferred that Southeastern artisans had copied such designs from stools or other wooden objects onto the wooden paddles with which they stamped their pottery. The idea is partially sustained by recent findings in Southeastern archeology which show that the complicated stamped pottery styles appear quite suddenly and full-blown. Prior to the appearance of the complicated styles, pottery was stamped, but the designs were simple lines or checks. This abrupt appearance of the new pottery designs does argue for a relatively sudden technological transference of the complicated carvings from other manufactures. Such a process could have occurred, however, entirely within Southeastern native traditions; and proof of a West Indian diffusion reverts, in final analysis, to similarity or lack of similarity between West Indian and Southeastern designs. The examples of design which Holmes shows, from the wooden stool and from Southeastern stamped pottery, are certainly suggestive of contact in their general similarity. Holmes' proposition, like some of the others, should be examined by more thorough and rigorous analysis.

We have considered the question almost entirely upon the basis of pottery similarity or dissimilarity, but there is one aspect of late Antillean culture that definitely does not reinforce the arguments favoring a connection with Weeden Island. This is the burial-mound trait. Neither in Carrier nor in any other West Indian culture do we have definite evidence of burial mounds.[96] This is a basic distinction between West Indian cultures and not only Weeden Island but many contemporary horticultural societies in the southeastern United States.

TIME-SPACE INTEGRATION

A graphic expression of the temporal and spatial relationships of Florida Gulf Coast culture periods and neighboring archeological culture areas in the Southeast is the chronology chart presented in figure 76. The Gulf Florida sequences are given in the three regional divisions as they have been developed in this report: the northwest, the central, and the Manatee. Gulf Coast and Georgia and Gulf Coast and Louisiana correlations follow the survey conclusions of Willey and Woodbury (1942) and of Ford and Willey (1941). The position of the Leon-Jefferson Period is from H. G. Smith (1948). Correlations of Gulf Coast with the Glades and East Florida are taken from Goggin (1947b; n.d.2), and from numerous conversations with Goggin during 1944-48. The placing of the "Caddo" area column in juxtaposition to the other sequences is after Krieger (1946). The chronological charts of Martin, Quimby, and Collier (1947) and J. B. Griffin (1946) have also been consulted. The estimated absolute dates are taken directly from Krieger (1946) for the centuries from A.D. 1200 to 1700. (See also Krieger, 1947.) These are the best archeological dating estimates for the Southeast, cross-tying as they do with the tree-ring calendar in the eastern Pueblo area of New Mexico. The effect of Krieger's dating has been to drop back the estimates for the later periods by 100 to 200 years.[97] For example, in the Lower Mississippi Valley column the beginnings of the Placquemine Period have been revised from a date of A.D. 1600 to approximately 1450, and the Coles Creek Period has been lowered from an initial date of around A.D. 1350 to about 1250. Marksville and

---

[96] Gower (1927, pp. 13 and 49) lists burial mounds as "Tainan" or Arawak. There is no clear-cut evidence anywhere in the West Indies for burial mounds as distinguished from rubbish hillocks in which burials were made.

[97] As this goes to press Krieger's recent (1949) dating estimates in eastern Texas place Early Alto (Gahagan) as coeval with Marksville (and Santa Rosa-Swift Creek) and place them all as of about A.D. 500.

Tchefuncte have been made earlier in accordance with these changes. The same is true for the Florida Gulf Coast where Fort Walton is now given a beginning date of 1500, and the preceding periods lowered to conform with this (cf. Ford and Willey, 1941, figs. 2 and 6). The earlier periods represented on the chart, the preceramic, Orange, Stallings Island, Deptford, and probably Tchefuncte, have all been foreshortened out of all proportion with the middle and late periods. This was done to make room for them on the chart. It probably would have been closer to the truth if these horizons had been lengthened to three or four times the duration of such periods as Santa Rosa-Swift Creek or Weeden Island.

All sequence equations have been made upon the basis of ceramic cross ties. In some instances this has been by means of trade wares; in others, stylistic resemblances indicative of relatively rapid diffusion have served. The equation of culture periods by ceramic types has, in some cases, been at variance with other aspects of the cultures involved. For example, the Troyville Period of Louisiana has been matched on the chronology chart (fig. 76) with the Weeden Island I Period of the Gulf Coast, and the ceramic correlation of the two periods is, indeed, high. The distribution of the burial-mound complex, on the other hand, does not conform to this equation. Weeden Island I, and also Weeden Island II, are burial-mound cultures, whereas Troyville and Coles Creek, their Louisiana contemporaries, are not. Sequence alignments by ceramics are even further violated when we consider the Safety Harbor Period which is also a burial-mound culture, although it is on the European-contact horizon. Clearly, in this case, the factor of time lag is operative upon the trait of mound burial. It is also possible, and even likely, that time lag has also affected the distribution of pottery trade wares or the diffusion of pottery-making and pottery-decorating ideas. But the working assumption underlying the attempt to arrive at contemporaneity between the sequence periods of two relative chronologies is the same as that upon which the structure of the Gulf Coast chronology has been erected. Pottery has been considered as a sensitive index which changes through time with relative rapidity. This susceptibility to rapid change should minimize the time-lag factor in its geographical distributions. Furthermore, the diffusion of new pottery concepts, from area to area, should have met with less ethnocentric resistance than would have been engendered by diffusions or attempted propagations of other ideas.

These inequities in the time-space arrangement of culture traits and trait complexes have given rise to another concept in Southeastern

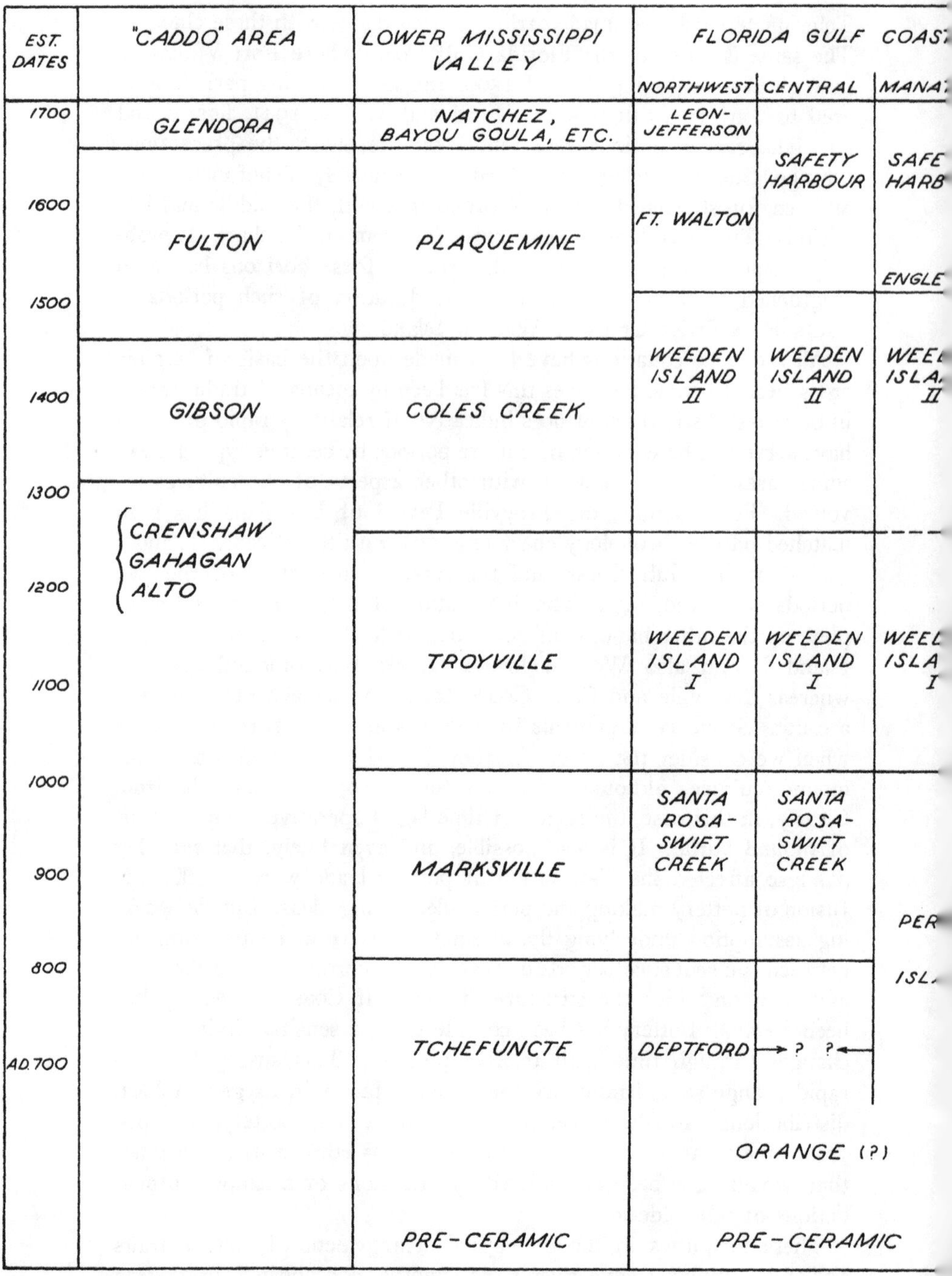

EST. DATES	"CADDO" AREA	LOWER MISSISSIPPI VALLEY	FLORIDA GULF COAS		
			NORTHWEST	CENTRAL	MANA
1700	GLENDORA	NATCHEZ, BAYOU GOULA, ETC.	LEON-JEFFERSON	SAFETY HARBOUR	SAFE HARB
1600	FULTON	PLAQUEMINE	FT. WALTON		
1500					ENGLE
1400	GIBSON	COLES CREEK	WEEDEN ISLAND II	WEEDEN ISLAND II	WEEL ISLA II
1300	CRENSHAW GAHAGAN ALTO				
1200					
1100		TROYVILLE	WEEDEN ISLAND I	WEEDEN ISLAND I	WEEL ISLA I
1000					
900		MARKSVILLE	SANTA ROSA-SWIFT CREEK	SANTA ROSA-SWIFT CREEK	PER
800					ISL
A.D. 700		TCHEFUNCTE	DEPTFORD →	? ? ←	
			ORANGE (?)		
		PRE-CERAMIC	PRE-CERAMIC		

FIG. 76.—Chart of comparative culture sequences showin

GEORGIA		EAST FLORIDA			GLADES AREA
CENTRAL	COASTAL	N. CENTRAL	N. ST. JOHNS	MELBOURNE	
OCMULGEE FIELDS	IRENE-LAMAR	ALACHUA	ST. AUGUSTINE	ST. AUGUSTINE	GLADES III
LAMAR	IRENE-LAMAR	ALACHUA	ST. JOHNS II	MALABAR II	GLADES III
MACON PLATEAU	SAVANNAH II	HICKORY POND	ST. JOHNS II	MALABAR II	GLADES III
SWIFT CREEK	SAVANNAH I WILMINGTON	CADES POND	ST. JOHNS I	MALABAR I	GLADES II
SWIFT CREEK	SWIFT CREEK	PRE-CADES POND	ST. JOHNS I	MALABAR I	GLADES II
? ←	DEPTFORD		ST. JOHNS I	MALABAR I	GLADES I
? ←	ST. SIMONS OR STALLINGS ISLAND	ORANGE	ORANGE	ORANGE	GLADES I
? ←	PRE-CERAMIC		PRE-CERAMIC	PRE-CERAMIC	?

orida Gulf Coast in relation to neighboring culture areas.

archeology, the culture stage. The formulation of stages must necessarily be preceded by the establishment of periods and horizons. The latter are horizontal time zones such as those indicated on the chronology chart (fig. 76). A culture stage may be, in certain circumstances, coextensive with a culture horizon, but usually it is a diagonal cross-sectioning of the time continuity. Ford and I applied a culture-stage type of synthesis to eastern United States archeology in 1941 (Ford and Willey, 1941). The stages which we employed were defined primarily by mound ceremonialism. Superficially, this was an inconsistency as "burial mounds" are essentially places for the disposal of the dead, while "temple mounds" are pediments for religious or political buildings. Two quite different cultural categories or activities were, thus, being contrasted in the same system. Yet, in this case, the labels "burial mound" and "temple mound" have a fundamental consistency. We were, in effect, contrasting community types by emphasizing their most conspicuous symbols. In this sense "burial mound," or the Burial Mound stage, represented not just a burial practice but a way of life differing significantly from the "temple mound" or Temple Mound stage. A third community type, the Archaic, was also defined as a stage and is, in this same sense, in comparable contrast to the other stages; although the term "Archaic" has a connotation quite different from that of the other two stage names.

The three major culture stages of the East may be applied to Gulf Florida and its neighboring areas in a very striking manner. The Archaic stage includes: (1) the pre-Tchefuncte period in the west; (2) the preceramic, Orange, Deptford, and, probably, early Perico Island Periods on the Florida Gulf; (3) the preceramic, Stallings Island, Deptford, and, probably, early Swift Creek Periods in Georgia; (4) the preceramic and Orange periods in east Florida; and (5) Glades I and probably part of the Glades II Period in the Glades area. The Burial Mound stage begins in the west with the Tchefuncte Period which belongs to the Burial Mound I subdivision of the stage. Possibly components of this stage will be revealed in the Deptford, early Swift Creek, and early St. Johns I cultures; but evidence for this is not clear. The Burial Mound II subdivision of the stage is more apparent. It includes: (1) the Marksville Period in the west; (2) the Santa Rosa-Swift Creek, late Perico Island, Weeden Island I and II, Englewood, and Safety Harbor Periods on the Florida Gulf; (3) the late Swift Creek, Wilmington, and Savannah I Periods in Georgia; and (4) the Cades Pond, Hickory Pond, St. Johns I, early St. Johns II, and Malabar II Periods in east Florida. Temple

Mound I stage is applicable to the Troyville-Coles Creek Periods in Louisiana, the Macon Plateau Period, and, perhaps, the Savannah II Period in Georgia. Only Temple Mound II, however, is seen in Florida where it is represented by the Fort Walton Period, probably the Alachüa Period and the late St. Johns II Period. The Temple Mound II stage is also well represented in Georgia by the Lamar and Irene-Lamar Periods. In Gulf Florida, the Safety Harbor culture was undergoing a transitional phase between the Burial Mound and Temple Mound stages. South, in the Glades, burial mounds make their appearance in the late Glades II and Glades III Periods, and temple mounds also appear in the Glades III Period. But other major aspects of Glades culture, including the subsistence orientation, remain more or less unchanged from Archaic stage standards.

SUMMARY RECONSTRUCTION

The prehistory of the Florida Gulf Coast can be most readily synthesized on three levels or stages of cultural attainment: the Archaic, the Burial Mound, and the Temple Mound.

1. During the Archaic stage Gulf Florida was first occupied by a hunting, fishing, and shellfish-gathering people who occupied villages along the shore. These Indians made flint and shell tools, weapons, and other implements but no pottery. They were undoubtedly related by culture, race, and, possibly, language to other Archaic-stage Indians of the southeastern United States. At this period, which we will call simply the preceramic, the Gulf Coast was not as densely inhabited as other areas of the Southeast, such as the lower St. Johns River in northeast Florida, the lower Savannah River, and the Tennessee River in Alabama. Fresh-water shellfish seem to have been the principal diet at this early time, and, as the rivers flowing into Gulf Florida were not so large or so rich in mussels as those named, adequate food resources for larger populations were not available.

Later, in the Archaic stage a distinctive fiber-tempered pottery was manufactured at many places throughout the Southeast. On the lower Savannah this fiber-tempered pottery period has been called the Stallings Island, on the Georgia Coast, the St. Simon's, and on the St. Johns, the Orange. Occasional fragments of this fiber ware have been found in Gulf Florida sites, suggesting that such a period may have been in existence here, but data are as yet too few to be definitive.

Toward the close of the Archaic stage the idea of ceramics becomes fully established in northwest Florida. This has been called the

Deptford Period after a culture of the same name on the Georgia Coast and lower Savannah River. Deptford pottery is sand-tempered, made in simple conoidal pot shapes, and decorated with check or simple linear-stamped impressions. It is found most abundantly in the eastern section of northwest Florida, diminishing toward the west. This distribution, coupled with its abundance in Georgia and South Carolina, suggests that the knowledge of this type of ware came to Florida from the northeast. Deptford sites are small shell-midden heaps, and it is doubtful if any important changes in the type of economy had occurred since preceramic times. Oysters and other marine shellfish apparently replaced fresh-water mussels as the dietary staple at about this time. This shift was brought about by environmental changes, and, undoubtedly, made the seacoast a more desirable place to live.

Contemporaneous with the Deptford Period another culture was flourishing in the south, around Tampa Bay. This is the Perico Island. The Perico Islanders were also potters, and manufactured a sand-tempered ware, less well made than the Deptford and only occasionally decorated with incisions and punctations. The Perico Island people must have been a part of the earlier preceramic population who occupied the Florida peninsula. The stimulus for their ceramic craft was probably derived from the Orange Period people on the St. Johns and from the Deptford Indians. The specialization of Perico Island culture, as seen in its pottery and shell tools, probably marks the beginning of the Glades cultural tradition which was to continue for centuries in southern Florida. A little later the Perico Islanders were to adopt the burial-mound complex and to trade with more advanced ceramic craftsmen in north Florida, but this takes us ahead of our story into the next stage.

It is possible that all these Archaic-stage Indians may have been closely affiliated as to racial group. This is a surmise based upon our knowledge of other Archaic peoples of the Southeast. These were medium- to long-headed Indians. If the old Florida Indians were medium- to long-headed we may expect to find this physical type in the south, an area which also retained many Archaic cultural traits long after they had disappeared in the northern part of the State. As this south Florida Glades area was in historic times occupied by the Calusa, Tekesta, and Ais, linguistic groups unaffiliated with the major stocks of the Southeast, it may be that the Archaic populations of Florida spoke these languages.

2. The first period of the Burial Mound stage in Gulf Florida is the Santa Rosa-Swift Creek. There are hints that certain ceramic traits

associated with this period, as well as the burial-mound idea, may have reached northwest Florida even earlier, during the Deptford Period; but the evidence on this is inconclusive. The appearance of the Santa Rosa-Swift Creek culture type may be linked with the arrival of a new people speaking a language different from those of the old Archaic-stage inhabitants. If so, the probabilities favor this language, or linguistic stock, being the Timucuan. Santa Rosa-Swift Creek culture is found throughout most of the Gulf area, occurring as far south as Tampa Bay. During this expansion it probably impinged upon and influenced the Perico Island culture. Living sites of the Santa Rosa-Swift Creek Period are also small villages, but these are much more numerous than the Deptford or Perico Island Period sites. Santa Rosa-Swift Creek population has been estimated at about 5,000 to 7,000 persons. The duration of the period is placed at 200 years, from A.D. 800 to 1000.

It is thought that the new elements responsible for the Santa Rosa-Swift Creek culture came into Florida from the west as the burial-mound and ceramic complexes of the Lower Mississippi Valley Marksville Period have much in common with Santa Rosa-Swift Creek. In turn, Santa Rosa-Swift Creek became the focus of Burial Mound stage influences for the rest of Florida and Georgia. Although local supporting evidence is lacking, maize horticulture was probably introduced into Gulf Florida as a part of the Santa Rosa-Swift Creek Complex, and from this time on farming was an important economic activity of the Gulf Florida Indians.

Western influences were not the only ones that were determinative for Santa Rosa-Swift Creek. In addition to the new pottery styles of the west (incision, punctation, rocker-stamped, and painted techniques), a complicated stamped tradition has a major role in the ceramic complex of the period. This is expressed in the Swift Creek ware, and the conception and skillful execution of the decorative designs of the style imply a mastery of the wood-carver's art. Origins of Swift Creek and other complicated stamped pottery styles were in south Georgia. Other streams of influence in Santa Rosa-Swift Creek are the negative-painted pottery type, which may have developed locally as a technological transfer; the polished-stone celt and monitor pipes, which came from the west or the north; use of mica, a northern import; and copper ornaments of the Ohio Hopewell type. These last were probably trade items. Shell tools also found their way into Santa Rosa-Swift Creek artifact assemblages from the Glades area to the south.

The Weeden Island I and II Periods were local developments out of the Santa Rosa-Swift Creek Period. The nature of sites and settlements and their distribution are much the same during these two periods as they were during the previous one, although population increased. An average of 10,000 to 15,000 people for the Gulf Coast is estimated, and the duration of the two periods is put at 250 years for each, spanning the gap from A.D. 1000 to 1500. Burial-mound practices were much the same during the Weeden Island Periods with only slight changes noticeable. Secondary burial is a little more common than during the Santa Rosa-Swift Creek Period. Pottery styles change, but show relationships to the previous period. There is a tendency for the complicated stamped tradition and the vessel forms associated with this tradition to drop out, especially in the Weeden Island II Period. Stonework is a little scarcer than previously, pipes are less common, copper artifacts are very rare, and shell tools and ornaments are not as frequent as in Santa Rosa-Swift Creek. Weeden Island trade contacts with both the north and the south seem less strong than they had been; with the west, contact continues and is reflected mainly in ceramics. There is also a very real possibility that Weeden Island ceramic ideas, as represented in effigy modeling, had an influence upon the development of Middle Mississippian styles. This is suggested by stylistic similarity and the earlier position of Weeden Island in relation to Middle Mississippi; but the course of such contact has not been plotted.

It is during the Weeden Island Periods that contacts with the West Indies are most likely to be found, if such existed during the sequence of pottery periods on the Gulf Coast. Evidence on this question is not sufficiently strong to postulate such diffusions, in either direction.

In general, the Weeden Island Periods were the culture climax or optimum prehistoric periods for the Gulf Coast. The subsistence technology at that time represented the maximum effective adjustment to the environment. Food economy was undoubtedly balanced between fishing, hunting, and shellfish gathering on the one hand and horticulture on the other.

3. The Temple Mound stage in Gulf Florida was chronologically late in its arrival compared to some other areas of the Southeast, and it was undoubtedly a part of the lower Southeastern spread of the Middle Mississippian intensive agriculturists. It is postulated that a new people came into northwest Florida at this time with the Fort Walton culture. These were Muskogean peoples who, moving south through Alabama and western Georgia, dislodged the Timucuans and pushed them east into the Florida peninsula. The Apalachee, Sawokli,

Chatot, and Pensacola were, following this argument, the bearers of the Fort Walton culture. At the same time, the Englewood and Safety Harbor cultures of the central Gulf Coast and Manatee regions were evolved locally out of Weeden Island and late Weeden Island contacts with Fort Walton. The Safety Harbor peoples were the sixteenth- and seventeenth-century Timucuans of the area.

Changes in community type were effected in the northwest during Fort Walton with the appearance of the temple mound and the disappearance of the old burial-mound ceremonialism. There are few temple-mound sites on the immediate coast, but more are known in the interior. This interior country, particularly in Leon and Jefferson Counties, is more suitable for intensive agriculture than the sandy soils of the coastal strip, and it is likely that with the institution of a new socioeconomic and political system population shifted inland to an environment more favorable to the modifications in food economy. This is partially corroborated by the accounts of the sixteenth-century Spanish who report that the larger towns of the northwest were in the interior. A population estimate for the Fort Walton culture has been set at between 7,500 and 12,000 persons. For Safety Harbor an estimate of 6,000 persons is made, giving a total Gulf Coast population for the sixteenth century of somewhere in the neighborhood of 15,000, about the same as the estimated figure for each of the Weeden Island Periods. Duration of the Fort Walton Period is given as A.D. 1500 to 1650, the later date coinciding with the establishment of the Spanish missions in the Gulf Coast territory and the beginning of the Leon-Jefferson Period. Leon-Jefferson lasted from 1650 to about 1725. During this time the Indian populations were considerably reduced.

Changes in ceramic types between Weeden Island and Fort Walton are fairly abrupt. The new styles are closely related to those of central Alabama although there is some evidence of old local continuity. Other artifact types are changed somewhat. Fort Walton burial is in cemeteries or in the floors and flanks of platform mounds rather than in burial mounds, but the earlier prevalent custom of secondary burial treatment continues. Englewood and Safety Harbor ceramic complexes are derived more directly out of Weeden Island, and the burial-mound practice seems to be universal in the south. Temple mounds do, however, come in during the Safety Harbor Period.

The Leon-Jefferson culture shows the breaking up of the Indian patterns and the substitution of Spanish colonization. Native handicrafts continue to some extent, and the pottery of the period can be derived from Fort Walton and from late influences out of Georgia.

TRENDS

A number of trends can be recapitulated from this record of Gulf Coast prehistory:

1. Food economy. Hunting, fishing, and gathering were succeeded by an economy that employed these older techniques together with maize horticulture. A late-period tendency is toward a more intensive horticulture, although the old food-gathering methods were still employed. This trend follows the general trend for the southeastern United States, and is historically conditioned by the diffusion of maize horticulture.

2. Settlements. Early settlements were small coastal villages. During the Santa Rosa-Swift Creek and Weeden Island Periods these villages remain much the same in size and location but they became much more numerous. In the late periods, especially Fort Walton, the small village community continues, but large towns also arise. There is a trend toward settlement in the interior rather than the coast at this time. These settlement trends are obviously conditioned by those of food economy.

3. Population. The population trend is steadily upward until a climax is reached during the Weeden Island Periods. It is doubtful if there were more people in the area during the Fort Walton and Safety Harbor Periods, but they were concentrated in larger communities.

4. Political organization. It is inferable that the trend was from numerous small autonomous units to larger political aggregates and, eventually, tribal federations. This trend was undoubtedly conditioned by population growth but is also explainable by historical factors. It is duplicated throughout the Southeast and, probably, the world, at least as far as early Neolithic sequences are concerned.

5. Ceremonialism. There is little reflection of ceremonialism in the Archaic periods, but the succeeding Burial Mound stage periods are rich in a ceremonialism which centers around a cult of the dead. There is a late shift away from this in Fort Walton when ceremonialism can more reasonably be said to have existed around the temple sites and the religious and political leadership which they symbolize. This trend is also noted throughout the Southeast.

6. Ceramic arts. Technical and artistic improvement is continued up through the Weeden Island I Period. From here on, technical

levels are maintained, but artistic quality may be lessened. This last judgment is, of course, subjective. It seems likely, though, that pottery was less intimately tied up with religious ritualism in the late periods, and this may account for an esthetic decline.

7. Other crafts. These are best developed in the Santa Rosa-Swift Creek Period after which work in stone, shell, and metals is less common. This pattern of occurrence, rather than trend, is probably explained by the following.

8. Trade. Outside exchange in raw materials and finished products was most vigorous during the Santa Rosa-Swift Creek Period. At least it is at this time that the most exotic goods are found in Gulf Florida sites. Trade, per se, should be distinguished from influence in this context. This pattern of occurrence is duplicated on the Hopewellian horizon in many parts of the eastern United States.

BIBLIOGRAPHY

ALLEN, JOHN H.

1846. Some facts respecting the geology of Tampa Bay, Florida. Amer. Journ. Sci., ser. 2, vol. 1, pp. 38-42.

ANONYMOUS.

1890. Pottery find in Florida. Amer. Antiquarian, vol. 12, pp. 185-186.

1925. Work in Florida. Expl. and Field-work Smithsonian Inst. in 1924, Smithsonian Misc. Coll., vol. 77, No. 2, pp. 93-98.

1926. Investigation of shell and sand mounds on Pinellas Peninsula, Florida. Expl. and Field-work Smithsonian Inst. in 1925, Smithsonian Misc. Coll., vol. 78, No. 1, pp. 125-132.

1937. Florida second biennial report of State Board of Conservation, Biennium ending June 30, 1936, pp. 109-152. Tallahassee.

1939a. Notes on two interesting mounds excavated in Hillsborough County. Third Bien. Rep. Florida State Board Conserv., Biennium ending June 30, 1938, pp. 25-30. Tallahassee.

1939b. Aboriginal stone quarries of Hillsborough County and sources of abrasives and pigment. Third Bien. Rep. Florida State Board Conserv., Biennium ending June 30, 1938, pp. 31-32. Tallahassee.

BARTRAM, WILLIAM.

1940. The travels of William Bartram. Edited by Mark Van Doren, New York.

BECKER, R. B.

1944. An early Indian clam bake. Proc. Florida Acad. Sci., vol. 7, No. 1, pp. 23-27.

BELL, JAMES.

1883. Mounds in Alachua County, Florida. Ann. Rep. Smithsonian Inst. for 1881, pp. 635-637.

BOYD, M. F.

1939. Mission sites in Florida. Florida Hist. Quart., vol. 17, No. 4, pp. 255-280.

BRINTON, DANIEL GARRISON.

1859. Floridian peninsula, its literary history, Indian tribes, and antiquities. Philadelphia.

1867. Artificial shell deposits of the United States. Ann. Rep. Smithsonian Inst. for 1866, pp. 356-358.

BROWER, CHARLES DE WOLFE.

1906. Shell heaps of Florida. Rec. Past, vol. 5, pt. 9, pp. 331-338.

BROWN, JOHN S.

n.d. Shell heaps of Cedar Keys, Florida. Ms. Bur. Amer. Ethnol. vault. (Circa 1920.)

CALDWELL, J. R., and MCCANN, CATHERINE.

1941. Irene Mound Site. Univ. Georgia Press, Athens.

CALDWELL, J. R., and WARING, A. J., JR.

1939. Newsletter of the Southeastern Archaeological Conference, vol. 1, No. 6. (Mimeo.) Lexington, Ky.

Calkins, W. W.

1877-1880. Notes of personal investigations among the shell mounds of Florida. Proc. Davenport Acad. Nat. Sci., 1876-78, vol. 2, pp. 225-229. Davenport, Iowa.

Claflin, William H., Jr.

1931. The Stallings Island Mound, Columbia County, Georgia. Peabody Mus. Pap., vol. 15, No. 1. Cambridge.

Coe, Joffre L.

n.d. Report on mound work in the region of Lake Apopka, Florida. Ms. Bur. Amer. Ethnol. vault. (September 1933.)

Conrad, T. A.

1846. Observations on the geology of a part of eastern Florida, with a catalogue of recent shells of the coast. Amer. Journ. Sci., ser. 2, vol. 2, pp. 36-48.

Cooke, C. W., and Mossom, S.

1929. Geology of Florida. 20th Ann. Rep. Florida State Geol. Surv., pp. 31-279.

Cushing, Frank Hamilton.

1897. Explorations of ancient key-dwellers remains on the Gulf Coast of Florida. Proc. Amer. Philos. Soc., vol. 35, pp. 329-448. Philadelphia, Pa.

Dall, William Healey.

1887. Notes on the geology of Florida. Amer. Journ. Sci., ser. 2, vol. 34, art. 19, pp. 161-170.

Dickinson, S. D.

1936. Ceramic relationships of the pre-Caddo pottery from the Crenshaw Site. Bull. Texas Arch. and Paleont. Soc., vol. 8.

Ecker, A.

1878. Zur Kenntniss des Körperbaues früherer Einwohner der Halbinsel Florida. Archiv. für Anthrop., vol. 10, pp. 101-114.

Escalente Fontaneda, D.

1944. Memoir. Written in Spain about 1575. Translated and annotated by Buckingham Smith, 1854. Miami, Florida (Gulf Coast).

Fairbanks, C. H.

1940. Newsletter of the Southeastern Archaeological Conference, vol. 2, No. 2. (Mimeo.) Lexington, Ky.

1942. The taxonomic position of Stallings Island. Amer. Antiquity, vol. 7, No. 3, pp. 223, 231.

1946. The Kolomoki mound group, Early County, Georgia. Amer. Antiquity, vol. 11, pp. 258-260.

Farber, G. C.

1887. Mound in Florida. Amer. Antiquarian, vol. 9, No. 5, pp. 307-308.

Featherstonhaugh, Thomas.

1897. Note on Florida archaeology. Amer. Anthrop., vol. 10, p. 200.

1899. Mound builders of central Florida. Harrisburg.

n.d. An investigation of the Brooker mounds, Florida. Ms., U.S. Nat. Mus., Access. No. 24012.

Fenneman, Nevin M.

1938. Physiography of the eastern United States. (First edition.) New York.

FEWKES, JESSE WALTER.
1924. Preliminary archeological explorations at Weeden Island, Florida. Smithsonian Misc. Coll., vol. 76, No. 13, pp. 1-26, 21 pls.

FORD, J. A., and QUIMBY, G. I.
1945. The Tchefuncte culture, an early occupation of the Lower Mississippi Valley. Mem. Soc. Amer. Archaeol., No. 3.

FORD, J. A., and WILLEY, GORDON R.
1939. Newsletter of the Southeastern Archaeological Conference, vol. 1, Nos. 3 and 4. (Mimeo.) Lexington, Ky.
1940. Crooks Site, a Marksville Period burial mound in La Salle Parish, Louisiana. Anthrop. Study No. 3, Dep. Conserv., Louisiana Geol. Surv.
1941. An interpretation of the prehistory of the eastern United States. Amer. Anthrop., vol. 43, No. 3, pp. 325-363.

GILLMAN, HENRY.
1878. Crania utilized as cinerary urns in a burial mound in Florida. Amer. Natur., vol. 12, pp. 753-754. Philadelphia, Pa.
1879. Remarkable burial custom from a mound in Florida: the crania utilized as a cinerary urn. Proc. Amer. Assoc. Adv. Sci., sect. B., vol. 27, pp. 309-312. Salem, Mass.

GOGGIN, JOHN M.
1939. A ceramic sequence in South Florida. New Mexico Anthrop., vol. 3, pp. 36-40.
1940. The distribution of pottery wares in the Glades archeological area of South Florida. New Mexico Anthrop., vol. 4, pp. 22-33.
1944a. A tentative formulation of pottery types for the Glades area. (Mimeo.) New Haven.
1944b. Archaeological investigations on the Upper Florida Keys. Tequesta, No. 4, pp. 13-38. Coral Gables, Fla.
1947a. Manifestations of a south Florida cult in northwestern Florida. Amer. Antiquity, vol. 12, No. 4, pp. 273-276.
1947b. A preliminary definition of archaeological areas and periods in Florida. Amer. Antiquity, vol. 13, pp. 114-127.
1948a. Some pottery types from central Florida. Gainesville Anthrop. Assoc. Bull. No. 1.
1948b. Florida archeology and recent ecological changes. Journ. Washington Acad. Sci., vol. 38, No. 7, pp. 225-233.
n.d. 1 The archaeology of the Glades area, south Florida. Ms.
n.d. 2 Culture and geography in Florida prehistory. Ph.D. thesis, Yale University, New Haven.

GOGGIN, JOHN M., and ROUSE, IRVING.
1948. A West Indian ax from Florida. Amer. Antiquity, vol. 13, No. 4, pl. 1, pp. 323-325.

GOWER, CHARLOTTE D.
1927. The northern and southern affiliations of Antillean culture. Mem. Amer. Anthrop. Assoc. No. 35.

GREENMAN, EMERSON F.
1938. Hopewellian traits in Florida. Amer. Antiquity, vol. 3, No. 4, pp. 327-332.

GRIFFIN, JAMES B.

1943. An analysis and interpretation of the ceramic remains from two sites near Beaufort, South Carolina. Bur. Amer. Ethnol. Bull. 133, No. 22.

1945. The significance of the fibre-tempered pottery of the St. Johns area in Florida. Journ. Washington Acad. Sci., vol. 35, No. 7, pp. 218-223.

1946. Cultural change and continuity in eastern United States archaeology. *In* Man in northeastern North America, Pap. R. S. Peabody Foundation, vol 3, pp. 37-95. Andover, Mass.

GRIFFIN, JOHN W.

1943. The Antillean problem in Florida archaeology. Florida Hist. Quart., vol. 22, No. 2, pp. 86-91.

1946. Historic artifacts and the Buzzard cult in Florida. Florida Hist. Quart., vol. 24, pp. 295-301.

1947. Comments on a site in the St. Marks National Wildlife Refuge, Wakulla County, Florida. Amer. Antiquity, vol. 13, No. 2, pp. 182-183.

n.d. Prehistoric Florida—A review. Ms. prepared for F-C. Cole Anniv. Vol.

HAAG, W. G.

1939. Newsletter of the Southeastern Archaeological Conference, vol. 1, No. 1. (Mimeo.) Lexington, Ky.

1942. Early horizons in the Southeast. Amer. Antiquity, vol. 7, No. 3, pp. 209-222.

HARPER, ROLAND M.

1914. Geography and vegetation of northern Florida. 6th Ann. Rep. Florida State Geol. Surv., pp. 165-437.

HEILPRIN, ANGELO.

1887. Explorations on the west coast of Florida, and in the Okechobee Wilderness. Trans. Wagner Free Inst., vol. 1, pp. 1-134. Philadelphia, Pa.

HEWITT, J. F.

1898. Archaeology of the west coast of Florida. Medical Bull., vol. 20, 135 pp. Philadelphia, Pa.

HOLMES, WILLIAM HENRY.

1894a. Earthenware of Florida: Collections of Clarence B. Moore. Journ. Acad. Nat. Sci. Philadelphia, vol. 10, pp. 105-128.

1894b. Caribbean influence on the prehistoric ceramic art of the southern States. Amer. Anthrop., vol. 7, pp. 71-78.

1903. Aboriginal pottery of the eastern United States. 20th Ann. Rep. Bur. Amer. Ethnol. 1898-99, pp. 1-237.

1914. Areas of American culture characterization tentatively outlined as an aid in the study of the antiquities. Amer. Anthrop., vol. 18, pp. 413-446.

HRDLIČKA, ALEŠ.

1907. Skeletal remains suggesting or attributed to Early man in North America. Bur. Amer. Ethnol. Bull. 33.

1922. Anthropology of Florida. Publ. Florida Hist. Soc., No. 1.

1940. Catalog of human crania in the United States National Museum collections: Indians of the Gulf States. Proc. U.S. Nat. Mus., vol. 87, pp. 315-464.

JENNINGS, JESSE D.

1941. Chickasaw and earlier Indian cultures of northeast Mississippi. Journ. Mississippi Hist., vol. 3, No. 3, pp. 155-226.

JENNINGS, J. D., and FAIRBANKS, C. H.

1939. Newsletter of the Southeastern Archaeological Conference, vol. 1, No. 2. (Mimeo.) Lexington, Ky.

KELLY, A. R.

1938. A preliminary report on archeological explorations at Macon, Ga. Bur. Amer. Ethnol. Bull. 119, No. 1.

KENWORTHY, CHARLES J.

1883. Ancient canals in Florida. Ann. Rep. Smithsonian Inst. for 1881, pp. 631-635.

KIMBALL, MARY R.

1872. Florida Indians. Bull. Essex Inst., vol. 4, pp. 18-19. Salem, Mass.

KRIEGER, ALEX D.

1944. The typological concept. Amer. Antiquity, vol. 9, No. 3, pp. 271-288.

1945. An inquiry into supposed Mexican influence on a prehistoric "cult" in the southern United States. Amer. Anthrop., vol. 47, No. 4, pp. 483-515.

1946. Culture complexes and chronology in northern Texas. Univ. Texas Publ. No. 4640. Austin.

1947. The eastward extension of Puebloan dating toward cultures of the Mississippi Valley. Amer. Antiquity, vol. 12, pp. 141-148.

KROEBER, A. L.

1939. Cultural and natural areas of native North America. Univ. Calif. Publ. in Amer. Archaeol. and Ethnol., vol. 38.

KUNZ, G. F.

1887. Gold and silver ornaments from mounds of Florida. Amer. Antiquarian, vol. 9, p. 219.

LAWSON, R. H.

1918. Explorations at Pensacola, Florida. Archaeol. Bull., vol. 9, No. 6, pp. 67-68.

LEBARON, J. FRANCIS.

1884. Prehistoric remains in Florida. Ann. Rep. Smithsonian Inst. for 1882, pp. 771-790.

LEIDY, JOSEPH.

1889. Notice of some fossil human bones. Trans. Wagner Free Inst., vol. 2, pp. 9-12.

LEMOYNE DE MORGUES, JACQUES.

1946. The narrative of Jacques Le Moyne de Morgues. The New World, pp. 33-97. Stefan Lorant, editor. New York.

LEWIS, T. M. N.

1931. A Florida burial ground. Wisconsin Arch., n. s., vol. 10, No. 4, pp. 123-129.

LEWIS, T. M. N., and KNEBERG, MADELEINE.

1946. Hiwassee Island. Univ. Tennessee Press.

MARTENS, J. H. C.
1931. Beaches of Florida. 21st and 22d Ann. Reps. Florida State Geol. Surv., pp. 69-119.

MARTIN, PAUL S., QUIMBY, G. I., and COLLIER, DONALD.
1947. Indians before Columbus. Chicago.

MASIUS, VERA.
n.d. Excavations at South Indian Field, Brevard County. Ms.

MOONEY, JAMES.
1928. The aboriginal population of America north of Mexico. Smithsonian Misc. Coll., vol. 80, No. 7.

MOORE, C. B.
1894a. Certain sand mounds of the St. Johns River, Florida, pt. 1. Journ. Acad. Nat. Sci. Philadelphia, vol. 10, pp. 130-248.
1894b. Certain sand mounds of the St. Johns River, Florida, pt. 2. Journ. Acad. Nat. Sci. Philadelphia, vol. 10.
1895a. Certain sand mounds of the Ocklawaha River, Florida. Journ. Acad. Nat. Sci. Philadelphia, vol. 10.
1895b. Two mounds on Murphy Island, Florida. Journ. Acad. Nat. Sci. Philadelphia, vol. 10.
1896. Certain river mounds of Duval County, Florida. Journ. Acad. Nat. Sci. Philadelphia, vol. 10.
1900. Certain antiquities of the Florida west coast. Journ. Acad. Nat. Sci. Philadelphia, vol. 11.
1901. Certain aboriginal remains of the northwest Florida coast, pt. 1. Journ. Acad. Nat. Sci. Philadelphia, vol. 11.
1902. Certain aboriginal remains of the northwest Florida coast, pt. 2. Journ. Acad. Nat. Sci. Philadelphia, vol. 12.
1903. Certain aboriginal mounds of the Florida central west coast. Journ. Acad. Nat. Sci. Philadelphia, vol. 12.
1905. Aboriginal remains of Black Warrior River, Lower Tombigbee River, Mobile Bay and Mississippi Sound, and miscellaneous investigations in Florida. Journ. Acad. Nat. Sci. Philadelphia, vol. 13.
1907. Moundville revisited: Crystal River revisited: Mounds of the lower Chattahoochee and lower Flint Rivers: Notes on the Ten Thousand Islands, Florida. Journ. Acad. Nat. Sci. Philadelphia, vol. 13.
1910. Antiquities of the St. Francis, White, and Black Rivers, Arkansas. Journ. Acad. Nat. Sci. Philadelphia, vol. 14.
1918. The northwestern Florida coast revisited. Journ. Acad. Nat. Sci. Philadelphia, vol. 16.

NEWELL, H. PERRY, and KRIEGER, A. D.
1949. The George C. Davis site, Cherokee County, Texas. Amer. Antiq., vol. 14, No. 4, pt. 2.

NEWMAN, M. T., and SNOW, C. E.
1943. Preliminary report on the skeletal material from Pickwick Basin, Alabama. Bur. Amer. Ethnol. Bull. 129, pp. 395-507.

OSGOOD, CORNELIUS.
1942. The Ciboney culture of Cayo Redondo, Cuba. Yale Univ. Publ. in Anthrop., No. 25. (Gulf Coast.)

QUIMBY, GEORGE, JR.
1942. The Natchezan culture type. Amer. Antiquity, vol. 7, No. 3, pp. 255-275.

RAINEY, F. G.
1935. Indian burial site at Crystal River, Florida. Florida Hist. Quart., vol. 13, No. 4, pp. 185-192.

RAU, C.
1878. Observations on a gold ornament from a mound in Florida. Ann. Rep. Smithsonian Inst. for 1877, pp. 298-302.

ROUSE, IRVING.
1939. Prehistory in Haiti, a study in method. Yale Univ. Publ. in Anthrop., No. 21.
1940. Some evidence concerning the origins of West Indian pottery making. Amer. Anthrop., vol. 42, No. 1, pp. 49-80.
1948. The Arawak. *In* Handbook of South American Indians, vol. 4, pt. 3, pp. 507-546, Bur. Amer. Ethnol. Bull. 143.

SCHOFF, H. L.
n.d. Letter on Pool Hammock, Florida, near Laurel, Sarasota County. Bur. Amer. Ethnol. vault. (January 1933.)

SCHOOLCRAFT, H. R.
1854. Antique pottery from the minor mounds occupied by the Indians in feasts to the dead, on the sea-coast of Florida and Georgia. Indian Tribes of the United States, pt. III, pp. 75-82.

SETZLER, FRANK M.
1933. Pottery of the Hopewell type from Louisiana. Proc. U. S. Nat. Mus., vol. 82, No. 2963, art. 22, pp. 1-21.

SHEPARD J.
1886. Shell heaps and mounds in Florida. Ann. Rep. Smithsonian Inst. for 1885, pt. 1, pp. 902-906.

SIMONS, M. H.
1884. Shell heaps of Charlotte Harbor, Florida. Ann. Rep. Smithsonian Inst. for 1882, pp. 794-796.

SIMPSON, J. C.
1941. Source material for Florida aboriginal artifacts. Proc. Florida Acad. Sci. 1940, vol. 5, pp. 32-34.

SLEIGHT, F. W.
1943. Archaeological needs for Florida. Amer. Antiquity, vol. 8, No. 4, pp. 387-392.

SMALL, JOHN K.
1924. The land where spring meets autumn. Journ. New York Bot. Gard., vol. 25, pp. 53-94.
1927. Among floral aborigines. Journ. New York Bot. Gard., vol. 28, pp. 1-20 and 25-40.

SMITH, HALE G.
1948. Two historical archaeological periods in Florida. Amer. Antiquity, vol. 13, No. 4, pt. 1, pp. 313-319.

SMITH, RHEA M.
1933. Anthropology in Florida. Florida Hist. Quart., vol. 11, No. 4, pp. 151-172.

SNOW, C. E.
1948. Indian Knoll skeletons from site Oh2, Ohio County, Kentucky. Rep. in Anthrop., vol. 4, No. 3, pt. 2. Univ. Kentucky.

STEARNS, R. E. C.
1870. Rambles in Florida. Amer. Nat., vol. 3, pp. 349-360, 397-405, 455-470.
1872. Remarks on mounds and shell heaps of Tampa Bay. Proc. California Acad. Sci., ser. 1, vol. 4, pp. 214-215.

STERNBERG, G. M.
1876. Indian burial mounds near Pensacola, Florida. Proc. Amer. Assoc. Adv. Sci., vol. 24, pt. 2, pp. 282-292. Salem, Mass.

STEWART, T. D.
1940. Some historical implications of physical anthropology in North America. Smithsonian Misc. Coll., vol. 100, pp. 15-50.
1946. A reexamination of the fossil human skeletal remains from Melbourne, Florida, with further data on the Vero skull. Smithsonian Misc. Coll., vol. 106, No. 10.

STIRLING, M. W.
1930. Prehistoric mounds in the vicinity of Tampa Bay, Florida. Expl. and Field-work Smithsonian Inst. in 1929, pp. 183-186.
1931. Mounds of the vanished Calusa Indians of Florida. Expl. and Field-work Smithsonian Inst. in 1930, pp. 167-172.
1935. Smithsonian archeological projects conducted under the Federal Emergency Relief Administration, 1933-34. Ann. Rep. Smithsonian Inst. for 1934, pp. 371-400.
1936. Florida cultural affiliations in relation to adjacent areas. *In* Essays in Anthropology, in honor of Alfred Louis Kroeber, pp. 351-357.

STONE, DORIS Z.
1939. Relationship of Florida archaeology to that of middle America. Florida Hist. Quart., vol. 17, No. 3, pp. 211-218.

STUBBS, SIDNEY A.
1940. The future of Florida archaeological research. Proc. Florida Acad. Sci., vol. 4, pp. 266-270.

SWANTON, JOHN R.
1922. Early history of the Creek Indians and their neighbors. Bur. Amer. Ethnol. Bull. 73.
1946. The Indians of the Southeastern United States. Bur. Amer. Ethnol. Bull. 137.

THOMAS, CYRUS.
1891. Catalogue of prehistoric works east of the Rocky Mountains. Bur. Amer. Ethnol. Bull. 12.
1894. Report on the mound explorations of the Bureau of Ethnology. 12th Ann. Rep. Bur. Amer. Ethnol.

UNITED STATES DEPARTMENT OF AGRICULTURE YEARBOOK.
1941. Climate and man.

VERNON, ROBERT O.
1942. Geology of Holmes and Washington Counties, Florida. Florida State Geol. Surv. Bull. No. 21.

VOGDES, A. W.
1879. Notes on a lost race of America. Amer. Nat., vol. 13, pp. 9-11.

VON BONIN, G., and MORANT, G. M.
1938. Indian races in the United States. A survey of previously published measurements. Biometrika, vol. 30, pp. 94-129.

VON EICKSTEDT, E. F.
1934. Rassenkunde und Rassengeschichte der Menschheit. F. Enke Verlag. Stuttgart, 935 pp.

WAINWRIGHT, R. D.
1916. Two months research in the sand and shell mounds of Florida. Archaeol. Bull., vol. 7, No. 6, pp. 139-144.
1918. Archaeological exploration in southern Florida, 1917. Archaeol. Bull., vol. 9, Nos. 3 and 4, pp. 28-32, 43-47.

WALKER, S. T.
1880a. Preliminary explorations among the Indian mounds in southern Florida. Ann. Rep. Smithsonian Inst. for 1879, pp. 392-413.
1880b. Report on the shell heaps of Tampa Bay, Florida. Ann. Rep. Smithsonian Inst. for 1879, pp. 413-422.
1883. The aborigines of Florida. Ann. Rep. Smithsonian Inst. for 1881, pp. 677-680.
1885. Mounds and shell heaps on the west coast of Florida. Ann. Rep. Smithsonian Inst. for 1883, pp. 854-868.

WARING, A. J., JR., and HOLDER, PRESTON.
1945. A prehistoric ceremonial complex in the southeastern United States. Amer. Anthrop., vol. 47, No. 1, pp. 1-34.

WEBB, WILLIAM S., and DEJARNETTE, DAVID L.
1942. An archeological survey of Pickwick Basin in the adjacent portions of the States of Alabama, Mississippi, and Tennessee. Bur. Amer. Ethnol. Bull. 129.

WILLEY, GORDON R.
1939. Ceramic stratigraphy in a Georgia village site. Amer. Antiquity, vol. 5, No. 2, pp. 140-147.
1945. The Weeden Island Culture: a preliminary definition. Amer. Antiquity, vol. 10, No. 3, pp. 225-254.
1948a. Culture sequence for the Manatee region of West Florida. Amer. Antiquity, vol. 13, No. 4, pp. 209-218.
1948b. The cultural context of the Crystal River negative painted style. Amer. Antiquity, vol. 13, No. 4, pt. 1, pp. 325-328.
1948c. A proto-type for the Southern Cult. Amer. Antiquity, vol. 13, No. 4, pt. 1, pp. 328-330.
n.d. Excavations in southeast Florida. Ms.

WILLEY, GORDON R., and PHILLIPS, PHILIP.
1944. Negative-painted pottery from Crystal River, Florida. Amer. Antiquity, vol. 10, No. 2, pp. 173-185.

WILLEY, GORDON R., and WOODBURY, R. B.
1942. A chronological outline for the northwest Florida coast. Amer. Antiquity, vol. 7, pp. 232-254.

WIMBERLY, STEVE B., and TOURTELOT, HARRY A.
1941. The McQuorquodale Mound: A manifestation of the Hopewellian phase in south Alabama. Geol. Surv. of Alabama, Mus. Pap. 19, 42 pp.

WISSLER, CLARK.
1938. The American Indian. New York.

Wyman, J.
1870. Explorations in Florida. Third Ann. Rep. Trustees Peabody Mus., Harvard Univ., pp. 8-9.
1875. Fresh-water shell mounds of the St. Johns River, Florida. Mem. Peabody Acad. Sci., vol. 1, No. 4. Salem, Mass.

EXPLANATION OF PLATES

Plate

1. Pit excavation at Carrabelle (Fr-2), Franklin County. *Top:* Excavating the isolated strati-block of pit II; *bottom:* test pit on completion, showing midden and shells to a depth of 1 meter.
2. Shell middens on the northwest Gulf Coast. *Top:* East Point midden, Franklin County; *bottom:* beginning a test pit at Mound Field (Wa-8), Wakulla County.
3. Lake Jackson site (Le-1), Leon County. *Top:* View of the lake bed from the bordering hills above the site; *bottom:* mound 6 (artificial height about 2.5 meters).
4. Burial types from the Thomas (Hi-1) and Cockroach Key (Hi-2) burial mounds. *Top:* Flexed and vertical bundle burials from Thomas; *center:* flexed burial from Cockroach Key; *bottom:* secondary bundle burials, vertical and horizontal, at Cockroach Key.
5. The Englewood mound (So-1). *Top:* Before clearing; *bottom:* excavations showing old sod line near bottom of cut on the 30-foot profile line.
6. Englewood (So-1) burials. *Top:* Flexed; *bottom:* bundle.
7. Perico Island (Ma-6). *Top, left:* The burial mound before excavation; *top, right:* typical flexed burial from the burial mound; *center, left:* excavating the burial mound; *center, right:* excavating the smaller midden; *bottom, left:* the cemetery site; *bottom, right:* three flexed burials in the cemetery.
8. Cockroach Key (Hi-2). *Top:* A small area (3.5 x 6 feet) with the bones of 15 secondary burials massed together, burial mound; *center:* looking north from the highest shell accumulation on Cockroach Key; *bottom:* the burial mound after clearing, looking north.
9. The northwest Gulf Coast. *Top:* Looking southward across the "trough" or depression between the dune ridges on Santa Rosa Island. The man in the center is standing in the midst of a typical midden site of the island; *bottom:* a view of Nine-Mile Point (Fr-9), Franklin County.
10. The northwest Gulf Coast. *Top:* Tucker site (Fr-4), Franklin County, looking down the cleared "right-of-way" over the shell midden; *bottom:* the destroyed Hall site (Wa-4) midden, Wakulla County.
11. The Pierce site (Fr-14), Franklin County. *Top:* Area of destroyed midden; *bottom:* cross section of flat-topped mound as seen from railroad cut. This mound may be Moore's Pierce mound C.
12. Deptford Period sherd types. All Deptford Linear Check Stamped from the northwest coast.
13. Deptford Period sherd types. *a-c,* Deptford Bold Check Stamped; *d-f,* Deptford Simple Stamped; *g,* St. Simons Plain. From the northwest coast.
14. Perico Island Period sherds. *a, d,* Perico Island Incised; *b, c, e,* Perico Island Linear Punctated; *f,* unclassified incised sherd on Biscayne-type

Plate

paste; *g*, Deptford Bold Check Stamped podal support; *h*, complicated stamped sherd; *i*, Glades Plain with unusual rim projection. All from Perico Island site. (Courtesy U.S. National Museum; Nos. 383990, 383996, 384005, 384000, 384004, 383989, 384027, 384032, 384030.)

15. Perico Island Period artifact types. *a*, flat-surface or *Strombus* shell celt; *b*, single-grooved columella pendant or plummet; *c*, *d*, inner and outer sides of concave-surface or *Busycon* celt; *e*, *f*, conch columella chisel and hammer; *g*, *h*, *Busycon* hammers; *i*, *l*, hammerstones; *j*, single-grooved stone plummet; *k*, grinding stone; *m*, bone dagger or point. All from Perico Island site except *e-h*, *j*, and *l*, which are from Shaws Point, Manatee County. (Courtesy U.S. National Museum; Nos. 384019, 384058, 384059, 384057, 384057, 384060, 384060, 384016, 384062, 384018, 384063, 384021.)

16. Perico Island Period artifact types. *a*, *b*, flat-surface or *Strombus* celts; *c*, concave-surface or *Busycon* celt; *d*, bipointed bone projectiles; *e*, shell bead; *f*, *j*, chipped-stone projectiles; *g*, double-grooved columella pendant or plummet; *h*, bone awl; *i*, pierced turtle-carapace fragment, probably from a gorget. All from the Cockroach Key site. (Courtesy U.S. National Museum; Nos. 384297, ?, 384297, 384302, and 384294, 384299, 384301, 384305, ?, 384300, 384306.)

17. Santa Rosa-Swift Creek Period sherd types. All Alligator Bayou Stamped from the northwest coast.

18. Santa Rosa-Swift Creek Period sherd types. *a-c*, Santa Rosa Stamped; *d-h*, Basin Bayou Incised; *i-j*, Santa Rosa Punctated. From the northwest coast.

19. Santa Rosa-Swift Creek Period sherd types. *a*, *b*, Crooked River Complicated Stamped; *c-e*, Alligator Bayou Stamped. From the northwest coast.

20. Santa Rosa-Swift Creek Period sherd types. All Swift Creek Complicated Stamped, Early Variety, from the northwest coast.

21. Santa Rosa-Swift Creek Period sherd types. *a-e*, New River Complicated Stamped; *f*, *g*, Gulf Check Stamped; *h*, West Florida Cord-marked, Early Variety; *i*, tetrapod base of a Franklin Plain vessel. From the northwest coast.

22. Santa Rosa-Swift Creek Period vessels. *a*, Pierce Zoned Red; *b*, plain miniature vessel, unclassified but probably of this period; *c*, *d*, *f*, *g*, Swift Creek Complicated Stamped, Early Variety; *e*, Franklin Plain. (Courtesy R. S. Peabody Foundation, Andover, from the following sites in order with catalog numbers: Pierce mound A, 39301; Yent, 39175; Anderson's Bayou, 38945; Green Point, 39248; Franklin County, 39238. Respective heights as follows: *a*, 14 cm.; *b*, 6 cm.; *c*, 19 cm.; *d*, 22 cm.; *e*, 10 cm.; *f*, 13 cm.; *g*, 18 cm.)

23. Santa Rosa-Swift Creek Period vessels. Crystal River Negative Painted. (*a*, courtesy R. S. Peabody Foundation, Green Point site, No. 39147; *b*, *c*, courtesy Heye Foundation, Crystal River site, Nos. 17/3523, 18/326. Respective rim diameters: *a*, 7 cm.; *b*, 9.7 cm.; *c*, 16.5 cm.)

24. Santa Rosa-Swift Creek Period artifacts. *a*, double-grooved shell plummet or pendant; *b*, socketed bone projectile point; *c*, *d*, chipped-stone projectile points; *e*, *g*, *h*, pottery pipes; *f*, shell gorget; *i*, *j*, copper ear

Plate

ornament plated with silver. (Artifacts *a-d* from northwest Florida middens. All others courtesy Heye Foundation with sites as follows: *e*, Huckleberry Landing, No. 17/1092; *f*, Crystal River; *i*, Crystal River, No. 17/62. Artifact *a* is 10 cm. long and *b-d* are to same scale; *i* and *j* are about 6 cm. in diameter; no scale for other objects.)

25. Weeden Island Period sherd types. *a-f*, Weeden Island Incised; *g, h*, Weeden Island Punctated. From the northwest coast.

26. Weeden Island Period sherd types. *a-e*, Weeden Island Incised; *f-h*, Weeden Island Zoned Red. From the Weeden Island site. (Courtesy U.S. National Museum; Nos. 369390, 325671, 325671, 325671, 325671, 369388, 369388, 369388.)

27. Weeden Island Period sherd types. *a, d, e, g, h*, Weeden Island Punctated; *b, c, f*, Papys Bayou Punctated. From the Weeden Island site. (Courtesy U.S. National Museum; Nos. 369390(*a*), 325671 (all others).)

28. Weeden Island Period sherd types. *b*, Papys Bayou Punctated; all others Weeden Island Punctated. From Thomas mound. (Courtesy U.S. National Museum; Nos. 384210, 384207, 384267, 384187, 384201, 384156, 384151, 384233.)

29. Weeden Island Period sherd types. *a*, Weeden Island Zoned Red; all others, Carrabelle Incised. From northwest Florida.

30. Weeden Island Period sherd types. All Carrabelle Punctated. From northwest Florida.

31. Weeden Island Period sherd types. *a, b*, Carrabelle Punctated; *c-f*, Indian Pass Incised. From northwest Florida.

32. Weeden Island Period sherd types. *a-d*, Keith Incised; *e-f*, Tucker Ridge-pinched; *g, h*, St. Petersburg Incised. From northwest Florida.

33. Weeden Island Period sherd types. *a-e*, Carrabelle Incised; *f-i*, Keith Incised; *j, k*, St. Petersburg Incised. From the Weeden Island site. (Courtesy U.S. National Museum; Nos. 369387, 325671, 325671, 325671, 325671, 325671, 325671, 330622, 325671, 325671, 325671.)

34. Weeden Island Period sherd types. All Swift Creek Complicated Stamped, Late Variety. From northwest Florida.

35. Weeden Island Period sherd types. *a-f*, Swift Creek Complicated Stamped, probably Late Variety; *g-j*, Tampa Complicated Stamped; *k*, Old Bay Complicated Stamped. From Thomas mound. (Courtesy U.S. National Museum; Nos. 384288, 384167, 384163, 384200, 384256, 384198, 384233, 384233, 384238, ?, 384172.)

36. Weeden Island Period sherd types. *a*, Swift Creek Complicated Stamped, probably Late Variety; *b, c*, Old Bay Complicated Stamped; *d, e*, Sun City Complicated Stamped; *f*, unidentified stamped sherd; *g, h*, Little Manatee Zoned Stamped; *i*, Ruskin Dentate Stamped. From the Weeden Island site. (Courtesy U.S. National Museum; Nos. 325671, 324671, 369389, 325671, 325671, 325671, 369390, 369390, 325670.)

37. Weeden Island Period sherd types. *a, b*, Ruskin Dentate Stamped; *c, d*, Thomas Simple Stamped; *e, f*, Little Manatee Zoned Stamped; *g*, Ruskin Linear Punctated. All from Thomas mound. (Courtesy U.S. National Museum; Nos. ?, ?, 384239, 384231, 384264, 384257, 384158.)

Plate

38. Weeden Island Period sherd types. *a*, Little Manatee Shell Stamped; *b-g*, Hillsborough Shell Stamped; *h*, unclassified fabric-marked sherd. From Thomas Mound. (Courtesy U.S. National Museum; Nos. 384144, 384266, 384226, ?, ?, 384195, ?, 384265.)
39. Weeden Island Period sherd types. *a, b*, Wakulla Check Stamped; *c-f*, Weeden Island Plain. From northwest Florida.
40. Weeden Island Period sherd types. *a-f*, Wakulla Check Stamped; *g*, Biscayne Check Stamped. From Thomas mound. (Courtesy U.S. National Museum; Nos. 38429, 384203, 384206, 384238, 384253, 384216, ?.)
41. Vessels of various periods. *a*, Oklawaha Plain; *b*, human-effigy vessel of the type Weeden Island Plain; *c*, human-figurine vessel in the Weeden Island style; *d*, Deptford Simple Stamped; *e*, compartment tray of the type Weeden Island Plain; *f*, Basin Bayou Incised. From the following sites: *a*, El Dorado Lake, Lake county; *b*, Warrior River, mound A; *c*, Aucilla River; *d*, Carrabelle midden and cemetery; *f*, Warrior River, mound B; *g*, Pearl Bayou mound. (Courtesy Heye Foundation; Nos. 17/4501, 17/3947, 8/4154, 8/4153, 17/3948, 17/4038.)
42. Artifacts of various periods. *a-f*, Weeden Island Period chipped-stone projectiles; *g*, bird-effigy pipe fragment of pottery belonging to the Weeden Island Period; *h*, Santa Rosa-Swift Creek Period stone celt; *i*, Weeden Island Period stone celt; *j, k*, Fort Walton Period stone celts. Celt form *j* also occurs in the Weeden Island Period. Artifacts *a-g*, from midden sites in northwest Florida; *h*, Jackson mound; *i*, Calhoun County; *j*, Fort Walton; *k*, Fort Walton. (Celts are shown courtesy R. S. Peabody Foundation; Nos. 40382, 40376, 18586, no number.)
43. Fort Walton Period sherd types. All Fort Walton Incised. From northwest Florida.
44. Fort Walton Period sherd types. All Lake Jackson Plain. From northwest Florida.
45. Fort Walton Period sherd types. *a-e*, Point Washington Incised; *f, g*, Fort Walton Incised. From northwest Florida.
46. Englewood Period and associated vessel types. *a, b*, Englewood Incised; *c*, Sarasota Incised; *d, e*, Englewood Plain; *f*, St. Petersburg Incised, although fluting on body is unusual; *g*, Biscayne Roughened. From the Englewood mound. (Courtesy U.S. National Museum; Nos. 383166, 383168, 383171, ?, 383169, 383167, 383165.)
47. Englewood Period sherd types. All Englewood Incised. From Englewood mound. (Courtesy U.S. National Museum; Nos. 383179, 383187, 383178, 383189, 383185, 383189, 383183.)
48. Englewood Period and associated sherd types. *a, b*, unclassified incised with sherd *b* showing evidences of a former strap-handle attachment; *c-f*, Lemon Bay Incised; *g, h*, Sarasota Incised. From Englewood mound. (Courtesy U.S. National Museum; Nos. 383181, 383184, 383181, 383185, 383189, 383183, 383185, 383182.)
49. Safety Harbor Period sherd types. All Safety Harbor Incised. From Safety Harbor burial mound. (Courtesy U.S. National Museum, No. 351520.)
50. Safety Harbor Period and associated sherd types: *a-d, f*, Pinellas Plain; *e*, Biscayne Check Stamped. From Safety Harbor burial mound. (Courtesy U.S. National Museum; Nos. 351520, 351520, 351522, 351520, 35121, 351522.)

Plate

51. Safety Harbor Period sherd types. All Pinellas Incised. From Safety Harbor burial mound. (Courtesy U.S. National Museum; No. 35120.)
52. Safety Harbor Period sherd types. *a,* Pinellas Incised; *b,* Pinellas Plain; *c-h,* Safety Harbor Incised. Intrusive sherds from the Thomas mound. (Courtesy U.S. National Museum; Nos. 384286, 384283, 384263, 384173, 38419, 384238, ?, 384241.)
53. Safety Harbor Period and associated vessel types. *a,* Pinellas Incised; *b, d, e,* Glades Plain; *c,* Lamar-like Complicated Stamped. Vessel *b* from Parrish mound 3; all others from Parrish mound 1. (Courtesy U.S. National Museum; Nos. 383190, 383228, 383192, 383191, 383193.)

54A. Safety Harbor Period and associated vessel types. *a, b,* Opposite sides of a Safety Harbor Incised vessel (see fig. 64); *c,* Lamar-like Complicated Stamped; *d,* Pasco Red; *e,* Safety Harbor Incised. All from Parrish mound 3. (Courtesy U.S. National Museum; Nos. 383225, 383224, 383226, 383227.)

54B. Safety Harbor Period chipped-stone projectiles and blades. From Parrish mound 3. (Courtesy U.S. National Museum; Nos. 383231 (*b, d*), 383230 (all others).)

55. Safety Harbor Period artifacts. Chipped-stone projectile points and blades. From the Safety Harbor village site. (Courtesy U.S. National Museum; Nos. 362383(*b*), 362385 (*c*), 351530 (all others).)
56. Safety Harbor Period artifacts. Chipped-stone projectile points. From Parrish mound 1. (Courtesy U.S. National Museum; No. 383201.)
57. Safety Harbor Period artifacts. *a-j, m-o,* chipped-stone projectiles and blades; *k-l, p-u,* chipped-stone scrapers; *v,* green-glaze European pipe; *w, x,* European trade pipes. From Safety Harbor village site and burial mound. (Courtesy U.S. National Museum; Nos. 351530 (*a-i*); others 351515, 351529, 362384, 362383, 362383, 362383, 351529, 362384, 351529, 351529, 362384, 351530, ?, ?, 362386.)
58. Safety Harbor Period artifacts. *a, b,* European combs of bone or tortoise shell; *c,* twisted cone of sheet gold; *d,* beads of sheet silver; *e,* green glass pentagonal bead; *f,* green glass pendant; *g,* copper ear ornament with hollow bulbar center. From Parrish mound 1. (Courtesy U.S. National Museum; Nos. 383199, 383198, 383206, 383204, 383205, 383203.)
59. Safety Harbor Period artifacts. *a,* European comb of bone or tortoise shell; *b,* European brass pendant; *c,* single-grooved stone plummet; *d, e,* chipped-stone projectiles; *f,* ground-stone tubular bead; *g, h,* shell beads; *i-l,* charred fragments of carved wood; *m-q,* charred fragments of hair cordage which have outer woven sheathing covering inner braided cord. From Parrish mound 2. (Courtesy U.S. National Museum; Nos. 383215, 383218, 383216, 383220, 383217, 383213, 383213, 383214 (all wood), 383221 (all cordage).)
60. Leon-Jefferson Period sherds and artifacts. *a-c,* Leon Check Stamped; *d-f,* complicated stamped ware, probably of the Jefferson Series; *g,* European crockery; *h,* iron spike; *i,* gun flint. From Jefferson County.

PIT EXCAVATION AT CARRABELLE (FR-2), FRANKLIN COUNTY

(For explanation, see p. 595.)

SHELL MIDDENS ON THE NORTHWEST GULF COAST

(For explanation, see p. 595.)

LAKE JACKSON SITE (LE-1), LEON COUNTY
(For explanation, see p. 595.)

BURIAL TYPES FROM THE THOMAS (HI-1) AND COCKROACH KEY (HI-2) BURIAL MOUNDS

(For explanation, see p. 595.)

THE ENGLEWOOD MOUND (So-1)

(For explanation, see p. 595.)

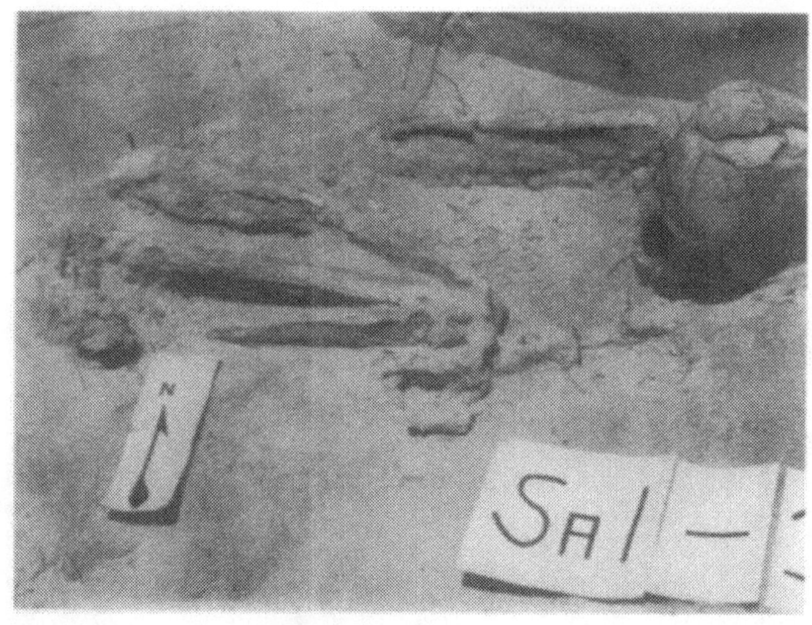

ENGLEWOOD (SO-1) BURIALS

(For explanation, see p. 595.)

PERICO ISLAND (MA-6)

(For explanation, see p. 595.)

Cockroach Key (Hi-2)

(For explanation, see p. 595.)

THE NORTHWEST GULF COAST

(For explanation, see p. 595.)

THE NORTHWEST GULF COAST

(For explanation, see p. 595.)

THE PIERCE SITE (FR-14), FRANKLIN COUNTY
(For explanation, see p. 595.)

DEPTFORD PERIOD SHERD TYPES

(For explanation, see p. 595.)

Deptford Period Sherd Types

(For explanation, see p. 595.)

Perico Island Period Sherds

(For explanation, see pp. 595-596.)

PERICO ISLAND PERIOD ARTIFACT TYPES

(For explanation, see p. 596.)

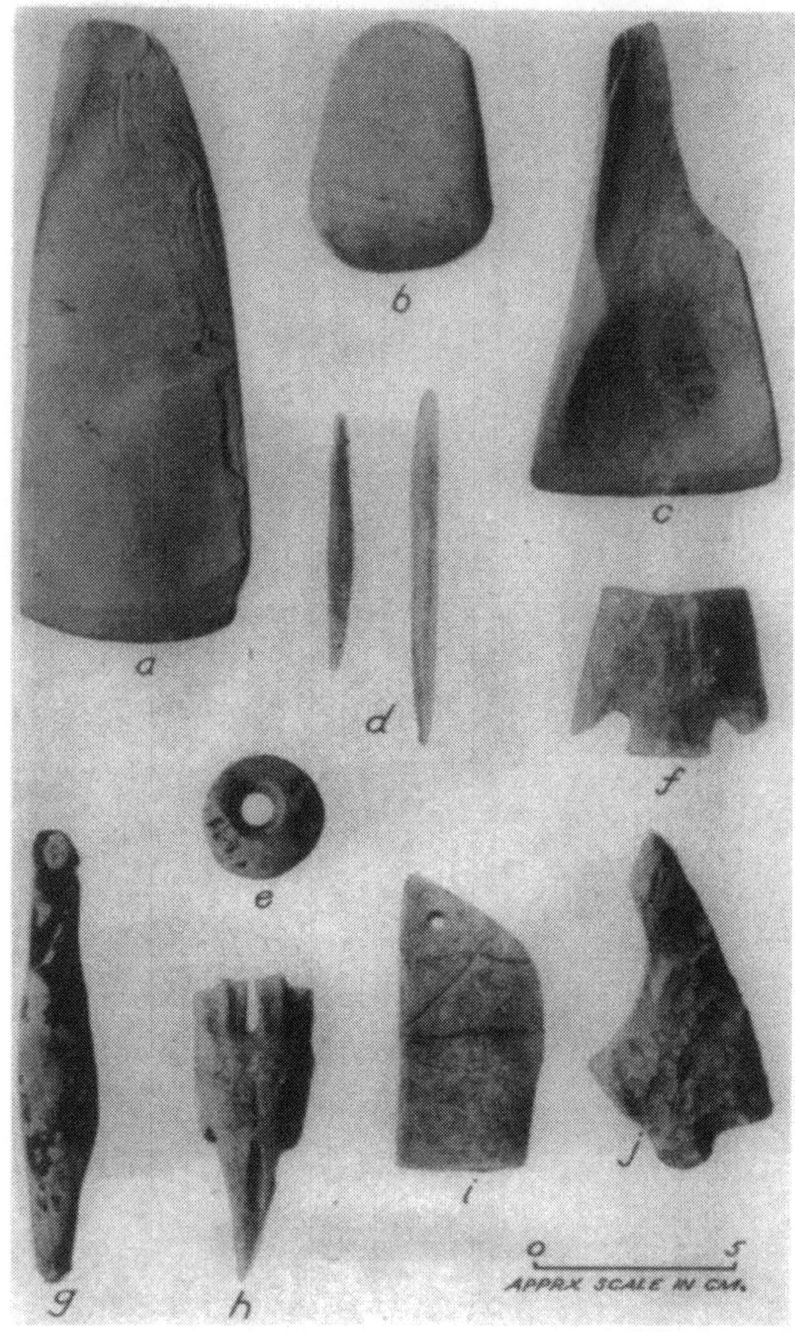

PERICO ISLAND PERIOD ARTIFACT TYPES

(For explanation, see p. 596.)

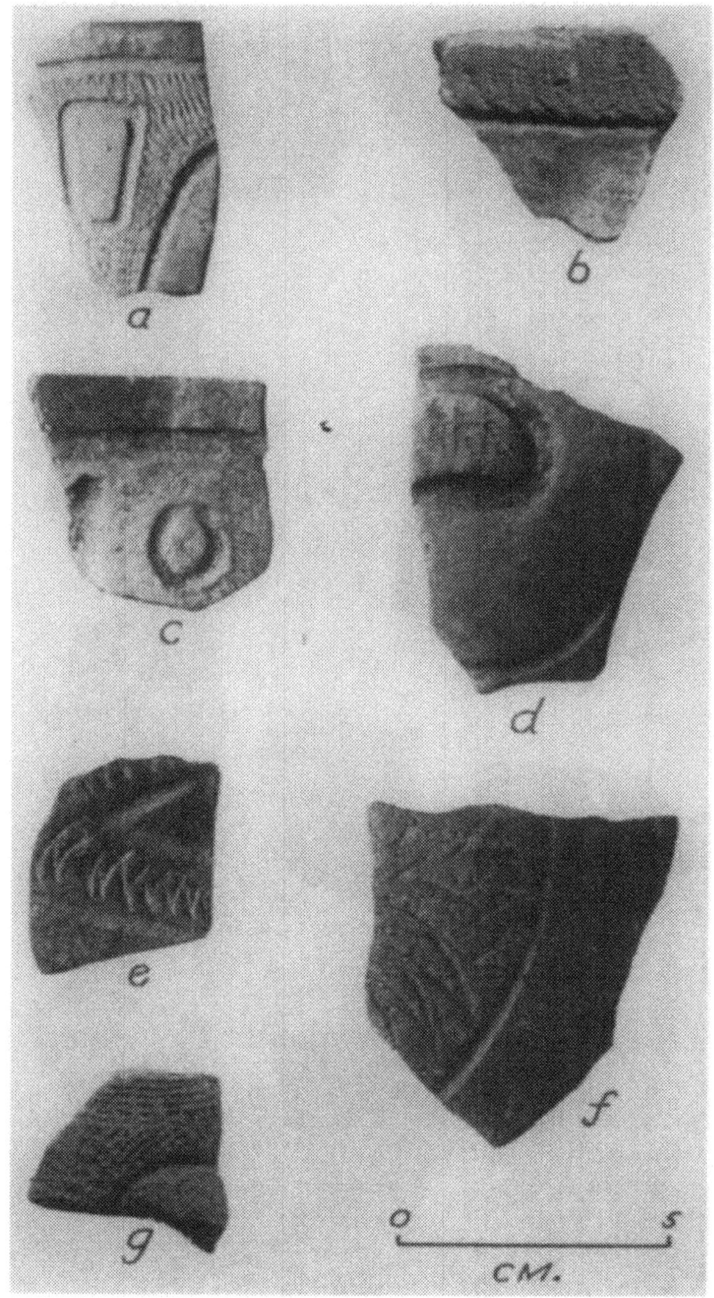

Santa Rosa-Swift Creek Period Sherd Types

(For explanation, see p. 596.)

SANTA ROSA-SWIFT CREEK PERIOD SHERD TYPES

(For explanation, see p. 596.)

Santa Rosa-Swift Creek Period Sherd Types

(For explanation, see p. 596.)

SANTA ROSA-SWIFT CREEK PERIOD SHERD TYPES

(For explanation, see p. 596.)

SANTA ROSA-SWIFT CREEK PERIOD SHERD TYPES

(For explanation, see p. 596.)

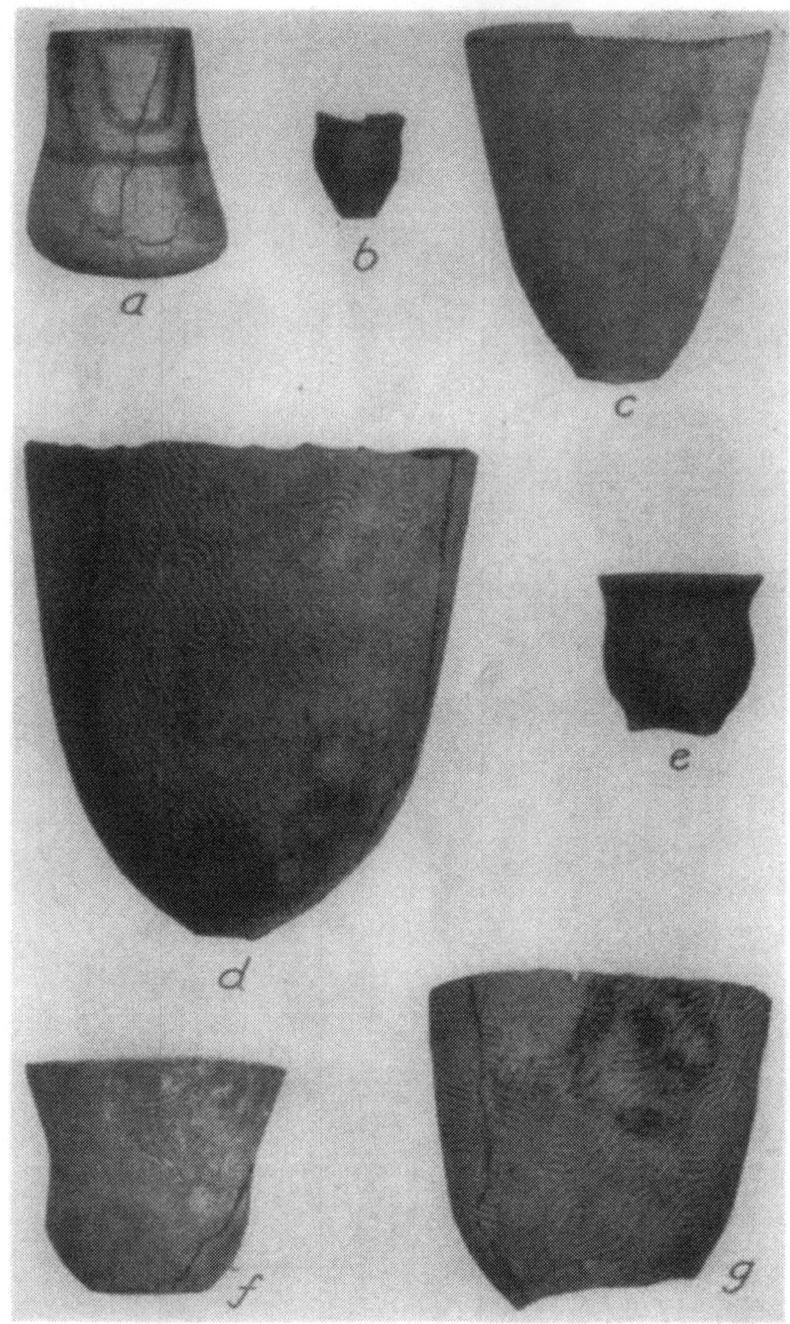

SANTA ROSA-SWIFT CREEK PERIOD VESSELS
(For explanation, see p. 596.)

SANTA ROSA-SWIFT CREEK PERIOD VESSELS

(For explanation, see p. 596.)

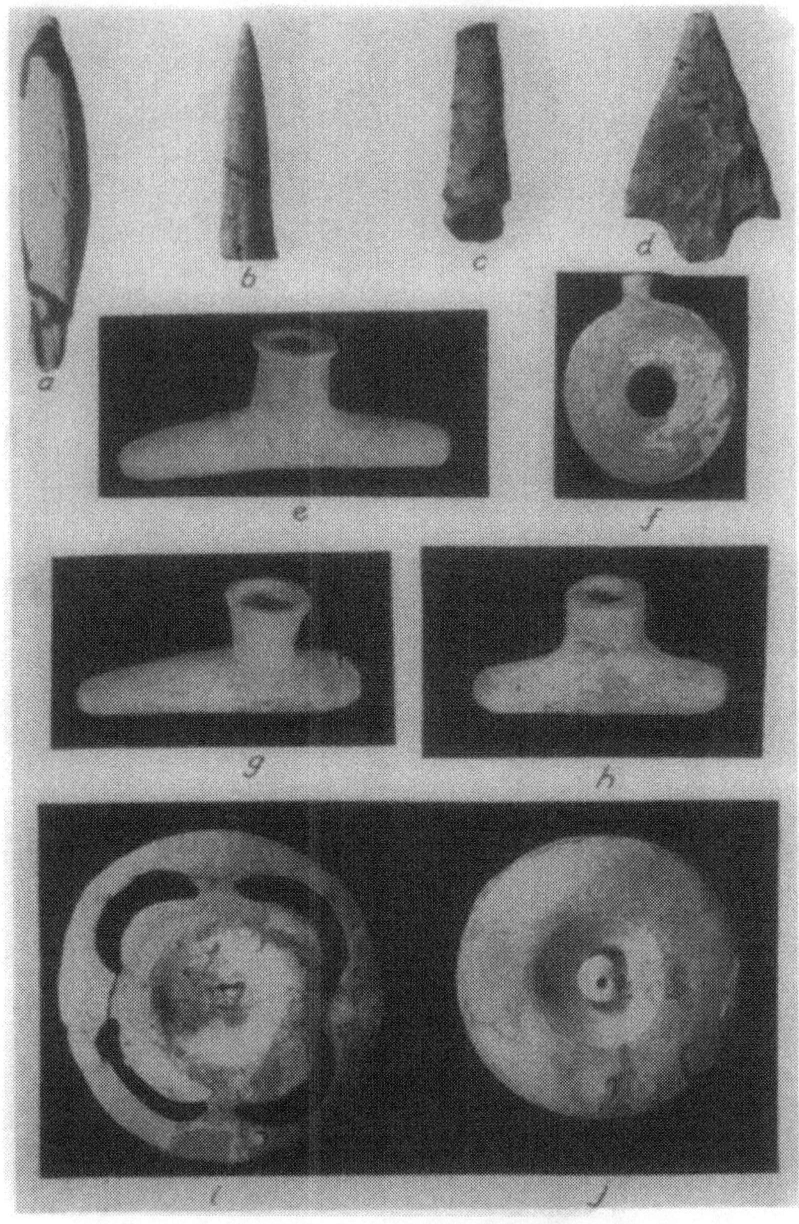

SANTA ROSA-SWIFT CREEK PERIOD ARTIFACTS

(For explanation, see pp. 596-597.)

WEEDEN ISLAND PERIOD SHERD TYPES

(For explanation, see p. 597.)

Weeden Island Period Sherd Types

(For explanation, see p. 597.)

WEEDEN ISLAND PERIOD SHERD TYPES

(For explanation, see p. 597.)

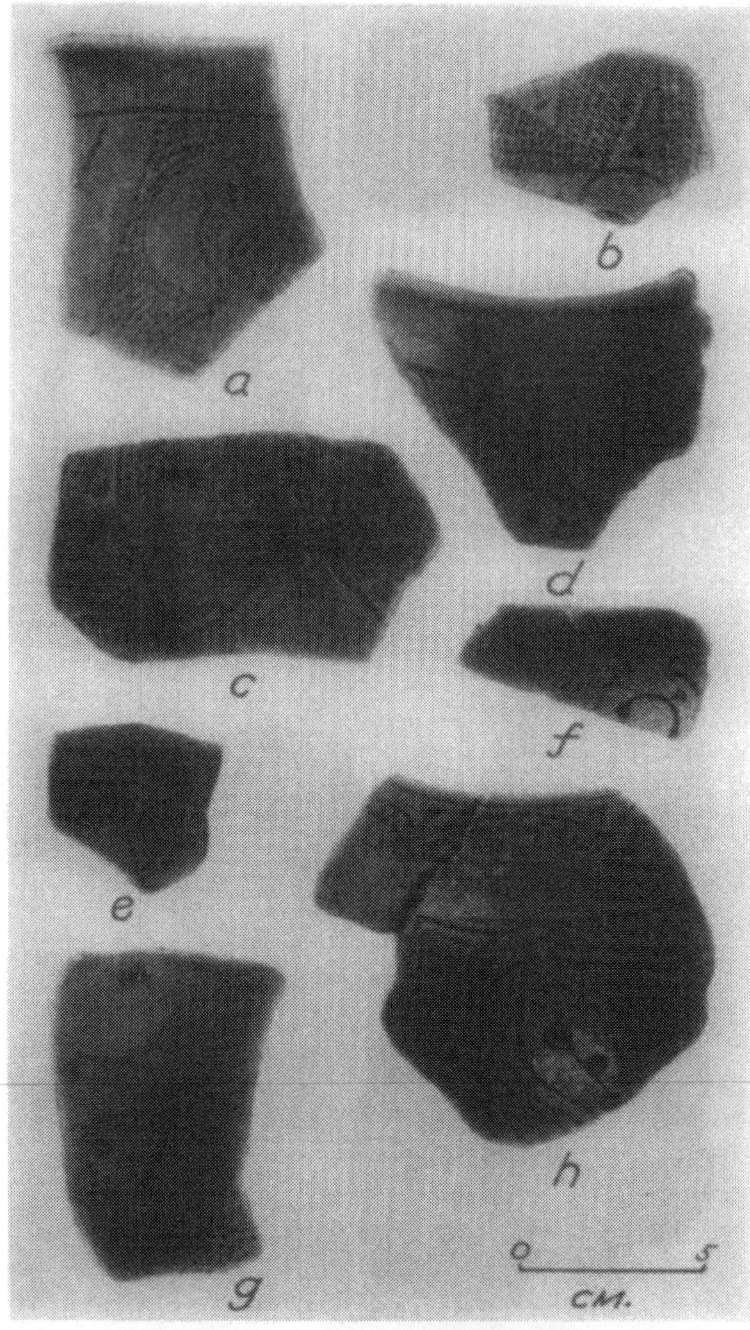

WEEDEN ISLAND PERIOD SHERD TYPES

(For explanation, see p. 597.)

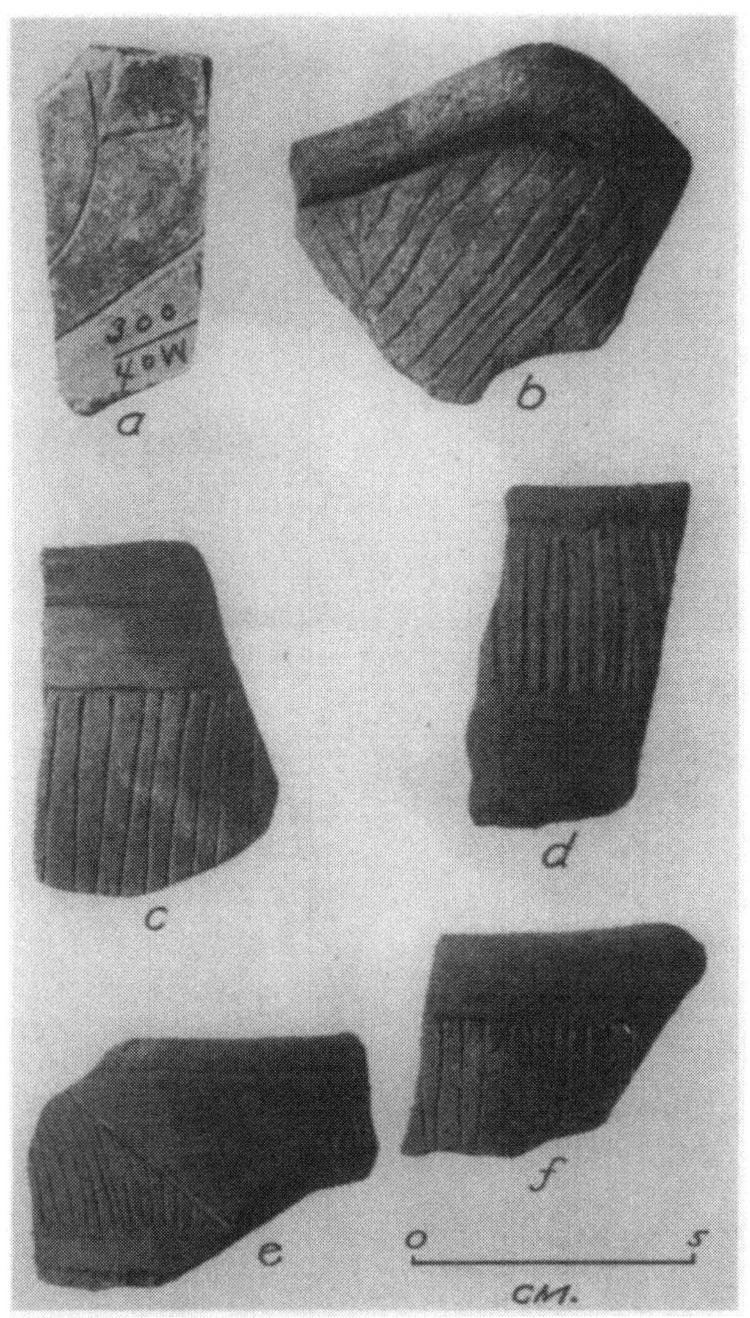

WEEDEN ISLAND PERIOD SHERD TYPES

(For explanation, see p. 597.)

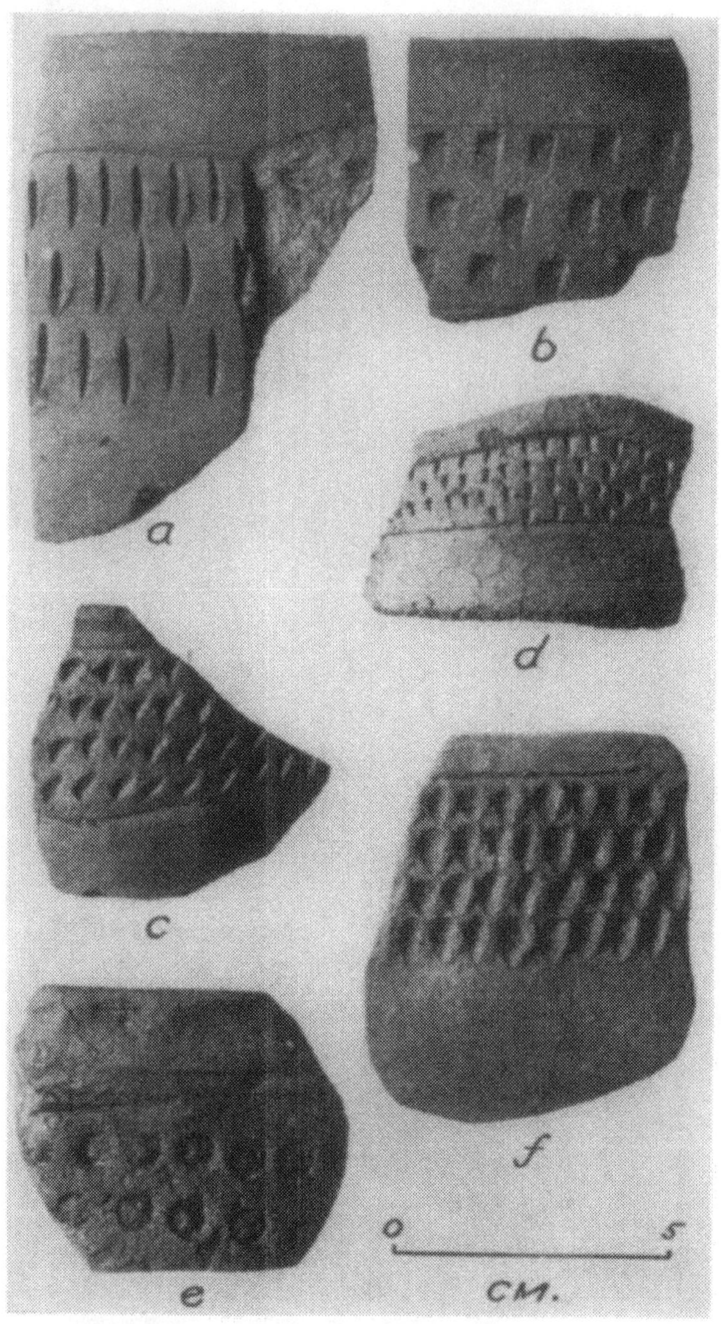

WEEDEN ISLAND PERIOD SHERD TYPES

(For explanation, see p. 597.)

WEEDEN ISLAND PERIOD SHERD TYPES

(For explanation, see p. 597.)

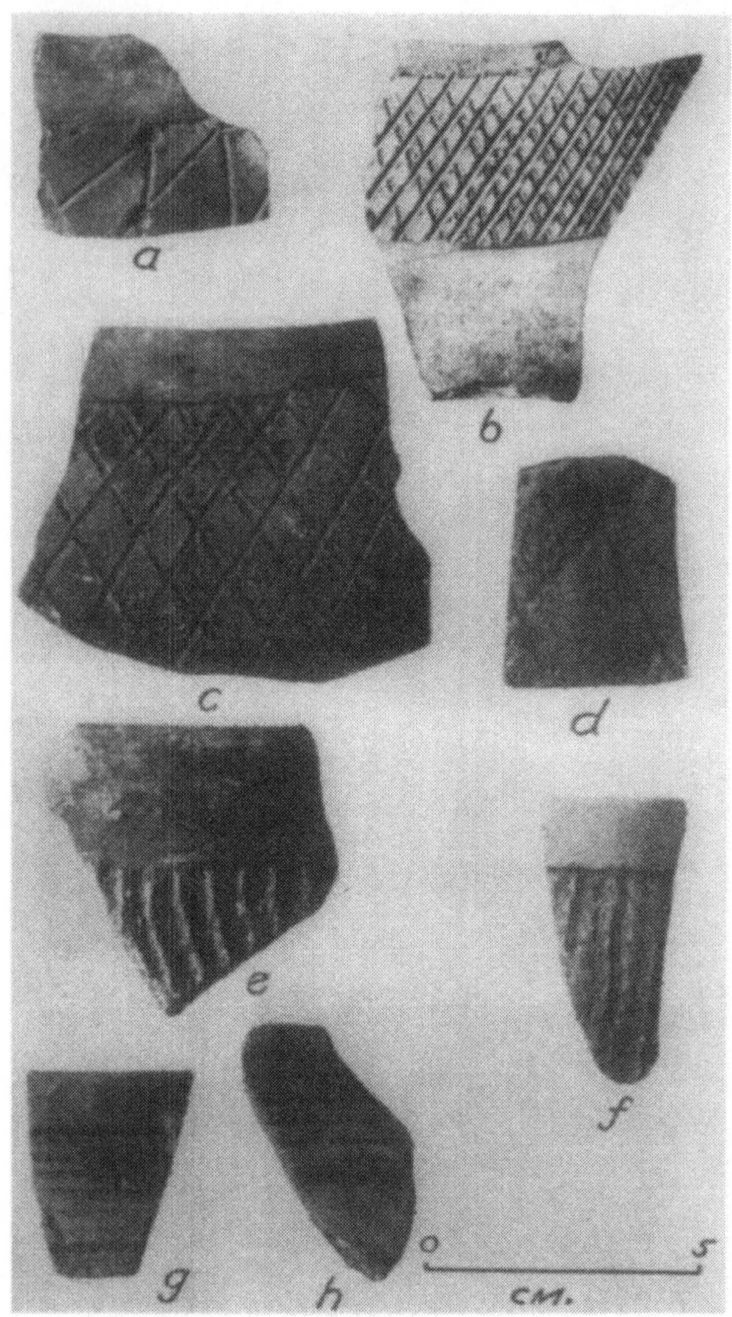

WEEDEN ISLAND PERIOD SHERD TYPES

(For explanation, see p. 597.)

WEEDEN ISLAND PERIOD SHERD TYPES

(For explanation, see p. 597.)

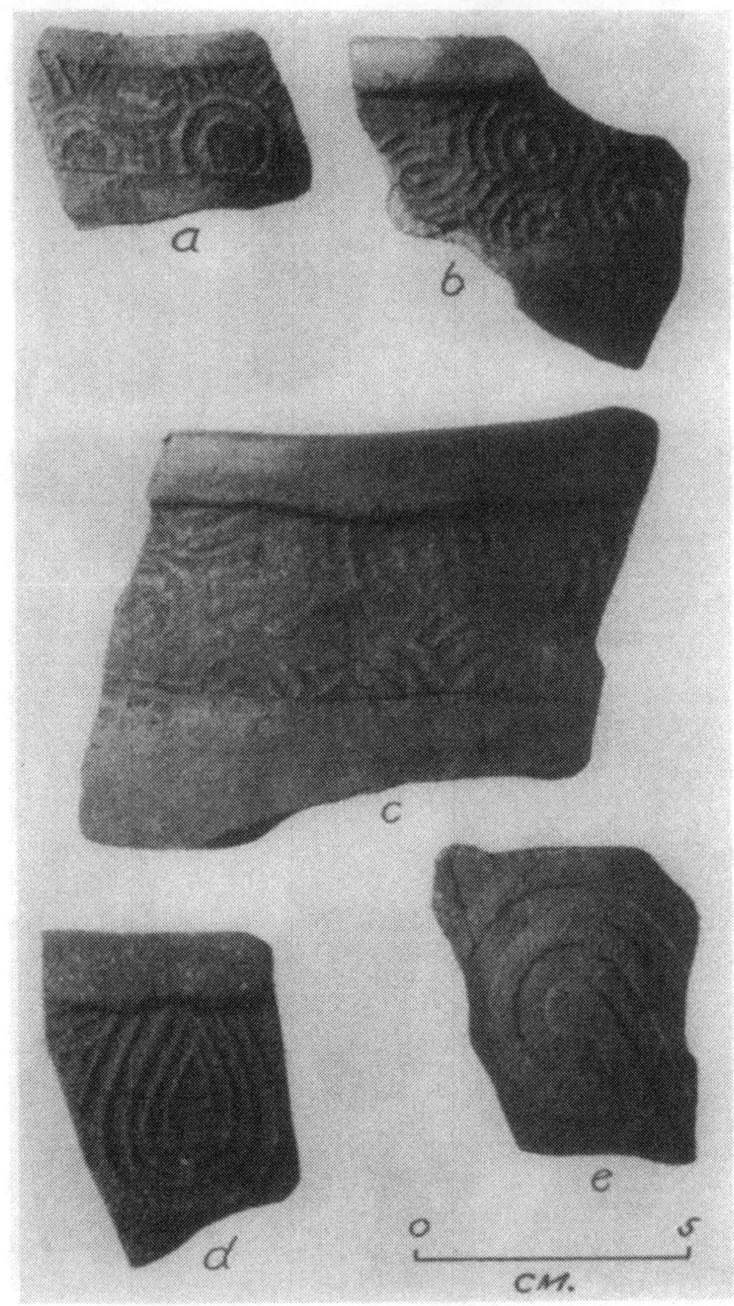

Weeden Island Period Sherd Types

(For explanation, see p. 597.)

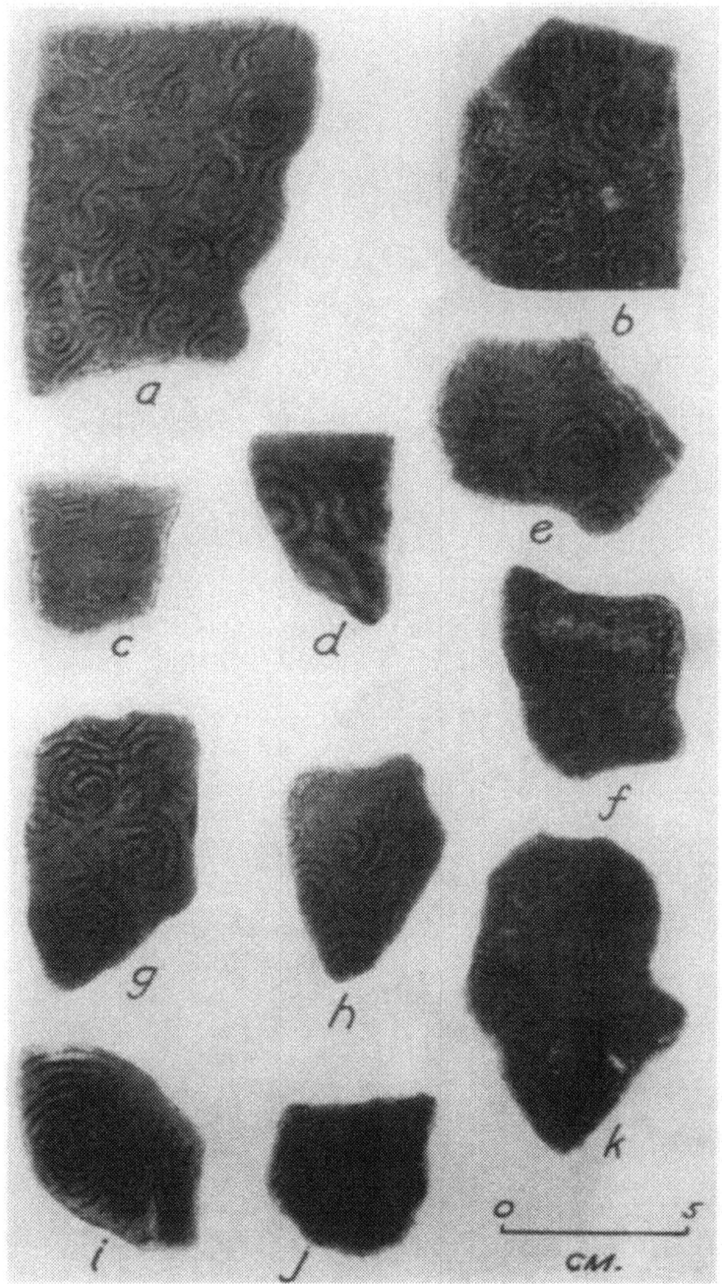

WEEDEN ISLAND PERIOD SHERD TYPES

(For explanation, see p. 597.)

WEEDEN ISLAND PERIOD SHERD TYPES

(For explanation, see p. 597.)

WEEDEN ISLAND PERIOD SHERD TYPES

(For explanation, see p. 597.)

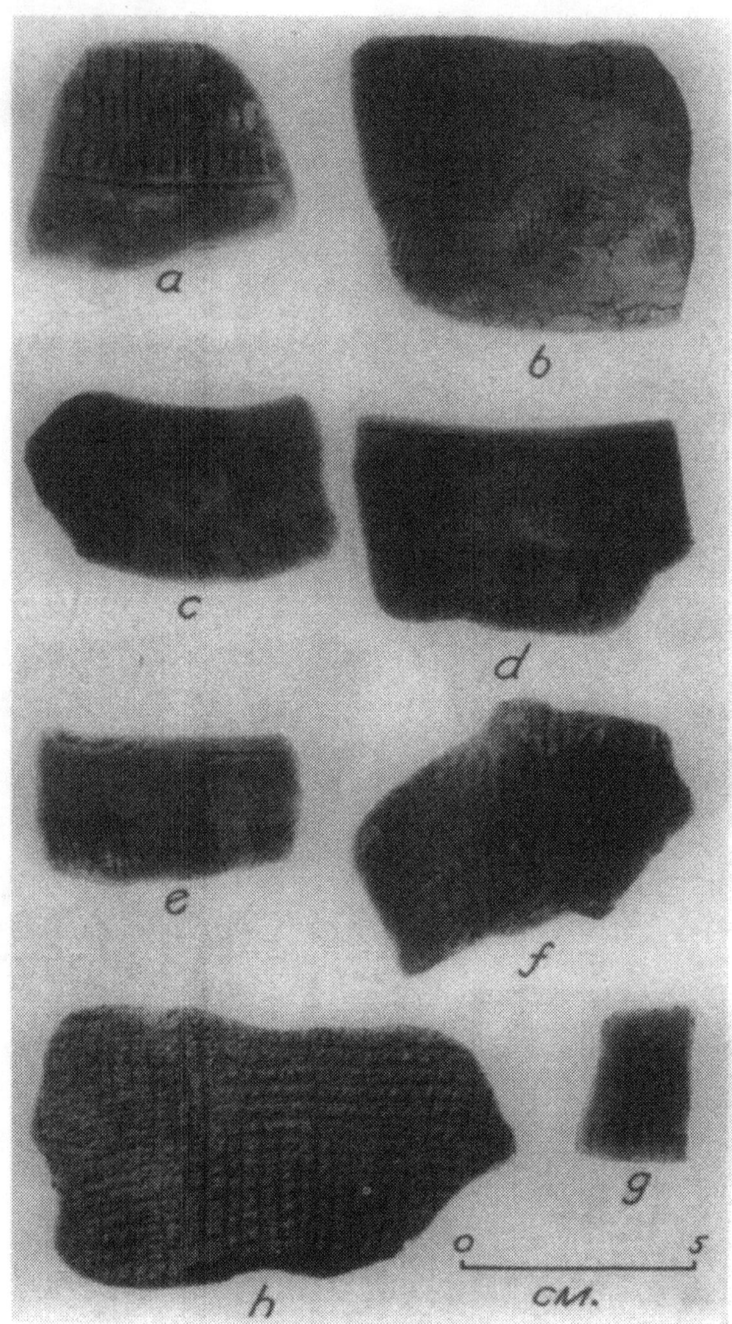

Weeden Island Period Sherd Types

(For explanation, see p. 598.)

Weeden Island Period Sherd Types

(For explanation, see p. 598.)

Weeden Island Period Sherd Types

(For explanation, see p. 598.)

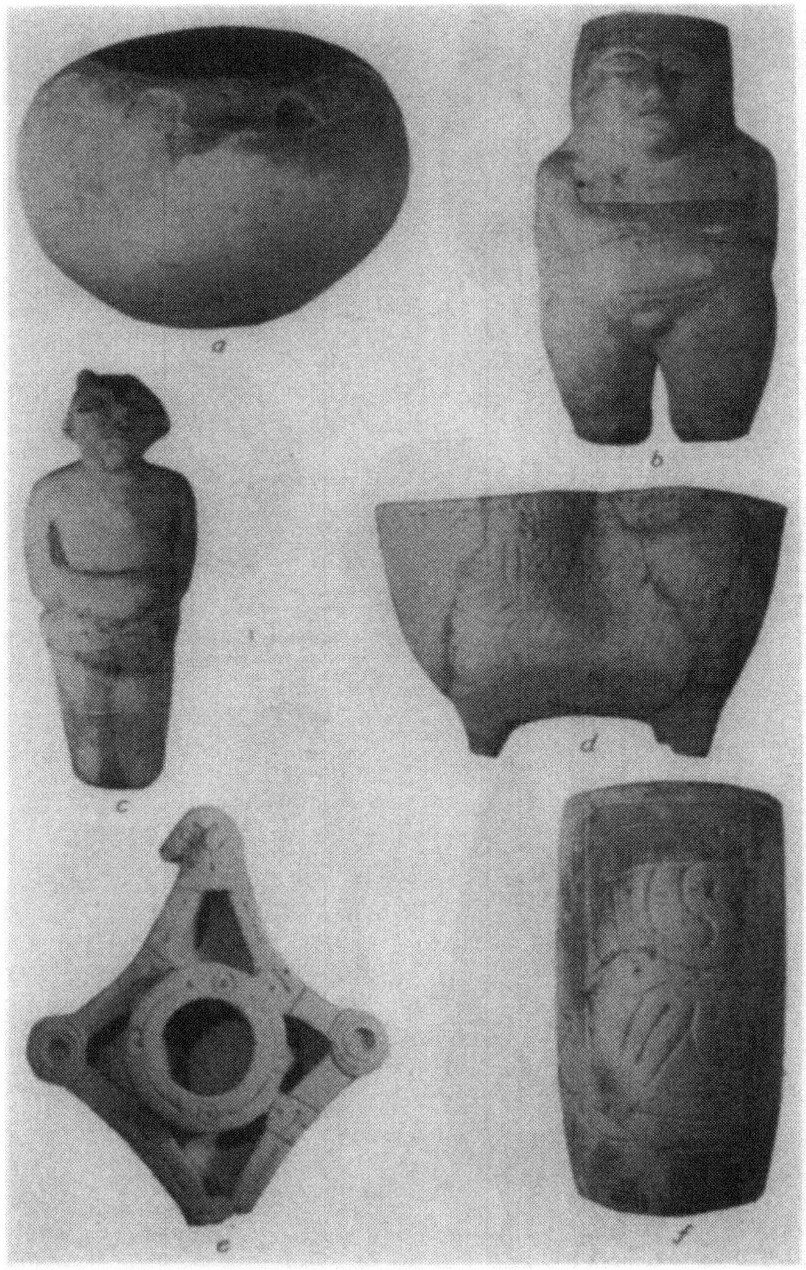

Vessels of Various Periods

(For explanation, see p. 598.)

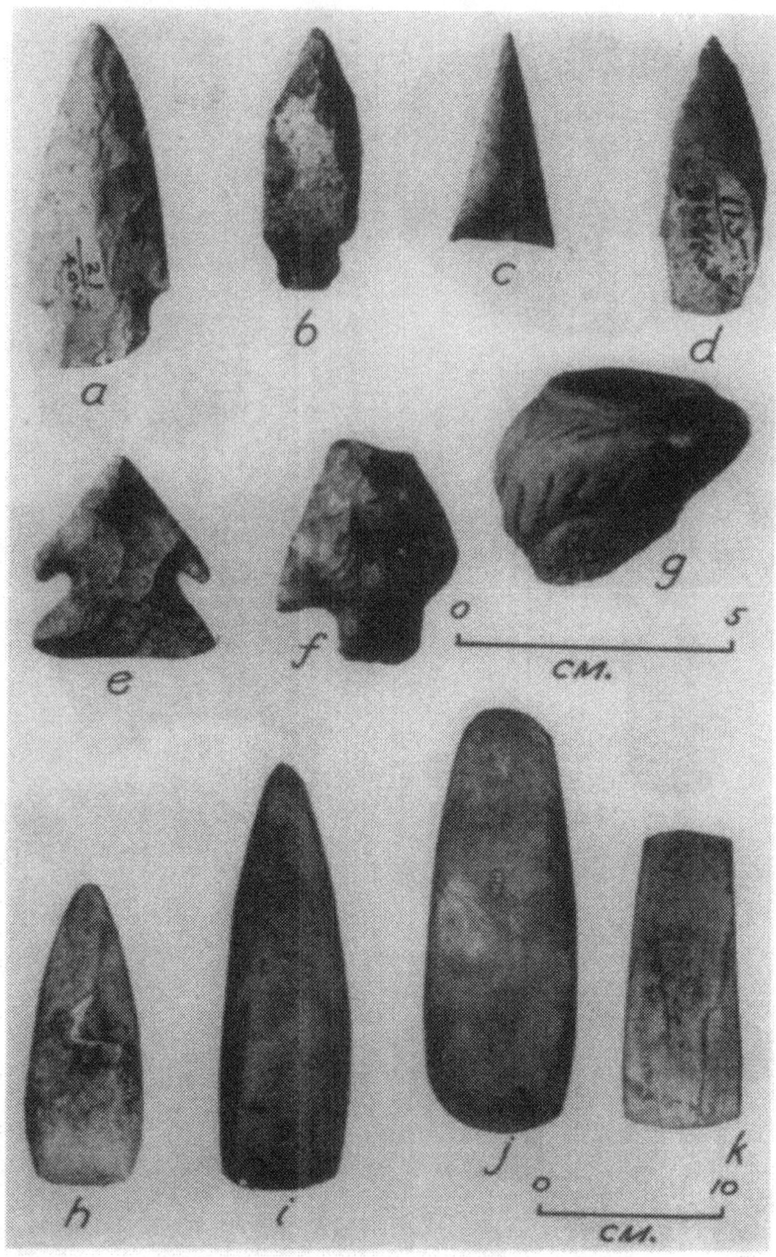

Artifacts of Various Periods

(For explanation, see p. 598.)

FORT WALTON PERIOD SHERD TYPES

(For explanation, see p. 598.)

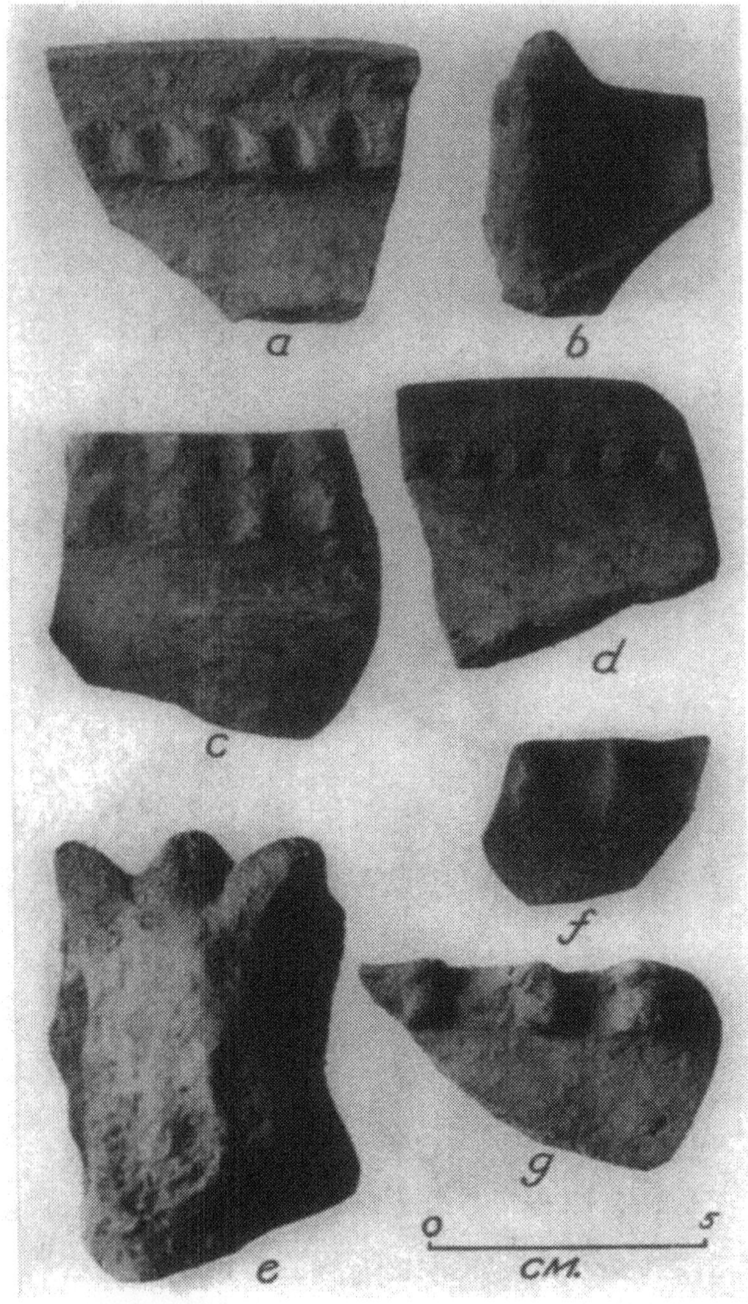

FORT WALTON PERIOD SHERD TYPES

(For explanation, see p. 598.)

FORT WALTON PERIOD SHERD TYPES
(For explanation, see p. 598.)

ENGLEWOOD PERIOD AND ASSOCIATED VESSEL TYPES

(For explanation, see p. 598.)

ENGLEWOOD PERIOD SHERD TYPES

(For explanation, see p. 598.)

ENGLEWOOD PERIOD AND ASSOCIATED SHERD TYPES

(For explanation, see p. 598.)

SAFETY HARBOR PERIOD SHERD TYPES

(For explanation, see p. 598.)

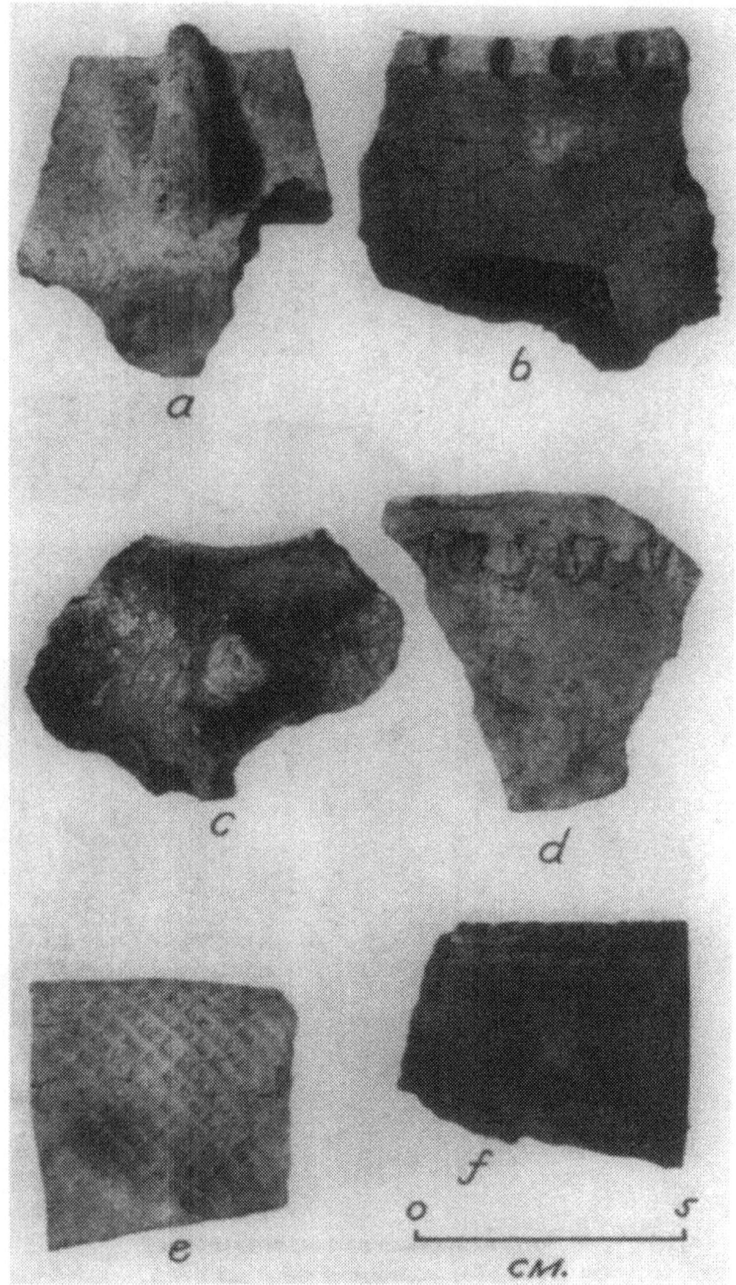

SAFETY HARBOR PERIOD AND ASSOCIATED SHERD TYPES

(For explanation, see p. 598.)

SAFETY HARBOR PERIOD SHERD TYPES

(For explanation, see p. 599.)

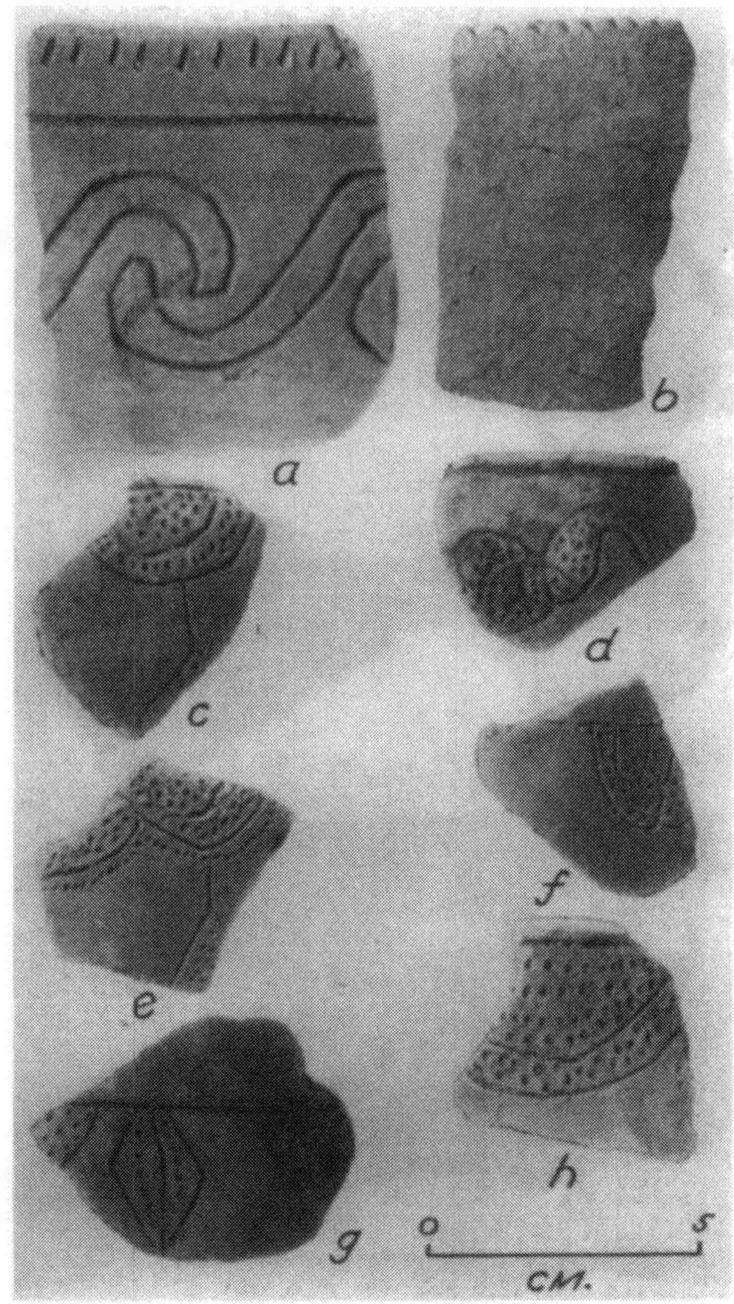

SAFETY HARBOR PERIOD SHERD TYPES

(For explanation, see p. 599.)

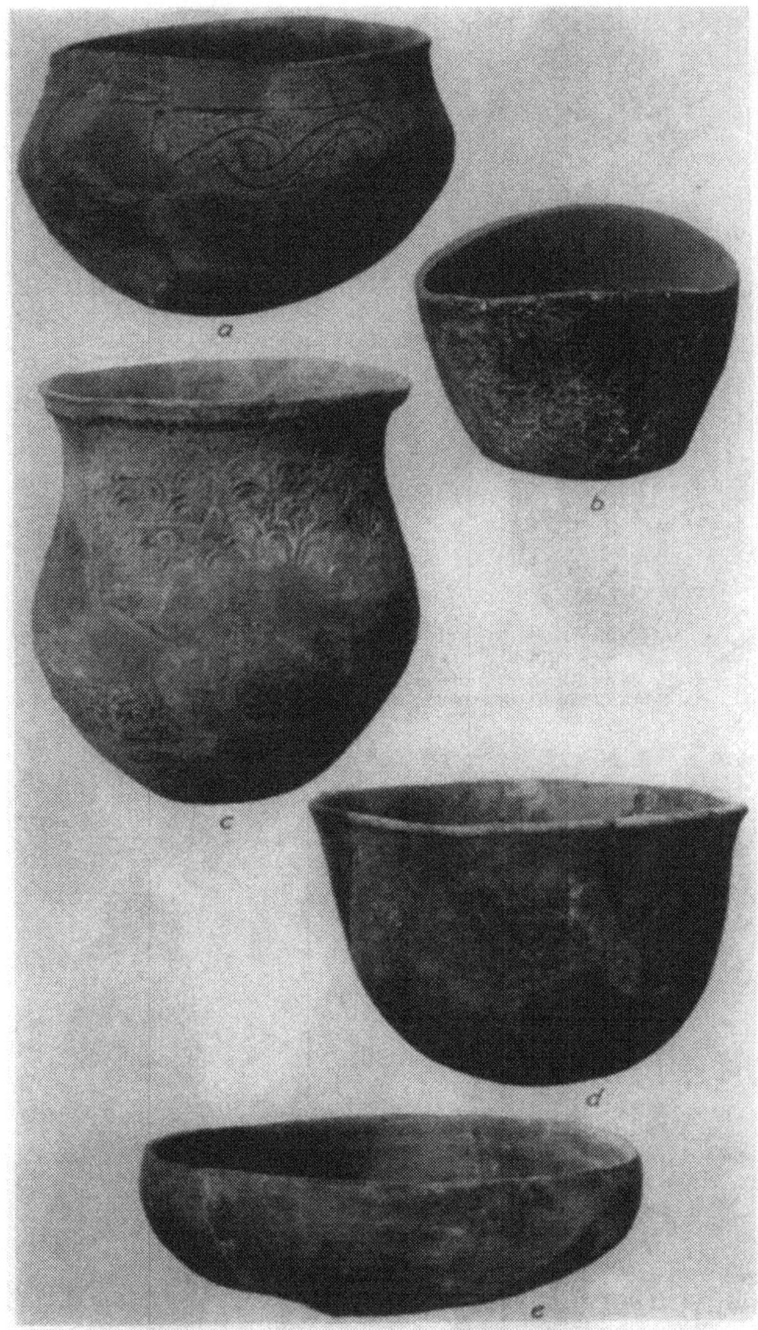

SAFETY HARBOR PERIOD AND ASSOCIATED VESSEL TYPES

(For explanation, see p. 599.)

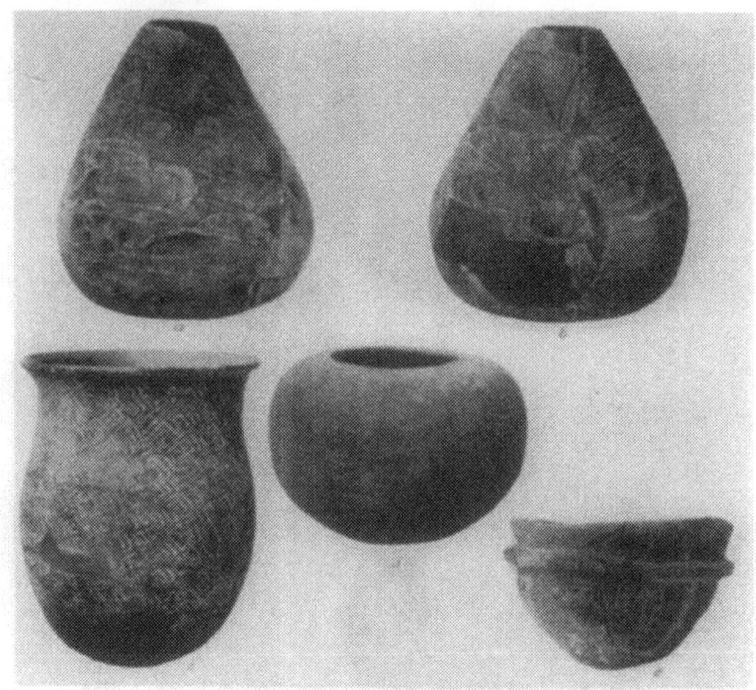

A. SAFETY HARBOR PERIOD AND ASSOCIATED VESSEL TYPES

B. SAFETY HARBOR CHIPPED-STONE PROJECTILES AND BLADES

(For explanation, see p. 599.)

Safety Harbor Period Artifacts

(For explanation, see p. 599.)

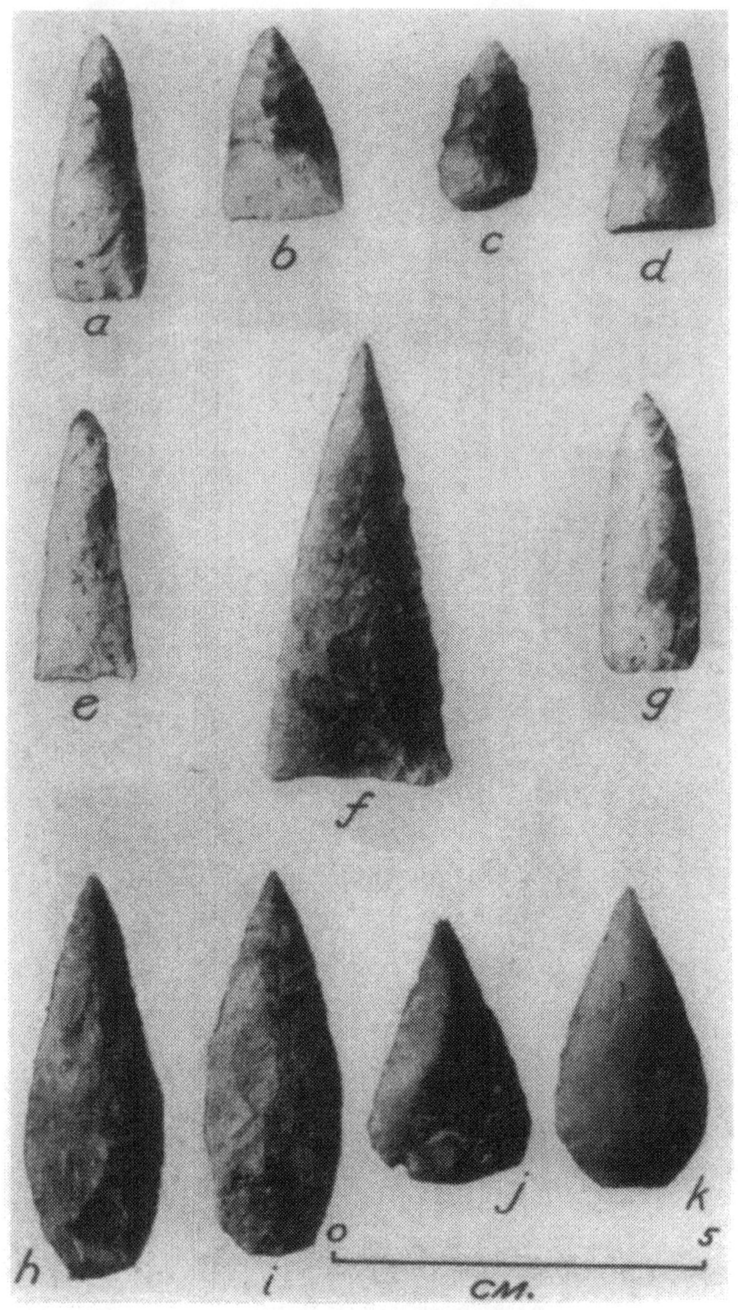

SAFETY HARBOR PERIOD ARTIFACTS

(For explanation, see p. 599.)

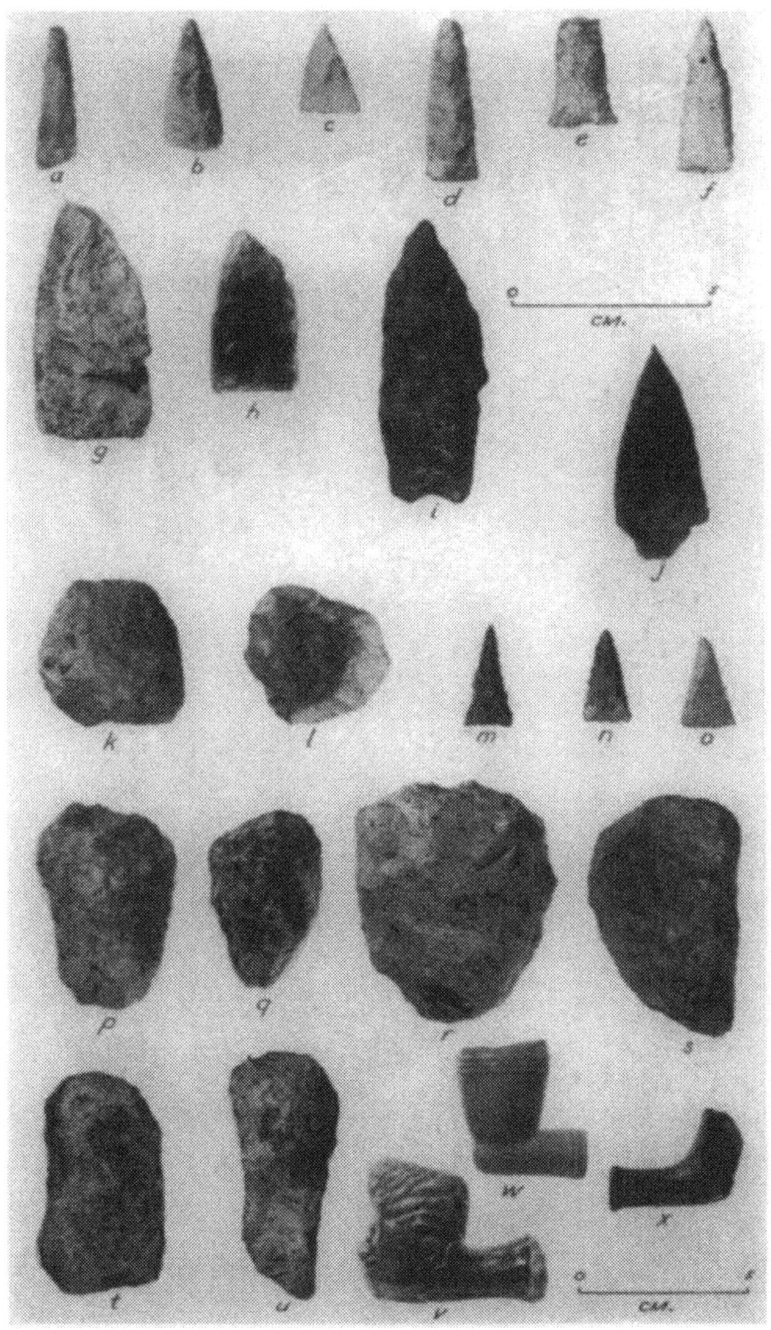

Safety Harbor Period Artifacts

(For explanation, see p. 599.)

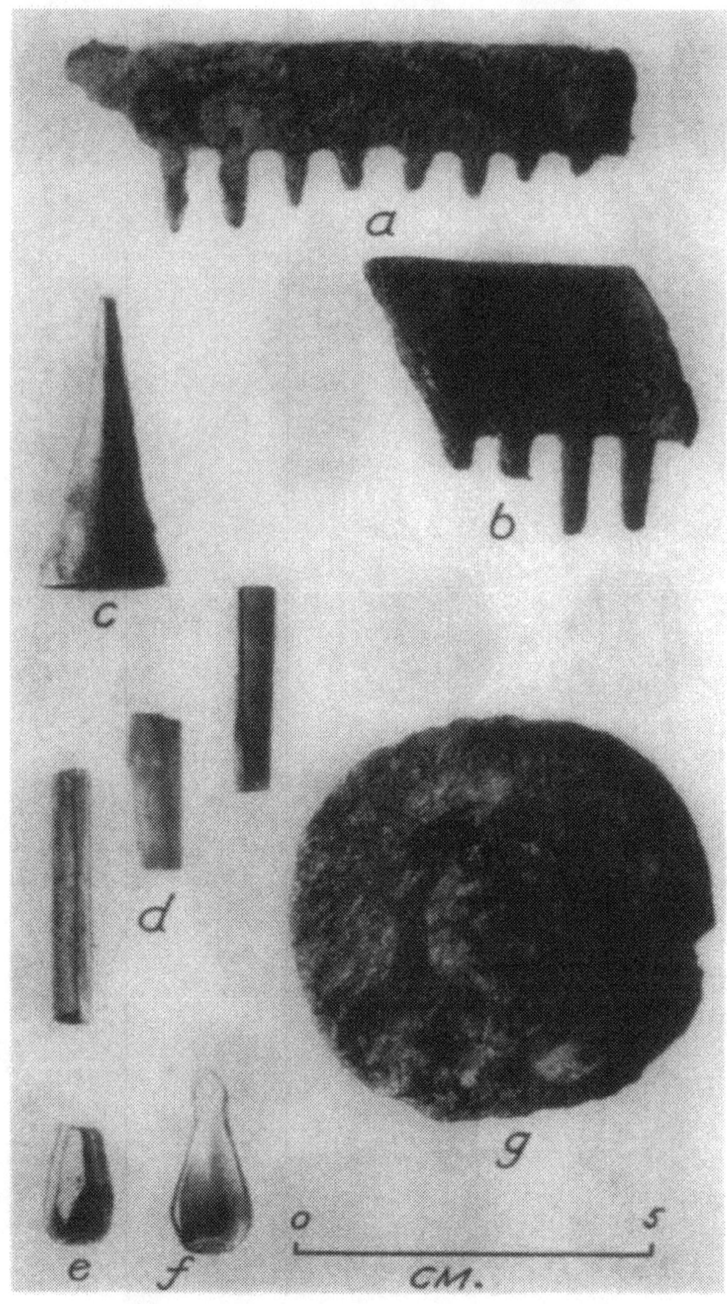

Safety Harbor Period Artifacts

(For explanation, see p. 599.)

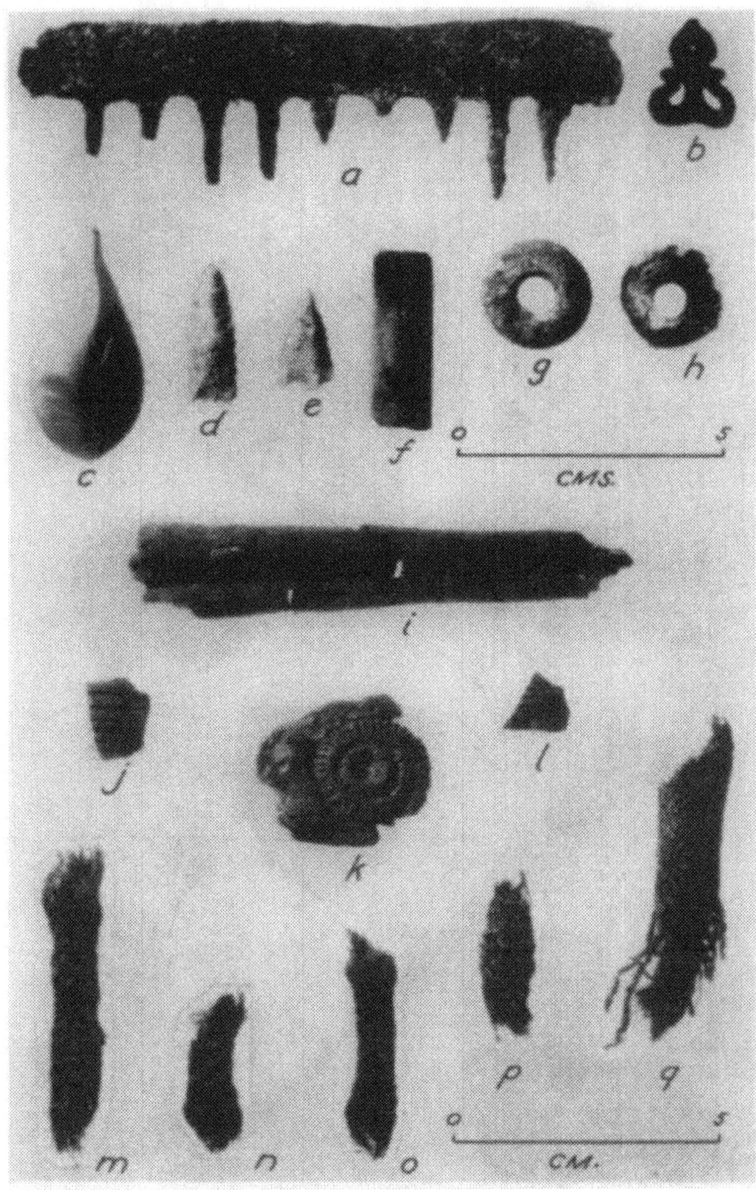

SAFETY HARBOR PERIOD ARTIFACTS

(For explanation, see p. 599.)

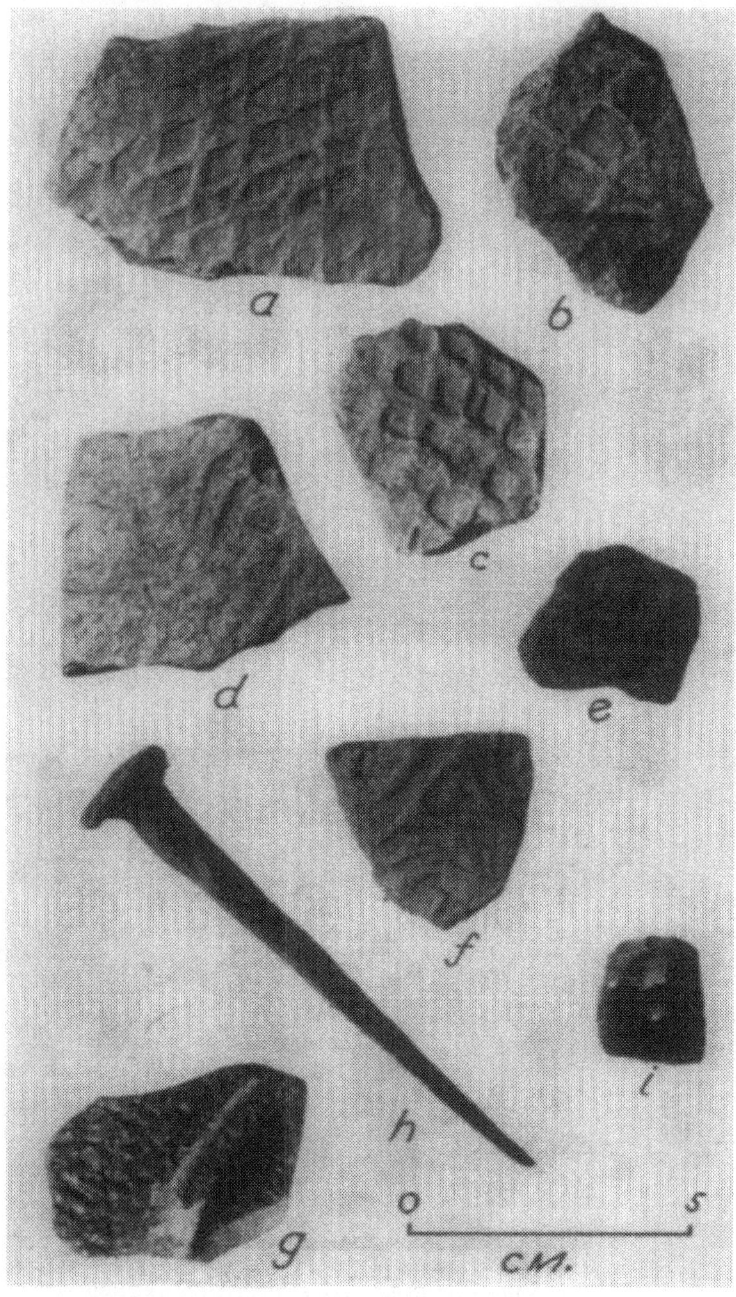

LEON-JEFFERSON PERIOD SHERDS AND ARTIFACTS

(For explanation, see p. 599.)

Printed in the USA
CPSIA information can be obtained
at www.ICGtesting.com
CBHW021308201124
17447CB00013B/1